150 Leading Cases

European Law

150 LEADING CASES

European Law

CONSULTANT EDITOR: LORD TEMPLEMAN
EDITOR: ALINA KACZOROWSKA
BCL, DEA, PhD, Barrister at the Paris Bar

OLD BAILEY PRESS

OLD BAILEY PRESS
200 Greyhound Road, London W14 9RY

First edition 1999

© The HLT Group Ltd 1999

All Old Bailey Press publications enjoy copyright protection and the copyright belongs to the HLT Group Ltd.

All rights reserved. No part of this publication may be reproduced or transmitted in any form or by any means, electronic, mechanical, photocopying, recording or otherwise, or stored in any retrieval system of any nature without either the written permission of the copyright holder, application for which should be made to the HLT Group Ltd, or a licence permitting restricted copying in the United Kingdom issued by the Copyright Licensing Agency.

Any person who infringes the above in relation to this publication may be liable to criminal prosecution and civil claims for damages.

ISBN 1 85836 320 9

British Library Cataloguing-in-Publication

A catalogue record for this book is available from the British Library.

Printed and bound in Great Britain

Contents

Acknowledgements *vii*

Preface *ix*

Table of Cases *xi*

Law of the European Union

1   The Evolution and the Constitution of the European Union   *1*

2   The Institutions of the European Union   *31*

3   Judicial Review in the European Community I: Direct Actions against Member States   *51*

4   Judicial Review in the European Community II: Direct Actions against European Community Institutions   *72*

5   Preliminary Rulings: Article 177 EC (now Article 234 EC)   *92*

6   Sources of Law and Principles of Interpretation   *109*

7   Fundamental Principles of European Community Law   *126*

8   Free Movement of Goods   *158*

9   Intellectual Property   *190*

10 Free Movement of Workers: Articles 49–51 EC Treaty (now Articles 39–42 EC Treaty)   *203*

11 Social Policy   *218*

12 The Right of Establishment and the Right to Supply and Receive Services: Articles 52–58 EC Treaty (now Articles 43–58 EC Treaty)   *242*

13 EC Competition Law   *261*

Law of the European Convention on Human Rights

14 The Right to Life: Article 2   *303*

15 The Right to Freedom from Torture and Inhuman and Degrading Treatment: Article 3   *311*

16 The Right to Liberty and Security of the Person: Article 5   *314*

17 The Right to Privacy and Family Life: Article 8   *321*

18 Freedom of Thought, Conscience and Religion: Article 9   *337*

19 The Right to Freedom of Expression: Article 10   *340*

20 The Right of Association with Others: Article 11   *348*

21 The Right to Marry: Article 12   353

22 The Right to Freedom from Discrimination: Article 14   359

23 The Right to Participate in Elections to Choose Legislature: Article 3 of Protocol 1   364

Appendix: Numbering of the Treaty on European Union and the EC Treaty articles before and after the entry into force of the Amsterdam Treaty   373

Acknowledgements

Extracts from the Treaties and documents of the European Economic Communities, and of the judgments and decisions of the European Court of Justice and the European Court of Human Rights, have been reproduced with the permission of the European Commission, the European Court of Justice, the European Court of Human Rights and the European Law Centre.

The publishers and editor would also like to thank the Incorporated Council of Law Reporting for England and Wales for their kind permission to reproduce extracts from the Weekly Law Reports, Butterworths for their kind permission to reproduce extracts from the All England Law Reports and Times Newspapers Limited for their kind permission to reproduce an extract from the Times Law Reports.

Preface

This work presents 150 of the most significant cases emanating from the courts of the European Communities and the institutions interpreting the European Convention on Human Rights. The book examines both recent cases (up to May 1999) – which take account of new developments, of changes in the law and of the European Court's clarifications of essential issues – and earlier 'landmark' cases in the light of subsequent events. The comments elucidating the nuances of the various judgments and identifying the salient facts and new approaches are intended to ensure that this publication can be used as an educative work which stands on its own. Additionally, the inclusion of verbatim quotations of important extracts from judgments make it an ideal companion to the Old Bailey Press *Law of the European Union* textbook.

Dramatic changes have taken place in European law. In relation to European human rights, the entry into force of Protocol No 11 to the European Convention on Human Rights on 1 November 1998 has reformed the Strasbourg system. The newly created European Court of Human Rights delivered its first judgments in February 1999.

In respect of the European Community, the Treaty of Amsterdam entered into force on 1 May 1999 bringing with it wide-ranging reforms and substantial changes. The least important but the most annoying consequence of its entry into force is the change in numbering of the articles of the Treaty on European Union and the EC Treaty. The change in numbering must be remembered. All the cases/judgments dealt with in this book refer only to the pre-Amsterdam Treaty numbering. Accordingly, in the text I have used the same references. In order to assist the reader I have at the beginning of each chapter (apart from general introductory chapters) set out both the old and new numbering of the principal articles governing the subject dealt with in that chapter. Additionally, this book has an appendix containing a correlation table. Also note that since the Treaty on European Union the EEC Treaty is to be referred to as the EC Treaty, and this has been used throughout.

I have two further particular points. First, please note that recent cases, although unreported, can be found at the following websites. For the Court of Justice of the European Communities: http://europa.eu.int/cj/en/index.htm. This website contains a weekly bulletin summarising recent judgments and opinions of the ECJ and CFI and recent case law – from June 1996. The website address of the European Court of Human Rights is: http://www.dhcour.coe.fr/. This Court's database, hudoc, contains almost all judgments and decisions of the Court from 1959. Second, please take into consideration that many quotations from judgments do not read well but they are precise quotations.

I would like to thank my charming friends from the Old Bailey Press – Professor Cedric Bell for his encouragement and help over the years, Helen O'Shea for her competence and great patience whilst dealing with me and my book, and my editor, Linda Clifford, whose constructive and analytical comments are greatly appreciated. I am also most grateful to Christopher Ireland, of Irelands Commercial Lawyers in Hampshire, for his intuitive reading of my original manuscript.

Alina Kaczorowska
August 1999

Table of Cases

Cases in bold type are the leading cases. Page numbers in bold indicate the main references to them.

Abdulaziz, Cabales and Balkandali v United Kindom (1985) 7 EHRR 471; judgment of 28 May 1985, Series A no 94   328, *359*
Accession of the Community to the European Convention for the Protection of Human Rights and Fundamental Freedoms, Re Opinion 2/94 [1996] ECR I–1759   *28, 39*
Accrington Beef Case C–241/95 [1996] ECR 6699   *105*
Adams v EC Commission Case 145/83 [1985] ECR 3539   *83*
Ahlström and Others v EC Council (Re Wool Pulp Cartel) Joined Cases 89, 104, 114, 116, 117 and 125–129/85 [1988] ECR 5193; [1988] 4 CMLR 901   *24*
Ahlström and Others v Commission (Re Wood Pulp Cartel) Joined Cases 89, 104, 114, 116, 117 and 125–129/85 [1993] 4 CMLR 407   *261, 268, 285*
Airey v Ireland (1979) Series A no 32   *328, 329*
Aktien-Zuckerfabrik Schoppenstedt v EC Council Case 5/71 [1971] ECR 975   *85*
AKZO Chemie BV v EC Commission Case 53/85 [1986] ECR 1965   *297*
AKZO Chemie BV v EC Commission Case C–62/82 [1991] ECR I–3359; [1993] 5 CMLR 197   *276*
Alpine Investments Case C–384/93 [1995] ECR I–1141   *257*
Amministrazione delle Finanze dello Stato v San Giorgio Case 199/82 [1983] ECR 3595   *70*
Amministrazione delle Finanze dello Stato v Simmenthal SpA Case 106/77 [1978] ECR 629; [1978] 3 CMLR 263   *69,* ***126****, 131, 132, 367*
Amylum (GR) and Tunnel Refineries Ltd v EC Council and EC Commission Cases 116 and 124/77 [1979] ECR 3497   *89*
Andoui and Cornuaille v Belgian State Joined Cases 115 and 116/81 [1982] ECR 1665   *215*
Apple and Pear Development Council v K J Lewis Ltd Case 222/82 [1984] 3 CMLR 733   *164*

Aragonesa de Publicidad Cases C–1 and 171/90 [1991] ECR I–4165   *174*
Arrowsmith v United Kingdom (1978) 19 DR 5   *316*
Asocarne Case C–10/95P [1995] ECR I–4149   *106*
Atlanta Fruchthandelsgesellschaft v BEF Case C–465/93 [1995] ECR I–3761   *108*
Automec (II) v EC Commission Case T–24/90 [1992] 5 CMLR 431   *262*
Awoyemi (Ibiyinka), judgment of 29 October 1998 (nyr)   *203*

B v France, judgment of 25 March 1992, Series A no 232–C   *355*
Bachmann (Hans-Martin) v Belgian State Case C–204/90 [1992] ECR I–249   *248*
Barber v Guardian Royal Exchange Case C–262/88 [1990] ECR I–889; [1990] 2 CMLR 513   *137, 234, 235*
Bauhuis v Netherlands Case 4/76 [1977] ECR 5   *160*
Baustahlgewebe GmbH v Commission of the European Communities Case C–185/95P, judgment of 17 December 1998 (nyr)   *286*
Bayer AG v EC Commission Case T–12/90 [1991] ECR II–219; [1993] 4 CMLR 30   *80*
Bayerische Motorenwerke AG (BMW) and Netherland BV v Ronald Karel Deenik Case C–63/97 [1999] 1 CMLR 1099   *190*
Becker v Finanzamt Münster-Innenstadt Case 8/81 [1982] ECR 53; [1982] 1 CMLR 499   *130, 142, 144*
'Belgian Linguistic' Case, Series A no 6   *340*
Berrehab v The Netherlands (1988) 11 EHRR 322; judgment of 21 June 1988, Series A no 138   *209*
Bethell (Lord) v EC Commission Case 246/81 [1982] ECR 2277; [1982] 3 CMLR 300   *82*
Bickel (Horst Otto) and Ulrich Franz Case C–274/96, judgment of 24 November 1998 (nyr)   *5*

Bilka-Kaufhaus GbmH v Karin Weber von Hartz Case 170/84 [1986] ECR 1607   *234*
Blackburn v Attorney-General [1971] CMLR 784   *27*
Blaizot et al v University of Liège Case 24/86 [1988] ECR 379   *137*
Bluhme (D) (Brown Bees of Laesø) Case C–67/97, judgment of 3 December 1998 (nyr)   *173*
Bollman Case 40/69 [1970] ECR 69   *112*
Bonsignore v Oberstadtdirektor of the City of Cologne Case 67/74 [1975] ECR 297   *204*
Bordessa Cases C–358 and 416/93 [1995] ECR I–361   *204*
Bork (P) International A/S v Foreningen af Arbejdsledere i Danmark Case 101/87 [1989] IRLR 41   *123*
Borker Case 138/80 [1980] ECR 1975   *97*
Bosman Case C–141/93 [1995] ECR I–4921   *93*
Boyle (Margaret) and Others v Equal Opportunites Commission Case C–411/96 [1998] 3 CMLR 1133   *218*
Brasserie du Pêcheur SA v Germany C–46/93 [1996] 1 CMLR 889   *60, 67*
Brincat v Italy, judgment of 26 November 1992, Series A no 249–A   *318*
Brinkmann Tabakfabriken GmbH v Skatteministeriet Case C–319/96 [1998] 3 CMLR 673   *65*
Bristol Cases C–427, 429 and 436/93 [1996] ECR I–3457   *196*
Brogan and Others v United Kingdom (1989) 11 EHRR 117   *314*
Brown (Mary) v Rentokil Ltd Case C–394/96 [1998] ECR I–4185; [1998] 2 CMLR 1049   *220*
Brüggemann and Scheuten v FRG No 6959/75 (1978) 10 DR 100   *308, 310*
Buckley v United Kingdom, judgment of 25 September 1996, Reports of Judgments and Decisions 1996–IV   *331*
Buscarini and Others v San Marino, judgment of 18 February 1999 (nyr)   *337*
Bussone v Ministry of Agriculture [1978] ECR 2429; [1979] 3 CMLR 18   *111*

Cable and Others v United Kingdom, judgment of 18 February 1999 (nyr)   *320*
Campbell v United Kingdom (1993) 15 EHRR 137   *327*
Cassis de Dijon Case see Rewe-Zentral AG v Bundesmonopolverwaltung für Branntwein
Centre d'insémination de la Crespelle Case C–387/93 [1994] ECR I–5077   *180*

Centros Ltd v Erhvervs-og Selskabsstyrelsen Case C–212/97, judgment of 9 March 1999 (nyr)   *242*
CILFIT v Minister of Health Case 283/81 [1982] ECR 3415; [1983] 1 CMLR 472   *97, 100*
Clemessy Case 280/82 [1986] ECR I–1907   *91*
CNL Sucal v Hag (Hag II) Case C–10/89 [1990] ECR I–3711   *199*
CNTA SA v EC Commission Case 74/74 [1975] ECR 533   *91*
Coditel SA v Ciné Vog Films Case 62/79 [1980] ECR 881   *197*
Codorniu SA v EC Council Case C–309/89 [1994] ECR I–1853; [1995] 2 CMLR 561   *72, 76*
Commercial Solvents Corporation v EC Commission Cases 6–7/73 [1974] ECR 223; [1974] 1 CMLR 309   *276, 279*
Commission of the European Communities (supported by the United Kingdom of Great Britain and Northern Ireland) v Kingdom of The Netherlands, Italian Republic and Kingdom of Spain Joined Cases C–157–160/94 [1997] ECR I–5699   *183*
Compassion in World Farming Case C–1/96 [1998] ECR I–1251   *175*
Conegate Ltd v HM Customs & Excise Case 121/85 [1986] ECR 1007; [1986] 1 CMLR 739   *175, 183*
Conforama Case C–312/89 [1993] 3 CMLR 746   *173*
Consten SA and Grundig-Verkaufs GmbH v EC Commission Cases 56 and 58/64 [1966] ECR 229; [1966] CMLR 418   *265*
Corbeau (Paul), Re Case C–320/91 [1993] ECR I–2533   *185*
Cossey v United Kingdom (1991) 13 EHRR 622   *354, 355, 356, 357*
Costa v ENEL Case 6/64 [1964] ECR 585; [1964] 3 CMLR 425   *69, 127, 129, 367*
Cowan v Trésor Public Case 186/87 [1989] ECR 195; [1990] 2 CMLR 613   *258, 260*
Coyne v United Kingdom, Reports of Judgmentsen and Decisions 1997–I   *319*
Criminal Proceedngs against Calfa Case C–348/96, judgment of 19 January 1999 (nyr)   *259*
Criminal Proceedings against X Joined Cases C–74 and 129/95 [1996] ECR I–6609   *155*
Crotty v An Taoiseach [1987] 2 CMLR 666   *26*

Da Costa v Netherlands Cases 28–30/62 [1963] CMLR 224   *99*

Danisco Sugar AB *v* **Almänna Ombudet** Case C–27/96 [1997] ECR I–6653 *115*
Dansk Denkavit *v* **Ministry of Agriculture** Case 29/87 [1988] ECR 2965; [1990] 1 CMLR 203 *177*
Dansk Supermarket Case 58/80 [1981] ECR 181 *137*
Data Delecta and Forsberg *v* MSL Dynamics Case C–43/95 [1996] ECR I–4661 *119, 120*
De Jong, Baljet and Van dem Brink *v* The Netherlands, judgment of 22 May 1984, Series A no 77 *317*
De Wilde, Ooms and Versyp, judgment of 18 June 1971, Series A no 12 *326, 341*
Defrenne (Gabrielle) *v* **Sabena (No 1)** Case 43/75 [1976] ECR 455; [1976] 2 CMLR 98 *136, 234, 235*
Dekker Case C–177/88 [1990] ECR I–3941 *222*
Demo-Studio Schmidt Case 210/81 [1983] ECR 3045 *264*
Denkavit Case C–283/94 [1996] ECR I–5063 *66*
Denkavit *v* France Case 132/78 [1979] 3 CMLR 605 *160*
Denkavit Italiana Case 61/79 [1980] ECR 1205 *137*
Denkavit Nederland Case 18/83 [1984] ECR 2171 *167*
Dietz, judgment of 24 October 1996 *235*
Dillenkofer (Erich) and Others *v* **Federal Republic of Germany** Joined Cases C–178, 179 and 189/94 [1996] ECR I–4845 *67*
Dirección General de Defensa de la Competencia *v* Associación Española de Banca Privado and Others Case C–67/91 [1992] ECR I–4785 *296, 298*
Dorsch Consult Ingenieurgesellschaft mbH *v* EC Council and EC Commission Case T–184/95 [1998] ECR II–667 *91*
Draempachl (Nils) *v* **Urania Immobilienservice OHP** Case C–180/95 [1997] ECR I–2195 *222*
Draft Treaty on a European Economic Area, Re the Opinion 1/91 [1992] 1 CMLR 245 *33*
Driessen en Zonen and Others *v* Minister von Verkeer en Waterstaat Cases C–13–16/92 [1993] ECR I–4751 *106*
Dudgeon *v* **United Kingdom** (1981) 4 EHRR 149; judgment of 22 October 1981, Series A no 45 *321, 330, 331*
Duinhof and Duijf *v* The Netherlands, judgment of 22 May 1984, Series A no 79 *319*

Eau de Cologne *v* Provide Case C–150/88 [1989] ECR 3891 *93*
European Commission *v* BASF and Others Cases T–79, 84–86, 91–92, 96 and 98/89 [1992] ECR II–315 *41*
EC Commission *v* BASF and Others Case C–137/92P [1994] ECR I–2555 *41*
EC Commission *v* Belgium Case 77/69 [1970] ECR 237 *56*
EC Commission *v* Belgium (Re State Employees) Case 149/79 [1980] ECR 3881 *207*
EC Commission *v* Belgium (No 2) Case 149/79 [1982] ECR 1845 *207*
EC Commission *v* **Belgium (Re Storage Charges)** Case 132/82 [1983] ECR 1649; [1983] 3 CMLR 600 *158*
EC Commission *v* Belgium Case 314/82 [1984] ECR 1543; [1985] 3 CMLR 134 *160*
EC Commission *v* **Belgium (Re Failure to Implement Directives)** Case C–225/86 [1988] ECR 579; [1989] 2 CMLR 797 *51*
EC Commission *v* Belgium Case C–133/94 [1996] ECR I–2323 *56*
EC Commission *v* **Belgium** Case C–263/96 [1997] ECR I–7453 *52*
EC Commission *v* Denmark Case 158/82 [1983] ECR 3573 *160*
EC Commission *v* **EC Council (Re the European Road Transport Agreement (ERTA))** Case 22/70 [1971] ECR 263; [1971] CMLR 335 *11, 18*
EC Commission *v* **EC Council (Re Generalised Tariff Preferences)** Case 45/86 [1987] ECR 1493 *33, 37*
EC Commission *v* EC Council Case C–155/91 [1993] ECR I–939 *33*
EC Commission *v* **EC Council** Case C–170/96 [1998] ECR I–2763 *9*
EC Commission *v* **Federal Republic of Germany** Case C–191/95, judgment of 29 September 1998 (nyr) *39*
EC Commission *v* France Case 270/83 [1986] ECR 273 *244*
EC Commission *v* France Case 307/84 [1986] ECR 1425 *245*
EC Commission *v* **French Republic** Case C–265/95 [1997] ECR I–6959 *161*
EC Commission *v* **French Republic** Case C–144/97 [1998] ECR I–613 *55*
EC Commission *v* Germany (Re German Beer Purity Law) Case 178/84 [1988] ECR 1227 *60*

Table of Cases

EC Commission *v* Germany (Re Restrictions on the Legal Profession) Case 427/85 [1988] ECR 1123; [1989] 2 CMLR 677   *253*

EC Commission *v* Germany (Re Animals Inspection Fees) Case 18/87 [1990] 1 CMLR 561   *159*

EC Commission *v* Germany Case C–131/93 [1994] ECR I–3303   *175*

EC Commission *v* Germany Case C–24/97 [1998] ECR I–2133   *9*

EC Commission *v* Greece Case 272/86 [1988] ECR 4875   *58*

EC Commission *v* Greece Case 68/88 [1989] ECR 2965   *224*

EC Commission *v* Greece Case C–347/88 [1990] ECR I–4747   *184*

EC Commission *v* Greece Case C–65/91 [1992] ECR I–5245   *58*

EC Commission *v* Greece (Re Electronic Cash Registers) Case C–137/91 [1992] 3 CMLR 117   *56*

EC Commission *v* Greece Cases C–109, 207 and 225/94 [1995] ECR I–1791   *54*

EC Commission *v* Hellenic Republic Case C–375/95 [1997] ECR I–5981   *186*

EC Commission *v* Ireland Case 249/81 [1982] ECR 4005; [1983] 2 CMLR 99   *164*

EC Commission *v* Italy Case 24/68 (Re Statistical Levy) [1969] ECR 193; [1971] CMLR 611   *159, 160*

EC Commission *v* Italy Case 39/72 [1973] ECR 101   *112*

EC Commission *v* Italy Case 168/85 [1986] ECR 2945; [1988] 1 CMLR 580   *61*

EC Commission *v* Italy Case 200/85 [1986] ECR 3953   *189*

EC Commission *v* Italy Case 225/85 [1986] ECR 2625   *207*

EC Commission *v* Italy Case 27/87 [1989] ECR 143   *68*

EC Commission *v* Italy Case C–120/88 [1991] ECR I–621   *61*

EC Commission *v* Italy Case C–33/90 [1991] ECR I–5987   *58*

EC Commission *v* Italy Case C–182/94 [1995] ECR I–1465   *53*

EC Commission *v* Luxembourg Case 58/81 [1982] ECR 2175   *56*

EC Commission *v* Luxembourg (Re Access to the Medical Profession) Case C–351/90 [1992] 3 CMLR 124   *245*

EC Commission *v* Luxembourg Case C–111/91 [1993] ECR I–817   *9*

EC Commission *v* Netherlands [1977] ECR 1355; [1978] 3 CMLR 630   *160*

EC Commission *v* Netherlands Case 96/81 [1982] ECR 1791   *52*

EC Commission *v* Spain Case C–119/89 [1989] ECR I–641 [1993] 1 CMLR 41   *61*

EC Commission *v* Spain Case C–375/92 [1994] ECR I–923   *58*

EC Commission *v* United Kingdom Case C–246/89 [1991] ECR I–4585   *60*

EC Commission *v* United Kingdom Case C–40/92 [1994] ECR I–989   *58*

EC Community *v* Volkswagen AG and Others European Commission Decision 98/273/EC of 28 January 1998 [1998] 5 CMLR 33   *298*

EC Council *v* European Parliament (Re The Community Budget) Case 34/86 [1986] ECR 2155; [1986] 3 CMLR 94   *46*

EEC Seed Crushers' and Oil Processors' Federation (FEDIOL) *v* EC Commission Case 191/82 [1983] ECR 2913   *77*

Emesa Sugar (Free Zone) NV *v* European Commission Cases C–363 and 364/48P(R) Order of the ECJ of 17 December 1998 (nyr)   *107*

EMI Electrola, Warner Brothers Inc *v* Christiansen Case 158/86 [1988] ECR 2605   *197*

Enderby Case C–123/92 [1993] ECR I–5535   *240*

Engel and Others *v* The Netherlands, judgment of 8 June 1976, Series A no 22   *317, 341*

Enka BV *v* Inspecteur der Invoerrechten en Accijnzen, Arnhem Case 38/77 [1977] ECR 2203   *149*

ENU Case C–107/91 [1993] ECR I–599   *83*

Eridania *v* EC Commission Cases 10 and 18/68 [1969] ECR 459   *74*

ERTA Case, The *see* EC Commission *v* EC Council

European Parliament *v* Council of the European Union Joined Cases C–164 and 165/97, judgment of 25 February 1999 (nyr)   *41*

European Parliament *v* EC Council (Re Common Transport Policy) Case 13/83 [1985] ECR 1513; [1985] 1 CMLR 138   *42*

European Parliament *v* EC Council (Re Comitology) Case 302/87 [1988] ECR 5615   *44, 46*

European Parliament *v* EC Council (Re Tchernobyl) Case C–70/88 [1990] ECR 2041; [1992] 1 CMLR 91   *42, 44*

European Parliament *v* EC Council Case C–65/90 [1992] ECR I–4593   *106*

European Parliament *v* EC Council (Cabotage II)
Case C–388/92 [1994] ECR I–2067 *106*
European Parliament *v* EC Council Case
C–360/96 [1996] ECR I–1195 *42*
European Parliament *v* EC Council Case C–42/97,
judgment of 23 February 1999 (nyr) *33*
Eurotunnel SA and Others *v* SeaFrance Case
C–408/95 [1997] ECR I–6315; [1998] 2
CMLR 293 ***103***

Findlay *v* United Kingdom (1997) 24 EHRR 221;
Reports of Judgments and Decisions 1997–V,
p276 *319, 320*
Firma Foto-Frost *v* Hauptzollamt Lübeck-Ost
Case 314/85 [1988] 3 CMLR 57 ***106***
Fisscher Case C–128/93 [1994] ECR I–4583
234
Foglia (Pasquale) *v* Mariella Novello (No 1)
Case 104/79 [1980] ECR 745; [1981] 1
CMLR 45 ***92, 93***
Foglia (Pasquale) *v* Mariella Novello (No 2) Case
244/80 [1981] ECR 3045 *93*
Foster and Others *v* British Gas plc Case
C–188/89 [1990] ECR I–33/3; [1990] 3
CMLR 833 ***141***
Fournier *v* France No 11406/85 (1988) 55 DR 130
371
France *v* European Parliament Cases 358/85 and
51/86 [1988] ECR 4821 *47*
France *v* European Parliament Case C–345/95
[1997] ECR I–5215 ***46***
France *v* United Kingdom (Re Fishing Mesh)
Case 141/78 [1979] ECR 2923; [1980] 1
CMLR 6 ***58***
Francovich *v* Italian Republic Joined Cases C–6
and 9/90 [1991] ECR I–5357; [1993] 2 CMLR
66 *61, 62, 63, 64, 65, 67,* ***68****, 156, 157*
Fratelli Costanzo *v* Comune di Milano Case
C–103/88 [1989] ECR 1839 *127, 149*
Freers and Speckmann Case C–278/93 [1996]
ECR I–1165 *241*
Futura Participation Case C–250/95 [1997] ECR
I–2471 *248*

GEMA *v* EC Commission Case 125/78 [1979]
ECR 3173 *264*
**Gencor Ltd *v* Commission of the European
Communities** Case T–102/96, judgment of 25
March 1999 (nyr) ***283***
German Communist Party Case *see* KPD *v* FRG
Germany *v* EC Commission Cases 52 and 55/65
[1966] ECR 159 *159*
Gibraltar Case C–298/89 [1993] ECR I–3605
106

Golder *v* United Kingdom (1975) 1 EHRR 524;
judgment of 21 February 1975, Series A no 18
325*, 341, 346*
Granaria Case 18/72 [1972] ECR 1172 *112*
**Grant (Lisa Jacqueline) *v* South West Trains
Ltd** Case C–249/96 [1998] ECR I–621;
[1998] 1 CMLR 993 ***227, 229***
Guerin Automobiles *v* EC Commission Case
C–282/95P [1997] 5 CMLR 447 *265*

H *v* Norway No 17004/90 (1992) (unrep) *310*
Haar Petroleum Case C–90/94 [1997] ECR
I–4085 *189*
Haegman Case 181/73 [1974] ECR 449 *110,
111*
**Handels-og Kontorfunktionaerernes Forbund *v*
Faellesforeninger for Danmarks
Brugsforeninger** Case C–66/96, judgment of
19 November 1998 (nyr) ***225***
Handels-og Kontorfunktionaerernes Forbund i
Danmark *v* Dansk Arbejdsgiverforening Case
C–179/88 [1990] ECR I–3979 *221*
Handyside *v* United Kingdom (1976) 1 EHRR
737; judgment of 7 December 1976, Series A
no 24 *322, 323,* ***340***
Harz *v* Deutsche Tradax GmbH Case 79/83
[1984] ECR 1921 ***151****, 152, 153*
Hauptzollampt Mainz *v* Kupferberg Case
104/81 [1982] ECR 3641; [1983] 1 CMLR 1
109
Hayes *v* Kronenberger Case 323/95 [1997] ECR
I–1711 *119, 120*
Hessische Knappschaft Case 44/65 [1965] ECR
1192 *4*
Hilti *v* EC Commission Case T–30/89 [1992] 4
CMLR 16 ***279***
HNL and Others *v* EC Council and EC
Commission Joined Cases 83 and 94/76, and
4, 15 and 40/77 [1978] ECR 1209 *63, 88*
Hoechst AG *v* EC Commission Cases 46/87 and
227/88 [1989] ECR 2859; [1991] 4 CMLR
430 ***290***
Hoever and Zachow Cases C–245 and 312/94
[1996] ECR I–4895 *9*
Huber *v* Switzerland, judgment of 23 October
1990, Series A no 188 *318*
Humblet *v* Belgium Case 6/60 [1960] ECR 1125
69, 125
Humblot *v* Directeur des Services Fiscaux Case
112/84 [1985] ECR 1367 *189*
Hunt *v* Clarke (1889) 58 LJQB 490 *345*

Iannelli & Volpi *v* Meroni Case 74/76 [1977] ECR
557; [1977] 2 CMLR 688 *63*

IFG v Freistaat Bayern Case 1/83 [1984] ECR 349; [1985] 1 CMLR 453 *160*
IHT Internationale Heiztechnik GmbH v Ideal Standard GmbH Case C–9/93 [1994] ECR I–2789 *199*
ILO Convention 170 on Chemicals at Work, Re, Opinion 2/91 [1993] 3 CMLR 800 *14*
Imperial Chemical Industries v Colmer (Inspector of Taxes) Case C–264/96 [1998] 3 CMLR 293 *246*
Imperial Chemical Industries Ltd v EC Commission (Dyestuffs) Case 48/69 [1972] ECR 619; [1972] CMLR 557 *267, 269*
Independent Television Publications Ltd v EC Commission Case T–76/89 [1991] 4 CMLR 745 *279*
Inter-Environmental Wallonie ASBL v Région Wallonne Case C–129/96 [1998] 1 CMLR 1057 *113*
International Chemical Corporation v Amministrazione delle Finanze Case 66/80 [1981] ECR 1191 *107*
Internationale Handelsgesellschaft GmbH v Einfuhr und Vorratsstelle für Getriede und Futtermittel (EVGF) Case 11/70 [1970] ECR 1125; [1970] CMLR 255 *129*
Irish Creamery Milk Supplier's Association v Ireland Joined Cases 36 and 71/80 [1981] ECR 147 *94*

Javico Case C–306/96 [1998] ECR I–28 April *202*
Johnston v Chief Constable of the Royal Ulster Constabulary Case 222/84 [1986] ECR 1651 *230, 235*
Johnston v Ireland (1986) 9 EHRR 203 *327*

Kalanke v Freie Hansestadt Bremen Case C–450/93 [1995] ECR I–3051 *229, 237*
Keck and Methouard, Criminal Proceedings against Cases C–267–268/91 [1993] ECR I–6097 *164, 173, 174, 175*
Kieffer (René) and Romain Thill Case C–114/96 [1997] ECR I–3629 *166*
Knudsen v Norway No 11045/84 (1985) 42 DR 247 *310*
Kokkinakis v Greece, judgment of 25 May 1993, Series A no 260–A *338*
Konig, judgment of 28 June 1987, Series A no 27 *346*
Koninklijke Scholten Honig NV v EC Council and EC Commission Case 43/77 [1979] ECR 3583 *89*

KPD v FRG No 250/57, 1 YB 222 (1957) *351*
KSH NV v EC Council and EC Commission Case 101/76 [1977] ECR 797 *74*
Kus v Landeshaupt Stadt Wiesbaden Case C–237/91 [1992] ECR I–6781 *209*

La Pyramide SARL Case C–378/93 [1994] ECR I–3999 *103*
Ladbroke Racing Ltd v EC Commission Case T–32/93 [1994] ECR II–1015 *83*
Larsson v Føtex Supermarked Case C–400/95 [1997] ECR I–2757 *221*
Laskey, Jaggard and Brown v United Kingdom, judgment of 19 February 1997 (nyr) *329*
Lawrie-Blum v Land Baden-Württemberg Case 66/85 [1986] EC 2121; [1987] 3 CMLR 767 *205*
Lestelle v EC Commission Case C–30/91P [1992] ECR I–3755 *296*
Letellier v France (1992) 14 EHRR 83; judgment of 26 June 1991, Series A no 27 *309*
Levez (BS) v T H Jennings (Harlow Pools) Ltd Case C–326/96, judgment of 1 December 1998 (nyr) *230*
Levin v Staatsecretaris van Justitie Case 53/81 [1982] ECR 1035 *206*
Ligur Carni Cases C–277, 318 and 319/91 [1993] ECR I–6621 *174*
Lindsay v United Kingdom No 8364/78 (1978) 15 DR 247 *366*
Lister v Forth Dry Dock and Engineering Co [1989] 2 WLR 634; [1989] 1 All ER 1134 *123*
Lithgow and Others v United Kingdom, judgment of 8 July 1986, Series A no 102 *328*
Loizidou v Turkey, judgment of 23 March 1995, Series A no 310 *367*
Luisi and Carbone v Ministero del Tesoro Cases 286/82 and 26/83 [1984] ECR 377 *258*
Lütticke (Alfons) v Hauptzollampt Saarlouis Case 57/65 [1966] ECR 205 *137, 179*
Luxembourg v European Parliament Case 230/81 [1983] ECR 255; [1983] CMLR 726 *47*
Luxembourg v European Parliament Case 108/83 [1984] ECR 1945 *47*
Luxembourg v European Parliament Cases 213/88 and C–39/89 [1991] ECR I–5643 *47*
McCann and Others v United Kingdom (1995) 21 EHRR 97; judgment of 27 September 1995, Series A no 324 *304*

Magorrian (Mary Teresa) and Irene Patricia Cunningham *v* **Eastern Health and Social Services Board and Depart of Health and Social Services** Case C–246/96 [1997] ECR I–7153 *233*
Mannington Mills Inc *v* Congoleum Corp 595 2d 1287 (3d Cir 1979) *285*
Matthews *v* **United Kingdom,** judgment of 18 February 1999 (nyr) *364*
Marchandise Case C–332/89 [1993] 3 CMLR 746 *173*
Marckx *v* **Belgium** (1979) 2 EHRR 330 *327, 333*
Marimex *v* Ministero delle Finanze Case 84/71 [1972] ECR 89 *130*
Marleasing SA *v* **La Comercial Internacional de Alimentacion SA** Case C–106/89 [1990] ECR 4135; [1992] 1 CMLR 305 *150, 151, 154, 157*
Marschall (Hellmutt) *v* **Land Nordrhein-Westfalen** Case C–409/95 [1997] ECR I–6363; [1998] 1 CMLR 547 *236*
Marshall *v* **Southampton and South-West Hampshire Area Health Authority (No 1)** Case 152/84 [1986] ECR 723; [1986] 1 CMLR 688 *95, 142, 143*
Mathieu-Mohin and Clerfayt *v* Belgium, judgment of 2 March 1987, Series A no 113 *367, 370, 371*
Mattheus (Lothar) *v* **Doego Fruchtimport und Tiefkühlkost** Case 93/78 [1978] ECR 2203 *3*
Matznetter, judgment of 10 November 1969, Series A no 10 *342*
Mehuy and Schott Case C–51/93 [1994] ECR I–3879 *167*
Métropole Télévision Cases T–528, 542, 543 and 546/93 [1996] ECR II–649 *78*
Michelletti Case C–369/90 [1992] ECR I–4239 *119*
Ministero delle Finanze *v* **IN.CO.GE '90 SRL and Others** Joined Cases C–10–22/97, judgment of 22 October 1998 (nyr) *130*
Modinos *v* Cyprus A 259 (1993) Com Rep *324, 332*
Molitaria Immolese Case 30/67 [1968] ECR 172 *74*
Molyneaux, ex parte [1986] 1 WLR 331 *27*
Monin Automobiles Case C–428/93 [1994] ECR I–1707 *103*
Morson and Jhanjan (Re Surinam Mothers) Cases 35 and 36/82 [1982] ECR 3723 *209*

Mulder *v* Ministry of Agriculture and Fisheries Case 120/86 [1988] ECR 2321; [1989] 2 CMLR 1 *87, 88*
Mulder and Others *v* **EC Council and EC Commission** Joined Cases C–104/89 and C–37/90 [1992] ECR I–3061 *87*
Musik-Vertrieb *v* GEMA Case 78/70 [1971] ECR 147 *197*
Mutsch Case 137/84 [1985] ECR 2681 *6*

National Panasonic (UK) Ltd *v* EC Commission Case 136/79 [1980] ECR 2033; [1980] 3 CMLR 169 *292*
Nederlandse Ondernemingen Case 51/76 [1977] ECR 113 *146, 149*
Nederlandse Spoowegen Case 38/75 [1975] ECR 1439 *130*
Neumeister, judgment of 27 June 1968, Series A no 8 *342*
Niemietz *v* Germany A 251–B (1992) *327*
Nilsson (Gunnar), per Olov Hagelgren, Solweig Arrborn Case C–162/97, judgment of 19 November 1998 (nyr) *179*
Nold and Others *v* **EC Commission** Case 4/73 [1974] ECR 491; [1974] 2 CMLR 338 *116*
Norddeutsches Vieh-und Fleischkontor Case 3/70 [1971] ECR 49 *112*
Norris *v* Ireland (1988) 13 EHRR 186 *324, 331–332*

Odigitria Case T–572/93 [1995] ECR II–2025 *89*
Officier van Justitie *v* **Kolpinghuis Nijmegen BV** Case 80/86 [1989] 2 CMLR 18 *154*
Officier van Justitie *v* Kortmann Case 32/80 [1981] ECR 251 *179*
Ogur *v* **Turkey,** judgment of 20 May 1999 (nyr) *303*
Olssen *v* Sweden (No 1), judgment of 24 March 1988, Series A no 130 *331*
Opel Austria Case T–115/94 [1997] ECR II–39 *116*
Open Door Counselling and Dublin Well Woman Centre *v* Ireland (1993) 15 EHRR 244 *309*
Ordre Des Avocats *v* Klopp [1984] ECR 2971 *255*
Orkem *v* EC Commission Case 374/87 [1989] ECR 3238 *297*
Oscar Bronner GmbH & Co KG *v* **Mediaprint Zeitungs-und Eitschriftenverlag GmbH & Co KG** Case C–7/97, judgment of 26 November 1998 (nyr) *278*

P v S and Cornwall County Council Case C–13/94 [1996] ECR I–2143   *228, 229*
Parfums Christian Dior SA and Parfums Christian Dior BV Case C–337/95 [1997] ECR I–6013; [1998] 1 CMLR 234   *192*
Partie Ecologiste 'Les Verts' v European Parliament Case 294/83 [1986] ECR 1339   *46, 107*
Pastätter Case C–217/89 [1990] ECR I–4585   *88*
Paton v United Kingdom (1980) 3 EHRR 408   *307*
Pesqueria Vasco-Montanesa Ord Cases T–452 and 453/93R [1994] ECR II–229   *82*
Pickstone v Freemans plc [1988] 2 All ER 803   *124*
Plaumann v EC Commission Case 25/62 [1964] ECR 95; [1964] CMLR 29   *73, 76*
Politi v Italian Ministry of Finance Case 43/71 [1971] ECR 1039   *130*
Ponente Carni v Amministrazione delle Finanze dello Stato Cases C–71 and 178/91 [1993] ECR I–1915   *131*
Practice Direction (Supreme Court: References to the Court of Justice of the European Communities) (1999) The Times 19 January   *100*
Pranti (Karl), Criminal Proceedings against Case 16/83 [1984] ECR 1299   *175*
Pretore di Salo v Persons Unknown Case 14/86 [1987] ECR 2545; [1989] 1 CMLR 71   *93, 155*
Procureur du Roi v Dassonville Case 8/74 [1974] ECR 837; [1974] 2 CMLR 436   *165, 168, 169, 172*
Procureur du Roi v Jean Noël Royer Case 48/75 [1976] ECR 497   *9*
Pubblico Ministero v Manghera Case 59/75 [1976] ECR 91   *184*
Pubblico Ministero v Ratti Case 148/78 [1979] ECR 1629; [1980] 1 CMLR 96   *114*, **146**, *149*
Punto Casa SpA v Sindaco del Commune di Capena Joined Cases C–69 and 258/93 [1994] ECR I–2355   *173*

R v Bouchereau Case 30/77 [1977] ECR 1999   *205, 260*
R v Henn and Darby Case 34/79 [1979] ECR 3795; [1980] CMLR 246   *176*, **181**
R v HM Treasury, ex parte British Telecommunications plc Case C–292/93 [1996] ECR I–1631   *66, 67, 68*

R v Immigration Appeal Tribunal, ex parte Antonissen Case C–292/89 [1991] 2 CMLR 373   *217*
R v Immigration Appeal Tribunal and Surinder Singh, ex parte Secretary of State for the Home Department Case C–370/90 [1992] 3 CMLR 335   *207*
R v Ministry of Agriculture, Fisheries and Food, ex parte Hedley Lomas (Ireland) Limited Case C–5/94 [1996] ECR I–2553; [1996] 2 CMLR 391   *66, 67*
R v Royal Pharmaceutical Society for Great Britain Cases 266 and 267/87 [1989] 2 CMLR 751   *169*
R v Secretary of State for Employment, ex parte Seymour-Smith and Perez Case C–167/97, judgment of 9 February 1999 (nyr)   *237*
R v Secretary of State for Foreign and Commonwealth Affairs, ex parte Rees-Mogg [1993] 3 CMLR 101; [1994] 1 All ER 457   *25*
R v Secretary of State for the Home Department, ex parte Mann Singh Shingara; R v Secretary of State for the Home Department, ex parte Abbas Radiom Joined Cases C–65 and 111/95, judgment of 17 June 1997 (nyr)   *210*
R v Secretary of State for Transport, ex parte Factortame [1990] 2 AC 85   *132*
R v Secretary of State for Transport, ex parte Factortame Case 213/89 [1990] 3 CMLR 867; ECR I–2433   *69, 134*
R v Secretary of State for Transport, ex parte Factortame (No 2) Case 213/89 [1991] 1 AC 603   *135*
R v Secretary of State for Transport, ex parte Factortame (No 4) Case C–46/93 [1996] 1 CMLR 889   *60, 67*
Rasmussen, Series A no 87   *360*
Rayner (J H) v Department of Trade [1990] 2 AC 418   *27*
Rees v United Kingdom (1987) 9 EHRR 56   *354, 355, 356, 357*
Rewe v Landwirtschaftskammer Saarland Case 33/76 [1976] ECR 1989   *70*
Rewe-Handelsgesellschaft Nord mbH v Hauptzollamt Kiel Case 158/80 [1981] ECR 1805   *38, 70, 130*
Rewe-Zentral AG v Bundesmonopolverwaltung für Branntwein Case 120/78 [1979] ECR 649; [1979] 3 CMLR 337   *165*, **170**, *244, 257*

Rewe-Zentralfinanz *v* Landwirtschaftskammer Westfalen-Lippe Case 39/73 [1973] ECR 1039   *159*
Reyners (Jean) *v* Belgian State Case 2/74 [1974] ECR 631; [1974] 2 CMLR 305   *63, 249*
Ringeisen, judgment of 16 July 1971, Series A no 13   *342*
Roe *v* Wade 410 US 113 (1973)   *309*
Royscot Leasing (and three other appellants) *v* Commissioners of Customs and Excise (1998) The Times 23 November   *102, 103*
Russo *v* AIMA Case 60/75 [1976] ECR 45   *70*
Rutili (Roland) *v* Minister of the Interior Case 36/75 [1975] ECR 1219; [1976] 1 CMLR 140   *149, 213*

SABEL BV *v* Puma AG, Rudolf Dassler Sport Case C–151/95 [1998] 1 CMLR 445   *197*
Sala (Maria Martinez) *v* Freistaat Bayern Case C–85/96 [1998] ECR I–2691   *6*
Saldanha (Stephen Austin) and MTS Securities Corporation *v* Hiross Holding AG Case C–122/96 [1997] ECR I–5325   *118*
Salumi Cases 66, 127 and 128/79 [1980] ECR 1258   *137*
Salumificio di Cornuda *v* Amministrazione delle Finanze dello Stato Case 130/78 [1979] ECR 867   *130*
Samenwerkende Elektriciteits Produktiebedrijven (SEP) NV *v* Commission of the European Communities Case C–36/92P [1994] ECR I–1911   *294*
San Michele and ors *v* EC Commission [1962] ECR 449   *292*
Sanz de Lera Case C–163/94 [1995] ECR I–4821   *204*
Sarrio *v* EC Commission Case T–334/94 [1998] ECR II–1727; [1998] 5 CMLR 195   *268*
Schiesser *v* Switzerland, judgment of 4 December 1979, Series A no 34   *319*
Schöenberger and Durmaz *v* Switzerland 11 EHRR 202   *327*
Schonenberg Case 88/77 [1978] ECR 473   *127*
Schröder (Aloys) and Others *v* Commission of the European Communities Case C–22/97, judgment of 10 December 1998 (nyr)   *90*
Schroeder Case 40/72 [1973] ECR 125   *111*
Schumacker Case C–279/93 [1995] ECR I–225   *248*
Segers *v* Bestuur van de Bedrifsvereniging voor bank-en verzekeringswezen Case C–79/85 [1986] ECR 2375   *244*
Sequela *v* Administration des Impôts Case 76/87 [1988] ECR 2397   *189*

SGEEM and Etroy *v* European Investment Bank Case C–370/89 [1993] ECR I–2583   *85*
Sheffield and Horsham *v* United Kingdom (1998) 27 EHRR 163   *353*
Silhouette International Schmied GmbH & Co Kg *v* Hartlauer Handelsgesellschaft mbH Case C–355/96 [1998] ECR I–4799   *200*
Simet Cases 25 and 26/65 [1967] ECR 40   *82*
Skanavi Case C–193/94, judgment of 29 February 1996   *204*
Socialist Party and Others *v* Turkey, judgment of 25 May 1998 (nyr)   *348*
Société Bautiaa Cases C–197 and 252/94 [1996] ECR I–505   *137*
Société d'Importation E Leclerc-SIMPLEC *v* TFI Publicité SA and M6 Publicité SA Case C–412/93 [1995] ECR I–179   *93*
Soering *v* United Kingdom (1989) 11 EHRR 439   *311*
Spagl *v* Hauptzollamt Rosenheim Case C–189/89 [1990] ECR I–4585   *88*
SPI and SAMI Cases 267–269/81 [1983] ECR 801   *130*
Spijker Kwasten BV *v* EC Commission Case 231/82 [1983] ECR 259   *74*
State, The *v* Jean Noel Royer Case 48/75 [1976] ECR 497; [1976] 2 CMLR 619   *215*
Stichting Greenpeace Council *v* EC Commission Case C–321/95 [1998] ECR I–1651   *73, 75*
Stögmüller, judgment of 10 November 1969, Series A no 9   *342*
Stoke-on-Trent City Council *v* B & Q plc Case C–169/91 [1993] 1 CMLR 426; [1993] 1 All ER 481   *172*
Suiker Unie *v* Commission Cases 40–48, 50, 54–56, 111, 113–114/73 [1975] ECR 1663; [1976] 1 CMLR 295   *261, 268*
Sunday Times *v* United Kingdom, judgment of 26 April 1979, Series A no 30   *322, 323, 324*
Sunday Times *v* United Kingdom (1980) 3 EHRR 317   *343*
Svenska Journalistforbunder *v* Council of the European Union Case T–174/95 [1998] 3 CMLR 645   *48*

Télémarketing Case 311/84   *279*
Terres Rouges Consultant SA *v* EC Commission, supported by the Council, Spain and France Case T–47/95 [1997] ECR II–481   *73*
Tête *v* France No 11123/84 (1987) 54 DR 52   *366, 367, 368, 370*
Tetra Pak International SA *v* EC Commission (No 2) Case C–333/94P [1997] 4 CMLR 662   *277*

Tezi Textiel v EC Commission Case 59/84 [1986] ECR 887   *81*
Thieffry (Jean) v Conseil de l'Ordre des Avocats à la Cour de Paris Case 71/76 [1977] ECR 765; [1977] 2 CMLR 373   *250*
Timex Corporation v EC Council and EC Commission Case 264/82 [1985] ECR 849   *76*
Toepfer (Alfred) and Getreideimport Gesellschaft v EC Commission Joined Cases 106 and 107/63 [1965] ECR 525; [1966] CMLR 111   *78*
TWD Textilewerke Deggendorf GmbH v Germany Case C–188/92 [1994] ECR I–833   *104, 105*
Tymen (Regina and Robert) Case 269/80 [1981] ECR 3079   *127*
Tyrer v United Kingdom (1978) 2 EHRR 1; judgment of 25 April 1978, Series A no 26   *369*

Union Deutsche Lebens-mittelwerke Case 97/85 [1987] ECR 2265   *74*
Union Nazionale Importatori e Commercianti Motoviecoli Esteri (UNICME) and Others v EC Commission Case 123/77 [1978] ECR 845   *79*
United Communist Party of Turkey and Others, Reports of Judgments and Decisions 1998–I, p17   *349, 350, 351, 365, 366, 367*
United Kingdom v EC Council (Re Hormones) Case 68/86 [1988] 2 CMLR 453   *31*
United Kingdom v EC Council (Re Working Time Directive) Case C–84/94 [1996] ECR I–5758   *120*
United States v Nippon Paper Indust Co 109 F3d (1sr Cir 1997)   *286*
Uruguay Round Agreements, Re Opinion 1/94 [1994] ECR I–5267; [1995] 1 CMLR 205   *16*

Valsabbia Case 209/83 [1984] ECR 3089   *82*
Van Binsbergen v Bestuur van de Bedrijfvereniging Voor de Metaalnijverheid Case 33/74 [1974] ECR 1299; [1975] 1 CMLR 298   *255*
Van Duyn v Home Office Case 41/74 [1974] ECR 1337; [1975] CMLR 1   ***147**, 215*

Van Gend en Loos v Nederlandse Administratie der Belastingen Case 26/62 [1963] ECR 1; [1963] CMLR 105   *69, 138, **139***
Vassen-Göbbels Case 61/65 [1966] ECR 377   *97*
Victoria Film A/S Case C–134/97 [1999] 1 CMLR 279   *96*
Vine Products Ltd v Green [1966] Ch 484   *344*
Vogt v Germany, judgment of 26 September 1995, Series A no 323   *351*
Völk v Etablissements Vervaecke SPRL Case 5/69 [1969] ECR 295   *274*
Von Colson and Kamann v Land Nordrhein-Westfalen Case 14/83 [1984] ECR 1891; [1986] 2 CMLR 430   *124, 143, 150, **151**, 152, 153, 155, 224*
Von Deetzen Case 170/86 [1988] ECR 2355   *88*
Vroege Case C–57/93 [1994] ECR I–4541   *234*

Wachauf Case 5/88 [1989] ECR 2609   *130*
Wagner Miret v Fondo de Garantia Salarial Case C–334/92 [1995] 2 CMLR 49   ***156***
Webb v EMO Air Cargo (UK) Ltd [1992] 4 All ER 929   *154*
Webb v EMO Air Cargo (UK) Ltd (No 2) [1995] 4 All ER 577   *153*
Weber Case T–482/93 [1996] ECR II–609   *73*
Wemhoff, judgment of 27 June 1968, Series A no 7   *342*
Wood Pulp Cartel Cases see Ahlström and Others v EC Council

X v Austria No 70451/75 (1976) 7 DR 87   *310*
X v Norway No 867/60 (1961) 6 CD 34   *310*
X, Y and Z v United Kingdom, judgment of 22 April 1997, Reports of Judgments and Decisions 1997–II   *355, 357*

Young, James and Webster v United Kingdom (1981) 4 EHRR 38; judgment of 13 August 1981, Series A no 44   *321, 323*
Yves Saint-Laurent et Givenchy Cases T–19 and 88/92 [1996] ECR II–1851, 1931 and 1961   *197*

Zuckerfabrik Südderdithmarschen v Haupzollamt Itzehoe Cases C–143/88 and C–92/89 [1991] ECR I–415   *108*

LAW OF THE EUROPEAN UNION

1 The Evolution and the Constitution of the European Union

Admission to the European Union

Lothar Mattheus v *Doego Fruchtimport und Tiefkühlkost* Case 93/78 [1978] ECR 2203 European Court of Justice

- *Application for membership of the Community – conditions of admission – art 237 EC Treaty – agreement between private parties tending to compel the ECJ to give a preliminary ruling (art 177 EC Treaty)*

Facts

The parties entered into a contract on 1 August 1977. According to their agreement the plaintiff would set up market survey systems in Spain and Portugal, to be operational by the date of the decision concerning the accession of those States to the European Community (formerly EEC). In consideration the defendant was to pay a half-yearly lump sum to cover the plaintiff's expenses. The contract contained the following clause:

> 'This agreement is definitively concluded for a period of five years. If the said accession should in fact or in law prove to be impracticable, the Principal [Duego] shall have the right to terminate this agreement. The decisive factor in determining whether the said accession is practicable in law shall be a decision of the ECJ. In the event of a justifiable termination the Agent shall lose his right to repayment of expenses.
>
> ...The courts in Essen shall have jurisdiction in matters arising out of this agreement'

On 29 January 1978 Mattheus wrote to the defendants requesting reimbursement of DM 527.85 expenses, the defendants terminated the contract under the above clause and were sued in the local court, Amtsgericht Essen, which made a reference to the ECJ for a preliminary ruling under art 177 asking three questions:

1. whether art 237 EC, standing alone or in conjunction with other articles of the EC Treaty, is to be interpreted as meaning that it imposes substantive legal limits on the accession of third countries over and above the formal conditions laid down in art 237 EC;
2. what are those limits; and
3. is the accession of Spain, Portugal and Greece for reasons of Community law not possible in the future.

Held

The ECJ has no jurisdiction to give a ruling on the questions referred to it by the national court.

Judgment

> 'In the words of the first paragraph of art 177 of the Treaty: "The Court of Justice shall have jurisdiction to give preliminary rulings concerning ... (a) the interpretation of the Treaty ...".
>
> According to the second paragraph of that article: "Where such a question is raised before any court or tribunal of a Member State, that court or tribunal may, if it considers that a decision on the question is necessary to enable it to give judgment, request the Court of Justice to give a ruling thereon."

The division of powers thus effected is mandatory; it cannot be altered, nor can the exercise of those powers be impeded, in particular by agreements between private persons tending to compel the courts of the Member States to request a preliminary ruling by depriving them of the independent exercise of the discretion which they are given by the second paragraph of art 177.

... As provided for in the first paragraph of art 237 of the EC Treaty: "Any European State may apply to become a member of the Community. It shall address its application to the Council, which shall act unanimously after obtaining the opinion of the Commission."

The second paragraph of the article reads: "The conditions of admission and the adjustments to this Treaty necessitated thereby shall be the subject of an agreement between the Member States and the applicant State. This agreement shall be submitted for ratification by all the Contracting States in accordance with their respective constitutional requirements."

These provisions lay down a precise procedure encompassed within well-defined limits for the admission of a new Member State, during which the conditions of accession are to be drawn up by the authorities indicated in the article itself.

Thus the legal conditions for such accession remain to be defined in the context of that procedure without its being possible to determine the content judicially in advance.

Therefore the Court of Justice cannot in proceedings pursuant to art 177 give a ruling on the form or subject-matter of the conditions which might be adopted.'

Comment

Article 177 EC specifies that only courts and tribunals may ask for preliminary rulings. This formula excludes the parties to a dispute referring directly to the ECJ and rules out any possibility in contracts for disputes on a point of Community law to be referred to the ECJ and thus impose upon the ECJ jurisdiction under art 177 EC (*Hessische Knappschaft* Case 44/65 [1965] ECR 1192).

Article 237 lays down a precise procedure encompassed within well defined limits for the admission of new Member States, during which the conditions for accession are drawn up by the authorities indicated in the article itself. Thus the legal conditions for such accession remain to be defined in the context of that procedure without it being possible to determine the content judicially in advance. The ECJ cannot give a ruling on the form or subject-matter of the conditions that may be applied. Therefore any decision on the merits of a State's admission remains within the discretion of the Council and escapes the jurisdiction of the ECJ. The latter is limited to reviewing whether the legal conditions and procedural requirements for admission were fulfilled by the Community institutions.

The Treaty on European Union modified the procedure of admission. Article O of the TEU stipulates that:

'Any European State may apply to become a Member of the Union. It shall address its application to the Council, which shall act unanimously after consulting the Commission and after receiving the assent of the European Parliament, which shall act by an absolute majority of its component members.

The conditions of admission and the adjustments to the Treaties on which the Union is founded which such admission entails shall be the subject of an agreement between the Member States and the applicant State. The agreement shall be submitted for ratification by all the Contracting States in accordance with their respective constitutional requirements.'

Under art O of TEU a candidate State accedes to the European Union which implies adhesion to all three Communities and not to each Community separately as provided in the founding Treaties: arts 98 ECSC, 237 EC and 205 Euroatom.

Citizenship of the European Union

Horst Otto Bickel, Ulrich Franz
Case C–274/96 Judgment of 24 November 1998 (not yet reported)
European Court of Justice

* *Citizenship of the European Union – free movement of persons – non-discrimination on the ground of nationality – language rules applicable to criminal proceedings*

Facts
Italian authorities commenced criminal proceedings against Mr Bickel, an Austrian national, who drove his lorry at Castelbello in the Trentino-Aldo Adige region of Italy under the influence of alcohol and Mr Franz, a German national, who, while visiting the same region of Italy, was found by a customs inspection in possession of a type of knife that is prohibited in Italy. Both offenders made a declaration before the District Magistrate of Bolzano that they had no knowledge of Italian and requested that the proceedings were conducted in German on the basis that the German-speaking citizens of the province of Bolzano were permitted to use German in relations with the judicial and administrative authorities located in that province or entrusted with responsibility at regional level. The referring court asked the ECJ whether the situation of both offenders was within the scope of EC Treaty and, if so, whether the right conferred on the German-speaking minority living in the province of Bolzano should be extended to nationals from other German-speaking Member States travelling or staying in that area.

Held
The ECJ held that the right conferred by national rules upon its linguistic minority was within the scope of the EC Treaty. It stated that the principle of non-discrimination embodied in art 6 EC Treaty precludes national rules which, in respect of a particular language (other than the principal language of the Member State concerned), confer on citizens whose language is that particular language and who are resident in a defined area the right to require that criminal proceedings be conducted in that language, without conferring the same right on nationals of other Member States travelling or staying in that area, whose language is the same.

Judgment
'Situations governed by Community law include those covered by the freedom to provide services, the right to which is laid down in art 59 of the Treaty. The Court has consistently held that this right includes the freedom for the recipients of services to go to another Member State in order to receive a service there. Article 59 therefore covers all nationals of Member States who, independently of other freedoms guaranteed by the Treaty, visit another Member State where they intend or are likely to receive services. Such persons (and they include both Mr Bickel and Mr Franz) are free to visit and move around within the host State.

In that regard, the exercise of the right to move and reside freely in another Member State is enhanced if the citizens of the Union are able to use a given language to communicate with the administrative and judicial authorities of a State on the same footing as its nationals. Consequently, persons such as Mr Bickel and Mr Franz, in exercising that right in another Member State, are in principle entitled, pursuant to art 6 of the Treaty, to treatment no less favourable than that accorded to nationals of the host State so far as concerns the use of languages which are spoken there.

In the submission of Mr Bickel and Mr Franz, if any discrimination contrary to art 6 of the Treaty is to be avoided, the right to have proceedings conducted in German must be extended to all citizens of the Union, since it is already available to nationals of one of the Member States.

The documents before the Court show

that the German-speaking nationals of other Member States, particularly Germany and Austria (such as Mr Bickel and Mr Franz) who travel or stay in the province of Bolzano cannot require criminal proceedings to be conducted in German despite the fact that the national rules provide that the German language is to have the same status as Italian.

In those circumstances, it appears that German-speaking nationals of other Member States travelling or staying in the province of Bolzano are at a disadvantage by comparison with Italian nationals resident there whose language is German ...

... The Italian government's contention that the aim of those rules is to protect the ethno-cultural minority residing in the province in question does not constitute a valid justification in this context. Of course, the protection of such a minority may constitute a legitimate aim. It does not appear, however, from the documents before the Court that that aim would be undermined if the rules in issue were extended to cover German-speaking nationals of other Member States exercising their right to freedom of movement.'

Comment

The ECJ confirmed that although the rules of criminal law and criminal procedure are within the competence of a Member State, that competence cannot be exercised contrary to fundamental principles of Community law – in particular the principle of equality of treatment as stated in art 6 EC Treaty. The ECJ based its reasoning on art 8 EC Treaty rather than on the principle of non-discrimination on the ground of nationality as the Court wished to emphasise the equality of treatment among the citizens of the EU. From this perspective, the reference to the citizenship of the EU permitted the ECJ to compare German-speaking nationals of the province of Bolzano with German-speaking nationals from other Member States. The ECJ considered that the latter when travelling or staying in that province were disadvantaged in comparison to the former. Therefore, the requirement of residence in the province of Bolzano as a condition for benefiting from a special linguistic regime was neither justified on the ground of objective criteria not related to nationality nor proportional to the aim of Italian rules intended to protect the ethno-cultural German-speaking minority residing in the province of Bolzano. The decision of the ECJ in the present case confirms that the Court pays special attention to the protection of rights and facilities of individuals in linguistic matters (see *Mutsch* Case 137/84 [1985] ECR 2681).

Maria Martinez Sala v *Freistaat Bayern* Case C–85/96 [1998] ECR I–2691 European Court of Justice

• *Citizenship of the European Union – principle of non-discrimination on the ground of nationality – free movement of persons – definition of 'worker' – art 4 of Regulation 1408/71 – child-raising allowance – definition of family benefit – art 7(2) of Regulation 1612/68 – definition of social advantage – requirement of possession of a residence permit or authorisation*

Facts

The German authorities of the Freistaat Bayern (State of Bavaria) refused to grant a child-raising allowance for a child of Mrs Martinez Sala, a Spanish national who had resided in Germany for many years. The basis of residence was: first, a residence permit (until May 1984); second, documents specifying that she had applied for an extension of her residence permit; third, a residence permit issued on 19 April 1994 and expiring on 18 April 1995; and fourth, a one-year extension (to 18 April 1996) of the residence permit which expired on 18 April 1995. Mrs Martinez Sala was born in 1956 and came to Germany in 1968. Between 1976 and 1986 she had various jobs and was in employment again from 12 September to 24 October 1989. After that she received social assistance from the German authorities. When she applied for child-raising allowance in January 1993 she did not have a residence permit. Her application was refused on the grounds that she was neither a German national nor in possession of a residence entitlement/residence permit. She challenged that decision before a German court which referred to the ECJ for a preliminary ruling on four questions, concerning:

1. whether a national of one Member State who resides in another Member State, where he is employed and receives social assistance has the status of worker;
2. whether a child-raising allowance is considered as a family benefit within the meaning of art 4(1)(h) of Regulation 1408/71; or
3. as a social advantage within the scope of art 7(2) of Regulation 1612/68;
4. whether it is necessary for a national of other Member States to produce a formal residence permit in order to receive a child-raising benefit in a host Member State.

Held
The ECJ held that Community law precludes a Member State from requiring nationals of other Member States authorised to reside in its territory to produce a formal residence permit in order to receive a child-raising allowance, whereas that Member State's own nationals are only required to be permanently or ordinarily resident in that Member State. The ECJ also stated that a benefit such as the child-raising allowance is considered as a family benefit within the meaning of art 4(1) of Regulation 1408/71, and as a social advantage within the meaning of art 7(2) of Regulation 1612/68. The ECJ left to a national court the decision as to whether a person such as the appellant should be considered as a worker within the meaning of art 48 EC Treaty.

Judgment
'[*The first question*]
In the present case the referring court has not furnished sufficient information to enable the Court to determine whether a person in the position of the appellant in the main proceedings is a worker within the meaning of art 48 of the Treaty and Regulation No 1612/68, by reason, for example, of the fact that she is seeking employment. It is for the national court to undertake that investigation.

[*The second and third questions*]
In its judgment of 10 October 1996 in *Hoever and Zachow* [1996] ECR I–4895 the Court has already held that a benefit such as the child-raising allowance provided for by the BErzGG [the Federal Law on the Grant of Child-raising Allowance and Parental Leave], which is automatically granted to persons fulfilling certain objective criteria, without any individual and discretionary assessment of personal needs, and which is intended to meet family expenses, must be treated as a family benefit within the meaning of art 4(1)(h) of Regulation No 1408/71.

The child-raising allowance in question here is an advantage granted, inter alia, to workers who work part-time. It is therefore a social advantage within the meaning of art 7(2) of Regulation No 1612/68.

[*The fourth question*]
Whilst Community law does not prevent a Member State from requiring nationals of other Member States lawfully resident in its territory to carry at all times a document certifying their right of residence, if an identical obligation is imposed upon its own nationals as regards their identity cards, the same is not necessarily the case where a Member State requires nationals of other Member States, in order to receive a child-raising allowance, to be in possession of a residence permit for the issue of which the administration is responsible.

For the purposes of recognition of the right of residence, a residence permit can only have declaratory and probative force. However, the case-file shows that, for the purposes of the grant of the benefit in question, possession of a residence permit is constitutive of the right to the benefit.

Consequently, for a Member State to

require a national of another Member State who wishes to receive a benefit such as the allowance in question to produce a document which is constitutive of the right to the benefit and which is issued by its own authorities, when its own nationals are not required to produce any document of that kind, amounts to unequal treatment.

In the sphere of application of the Treaty and in the absence of any justification, such unequal treatment constitutes discrimination prohibited by art 6 of the EC Treaty.

The German government, while accepting that the condition imposed by the BErzGG constituted unequal treatment within the meaning of art 6 of the Treaty, argued that the facts of the case being considered in the main proceedings did not fall within either the scope ratione materiae or the scope ratione personae of the Treaty so that the appellant in the main proceedings could not rely on art 6.

As regards the scope ratione materiae of the Treaty, reference should be made to the replies given to the first, second and third questions, according to which the child-raising allowance in question in the main proceedings indisputably falls within the scope ratione materiae of Community law.

As regards its scope ratione personae, if the referring court were to conclude that, in view of the criteria provided in reply to the first preliminary question, the appellant in the proceedings before it has the status of worker within the meaning of art 48 of the Treaty and of Regulation No 1612/68 or of employed person within the meaning of Regulation No 1408/71, the unequal treatment in question would be incompatible with arts 48 and 51 of the Treaty.

Should this not be the case, the Commission submits that, in any event, since 1 November 1993 when the Treaty on European Union came into force, the appellant in the main proceedings has a right of residence under art 8a of the EC Treaty, which provides that: "Every citizen of the Union shall have the right to move and reside freely within the territory of the Member States, subject to the limitations and conditions laid down in this Treaty and by the measures adopted to give it effect."

According to art 8(1) of the EC Treaty, every person holding the nationality of a Member State is to be a citizen of the Union.

As a national of a Member State lawfully residing in the territory of another Member State, the appellant in the main proceedings comes within the scope ratione personae of the provisions of the Treaty on European citizenship.

Article 8(2) of the Treaty attaches to the status of citizen of the Union the rights and duties laid down by the Treaty, including the right, laid down in art 6 of the Treaty, not to suffer discrimination on grounds of nationality within the scope of application ratione materiae of the Treaty.

It follows that a citizen of the European Union, such as the appellant in the main proceedings, lawfully resident in the territory of the host Member State, can rely on art 6 of the Treaty in all situations which fall within the scope ratione materiae of Community law, including the situation where that Member State delays or refuses to grant to that claimant a benefit that is provided to all persons lawfully resident in the territory of that State on the ground that the claimant is not in possession of a document which nationals of that same State are not required to have and the issue of which may be delayed or refused by the authorities of that State.'

Comment

In the present case the ECJ, for the first time, invoked the concept of citizenship of the European Union embodied in art 8 EC Treaty. It stated that a national of a Member State lawfully residing in the territory of another Member State may rely on art 8(2) EC Treaty in all situations within the scope of application ratione materiae of Community law. The ECJ made reference to art 8(2) EC Treaty in response to the argument submitted by the German authorities that Mrs Marinez Sala was not a worker within the meaning of art 48 EC Treaty and therefore outside the scope of application of art 6 EC Treaty. The ECJ replied that even if she was not a worker (and that is to be determined by the German court) she is a citizen of the European Union and as such is entitled to move and to reside freely within the territories of the Member States as well as not to be subject to discrimination based on nationality prohibited by art 6 EC Treaty. Two important implications of the present decisions of the ECJ are that, first, art 8(2) is directly effective and, second, the scope of application of the principle of non-discrimination on the grounds of nationality embodied in art 6 EC Treaty has been considerably extended via the application of art 8(2) EC Treaty.

In relation to other issues referred by the German court, the ECJ confirmed its prior solutions, that a child-raising allowance is in principle a family benefit (see *Hoever and Zachow* Cases C–245 and 312/94 [1996] ECR I–4895) within the meaning of art 4(1) of Regulation 1408/71, although this benefit is also a social advantage within the meaning of art 7(2) of Regulation 1612/68 as it is related to the contract of employment even on a part-time basis. Community law has already recognised the possibility of a double qualifications for certain benefits in *EC Commission* v *Luxembourg* Case C–111/91 [1993] ECR I–817.

The question of a residence permit was answered by the ECJ in conformity with its previous case law. A Member State may impose upon nationals from other Member States residing in its territory the requirement of carrying at all times a document certifying their right of residence if an identical obligation is imposed upon its own nationals (recently confirmed in *EC Commission* v *Germany* Case C–24/97 [1998] ECR I–2133). Such a document can only have declaratory and probative force (*Royer* Case 48/75 [1976] ECR 497).

Co-operation in justice and home affairs

EC Commission v *EC Council* Case C–170/96 [1998] ECR I–2763
European Court of Justice

- *Jurisdiction of the ECJ in the area of justice and home affairs – art K.3 of the TEU – art L of the TEU – art 100c EC Treaty – act of the Council – joint action regarding airport transit visas – legal basis*

Facts
The Commission supported by the European Parliament brought an action for annulment of the Joint Action of 4 March 1996 adopted by the Council on the basis of art K.3 of the Treaty on European Union on airport transit arrangements (OJ 1996 L63 p8). The French Republic, the Kingdom of Denmark and the United Kingdom intervened in support of the Council. The Commission argued that the Council should have acted on the basis of art 100c and not art K.3 of the TEU. In the context of art K.3 of the TEU the ECJ had to determine whether or not it had jurisdiction to adjudicate the question.

Held
The ECJ held that it had jurisdiction to review the content of the joint action in question. The ECJ dismissed the application submitted by the Commission.

Judgment
'[*Jurisdiction of the Court*]
It should first be noted that by its application the Commission seeks a declaration that, in light of its objective, the Act adopted by the Council falls within the scope of art 100c of the EC Treaty, so that it should have been based on that provision.

Next, art M of the Treaty on European Union makes it clear that a provision such as art K.3(2), which provides for the adoption of joint action by the Council in the areas referred to in art K.1 of the Treaty on European Union, does not affect the provisions of the EC Treaty.

In accordance with art L of the Treaty on European Union, the provisions of the EC Treaty concerning the powers of the Court of Justice and the exercise of those powers apply to art M of the Treaty on European Union.

It is therefore the task of the Court to ensure that acts which, according to the Council, fall within the scope of art K.3(2) of the Treaty on European Union do not encroach upon the powers conferred by the EC Treaty on the Community.

It follows that the Court has jurisdiction to review the content of the Act in the light of art 100c of the EC Treaty in order to ascertain whether the Act affects the powers of the Community under that provision and to annul the Act if it appears that it should have been based on art 100c of the EC Treaty.

[*Transit arrangements*]
The airport transit visa is concerned with the situation of a passenger arriving on a flight from a third country and remaining in the airport of the Member State in which the aircraft landed in order to take off in the same or another aircraft bound for another third country. The requirement of such a visa under art 1 of the Act therefore presupposes that the holder will remain in the international area of that airport and will not be authorised to move within the territory of that Member State.

That interpretation is borne out by art 3 of the Act, which provides that nationals of third countries are not required to have an airport transit visa when passing through the international areas of airports in Member States if they already hold an entry or transit visa.

It follows that an airport transit visa does not authorise its holder to cross the external borders of Member States in the sense contemplated by art 100c of the EC Treaty. Consequently, the Act does not fall within the ambit of that provision.'

Comment
Article L of the TEU excludes the jurisdiction of the ECJ in areas of Common Foreign and Security Policy (Pillar 2 of the TEU) and Co-operation in Justice and Home Affairs (Pillar 3 of the TEU). For that reason, the government of the UK argued that the ECJ had no jurisdiction to review a measure adopted on the basis of art K.3 TEU (Pillar 3 of the TEU). The ECJ decided otherwise. The Court upheld the arguments of the Commission. The Commission argued that because the contested measures should have been adopted on the basis of art 100c EC Treaty, which provision is within the jurisdiction of the Court, and because art M of the TEU stipulates that a provision such as art K.3(2) of the TEU, which provides for the adoption of joint action in the areas specified in art K.1 of the TEU, must not affect the provisions of EC Treaty, the ECJ should have jurisdiction to review that measure. The ECJ held that it had jurisdiction to examine whether or not a measure based on art K.3 encroached upon the powers conferred to the ECJ in relation to art 100c EC Treaty.

This case illustrates the difficulty created by the Treaty of Maastricht in relation to entry and stay of nationals of third countries in the territory of the EU resulting from the division of competence between the Community (art 100c EC Treaty) and Co-operation in Justice and Home Affairs (art K.3) covered by the Pillar 3. Fortunately, the Treaty of Amsterdam brings the areas of visa policy, the terms of issuing residence permits to immigrants, etc, within the realm of Community rules.

Competence of the European Community

EC Commission v EC Council (Re the European Road Transport Agreement) Case 22/70 [1971] ECR 263; [1971] CMLR 335 European Court of Justice

- Legal personality of the EC – external relations – capacity of the EC to conclude agreements with third countries – implied powers of the EC – action for annulment under art 173 EC Treaty – reviewable acts under art 173 EC Treaty – common transport policy – distribution of powers amongst institutions

Facts
In 1962 five of the original Member States of the Community entered into an international agreement (AETR) with several non-Community states designed to establish a legal regime for the organisation of road transportation throughout Europe.

Prior to the entry into force of the agreement, the European Commission drafted proposals for the implementation of the Community transport policy, as required by art 75 of the EC Treaty. These proposals were enacted by the Council of Ministers as Council Regulation 543/69 (1969).

At a meeting in March 1970, the Council of Ministers discussed the shape of Community policy for imminent negotiations for the revision of the AETR, due to be held in April 1970. A common position was agreed in the Council, and subsequent negotiations were to be conducted in the light of the general policy framework.

The Commission took the view that the discussions held in the Council encroached upon its area of responsibility. The Commission brought an action in the Court of Justice of the European Communities (ECJ) to annul the Council proceedings on the grounds that the Member States no longer exercised the capacity to enter into negotiations for international agreements in matters which fell within the scope of the Community Treaties.

Held
The ECJ held that, if a particular subject matter falls within the scope of the Community Treaties, Member States can no longer exercise the capacity to conduct negotiations on any subject which would interfere with the formulation of policy. The Court defined the competence of the Community by reference to the general principles of the EC Treaty. Member States therefore, no longer possess the right, acting individually or collectively, to enter international obligations with third countries which would affect the proper exercise of the functions assigned to the Community acting through the European Commission. In relation to the substance of the dispute, the ECJ held that the AETR agreement had been in the process of negotiation since 1962, a considerable time before the issue of Regulation 543/69. Despite the Commission's claim that the Council had infringed art 75, the Commission had in fact made no attempt to make any submission to the Council under art 75(1)(c) nor did the Commission make any application to the Council in pursuance of its right to carry out these negotiations under art 228(1). In the light of the above and the fact that a shift in the negotiating power may have jeopardised the successful outcome of the negotiations, the ECJ dismissed the application.

Judgment
'[Implied powers]
In the absence of specific provisions of the Treaty relating to the negotiation and conclusion of international agreements in the sphere of transport policy – a category into which the AETR falls by its very nature – one must turn to the general system of Community law in the sphere of relations with third countries.

Article 210 provides that: "The Community shall have legal personality."

This provision, placed at the head of Part Six of the Treaty, devoted to "General and Final Provisions", means that in its external relations the Community enjoys the capacity to establish contractual links with third countries over the whole field of objectives defined in Part One of the Treaty, which Part Six supplements.

To determine in a particular case the Community's authority to enter into international agreements, regard must be had to the whole scheme of the Treaty no less than to its substantive provisions.

Such authority arises not only from an express conferment by the Treaty – as is the case with arts 113 and 114 for tariff and trade agreements and with art 238 for associations agreements – but may equally flow from other provisions of the Treaty and from measures adopted, within the framework of those provisions, by the Community institutions.

In particular, each time the Community, with a view to implementing a common policy envisaged by the Treaty, adopts provisions laying down common rules, whatever form these may take, the Member States no longer have the right, acting individually or even collectively, to undertake obligations with third countries which affect those rules.

As and when such common rules come into being, the Community alone is in a position to assume and carry out contractual obligations towards third countries affecting the whole sphere of application of the Community legal system.

With regard to the implementation of the provisions of the Treaty the system of internal Community measures may not therefore be separated from that of external relations.

Under art 5, the Member States are required on the one hand to take all appropriate measures to ensure fulfilment of the obligations arising out of the Treaty or resulting from action taken by the institutions and, on the other hand, to abstain from any measure which might jeopardise the attainment of the objectives of the Treaty.

If these two provisions are read in conjunction, it follows that to the extent to which Community rules are promulgated for the attainment of the objectives of the Treaty, the Member States cannot, outside the framework of the Community institutions, assume obligations which might affect those rules or alter their scope.

According to art 74, the objectives of the Treaty in matters of transport are to be pursued within the framework of a common policy.

With this view, art 75(1) directs the Council to lay down common rules and, in addition, "any appropriate provisions".

By the terms of subparagraph (a) of the same provision, those common rules are applicable "to international transport to or from the territory of a Member State or passing across the territory of one or more Member States".

This provision is equally concerned with transport from or to third countries, as regards that part of the journey which takes place on Community territory.

It thus assumes that the powers of the Community extend to relationships arising from international law, and hence involve the need in the sphere in question for agreements with the third countries concerned.

Although it is true that arts 74 and 75 do not expressly confer on the Community authority to enter into international agreements, nevertheless the bringing into force, on 25 March 1969, of Regulation No 543/69 of the Council on the harmonisation of certain social legislation relating to road transport (OJ L77 p49) necessarily vested in the Community power to enter into any agreements with third countries relating to the subject-matter governed by that regulation.

The grant of power is moreover expressly recognized by art 3 of the said regulation which prescribes that: "The Community shall enter into any negotiations with third countries which may prove necessary for the purpose of implementing this regulation."

Since the subject-matter of the AETR falls within the scope of Regulation No 543/69, the Community has been empowered to negotiate and conclude the agreement in question since the entry into force of the said regulation.

These Community powers exclude the possibility of concurrent powers on the part of Member States, since any steps taken outside the framework of the Community institutions would be incompatible with the unity of the Common Market and the uniform application of Community law.

[*Reviewable act*]
The Council considers that the proceedings of 20 March 1970 do not constitute an act, within the meaning of the first sentence of the first paragraph of art 173, the legality of which is open to review.

Neither by their form nor by their subject-matter or content, it is argued were these proceedings a regulation, a decision or a directive within the meaning of art 189 ...

... Under art 173, the Court has a duty to review the legality "of acts of the Council ... other than recommendations or opinions".

Since the only matters excluded from the scope of the action for annulment open to the Member States and the institutions are 'recommendations or opinions' – which by the final paragraph of art 189 are declared to have no binding force – art 173 treats as acts open to review by the Court all measures adopted by the institutions which are intended to have legal force.

... An action for annulment must therefore be available in the case of all measures adopted by the institutions, whatever their nature or form, which are intended to have legal effects ...

... It thus seems that in so far as they [Council's proceedings] concerned the objective of the negotiations as defined by the Council, proceedings of 20 March 1970 could not have been simply the expression or the recognition of a voluntary co-ordination, but were designed to lay down a course of action binding on both the institutions and the Member States, and destined ultimately to be reflected in the tenor of the regulation.

In the part of its conclusions relating to the negotiating procedure, the Council adopted provisions which were capable of derogating in certain circumstances from the procedure laid down by the Treaty regarding negotiations with third countries and the conclusion of agreements.

Hence, the proceedings of 20 March 1970 had definite legal effects both on relations between the Community and the Member States and on the relationship between institutions.'

Comment

In this case the Court not only settled the first dispute brought by the Commission against the Council but also adopted a radical approach towards the expansion of Community competence by establishing important general principles in this area, first, on the attribution of powers to the EC and, second, on their exclusive nature. With regard to attributed powers, the ECJ stated that in order to determine in a particular case the Community competence to enter into international agreements 'regard must be had to the whole scheme of the Treaty no less than its substantive provisions'. The ECJ endorsed the doctrine of parallelism under which the external competence is not limited to express provisions of the Treaty but may also derive from other provisions of the Treaty and from internal measures adopted within the framework of those provisions.

On the exclusive nature of Community powers the ECJ stated that where the Community has adopted Community rules within the framework of a common policy, the Member States are not allowed, individually or collectively, to enter into agreements with third States in the areas affected by those rules.

In the present case the ECJ considerably extended the category of reviewable acts under art 173 EC Treaty. The Court held that any act which has binding legal effect, irrespective of its form and nature, may be challenged under art 173 EC Treaty.

Re ILO Convention 170 on Chemicals at Work Opinion 2/91 [[1993] 3 CMLR 800 European Court of Justice

- *Compatibility of an international treaty with the EC Treaty – Community external competence – treaty-making powers of the EC – extension to all areas where there are common policies or positive measures – joint action – minimum standards – art 118a EC Treaty*

Facts

All the members of the European Community are members of the International Labour Organisation. The Community is not a full member of this organisation in its own right. An international convention on safety in the use of chemicals at work was negotiated within the ILO.

Since competence for matters covered by the Convention was spread among the Member States and the EC/EU, the European Commission requested an opinion from the ECJ as to whether the EC/EU had status to adhere to the Convention. This question goes to the heart of the nature of the competence conferred on the EC.

Held

The treaty-making powers of the Community operated in all spheres falling inside a 'common policy' and also in those areas where there were positive measures enacted by the Community. Where competence was shared between the Member States, on the one hand, and the Community on the other, the Community's approval was required. Hence, the negotiation and conclusion of an international agreement in such areas required joint action on the part of the Community and the Member States.

Judgment

'... Convention 170 concerns safety in the use of chemicals at work. According to the preamble, its essential objective is to prevent or reduce the incidence of chemically induced illnesses and injuries at work by ensuring that all chemicals are evaluated to determine their hazards, by providing employers and workers with the information necessary for their protection, and finally, by establishing principles for protective programmes.

The field covered by Convention 170 falls within the "social provisions" of the [EC] Treaty which constitute Chapter 1 of Title III on social policy.

Under art 118a [EC], member States are required to pay particular attention to encouraging improvements, as regards the health and safety of workers, and to set as their objective the harmonisation of conditions in this area, while maintaining the improvements made. In order to help achieve this objective, the Council has the power to adopt minimum requirements by means of directives. It follows from art 118a(3) [EC] Treaty that the provisions adopted pursuant to that article are not to prevent any Member State from maintaining or introducing more stringent measures for the protection of working conditions compatible with the Treaty.

The Community thus enjoys an internal legislative competence in the area of social policy. Consequently, Convention 170, whose subject-matter coincides, moreover, with that of several directives adopted under art 118a [EC], falls within the Community's area of competence.

For the purpose of determining whether this competence is exclusive in nature, it should be pointed out that the provisions of Convention 170 are not of such a kind as to affect rules adopted pursuant to art 118a [EC]. If, on the one hand, the Community decides to adopt rules which are less stringent than those set out in an ILO convention, Member States may, in accordance with art 118a(3), adopt more stringent measures for the protection of working conditions or apply for that purpose the provisions of the relevant ILO convention. If, on the other hand, the Community decides to adopt more stringent measures than those provided for under an ILO convention, there is nothing to prevent the full application of Community law by the Member States under art 19(8) of the ILO Constitution, which allows Members to adopt more stringent measures than those provided for in conventions or recommendations adopted by that organisation.

The Commission notes, however, that it is sometimes difficult to determine whether a specific measure is more favourable to workers than another. Thus, in order to avoid being in breach of the provisions of an ILO convention, Member States may be tempted not to adopt provisions better suited to the social and technological conditions which are specific to the Community. The Commission therefore takes the view, in so far as this attitude risks impairing the development of Community law, the Community itself ought to have exclusive competence to conclude Convention 170.

That argument cannot be accepted. Difficulties, such as those referred to by the Commission, which might arise for the legislative function of the Community cannot constitute the basis for exclusive Community competence.

Nor, for the same reasons, can exclusive competence be founded on the Community provisions adopted on the basis of art 100 [EC] Treaty, such as, in particular, Council Directive 80/1107 on the protection of workers from the risks related to exposure to chemical, physical and biological agents at work and individual directives adopted pursuant to art 8 of Directive 80/1107, all of which lay down minimum requirements.

A number of directives adopted in the areas covered by Part III of Convention 170 do, however, contain rules, which are more than minimum requirements. This is the case, for instance, with regard to Council Directive 67/548 on the approximation of laws, regulations and administrative practices relating to the classification, packaging and labelling of dangerous substances adopted pursuant to art 100 [EC] and amended by, inter alia, Directive 79/831 and Directive 88/379 on the approximation of the laws, regulations and administrative provisions of the Member States relating to the classification, packaging and labelling of dangerous preparations, adopted pursuant to art 100a [EC].

Those directives contain provisions which in certain respects constitute measures conferring on workers, in their conditions of work, more extensive protection than that accorder under the provisions contained in Part III of Convention 170. This is so, in particular, in the case of the very detailed rules on labelling set out in the above-mentioned Directive 88/379.

The scope of Convention 170, however, is wider than that of the directives mentioned. The definition of chemicals (art 2(a)), for instance, is broader than that of products covered by the directives. In addition (and in contrast to the provisions contained in the directives), arts 6(3) and 7(3) of the Convention regulate the transport of chemicals.

While there is no contradiction between these provisions of the Convention and those of the directives mentioned, it must nevertheless be accepted that Part III of Convention 170 is concerned with an area which is already covered to a large extent by Community rules progressively adopted since 1967 with a view to achieving an ever greater degree of harmonisation and designed, on the one hand, to remove barriers to trade resulting from differences in legislation from one Member State to another and, on the other hand, to provide, at the same time, protection for human health and the environment.

In those circumstances, it must be considered that the commitments arising from Part III of Convention 170, falling within the area covered by the directives cited above are of such a kind as to affect the Community rules laid down in those directives and that consequently Member States cannot undertake such commitments outside the framework of the Community institutions.

... It follows from all the foregoing considerations that the conclusion of ILO Convention 170 is a matter which falls within the joint competence of the Member States and the Community.'

Comment

In the present opinion the ECJ made a distinction between common rules and minimum rules. In many areas the Community harmonisation measures are based on minimum standards with a possibility for a Member State to apply higher standards (for example in environmental matters). The ILO Convention contains minimum rules on safety in the use of chemicals at work which will not affect any national or Community legislation providing for more favourable protection of workers. Under art 118a EC Treaty the Community is entitled to adopt measures in respect of health and safety of workers. Under this provision, Member States are permitted to maintain and introduce more stringent requirements for the protection of working conditions than the minimum standards adopted by the Council in this area.

In relation to exclusive competence of the Community in this area the ECJ stated that Convention 170, as containing the 'minimum rules' would not affect rules adopted at the Community level. Therefore, if national rules were more stringent than both the Community measures and Convention 170, national rules prevail. This is expressly authorised by both instruments. The Commission argued that the Community should have exclusive competence in the matter for two reasons. First, that sometimes it is difficult to determine which rule is more favourable to the workers, which may prevent Member States from adopting measures under art 118a EC Treaty as being contrary to the Convention and, second, in the event that a Community rule was below the standard contained in the Convention, Member States would be in breach of Community law if they applied the Convention. The ECJ rejected those arguments and stated such difficulties cannot constitute the basis for exclusive Community competence and that, for the same reason, such a competence cannot be founded on Community rules which lay down minimum requirements.

Re Uruguay Round Agreements
Opinion 1/94 [1994] ECR I–5267
European Court of Justice

* *Exclusive competence of the EC – common commercial policy – TRIPs and GATS agreements – scope of implied external powers of the EC – duty of co-operation between Member States and the Community institutions in the area of shared competence*

Facts

The Commission requested the opinion of the ECJ under art 228(6) EC Treaty as to the exclusive competence of the Community to conclude a number of multilateral agreements, in particular GATS and TRIPs of the Uruguay round of negotiations conducted within the framework of the General Agreement on Tariffs and Trade (GATT).

The GATS and TRIPs agreements are modelled on GATT rules. GATS applies to trade in all services apart from services supplied in the exercise of governmental authority and regulates four forms of services, that is, cross-border supply of services, consumption abroad, commercial presence and movement of persons. As a result, it covers not only supply of services but also establishment of the supply of services. The TRIPs agreement encompasses all intellectual property rights. The Commission asked the following questions:

1. whether the EC has exclusive competence to conclude Multilateral Agreements on Trade in Goods, in so far as those Agreements covered products under the ESCS and Euratom Treaties;
2. whether the EC has exclusive competence under art 113 EC or alternatively under other provisions of EC Treaty, to conclude the General Agreement on Trade in Services (GATS) and the Agreement on Trade-related Aspects of Intellectual Property Rights (TRIPs) within the framework of the GATT agreements.

Held

The ECJ held that the EC had exclusive competence under art 113 EC to conclude Multilateral Agreements on Trade in Goods, including the Agreement on Agriculture and goods subject of the Euratom and ESCS Treaties. In relation to the Multilateral Agreements on Trade in Goods (the Tokyo Round Agreement on Technical Barriers to Trade was concluded jointly by the EEC and the Member States), the ECJ confirmed the exclusive competence of the EC in this area. On trade in ESCS and Euratom products with third countries the ECJ restated its previous position that this is covered under art 113 and as such is within the exclusive competence of the EC, apart from agreements relating specifically to ESCS products.

The ECJ held that many areas were excluded from the scope of art 113 EC: international transport; all services except the cross-frontier supplies of services; the TRIPs agreement apart from its provisions regarding the prohibition of the release into free circulation of counterfeit goods already governed by Regulation 3842/86. The Court stated that competence to conclude GATS and TRIPs is shared between the EC and the Member States.

Judgment

'[*Article 113 of the EC Treaty, GATS and TRIPs*]

Relying essentially on the non-restrictive interpretation applied by the Court's case law to the concept of the common commercial policy (see Opinion 1/78, paragraphs 44 and 45), the links or overlap between goods and services, the purpose of GATS and the instruments used, the Commission concludes that services fall within the common commercial policy, without any need to distinguish between the different modes of supply of services and, in particular, between the direct, cross-frontier supply of services and the supply of services through a commercial presence in the country of the person to whom they are supplied. The Commission also maintains that international agreements of a commercial nature in relation to transport (as opposed to those relating to safety rules) fall within the common commercial policy and not within the particular title of the Treaty on the common transport policy.

It is appropriate to consider, first, services other than transport and, subsequently, the particular services comprised in transport.

As regards the first category, it should be recalled at the outset that in Opinion 1/75 the Court, which had been asked to rule on the scope of Community competence as to the arrangements relating to a local cost standard, held that "the field of the common commercial policy, and more particularly that of export policy, necessarily covers systems of aid for exports and more particularly measures concerning credits for the financing of local costs linked to export operations" ([1975] ECR 1362). The local costs in question concerned expenses incurred for the supply of both goods and services. Nevertheless, the Court recognized the exclusive competence of the Community, without drawing a distinction between goods and services.

In its Opinion 1/78 (paragraph 44), the Court rejected an interpretation of art 113 "the effect of which would be to restrict the common commercial policy to the use of instruments intended to have an effect only on the traditional aspects of external trade". On the contrary, it considered that "the question of external trade must be governed from a wide point of view", as is confirmed by "the fact that the enumeration in art 113 of the subjects covered by commercial policy ... is conceived as a non-exhaustive enumeration" (Opinion 1/78, paragraph 45).

The Commission points out in its request for an opinion that in certain developed countries the services sector has become the dominant sector of the economy and that the global economy has been undergoing fundamental structural changes. The trend is for basic industry to be transferred to developing countries, whilst the developed economies have tended to become, in the main, exporters of services and of goods with a high value-added content. The Court notes that this trend is borne out by the WTO Agreement and its annexes, which were the subject of a single process of negotiation covering both goods and services.

Having regard to this trend in international trade, it follows from the open nature of the common commercial policy, within the meaning of the Treaty, that trade in services cannot immediately, and as a matter of principle, be excluded from the scope of art 113, as some of the governments which have submitted observations contend.

In order to make that conclusion more specific, however, one must take into account the definition of trade in services given in GATS in order to see whether the overall scheme of the Treaty is not such as to limit the extent to which trade in services can be included within art 113.

Under art 1(2) of GATS, trade in services is defined, for the purposes of that Agreement, as comprising four modes of services: (1) cross-frontier supplies not involving any movement of persons; (2) consumption abroad, which entails the movement of the consumer into the territory of the WTO member country in which the supplier is established; (3) commercial presence, ie the presence of a subsidiary or branch in the territory of the WTO member country in which the service is rendered; (4) the presence of natural persons from a WTO member country, enabling a supplier from one member country to supply services within the territory of any other member country.

As regards cross-frontier supplies, the service is rendered by a supplier established in one country to a consumer residing in another. The supplier does not move to the consumer country; nor, conversely, does the consumer move to the supplier's county. This situation is, therefore, not unlike trade in goods, which is unquestionably covered by the common commercial policy within the meaning of the Treaty. There is thus no particular reason why such a supply should not fall within the concept of the common commercial policy,

The same cannot be said of the other three modes of supply of services covered by GATS, namely, consumption abroad, commercial presence and the presence of natural persons.

As regards natural persons, it is clear from art 3 of the Treaty, which distinguishes between "a common commercial policy" in paragraph (b) and "measures concerning the entry and movement of persons" in paragraph (d), that the treatment of nationals of non-member countries on crossing the external frontiers of Member States cannot be regarded as falling within the common commercial policy. More generally, the existence in the Treaty of specific chapters on the free movement of natural and legal persons shows that those matters do not fall within the common commercial policy.

It follows that the modes of supply of services referred to by GATS as "consumption abroad", "commercial presence" and the "presence of natural persons" are not covered by the common commercial policy.

Turning next to the particular services comprised in transport, these are the subject of a specific title (Title IV) of the Treaty, distinct from Title VII on the common commercial policy. It was precisely in relation to transport policy that the Court held for the first time that the competence of the Community to conclude international agreements "arises not only from an express conferment by the Treaty – as is the case with arts 113 and 114 for tariff and trade agreements and with art 238 for association agreements – but may equally flow from other provisions of the Treaty and from measures adopted, within the framework of those provisions, by the Community institutions" (Case 22/70 *EC Commission* v *EC Council,* paragraph 16, the "AETR judgment"). The idea underlying that decision is that international agreements in transport matters are not covered by art 113.

The scope of the AETR judgment cannot be cut down by drawing a distinction between agreements on safety rules, such as those relating to the length of driving periods of professional drivers, with which the AETR judgment was concerned, and agreements of a commercial nature.

The AETR judgment draws no such distinction. The Court confirmed that analysis in Opinion 1/76 concerning an agreement intended to rationalise the economic situation in the inland waterways sector – in other words, an economic agreement not concerned with the laying down of safety rules. Moreover, numerous agreements have been concluded with non-member countries on the basis of the Transport Title; a long list of such agreements was given by the United Kingdom in its observations.

In support of its view the Commission has further cited a series of embargoes based on art 113 and involving the suspension of transport services: Measures against Iraq: Council Regulation 2340/90 preventing trade by the Community as regards Iraq and Kuwait, Council Regulation 3155/90 extending and amending Regulation 2340/90 preventing trade by the Community as regards Iraq and Kuwait, and Council Regulation 1194/91 amending Regulations 2340/90 and 3155/90 preventing trade by the Community as regards Iraq and Kuwait; measures against the Federal Republic of Yugoslavia (Serbia and Montenegro); measures against Haiti: Council Regulation 1608/93 introducing an embargo concerning certain trade between the European Economic Community and Haiti. Those precedents are not conclusive. As the European Parliament has rightly observed, since the embargoes related primarily to the export and import of products, they could not have been effective if it had not been decided at the same time to suspend transport services. Such suspension is to be seen as a necessary adjunct to the principal measure. Consequently, the precedents are not relevant to the question whether the Community has exclusive competence pursuant to art 113 to conclude international agreements in the field of transport.

In any event, the Court has consistently held that a mere practice of the Council cannot derogate from the rules laid down in the Treaty and cannot, therefore, create a precedent binding on Community institutions with regard to the correct legal basis (see Case 68/86 *United Kingdom* v *EC Council,* paragraph 24).

It follows that only cross-frontier suppliers are covered by art 113 of the Treaty and that international agreements in the field of transport are excluded from it.

TRIPs
The Commission's argument in support of its contention that the Community has exclusive competence under art 113 is essentially that the rules concerning intellectual property rights are closely linked to trade in the products and services to which they apply.

It should be noted, first, that section 4 of Part III of TRIP's, which concerns the means of enforcement of intellectual property rights, contains specific rules as to measures to be applied at border crossing points. As the United Kingdom has pointed out, that section has its counterpart in the provisions of Council Regulation (EEC) No 3842/86 laying down measures to prohibit the release for free circulation of counterfeit goods. Inasmuch as that regulation concerns the prohibition of the release into free circulation of counterfeit goods, it was rightly based on art 113 of the Treaty: it relates to measures to be taken by the customs authorities at the external frontiers of the Community. Since measures of that type can be adopted autonomously by the Community institutions on the basis of art 113 of the EC Treaty, it is for the Community alone to conclude international agreements on such matters.

However, as regards matters other than the provisions of TRIPs on the release into free circulation of counterfeit goods, the Commission's arguments cannot be accepted.

Admittedly, there is a connection between intellectual property and trade in goods. Intellectual property rights enable those holding them to prevent third parties from carrying out certain acts. The power to prohibit the use of a trade mark, the manufacture of a product, the copying of a design or the reproduction of a book, a disc or a videocassette inevitably has effect on trade. Intellectual property rights are moreover specifically designed to produce such effects. That is not enough to bring them within the scope of art 113. Intellectual property rights do not relate specifically to international trade; they affect internal trade as much as, if not more than, international trade.

As the French government has rightly observed, the primary objective of TRIPs is to strengthen and harmonise the protection of intellectual property on a word-wide scale. The Commission has itself conceded that, since TRIPs lays down rules in fields in which there are no Community harmonisation measures, its conclusion would make it possible at the same time to achieve harmonisation within the Community and thereby to contribute to the establishment and functioning of the Common Market.

It should be noted here that, at the level of internal legislation, the Community is competent, in the field of intellectual property, to harmonise national laws pursuant to art 100 and may use art 235 as the basis for creating new rights superimposed on national rights, as it did in Council Regulation (EC) No 40/94 on the Community trade mark. Those measures are subject to voting rules (unanimity in the case of art 100 and 235) or rules of procedure (consultation of the Parliament in the case of arts 100 and 235, the joint decision-making procedure in the case of art 100a) which are different from those applicable under art 113.

If the Community were to be recognised as having exclusive competence to enter into agreements with non-member countries to harmonise the protection of intellectual property and, at the same time, to achieve harmonization at Community level, the Community institutions would be able to escape the internal constraints to which they are subject in relation to procedures and rules as to voting.

Institutional practices in relation to autonomous measures or external agreements adopted on the basis of art 113 cannot alter this conclusion.

... it must be held that, apart from those of its provisions which concern the prohibition of the release into free circulation of counterfeit goods, TRIPs does not fall within the scope of the common commercial policy.

[*The Community's implied external powers, GATS and TRIPs*]
In the event of the Court rejecting its main contention that the Community has exclusive competence pursuant to art 113, the Commission maintains in the alternative that the Community's exclusive competence to conclude GATS and TRIPs flows implicitly from the provisions of the Treaty establishing its internal competence, or else from the need to enter into international commitments with a view to achieving an internal Community objective. The Commission also argues that, even if the Community does not have adequate powers on the basis of specific provisions of the Treaty or legislative acts of the institutions, it has exclusive competence by virtue of arts 100a and 235 of the Treaty. The Council and the Member States which have submitted observations acknowledge that the Community has certain powers, but deny that they are exclusive.

GATS
With particular regard to GATS, the Commission cites three possible sources for exclusive external competence on the part of the Community: the powers conferred on the Community institutions by the Treaty at internal level, the need to conclude the agreement in order to achieve a Community objective, and, lastly, arts 100a and 235.

The Commission argues, first, that there is no area or specific provision in GATS in respect of which the Community does not have corresponding powers to adopt measures at internal level. According to the Commission, those powers are set out in the chapter on the right of establishment, freedom to provide services and transport. Exclusive external competence flows from those internal powers.

This argument must be rejected.

It was on the basis of art 75(1)(a) which, as regards that part of a journey which takes place on Community territory, also concerns transport from or to non-member countries, that the Court held in the AETR judgment (at paragraph 27), that "the powers of the Community extend to relationships arising from international law, and hence involve the need in the sphere in question for agreements with the third countries concerned".

However, even in the field of transport, The Community's exclusive external competence does not automatically flow from its power to lay down rules at internal level. As the Court pointed out in the AETR judgment (paragraphs 17 and 18), the Member States, whether acting individually or collectively, only lose their right to assume obligations with non-member countries as and when common rules which could be affected by those obligations come into being. Only insofar as common rules have been established at internal level does the external competence of the Community become exclusive. However, not all transport matters are already covered by common rules.

... Unlike the chapter on transport, the chapters on the right of establishment and on freedom to provide services do not contain any provision expressly extending the competence of the Community to "relationships arising from international law". As has rightly been observed by the Council and most of the Member States which have submitted observations, the sole objective of those chapters is to secure the right of establishment and freedom to provide services for nationals of Member States. They contain no provisions on the problem of the first establishment of nationals of non-member countries and the rules governing their access to self-employed activities. One cannot therefore infer from those chapters that the Community has exclusive competence to conclude an agreement with non-member countries to liberalise the subject of cross-border supplies within the meaning of GATS, which are covered by art 113.

Referring to Opinion 1/76 (paragraphs 3 and 4), the Commission submits, second, that the Community's exclusive external competence is not confined to cases in which use has already been made of internal powers to adopt measures for the attainment of common policies. Whenever Community law has conferred on the institutions internal powers for the purposes of attaining specific objectives, the international competence of the Community implicitly flows, according to the Commission, from those provisions. It is enough that the Community's participation in the international agreement is necessary for the attainment of one of the objectives of the Community.

The Commission puts forward here both internal and external reasons to justify participation by the Community, and by the Community alone, in the conclusion of GATS and TRIPs. At internal level, the Commission maintains that, without such participation, the coherence of the internal market would be impaired. At external level, The European Community cannot allow itself to remain inactive on the international stage: the need for the conclusion of the WTO Agreement and its annexes, reflecting a global approach to international trade (embracing goods, services and intellectual property), is not in dispute.

That application of Opinion 1/76 to GATS cannot be accepted.

Opinion 1/76 related to an issue different from that arising from GATS. It concerned rationalisation of the economic situation in the inland waterways sector in the Rhine and Moselle basins, and throughout all The Netherlands inland waterways and the German inland waterways linked to the Rhine basin, by elimination of short-term over-capacity. It was not possible to achieve that objective by the establishment of autonomous common rules, because of the traditional participation of vessels from Switzerland in navigation on the waterways in question. It was necessary, therefore, to bring Switzerland into the scheme envisaged by means of an international agreement (see Opinion 1/76, paragraph 2). Similarly, in the context of conservation of the resources of the seas, the restriction, by means of internal legislative measures, of fishing on the high seas by vessels flying the flag of a Member State would hardly be effective if the same restrictions were not to apply to vessels flying the flag of a non-member country bordering on the same seas. It is understandable, therefore, that external powers may be exercised, and thus become exclusive, without any internal legislation having first been adopted.

That is not the situation in the sphere of services: attainment of freedom of establishment and freedom to provide services for nationals of the Member States is not inextricably linked to the treatment to be afforded in the Community to nationals of non-member countries or in non-member countries to nationals of Member States of the Community.

Third, the Commission refers to arts 100a and 235 of the Treaty as the basis of exclusive external competence.

As regards art 100a, it is undeniable that, where harmonising powers have been exercised, the harmonisation measures thus adopted may limit, or even remove, the freedom of the Member States to negotiate with non-member countries. However, an internal power to harmonise which has not been exercised in a specific field cannot confer exclusive competence in the field on the Community.

Article 235, which enables the Community to cope with any insufficiency in the powers conferred on it, expressly or by implication, for the achievement of its objectives, cannot in itself vest exclusive competence in the Community at international level. Save where internal powers can only be effectively exercised at the same time as external powers (see Opinion 1/76 and paragraph 85 above) internal competence can give rise to exclusive external competence only if it is exercised. This applies a fortiori to art 235.

... It follows that competence to conclude GATS is shared between the Community and the Member States.

TRIPs
In support of its claim that the Community has exclusive competence to conclude TRIPs, the Commission relies on the existence of legislative acts of the institutions which could be affected within the meaning of the AETR judgment if the Member States were jointly to participate in its conclusion, and, as with GATS, on the need for the Community to participate in the agreement in order to achieve one of the objectives set out in the Treaty (the "Opinion 1/76 doctrine"), as well as on arts 100a and 235.

The relevance of the reference to Opinion 1/76 is as just disputable in the case of TRIPs as in the case of GATS: unification or harmonisation of intellectual property rights in the Community context does not necessarily have to be accompanied by agreements with non-member countries in order to be effective.

Moreover, arts 100a and 245 of the Treaty cannot in themselves confer exclusive competence on the Community, as stated above.

It only remains, therefore, to consider whether the subordinate legislative acts adopted in the Community context could be affected within the meaning of the AETR judgment if the Member States were to participate in the conclusion of TRIPs, as the Commission maintains.

Suffice it to say on that point that the harmonisation achieved within the Community in certain areas covered by TRIPs is only partial and that, in other areas, no harmonisation has been envisaged. There has been only partial harmonisation as regards trade marks, for example: it is apparent from the third recital in the preamble to the First Council Directive 89/104 to approximate the laws of the Member States relating to trade marks that it is confined to the approximation of national laws "which most directly affect the functioning of the internal market". In other areas covered by TRIPs, no Community harmonisation measures have been adopted. That is the position as regards the protection of undisclosed technical information, as regards industrial designs, in respect of which proposals have merely been submitted, and as regards patents. With regard to patents, the only acts referred to by the Commission are conventions which are intergovernmental in origin, and not Community acts: the Munich Convention of 5 October 1973 on the Grant of European Patents and the Luxembourg

Agreement of 15 December 1989 relating to Community Patents, which has not yet, however, entered into force.

Some of the governments which have submitted observations have argued that the provisions of TRIPs relating to measures to be adopted to secure the effective protection of intellectual property rights, such as those ensuring a fair and just procedure, the rules regarding the submission of evidence, the right to be heard, the giving of reasons for decision, the right of appeal, interim measures and the award of damages, fall within the competence of the Member States. If that argument is to be understood as meaning that all those matters are within some sort of domain reserved to the Member States, it cannot be accepted. The Commission is certainly competent to harmonise national rules on those matters, insofar as, in the words of art 100 of the Treaty, they "directly affect the establishment or functioning of the Community Market". But the fact remains that the Community institutions have not hitherto exercised their powers in the field of the "enforcement of intellectual property rights", except in Regulation No 3842/86 (paragraph 55) laying down measures to prohibit the release for free circulation of counterfeit goods.

It follows that the Community and its Member States are jointly competent to conclude TRIPs.

[*The duty of co-operation between the Member States and the Community institutions*]

... it must be stressed, first, that any problems which may arise in implementation of the WTO Agreement and its annexes as regards the co-ordination necessary to ensure unity of action where the Community and the Member States participate jointly cannot modify the answer to the question of competence, that being a prior issue. As the Council has pointed out, resolution of the issue of the allocation of competence cannot depend on problems which may possibly arise in administration of the agreements.

Next, where it is apparent that the subject-matter of an agreement or convention falls in part within the competence of the Community and in part within that of the Member States, it is essential to ensure close co-operation between the Member States and the Community institutions, both in the process of negotiation and conclusion and in the fulfilment of the commitments entered into. That obligation to co-operate flows from the requirement of unity in the international representation of the Community (Ruling 1/78, paragraphs 34 to 36, and Opinion 2/99, paragraph 36).'

Comment

The distinction between exclusive external competence of the Community and competence which it shares with the Member States is very important. If the external competence is exclusive, Member States are prevented from acting unilaterally or collectively in this area. They are confined to the processes available within the Community institutional system in relation to the adoption of external measures. Exclusive competence of the Community may be based on express EC Treaty provisions conferring upon the Community external powers (for example art 113 in relation to the common commercial policy), and on express provisions in internal measures (regulations, directives, etc). It may also be implied from internal provisions adopted by Community institutions, and finally it may be implied if, taking into account particular circumstances, internal powers can only be effectively exercised at the same time as external powers. In particular, the last-mentioned possibility has been examined by the ECJ in the present opinion.

In respect of implied exclusive external competence the Court stated that such a competence did not automatically flow from the Community's internal power. Such competence results only when there are common rules which could be affected by continued Member State external competence. The external competence of the Community becomes exclusive without internal legislation where the conclusion of an international agreement is necessary to achieve Treaty objectives which cannot be achieved by internal rules, that is, without third part participation. However, until the competence is exercised, the Member States may enter into international agreements.

Extra-territorial application of Community law

Ahlström and Others* v *EC Commission (Re Wood Pulp Cartel) Joined Cases 89, 104, 114, 116, 117 and 125–129/85 [1988] ECR 5193; [1988] 4 CMLR 901 European Court of Justice

• *Extra-territorial application of EC Treaty – effects doctrine – undertakings from third countries – art 85(1) EC Treaty – concerted price-fixing*

Note: Only the issue of territorial jurisdiction is dealt with here. See, further, Chapter 13 on EC Competition Law. For this reason the case reference is different. There are two judgments of the ECJ in the same case.

Facts
The Commission found more than 40 suppliers of wood pulp in violation of Community competition law despite the fact that none of these was resident within the European Community. Fines were imposed on 36 of these undertakings for violation of art 85(1) EC Treaty. A number of these undertakings appealed against the decision to the ECJ. One of their arguments was that EC competition law was not capable of having extra-territorial effect and therefore the fines were unlawful.

Held
The ECJ confirmed the extra-territorial application of EC competition law.

Judgment
'It should be noted that the main sources of supply of wood pulp are outside the Community, in Canada, the United States, Sweden and Finland and that the market therefore has a global dimension. Where wood pulp producers established in those countries sell directly to purchasers established in the Community and engage in price competition in order to win orders from those customers, that constitutes competition within the Common Market.

It follows that where those producers concert on the prices to be charged to their customers in the Community and put that concertation into effect by selling at prices which are actually co-ordinated, they are taking part in concertation which has the object and effect of restricting competition within the Common Market within the meaning of art 85 of the Treaty.

Accordingly, it must be concluded that by applying the competition rules in the Treaty in the circumstances of this case to undertakings whose registered offices are situated outside the Community, the Commission has not made an incorrect assessment of the territorial scope of art 85.

The applicants have submitted that the decision is incompatible with public international law on the grounds that the application of the competition rules in this case was founded exclusively on the economic repercussions within the Common Market of conduct restricting competition which was adopted outside the Community.

It should be observed that an infringement of art 85, such as the conclusion of an agreement which has had the effect of restricting competition within the Common Market, consists of conduct made up of two elements: the formation of the agreement, decision or concerted practice and the implementation thereof. If the applicability of prohibitions laid down under competition law were made to depend on the place where the agreement, decision or concerted practice was formed, the result would obviously be to give undertakings an easy means of evading these prohibitions. The decisive factor is therefore the place where it is implemented.

The producers in this case implemented their pricing agreement within the Common Market. It is immaterial in that respect whether or not they had recourse to subsidiaries, agents, sub-agents, or branches within the Community in order to make their contacts with purchasers within the Community.

Accordingly, the Community's jurisdiction to apply its competition rules to such conduct is covered by the territoriality principle as universally recognised in public international law.'

Comment

Extra-territorial jurisdiction was developed to respond to the internationalisation of criminal activities at the end of the nineteenth century. It has also found its application in anti-trust cases, especially in the US anti-trust laws and the EC competition rules.

In certain circumstances the exercise of extra-territorial jurisdiction by the EC is justified when the effect of some anti-competitive conduct of foreign undertakings is realised or felt within the territory of the Union. In the present case the ECJ held that activities of undertakings concerned, although situated outside the territory of the EC, were within the scope of application of EC competition rules because implementation of their agreement had effect within the Community. Their concerted practice had intended a direct and substantial effect on trade within the Community through a reduction in competition in terms of price in sales of wood pulp to Community undertakings. As a result, the concerted practice restricted competition within the EC.

The extra-territorial application of EC competition law creates many problems. The investigation of alleged breaches of EC competition rules outside the territory of the Union often necessitates co-operation of competent authorities of a third State. Even more challenging is the actual enforcement outside the territory of decisions of the Commission and judgments of the ECJ in competition cases because a third State, where the undertaking is located, has no obligation to co-operate or assist the Commission.

Relationship between the European Community law and the constitution of the United Kingdom

R v *Secretary of State for Foreign and Commonwealth Affairs, ex parte Rees-Mogg* [1993] 3 CMLR 101; [1994] 1 All ER 457 Queen's Bench Divisional Court

• Ratification of the Treaty on European Union – compatibility of the Maastricht Treaty with UK constitution – delegation of the royal prerogative

Facts

The applicant brought an action for a declaration that the United Kingdom's purported ratification of the Maastricht Treaty, in the form of the European Communities (Amendment) Act 1993, infringed the UK constitution on three grounds. First, by ratifying the Protocol on Social Policy, the UK government was in breach of s6 of the European Parliamentary Elections Act 1978. Second, by ratifying the Protocol, the government was altering the content of Community law without adequate approval. Finally, if the government ratified Title V of the Maastricht Treaty, it would unlawfully transfer part of the royal prerogative, namely the right to conduct foreign and security policy, to the institutions of the Community without adequate statutory approval.

Of these arguments, only the last is dealt with (being the only one of importance) in the judgment extract set out below. This is the question of whether the UK government can delegate sovereign powers previously exercised by the Crown to the European Community.

Held

The first argument was rejected, as a point of construction of statutes, on the ground that the Protocol formed part of the Treaty on European Union itself and could be validly ratified by the 1993 Act notwithstanding the terms of the earlier statute. On the second point, the Court held that approval of the Protocol provided the UK with an option to decide whether or not to participate in the formulation of social policy at the European Union level.

On the final point, the applicant was also unsuccessful.

Judgment

'Title V of the Union Treaty establishes a common foreign and security policy among the Member States. The objectives are set in art J.1(4). Article J.1(4) provides:

"The Member States shall support the Union's external and security policy actively and unreservedly in a spirit of loyalty and mutual solidarity. They shall refrain from any action which is contrary to the interests of the Union or likely to impair its effectiveness as a cohesive force in international relations. The Council shall ensure that these principles are complied with."

Under art J.2(2) the Council is obliged to define a common position, whenever it deems it necessary. Member States must then ensure that their policies conform to the common position. Article J.4(1) provides:

"The common foreign and security policy shall include all questions related to the security of the Union, including the eventual framing of a common defence policy, which might in time lead to a common defence."

Under art J.5(1) the Presidency represent the Union in matters coming within the common foreign and security policy. There are other important provisions. But we have quoted enough to give the flavour. Unless otherwise agreed under art J.3(2), the decisions of the Council must be taken unanimously.

Title V is not, of course, included in s1(1) of the 1993 Act, since it is an inter-government agreement, which could have no impact on United Kingdom domestic law. The arguments advanced by [counsel for the applicant] under this head are therefore of a very different nature from the arguments so far considered. By English common law, the Crown is, he says, incapable of abandoning, or transferring, any of its ancient prerogative powers, without statutory enactment.

In support of his general proposition, [counsel for the applicant] quotes a number of old authorities, starting with *Saltpetre* (1606) 12 Coke's Report 12. He also relies on a very recent decision of the Irish Supreme Court in relation to the Single European Act whereby the Court held, by a majority, that it was not competent for the Government of Ireland to ratify Title III of the Act without a referendum; see *Crotty* v *An Taoiseach* [1987] 2 CMLR 666. We quote from the headnote:

"It would be quite incompatible with the freedom of action in foreign relations conferred on the Government by the Irish Constitution for the Government to quality it or inhibit it in any manner by formal agreement with other states to do so. That freedom does not carry with it the power to abdicate the freedom to enter into binding agreements with other states to exercise the power to decide matters of foreign policy in a particular way or to refrain from exercising it save by particular procedures and so to bind the state in its freedom of action in its foreign policy. Title III of the Single European Act requires such limitations on the Government's freedom of action in foreign relations and therefore may not be ratified without a referendum."

[Counsel for the applicant] submits that, by the same token, the effect of Title V of the Union Treaty is, or will be, that the Crown has transferred its prerogative power in relation to foreign policy, security, and ultimately defence, to the Council without statutory enactment. But we do not consider that the *Crotty* case affords any real assistance, because the issues there turned solely on the provisions of the Irish Constitution.

[Counsel for the respondent]'s first answer is that the questions raised under this head are simply not justiciable in the English courts. A similar point arose in *Blackburn* v *Attorney-General* [1971] CMLR 784. In that case Mr Raymond Blackburn sought a declaration that by signing the Treaty of Rome the government would be surrendering forever a part of the sovereignty of the Crown in Parliament, and that by so doing it would be in breach of the law. There was an application to strike out the action. The application succeeded both at first instance and on appeal. Lord Denning set out the general principle in relation to treaties and continued:

> "Mr Blackburn acknowledged the general principle, but he urged that this proposed treaty is a category by itself, in that it diminishes the sovereignty of Parliament over the people of this country. I cannot accept the distinction. The general principle applies to this treaty as to any other. The treaty-making power of this country rests not in the courts, but in the Crown; that is, Her Majesty acting upon the advice of her Ministers. When her Ministers negotiate and sign a treaty, even a treaty of such paramount importance as this proposed one, they act on behalf of the country as a whole. They exercise the prerogative of the Crown. Their action in so doing cannot be challenged or questioned in these courts."

The authority of *Blackburn* v *Attorney-General* has recently been confirmed by the House of Lords in *J H Rayner* v *Department of Trade* [1990] 2 AC 418. [Counsel for the respondent] submits that what was true in 1971 before the Treaty of Rome was signed is as true today in relation to Title V of the Union Treaty. Since no question of domestic law is involved, the court has no jurisdiction even to consider the questions raised by [counsel for the applicant] under this head.

It would be possible for us to accept this argument and leave it at that. But [counsel for the applicant] pointed out in reply that the principle of non-justiciability is not universal and absolute. There are exceptions. Thus it is clear from s6 of the 1978 Act that the court would be entitled, and indeed bound, if required, to consider whether any treaty which the government proposed to ratify involved an increase in the powers of the European Parliament. Fortunately we have not been concerned with that problem in this case.

Similarly in *ex parte Molyneaux*, Taylor J, as he then was, considered the text of the inter-governmental conference established between the government of the United Kingdom and the government of the Republic of Ireland in November 1985, to see if it contravened any statute or rule of common law, or any constitutional convention. He held that it did not.

So we will assume, contrary to [counsel for the respondent's] argument, that we are entitled to consider the questions raised by [counsel for the applicant]. We will also assume (what was not in dispute) that the government could not lawfully transfer any part of the Crown's prerogative powers in relation to foreign affairs without statutory enactment. Where does that take us? It takes us to this: that even if one reads Title V with an eye most favourable to [counsel for the applicant's] argument, it cannot be regarded as a transfer of prerogative powers. As [counsel for the respondent] succinctly put it, Title V does not entail an abandonment or transfer of prerogative powers but an exercise of those powers. We agree. So far as we know, nobody has ever suggested that the Charter of the United Nations, for example, or of the North Atlantic Treaty Organisation, involves a transfer of prerogative power. Title V should be read in the same light. In the last resort, as was pointed out in argument, though not pursued, it would presumably be open to the government to denounce the Treaty, or at least to fail to comply with its international obligations under Title V.

It follows that we reject [counsel for the

applicant's] third argument, either on the ground that the questions raised are not justiciable, or, if they are, that it fails on the merits.

For the reasons given the applicant is not entitled to any of the declarations for which he asks.'

Comment

The final ratification of the Treaty on European Union by the UK was delayed by a judicial review of its terms in the present case. From a jurisprudential point of view, the third argument submitted by the applicant was the most interesting. The court refused to accept that the transfer of limited political competence in these spheres could be construed as an abandonment or irrevocable transfer of the royal prerogative. Consequently, the applicant's petition for a declaration was rejected. The Treaty on European Union was ratified in the United Kingdom on 2 August 1993.

Relationship between European Community law and the European Convention for the Protection of Human Rights and Fundamental Freedoms

Accession of the European Community to the European Convention for the Protection of Human Rights and Fundamental Freedoms Opinion 2/94 [1996] ECR I-1759 European Court of Justice

- *European Convention on Human Rights – admissibility of the request for an opinion – art 228(6) EC Treaty – compatibility of accession with the EC Treaty – arts 164 and 219 EC Treaty – competence of the EC to accede to the ECHR – art 235 EC Treaty*

Facts

The Council requested the opinion of the ECJ under art 228 EC Treaty on the question whether the accession of the EC to the ECHR would be compatible with the EC Treaty. Fourteen governments submitted observations; the majority were in favour of accession, and against it were France, Ireland, Portugal, Spain and the UK. The ECJ had to answer three questions: first, concerning the admissibility of the request taking into account that the conclusion of an agreement was hypothetical as there had been no negotiation of any kind nor a draft; second, on the compatibility of accession with EC Treaty, in particular with rules on jurisdiction of the ECJ; and, third, on the competence of the Community to accede to the ECHR.

Held

The ECJ held that it had jurisdiction under art 228 EC Treaty to deliver an opinion. The ECJ held it had no sufficient information to decide whether accession by the EC to the ECHR would infringe its jurisdiction under arts 164 and 219 EC Treaty. The Court stated that the Community had no competence to accede to the ECHR.

Judgment

'[*Admissibility of the request for an opinion*]
... As regards the question of competence, in paragraph 35 of Opinion 1/78 the Court held that, where a question of competence has to be decided, it is in the interests of the Community institutions and of the States concerned, including non-member countries, to have that question clarified from the outset of negotiations and even before the main points of the agreement are negotiated.

The only condition which the Court referred to in that Opinion is that the purpose of the envisaged agreement be known before negotiations are commenced.

There can be no doubt that, as far as this request for an opinion is concerned, the purpose of the envisaged agreement is known. Irrespective of the mechanism by which the Community might accede to the

Convention, the general purpose and subject-matter of the Convention and the institutional significance of such accession for the Community are perfectly well known.

The admissibility of the request for an opinion cannot be challenged on the ground that the Council has not yet adopted a decision to open negotiations and that no agreement is therefore envisaged within the meaning of art 228(6) of the Treaty.

While it is true that no such decision has yet been taken, accession by the Community to the Convention has been the subject of various Commission studies and proposals and was on the Council's agenda at the time when the request for an Opinion was lodged. The fact that the Council has set the art 228(6) procedure in motion presupposes that it envisaged the possibility of negotiating and concluding such an agreement. The request for an opinion thus appears to be prompted by the Council's legitimate concern to know the exact extent of its powers before taking any decision on the opening of negotiations.

Furthermore, insofar as the request for an opinion concerns the question of Community competence, its import is sufficiently clear and a formal Council decision to open negotiations was not indispensable in order further to define its purpose.

Finally, if the art 228(6) procedure is to be effective it must be possible for the question of competence to be referred to the Court not only as soon as negotiations are commenced (Opinion 1/78, paragraph 35) but also before negotiations have formally begun.

... It follows that the request for an Opinion is admissible insofar as it concerns the competence of the Community to conclude an agreement of the kind envisaged.

[*Compatibility of accession with arts 164 and 219 EC Treaty*]

... In order fully to answer the question whether accession by the Community to the Convention would be compatible with the rules of the Treaty, in particular with arts 164 and 219 relating to the jurisdiction of the Court, the Court must have sufficient information regarding the arrangements by which the Community envisages submitting to the present and future judicial control machinery established by the Convention.

As it is, the Court has been given no detailed information as to the solutions that are envisaged to give effect in practice to such submission of the Community to the jurisdiction of an international court.

It follows that the Court is not in a position to give its opinion on the compatibility of Community accession to the Convention with the rules of the Treaty.

[*Competence of the Community to accede to the Convention*]

... Article 235 is designed to fill the gap where no specific provisions of the Treaty confer on the Community institutions express or implied powers to act, if such powers appear none the less to be necessary to enable the Community to carry out its functions with a view to attaining one of the objectives laid down by the Treaty.

That provision, being an integral part of an institutional system based on the principle of conferred powers, cannot serve as a basis for widening the scope of the Treaty as a whole and, in particular, by those that define the task and the activities of the Community. On any view, art 235 cannot be used as a basis for the adoption of provisions whose effect would, in substance, be to amend the Treaty without following the procedure which it provides for that purpose.

It is in the light of those considerations that the question whether accession by the Community to the Convention may be based on art 235 must be examined.

It should first be noted that the importance of respect for human rights has been emphasised in various declarations of the Member States and of the Community institutions ... Reference is also made to respect for human rights in the preamble to the Single European Act and in the preamble to, and in art F(2), the fifth indent of art J.1(2) and art K.2(1) of, the Treaty on European Union. Article F provides that the union is to respect fundamental rights, as guaranteed, in particular, by the Convention. Article 130u(2) of the EC Treaty provides that Community policy in the area of development co-operation is to contribute to the objective of respecting human rights and fundamental freedoms.

Furthermore, it is well settled that fundamental rights form an integral part of the general principles of law whose observance the Court ensures. For that purpose, the Court draws inspiration from the constitutional traditions common to the Member States and from the guidelines supplied by international treaties for the protection of human rights on which the Member States have collaborated or to which they are signatories. In that regard, the Court has stated that the Convention has special significance (see, in particular, the judgment in Case C–260/89 AETR, paragraph 41).

Respect for human rights is therefore a condition of the lawfulness of Community acts. Accession to the Convention entails a substantial change in the present Community system for the protection of human rights in that it would entail the entry of the Community into a distinct international institutional system as well as integration of all the provisions of the Convention into the Community legal order.

Such a modification of the system for the protection of human rights in the Community, with equally fundamental institutional implications for the Community and for the Member States, would be of constitutional significance and would therefore be such as to go beyond the scope of art 235. It could be brought about only by way of Treaty amendment.

It must therefore be held that, as Community law now stands, the Community has no competence to accede to the Convention.'

Comment

The importance of fundamental human rights has prompted the Council, the Commission and the European Parliament to sign a Joined Declaration on 5 April 1977 which expresses their attachment to the protection of human rights. Although the Declaration is solely a political statement it has initiated a new approach, that is the need for the Community to incorporate the European Convention on human rights into Community law. This initiative was blocked by the Member States at the Maastricht Conference and in the present Opinion 2/94 the ECJ held that the EC had no competence to accede to the ECHR without a Treaty amendment.

In the present opinion the ECJ clarified the extent to which art 235 EC Treaty can be used to extend the implied external competence of the Community. The ECJ stated that art 235 EC Treaty cannot constitute a legal base for accession to the ECHR since such accession being of constitutional significance is beyond its scope of application.

In this context it is interesting to note that the General Affairs Council discussed on 17–18 May 1999 the possibility of drafting an EU charter of fundamental rights. It stated that such a charter could enshrine the fundamental rights and freedoms set out in the ECHR, as well as basic procedural rights. The Cologne European Council (3–4 June 1999) has launched the process.

2 The Institutions of the European Union

The Council of the European Union

United Kingdom v *EC Council (Re Hormones)* Case 68/86 [1988] 2 CMLR 453 European Court of Justice

• Legal basis for the adoption of measures – objective criteria determining the choice of legal basis – arts 100 and 43 EC Treaty – voting in the Council – agriculture – use of hormones

Facts
The United Kingdom brought an action for annulment of a Council directive prohibiting the use of particular types of hormones in the rearing of livestock. The measure had been adopted by the Council despite the votes of the United Kingdom and Denmark against its adoption. The United Kingdom argued that the legal authority for the adoption of the measure was art 100 EC Treaty, which requires unanimity. In the Council, the other Member States claimed that art 43 EC Treaty was the correct legal basis for the measure. This provision permitted the adoption of legislation by means of a qualified majority. If the proper legal basis for the measure was art 100, the measure was void due to the negative votes of the UK and Denmark, but if the measure could be justified under art 43, the measure would be validly constituted.

Held
The ECJ held that the Council acted properly in adopting the measure under art 43 EC Treaty. This provision was sufficiently broad as to permit legislation which dealt not only directly, but also indirectly, with issues relating to agriculture. The choice of the legal basis for legislation must be made on objective criteria, which may be subject to judicial review. The fact that, in the past, the Council had followed a practice of citing a double basis for the adoption of such measures could not constitute a precedent capable of modifying the express terms of a Treaty provision.

Judgment
'... in order to determine whether the submission based on the alleged insufficiency of the legal basis of the directive at issue is well-founded it is necessary to consider whether the Council had the power to adopt it on the basis of art 43 alone.

By virtue of art 38 of the Treaty, the provisions of arts 30 to 46 apply to the products listed in Annex II of the Treaty. Article 43, moreover, must be interpreted in the light of art 39, which sets out the objectives of the Common Agricultural Policy, and art 40, which governs its implementation, providing inter alia that in order to attain the objectives set out in art 39 a common organisation of agricultural markets is to be established and that organisation include all measures required to attain those objectives.

The agricultural policy objectives set out in art 39 of the Treaty include in particular the increasing of productivity by promoting technical progress and by ensuring the rational development of agricultural production and the optimum utilisation of the factors of production. Moreover, art 39(2)(b) and (c) provide that in working out the Common Agricultural Policy account must be taken of the need to effect the appropriate adjustments by degrees and the fact that in the Member States agriculture constitutes a sector closely linked with the economy as a whole. It follows that agricultural policy objectives must be conceived in such a manner as to enable the Community institutions to carry out their duties in the light of developments in agriculture and in the economy as a whole.

Measures adopted on the basis of art 43 of the Treaty with a view to achieving those objectives under a common organisation of the market as provided for in art 40(2) may include rules governing conditions and methods of production, quality and marketing of agricultural products. The common organisation of the market contain many rules in that regard.

Efforts to achieve objectives of the Common Agricultural Policy, in particular under common organisations of the markets, cannot disregard requirements relating to the public interest such as the protection of consumers or the protection of the health and life of humans and animals, requirements which the Community institutions must take into account in exercising their powers.

Finally, it must be observed that according to art 42 of the Treaty the rules on competition are to apply to production of and trade in agricultural products only to the extent determined by the Council within the framework of provisions adopted pursuant to art 43. Consequently, in adopting such provisions the Council must take into consideration the requirements of competition policy.

It follows from the provisions discussed above, taken as a whole, that art 43 of the Treaty is the appropriate legal basis for any legislation concerning the production and marketing of agricultural products listed in Annex II of the Treaty which contributed to the achievement of one or more of the objectives of the Common Agricultural Policy set out in art 39 of the Treaty. There is no need to have recourse to art 100 of the Treaty where such legislation involves the harmonisation of provisions of national laws in that field.

As the Court pointed out (in earlier cases), art 38(2) of the Treaty gives precedence to specific provisions in the agricultural field over general provisions relating to the establishment of the common market. Consequently, even where the legislation in question is directed both to objectives of agricultural policy and to other objectives which, in the absence of specific provisions, are pursued on the basis of art 100 of the Treaty, that article, a general one under which directives may be adopted for the approximation of the laws of the Member States, cannot be relied on as a ground for restricting the field of application of art 43 of the Treaty.

It is on the basis of the foregoing considerations that it must be determined whether or not the contested directive falls within the scope of art 43 of the Treaty as described above.

In that regard, it must first be observed that there are common organisations of the markets in the sectors of beef and veal, pigmeat and sheepmeat and goatmeat, and that (the regulations establishing these organisations) provide for the adoption of Community measures designed to promote better organisation of production, processing and marketing, and to improve quality.

The directive at issue essentially contains, on the one hand, rules on the administration of certain substances having a hormonal action on farm animals whose meat is covered by the aforementioned common organisations of the markets and, on the other hand, rules concerning the requisite control measures. Those measures relate in particular to trade between Member States in live animals and meat and to imports of those products into the Community.

The aim of the directive, according to the recital in its preamble, is to protect human health and consumers interests with a view to eliminating the distortion of conditions of competition and bringing about an increase in "consumption of the production in question".

In view of the content and objectives of

the directive, it must be found that, in regulating conditions for the production and marketing of meat with a view to improving its quality, it comes into the category of measures provided for by the aforementioned common organisations of the markets in meat and thus contributes to the achievement of the objectives of the Common Agricultural Policy which are set out in art 39 of the Treaty.

It follows from the foregoing that the directive at issue falls within the sphere of the Common Agricultural Policy and that the Council had the power to adopt it on the basis of art 43 alone. That finding cannot be affected by the fact, on which the applicant places some reliance, that the Council departed from its practice of basing measures in the field in question on arts 43 and 100 of the Treaty.

On that point, it should be borne in mind, as the Court held in its judgment in Case 45/87 *EC Commission* v *EC Council*, in the context of the organisation of the powers of the Community that the choice of the legal basis for the measure must be based on objective factors which are amenable to judicial review. A mere practice on the part of the Council cannot derogate from the rules laid down in the Treaty. Such a practice cannot therefore create a precedent binding on Community institutions with regard to the correct legal basis.

The applicant's first submission must therefore be rejected.'

Comment

The choice of a legal basis for a particular measure must be based on objective factors which are amenable to judicial review. The aim and content of that measure should be taken into account in order to select a proper legal basis (*EC Commission* v *EC Council* Case C–155/91 [1993] ECR I–939, recently *European Parliament* v *EC Council* Case C–42/97, judgment of 23 February 1999, nyr). In the present case, the primary objective of the measure is a common organisation of agricultural markets and the secondary objective is the harmonisation of provisions of national law in the area of agriculture. Consequently ECR I–939, the theory of the principal and accessory should be applied in order to select the proper legal basis for the adoption of that measure.

The choice of a legal basis determines the mode of voting in the Council. Article 43 EC Treaty permits the adoption of a measure by means of a qualified majority whilst art 100 EC Treaty requires unanimity. Therefore, the choice of legal basis has important implications. In the present case the UK and Denmark voted against its adoption which means that if the proper legal basis had been art 100 EC Treaty, the measure would have never been adopted.

The Court of Justice of the European Communities (ECJ)

Re the Draft Treaty on a European Economic Area Opinion 1/91 [1992] 1 CMLR 245 European Court of Justice

• *Consultative jurisdiction – infringement of the powers of the ECJ – international agreement between the EC and EFTA – creation of the European economic area – modifications required for approval of the EEA agreement*

Facts

The European Community and the European Free Trade Association (EFTA) entered into an international agreement to create the European Economic Area. This agreement extended the scope of the EC Treaty's four freedoms and the existing principles of competition law to the Member States of the EFTA on a reciprocal basis.

The agreement also established a separate Court to supervise the implementation and enforcement of these provisions. This Court was to consist of judges of the ECJ and other appointees named by the contracting parties to the agreement. This Court was required to take into consideration all the jurisprudence of the ECJ to the date of the signing of the agreement, but not necessarily after that date. The Court would also have the power to refer a matter to the ECJ for a preliminary ruling but any decision was not necessarily binding on the referring judge.

The judges of the ECJ expressed a number of reservations about the legal implications of such an agreement, especially on the competence of the ECJ. As a result, the Commission requested an opinion from the ECJ on the compatibility of the agreement with the EC Treaty.

Held
The ECJ rejected a number of parts of the agreement on the ground that they undermined the ECJ's authority as conferred by the EC Treaty. In particular, the ECJ stressed that the two treaties sought to achieve separate purposes. For that reason, homogeneity of the rules of law throughout the EEA is not secured by the fact that the provisions of Community law and those of the corresponding provisions of the agreement are identical in their content or wording

The EEA Treaty was accordingly suspended and subsequently amended to take into consideration the concerns of the ECJ.

Judgment
'The EEA is to be established on the basis of an international treaty which, essentially, merely creates rights and obligations as between the Contracting Parties and provides for no transfer of sovereign rights to the intergovernmental institutions which it sets up.

In contrast, the [EC] Treaty, albeit concluded in the form of an international agreement, none the less constitutes the constitutional charter of the Community based on the rule of law. As the Court of Justice has consistently held, the Community treaties established a new legal order for the benefit of which the States limited their sovereign rights, in even wider fields, and the subject of which comprise not only Member States but also their nationals. The essential characteristics of the Community legal order which has thus been established are in particular its primacy over the law of the Member States and the direct effect of a whole series of provisions which are applicable to their nationals and to the Member States themselves.

It follows from those considerations that homogeneity of the rules of law throughout the EEA is not secured by the fact that the provisions of Community law and those of the corresponding provisions of the agreement are identical in their content or wording.

It must therefore be considered whether the agreement provides for other means of guaranteeing that homogeneity.

Article 6 of the Agreement pursues that objective by stipulating that the rules of the Agreement must be interpreted in conformity with the case law of the Court of Justice on the corresponding provisions of Community law.

However, for two reasons that interpretation mechanism will not enable the desired legal homogeneity to be achieved.

First, art 6 is concerned only with rulings of the Court of Justice given prior to the date of signature of the Agreement. Since the case law will evolve, it will be difficult to distinguish the new case law from the old and hence the past from the future.

Secondly, although art 6 of the Agreement does not clearly specify whether it refers to the Court's case law as a whole, and in particular the case law on the direct effect and primacy of Community law, it appears from Protocol 35 to the agreement that, without recognising the principles of direct effect and primacy which that case law entails, the Contracting Parties undertake merely to introduce into their respective legal orders a statutory provision to the effect that EEA rules are to prevail over contrary legislative provisions.

It follows that compliance with the case law of the Court of Justice, as laid down in art 6 of the Agreement, does not extend to essential elements of that case law which are irreconcilable with the homogeneity of the law throughout the EEA, either as regards the past or for the future.

It follows from the foregoing considerations that the divergencies which exist between the aims and context of the Agreement, on the one hand, and the aims and context of Community law, on the other, stand in the way of the achievement of the objective of homogeneity in the interpretation and application of the law in the EEA.

It is in light of the contradiction which has just been identified that it must be considered whether the proposed system of courts may undermine the authority of the Community legal order in pursuing its particular objectives.

The interpretation of the expression "Contracting Party" which the EEA Court will have to give in the exercise of its jurisdiction will be considered first, followed by the effect of the case law of that court on the interpretation of Community law.

As far as the first point is concerned, it must be observed that the EEA Court has jurisdiction under art 96(1)(a) of the Agreement with regard to settlement of dispute between the Contracting Parties and that, according to art 117(1) of the Agreement, the EEA Joint Committee or a Contracting Party may bring such a dispute before the EEA Court.

The expression "Contracting Parties" is defined in art 2(c) of the Agreement. As far as the Community and its Member States are concerned, it covers the Community and the Member States, or the Community, or the Member States, depending on the case. Which of the three possibilities is to be chosen is to be deduced in each case from the relevant provisions of the Agreement and from the respective competencies of the Community and the Member States as they follow from the [EC] Treaty and the ECSC Treaty.

This means that, when a dispute relating to the interpretation or application of one or more provisions of the Agreement is brought before it, the EEA Court may be called upon to interpret the expression "Contracting Party" within the meaning of art 2(c) of the Agreement, in order to determine either, for the purposes of the provision at issue, the expression "Contracting Party" means the Community, the Community and the Member States, or simply the Member States. Consequently, the EEA Court will have to rule on the respective competencies of the Community and the Member States as regards matters governed by the provisions of the Agreement.

It follows that the jurisdiction conferred on the EEA Court under art 2(c), art 96(1)(a) and art 117(1) of the Agreement is likely adversely to affect the allocation of responsibilities defined in the Treaties and, hence, the autonomy of the Community legal order, respect for which must be assured by the Court of Justice pursuant to art 164 of the [EC] Treaty. This exclusive jurisdiction of the Court of Justice is confirmed by art 219 of the [EC] Treaty under which Member States undertake not to submit a dispute concerning the interpretation or application of that Treaty to any method of settlement other than those provided for in the Treaty.

Consequently, to confer that jurisdiction on the EEA Court is incompatible with Community law.

As for the second point, it must be observed in limine that international agreements concluded by means of the procedure set out in art 228 of the Treaty are binding on the institutions of the Community and its Member States and that, as the Court of Justice has consistently held, the provisions of such agreements and the measures adopted by institutions set up by such agreements become an integral part of the Community legal order when they enter into force.

In this connection, it must be pointed out that the agreement is an act of one of the institutions of the Community within the meaning of indent (b) of art 117(1) [EC] and that therefore the court has jurisdiction to give preliminary rulings on its interpretation. It also has jurisdiction to rule on the Agreement in the event that the Member

States of the Community fail to fulfil their obligations under the Agreement.

Where, however, an international agreement provides for its own system of courts, including a court with jurisdiction to settle disputes between the Contracting Parties to the agreement, and, as a result, to interpret its provisions, the decisions will also be binding on the Community institutions, including the Court of Justice. Those decisions will also be binding in the event that the Court of Justice is called upon to rule, by way of preliminary ruling or in a direct action, on the interpretation of the international agreement, in so far that agreement is an integral part of the Community legal order.

An international agreement providing for such a system of courts is in principle compatible with Community law. The Community's competence in the field of international relations and its capacity to conclude international agreements necessarily entail the power to submit to the decisions of a court which is created or designated by such an agreement as regards the interpretation and application of its provisions.

However, the Agreement at issue takes over an essential part of the rules – including the rules of secondary legislation – which govern economic and trading relations within the Community and which constitute, for the most part, fundamental provisions of the Community legal order.

Consequently, the Agreement has the effect of introducing into the Community legal order a large body of rules which is juxtaposed to a corpus of identically-worded Community rules.

Furthermore, in the preamble to the Agreement and in art 1, the Contracting Parties express the intention of securing the uniform application of the provisions of the Agreement throughout their territory.

However, the objective of uniform application and equality of conditions of competition which is pursued in this way and reflected in art 6 and art 104(1) of the Agreement necessarily covers the interpretation both of the provisions of the Agreement and of the corresponding provisions of the Community legal order.

Although, under art 6 of the Agreement, the EEA Court is under a duty to interpret the provisions of the Agreement in the light of the relevant rulings of the Court of Justice given prior to the date of signature of the Agreement, the EEA Court will no longer be subject to any such obligation in the case of decisions given by the Court of Justice after that date.

Consequently, the Agreement's objective of ensuring homogeneity of the law throughout the EEA will determine not only the interpretation of the rules of the Agreement but also the interpretation of the corresponding rules of Community law.

It follows that in so far as it conditions the future interpretation of the Community rules on free movement and competition the machinery of courts provided for in the Agreement conflicts with art 164 of the [EC] Treaty and, more generally, with the very foundations of the Community.'

Comment

Unlike its name the consultative jurisdiction of the ECJ results in binding decisions although it is not necessary that a dispute exists on the matter brought to the attention of the ECJ even though in practice this is often the case. The consultative jurisdiction is provided for all three Communities: arts 95(3) and (4) ECSC, 103 and 104 Euratom and 228(6) EC. The Council, the Commission or a Member State may ask the ECJ for its opinion as to whether the envisaged agreement is compatible with the provisions of the Treaty. If the ECJ considers that the agreement in question is contrary to EC law the only possibility for that agreement to enter into force, apart from its renegotiation, is to revise the Treaty in accordance with art N TEU. The consultative jurisdiction of the ECJ has become quite popular in recent years.

In the context of the present case it is interesting to note that the EEA Agreement is the most important and the most sophisticated agreement concluded under art 228 as it has created a sui generis form of integration.

EFTA was the biggest commercial partner of the EC but after the accession of Austria, Finland and Sweden to the EU on 1 January 1995, which resulted in their desertion from EFTA, the latter has become an obscure and insignificant organisation.

The Treaty establishing the European Economic Area (EEA) was signed on 2 May 1992 in Oporto between the twelve Member States of the European Economic Communities (EEC, ESCS but not the Euratom) and the seven Members of the European Free Trade Area: Austria, Finland, Iceland, Liechtenstein, Norway, Sweden and Switzerland. Its main objective was the creation of the biggest trade area in the world which would account for 46 per cent of the world trade. It was beneficial for both parties: for EFTA countries it secured access to a single market which was essential for their economic survival; for the EC it ensured the expansion of its economy and constituted a counterbalance for the influence of NAFTA (North American Free Trade Agreement) and Japan in international markets.

There were a number of obstacles to the ratification of the original EEA Treaty.

First, the ECJ challenged the creation of the EEA in the present opinion.

Second, the Swiss rejected the EEA in a referendum held in December 1992. The non-participation of Switzerland in the EEA necessitated amendments to the original agreement. The Commission presented a modified text of the EEA Treaty on 9 March 1993 which was embodied in a Protocol annexed to the Treaty and signed on 17 March 1993. The EEA Treaty as amended entered into force on 1 January 1995.

Under the EEA six institutions were set up: the EEA Council, the EEA Joint Committee, the EEA Joint Parliamentary Committee, the EEA Consultative Committee, the EEA Surveillance Authority and the EFTA Court. The main difference in the functioning of the EEA bodies and the EU is that the decision-making procedures of the EEA institutions are based upon consensus between the EU and its Member States and the EFTA countries. Furthermore, the EEA institutions are classical inter-governmental bodies as they have no legislative power.

Presently, there are only three EFTA countries within the EEA: Iceland, Liechtenstein and Norway.

The European Commission

EC Commission v EC Council (Re Generalised System of Tariff Preferences) Case 45/86 [1987] ECR 1493 European Court of Justice

- *Absence of a precise legal basis – measures based on a twin legal basis – single legal basis sufficient – arts 113 and 235 EC Treaty – objective factors – common commercial policy – Community system of generalised tariffs*

Facts
The Commission challenged the legality of two Council regulations dealing with the issue of tariff preferences for products from third world countries on the ground that they were adopted without their legal basis being expressly stated as required by art 190 EC Treaty. In addition, the fact that the Council had resorted to unanimous voting in relation to the adoption of the measures implied that art 235 EC Treaty was the legal basis the Council had in mind. The Commission argued that the measure should have been adopted on the authority of art 113 EC Treaty alone.

Held
The ECJ sustained the arguments of the Commission and found the measures in question void. Where the illegality was not merely formal, the fact that a measure was adopted on the incorrect legal basis was sufficient to render it void.

Judgment

'Article 190 of the Treaty provides that "Regulations, directives and decisions of the Council and of the Commission shall state the reasons on which they are based". According to the case law of the Court (in particular the judgment in Case 158/80 *Rewe-Handelsgesellschaft Nord mbH v Hauptzollamt Kiel* [1981] ECR 1805), in order to satisfy the requirements to state reasons, Community measures must include a statement of facts and the law which led the institution in question to adopt them, so as to make possible review by the Court and so that the Member States and the nationals concerned may have knowledge of the conditions under which the Community institutions have applied the Treaty.

It is therefore necessary to consider whether the contested regulations satisfy those requirements.

In that connection the Council contends that, although the indication of the legal basis is not precise, the recitals in the preambles to the regulations, taken as a whole, provide sufficient alternative information as to the aims pursued by the Council, that is to say both commercial aims and aims of development-aid policy.

However, those indications are not sufficient to identify the legal basis by virtue of which the Council acted. Although the recitals on the preambles to the regulations do refer to improving access for developing countries to the markets of the preference-giving countries, they merely state that adaptations to the Community system of generalised preferences have proved to be necessary in the light of experience in the first fifteen years. Moreover, according to information given to the Court by the Council itself, the wording "having regard to the Treaty" was adopted as a result of differences of opinion about the choice of the appropriate legal basis. Consequently, the wording chosen was designed precisely to leave the legal basis of the regulations in questions vague.

Admittedly, failure to refer to a precise provision of the Treaty need not necessarily constitute and infringement of essential procedural requirements when the legal basis for the measure may be determined from other parts of the measure. However, such explicit reference is indispensable where, in its absence, the parties concerned and the Court are left uncertain as to the precise legal basis.

In answer to a question put by the Court the Council has stated that when it adopted the contested regulations it intended to base them on both arts 113 and 235 of the [EC] Treaty. It has explained that it departed from the Commission's proposal to base the regulations on art 113 alone because it was convinced that the contested regulations had not only commercial policy aims, but also major development policy aims. The implementation of development policy goes beyond the scope of art 113 of the Treaty and necessitates recourse to art 235.

It must also be observed that in the context of the organisation of the powers of the Community the choice of the legal basis for a measure may not depend simply on an institution's conviction as to the objective pursued but must be based on objective factors which are amenable to judicial review.

In this case, the dispute as to the correct legal basis was not purely formal in scope since arts 113 and 235 of the [EC] Treaty lay down different rules governing the Council's decision-making process, and the choice of the legal basis was therefore liable to affect the determination of the content of the contested legislation.

It follows from the very wording of art 235 that its use as the legal basis for a measure is justified only where no other provision of the Treaty gives the Community institutions the necessary power to adopt the measure in question.

It must therefore be considered whether in this case the Council was competent to adopt the contested regulations pursuant to art 113 of the Treaty alone, as the Commission maintains.'

After due consideration of this question, the ECJ concluded that art 113 would have been a sufficient basis for the regulations and the Council was not justified in adopting the measure on the basis of art 235, and continued:

> 'It is clear from the foregoing that the contested regulations do not satisfy the requirements laid down in art 190 of the Treaty with regard to the statement of reasons and that, moreover, they were not adopted on the correct legal basis. Consequently, they must be declared void.'

Comment
Article 235 EC provides that if action by the Community is necessary in order to achieve one of the objectives of the common market but the Treaty has not assigned appropriate competences to the EC in this area, the Council is empowered to take that necessary measure acting unanimously on a proposal from the Commission and after consulting the European Parliament. Article 235 EC provides the EC with residual legislative powers which were used extensively to take measures in important areas outside the scope of the founding Treaty (such as environmental protection, regional aid, research and technology). On the basis of art 235 EC Treaty the Community extended its competences without revising the Treaty itself.

In the past, the Council leant, probably, too frequently, upon art 235 EC for two reasons. First, the Paris summit in October 1972 decided that in order to establish an economic and monetary union, as well as promote the social dimension of the Community, all provisions of the EC Treaty, including art 235, should be widely used. As a result, in the 1970s the Council referred to art 235 EC extensively and systematically. On 15 March 1992, 677 measures both internal and external were adopted on the basis of this provision, and 407 are still operational (Question No 1130/92, OJ C285 of 3.11.1992). The second reason is that art 235 EC requires unanimity and thus the Member States felt well protected in adopting measures as none of them were contrary to their vital national interests.

The Commission has challenged before the ECJ the legal basis of certain measures adopted by the Council under art 235 EC. In the present case the ECJ held that a measure can only be adopted under art 235 if there is no other appropriate provision in the Treaty which would provide a legal basis for Community action.

Amendments to the founding Treaty have considerably extended the competences of the Community and thus limited the role of art 235 EC Treaty. In Opinion 2/94 (ECHR) ([1996] ECR I–1759, para 30) the ECJ held that:

> 'Article 235, cannot be used as a basis for the adoption of provisions whose effect would, in substance be to amend the Treaty without following the procedure which it provides for that purpose.'

EC Commission v *Federal Republic of Germany* Case C–191/95 Judgment of 29 September 1998 (not yet reported) European Court of Justice

• *Action for failure to act – reasoned opinion – principle of collegiate responsibility of the Commission – company law – Directives 68/151 and 78/660 – annual accounts – penalties for failure to disclose companies' annual accounts – different grounds of complaint in the letter of formal notice and the application for a declaration under art 169 EC Treaty*

Facts
The Commission decided to issue a reasoned opinion against the government of the Federal Republic of Germany for failure to provide for appropriate penalties in cases where companies limited by shares failed to disclose their annual accounts, as prescribed in particular by the First Council Directive 68/151/EEC of 9 March 1968 and the Fourth Council Directive 78/660/EEC of 25 July 1978. When Germany did not comply with the opinion the

Commission decided, in conformity with art 169 EC Treaty, to bring proceedings before the ECJ against the German government. Both decisions were challenged by the German government as not being the subject of collective deliberations by the college of Commissioners. Germany argued that the issue of the reasoned opinion and commencement of proceedings were delegated. In addition, Germany maintained that the action was inadmissible because the contents of the application for a declaration of its failure to fulfil obligations under art 169 EC Treaty differed from those of the letter of formal notice.

Held

The plea of inadmissibility submitted by the government of Germany was rejected by the ECJ.

Judgment

'[*Principle of collegiality*]

It is important to remember, at the outset, that the functioning of the Commission is governed by the principle of collegiate responsibility.

It is common ground that the decisions to issue the reasoned opinion and to commence proceedings are subject to that principle of collegiate responsibility.

The principle of collegiality is based on the equal participation of the Commissioners in the adoption of decisions, from which it follows in particular that decisions should be the subject of collective deliberation and that all the members of the college of Commissioners should bear collective responsibility at political level for all decisions adopted.

Nevertheless, the formal requirements for effective compliance with the principle of collegiality vary according to the nature and legal effects of the acts adopted by that institution.

The issue of a reasoned opinion constitutes a preliminary procedure, which does not have any binding legal effect for the addressee of the reasoned opinion. The purpose of that pre-litigation procedure provided for by art 169 of the Treaty is to enable the Member State to comply of its own accord with the requirements of the Treaty or, if appropriate, to justify its position.

If that attempt at settlement is unsuccessful, the function of the reasoned opinion is to define the subject-matter of the dispute. The Commission is not, however, empowered to determine conclusively, by reasoned opinions formulated pursuant to art 169, the rights and duties of a Member State or to afford that State guarantees concerning the compatibility of a given line of conduct with the Treaty. According to the system embodied in arts 169 to 171 of the Treaty, the rights and duties of Member States may be determined and their conduct appraised only by a judgment of the Court.

The reasoned opinion therefore has legal effect only in relation to the commencement of proceedings before the Court so that where a Member State does not comply with that opinion within the period allowed, the Commission has the right, but not the duty, to commence proceedings before the Court.

The decision to commence proceedings before the Court, whilst it constitutes an indispensable step for the purpose of enabling the Court to give judgment on the alleged failure to fulfil obligations by way of a binding decision, nevertheless does not per se alter the legal position in question.

Both the Commission's decision to issue a reasoned opinion and its decision to bring an action for a declaration of failure to fulfil obligations must be the subject of collective deliberation by the college of Commissioners. The information on which those decisions are based must therefore be available to the members of the college. It is not, however, necessary for the college itself formally to decide on the wording of the acts which give effect to those decisions and put them in final form.

In this case it is not disputed that the members of the college had available to them all the information they considered would assist them for the purposes of adopting the decision when the college decided, on 31 July 1991, to issue the reasoned opinion, and approved, on 13 December 1994, the proposal to bring the present action.

In those circumstances, it must be held that the Commission complied with the rules relating to the principle of collegiality when it issued the reasoned opinion with regard to the Federal Republic of Germany and brought the present action.

[*Inadmissibility based on the difference between the content of the application and the letter of formal notice*]
The fact that the Commission did not persist in the complaints based on the fact that a large proportion of companies limited by shares were failing to comply with the disclosure requirements, whilst it detailed the complaints based on the need to provide appropriate sanctions, which it had already set out more generally in the letter of formal notice, merely limited the subject-matter of the action.'

Comment
The Commission is a collegiate body. This means that each member of the Commission is not empowered to take any decision on his own and that once he makes a decision, issues a declaration etc he expresses the position of the entire Commission. This principle entails that each measure must be formally approved by the college, its violation may render that measure invalid (*EC Commission* v *BASF* Case C–137/92P [1994] ECR I–2555 in which the ECJ confirmed the decision of the CFI (*BASF* Cases T–79, 84–86, 91–92, 94, 96 and 98/89 [1992] ECR II–315)).

In the present case the ECJ held that compliance with the principle of collegiality varies according to the nature and legal effect of the act. In the case of acts which have no binding legal effect it is not necessary for the college 'itself formally to decide on the wording of the acts which give effect to those decisions and put them in final form'

The European Parliament

European Parliament* v *Council of the European Union Joined Cases C–164 and 165/97 Judgment of 25 February 1999 (not yet reported) European Court of Justice

- *Parliament's prerogatives – choice of legal basis – arts 43 and 130s EC Treaty – environment – protection of forests against atmospheric pollution and fire*

Facts
The European Parliament (EP) brought proceedings against the Council for annulment of two Regulations, Nos 307/97 and 308/97, concerning the protection of forests against pollution and fire. The EP argued that both Regulations were adopted on an inappropriate legal basis, ie art 43 EC Treaty instead of art 130s EC Treaty. Consequently, the EP prerogatives in respect of the procedure involving its participation in the drafting of legislation were undermined.

Held
The ECJ annulled both Regulations. It held that the challenged Regulations should continue to have effect pending the adoption, within a reasonable time, of regulations enacted on the proper legal basis.

Judgment
'It must be borne in mind that in the context of the organisation of the powers of the Community, the choice of a legal basis for a measure must be based on objective factors which are amenable to judicial review. Those factors include, in particular, the aim and content of the measure.

It is clear from the provisions of the amended regulations that the aims of the Community schemes for the protection of forests are partly agricultural since they are intended in particular to contribute to safeguarding the productive potential of agriculture, and partly of a specifically environmental nature since their primary objective is to maintain and monitor forest ecosystems.

With more particular reference to the common agricultural policy and the Community environmental policy, there is nothing in the case-law to indicate that, in principle, one should take precedence over the other. It makes clear that a Community measure cannot be part of Community action on environmental matters merely because it takes account of requirements of protection referred to in art 130r(2) of the EC Treaty. Articles 130r and 130s leave intact the powers held by the Community under other provisions of the Treaty and provide a legal basis only for specific action on environmental matters. In contrast, art 130s of the Treaty must be the basis for provisions which fall specifically within the environmental policy, even if they have an impact on the functioning of the internal market or if their objective is the improvement of agricultural production.

In this case, although the measures referred to in the regulations may have certain positive repercussions on the functioning of agriculture, those indirect consequences are incidental to the primary aim of the Community schemes for the protection of forests, which are intended to ensure that the natural heritage represented by forest ecosystems is conserved and turned to account, and does not merely consider their utility to agriculture. Measures to defend the forest environment against the risks of destruction and degradation associated with fires and atmospheric pollution inherently form part of the environmental action for which Community competence is founded on art 130s of the Treaty.

The contested regulations do not constitute rules on the production and marketing of agricultural products for which, to the extent to which those rules contribute to the attainment or one or more objectives of the common agricultural policy set out in art 39 of the Treaty, art 43 of the Treaty would have been the appropriate legal basis.

The Parliament is therefore correct in its assertion that, by basing the contested regulations on art 43 of the Treaty although art 130s was the appropriate legal basis, the Council has infringed essential procedural requirements and undermined its prerogatives.'

Comment

The ECJ confirmed its position as to the choice of a legal basis in respect of a Community measure. The ECJ stated that when the aims of contested regulations are partly agricultural and partly of a specifically environment nature then in order to determine the appropriate legal basis the Council has to apply the theory of the principal and accessory (see *European Parliament* v *EC Council (Re Tchernobyl)* Case C–70/88 [1990] ECR 2041; [1992] 1 CMLR 91) unless the measure is intended to pursue both objectives. In that case the measure must be based on two legal basis (see *European Parliament* v *EC Council* Case C–360/96 [1996] ECR I–1195).

The choice of a legal basis determines the participation of the EP in the adoption of a measure. In the present case both regulations should have been based on art 130s of the Treaty and therefore adopted by the Council under the procedure for co-operation with the Parliament provided for in art 189c of that Treaty. Their adoption on the basis of art 43 EC means that the Parliament was merely consulted.

European Parliament v *EC Council (Re Common Transport Policy)* Case 13/83 [1985] ECR 1513; [1985] 1 CMLR 138 European Court of Justice

• *Action for failure to act – right of the European Parliament to commence proceedings under art 175 EC Treaty – objections raised by the Council against the right of Parliament to initiate such proceedings – challenge dismissed – common transport policy*

Facts

The European Parliament (EP) brought an action under art 175(1) of the EC Treaty against the EC Council, alleging that the Council had infringed the terms of the EC Treaty by failing to introduce a common policy for transport, in particular to establish a framework for the negotiation of such a policy.

The Council objected to the admissibility of the action arguing, inter alia, that the EP had no locus standi under art 175 of the EC Treaty to initiate such proceedings. Article 175 merely refers to 'other institutions of the Community' in relation to competence to raise an action in the ECJ for failure to act. No express reference is made to the position of the EP in such proceedings. In addition, the Council also alleged that the conditions laid down in art 175 for bringing such an action had not been satisfied.

Held

The ECJ rejected the contention that the EP possessed no competence to bring an action under art 175. The fact that the EP lacked capacity to commence actions under other provisions of the Treaty was irrelevant in construing art 175 which conferred rights of action to the 'other institutions of the Community', other than the Council and the Commission. The ECJ also rejected the allegations that the procedure followed in the raising of the action did not satisfy the conditions set out in art 175.

Judgment

'[*Capacity of the EP to bring proceedings under art 175 EC Treaty*]

The Council explains first of all that in its opinion the present action is to be seen as part of the Parliament's efforts to increase its influence in the decision-making process within the Community. Those efforts, although legitimate, should not seek to exploit the action for failure to act provided for by art 175 since collaboration between the Community institutions is not governed by that provision. The political aims of the Parliament must be pursued by other means.

In the light of that the Council, while recognising that art 175 gives a right of action in respect of omissions of the Council and Commission to Member States and the "other institutions of the Community", enquires whether the right of review conferred on the Parliament by the Treaty is not exhausted by the powers provided for in arts 175, 143 and 144 of the Treaty, which govern the ways in which the Parliament may exercise influence on the activities of the Commission and the Council. If so, the Parliament can have no right of review over the Council which may exercised by means of an action for failure to act.

The Council adds that upon systematic interpretation of the Treaty the Parliament has no capacity to bring proceedings. The Parliament has no right of action under art 173, which enables a review of the legality of measures of the Council and Commission to be obtained by means of an action for annulment. In so far as the Treaty deprives the Parliament of the right to review the legality of measures of the two institutions it would be illogical to allow it a right of action in the case of unlawful failure by one of those institutions to act. Accordingly, only through an express attribution of powers would it have been possible to confer on the Parliament a right to bring an action for failure to act.

The European Parliament and the Commission contest that argument on the basis of the actual wording of art 175, which in their view does not lend itself to any interpretation which would prevent the Parliament from bringing an action for failure to act. Both institutions also consider that recognition of such a power is in no way incompatible with the division of powers provided for by the Treaty.

The Court would emphasise that the first paragraph of art 175, as the Council recognised, expressly gives a right of action for failure to act against the Council and Commission, inter alia, to "the other institutions of the Community". It this gives the same right of action to all the Community institutions. It is not possible to restrict the exercise of that right by one of them without adversely affecting its status as an institution under the Treaty, in particular art 4(1).

The fact that the European Parliament is at the same time the Community institution whose task is to exercise a political review of the activities of the Commission, and to a certain extent those of the Council, is not capable of affecting the interpretation of the provisions of the Treaty on the rights of action of the institutions.

Accordingly the first objection of inadmissibility must be rejected.'

Comment
The ECJ confirmed that the EP may bring an action against the Council or Commission for failing to act under the terms of art 175 EC Treaty.

European Parliament v EC Council (Re Tchernobyl) Case C–70/88 [1990] ECR 2041; [1992] 1 CMLR 91 European Court of Justice

- *Action for annulment under art 173 EC Treaty – no express right granted to the European Parliament to initiate such an action – locus standi – a semi-privileged applicant – the prerogatives of the European Parliament*

Facts
Before the present case, the European Parliament (EP) had brought a number of actions in an attempt to establish its locus standi under art 173 of the EC Treaty to bring an action for annulment against the other institutions of the Community, particularly the Council and the Commission (see *European Parliament v EC Council (Re Comitology)* Case 302/87 [1988] ECR 5615). Article 173 (before its amendment by the Treaty of Maastricht) expressly reserved the right to bring actions for annulment of the acts of Community institutions to the Council, the Commission and the Member States as privileged applicants.

In the present case the EP challenged an act of the Council. During the consultation stage of the legislative process, Parliament had expressed its disagreement over the legal basis proposed by the Commission for enacting such legislation. Despite these reservations, the Council proceeded to adopt the regulation on the contested legal basis.

The EP brought an action for annulment of the regulation on the ground that it had been adopted on the basis of inappropriate legal authority. However, technically the action was raised under art 146 of the Euratom Treaty and art 173 of the EC Treaty, although both provisions are worded in identical terms.

Held
The ECJ reversed its earlier jurisprudence in a dramatic turnabout, and found that the European Parliament did possess sufficient standing under art 173 to bring an action to challenge the disputed regulation.

Judgment
It was appropriate to observe, as a preliminary ruling matter, that since the disputed measure was based upon a provision of the Euratom Treaty, the admissibility of the action seeking the annulment of that measure was to be assessed in the light of that Treaty.

It was clear from the judgment in Case 302/87 *Comitology* that the Parliament had no right to bring an action for annulment under the provisions of art 173 of the EC Treaty or those of art 146 of the Euratom Treaty which was identically worded.

As pointed out by that judgment, not only did the Parliament have the right to bring an action for failure to act but also the Treaties provided various means by which acts of the Council or the Commission adopted in infringement of the prerogatives of the Parliament could be reviewed by the Court. None the less the background and the arguments had revealed that however useful and varied the various means of redress laid down by the Euratom and EC Treaty might be, they could prove to be inefficient or uncertain.

In the first place, an action for failure to act could not be used to dispute the legal basis of an act which had already been adopted. Moreover, the submission of a preliminary question relating to the validity of a given act or the bringing of acts before the Court by states or individuals with a view to annulment of such an act, were mere possibilities upon which the Parliament could not rely. Finally, although it was for the Commission to ensure the observance of the powers of the Parliament, that task could not go so far as to require the Commission to accept a position of the Parliament and to present an application for annulment which for its own part, it might view as ill-founded.

It followed from the foregoing that the existence of the various legal remedies was not sufficient to guarantee in all circumstances, the annulment of an act of the Council or of the Commission which had infringed the powers of the Parliament. These powers were one of the elements in the institutional balance established by the Treaties. The Treaties had established a system of division of powers between the various institutions of the Community, which conferred upon each of them its own task in the institutional structure of the Community and in the achievement of the tasks conferred upon it.

Respect for the institutional balance implied that each institution should be able to exercise its powers while observing those of the others. It required also that any infringement of that rule, should it arise, should be able to be punished.

The Court, which was responsible pursuant to the Treaties for ensuring the observance of the law in their interpretation and application, had therefore to ensure that he institutional balance was maintained and consequently had to provide judicial review over the observation of the powers of the Parliament where a case was brought before it by the latter, by means of an action suitable to the objective which it was seeking to attain.

In carrying out that task, the Court obviously could not include the Parliament among the institutions which might bring an action pursuant to art 173 of the EC Treaty or art 146 of the Euratom Treaty, without having to demonstrate a specific interest in the proceedings.

It was, however, for it to ensure the full application of the provisions of the Treaty relating to the institutional balance and to act in such a way that the European Parliament, like the other institutions, could not have its powers infringed without having the possibility of a legal action provided for by the Treaties and which could be used in a certain and effective manner.

The absence from the Treaties of a provision enabling the Parliament to bring an action for annulment might constitute a procedural lacuna; however, that could not prevail over the fundamental interest in the maintenance and observation of its institutional balance laid down by the Treaties establishing the European Communities.

Consequently, an action for the annulment of an act of the Council or the Commission brought before the Court by the Parliament was admissible provided that that action sought only to safeguard its powers and that it was based exclusively on grounds based upon the infringement of those powers. Subject to that reservation, an action for annulment by the European Parliament was to be brought in accordance with the rules laid down in the Treaties for an action for annulment brought by other institutions.

The various powers conferred upon the Parliament by the Treaties included participation in the procedure for drawing up legislative acts in the context of the co-operation procedure laid down in the EC Treaty.

In the present case, the Parliament maintained that the disputed regulation was based on art 31 of the Euratom Treaty, which provided only for consultation of the Parliament, although it ought to have been based on art 100a of the EC Treaty which required the opening of the co-operation procedure with the Parliament.

The Parliament therefore concluded that

the choice by the Council of the legal basis for the disputed regulation had resulted in a failure to observe its powers by depriving it of the possibility, provided for in the co-operation procedure, of taking a more active part in the drawing up of the act than was possible in the context of the consultation procedure.

The Parliament having raised the question of an infringement of its powers following the choice of the legal basis of the disputed act, it follows from the foregoing that the present action is admissible.

Comment
Until the entry into force of the TEU the EP was denied locus standi under art 173 EC. It was logical in the sense that acts adopted by the EP were not reviewable under art 173 EC. However, once the ECJ permitted acts of the EP to be reviewed (*Partie Ecologiste 'Les Verts'* v *European Parliament* Case 294/83 [1986] ECR 1339 and *EC Council* v *European Parliament (Budget)* Case 34/86 [1986] ECR 2155), the EP argued that its locus standi under art 173 EC Treaty should be recognised. In *European Parliament* v *EC Council (Comitology)* Case 302/87 the ECJ had refused to confer the EP even limited locus standi although Advocate-General Darmon suggested that the EP should have limited locus standi to maintain the institutional balance of power, especially in cases where its interests or rights were directly affected by acts of the Commission or the Council since in such circumstances the position of the EP would be worse than that of a non-privileged applicant.

Two years later the ECJ reversed its position. In the present case the ECJ referred to the suggestions of Advocate-General Darmon and decided that the action of the EP was admissible under art 173 EC taking into account that the EP prerogatives (which in this case concerned the right of the EP to influence the legislative process leading to the adoption of a measure) were infringed. In the present case the ECJ imposed an important restriction upon the EP. This is that the EP may submit an application for annulment only in order to protect its prerogatives and based solely on the violation of its prerogatives.

France v European Parliament Case C–345/95 [1997] ECR I–5215
European Court of Justice

• *Seat of the European Parliament – periods of monthly plenary ordinary sessions – Edinburgh Decision*

Facts
The French government supported by Luxembourg brought an action for annulment of the vote of the European Parliament (EP) of 20 September 1995 adopting the calendar for its part-sessions for 1996 which reduced the number of plenary part-sessions to be held in Strasbourg in 1996 from 12 to 11. The French government argued that the vote in question was adopted in breach of the Edinburgh Decision, in breach of essential procedural requirements and was also contrary to art 190 EC Treaty. The Edinburgh Decision adopted by the European Council on 12 December 1992 was intended to determine the location of the seats of the Community institutions and of certain bodies and departments of the European Communities. Article 1(a) of that decision specified that:

> 'The European Parliament shall have its seat in Strasbourg where the 12 periods of monthly plenary sessions, including the budget session, shall be held. The periods of additional plenary sessions shall be held in Brussels. The Committees of the European Parliament shall meet in Brussels. The General Secretariat of the European Parliament and its departments shall remain in Luxembourg' (OJ C341 23.12.92 p1).

The Edinburgh Decision was confirmed and complemented by the European Council Decision adopted at the Brussels meeting on 29–30 October 1993 (OJ C323 30.11.93 p1)

Held
The ECJ annulled the vote of the EP of 20 September 1995 adopting the calendar of its

part-time sessions for 1996 to the extent that it did not provide for 12 ordinary plenary part-sessions in Strasbourg in 1996.

Judgment

'By adopting the Edinburgh Decision, therefore, the governments of the Member States have now discharged their obligation by definitively locating the seat of the Parliament in Strasbourg, whilst maintaining several places of work for that institution.

Given a plurality of working places, the exercise of that competence involved not only the obligation to determine the location of the seat of the Parliament but also the implied power to give precision to that term by indicating the activities which must take place there ...

... The Edinburgh Decision must thus be interpreted as defining the seat of the Parliament as the place where 12 ordinary plenary part-sessions must take place on a regular basis, including those during which the Parliament is to exercise the budgetary powers conferred upon it by the Treaty. Additional plenary part-sessions cannot therefore be scheduled for any other place of work unless the Parliament holds the 12 ordinary plenary part-sessions in Strasbourg, where it has its seat.

Contrary to the Parliament's contention, the governments of the Member States have not, by so defining its seat, encroached upon the power of the Parliament to determine its own internal organization, conferred by arts 25 of the ECSC Treaty, 142 of the EC Treaty and 112 of the EAEC Treaty.

Whilst the Parliament is authorised, under that power of internal organisation, to take appropriate measures to ensure the proper functioning and conduct of its proceedings, its decisions in that regard must respect the competence of the governments of the Member States to determine the seat of the institutions ...

... Whilst it is true that the Edinburgh Decision does place certain constraints on the Parliament as regards the organisation of its work, those constraints are inherent in the need to determine its seat while maintaining several places of work for the institution.'

Comment

Articles 216 EC, 77 ECSC and 189 Euratom provide that the seat of Community institutions should be determined by common accord of the Member States. In practice, the determination of the permanent seats of the Community institutions has always been subject to fierce competition among the Member States. The Decision of 8 April 1965 (OJ L152 13.7.67 p18) offered a temporary solution by locating the seats of the institutions in three different places: Luxembourg, Brussels and Strasbourg. This compromise led to many political, financial and legal difficulties, especially with respect to where the session of the EP were to be held (*Luxembourg* v *European Parliament* Case 230/81 [1983] ECR 255; *Luxembourg* v *European Parliament* Case 108/83 [1984] ECR 1945; *France* v *European Parliament* Cases 358/85 and 51/86 [1988] ECR 4821; *Luxembourg* v *European Parliament* Cases C–213/88 and C–39/89 [1991] ECR I–5643).

It seemed that the Edinburgh Decision had settled all controversies regarding the seat of the EP. This is not, however, the case as the EP did not hesitate to challenge the Edinburgh Decision arguing that the latter was adopted in breach of art 216 EC as it encroached upon the power of the EP to determined its own internal organisation conferred by art 142 EC.

The ECJ held that by adopting the Edinburgh Decision the Member States discharged their obligation consisting of definitely locating the seat of the EP in Strasbourg whilst maintaining several places of work for that institution.

Public access to deliberations of the institutions

Svenska Journalistforbunder v *Council of the European Union*
Case T–174/95 [1998] 3 CMLR 645
Court of the First Instance

• Access to information – principle of transparency – scope of the exception concerning the protection of public security – confidentiality of the Council's proceedings – statement of reasons – publication of the defence on the Internet – abuse of procedure

Facts

The applicant, the Swedish Journalist's Union, applied to the Council of the European Union for access to 20 documents relating to the setting up of Europol. Initially, the applicant was allowed access to two documents and after a meeting of the information working party of COREPER to two further documents. The Council of the European Union refused access to the remaining documents on the grounds that 'their release could be harmful to the public interest (public security) and ... [that] they relate to the Council's proceedings, including the position taken by the members of the Council, and are therefore covered by the duty of confidentiality'. The applicant published the edited version of the Council's justification for refusal on the Internet and invited the public to send their comments to the Council's agents, whose telephone and fax numbers were given. The applicant challenged the decision of the Council refusing access to these documents.

Held

The decision of the Council refusing the applicant access to the remaining documents was annulled as it did not comply with the requirements for reasoning laid down in art 190 EC. The Court of First Instance held that the applicant was to bear its own costs of the proceedings, taking into account that it abused the procedure by inviting the public to send their comments to the Council's agents which action was intended to put pressure on the Council, to provoke public criticism of its agents in the performance of their duty and, finally, to allow third party access to the case file of the procedural documents, without the express authorisation of the President of the Court, which was contrary to the Court's procedural rules.

Judgment

'[*Access to the Council's documents*]
... The duty to state reasons in individual decisions has the double purpose of permitting, on the one hand, interested parties to know the reasons for the adoption of the measure so that they can protect their own interests and, on the other hand, enabling the Community court to exercise its jurisdiction to review the validity of the decision.

... In the contested decision the Council indicated only that the disclosure of the 16 documents in question would prejudice the protection of the public interest (public security) and that the documents related to the proceedings of the Council, particularly the views expressed by members of the Council, and for that reason fell within the scope of the duty of confidentiality.

... the Court notes that although the initial refusal contained in the letter of 1 June 1995 was based only upon "the principle of confidentiality as set in art 4(1) of Decision 93/731" the Council was nevertheless able to grant access to two further documents in the course of its consideration of the confirmatory request, namely a report on the activities of the Europol Drugs Unit (document No 4533/95) and a provisional agenda for a meeting of Committee K.4 (document No 4135/95), documents clearly relating to the activities of the Council within the scope of Title VI of the EU Treaty. If the fact that such documents related to Title VI of the EU Treaty meant that they were automatically covered by the exception based upon the protection of the public interest (public security), the Council had no entitlement to grant access to the documents. Moreover, given that the Council considered that it was entitled to grant access to these two documents, having first balanced the interests involved, it follows that the Council must necessarily have considered that all of the documents relating to Title VI did not automatically fall within the scope of the first exception based upon the protection of the public interest (public security). Furthermore, the Council itself admitted that it had not considered that all of the documents connected with Europol were covered by the exception relating to public security.

Finally, so far as concerns the exception in favour of the protection of the confidentiality of its proceedings, the Council did not specifically indicate in the contested decision that all of the documents included in the applicant's request were covered by the exception based upon the protection of the public interest. The applicant could not therefore rule out the possibility that access to some of the documents in question was being refused because they were covered only by the exception based upon the protection of the confidentiality of its proceedings.

The terms of the contested decision do not, however, permit the applicant and, therefore, the Court to check whether the Council has complied with its duty to carry out a genuine balancing of the interests concerned as the application of art 4(2) of Decision 93/731 requires. In fact, the contested decision mentions only the fact that the requested documents related to proceedings of the Council, including the views expressed by members of the Council, without saying whether it had made any comparative analysis which sought to balance, on the one hand, the interest of the citizens seeking the information and, on the other hand, the criteria for confidentiality of the proceedings of the Council.

It follows from all of the foregoing that the contested decision does not comply with the requirements for reasoning as laid down in art 190 of the Treaty and must therefore be annulled without there being any need to consider the other grounds raised by the applicant or to look at the contents of the documents themselves.

[*Publication of the defence on the Internet*]
Under the rules which govern procedure in cases before the Court of First Instance, parties are entitled to protection against the misuse of pleadings and evidence. Thus, in accordance with the third subparagraph of art 5(3) of the Instructions to the Registrar of 3 March 1994, no third party, private or public, may have access to the case-file or to the procedural documents without the express authorisation of the President, after the parties have been heard. Moreover, in accordance with art 116(2) of the Rules of Procedure, the President may exclude secret or confidential documents from those furnished to an intervener in a case.

It follows that a party who is granted access to the procedural documents of other parties is entitled to use those documents only for the purpose of pursuing his own case and for no other purpose, including that of inciting criticism on the part of the public in relation to arguments raised by other parties in the case.

In the present case, it is clear that the actions of the applicant in publishing an edited version of the defence on the Internet in conjunction with an invitation to the public to send their comments to the Agents of the Council and in providing the telephone and telefax numbers of those Agents, had as their purpose to bring pressure to bear upon the Council and to provoke public criticism of the Agents of the institution in the performance of their duties.

These actions on the part of the applicant involved an abuse of procedure which will be taken into account in awarding costs (see below, paragraph 140), having regard, in particular, to the fact that this incident led to a suspension of the proceedings and made it necessary for the parties in the case to lodge additional submissions in this respect.'

Comment

The implementation of the principle of transparency means that citizens of the EU generally have access to documents of EC institutions. Under Council Decision 93/731 the public has access to Council and Commission documents, whilst the European Parliament Decision 97/632/ECSC/EEC/Euroatom ensures wide access to European Parliament documents. However, access to EC institutions' documents may be refused in certain circumstances (see the judgment above). Grounds for refusal must be given and must indicate the means of redress that are available to the applicant.

3 Judicial Review in the European Community I: Direct Actions against Member States

Actions against a Member State by the European Commission under art 169 EC Treaty (now art 226 EC Treaty)

EC Commission v Belgium (Re Failure to Implement Directives)
Case C–225/86 [1988] ECR 579; [1989] 2 CMLR 797 European Court of Justice

• Action against Belgium for failure to comply with Community law – defence based on constitutional fetters – defence rejected – immediate remedial action required

Facts
In February 1982, the ECJ ruled that Belgium was in violation of its Treaty obligations by failing to adopt a number of Community directives within the prescribed period. By July 1985, Belgium has still not complied with the judgment of the ECJ. The directives were still not implemented. The Commission brought another action before the ECJ, this time requiring the Court to compel Belgium to comply with the judgment and adopt the appropriate legislation. The Belgian government claimed that its failure to comply with the judgment of the ECJ was attributable to the constitutional limitations placed on the central government by the Belgian constitution. In particular, the central government had no power to compel provincial governments to comply with the judgments of the ECJ as far as the implementation of legislation was concerned.

Held
The ECJ held that the fact that a government is constitutionally unable to compel a constituent part of its territory to comply with a judgment of the ECJ did not absolve that Member State of its responsibilities under Community law. The ECJ stated that although the Community Treaties did not specify a period within which a Member State must comply with judgment of the ECJ, remedial action must be commenced immediately after the judgment had been rendered.

Judgment
'The Belgian government states that the delay is the result of special difficulties arising out of the transfer of a substantial number of powers to the new regional institutions created by the Loi Speciale de Reforms Institionelles of 8 August 1980.

In reply to the question asked by the Court, the Belgian government stated that the national authorities has power to implement only part of Directive 78/176. At the hearing the Agent of the Belgian government stated that the Royal Decree on the discharge of waste water into surface water had been adopted on 4 August 1986, and therefore at the level of the powers of the national authorities all the measures had been adopted to comply with the aforesaid judgments.

In so far as the regional level was concerned the Belgian government informed the Court that on 2 July 1981, the Flemish region had adopted a decree on the management of waste and had issued a series of implementing decrees which covered the four directives. However, the Belgian government admitted that the directives still had not been wholly implemented in the Walloon region and the Brussels region in spite of the efforts made by those two regions to that end. In that connection, the Agent of the Belgian government stated at the hearing that the Belgian legislation did not empower the State to compel the regions to implement Community legislation or to substitute itself for them and directly implement the directives in the event of persistent delay on their part.

As the Court stated in its judgment in Case 96/81 *EC Commission* v *Netherlands*, each Member State is free to delegate powers to its domestic authorities as it considers fit and to implement directives by means of measures adopted by regional or local authorities. That division of powers does not however release it from the obligation to ensure that the provisions of the directive are properly implemented in national law.

Furthermore, the Court has consistently held that a Member State may not plead provisions, practices or circumstances existing in its internal legal system in order to justify failure to comply with its obligations under Community law.

In its judgment of 2 February 1982, the Court held that by not adopting within the prescribed periods the provisions needed to comply with the directives, the Kingdom of Belgium had failed to fulfil its obligations under the Treaty. The Kingdom of Belgium was required under art 171 of the Treaty to take the necessary measures to comply with judgments of the Court. Article 171 does not specify the period within which such measures must be adopted. However, action to comply with a judgment must be commenced immediately and must be completed as soon as possible, which was not the case here since several years have passed since the judgments in question were delivered.

It must therefore be held that the Kingdom of Belgium has failed to fulfil its obligations under the Treaty.'

Comment

The ingeniousness of Member States in constructing defences under art 169 EC is astonishing. Over the years, they have attempted to plead every justification imaginable for their failure to fulfil their obligations under the Treaty. In the present case, the ECJ rejected a defence based on a Member State's constitutional and institutional organisation. The ECJ stated that a Member State cannot invoke provisions, practices or circumstances existing in its internal legal system in order to justify its failure to fulfil an obligation arising under Community law.

EC Commission v *Belgium* Case C–263/96 [1997] ECR I–7453 European Court of Justice

• *Action against a Member State – failure to implement a directive – defence based on circumstances existing in the Community legal order – defence rejected*

Facts

Belgium failed to implement Directive 89/106 on construction products within the prescribed time-limit. Belgium argued that Directive 89/106 required the adoption of further implementing measures at the Community level. This point has been confirmed by the Moliter group charged which the task of simplifying legislative and administrative acts adopted by the Community institutions and the organisation responsible for the pilot project SLIM concerning the simplification of legislation affecting the functioning of the internal market. The government of Belgium stated that the delays in the adoption of further implementing measures by the Community institutions justified non-implementation of the Directive, and that its failure did not adversely affect the creation of the internal market in construction products taking into account the fact that the latter due to the delays on the part of the Community had not yet been established.

Second, the government of Belgium stated that the difficulties it faced with respect to the implementation of the Directive originated from circumstances existing in the Community legal order, namely because further implementing measures based on non-binding Community acts were necessary in order to complete the Directive in question. Therefore, implementation of the Directive would be very difficult because the Directive as it stood then was incomplete. As a result, the failure to transpose it into national law was justified.

Finally, the Belgian government argued that the Directive in question had been modified by subsequent directives on several occasion and that its final version would be adopted by Belgium in the light of the recommendations adopted within the framework of the SLIM programme.

Held
The ECJ held that a Member State is in breach of its obligation arising out of the Treaty even though difficulties regarding the implementation of the directive in question within the prescribed time-limit result from circumstances existing in the Community legal order. The ECJ held Belgium in breach of Community law.

Judgment

'In its defence the Belgian government states, first that a draft Royal decree has now been drawn up but that a number of problems concerning recognition and supervision, notification of bodies and the creation of fund in accordance with art 7 of the Law of 25 March 1996 remain to be resolved. In that connection a working group bringing together representatives of the Ministry of Economic Affairs and of the Ministry of Transport and Infrastructure is in the process of being set up and the measures necessary for the transposition of the directive should be adopted within six months.

Secondly, the Belgian government emphasises that the directive has still not been implemented at Community level. It refers in that connection to certain documents. First, a report drawn up by the group of experts on legislative and administrative simplification (Molitor Group) indicates that, seven years after adoption of the directive, the construction sector is still not in a position to use the EC trade mark for construction products. Moreover, in a report on the directive submitted on 15 May 1996 under art 23 thereof, the Commission itself acknowledged that there were still obstacles to the practical implementation of the directive and concluded that for a large number of products harmonised standards would not be available for five years. In the same vein the Economic and Social Committee in its opinion on "Technical standards and mutual recognition" (OJ 1996 C212 p7) cited the poor operation of the directive and the lack of harmonised standards. Finally, the Council has supported the setting up of the pilot project known as SLIM (simpler legislation for the single market) whose objective is to examine whether the obligations and burdens weighting on undertakings and which constitute an impediment on account of their over complexity may be eased by simplifying legislative or administrative provisions.

The Belgian government concludes that the delay in the transposition of the directive has had no ill consequence on the process of achieving the single market or on the process of implementing the directive.

The Commission objects that, even though there has been a delay in the application of the directive, that does not prevent its transposition. Referring to the judgment in *EC Commission* v *Italy* Case C–182/94 [1995] ECR I–1465, it also emphasised the fact that the possibility of an amendment to a directive in the near future cannot justify the failure to transpose.

Thirdly, the Belgian government stresses that some of the problems connected with the transposition of the directive stem from Community law itself.

In its resolution of 21 December 1989 on a global approach to conformity assessment

(OJ 1990 C10 p1), for instance, the Council advocated systematic recourse to European standards (EN 45000) for the approval of certification and inspection and testing laboratories. That resolution led to the drawing up of a guide on the application of Community directives on technical harmonisation drawn up on the basis of the provisions of the new approach and the global approach (first version – 1994) and the general procedures were laid down in the document on methods of co-ordination for procedures for notification and management of bodies notified. Effect was given to the Council resolution and the documents cited, as regards the directive, by means of the document "Construct 95/149" of 3 November 1995, approved in December 1995 by the Standing Committee on construction referred to in art 19 of the directive.

According to the Belgian government, since these documents had no binding force, the Community legal basis is insufficient to permit the directive to be transposed in such a way as to take account both of the Council Resolution of 21 December 1989 and of the technical approval guide of 3 November 1995. In those circumstances the directive needs to be amended.

Fourthly, the Belgian Government points out that the directive has already been modified by Council Directive 93/68/EEC of 22 July 1993 amending Directives 87/404/EEC (simple pressure vessels), 88/378/EEC (safety of toys), 89/106/EEC (construction products), 89/336/ EEC (electromagnetic compatibility) 89/392/EEC (machinery), 89/686/EEC (personal protective equipment), 90/384/EEC (non-automatic weighing instruments), 90/385/EEC (active implantable medicinal devices), 90/396/EEC (appliances burning gaseous fuels), 91/263/EEC (telecommunications terminal equipment), 92/42/EEC (new hot-water boilers fired with liquid or gaseous fuels) and 73/23/EEC (electrical equipment designed for use within certain voltage limits) (OJ 1993 L220 p1). Article 14 thereof required the Member States to transpose the directive by 1 July 1994.

Moreover, the Belgian government observes that the SLIM report, submitted to the Council on 26 November 1996, could also result in an amendment to the directive.

It concludes that, under those conditions, the solution adopted by the Kingdom of Belgium, namely the adoption of an enabling law accompanied by a Royal decree, is the most appropriate method of transposition. Those legal instruments enable a swift and flexible response to changes in circumstances without the need for a cumbersome procedure of legislative amendment.

The Court notes that, after expiry of the period prescribed by the reasoned opinion, no provision had been adopted by the Kingdom of Belgium in order to meet its obligation to transpose the directive.

Although it is true, as the Kingdom of Belgium has pointed out, that a law was adopted on 25 March 1996 with that intention, it should be observed that, since it contains no substantive provisions transposing the directive but merely empowers an authority subsequently to adopt the requisite substantive provisions, that law cannot be regarded as effecting a complete and accurate transposition of the directive.

With regard to the first argument relied on by the Belgian government, the Court has consistently held that a Member State may not rely on circumstances in its internal legal system to justify its failure to comply with obligations and time-limits laid down in a directive (*EC Commission* v *Greece* Cases C–109, 207 and 225/94 [1995] ECR I–1791, paragraph 11).

As to the second argument, non-implementation of the directive at Community level cannot prevent the Kingdom of Belgium from adopting the laws and regulations necessary for transposition of the directive.

Furthermore, the binding force conferred on directives by the third paragraph of art 189 of the Treaty precludes any calling in question by a Member State, for opportunistic reasons, of the period prescribed by any directive for its transposition.

Finally, where the finding of a failure by a

Member State to fulfil its obligations is not bound up with a finding as to the damage flowing there from, a Member State may not rely on the argument that the failure to adopt measures to transpose a directive has had no adverse consequences for the functioning of the internal market or of that directive.

As to the third argument that the Council Resolution of 21 December 1989 and the technical approval guide of 3 November 1995 were without binding force, suffice it to state that the failure alleged against that State is constituted by the failure to transpose the directive. The fact that those documents are of no binding effect is therefore of no relevance to the alleged failure to fulfill obligations.

As to the fourth argument, concerning the various amendments made to the directive, Directive 93/68 neither amends nor abrogates the obligation to transpose it. The adoption of the latter directive therefore has no effect on the alleged failure to fulfil obligations. The same is true a fortiori of the purely putative adoption of another amending directive.

As regards the choice of a framework law accompanied by a Royal decree, it should be recalled that, in regard to the implementation of directives, art 189 of the Treaty leaves to the Member States the choice of forms and methods, provided that the result prescribed by the directive is achieved. However, in the present case, the framework law was not accompanied by any Royal decree, notwithstanding standing the flexibility afforded, according to the Belgian government, by such a legal instrument.

It must therefore be concluded that the result prescribed by the directive was not achieved, since an essential component of its transposition is lacking

Consequently, it must be held that, by not adopting all the laws, regulations and administrative provisions necessary to comply with the directive, the Kingdom of Belgium has failed to fulfil its obligations under that directive.'

Comment

The originality of the defences submitted by Belgium requires a comment. Notwithstanding arguments submitted by Belgium, the ECJ held that non-adoption on the part of the Community institutions of further implementing measures cannot justify a failure to transpose a directive by a Member State to which it is addressed. The ECJ rejected the defence based on circumstances existing in the Community legal order. In this respect, the ECJ emphasised that the obligation of implementation which results from art 189 cannot be modified according to the circumstances, even though difficulties have their root in the Community legal order. The ECJ underlined that the obligations arising out of the EC Treaty are assessed objectively, that is they are not conditional upon the existence of loss and therefore a Member State may not rely on the argument that the failure to adopt measures to transpose a directive has had no adverse impact on the functioning of the internal market or of that directive. The failure to fulfil an obligation results solely from non-implementation of a directive within a prescribed time-limit. It also means that a directive must be transposed as it stands, regardless of the fact that it may be subject to future modifications and amendments.

EC Commission v *French Republic*
Case C–144/97 [1998] ECR I–613
European Court of Justice

* *Action against a Member State – failure to implement a directive – defence based on internal legislative difficulties – dissolution of French Parliament – defence rejected*

Facts

The Commission brought proceedings against the French Republic for failure to implement Directive 92/74/ECC of 22 September 1992 widening the scope of Directive 81/85/ECC on the approximation of provisions laid down by law, regulation or administrative action relating to veterinary medicinal products and homeopathic veterinary medicinal products. The French government stated that it had already prepared a draft law and a draft decree transposing Directive 92/74/EEC but it was impossible to enact legislation in this respect because, by decree of 21 April 1997, the President of the French Republic dissolved the French Parliament.

Held
The ECJ held that the dissolution of a national Parliament which made it impossible for a Member State to implement the directive in question within the prescribed time-limit cannot amount to a defence under art 169 EC Treaty. The ECJ held France in breach of Community law.

Judgment
'Under the Directive the Member States had to bring into force the laws, regulations and administrative provisions needed in order to comply with the Directive by 31 December 1993 and to inform the Commission thereof forthwith.

The French Republic states that a draft law and a draft decree transposing the Directive have been drawn up. It adds that the draft law could not be put to a parliamentary vote because, by decree of 21 April 1997, the President of the French Republic decided to dissolve the National Assembly.

It is, however, settled case-law that a Member State cannot rely on provisions, practices or circumstances existing in its internal legal order in order to justify its failure to respect the obligations and time-limits laid down by a directive.

Since the Directive was not transposed within the period prescribed therein, the infringement pleaded by the Commission in that regard must be considered to be established.'

Comment
The interest of this case lies in the fact that the French government decided to justify its failure to implement the Directive in question on internal legislative difficulties knowing that the ECJ has been very consistent in rejecting this defence (see *EC Commission* v *Luxembourg* Case 58/81 [1982] ECR 2175; *EC Commission* v *Belgium* Case 77/69 [1970] ECR 237; *EC Commission* v *Belgium* Case C–133/94 [1996] ECR I–2323.

EC Commission v *Greece (Re Electronic Cash Registers)* Case C–137/91 [1992] 3 CMLR 117 European Court of Justice

• *Obligation to co-operate with the Commission during investigations under art 169 EC Treaty – breach of arts 5 EC and 30 EC Treaty by Greece – separate proceedings based on art 5 EC Treaty*

Facts
In 1988 Greece enacted a law requiring certain retailers to use electronic cash registers. All such registers were to be approved by the appropriate national authorities which adopted a policy of refusing to certify any register containing less than 35 per cent add-on value from Greece. Another Member States complained to the Commission that this policy obstructed imports of cash registers made by its manufacturers and was therefore in breach of art 30 EC Treaty.

The Commission began an investigation and, in the course of its initial stage, sent two telex messages to the Greek Permanent Representation in Brussels, requesting further information. No reply was received in response and the Commission issued a formal notice under art 169 EC Treaty informing Greece of the alleged breach of EC law and asking it to submit its observations on the compatibility of the national law with its Community obligations in respect of the disputed matter.

Again no reply was received by the Commission and, as a final step, the Commission delivered the formal pre-litigation reasoned opinion as required by art 169(1) EC Treaty prior to bringing Court proceedings. Once again, Greece failed to respond. The Commission instituted proceedings before the ECJ based on art 5 EC Treaty.

Held
The ECJ held that Greece had violated art 5 EC Treaty merely by failing to co-operate with the Commission during the investigation. Article 5 EC Treaty imposes a positive duty on Member States to assist the Commission in its investigations into alleged violations of Community law, and failure to do so is itself a breach of Community law.

Judgment
'The Commission states that, following a complaint from the authorities of a Member State concerning the arrangements in force in Greece relating to the purchase of electronic cash registers by commercial enterprises, it sent two telexes on December 7, 1988 and February 23, 1989, respectively, to the defendant's Permanent Representation to the European Communities asking for information and explanations concerning such arrangements. As the Hellenic Republic never replied to those telexes, the Commission considers that it infringed art 5 [EC].

Greece rejects this complaint. It points out that the Greek government gave the Commission all the necessary information concerning the arrangements in question at a meeting in Athens in September 1990. It adds that in January 1991 it sent the Commission the text of Act 1914/1990, which is said to put an end to the infringement by the defendant of art 30 [EC] Treaty. Therefore, the Commission was fully informed before the action was brought and it had no further interest in applying to the Court for a declaration that art 5 had been infringed.

In this connection it should be observed that the defendant did not supply the information in question until almost two years after it was requested and, in any case, after expiry of the time limit fixed by the reasoned opinion.

The failure to reply to the Commission's questions within a reasonable period made the task which it has to perform more difficult and therefore amounts to a violation of the obligation of co-operation laid down by art 5 [EC].

The defendant does not dispute the Commission's complaint that Act 1809/1988 is contrary to art 30 [EC] because it requires, as a condition for the approval of electronic cash registers by the Greek authorities, that not less than 35 per cent of the cost of the machine should consist of national value added. An Act which is said to rectify the position was brought in only after the time-limit fixed by the reasoned opinion had expired.

It follows that Greece has failed to fulfil its obligations under art 5 and 30 [EC] by not providing the Commission with the information which it had asked for and by imposing an obligation on enterprises to purchase exclusively electronic cash registers comprising in their manufacture not less than 35 per cent value added in Greece.'

Comment
Article 5 EC Treaty was considered for a long time as an interpretive device requiring Member States to act in good faith. Gradually, its scope of application has been extended. First, art 5 EC has served to strengthen the binding effect of Community obligations imposed upon Member States. Second, the ECJ has imposed, by virtue of art 5 EC, an obligation on national courts to interpret national law in conformity with Community law; and, finally, art 5 EC has become an independent and autonomous source of obligation. As a result, a breach of art 5 EC gives rise to the liability of the Member States under art 169 EC. In the present case the ECJ explained the autonomous function of art 5 EC.

Article 5 EC Treaty imposes a positive duty on Member States to co-operate with the Commission in its investigations into alleged violations of Community law. Failure to do so is in itself sufficient reason to give rise to the liability of a Member State under art 169 EC (*EC Commission* v *Italy* Case C–33/90 [1991] ECR I–5987; *EC Commission* v *Greece Case* C–65/91 [1992] ECR I–5245) regardless of whether a Member State refuses or simply ignores the request of the Commission for information (*EC Commission* v *Greece* Case 272/86 [1988] ECR 4875; *EC Commission* v *Spain* Case C–375/92 [1994] ECR I–923) or omits to forward necessary indications allowing the Commission to exercise its control of the observance by the Member States of Community law (*EC Commission* v *United Kingdom* Case C–40/92 [1994] ECR I–989).

Action by a Member States against another Member State under art 170 EC Treaty (now art 227 EC Treaty)

France v *United Kingdom (Re Fishing Mesh)* Case 141/78 [1979] ECR 2923; [1980] 1 CMLR 6
European Court of Justice

• *Direct action by one Member State against another Member State – incompatibility of national measures with EC law – the duty of co-operation – art 5 EC Treaty – conservation of fishing stock*

Facts
The United Kingdom enacted an Order in Council which regulated the size of the mesh of fishing nets in an attempt to conserve fishing stocks. Fishing policy is a matter within the competence of the Community and the Council of the European Union had earlier passed a resolution allowing Member States to introduce conservation measures, but only on the condition that prior consultations were held with the Commission. The United Kingdom failed to enter into such consultations prior to the enactment of the Order.

France complained to the Commission that the order had been enacted without the prior approval of the Commission and was therefore contrary to Community law. The Commission delivered a reasoned opinion which supported the contentions of the French government, but did not assume responsibility for continuing the action. The French government brought the matter before the ECJ in the form of a direct action against the United Kingdom based on art 170 EC Treaty.

Held
The ECJ held that the British Order in Council had indeed been enacted without the necessary formalities being observed and consequently the United Kingdom was held in breach of Community law.

Judgment
'The French Republic claims in particular that the disputed order, which was adopted in a matter reserved for the competence of the Community, was brought into force in disregard of the requirements set out in Annex VI to the Resolution adopted by the Council at The Hague at its meetings on 30 October and 3 November 1976, under which, pending the implementation of the appropriate Community measures, Member States might, as an interim measure, adopt unilateral measures to ensure the protection of fishery resources on condition that they had first consulted the Commission and sought its approval. As these requirements were not observed by the government of the United Kingdom the measure adopted is contrary to Community law. In the alternative, the French government also claims that the disputed order is, with regard to the measure adopted, excessive and thus does not constitute a reasonable measure of protection.

… The Commission has rightly claimed that that resolution, in particular field to which it applies, makes specific the duties of co-operation which the Member States assumed under art 5 of the [EC] Treaty when they acceded to the Community.

Performance of these duties is particularly necessary in a situation in which it has appeared impossible, by reason of divergences of interest which it has not yet been possible to resolve, to establish a common policy and in a field such as that of the conservation of the biological resources of the sea in which worthwhile results can only be attained thanks to the co-operation of all Member States.

It follows from the foregoing that the institution of measures of conservation by a Member State must first be notified to the other Member States and to the Commission and that such measures are in particular subject to the requirements laid down by Annex VI to the Hague Resolution. In other words, a Member State proposing to bring such measures into force is required to seek the approval of the Commission, which must be consulted at all stages of the procedure.

It is common ground that these requirements have not been satisfied in this case. The government of the United Kingdom, however, claims that it was not required to follow that procedure since it applies exclusively in the case of "unilateral measures" of conservation of resources adopted by a Member State and that the measures which are subject of the disputed order are not "unilateral measures", inasmuch as they were adopted in order to ensure, within the jurisdiction of the United Kingdom, the undertakings arising for the United Kingdom from the North-East Atlantic Fisheries Convention and the resolutions adopted thereunder.

Annex VI of the Hague Resolution, in the words of which "the Member States will not take any unilateral measures in respect of the conservation of resources", except in certain circumstances and with due observance of the requirements set out above must be understood as referring to any measure of conservation emanating from the Member States and not from the Community authorities. The duty of consultation arising under that resolution thus covers measures adopted by a Member State to comply with one of its international obligations in this matter. Such consultation was all the more necessary in this case since it is common ground, as has been emphasised by the French government and the Commission and accepted by the government of the United Kingdom itself, that the order in question, although carrying our certain recommendations of the North-East Atlantic Fisheries Convention, nevertheless in some respects goes beyond the requirements flowing from those recommendations.

It follows from the foregoing that, by not previously notifying the other Member States and the Commission of the measure adopted and seeking the approval of the Commission, the United Kingdom has failed to fulfil its obligations under art 5 of the [EC] Treaty, Annex VI to the Hague Resolution and arts 2 and 3 of Regulation 101/76.'

Comment

Articles 170 EC Treaty and 142 Euratom Treaty, recognise the autonomous right of a Member State to act against another Member State that has failed to fulfil its obligations arising from Community law. The Commission is very much involved in such proceedings: first, before a Member State brings an action, the Commission must be seised of the disputed matter; and second, the Commission must proceed in exactly the same manner as under art 169 EC, ie it investigates the matter, gives both parties an opportunity to submit their arguments orally and in writing and finally delivers a reasoned opinion within three months of the date on which the matter was brought to its attention.

The involvement of the Commission serves two purposes. On the one hand the Commission during the period of three months acts as an intermediary between the Member States concerned; it attempts to settle the case and find an acceptable solution to the crisis. Indeed, hostility between two Member States undermines the unity of the Community as a whole and may even paralyse its proper functioning. The period of three months is in reality the 'cooling off' period during which the Commission endeavours to resolve the matter in the light of the Community interest. On the other hand, the participation of the Commission in proceedings under art 170 EC emphasises its privileged role as a 'guardian' of the Treaty as well as the exceptional nature of an action against a Member State by another Member State. The case law in respect of art 170 EC confirms this point. Actions under art 170 EC are extremely rare and in general never reach the ECJ. So far the ECJ has delivered only one judgment under art 170 EC and that was in the present case.

Non-contractual liability of a Member State for breach of Community law

Brasserie du Pêcheur SA v Federal Republic of Germany; R v Secretary of State for Transport, ex parte Factortame Ltd and Others (No 4) Joined Cases C–46 and 48/93 [1996] 1 CMLR 889 European Court of Justice

- *Non–contractual liability of a Member State – acts and omissions of the national legislature – conditions of liability, fault – supremacy of Community law*

Facts
Brasserie du Pêcheur v Germany Case C–46/93
Brasserie, a French brewer, was forced to cease exports to Germany as its beer did not comply with the purity standards imposed by the Biersteuergesets (Law on Beer Duty, BGBl.I p144). In *EC Commission v Germany* Case 178/84 [1987] ECR 1227 the ECJ had already ruled that such a ban was incompatible with art 30 EC.

R v Secretary of State for Transport, ex parte Factortame (No 4) Case C–48/93
The United Kingdom government enacted the Merchant Shipping Act 1988 which made the registration of fishing vessels dependent upon conditions as to the nationality, residence and domicile of their owners. Factortame, being a Spanish-owned company, were deprived of their right to fish. In *Factortame (No 3)* Case C–221/89 [1991] ECR I–3905 the ECJ held such regulations as contrary to EC law, this was confirmed in *EC Commission* v *United Kingdom* Case C–246/89 [1991] ECR I–4585.

Held
The ECJ held that Member States could be liable under Community law for breaches of EC Treaty and Community measures in certain defined circumstances. The breach itself must be manifest and serious, and the injury sustained by the individual must have been caused by an illegal act committed by the authorities of a Member State. However, an applicant suing a Member State need not prove that the authorities were at fault.

It is for the national courts to determine the types of injury for which reparation may be awarded, as well as the criteria for quantifying the loss or damage. Nevertheless, under no circumstances could a Member State, in determining the measure of damages, apply criteria which are less favourable to EC cases than to equivalent domestic cases. The manner in which damages are assessed must not be such as to make it impossible or excessively difficult for full compensation to be obtained.

Judgment
'[*State liability for acts and omissions of the national legislature contrary to Community law (first question in both cases)*]
The German, Irish and Netherlands governments contend that Member States are required to make good loss or damage caused to individuals only where the provisions breached are not directly effective: in *Francovich and Others* the Court simply sought to fill a lacuna in the system for safe-

guarding rights of individuals. In so far as national law affords individuals a right of action enabling them to assert their rights under directly effective provisions of Community law, it is unnecessary, where such provisions are breached, also to grant them a right to reparation founded directly on Community law.

This argument cannot be accepted.

The Court consistently held that the right of individuals to rely on the directly effective provisions of the Treaty before national courts is only a minimum guarantee and is not sufficient in itself to ensure the full and complete implementation of the Treaty (see, in particular, Case 168/85 *EC Commission* v *Italy* [1986] ECR 2945, [1988] 1 CMLR 580, paragraph 11; Case C–120/88 *EC Commission v Italy* [1991] ECR I–621, paragraph 10; and C–119/89 *EC Commission* v *Spain* [1991] ECR I–641, [1993] 1 CMLR 41). The purpose of that right is to ensure that provisions of Community law prevail over national provisions. It cannot, in every case, secure for individuals the benefit of the rights conferred on them by Community law and, in particular, avoid their sustaining damage as a result of a breach of Community law attributable to a Member State. As appears from paragraph 33 of the judgment in *Francovich and Others*, the full effectiveness of Community law would be impaired if individuals were unable to obtain redress when their rights were infringed by a breach of Community law.

This will be so where an individual who is a victim of the non-transposition of a directive and is precluded from relying on certain of its provisions directly before the national court because they are insufficiently precise and unconditional, brings an action for damages against the defaulting Member State for breach of the third paragraph of art 189 of the Treaty. In such circumstances, which obtained in the case of *Francovich and Others*, the purpose of reparation is to redress the injurious consequences of a Member State's failure to transpose a directive as far as beneficiaries of that directive are concerned.

It is all the more so in the event of infringement of a right directly conferred by a Community provision upon which individuals are entitled to rely before the national courts. In that event, the right to reparation is the necessary corollary of the direct effect of the Community provision whose breach caused the damage sustained.

In this case, it is undisputed that the Community provisions at issue, namely art 30 of the Treaty in Case C–46/93 and art 52 in Case C–48/93, have direct effect in the sense that they confer on individuals rights upon which they are entitled to rely directly before the national courts. Breach of such provisions may give rise to reparation.

... It must, however, be stressed that the existence and extent of State liability for damage ensuing as a result of a breach of obligations incumbent on the State by virtue of Community law are questions of Treaty interpretation which fall within the jurisdiction of the Court.

In this case, as in *Francovich and Others*, those questions of interpretation have been referred to the Court by national courts pursuant to art 177 of the Treaty.

Since the Treaty contains no provision expressly and specifically governing the consequences of breaches of Community law by member States, it is for the Court, in pursuance of the task conferred on it by art 164 of the Treaty of ensuring that in the interpretation and application of the Treaty the law is observed, to rule on such a question in accordance with generally accepted methods of interpretation, in particular by reference to the fundamental principles of the Community legal system and, where necessary, general principles common to the legal systems of the Member States.

Indeed, it is to the general principles common to the laws of the Member States that the second paragraph of art 215 of the Treaty refers as the basis of the non-contractual liability of the Community for damage caused by its institutions or by its servants in the performance of their duties.

The principle of non-contractual liability of the Community expressly laid down in art 215 of the Treaty is simply an expression of the general principles familiar to the legal systems of the Member States that an unlawful act or omission gives rise to an obligation to make good the damage caused. That provision also reflects the obligation on public authorities to make good damage caused in the performance of their duties.

In any event, in many national legal systems the essentials of the legal rules governing State liability have been developed by the courts.

In view of the foregoing considerations, the Court held in *Francovich and Others* at paragraph 35, that the principle of State liability for loss and damage caused to individuals as a result of breaches of Community law for which it can be held responsible is inherent in the system of the Treaty.

It follows that the principle holds good for any case in which a Member State breaches Community law, whatever be the organ of the State whose act or omission was responsible for the breach ...

Consequently, the reply to the national courts must be that the principle that Member States are obliged to make good damage caused to individuals by breaches of Community law attributable to the State is applicable where the national legislature was responsible for the breach in question.

[*Conditions under which the State may incur liability for acts or omission of the national legislature contrary to Community law (second question in Case C–46/93 and first question in Case C–48/93*]

... Although Community law imposes State liability, the conditions under which that liability gives rise to reparation depend on the nature of the breach of Community law giving rise to the loss and damage (*Francovich and Others*).

In order to determine those conditions, account should be taken of the principles inherent in the Community legal order which form the basis for State liability, namely, first, the full effectiveness of community rules and the effective protection of the rights which they confer and, second, the obligation to co-operate imposed on Member States by art 5 of the Treaty (*Francovich and Others*).

In addition, as the Commission and the several governments which submitted observations have emphasised, it is pertinent to refer to the Court's case law on non-contractual liability on the part of the Community.

First, the second paragraph of art 215 of the Treaty refers, as regards the non-contractual liability of the Community, to the general principles common to the laws of the Member States, from which, in the absence of written rules, the Court also draws inspiration in other areas of Community law.

Second, the conditions under which the State may incur liability for damage caused to individuals by breach of Community law cannot, in the absence pf particular justification, differ from those governing the liability of the Community in like circumstances. The protection of the rights which individuals derive from Community law cannot vary depending on whether a national authority or a Community authority is responsible for the damage.

The system of rules which the Court has worked out with regard to art 215 of the Treaty, particularly in relation to liability for legislative measures, takes into account, inter alia, the complexity of the situations to be regulated, difficulties in the application or interpretation of the texts and, more particularly, the margin of discretion available to the author of the act in question.

Thus, in developing its case law on the non-contractual liability of the Community, in particular as regards legislative measures involving choices of economic policy, the Court has had regard to the wide discretion available to the institutions in implementing Community policies.

The strict approach taken towards the liability of the Community in the exercise of its legislative activities is due to two considerations. First, even where the legality of measures is subject to judicial review, exercise of the legislative function must not be hindered by the prospect of actions for damages whenever the general interest of the Community requires legislative measures to be adopted which may adversely affect individual interest. Second, in a legislative context characterised by the exercise of a wide discretion, which is essential for implementing a Community policy, the Community cannot incur liability unless the institution concerned has manifestly and gravely disregarded the limits on the exercise of its powers (Joined Cases 83 and 94/76, and 4, 15 and 40/77 *HNL and Others v EC Council and EC Commission* [1978] ECR 1209, paragraphs 5 and 6).

That said, the national legislature – like the Community institutions – does not systematically have a wide discretion when it acts in a field governed by Community law. Community law may impose upon it obligations to achieve a particular result or obligations to act or refrain from acting which reduce its margin of discretion, sometimes to a considerable degree. This is so, for instance, where, as in the circumstances to which the judgment in *Francovich an Others* relates, art 189 of the Treaty places the Member States under an obligation to take, within a given period, all the measures needed in order to achieve the result required by a directive. In such a case, the fact that it is for national legislature to take the necessary measures has no bearing on the Member State's liability for failing to transpose the directive.

In contrast, where a Member State acts in a field where it has a wide discretion, comparable to that of the Community institutions in implementing Community policies, the conditions under which it may incur liability must, in principle, be the same as those under which the Community institutions incur liability in a comparable situation.

In the case which gave rise to the reference in Case C–46/93, the German legislature had legislated in the field of foodstuffs, specifically beer. In the absence of Community harmonization, the national legislature had a wide discretion in that sphere in laying down rules on the quality of beer put on the market.

As regards the facts in Case C–48/93, the United Kingdom legislature also had a wide discretion. The legislation at issue was concerned, first with the registration of vessels, a field which, in view of the state of development of Community law, falls within the jurisdiction of the Member States and, secondly, with regulating fishing, a sector in which implementation of the common fisheries policy leaves a margin of discretion to the Member States.

Consequently, in each case the German and United Kingdom legislatures were faced with situations involving choices comparable to those made by the Community institutions when they adopt legislative measures pursuant to a Community policy.

In such circumstances, Community law confers a right to reparation where three conditions are met: the rule of law infringed must be intended to confer rights on individuals; the breach must be sufficiently serious; there must be a direct causal link between the breach of the obligation resting on the State and the damage sustained by the injured parties.

Firstly, those conditions satisfy the requirements of the full effectiveness of the rules of Community law and of the effective protection of the rights which those rules confer.

Secondly, those conditions correspond in substance to those defined by the Court in relation to art 215 in its case law on liability of the Community for damage caused to individuals by unlawful legislative measures adopted by its institutions.

The first condition is manifestly satisfied in the case of art 30 of the Treaty, the relevant provision in Case C–46/93, and in the case of art 52, the relevant provision in Case C–48/93. Whilst art 30 imposes a prohibition on member States, it nevertheless gives rise to rights for individuals which the national courts must protect (Case 74/76 *Iannelli & Volpi* v *Meroni* [1977] ECR 557, [1977] 2 CMLR 688, paragraph 13). Likewise, the essence of art 52 is to confer rights on individuals (Case 2/74 *Reyners* [1974] ECR 631, [1974] 2 CMLR 305, paragraph 25).

As to the second condition, as regards

both Community liability under art 215 and Member States' liability for breaches of Community law, the decisive test for finding that a breach of Community law is sufficiently serious is whether the Member State or the Community institution concerned manifestly and gravely disregarded the limits on its discretion.

The factors which the competent court may take into consideration include the clarity and precision of the rule breached, the measure of discretion left by that rule to the national or Community authorities, whether the infringement and the damage caused was intentional or involuntary, whether any error of law was excusable or inexcusable, the fact that the position taken by a Community institution may have contributed towards the omission, and the adoption or retention of national measures or practices contrary to Community law.

On any view, a breach of Community law will clearly be sufficiently serious if it has persisted despite a judgment finding the infringement in question to be established, or a preliminary ruling or settled case law of the Court on the matter from which it is clear that the conduct in question constituted an infringement.

While, in the present cases, the Court cannot substitute its assessment for that of the national courts, which have sole jurisdiction to find the facts in the main proceedings and decide how to characterise the breaches of Community law at issue, it will be helpful to indicate a number of circumstances which the national courts might take into account ...

[*The possibility of making reparation conditional upon the existence of fault*]

... where a breach of Community law is attributable to a Member State acting in a field in which it has a wide discretion to make legislative choices, a finding of a right to reparation on the basis of Community law will be conditional, inter alia, upon the breach having been sufficiently serious.

So, certain objective and subjective factors connected with the concept of fault under a national legal system may well be relevant for the purposes of determining whether or not a given breach of Community law is serious.

The obligation to make reparation for loss or damage caused to individuals cannot, however, depend upon a condition based on any concept of fault going beyond that of a sufficiently serious breach of Community law. Imposition of such a supplementary condition would be tantamount to calling in question the right to reparation founded on the Community legal order.

Accordingly, the reply to the question from the national court must be that, pursuant to the national legislation which it applies, reparation of loss or damage cannot be made conditional upon fault (intentional or negligent) on the part of the organ of the State responsible for the breach, going beyond that of a sufficiently serious breach of Community law.'

Comment

In the present cases the ECJ elucidated many outstanding questions left unanswered in *Francovich*. First, the Court abolished the disparity between the conditions governing liability of the Community institutions based on art 215(2) EC Treaty and the conditions under which the Member State may incur liability for damage caused to individuals in like circumstances. Second, the ECJ clarified the conditions of liability:

1. the rule of law which has been infringed must be one which is intended to confer rights on individuals;
2. the breach must be sufficiently serious to merit an award of damages. To be held liable a Member State must have 'manifestly and gravely' disregarded its obligation to be held liable. In order to assess whether this condition is satisfied, national courts should take into consideration a number of factors such as: the clarity and precision of the EC rule breached; the element of discretion in the adoption of normative acts by national authorities; whether or not the infringement was intentional or accidental; whether any error of law was excusable; and whether any

action or advice on the part of the Commission had contributed to the breach, etc;
3. there must be a direct causal link between the Member State's default and the loss suffered by the applicant.

These conditions of State liability apply to all breaches of Community law, whether legislative, executive or administrative. A State is liable regardless of the organ of State whose act or omission infringed Community law. Also, it is irrelevant whether the provision in question is directly effective or not. Whichever is breached, a Member State may be liable. The ECJ emphasised that direct effect constitutes a minimum guarantee and thus *Francovich* liability is a necessary corollary of the effet utile of Community law.

The ECJ has placed the onus upon national courts to uphold such rights under national rules for public tortious liability by imposing upon them the duty to 'verify whether or not the conditions governing state liability for a breach of Community law are fulfilled'. The court laid down the criteria which might be used by national courts in order to determine the measure of damage. National courts are charged with ensuring that the protection of Community law rights is given equal status and may not be less favourable than the protection afforded to similar rights arising under domestic law. National courts may not impose any procedure that makes it more difficult or even impossible for an individual to rely upon those rights. The UK's rule on the award of exemplary damages against a public official for oppressive, arbitrary or unconstitutional behaviour should be carried over to claims for breaches of EC law.

Brinkmann Tabakfabriken GmbH v *Skatteministeriet* Case C–319/96 [1998] 3 CMLR 673 European Court of Justice

• *Non-contractual liability of a Member State for breach of Community law – taxation – erroneous interpretation of Directive 79/32/EEC – cigarettes – smoking tobacco*

Facts
The Danish Eastern Regional Court referred to the ECJ two questions. The first concerned the classification of a product consisting of rolls of tobacco which in order to be smoked must be inserted into a cigarette-paper tube (sold separately from the rolls of tobacco) or wrapped in normal cigarette paper. The second concerned the non-contractual liability of Denmark for erroneously classifying the product in question as a cigarette for tax purposes and carrying out the decision adopted in respect of the classification of the product. This product was taxed in Germany as smoking tobacco while in Denmark it was considered as a cigarette. Different classification of the product in Germany and in Denmark resulted in different tax levied on that product, lower tax in Germany, higher tax in Denmark. Brinkmann, a producer of the product, brought an action against Denmark for loss it suffered in Denmark as a result of a higher rate of taxation. It argued that Danish authorities did not properly implement Directive 79/32 which contains the definitions of cigarettes and smoking tobacco.

Held
The ECJ confirmed that Denmark erroneously classified the product as a cigarette. The product should be classified as smoking tobacco within the meaning of Directive 79/32/EEC. The Court held that the Danish authorities should not be liable for damage sustained by Brinkmann because in interpreting erroneously Directive 79/32/EEC and not suspending the operation of the decision adopted they did not commit a sufficiently serious breach of Directive 79/32/EEC.

Judgment
'[*First question*]
First of all, the Second Directive, already contained a precise definition of cigarettes stating their three distinctive features to be

as follows: (a) they are rolls of tobacco; (b) which are capable of being smoked as they are; and (c) which are not cigars or cigarillos.

It is common ground that a product such as Westpoint exhibits the first and third characteristics. It does not, however, exhibit the second because the roll of tobacco at issue cannot be smoked as it is but must first be inserted into a cigarette-paper tube or wrapped in normal cigarette paper.

A product of the kind at issue in the main proceedings thus falls within the scope of art 4(1) of the Second Directive, which defines smoking tobacco. The rolls of tobacco at issue here in fact consist of tobacco which has been cut and is capable of being smoked without further industrial processing.

[Second question]
In this case, there is no disputing that arts 3(1) and 4(1) of the Second Directive which contain the definitions of cigarettes and smoking tobacco were not properly transposed into national law, as the competent Minister authorised by the relevant law to lay down the necessary provisions has not adopted any rule of law in implementation thereof.

However, it must be emphasised that there is no direct causal link in this case between the breach of Community law and the damage allegedly suffered by Brinkmann. Indeed, the Danish authorities gave immediate effect to the relevant provisions of the Second Directive containing precise definitions of tobacco products. Accordingly, the fact that the definitions in the Second Directive were not implemented by ministerial decree does not in itself give rise to liability on the part of the State.

It remains to be determined whether the Danish authorities committed a sufficiently serious breach of the relevant provisions of the Second Directive, having regard to the degree of clarity and precision of those provisions.

In this case, they did not. Indeed, Westpoint does not correspond exactly to either of the definitions in the Directive. Rather, the product is one which did not exist at the time when the Second Directive was adopted and which sought to give consumers the advantages of a cigarette while benefiting from the lower tax applicable to smoking tobacco. In those circumstances, the interpretation given by the Danish authorities to the relevant definitions was not manifestly contrary to the wording of the Second Directive or in particular to the aim pursued by it.'

Comment

The ECJ confirmed that even though Directive 79/32/EEC was not properly transposed into national law, the Danish authorities did refer to the Directive in order to classify the product although that classification was erroneous. Non-implementation of the Directive does not automatically give rise to non-contractual liability of a Member State. The erroneous interpretation itself was justified, taking into account that the product in question was neither a cigarette nor smoking tobacco. In the present case the ECJ confirmed its previous ruling in *R v Minister of Agriculture, Fisheries and Food, ex parte Hedley Lomas (Ireland) Ltd* Case C–5/94 [1996] ECR I–2553 that when a Member State enjoys a wide discretion in the manner of implementation of a directive then it must have 'manifestly and gravely' disregarded the limits of its discretion in order to be liable for damages suffered by individuals..

It is also interesting to note that in the present case the ECJ classified the product and therefore solved the dispute within the preliminary ruling proceedings. This attitude of the ECJ is not unusual (see *R v HM Treasury, ex parte British Telecommunicaions plc* Case C–292/93 [1996] ECR I–1631 and *Denkavit* Case C–283/94 [1996] ECR I–5063), although contrary to the letter and spirit of art 177 EC Treaty.

Erich Dillenkofer and Others v Federal Republic of Germany Joined Cases C–178, 179 and 189/94 [1996] ECR I–4845 European Court of Justice

- *Non-contactual liability of a Member State – non-implementation of Directive 90/314/EEC*

Facts
Erich Dillenkofer and others brought proceedings against Germany for non-implementation of Directive 90/314/EEC on package travel, package holidays and package tours within the prescribed time-limit. The plaintiffs had to make an 'advance payment' of 10 per cent towards the travel price, with a maximum of DM 500 to the travel organiser. The travel organiser became insolvent and they lost the deposit. The requirement of a deposit is contrary to Directive 90/314/EEC intended to protect customers against the risk of the organiser's insolvency. The plaintiffs suffered damages because of the failure of Germany to transpose the Directive within the prescribed time-limit and asked for compensation.

Held
The ECJ held that non-implementation of a directive within the prescribed time limit constitutes per se a serious breach of Community law and consequently gives rise to a right of reparation for individuals suffering injury if the result prescribed by the directive entails the grant to individuals of rights whose content is identifiable and a causal link exists between the breach of the State's obligation and the loss and damage suffered. Germany was liable for damages suffered by the plaintiffs.

Judgment
'[*Conditions under which a Member State incurs liability*]
The crux of these questions is whether a failure to transpose a directive within the prescribed period is sufficient per se to afford individuals who have suffered injury a right to reparation or whether other conditions must also be taken into consideration. In order to reply to those questions, reference must first be made to the Court's case law on the individual's right to reparation of damage caused by a breach of Community law for which a Member State can be held responsible.

The Court has held that the principle of State liability for loss and damage caused to individuals as a result of breaches of Community law for which the State can be held responsible is inherent in the system of the Treaty (*Francovich, Brasserie du Pêcheur, Factortame, British Telecommunications* and *Hedley Lomas*). Furthermore, the Court has held that the conditions under which State liability gives rise to a right to reparation depend on the nature of the breach of Community law giving rise to the loss and damage.

When the Court held that the conditions under which State liability gives rise to a right to reparation depended on the nature of the breach of Community law causing the damage, that meant that those conditions are to be applied according to each type of situation.

On the one hand, a breach of Community law is sufficiently serious if a Community institution or a Member State, in the exercise of its rule-making powers, manifestly and gravely disregards the limits on those powers. On the other hand, if, at the time when it committed the infringement, the Member State in question was not called upon to make any legislative choices and had only considerably reduced, or even no, discretion, the mere infringement of Community law may be sufficient to establish the existence of a sufficiently serious breach.

So where, as in *Francovich*, a Member State fails, in breach of the third paragraph of art 189 of the Treaty, to take any of the measures necessary to achieve the result prescribed by a directive within the period it lays down, that Member State manifestly and gravely disregards the limits on its discretion.

Consequently, such a breach gives rise to a right to reparation on the part of individuals if the result prescribed by the directive entails the grant of rights to them, the content of those rights is identifiable on the basis of the provisions of the directive and a causal link exists between the breach of the State's obligation and the loss and damage suffered by the injured parties: no other conditions need be taken into consideration.

In particular, reparation of that loss and damage cannot depend on a prior finding by the Court of an infringement of Community law attributable to the State, nor on the existence of intentional fault or negligence on the part of the organ of the State to which the infringement is attributable.'

Comment

In the present case the ECJ clarified the conditions for non-contractual liability of a Member State. The Court confirmed that when a Member State is not called upon to make any legislative choices and has only considerably reduced, or even no, discretion, the mere breach of EC law may be sufficient to establish the existence of a breach sufficiently serious to give rise to non-contractual liability (see *R v HM Treasury, ex parte British Telecommunications plc* Case C–392/93 [1996] ECR I–1631). In the case of non-implementation of a directive within the prescribed time-limit a Member State 'manifestly and gravely' disregards the limits of its discretion and therefore will be held liable.

Francovich v Italian Republic
Joined Cases C–6 and 9/90 [1991] ECR I–5357; [1993] 2 CMLR 66
European Court of Justice

• *Non-contractual liability of a Member State – failure to implement a directive – injury to private party – conditions of liability*

Facts

As a result of the bankruptcy of his employer, Francovich lost 6,000,000 lira. He sued his former employer but could not enforce judgment against him (the latter was insolvent). He decided to commence proceedings against the Italian State for sums due under Council Directive 80/987, which was not implemented in Italy, although the prescribed time-limit had already elapsed, or for compensation in lieu. Directive 80/987 on protection of employees in the event of the insolvency of their employers required that the Member State set up a scheme under which employees of insolvent companies would receive at least some of their outstanding wages. In *EC Commission v Italy* Case 22/87 [1989] ECR 143 the ECJ under art 169 EC held Italy in breach of EC law for non-implementation of Directive 80/987. The Italian court made reference to the ECJ under art 177 to determine whether the provision of the Directive in relation to payment of wages was directly effective, and whether the Italian State was liable for damages arising from its failure to implement the Directive.

Held

The ECJ held that the provision in question was not sufficiently clear to be directly effective. However, the ECJ stated that while the plaintiff could not rely on the direct effect of the Directive to establish liability, he could succeed against the State on the ground that Member States are liable to private individuals for injury caused to them by failing to properly implement a Community measure.

This liability was not absolute. In particular, in order to establish liability, the Directive had to confer rights on individuals and the content of these rights had to be identified within the context of the measure. The third condition for liability was the existence of a causal link between the failure of the Member State to comply with its Community obligations and the injury suffered by the individual.

Judgment

'[*The existence of State liability as a matter of principle*]

It must be recalled first of all that the [EC] Treaty has created its own legal system which is an integral part of the legal systems of the Member States and which courts are bound to apply; the subjects of that legal system are not only Member States but also their nationals. Just as it imposes obligations on individuals. Community law is also intended to create rights which become part of their legal patrimony; those rights arise not only where they are expressly granted by the Treaty but also by virtue of obligations which the Treaty imposes in a clearly defined manner both on individuals and on the Member States and the Community institutions (see the judgment in Case 26/62 *Van Gend en Loss* [1963] ECR 1 and Case 6/64 *Costa* v *ENEL* [1964] ECR 585).

Furthermore, it has been consistently held that the national courts whose task it is to apply the provisions of Community law in cases within their jurisdiction must ensure that those rules have full effect and protect the rights which they confer on individuals (see in particular the judgment in Case 106/77 *Amministrazione delle Finanze dello Stato* v *Simmenthal* [1978] ECR 629, paragraph 16, and Case C–213/89 *Factortame* [1990] ECR I–2433, paragraph 19).

It must be held that the full effectiveness of Community rules would be impaired and the protection of the rights which they grant would be weakened if individuals were unable to obtain compensation when their rights are infringed by a breach of Community law for which a member State can be held responsible.

The possibility of compensation by the Member State is particularly indispensable where, as in this case, the full effectiveness of Community rules is subject to prior action on the part of the state and consequently individuals cannot, in the absence of such action, enforce the rights granted to them by Community law before the national courts.

It follows that the principle of State liability for harm caused to individuals by breaches of Community law for which the State can be held responsible is inherent in the system of the Treaty.

Further foundation for the obligation on the part of Member States to pay compensation for such harm is to be found in art 5 of the Treaty, under which the Member States are required to take all appropriate measures, whether general or particular, to ensure fulfilment of their obligations under Community law. Among these is the obligation to nullify the unlawful consequences of a breach of Community law (see, in relation to the analogous provision of art 86 of the ECSC Treaty, the judgment in Case 6/60 *Humblet* v *Belgium* [1960] ECR 1125).

It follows from all the foregoing that it is a principle of Community law that the Member States are obliged to pay compensation for harm caused to individuals by breaches of Community law for which they can be held responsible.

[*Preconditions of State liability*]

Although State liability is thus required by Community law, the conditions under which that liability gives rise to a right to compensation depend on the nature of the breach of Community law giving rise to the harm.

Where, as in this case, a Member State fails to fulfil its obligation under the third paragraph of art 189 of the Treaty to take all the measures necessary to achieve the result prescribed by a directive the full effectiveness of that rule of Community law requires that there should be a right to compensation where three conditions are met.

The first of those conditions is that the result prescribed by the directive should entail the grant of rights to individuals. the second condition is that it should be possible to identify the content of those rights on the basis of the provisions of the directive. Finally, the third condition is the existence of a causal link between the breach of the State's obligation and the harm suffered by the injured parties.

Those conditions are sufficient to give rise to a right on the part of individuals to obtain compensation, a right which is founded directly on Community law.

Subject to that reservation, it is in accordance with the rules of national law on liability that the State must make reparation for the consequences of the harm caused. In the absence of any Community legislation, it is a matter for the internal legal order of each Member State to determine the competent court and lay down the detailed procedural rules for legal proceedings intended fully to safeguard the rights which individuals derive from Community law (see the judgments in Case 60/75 *Russo* v *AIMA* [1976] ECR 45, Case 33/76 *Rewe* v *Landwirtstchaftskammer Saarland* [1976] ECR 1989 and Case 158/80 *Rewe* v *Hauptzollamt Kiel* [1981] ECR 1805).

It must also be pointed out that the substantive and procedural conditions laid down by the national law of the various Member Stated on compensation for harm may not be less favourable than those relating to similar internal claims and may not be so framed as to make it virtually impossible or excessively difficult to obtain compensation (see, in relation to the analogous issue of the repayment of taxes levied in breach of Community law, inter alia, the judgment in Case 199/82 *Amministrazione delle Finanze dello Stato* v *San Giorgio* [1983] ECR 3595).

In this case, the breach of Community law by a Member State by virtue of its failure to transpose Directive 80/987 within the prescribed period has been confirmed by a judgment of the Court. The result required by that directive entails the grant to employees of a right to a guarantee of payment of their unpaid wage claims. As is clear from the examination of the first part of the first question, the content of that right can be identified on the basis of the provisions of the directive.

Consequently, the national court must, in accordance with the rules of national law on liability, uphold the right of employees to obtain compensation for harm caused to them as a result of the failure to transpose the directive.

The answer to be given to the national court must therefore be that a Member State is required to pay compensation for the harm suffered by individuals as a result of the failure to implement Directive 80/987.'

Comment

The principle that a Member State should be liable in damages to individuals who have suffered loss as a result of its infringement of Community law is today one of the cornerstones of Community law. Its origin can be found in *Russo* v *Aima* Case 69/75 [1976] ECR 45 in which the ECJ held that a Member State should compensate damage caused by its own breach of Community law but referred to national law to lay down the necessary conditions applicable to tortious liability.

In the present case the ECJ for the first time established Member States' liability in tort. The ECJ justified the new principle on the basis of supremacy of Community law, effet utile and art 5 EC which requires Member States to take all appropriate measure to ensure the fulfilment of their obligations arising out of the Treaty. The less obvious justification, not mentioned in the present case, is that many Member States in the late 1980s delayed the implementation of EC directives which were mainly used to complete the internal market. There was no effective remedy since penalties against defaulting Member States were introduced in the amended art 171 EC by the TEU. The best way to ensure implementation of an EC directive was to allow individuals to enforce their rights before national courts, that is to permit them to sue a defaulting Member State for loss that they had suffered, especially in cases where the EC directives were not directly effective or when individuals had no remedy based on indirect horizontal effect.

In this case the ECJ has established three conditions necessary to give rise to liability in the case of total failure of a Member State to implement a directive:

1. the result required by the directive must include the conferring of rights for the benefit of individuals;

2. the content of those rights must be clearly identifiable by reference to the directive;
3. there must be a causal link between the breach of the State's obligation and the damage suffered by the individual.

4 Judicial Review in the European Community II: Direct Actions against European Community Institutions

Article 173 EC Treaty (now art 230 EC Treaty): individual and direct concern

Codorniu SA v EC Council Case C–309/89 [1994] ECR I–1853; [1995] 2 CMLR 561 European Court of Justice

• Action for annulment – individual concern – locus standi – possibility to challenge 'real' regulation under art 173 EC Treaty – regulation reserving the use of the term 'crémant' to sparkling quality wines produced in two specific Member States – proprietor of a trade mark containing such a term traditionally using it for sparkling wines produced in another Member State

Facts
Codorniu, a Spanish producer of quality sparkling wines has been a holder of a graphic trade mark since 1924 in relation to one of its wine's designed as 'Gran Crémant de Codorniu'. In certain regions of French and Luxembourg the word 'crémant' was also used for certain quality wine. The producers in those countries asked the Community to adopt a regulation which would reserve the word 'crémant' only for their sparkling wine. Council Regulation 2045/89 restricted the use of the word 'crémant' to wines originated in France and Luxembourg in order to protect the traditional description used in those areas. Codorniu challenged the Regulation.

Held
The ECJ held that Codorniu was differentiated from other producers of wine since it had registered and used the word 'crémant' since 1924. Although Regulation 2045/89 was a true Regulation it did not prevent it from being of individual concern to Codorniu which was badly affected by the Regulation. Also the restriction of the word 'crémant' to wine originating from certain regions of France and Luxembourg could not be objectively justified, and in addition it was contrary to art 7(1) EEC which prohibits discrimination based on nationality.

Judgment
'Codorniu alleges that the contested provision [of Regulation 2045/89] is in reality a decision adopted in guise of a regulation. It has no general scope but affects a well determined class of producers which cannot be altered. Such producers are those who on 1 September 1989 traditionally designated their sparking wines with the term 'crémant'. For that class the contested provision has no general scope. Furthermore, the direct result of the contested provision will be to prevent Codorniu from using the term 'Gran Crémant' which will involve a loss of 38 per cent of its turnover. The effect of that damage is to distinguish it, within the meaning of the second paragraph of art 173 of the Treaty, from any other trader. Codorniu alleges that the Court has already

recognised the admissibility of an action for annulment brought by a natural or legal person against a regulation in such circumstances.

Under the second paragraph of art 173 of the Treaty the institution of proceedings by a natural or legal person for a declaration that a regulation is void is subject to the condition that the provision of the regulation at issue in the proceedings constitutes in reality a decision of direct and individual concern to that person.

As the Court has already held, the general applicability, and thus the legislative nature of a measure, is not called into question by the fact that it is possible to determine more or less exactly the number or even the identity of the persons to whom it applies at any given time, as long as it is established that it applies to them by virtue of an objective legal or factual situation defined by the measure in relation to its purpose.

Although, it is true that according to the criteria in the second paragraph of art 173 of the Treaty, the contested provision is, by nature and by virtue of its sphere of application, of a legislative nature in that it applies to the traders concerned in general, that does not prevent it from being of individual concern to some of them.

Natural or legal persons may claim that a contested provision is of individual concern to them only if it affects them by reason of certain attributes which are peculiar to them or by reason of circumstances in which they are differentiated from all other persons.

Codorniu registered the graphic trade mark 'Gran Crémant de Codorniu' in Spain in 1924 and traditionally used that mark both before and after registration. By reserving the right to use the term 'crémant' to French and Luxembourg producers, the contested provision prevents Codorniu from using its graphic trade mark.

It follows that Codorniu has established the existence of a situation which from the point of view of the contested provision differentiates it from all other traders.'

Comment
The restrictive interpretation of individual concern has been widely criticised. It was argued that the ECJ should take a more realistic approach and carry out an economic analysis of the situation of an undertaking, its degree of dependence vis-à-vis the effect that the measure in question had on the market in order to assess whether that measure differentiates and individualises the applicant from other undertakings. It was thought that the present case represented the real breakthrough. In the present case the applicant was prevented from using its trade mark which, from a point of view of its economic interests, resulted in putting it in such a disadvantageous position that it was differentiated from other undertakings and thus individually concerned by the contested Regulation. Unfortunately, it seems that a more liberal approach toward locus standi in general and individual concern in particular has been rejected (see especially *Stichting Greenpeace Council* v *EC Commission* Case C-321/95 [1998] ECR I-1651; *Weber* Case T-482/93 [1996] ECR II-609; *Terres Rouges Consultant SA* v *EC Commission, supported by the Council, Spain and France* Case T-47/95 [1997] ECR II-481, etc). It seems that the present case constitutes an exception justified on the ground of ownership of a trade mark.

Plaumann v EC Commission Case 25/62 [1964] ECR 95; [1964] CMLR 29 European Court of Justice

* *Action for annulment – locus standi – individual concern – definition of individual concern – the 'closed class' test*

Facts
Plaumann was an importer of clementines. Under the Common Customs tariff he paid 13 per cent customs duty as any importer of clementines from outside the Community. The government of Germany asked the Commission for authorisation under art 25(3) EC Treaty to suspend this duty. The Commission refused and issued a decision in this respect. Plaumann challenged this decision.

Held
The ECJ held that Plaumann was not individually and directly concerned by the Commission's decision, although he was affected as any importer of clementines by the decision. His commercial activities were such as may be practised at any time by any person and thus he did not distinguish himself from others in relation to the challenged directive as in the case of the addressee. Individual concern may only be invoked if persons other than the addressees of the decision demonstrate that 'that decision affects them by reason of certain attributes which are peculiar to them or by reason of circumstances in which they are differentiated from all other persons by virtue of these factors distinguishing them individually just as in the case of the person addressed'.

Judgment

'Under the second paragraph of art 173 of the Treaty private individuals may institute proceedings for annulment against decisions which, although addressed to another person, are of direct and individual concern to them, but in the present case the defendant denies that the contested decision is of direct and individual concern to the applicant.

It is appropriate in the first place to examine whether the second requirement of admissibility is fulfilled because, if the applicant is not individually concerned by the decision, it becomes unnecessary to enquire whether he is directly concerned.

... Persons other than those to whom a decision is addressed may only claim to be individually concerned if that decision affects them by reason of certain attributes which are peculiar to them or by reason of circumstances in which they are differentiated from all other persons and by virtue of these factors distinguishes them individually just as in the case of the person addressed. In the present case the applicant is affected by the disputed decision as an importer of clementines, that is to say, by reason of a commercial activity which may at any time be practised by any person and is not therefore such as to distinguish the applicant in relation to the contested decision as in the case of the addressee.

For these reasons the present action for annulment must be declared inadmissible.'

Comment

The most confusing and complicated question under art 173 EC is the issue of individual concern, mostly because of inconsistency in the decisions of Community courts in this area. In the present case the ECJ defined individual concern. The ECJ has restrictively interpreted 'certain peculiar attributes' or 'circumstances which differentiate' the applicant challenging a decision addressed to another person or a regulation in the form of a decision. As a result, the ECJ refused to recognise that a person was individually concerned in the following situations: in the *Plaumann* case when the Decision concerned specific activities, that is importers of clementines, when the number of the affected persons was limited, ie only 30 importers of clementines; when an undertaking was the only one concerned by a measure in a particular Member State (*Spijker Kwasten BV* v *EC Commission* Case 231/82 [1983] ECR 259; *Union Deutsche Lebens-mittelwerke* Case 97/85 [1987] ECR 2265); when an undertaking operated in a determined zone and the regulation expressly applied to that geographically delimited zone (*Molitaria Immolese* Case 30/67 [1968] ECR 172); when an undertaking was a direct competitor of another undertaking to which the decision was addressed (*Eridania* Cases 10 and 18/68 [1969] ECR 459); when the number of undertakings concerned was limited to three undertakings in a Member State but potential producers would not be in a position to enter the market for at least two years taking into account the technological requirements involving the production of isoglucose (*KSH NV* v *EC Council and EC Commission* Case 101/76 [1977] ECR 797).

In all those cases the applicants were considered as being members of the 'open class', that is anyone may at any time practice the commercial activity in question and potentially join the group of producers of particular goods. The case law of the ECJ indicates that in order to be individually concerned a person must prove that at the time the measure was passed it was possible to identify all potential applicants. It only happens if the membership of that class was fixed at that time which means, in practice, that only in respect of retrospective measures is it possible to invoke individual concern.

Stichting Greenpeace Council (Greenpeace International) and Others v *EC Commission* Case C–321/95 [1998] ECR I–1651 European Court of Justice

- Action for annulment – direct and individual concern – locus standi of a nature conservancy foundation on behalf of its members – environment – appeal

Facts
Geeenpeace International, a nature conservancy foundation with its headquarters in The Netherlands, brought an appeal against the order of the Court of First Instance (CFI) of 9 August 1995 which declared inadmissible their action for annulment of the Commission's decisions taken between 7 March 1991 and 29 October 1993 to disburse to the Kingdom of Spain ECU 12,000,000 from the European Regional Development Fund pursuant to Council Decision C(91) 440 concerning financial assistance for the construction of two power stations in the Canary Islands. The applicant argued: first, that the CFI erred in the interpretation and application of art 173(4) as it failed to take into consideration the nature and specific character of the environmental interests underpinning its action; second, that the CFI was wrong to take the view that reference to national laws on locus standi was irrelevant for the purposes of art 173; third, that the order of the CFI was contrary to the case law of the ECJ as well as the declaration of EC institutions and Member States on environmental matters; and, fourth, the applicant set up its own criteria for locus standi for a non-privileged applicant in environmental matters which criteria, according to the applicants, were satisfied in the present case.

Held
The ECJ confirmed the order of the CFI rejecting the action for annulment brought by Greenpeace International.

Judgment
'The interpretation of the fourth paragraph of art 173 of the Treaty that the Court of First Instance applied in concluding that the appellants did not have locus standi is consonant with the settled case law of the Court of Justice.

As far as natural persons are concerned, it follows from the case law, cited at paragraph 48 of the contested order, that where, as in the present case, the specific situation of the applicant was not taken into consideration in the adoption of the act, which concerns him in a general and abstract fashion and, in fact, like any other person in the same situation, the applicant is not individually concerned by the act.

The same applies to associations which claim to have locus standi on the basis of the fact that the persons whom they represent are individually concerned by the contested decision. For the reasons given in the preceding paragraph, that is not the case.

In appraising the appellants' arguments purporting to demonstrate that the case law of the Court of Justice, as applied by the Court of First Instance, takes no account of the nature and specific characteristics of the environmental interests underpinning their action, it should be emphasised that it is the decision to build the two power stations in question which is liable to affect the environmental rights arising under Directive 85/337 that the appellants seek to invoke.

In those circumstances, the contested decision, which concerns the Community financing of those power stations, can affect those rights only indirectly.

As regards the appellants' argument that application of the Court's case law would mean that, in the present case, the rights which they derive from Directive 85/337 would have no effective judicial protection at all, it must be noted that, as is clear from the file, Greenpeace brought proceedings before the national courts challenging the administrative authorisations issued to Unelco concerning the construction of those power stations.

Although the subject-matter of those proceedings and of the action brought before the Court of First Instance is different, both actions are based on the same rights afforded to individuals by Directive 85/337, so that in the circumstances of the present case those rights are fully protected by the national courts which may, if need be, refer a question to this Court for a preliminary ruling under art 177 of the Treaty.

The Court of First Instance did not therefore err in law in determining the question of the appellants' locus standi in the light of the criteria developed by the Court of Justice in the case law set out at paragraph 7 of this judgment.'

Comment

This is the first decision of the ECJ following *Codorniu* Case C–309/89 [1994] ECR I–1853 in respect of locus standi of non-privileged applicants under art 173(4) EC Treaty. The ECJ decided to apply the restrictive approach based on a 'closed class' test introduced by *Plaumann* Case 25/62 [1964] ECR 95. The ECJ rejected the opinion of Advocate-General Cosmas suggesting the evolution of conditions of admissibility in respect of actions brought by non-privileged applicants under art 173(4) ECJ in matters relating to the protection of environment. Also, the ECJ confirmed its case law in respect of the right of associations, including those active in the field of the protection of the environment, to bring an action for annulment under art 173 EC Treaty. In conformity with the opinion of the Advocate-General the ECJ rejected the possibility for an association to have locus standi under art 173 EC Treaty. According to the ECJ this possibility would lead to the development of an actio popularis contrary to the philosophy of art 173 EC Treaty.

Timex Corporation v *EC Council and EC Commission* Case 264/82 [1985] ECR 849 European Court of Justice

• *Action for annulment – locus standi – regulation introducing anti-dumping duties – participation of the applicants in the adoption of contested act*

Facts

Timex challenged Regulation 3017/79 which had imposed an anti-dumping duty on cheap mechanical watches coming from the Soviet Union. The Regulation was adopted as a result of a complaint lodged on behalf of Timex and taking into account information forwarded by the applicant. Timex sought to annul Regulation 3017/79, arguing that the new duty was too low.

Held

The ECJ held that Timex was individually concerned because its complaint led to the opening of the investigation procedure and subsequently to the adoption of Regulation 3017/79. The challenged Regulation constituted a decision in respect of Timex as the anti-dumping duty was fixed on the basis of 'the extent of the injury caused to Timex by the dumped importers'.

Judgment

'Timex and the parties intervening in its support contend that the action is admissible because the contested Regulation constitutes in reality a decision which is of direct and individual concern to Timex within the meaning of the second paragraph of art 173 of the [EC] Treaty. They submit that the Regulation was adopted as a result of a complaint lodged on behalf of Timex, amongst others, and that it therefore constitutes the culmination of an administrative proceedings initiated at Timex's request. Its interest in bringing proceedings is all the more evident in so far as it is the only remaining manufacturer of mechanical wristwatches in the United Kingdom and the anti-dumping duty was fixed exclusively by reference to its economic situation.

The question of admissibility raised by the Council and the Commission must be resolved in the light of the system established by Regulation 3017/79 and, more particularly, of the nature of the anti-dumping measures provided for by that Regulation, regard being had to the provisions of the second paragraph of art 173 of the [EC] Treaty.

Article 13(1) of Regulation 3017/79 provides that "Anti-dumping or countervailing duties, whether provisional or definitive, shall be imposed by Regulation." In the light of the criteria set out in the second paragraph of art 173, the measures in question are, in fact, legislative in nature and scope, inasmuch as they apply to traders in general; nevertheless, their provisions may be of direct and individual concern to some of those traders. In this regard, it is necessary to consider in particular the part played by the applicant in the anti-dumping proceedings and its position on the market to which the contested legislation applies.

It should be pointed out first of all that the complaint under art 5 of Regulation No 3017/79 which led to the adoption of Regulation No 1882/82 was lodged by the British Clock and Watch Manufacturers' Association Limited on behalf of manufacturers of mechanical watches in France and the United Kingdom, including Timex. According to the documents before the Court, that association took action because a complaint which Timex had lodged in April 1979 had been rejected by the Commission on the ground that it came from only one Community manufacturer.

The complaint which led to the opening of the investigation procedure therefore owes its origin to the complaint originally made by Timex. Moreover, it is clear from the preamble to Commission Regulation No 84/82 and the preamble to Council Regulation No 1882/82 that Timex's views were heard during that procedure.

It must also be remembered that Timex is the leading manufacturer of mechanical watches and watch movements in the Community and the only remaining manufacturer of those products in the United Kingdom. Furthermore, as is also clear from the preambles to Regulations Nos 84/82 and 1882/82, the conduct of the investigation procedure was largely determined by Timex's observations and the anti-dumping duty was fixed in the light of the effect of the dumping on Timex. More specifically, the preamble to Regulation No 1882/82 makes it clear that the definitive anti-dumping duty was made equal to the dumping margin which was found to exist "taking into account the extent of the injury to Timex by the dumping imports". The contested Regulation is therefore based on the applicant's own situation.

It follows that the contested Regulation constitutes a decision which is of direct and individual concern to Timex within the meaning of the second paragraph of art 173 of the [EC] Treaty. As the Court held in its judgment of 4 October 1983 in *EEC Seed Crushers' and Oil Processors' Federation (FEDIOL) v EC Commission* Case 191/82 [1983] ECR 2913, the applicant is therefore entitled to put before the Court any matters which would facilitate a review as to whether the Commission has observed the procedural guarantees granted to complainants by Regulation No 3017/79 and whether or not it has committed manifest errors in its assessment of the facts, has omitted to take any essential matters into consideration or has based the reasons for its decision on considerations amounting to a misuse of powers. In that respect, the Court is required to exercise its normal powers of review over a discretion granted to a public authority, even though it has no jurisdiction to intervene in the exercise of the discretion reserved to the Community authorities by the aforementioned Regulation.'

Comment

Non-contentious procedures involve more or less direct participation of undertakings in the adoption of the measures. If an applicant assists the Commission in the preparation of the measure then his association with the adoption of the measure differentiates him from others and his individual concern is self-evident. This is mostly used in competition, anti-dumping and State-aid cases. In the context of the common market, dumping occurs when a non-EC undertaking sells its products below domestic market prices and at the same time at a price below the real cost of the goods. This strategy is used to penetrate the market and eliminate the existing competitors. The undertaking affected by such dumping can complain to the Commission which may adopt a provisional regulation and request the Council to issue a definite regulation imposing an anti-dumping duty to counterbalance the competitive advantage of the foreign undertaking and which is determined in the light of the effect of the dumping on EC undertakings, especially the one that lodged a complaint.

It is interesting to mention that in *Métropole Télévision* Cases T–528, 542, 543 and 546/93 [1996] ECR II–649 the Commission argued that the applicant was not individually concerned as it did not participate in the preparation of the measure. The CFI replied that effective participation in the adoption of a measure cannot be required in order to establish an individual concern as it would amount to the introduction of an additional requirement which is not provided for in art 173 EC. Therefore, the CFI has rightly indicated that the participation in the adoption of a measure constitutes solely a factor facilitating the recognition of an individual concern but it is not a necessary requirement.

Alfred Toepfer and Getreideimport Gesellschaft v *EC Commission*
Joined Cases 106 and 107/63 [1965] ECR 525; [1966] CMLR 111
European Court of Justice

* Action for annulment – locus standi – applications by individuals against a decision addressed to another person – decision of direct concern to them – concept

Facts

Toepfer applied for an import licence for maize on 1 October 1962, being the very day on which the German authorities mistakenly reduced the levy for imports of maize from France to zero. The German intervention agency realised the mistake and refused to grant licences from 2 October 1962. Three days later the Commission authorised German authorities to impose the levy as from 2 October 1962. Toepfer challenged the Commission's decision on the grounds that he was individually and directly concerned.

Held

The ECJ held that Toepfer was individually concerned because the number and identity of those individually concerned 'had become fixed and ascertainable before the contested decision was made'.

Judgment

'The only persons concerned by the said measures were importers who had applied for an import licence during the course of the day of 1 October 1962. The number and identity of these importers had already become fixed and ascertainable before 4 October, when the contested decision was made. The Commission was in a position to know that its decision affected the interests and the position of the said importers alone.

The factual situation thus created differentiates the said importers, including the applicants, from all other persons and distinguishes them individually just as in the case of the person addressed.

Therefore, the objection of inadmissibility which has been raised is unfounded and the applications are admissible.'

Comment
The applicant was a member of a 'closed group' as the decision affected his interests and position in a significantly different way from other importers who might wish to apply for a licence after the adoption of the decision but during the remaining period of the ban. Therefore, only those who applied on 1 October were individually concerned since from 2–4 October applications were refused and on the 4 October the Commission issued its decision. As a result, Toepfer was within the closed group who applied on 1 October; the larger group, that is those who applied between 2–4 October, was open since they were refused licences and could reapply thereafter without loss to them as the levy would be the same after 2 October.

Unione Nazionale Importatori e Commercianti Motoviecoli Esteri (UNICME) and Others v *EC Council* Case 123/77 [1978] ECR 845 European Court of Justice

- *Action for annulment – locus standi – direct concern – Regulation 1692/77 – protective measures on the importation of motorcycles from a third country – discretion of a Member State in relation to import licences*

Facts
Under Council Regulation 1692/77 (EEC) concerning protective measures on the importation of motorcycles originating in Japan into Italy, Italian authorities were to issue a limited number of import authorisations. The applicants, Italian importers of such motorcycles and their trade association, UNICME, challenged the Regulation.

Held
The ECJ held that the applicants were not directly concerned since the Italian government had a discretion as to the grant of import licences. As a result, they were concerned not by the Regulation but by the subsequent refusal of import licences by the Italian authorities.

Judgment
'The system [introduced by Regulation 1692/77] would only affect the interests of the importers in the event of the necessary authorisation being refused them.

Consequently Regulation No 1692/77 would only be of concern to the applicants if, pursuant to that measure, they were refused an import authorisation.

In that case they will be able to raise the matter before the national court having jurisdiction, if necessary raising before that court their questions concerning the validity of the Regulation, which the court will, if it thinks fit, be able to deal with by means of the procedure under art 177 of the Treaty.

In the present case the condition laid down in art 173, to the effect that the contested measure must be of direct and individual concern to the applicants, is not fulfilled.

The applicants claim that, taken together, they represent all the importers affected by the import system introduced for motorcycles originating in Japan.

They state that even before Regulation No 1692/77 was adopted it could have been established that they were the only persons concerned and that they were all concerned.

The possibility of determining more or less precisely the number or even the identity of the persons to whom a measure applies by no means implies that it must be regarded as being of individual concern to them.

In the present case the fact that all the applicants might possibly be refused an import authorisation pursuant to Regulation No 1692/77 does not provide a sufficient basis for regarding the regulation as being of individual concern to them in the same way as if a decision had been addressed to them.

On the contrary the Regulation will not produce effects in individual cases until it is implemented by the Italian authorities.

Consequently, the second condition laid down by art 173 likewise remains unfulfilled.'

Comment
In the present case the application was rejected on the ground of lack of direct concern. Italian authorities enjoyed a large measure of discretion in the implementation of a Community measure.

Time-limit under art 173 EC Treaty

Bayer AG v *EC Commission* Case T–12/90 [1991] ECR II–219; [1993] 4 CMLR 30 Court of First Instance

• *Action for annulment – time-limit for initiating proceedings – excuses for failing to raise proceedings in time – regularity of notification – excusable error – unforeseeable circumstances and force majeure*

Facts
The Commission sent notification to the applicant company fining it for a number of infringements of art 85 EC Treaty.

The company brought an action under art 173(2) EC Treaty to have Commission's decision judicially reviewed. In response, the Commission argued that the application was inadmissible as time-barred under art 173(3) and the ECJ's rules of procedure.

The applicant argued that the action was not time-barred and relied on three separate contentions to support this argument. First, it was submitted that the Commission was guilty of a number of irregularities in the notification. In particular, the Commission notified the decision to the company and not to the company's legal department with which it had conducted all previous correspondence. Second, the company claimed that its internal organisational breakdown was an excusable error. Finally, the applicants pleaded unforeseeable circumstances in order to justify the delay in submitting the application under art 173 EC Treaty.

Held
The Court of First Instance rejected all three arguments submitted by the applicants. The Court stated that the Commission was not guilty of any procedural irregularities in the notification and had complied with the necessary formalities contained in its rules of procedure. Both the arguments relating to excusable error and force majeure were also rejected as the delay had been caused by fault on the part of the applicants.

Judgment
'[*Irregularity of the notification*]
With regard to the regularity of the notification, this Court notes that, according to the settled case law of the Court of Justice, a registered letter with acknowledgment of receipt is a suitable method of giving notice insomuch as it enables the date from which time begins to run to be determined. Furthermore, a decision is duly notified once it has been communicated to the person to whom it is addressed and that person is in a position to take cognisance of it.

In the present case, this Court has found that the Commission sent the decision to Bayer by registered letter with postal acknowledgment of receipt and that letter duly arrived at Bayer's registered office at Leverkusen on December 28, 1989. It follows that Bayer was in position on that date to take cognisance of the contents of the letter and thus of the tenor of the decision ...

It follows from the foregoing that the applicant's first plea in law in defence must be dismissed.

[Excusable error]
The Court considers, first of all, in view of the obligations incumbent on any normally experienced trader, that the fact that the Commission notified the contested decision to the applicants registered office, whereas it had previously addressed all its communications directly to the applicant's legal department, cannot constitute an exceptional circumstance such as to render excusable the applicant's error.

Secondly, the Court finds that the argument that Bayer had taken every step within its power to avoid any error in the forwarding of mail addressed to it is, assuming it is true, entirely irrelevant in the present case insomuch as it is clear from the documents before the Court, and it is not denied, that errors were in fact committed within the undertaking when the registered letter was received.

... It follows from the foregoing that Bayer may not rely either on the inadequate functioning of its internal organisation or on a failure to apply its own internal instructions in support of its claim that the error which is committed was excusable, insomuch as it is undisputed that those instructions were not followed and that, in any event, the Commission in no way contributed to the inadequate functioning of Bayer's organisation.

[Unforeseeable circumstances and force majeure]
Finally, Bayer considers that it may rely on the existence of unforeseeable circumstances or force majeure within the meaning of the second paragraph of art 42 of the rules of procedure of the Court of Justice. Having fulfilled in all respects its obligations of organisation and control, it cannot be held to have been at fault or, therefore, in view of the Commission's conduct as a whole, to have been responsible for the failure to comply within the prescribed period.

The Court observes that, for the purpose of determining whether the applicant has established the existence of unforeseeable circumstances or force majeure, there must, as the Court of Justice has consistently held, be abnormal difficulties, independent of the will of the person concerned and apparently inevitable, even if all due care is taken.

Bayer, however, in support of that plea in law, has relied on arguments identical to those put forward in support of its plea based on the existence in the circumstances of excusable error on its part. In view of what has bee stated above in connection with the alleged existence of excusable error, it appears clearly, and a fortiori, that the above-mentioned conditions for the existence of unforeseeable circumstances or force majeure, within the meaning of art 42 of the rules of procedure of the Court of Justice, such as to justify the transgression of the time-limit for initiating proceedings, are not fulfilled in this case.

It follows from the foregoing that the three pleas in law submitted by Bayer in its defence must be dismissed.'

Comment

The time-limit is one month under the ECSC Treaty and two months under the EC and Euratom Treaties. It is regrettable from the point of view of legal certainty that the various amendments to the founding Treaties have omitted to provide a situation where all three have the same the time-limit for bringing an action for annulment.

The time-limit begins to run from the date of publication of an act in the Official Journal of the European Communities, or from its notification to the applicant. If the act was published, by virtue of art 81 of the Rules of Procedure of the ECJ and the CFI, the commencement of the time-limit is extended by 15 days, and further extension is granted to take into consideration the distance of the applicant from the Community courts. In the case of an applicant from the United Kingdom the extension amounts to an additional ten days. Therefore, for a UK applicant the time-limit is two months, plus 15 days, plus ten days. In the absence of publication or notification the time-limit starts at the day when the act came to the knowledge of the applicant (*Tezi Textiel* Case 59/84 [1986] ECR 887). However, in the absence of a formal notification and provided that the applicant knew the content of the final position adopted by an EC institution, the time-limit starts to run at the time the definite decision came to his knowledge (*Pesqueria Vasco-Montanesa Ord* Cases T–452 and 453/93R [1994] ECR II–229).

The time-limit is rigorously enforced by the Community courts. Once it elapses, the application is deemed inadmissible d'office, that is the act is immune from annulment. This is justified by the principle of legal certainty and equality in the administration of justice (*Valsabbia* Case 209/83 [1984] ECR 3089).

In *Simet* Cases 25 and 26/65 [1967] ECR 40 the ECJ accepted an exception to the strict observance of the time-limit based on force majeure.

Article 175 EC Treaty (now art 232 EC Treaty)

Lord Bethell v EC Commission Case 246/81 [1982] ECR 2277; [1982] 3 CMLR 300 European Court of Justice

- *Action for failure to act – meaning of 'failure to act' – locus standi – conditions of admissibility – relationship between arts 173 and 175 EC Treaty*

Facts
Lord Bethell, a Member of the European Parliament and Chairman of the Freedom of the Skies Committee, complained to the Commission about anti-competitive practices of a number of European airlines in relation to passenger fares. He argued that the Commission was under a duty to submit proposals under art 89 EC in order to curtail those practices. Dissatisfied with the answer from the Commission he brought an action against the Commission under art 175 EC for failure to act, claiming that the Commission's reply amounted in fact to a failure to act, and alternatively under art 173 EC arguing that this answer should be annulled.

Held
The ECJ held that Lord Bethell had neither locus standi to challenge the Commission's alleged failure to act under art 175 EC Treaty nor to seek annulment of the Commission's answer under art 173 EC Treaty.

Judgment
'It appears from the provisions quoted [art 175 EC Treaty] that the applicant, for his application to be admissible, must be in a position to establish either that he is the addressee of a measure of the Commission having specific legal effects with regard to him, which is, as such, capable of being declared void, or that the Commission, having been duly called upon to act in pursuance of the second paragraph of art 175, has failed to adopt in relation to him a measure which he was legally entitled to claim by virtue of the rules of Community law.

In reply to a question from the Court the applicant stated that the measure to which he believed himself to be entitled was "a response, an adequate answer to his complaint saying either that the Commission was going to act upon it or saying that it was not and, if not, giving reasons". Alternatively the applicant took the view that the letter addressed to him on 17 July 1981 by the Director-General for Competition was to be described as an act against which proceedings may be instituted under the second paragraph of art 173.

The principal question to be resolved in this case is whether the Commission had, under the rules of Community law, the right and the duty to adopt in respect of the applicant a decision in the sense of the request made by the applicant to the Commission in his letter of 13 May 1981. It is apparent from the content of that letter and from the explanations given during the proceedings that the applicant is asking the Commission to undertake an investigation with regard to the airlines in the matter of the fixing of air fares with a view to a possible application to them of the provisions of the Treaty with regard to competition.

It is clear therefore that the applicant is asking the Commission, not to take a decision in respect of him, but to open an inquiry with regard to third parties and to take decisions in respect of them. No doubt the applicant, in his double capacity as a user of the airlines and a leading member of an organisation of users of air passenger services, has an indirect interest, as other users may have, in such proceedings and their possible outcome, but he is nevertheless not in the precise legal position of the actual addressee of a decision which may be declared void under the second paragraph of art 173 or in that of the potential addressee of a legal measure which the Commission has a duty to adopt with regard to him, as is the position under the third paragraph of art 175.

It follows that the application is inadmissible from the point of view of both art 175 and art 173.'

Comment

The ECJ held that the application of Lord Bethell would be admissible only if the Commission 'having been duly called upon ... has failed to adopt in relation to him a measure which he was legally entitled to claim by virtue of the rules of Community law'. Lord, Bethell, although indirectly concerned by the measure as a user of the airlines and Chairman of the Freedom of the Skies Committee which represented users, was nevertheless not in the legal position of a potential addressee of a decision and therefore the Commission had no duty to adopt such a decision with regard to him. Also, his application under art 173 EC was rejected for the same reason. The analogy between locus standi of non-privileged applicants under arts 173 EC and 175 EC was confirmed by the ECJ in the present case.

The similarity between arts 173 EC and 175 EC means that an application under art 175 EC is admissible if the applicant is directly and individually concerned by a measure which an EC institution failed to adopt, including a decision addressed to a third party but of individual and direct concern to the applicant. In *ENU* Case C–107/91 [1993] ECR I–599 the ECJ recognised this possibility within the framework of the Euratom Treaty and in *Ladbroke Racing Ltd v EC Commission* Case T–32/93 [1994] ECR II–1015 the Court of First Instance extended it to the EC Treaty).

Actions for damages against European Community institutions: art 215(2) EC Treaty (now art 288(2) EC Treaty)

Adams v *EC Commission* Case 145/83 [1985] ECR 3539 European Court of Justice

• *Action for non-contractual liability of European Commission – requirements of art 214 EC Treaty – duty of confidentiality, fault or negligence – damage – contributory negligence*

Facts

Adams was employed by the Swiss-based multinational Hoffman-La Roche. He forwarded confidential information to the Commission concerning breaches of art 86 by his employer for which the latter was heavily fined. During the proceedings Hoffman-La Roche asked the Commission to disclose the name of the informant. The Commission refused but forwarded to Hoffman-La Roche certain documents which enabled them to identify Adams as the source of leaked information which was contrary to the duty of confidentiality contained in art 214 EC. In the meantime Adams moved to Italy where he set up his own business. Hoffman-La Roche due to its international connections destroyed the business established by Adams in Italy. The Commission failed to inform Adams that his former employer was planning to persecute him. On his return to Switzerland Adams was arrested by the Swiss police for economic espionage and held in solitary confinement. His wife committed suicide. Adams brought proceedings before the ECJ against the Commission for loss of earnings and loss of reputation as a result of his conviction and imprisonment.

Held

The ECJ held that the Commission was liable for the breach of duty of confidentiality as it had allowed Adams to be identified as an informer, and awarded Adams £200,000 in damages for his mental anguish and lost earnings, and £176,000 for costs, half the sum he had demanded. The reason for the reduction was Adams' contributory negligence. The ECJ held that Adams contributed to the resulting damage by failing to warn the Commission that he could be identified from the confidential documents, and by failing to enquire about progress of proceedings especially before returning to Switzerland.

Judgment

'[*Duty of confidentiality*]
... As regards the existence of a duty of confidentiality it must be pointed out that art 214 of the [EC] Treaty lays down an obligation, in particular for the member and the servants of the institutions of the Community "not to disclose information of the kind covered by the obligation of professional secrecy, in particular information about undertakings, their business relations or their cost components". Although that provision primarily refers to information gathered from undertakings, the expression "in particular" shows that the principle in question is a general one which applies also to information supplied by natural persons, if that information is "of the kind" that is confidential. That is particularly in the case of information supplied on a purely voluntary basis but accompanied by a request for confidentiality in order to protect the informant's anonymity. An institution which accepts such information is bound to comply with such a condition.

As regards the case before the Court, it is quite clear from the applicant's letter of 25 February 1973 that he requested the Commission not to reveal his identity. It cannot therefore be denied that the Commission was bound by a duty of confidentiality towards the applicant in that respect. In fact the parties disagree not so much as to the existence of such a duty but as to whether the Commission was bound by a duty of confidentiality after the applicant had left his employment with Roche.

In that respect it must be pointed out that the applicant did not qualify his request by indicating a period upon which the expiry of which the Commission would be released from its duty of confidentiality regarding the identity of its informant. No such indication can be inferred from the fact that the applicant was prepared to appear before any court after he had left Roche. The giving of evidence before a court implies that the witness has been summoned, that he is under a duty to answer the questions put to him, and is, in return, entitled to all guarantees provided by a judicial procedure. The applicant's offer to confirm the accuracy of his information under such conditions cannot therefore be interpreted as a general statement releasing the Commission from its duty of confidentiality. Nor can any such intention be inferred from the applicant's subsequent conduct.

It must therefore be stated that the Commission was under a duty to keep the applicant's identity secret even after he had left his employer.

[*Damages*]
It must therefore be concluded that in principle the Community is bound to make good the damage resulting from the discovery of the applicant's identity by means of the documents handed over to Roche by the Commission. It must however be recognised that the extent of the Commission's liability is diminished by reason of the applicant's own negligence. The applicant failed to inform the Commission that it was possible to infer his identity as the informant

from the documents themselves. although he was in the best position to appreciate and to avert that risk. Nor did he ask the Commission to keep him informed of the progress of the investigation of Roche, and in particular of any use that might be made of the documents for that purpose. Lastly, he went back to Switzerland without attempting to make any inquiries in that respect, although he must have been aware of the risks to which his conduct towards his former employer had exposed him with regard to Swiss legislation.

Consequently, the applicant himself contributed significantly to the damage which he suffered. In assessing the conduct of the Commission on the one hand and that of the applicant on the other, the Court considers it equitable to apportion responsibility for that damage equally between the two parties.

It follows from all the foregoing considerations that the Commission must be ordered to compensate the applicant to the extent of one half of the damage suffered by him as a result of the fact that he was identified as the source of information regarding Roche's anti-competitive practice. For the rest, however, the application must be dismissed. The amount of the damages is to be determined by agreement between the parties or, failing such agreement, by the Court.'

Comment

There is an important distinction between the liability of Community institutions for unlawful conduct and liability for legislative acts adopted by them. In the present case the Commission was found liable for breach of the principle of confidentiality. Consequently, the applicant had to establish that the action of the Community was contrary to law, that he suffered damage as a result of the wrongful conduct of the Commission and that there was a causal link between the conduct of the institution and the alleged damage (see *SGEEM and Etroy* v *European Investment Bank* Case C–370/89 [1993] ECR I–2583).

Community law recognises contributory negligence. In the present case the ECJ held that the applicant through his own negligence contributed to the resulting damage and reduced the amount of damages proportionally to his responsibility for the loss.

Aktien-Zuckerfabrik Schöppenstedt v *EC Council* Case 5/71 [1971] ECR 975 European Court of Justice

• *Non-contractual liability of EC institutions – autonomous nature of action under art 215(2) EC Treaty – wrongful act – conditions for liability for legislative acts involving measures of economic policy – Regulation 769/68 – damages*

Facts

A German sugar producer argued that Regulation 769/68 on sugar prices infringed art 40(3) EC Treaty according to which any common price policy should be based on common criteria and uniform methods of calculation. He claimed damages under art 215(2) EC Treaty.

Held

The ECJ dismissed the claim.

Judgment

'In the present case the non-contractual liability of the Community presupposed at the very least the unlawful nature of the act alleged to be the cause of the damage. Where legislative action involving measures of economic policy is concerned, the Community does not incur non-contractual liability for damage suffered by individuals as a consequence of that action, by virtue of the provisions contained in art 215, second paragraph, of the Treaty, unless a sufficiently flagrant violation of a superior rule of law for the protection of individuals has occurred. For that reason the Court, in the present case, must first consider whether such a violation has occurred.

Regulation No 769/68 was adopted pursuant to art 37(1) of Regulation No 1009/67 which requires the Council to adopt provisions concerning the measures needed to offset the difference between national sugar prices and prices valid from 1 July 1968, and it authorises the Member States in which the price of white sugar is higher than the target price to grant compensation for such quantities of white sugar and raw sugar which are in free circulation in its territory at 0.00 hours on 1 July 1968. The applicant points out that as regards Member States with a low price this regulation provides for the payment of dues on sugar stocks only if the previous prices were less than the intervention price valid from 1 July 1968 and concludes from this that by adopting different criteria for the right to compensation of sugar producers in a Member State with high prices, the regulation infringes the provision of the last subparagraph of art 40(3) of the Treaty according to which any common price policy shall be based on common criteria and uniform methods of calculation.

The difference referred to does not constitute discrimination because it is the result of a new system of common organisation of the market in sugar which does not recognise a single fixed price but has a maximum and minimum price and lays down a framework of prices within which the level of actual price depends on the development of the market. Thus it is not possible to challenge the justification of transitional rules which proceeded on the basis that where the previous prices were already within the framework set up they must be governed by market forces and which therefore required the payment of dues only in cases where the previous prices were still too low to come within the new framework of prices and authorised compensation only in cases where the previous prices were too high to come within the said framework.

In addition, having regard to the special features of the system established with effect from 1 July 1968, the Council by adopting Regulation No 769/68 satisfied the requirements of art 37 of Regulation No 1009/67.

It is also necessary to dismiss the applicant's claim that Regulation No 769/68 infringed the provisions of art 40 of the Treaty because the method of calculating the compensation and dues for the raw sugar stocks was derived from that adopted for white sugar, which could, according to the applicant, result in the unequal treatment of the producers of raw sugar. Although, relying on hypothetical cases, the applicant stated that the calculation methods selected did not necessarily lead to uniform results with regard to producers of raw sugar, it was not proved that this could have been the case on 1 July 1968.

The applicant's action founded upon the Council's liability does not therefore satisfy the first condition mentioned above and must be dismissed.'

Comment

In the present case the ECJ established additional conditions for liability of Community institutions for legislative acts in the following terms:

'When legislative action involving measures of economic policy is concerned, the Community does not incur non-contractual liability for damage suffered by individuals as a consequence of that action, by virtue of the provisions contained in art 215, second paragraph, of the Treaty, unless a sufficiently flagrant violation of a superior rule of law for the protection of the individual has occurred.'

This is referred to as the Schöppenstedt formula. It means that the applicant must establish three general conditions and three special conditions. The three general conditions are: unlawful conduct on the part of the Community; damage to the applicant; and a causal link between the conduct of the Community institution and the alleged damage. The three special conditions are that there must be a breach of a superior rule of law, the breach must be sufficiently serious and the superior rule must be one for the protection of individuals.

This formula enhances the fact that EC institutions are particularly protected against actions in damages under art 215(2) EC. for the very simple reason that all legislative acts imply that their authors enjoy a large margin of discretion. Indeed, it is not important whether a legislative act concerns economic policies sensu stricto or other areas such as transport, social policy etc, what is important is that an institution has a wide discretion and must exercise it in the interest of the Community. It must make choices in conducting the Community policies in the areas of competences of the Community in order to attain the objectives which are essential for integration of national policies and especially to harmonise national laws in specific areas regardless of the fact that those legislative measures may adversely affect individual interests. The prospect of continual applications for damages must not hinder the Community in its policy-making. For that reason the requirements contained in the Schöppenstedt formula are very restrictive and rigorous.

Mulder and Others v *EC Council and EC Commission* Joined Cases C–104/89 and C–37/90 [1992] ECR I–3061 European Court of Justice

- *Action for non-contractual liability of the Council and the Commission – legislative measure involving economic policy choices – common agricultural policy – sufficiently serious breach – principle of protection of legitimate expectations – duty to mitigate any loss – abnormal and special damage*

Facts
Mulder and other farmers submitted an application under art 215(2) claiming that they suffered loss as a result of various Community regulations dealing with over-production and cuts-back in dairy products. Under Regulation 1078/77 (1977) they were paid a premium for five years for not selling milk and milk products. At the end of this five years period they applied for 'special reference quantities' which would have allowed them to come back into the market. Under Regulation 857/84 they failed to obtain the 'special reference quantities'. They were unable to sell any milk, and consequently, they were put out of business. They successfully challenged Regulation 857/84 under art 173 EC (*Mulder* v *Minister of Agriculture and Fisheries* Case 120/86 [1989] 2 CMLR 1). The farmers argued that the failure to obtain 'special reference quantities' upon the expiry of the scheme was contrary to Community law on the ground that such action contravened the principle of legitimate expectations.

Held
The ECJ held that the Community incurred liability in relation to the regulation allocating 'special reference quantities' but not in respect of the second regulation. In the case of the regulation concerning the allocation of 'special reference quantities', although the ECJ held that the group of people affected was clearly defined, it comprised more than 12,000 farmers who were entitled to claim approximately ECU 250 million. The ECJ reduced the damages awarded by the amount of profit which the producers could reasonably have earned from alternative activities on the grounds of the duty to mitigate any loss.

Judgment
'[*Wrongful acts – general legislative measures*]
The second paragraph of art 215 of the Treaty provides that, in the case of non-contractual liability, the Community in accordance with the general principles common to the laws of the Member States, is to make good any damage caused by its institutions in the performance of their duties. The scope of that provision has been specified in the sense that the Community does not incur liability on account of a legislative measure involving choices of economic policy unless a sufficiently serious breach of a superior rule of law for the protection the individuals occurred (see in particular, the judgment in *HNL* v *EC Council and EC Commission* Joined Cases 83 and 94/76, 4, 15 and 40/77

[1978] ECR 1209, paragraphs 4,5, and 6). More specifically, in a legislative field such as the one in question, which is characterised by the exercise of a wide discretion essential for the implementation of the Common Agricultural Policy, the Community cannot incur liability unless the institution concerned has manifestly and gravely disregarded the limits on the exercise of its powers (see in particular the judgment in *HNL* v *EC Commission and EC Council*, paragraph 6).

The Court has also consistently held that, in order for the Community to incur non-contractual liability, the damage alleged must go beyond the bounds of the normal economic risks inherent in the activities in the sector concerned.

... Those conditions are fulfilled in the case of Regulation No 857/84 as supplemented by Regulation No 1371/84.

In contrast, contrary to the applicants' assertions, the Community cannot incur liability on account of the fact that Regulation No 764/89 introduced the 60 per cent rule.

Admittedly, that rule also infringes the legitimate expectation of the producers concerned with regard to the limited nature of their non-marketing or conversion undertaking, as the Court held in the judgments in *Spagl* and *Pastätter* [*Spagl* v *Haumpzollamt Rosenheim* Case C–189/89 [1990] ECR I–4359 and *Pastätter* Case C–217/89 [1990] ECR I–4585]. However, the breach of the principle of the protection of legitimate expectations which was held to exist cannot be described as being sufficiently serious within the meaning of the case law on the non-contractual liability of the Community.

In that regard, it must be borne in mind first that, unlike the 1984 rules, which made it impossible for the producers concerned to market milk, the 60 per cent rule enabled those traders to resume their activities as milk producers. Consequently, in the amending regulation, Regulation No 764/89, the Council did not fail to take the situation of the producers concerned into account.

Secondly, it must be observed that, by adopting Regulation No 764/89 following the judgment of 28 April 1988 in *Mulder* and *Von Deetzen* [*Mulder* Case 120/86 [1988] ECR 2321 and *Von Deetzen* Case 170/86 [1988] ECR 2355], the Community legislature made an economic policy choice with regard to the manner in which it was necessary to implement the principles set out in those judgments. That was based, on the one hand, on the "overriding necessity of not jeopardising the fragile stability that currently obtains in the milk products sector" (fifth recital in the preamble to Regulation No 764/89) and, on the other, on the need to strike a balance between the interests of the producers concerned and the interests of the other producers subject to the scheme. The Council made that choice in such a way as to maintain the level of other producers' reference quantities unchanged while increasing the Community reserve by 600,000 tonnes, or 60 per cent of aggregate foreseeable applications for the allocation of special reference quantities, which, in its view, was the highest quantity compatible with the aims of the scheme. Accordingly the Council took account of a higher public interest, without gravely and manifestly disregarding the limits of its discretionary power in this area.

In the light of the foregoing, it must therefore be held that the Community is bound to make good the damage suffered by the applicants as a result of the application of Regulation No 857/84, as supplemented by Regulation No 1371/84, cited above, but not the damage resulting from the application of Regulation No 764/89, cited above.

[*Duty to mitigate any loss*]
As regards the extent of the damage which the Community should make good, in the absence of particular circumstances warranting a different assessment, account should be taken of the loss of earnings consisting in the difference between, on the one hand, the income which the applicants would have obtained in the normal course of events from the milk deliveries which they would have made if, during the period between 1 April 1984 (the date of entry into

force of Regulation No 857/84) and 29 March 1989 (the date of entry into force of Regulation No 764/89), they had obtained the reference quantities to which they were entitled and, on the other hand, the income which they actually obtained from milk deliveries made during that period in the absence of any reference quantity, plus any income which they obtained, or could have obtained, during that period from any replacement activities.

... As regards income from any replacement activities which is to be deducted from the hypothetical income referred above, it must be noted that that income must be taken to include not only that which the applicants actually obtained from replacement activities, but also that income which they could have obtained had they reasonably engaged in such activities. This conclusion must be reached in the light of a general principle common to the legal systems of the Member States to the effect that the injured party must show reasonable diligence in limiting the extent of his loss or risk having to bear the damage himself. Any operating losses incurred by the applicants in carrying out such a replacement activity cannot be attributed to the Community, since the origin of such losses does not lie in the effects of the Community rules.

It follows that the amount of compensation payable by the Community should correspond to the damage which it caused. The defendant institutions' contention that the amount of the compensation should be calculated on the basis of the amount of the non-marketing premium paid to each of the applicants must therefore be rejected. It must be noted in this regard that that premium constitutes the quid pro quo for the non-marketing undertaking and has no connection with the damage which the applicants suffered owing to the application of the rules on the additional levy, which were adopted at a later date.'

Comment
The ECJ confirmed the Schöppenstedt formula. The Court held that in relation to legislative acts involving choices in economic policy the Community institutions enjoyed a wide discretion and thus they were liable only if they had manifestly and gravely disregarded the limits of the exercise of their powers. As a result, in order to incur non-contractual liability the damage must go beyond the bounds of normal economic risks inherent in the activities relevant to a particular sector. However, in the present case the ECJ softened its approach towards the assessment of the criterion of sufficiently serious breach.

The restrictive interpretation reached its apogee in *G R Amylum NV and Tunnel Refineries Limited* v *EC Council and EC Commission* Cases 116 and 124/77 [1979] ECR 3497 and *Koninklijke Scholten Honig NV* v *EC Council and EC Commission* Case 43/77 [1979] ECR 3583, the so-called *Isoglucose* cases in which a regulation imposing levies on the production of isogluose, successfully challenged under art 173 EC prior to the application for damages, had such effect on the remaining three or four isoglucose undertakings in the Community that, for example, Koninklijke had to close down its business. The ECJ held that only if the conduct of an EC institution was 'verging on the arbitrary' (which was not the case) it would be considered as a sufficiently serious breach. The ECJ refused to award damages. The interests of the Community prevailed. The EC was entitled to limit the production of isoglucose and stabilise the market although some mistakes were made which resulted in the annulment of the Regulation.

In the present case the Court held that in the absence of 'the peremptory public interest' the Community cannot justify a measure which is gravely illegal and thus the Community would incur liability in such circumstances. Nevertheless, the change of approach of the Community courts in application of the Schöppenstedt formula has not eliminated the requirement that only grave illegality, in the absence of the peremptory public interest of the Community, would permit applicants to successfully claim damages under art 215(2) EC (*Odigitria* Case T–572/93 [1995] ECR II–2025).

As to the amount of damages, it is generally negotiated between the parties. In the case of a large number of applicants, the Commission and the Council submit a collective offer of indemnification as happened in the present case (the Council and the Commission adopted a regulation regarding the modality of indemnification OJ C198 5.08.92 p4).

However, the ECJ reduced the amount of damages. The Court justified the reduction on the basis of the duty upon the applicants to mitigate any loss, although the Court made no suggestion as to alternative activities but the term 'reasonable' implies that fundamentally different activities from their previous business were not considered as alternatives.

Aloys Schröder and Others v *Commission of the European Communities* Case C–22/97 Judgment of 10 December 1998 (not yet reported) European Court of Justice

- *Non-contractual liability of EC institutions – general legislative measures – the requirement of fault – control of classical swine fever – rights to defence – principle of proportionality – appeal against judgment of the Court of First Instance*

Facts
The applicants brought an appeal against the judgment of the Court of First Instance dismissing their action for damages under arts 178 and 215(2) EC. Treaty. The applicants claimed that they had suffered damage as a result of a number of decisions adopted by the Community in order to fight classical swine fever in Germany which restricted intra-Community and internal trade in swine in Member States affected by the epidemic. The applicants reared swine in the zone affected by the epidemic but their animals were not affected by swine fever.

The appellants based their appeal, first, on certain procedural errors before the Court of First Instance, which in their submission thus breached their rights of defence. Second, that the Court of First Instance erred in law by regarding the Commission's decisions as legislative rather than administrative measures and made incorrect assessments with respect to the principle of non-discrimination, their right to property and right to pursue a trade or occupation, and the principle of proportionality. Third, the appellants argued that the Court of First Instance disregarded the fact that the Commission's acts had no valid legal basis.

Held
The ECJ dismissed the appeal.

Judgment
'As regards the rights of the defence, it must be pointed out that the right to be heard in the context of judicial proceedings does not mean that the court has to incorporate in full in its decision all the submissions put forward by each party. The court, after listening to the submissions of the parties and assessing the evidence, has to decide whether or not to grant the relief sought in the application and give reasons for its decision.

The appellants' submissions under the first plea in law do not disclose any breach of those principles by the Court of First Instance. The first plea does not contain any point of law requiring analysis, but merely records disagreement on the facts found by the Court of First Instance. In particular, the appellants have not shown that the alleged failure by the Court of First Instance to consider certain parts of their arguments affected the outcome of the proceedings and so adversely affected their interests.

What the appellants are really seeking by means of the various allegations under this plea is to obtain from this Court a new assessment of the facts found by the Court of First Instance. However, under art 168a of the EC Treaty and the first paragraph of art 51 of the EC Statute of the Court of Justice, an appeal may only be based on pleas relating to the breach of rules of law, any assessment of the facts being excluded. The plea seeking a review of the facts by the Court of Justice is therefore inadmissible.

In their second and third pleas the appellants are essentially merely repeating arguments already put forward by them at first instance. However, no precise criticism of the legal reasoning of the Court of First Instance has been adduced.

Consequently, the second and the third pleas must be held to be inadmissible.'

Comment

The ECJ confirmed that the protection of public health justified the wide exercise of discretionary powers by the Commission. Consequently, the Commission was not found liable under art 215(2) EC Treaty. There are two interesting points raised by the present case. First, the ECJ imposed important limitations upon the exercise of the right of defence whilst the applicants tried to extend its scope of application. The ECJ held that the right to defence cannot call into question the power of judges to choose the arguments necessary to support their conclusions and necessary to give reasons for their decision. Second, the ECJ held that the determination of the nature of an act, whether administrative or legislative, was irrelevant since liability of EC institutions merely requires illegality of the challenged act. In this respect, the ECJ ignored liability without fault (see *Clemessy* Case 280/82 [1986] ECR I–1907; *Dorsch Consult Ingenieurgesellschaft mbH* v *EC Council and EC Commission* Case T–184/95 [1998] ECR II–667) and liability of EC institutions for a lawful act which had been adopted in such circumstances as to cause damages to the applicant (*CNTA SA* v *EC Commission* Case 74/74 [1975] ECR 533).

5 Preliminary Rulings: Article 177 EC (now Article 234 EC)

Preliminary ruling on interpretation of Community law

Pasquale Foglia v Mariella Novello (No 1) Case 104/79 [1980] ECR 745; [1981] 1 CMLR 45 European Court of Justice

• *Discretionary referral – genuine dispute between the parties to national proceedings – charges having equivalent effect to custom duties – art 30 EC Treaty*

Facts
Foglia, an Italian wine merchant, entered into a contract with Novello, an Italian national, for the delivery of liqueur wine to a person residing in France. They inserted an express clause providing that Novello would not pay any unlawfully levied taxes. The French authorities imposed a tax on the importation of the wine to France which Foglia paid although his contract which a shipper Danzas also provided that he should not be liable for any charges imposed in breach of the free movement of goods. Foglia brought proceedings against Novello who refused to reimburse the French tax levied on wine.

Held
The ECJ declined to exercise jurisdiction under art 177 EC on the ground that there was no real dispute between the parties to national proceedings. The Court held that the parties were concerned to obtain a ruling that the French tax system was invalid in relation to liqueur wine.

Judgment
'In their written submissions to the Court of Justice the two parties to the main action have provided an essentially identical description of the tax discrimination which is a feature of the French legislation concerning the taxation of liqueur wines; the two parties consider that the legislation is incompatible with Community law. In the course of the oral procedure before the Court Foglia stated that he was participating in the procedure before the Court in view of the interest of his undertaking as such and as an undertaking belonging to a certain category of Italian traders in the outcome of the legal issues involved in the dispute.

It thus appears that the parties to the main action are concerned to obtain a ruling that the French tax system is invalid for liqueur wines by the expedient of proceedings before an Italian court between two private individuals who are in agreement as to the result to be attained and who have inserted a clause in their contract in order to induce the Italian court to give a ruling on the point. The artificial nature of this expedient is underlined by the fact that Danzas did not exercise its rights under French law to institute proceedings over the consumption tax although it undoubtedly had an interest in doing so in view of the clause in the contract by which it was bound and moreover by the fact that Foglia paid without protest that undertaking's bill which included a sum paid in respect of that tax.

The duty of the Court of Justice under art 177 of the [EC] Treaty is to supply all courts in the Community with the information on the interpretation of Community law which is necessary to enable them to settle genuine disputes which are brought before them. A situation in which the Court was obliged by the expedient of arrangements like those described above to give rulings would jeopardise the whole system of legal remedies available to private individuals to enable them to protect themselves against tax provisions which are contrary to the Treaty.

This means that the questions asked by the national court, having regard to the circumstances of this case, do not fall within the framework of the duties of the Court of Justice under art 177 of the Treaty.

The Court of Justice accordingly has no jurisdiction to give a ruling on the questions asked by the national court.'

Comment
The ECJ held that the parties to national proceedings were concerned to obtain a ruling on the legality of the French legislation by the expedient of proceedings before an Italian court. Both parties had the same interest in the outcome of the dispute which was to obtain a ruling on the invalidity of the French legislation and, since under their contracts they were not liable for any unlawful charges imposed by France, their action was a collusive and artificial device aimed at obtaining a ruling and not a genuine dispute which the ECJ could settle.

When the Italian court asked the ECJ to provide clarification on its preliminary judgment in *Foglia* v *Novello* Case 104/79, the ECJ accepted the second reference in the same case but once again declined its jurisdiction to give a preliminary ruling on the same grounds (*Foglia* v *Novello (No 2)* Case 244/80 [1981] ECR 3045). The existence of a real dispute in the proceedings before a national court is determined from the point of view of art 177 EC. Thus, neither the fact that the parties challenge national legislation of one Member State before a court of another Member State, nor their agreement to 'organise' the proceedings before a national court leading to the preliminary ruling, is sufficient to exclude a real dispute from the scope of art 177 EC (see *Société d'Importation E Leclerc-SIPLEC* v *TF1 Publicité SA and M6 Publicité SA* Case C–412/93 [1995] ECR I–179; *Bosman* Case C–141/93 [1995] ECR I–4921, *Eau de Cologne* v *Provide* Case C–150/88 [1989] ECR 3891).

Pretore di Salo v *Persons Unknown*
Case 14/86 [1989] 1 CMLR 71
European Court of Justice

- *Preliminary ruling – jurisdiction of the ECJ – determination of a court or tribunal – timing of the reference – framing of the question referred – Directive 78/659/EEC*

Facts
The Italian authorities instituted criminal proceedings against unidentified persons responsible for the pollution of a river in Italy. The prosecution was based on provisions of the Italian Criminal Code, and the question was raised whether this statute was consistent with Council Directive 78/659 which regulated the quality of water and the amount of pollution that may be released into water sources.

The Pretore asked the ECJ for a preliminary ruling under art 177 as to whether the Italian laws for the protection of waters from pollution were consistent with the Directive. This gave rise to a number of issues, including the necessary status of the referring court to obtain a preliminary ruling, the proper timing of such request, and the role of the ECJ in ascertaining the facts of a dispute.

Held
The ECJ held that: (1) the reference from the magistrate came from 'a court or tribunal' within the meaning of art 177; (2) the reference was not premature and did not preclude a later reference if such a request was subsequently received from the tribunal; (3) the

question of compatibility of Italian law with Community law was too generally framed but, in such cases, the ECJ is empowered to reformulate the question; and (4) Directive 78/659 could not aggravate liability of a person violating the Directive.

Judgment

'[*First question*]
Without expressly arguing that the Court does not have jurisdiction to reply to the questions referred to it, the Italian government draws the Court's attention to the nature of the function performed in this case by the Pretore, which are both those of a public prosecutor and those of an examining magistrate. The Pretore carries out preliminary investigations in his capacity as public prosecutor and, where these disclose no grounds for continuing the proceedings, makes an order accordingly in the place of an examining magistrate. That order is not a judicial act because it cannot acquire the force of res judicata or create an irreversible procedural situation and because no reason need be given for it, whereas art 111 of the Italian Constitution imposes an obligation to state reasons in the case of judicial acts.

It must be observed that the Pretori are judges who, in proceedings such as those in which the questions referred to the Court in this case were raised, combine the functions of a public prosecutor and an examining magistrate. The Court has jurisdiction to reply to a request for a preliminary ruling if that request emanates from a court or tribunal which has acted in the general framework of its task as judging, independently and in accordance with law, cases coming within the jurisdiction conferred on it by law, even though certain functions of that court or tribunal in the proceedings which give rise to the reference for a preliminary ruling are not, strictly speaking, of a judicial nature.

[*Second question*]
At the hearing, the Italian government also maintained that, having regard to the present stage of the proceedings, at which the facts have not been sufficiently established and those who may be responsible have not yet been identified, a reference for a preliminary ruling is premature.

The European Commission considers that the reference for a preliminary ruling is inadmissible because in criminal proceedings against persons unknown it is possible that a decision may never be given on the substance of the case. All that is required for that to be the case is for those responsible never to be identified. At the hearing, the Commission also relied on another argument in support of the proposition that the Court does not have jurisdiction: if, after the Court's decision, the persons responsible were identified, they would be prevented from defending before the Court the interpretation of Community law most in conformity with their interests. That would constitute a violation of the right to a fair hearing.

It must be pointed out first that, as the Court decided in Joined Cases 36 and 71/80 *Irish Creamery Milk Supplier's Association v Ireland* [1981] ECR 147, if the interpretation of Community law is to be use to the national court, it is essential to define the legal context in which the interpretation requested should be placed. In that perspective, it might be convenient in certain circumstances for the facts of the case to be established and for questions of purely national law to be settled at the time when the reference is made to the Court of Justice so as to enable the latter to take cognisance of all the matters of fact and law which may be relevant to the interpretation of Community law which it is called upon to give.

However, as the Court already held, those considerations do not in any way restrict the discretion of the national court, which alone has a direct knowledge of the facts of the case and of the arguments of the parties, which will have to take responsibility for giving judgment in the case and which is therefore in the best position to appreciate at what stage of the proceedings it requires a preliminary ruling from the Court of Justice. The decision at what stage in the proceedings a question should be referred to the

Court of Justice for a preliminary ruling is therefore dictated by considerations of procedural economy and efficiency to be weighed only by the national court and not the Court of Justice.

It should be pointed out that the Court consistently held that the fact that judgments delivered on the basis of references for a preliminary ruling are binding on the national court does not preclude the national court to which such a reference is addressed from making a further reference to the Court of Justice if it considers it necessary in order to give judgment in the main proceedings. Such a reference may be justified when the national court encounters difficulties in understanding or applying the judgment, when it refers a fresh question of law to the Court, or again, when it submits new considerations which might lead the Court to give a different answer to a question submitted earlier.

It follows that where the accused are identified after the reference for a preliminary ruling and if one of the above mentioned conditions arises, the national court may once again refer a question to the Court of Justice and thereby ensure that due respect is given to the right to a fair hearing.

In those circumstances, the objections raised by the Commission and the Italian government concerning the jurisdiction of the Court must be rejected.

[*Third question*]
As the Court consistently held, it may not, in proceedings under art 177 [EC] Treaty, rule on the conformity of national measures with Community law. The Court may, however, extract from the wording of the question formulated by the national court, and having regard to the facts stated by the latter, those elements which concern the interpretation of Community law for the purpose of enabling that court to resolve the legal problems before it. In this case, however, in view of the generality of the question and the absence of any specific elements which would make it possible to identify the doubts entertained by the national court, it is not possible for the Court to reply to the first question referred to it.

[*Fourth question*]
According to the national court's order for reference, the Community rules are relevant to the questions of criminal law raised before it

"... in view of the fact that such rules constitute an essential basis for the criteria to be applied in the investigations, in view of the decisive importance for the purpose of the requirements laid down by the rules of criminal law in force and in view of the undeniable possibilities which may emerge from the directive of broadening the sphere of the protection afforded by the criminal law."

The national court is therefore essentially seeking to ascertain whether Directive 78/659 may, of itself and independently of the internal law of a Member State, have the effect of determining or aggravating the liability in criminal law of persons who act in contravention of that directive.

In that regard, the Court already held in Case 152/84 *Marshall* v *Southampton and South West Hampshire Area Health Authority* [1986] ECR 723 that "a directive may not of itself impose obligations on an individual and that a provision of a directive may not be relied upon as such against such a person." A directive which has not been transposed into the internal legal order of a Member State may not therefore give rise to obligations on individuals either in regard to other individuals or, a fortiori, in regard to the State itself.

Consequently, the reply to the [fourth] question must be that Council Directive 78/659 cannot, of itself and independently of a national law adopted by a Member State for its implementation, have the effect of determining or aggravating the liability in criminal law of persons who act in contravention of the provisions of that directive.'

Comment

In the present case the ECJ held that a body which exercises not only a judicial function but also other tasks may be considered as a court or tribunal within the meaning of art 177 EC. An Italian Pretore, a magistrate who initially acts as a public prosecutor and then as an examining magistrate, was considered as a court or a tribunal within the meaning of art 177 EC on the ground that the request emanated from a body that acted in the general framework of its task of judging, independently and in accordance with the law, despite the fact that certain functions performed by that body were not sensu stricto of a judicial nature.

Court or tribunal within the meaning of art 177 EC Treaty

Victoria Film A/S Case C–134/97 [1999] 1 CMLR 279 European Court of Justice

* Preliminary ruling – lack of jurisdiction of the ECJ – court or tribunal under art 177 EC Treaty – act of accession of the Kingdom of Sweden – transitional provisions – exemptions – services provided by authors, artists and performers

Facts
There was a tax dispute between Victoria Film A/S and Swedish tax authorities concerning certain transitional exemptions relating to turnover tax provided for in art 28(3)(b) of the Sixth Council Directive 77/388/EEC and the application of arts 2(1), 6(1) and 17 of that Directive allowing the suppliers of exclusive rights to exhibit motion pictures to deduct the VAT component of goods and services included in the price charged on the assignment of those rights. The Skatterättsnämnden (Swedish Revenue Board), which assesses the situation of the applicant from the point of view of internal taxation and delivers only preliminary decisions prior to binding decisions of the Swedish tax authorities, referred the above-mentioned questions for a preliminary ruling to the ECJ. The European Commission argued that the ECJ had no jurisdiction because the Swedish Revenue Board was not a court or a tribunal within the meaning of art 177 EC Treaty as its activities were administrative in nature.

Held
The ECJ held that it had no jurisdiction to answer the questions referred by the Swedish Revenue Board.

Judgment
'By decision of 20 February 1997, Skatterättsnämnden (Revenue Board) referred to the Court for a preliminary ruling under art 177 of the EC Treaty three questions on the interpretation of the Act concerning the conditions of accession of the Republic of Austria, the Republic of Finland and the Kingdom of Sweden and the adjustments to the Treaties on which the European Union is founded, in conjunction with art 28(3)(b) of Sixth Council Directive (77/388/EEC) of 17 May 1977 and point 2 of Annex F thereto.

Those questions have been raised in the context of an application for a preliminary decision submitted by Victoria Film A/S ("Victoria") to Skatterättsnämnden.

Skatterättsnämnden can, upon application by a taxable person, give a preliminary decision on matters of taxation.

The Commission submits that the Court has no jurisdiction to reply to the questions referred by Skatterättsnämnden. In particular, it submits that the latter is not a court or tribunal for the purposes of art 177 of the Treaty, since its activities seem to be rather administrative in nature.

In this connection, it should be observed that it has been consistently held that a national court may refer a question to the Court only if there is a case pending before it and if it is called upon to give judgment in proceedings intended to lead to a decision of a judicial nature.

It should be borne in mind, in particular, that at the time when an application for a preliminary decision is lodged with Skatterättsnämnden the taxpayer's situation has not been the subject of any decision by the tax authorities. Skatterättsnämnden does not therefore have as its task to review the legality of the decisions of the tax authorities but rather to adopt a view, for the first time, on how a specific transaction is to be assessed to tax.

Where, upon application by a taxable person, Skatterättsnämnden gives a preliminary decision on a matter of assessment or taxation, it performs a non-judicial function which, moreover, in other Member States is expressly entrusted to the tax authorities.'

Comment

In most cases the question whether or not a particular body is a court or a tribunal is self-evident. However, on a few occasions the ECJ has to determine the status of a referring body in the context of art 177 EC. The uniformity in the application of Community law throughout the Community requires that the definition of a court or a tribunal for the purposes of art 177 EC is independent from national concepts, which vary from one Member State to another, and has an autonomous, Community meaning. The case law of the ECJ has gradually determined the criteria permitting identification of a body which is considered as 'a court or a tribunal' under art 177 EC. Apart from all judicial bodies expressly recognised as such under national law of Member States, the ECJ held that other bodies can refer under art 177 EC provided they meet certain requirements. In *Vassen-Göbbels* Case 61/65 [1966] ECR 377 the ECJ held that technical factors – such as whether the type of procedure is adversarial or not, the involvement of national authorities in the appointments of the members of that body, the mandatory jurisdiction of that body imposed by national law upon the parties to the dispute – were all relevant for the purpose of art 177 EC.

In the present case the ECJ confirmed its case law in respect of determination of a court or tribunal within the meaning of art 177 EC Treaty. The fact that the Swedish Revenue Board did not exercise judicial function excluded it from the scope of art 177 EC. Similarly, in *Borker* Case 138/80 [1980] ECR 1975, Paris Conseil de l'Ordre des Avocats à la Cour (Paris Bar Council) was not considered as a court or tribunal within the meaning of art 177 EC because that body was not exercising any judicial function but in fact 'made a request for a declaration relating to a dispute between a member of the Bar and the courts or tribunals of another Member State'.

Compulsory reference

CILFIT v *Minister of Health* Case 283/81 [1982] ECR 3415; [1983] 1 CMLR 472 European Court of Justice

• *Compulsory reference – court or tribunal of last resort – question previously referred – doctrine of acte clair – health inspection levy in breach of art 30 EC Treaty – interpretation of EC law*

Facts

The Italian Ministry of Health imposed an inspection levy on imports of wool coming from other Member States. An Italian importer of wool challenged the levy. The Italian court considered that the case law on this matter was reasonably clear but as a court of final instance it was uncertain whether or not it should refer the question of legality of this fixed health inspection levy to the ECJ. The Italian court asked the ECJ whether it was obliged to refer under art 177(3) EC when the Community law was sufficiently clear and precise and there were no doubts as to its interpretation.

Held

The ECJ held that courts of last resort like any other courts or tribunals have the discretion to assess whether a referral is necessary to enable them to give judgment They are not obliged to refer if a question concerning the interpretation of Community law raised before them is not relevant to the dispute, that is, if it can in no way affect the outcome of the case.

The ECJ confirmed the principle that if the ECJ had already dealt with a point of law in question, even though the questions were not strictly identical, the court of last resort is not obliged to refer. Finally, the ECJ held that there is no obligation to refer if the correct application of Community law may be so obvious as to leave no scope for any reasonable doubt as to the manner in which the question raised is to be resolved. Before it comes to the conclusion that such is the case, the national court or tribunal must be convinced that the matter is equally obvious to the courts of the other Member States and to the Court of Justice.

Judgment

'In order to answer that question, it is necessary to take account of the system established by art 177, which confers jurisdiction on the Court of Justice to give preliminary rulings on, inter alia, the interpretation of the Treaty and the measures adopted by the institutions of the Community.

The second paragraph of that Article provides that any court or tribunal of a Member State may, if it considers that a decision on a question of interpretation is necessary to enable it to give judgment, request the Court of Justice to give a ruling thereon. The third paragraph of that Article provides that, where a question of interpretation is raised in a case pending before a court or tribunal of a Member State against whose decision there is no judicial remedy under national law, the court or tribunal shall bring the matter before the Court of Justice.

That obligation to refer a matter to the Court of Justice is based on co-operation, established with a view to ensuring the proper application and uniform interpretation of Community law in all Member States, between national courts, in their capacity as courts responsible for the application of Community law, and the Court of Justice. More particularly, the third paragraph of art 177 seeks to prevent the occurrence within the Community of divergencies in judicial decisions on question of Community law. The scope of that obligation must therefore be assessed, in view of those objectives, by reference to the powers of the national courts, on the one hand, and those of the Court of Justice, on the other, where such a question of interpretation is raised within the meaning of art 177.

In this connection, it is necessary to define the meaning for the purposes of Community law of the expression "where any such question is raised" in order to determine the circumstances in which a national court or tribunal against whose decision there is no judicial remedy under national law is obliged to bring a matter before the Court of Justice.

In this regard, it must in the first place be pointed out that art 177 does not constitute a means of redress available to the parties to a case pending before a national court or tribunal. Therefore the mere fact that a party contends that the dispute gives rise to a question concerning the interpretation of Community law does not mean that the court or tribunal concerned is compelled to consider that a question had been raised within the meaning of art 177. On the other hand, a national court or tribunal may, in an appropriate case, refer a matter to the Court of Justice of its own motion.

Secondly, it follows from the relationship between the second and third paragraphs of art 177 that the courts or tribunals referred to in the third paragraph have the same discretion as any other national court or tribunal to ascertain whether a decision on a question of Community law is necessary to enable them to give judgment. Accordingly, those court or tribunals are not obliged to refer to the Court of Justice a question concerning the interpretation of Community law raised before them if that question is not relevant, that is to say, if the answer to that question, regardless of what it may be, can in no way affect the outcome of the case,

If, however, those courts or tribunals consider that recourse to Community law is necessary to enable them to decide a case, art 177 imposes an obligation on them to refer to the Court of Justice any question of interpretation which may arise.

The question submitted by the [Italian court] seeks to ascertain whether, in certain circumstances, the obligation laid down in the third paragraph of art 177 might nonetheless be subject to certain restrictions.

It must be remembered in this connection that in its judgment in *Da Costa* v *Netherlands* (Cases 28–30/62 [1963] CMLR 224), the Court ruled that:

> "Although the third paragraph of art 177 unreservedly requires courts or tribunals of Member States against whose decision there is no judicial remedy under national law ... to refer to the Court every question of interpretation raised before them, the authority of an interpretation under art 177 already given by the Court may deprive the obligation of its purpose and thus empty it of its substance. Such is the case especially when the question raised is materially identical with a question which has already been the subject of a preliminary ruling in a similar case."

The same effect, as regards the limits set to the obligation laid down by the third paragraph of art 177, may be produced where previous decisions of the Court have already dealt with the point of law in question, irrespective of the nature of the proceedings which led to those decisions, even though the questions at issue are not strictly identical.

However, it must not be forgotten that in all such circumstances national courts and tribunals, including those referred in the third paragraph of art 177, remain entirely at liberty to bring a matter before the Court of Justice if they consider it appropriate to do so.

Finally, the correct application of Community law may be so obvious as to leave no scope for any reasonable doubt as to the manner in which the question raised is to be resolved. before it comes to the conclusion that such is the case, the national court or tribunal must be convinced that the matter is equally obvious to the courts of the other Member States and to the Court of Justice. Only if those conditions are satisfied may the national court or tribunal refrain from submitting the question to the Court of Justice and take upon itself the responsibility for resolving it.

However, the existence of such a possibility must be assessed on the basis of the characteristic features of Community law and the particular difficulties to which its interpretation gives rise.

To begin with, it must be borne in mind that Community legislation is drafted in several languages and that different language versions are equally authentic. An interpretation of a provision of Community law thus involves a comparison of the different language versions.

It must also be borne in mind, even where the different language versions are entirely in accord with one another, that Community law uses terminology which is peculiar to it. Furthermore, it must be emphasised that legal concepts do not necessarily have the same meaning in Community law and in the law of the various Member States.

Finally, every provision of Community law must be placed in its context and interpreted in the light of the provisions of Community law as a whole, regard being had to the objectives thereof and to the state of its evolution at the date on which the provision in question is to be applied.

In the light of all those considerations, the answer to the question submitted by the [Italian court] must be that the third paragraph of art 177 of the [EC] Treaty is to be interpreted as meaning that a court or tribunal against whose decision there is no judicial remedy under national law is required, where a question of Community law is raised before it, to comply with its obligation to bring the matter before the Court of Justice, unless it has established that the question is irrelevant or that the Community provision in question has already been interpreted by the Court or that the correct application of Community law is so obvious as to leave no scope for any reasonable doubt. The existence of such a possibility must be assessed in the light of the specific characteristics of Community law, the particular difficulties to which its interpretation give rise and the risk of divergences in judicial decisions within the Community.'

Comment

The ECJ endorsed the French doctrine of acte clair, according to which the court before which the exception prejudicielle is raised concerning the interpretation or validity of a particular provision must refer it to a competent court in order to resolve that question, but only if there is real difficulty concerning its interpretation or validity or if there is a serious doubt in this respect. However, if this provision is clear, if its validity is obvious, the court may apply it immediately.

It stems from *CILFIT* that it is not necessary for a court of last resort to refer if:

1. the question of Community law is irrelevant to the dispute;
2. the question of Community law has already been interpreted by the ECJ even though it may not be identical. However, it does not mean that national courts whatever their position in the hierarchy of national courts are prevented from referring an identical or a similar question to the ECJ. In *CILFIT* the ECJ clearly stated that all courts remain entirely at liberty to refer a matter before them if they consider it appropriate to do so.
3. the correct application of Community law is so obvious as to leave no scope for reasonable doubt, this incorporates the French theory of acte clair. However, the ECJ added that before a national court concludes that such is the case it must be convinced that the question is equally obvious to courts in other Member States and to the ECJ itself. Furthermore, the ECJ added three requirements which a national court must take into consideration when deciding that the matter is clear and free of doubts. Firstly, it must assess such possibility in the light of the characteristic features of Community law and especially the difficulties that its interpretation raise, ie that it is drafted in several languages and all version are equally authentic. Secondly, it must be aware that Community law uses peculiar terminology and has legal concepts which have different meaning in different Member States. Finally, a national court must bear in mind that every provision of Community law must be placed in its context and interpreted in the light of the provisions of Community law as a whole, its objectives and the state of its evolution at the date on which that provision is to be applied.

In practice the endorsement by the ECJ of the doctrine of acte clair has sensibly extended the discretion of the courts of last resort. It has also increased the risk of conflicting decisions being rendered by the highest courts in each Member State.

Optional jurisdiction

Practice Direction (Supreme Court: References to the Court of Justice of the European Communities) (1999) The Times 19 January (European Law Report)

Summary
Courts referring issues to the Court of Justice of the European Communities under art 177 of the EC Treaty (OJ 1992 No C224 p6) should ensure that the reference was in the form most helpful to the Court at Luxembourg which had to answer the questions posed.

Lord Bingham CJ:

'1. Before making a reference to the European Court of Justice under art 177 of the EC Treaty the Court of Appeal and the High Court should pay close attention to (a) the terms of that article, (b) Order 114 of the Rules of the Supreme Court and (c) Prescribed Form 109 (see *The Supreme Court Practice 1999* volume 2, paragraph 1A–114).

Close attention should also be paid to the *Guidance of the European Court of Justice on References by National Courts for Preliminary Rulings* incompletely reproduced at ([1997] 1 CMLR 78), and fully set out in Schedule B below.

2. It was the responsibility of the court, not the parties, to settle the terms of the reference. That should identify as clearly, succinctly and simply as the nature of the case

permitted the question to which the referring court sought an answer. It was very desirable that language should be used which lent itself ready to translation.

3. The referring court should, in a single document scheduled to the order:

(i) identify the parties and summarise the nature and history of the proceedings;

(ii) summarise the salient facts, indicating whether those were proved or admitted or assumed;

(iii) make reference to the rules of national law (substantive and procedural) relevant to the dispute;

(iv) summarise the contentions of the parties so far as relevant;

(v) explain why a ruling of the European Court was sought, identifying the EC provisions whose effect was in issue;

(vi) formulate, without avoidable complexity, the question(s) to which an answer was requested.

Where the document was in the form of a judgment, as would often be convenient, passages which were not relevant to the reference should be omitted from the text scheduled to the order.

Incorporation of appendices, annexures or enclosures as part of the document should be avoided, unless the relevant passages lent themselves ready to translation and were clearly identified.

4. The referring court should ensure that the order of reference, when finalised, was promptly passed to the Senior Master of the Queen's Bench Division so that it might be transmitted to Luxembourg without avoidable delay ...

Schedule B
Guidance of the European Court of Justice on References by National Courts for Preliminary Rulings.

... It had to be emphasised that the Note was for guidance only and had no binding or interpretive effect in relation to the provisions governing the preliminary ruling procedure.

1. Any court or tribunal of a Member State might ask the Court of Justice to interpret a rule of Community law, whether contained in the Treaties or in acts of secondary law, if it considered that that was necessary for it to give judgment in a case pending before it.

Courts or tribunals against whose decisions there was no judicial remedy under national law had to refer questions of interpretation arising before them to the Court of Justice, unless the Court had already ruled on the point or unless the correct application of the rule of Community law was obvious.

2. The Court of Justice had jurisdiction to rule on the validity of acts of the Community institutions. National courts or tribunals might reject a plea challenging the validity of such an act.

But where a national court, even one whose decision was still subject to appeal, intended to question the validity of a Community act, it had to refer that question to the Court of Justice.

Where, however, a national court or tribunal had serious doubts about the validity of a Community act on which a national measure was based, it might, in exceptional cases, temporarily suspend application of the latter measure or grant other interim relief with respect to it.

It had then to refer the question of validity to the Court of Justice, stating the reasons for which it considered that the Community act was not valid.

3. Questions referred for a preliminary ruling had to be limited to the interpretation or validity of a provision of Community law, since the Court of Justice did not have jurisdiction to interpret national law or assess its validity.

It was for the referring court or tribunal to apply the relevant rule of Community law in the specific case pending before it.

4. The order of the national court or tribunal referring a question to the Court of Justice for a preliminary ruling might be in any form allowed by national procedural law.

Reference of a question or questions to the Court of Justice generally involved stay of the national proceedings until the Court had given its ruling, but the decision to stay proceedings was one which it was for the national court alone to take in accordance with its own national law.

5. The order of reference containing the question or questions referred to the Court would have to be translated by the Court's translators into the other official languages of the Community.

Questions concerning the interpretation or validity of Community law were frequently of general interest and the Member States and Community institutions were entitled to submit observations. It was therefore desirable that the reference should be drafted as clearly and precisely as possible.

6. The order for reference should contain a statement of reasons which was succinct but sufficiently complete to give the Court, and those to whom it had to be notified, the Member States, the Commission and in certain cases the Council and the European Parliament, a clear understanding of the factual and legal context of the main proceedings.

In particular, it should include:

(i) a statement of the facts which were essential to a full understanding of the legal significance of the main proceedings.

(ii) an exposition of the national law which might be applicable.

(iii) a statement of the reasons which had prompted the national court to refer the question or questions to the Court of Justice; and

(iv) where appropriate, a summary of the arguments of the parties.

The aim should be to put the Court of Justice in a position to give the national court an answer which would be of assistance to it.

The order for reference should also be accompanied by copies of any documents needed for a proper understanding of the case, especially the text of the applicable national provisions.

However, as the case-file or documents annexed to the order for reference were not always translated in full into the other official languages of the Community, the national court should ensure that the order for reference itself included all the relevant information.

7. A national court or tribunal might refer a question to the Court of Justice as soon as it found that a ruling on the point or points of interpretation or validity was necessary to enable it to give judgment.

It had to be stressed, however, that it was not for the Court of Justice to decide issues of fact or to resolve disputes as to the interpretation or application of rules of national law.

It was therefore desirable that a decision to refer should not be taken until the national proceedings had reached a stage where the national court was able to define, if only as a working hypothesis, the factual and legal context of the question.

On any view, the administration of justice was likely to be best served if the reference was not made until both sides had been heard.

8. The order for reference and the relevant documents should be sent by the national court directly to the Court of Justice, by registered post, addressed to: The Registry, Court of Justice of the European Communities, L–2925 Luxembourg (Tel: 00 352 4303 1).

The Court Registry would remain in contact with the national court until judgment was given, and would send copies of the various documents, written observations, report for the hearing, opinion of the advocate-general. The Court would also send its judgment to the national court.

The Court would appreciate being informed about the application of its judgment in the national proceedings and being sent a copy of the national court's final decision.

9. Proceedings for a preliminary ruling before the Court of Justice were free of charge. The Court did not rule on costs.'

© Times Newspapers Limited 1998

Comment

This Practice Direction should be examined in the light of the recent decision of the Court of Appeal in *Royscot Leasing Ltd (and three other appellants)* v *Commissioners of Customs and Excise* (1998) The Times 23

November (European Law Report) in which the Commissioners of Customs and Excise asked the Court of Appeal to withdraw the referral for a preliminary ruling to the ECJ on value-added tax appeals against the four above-mentioned applicants. The Court of Appeal held that although it was entitled to order the withdrawal of a reference to the ECJ on its own initiative it should do so only when it was manifest that the reference would not fulfil any useful purpose. Consequently, the court should exercise its power of withdrawal only in exceptional cases.

In *Royscot* the Court of Appeal refused to withdraw the referral for the following reasons. First, the fact that the ECJ did not invite the referring court to withdraw its reference showed that the question could not be regarded as acte clair. In this respect it is interesting to note that when the referred questions does not concern a genuine dispute or has no real connection with Community law, the ECJ has developed a new manner to deal with them. Instead of declaring them inadmissible under art 177 EC, the ECJ under art 92 of its Rules of Procedure issues an order which declares them manifestly inadmissible (see *Monin Automobiles* Case C–428/93 [1994] ECR I–1707; *La Pyramide SARL* Case C–378/93 [1994] ECR I–3999). Second, the Court of Appeal emphasised that the greater the progress that the case had made in the ECJ since the referral, the greater was the significance of any absence of a suggestion by the ECJ that the referral should be withdrawn. In *Royscot* the oral hearing on the referral was due shortly in Luxembourg and it was clear that a fair amount of work had manifestly been done on the case.

Preliminary rulings on validity of Community acts

Eurotunnel SA and Others v *SeaFrance* Case C–408/95 [1997] ECR I–6315; [1998] 2 CMLR 293 European Court of Justice

• *Administrative law – assessment of validity of transitional arrangements for tax-free shops – conditions for a natural or legal person to challenge the validity of Community acts in the context of preliminary rulings when no action for annulment has been brought pursuant to art 173 EC within the prescribed time-limit – obligation to consult again the European Parliament if the Council substantially amends a proposal after receiving the Parliament's opinion within the consultation procedure*

Facts

French companies (Eurotunnel SA and France Manche SA) and English companies (Eurotunnel plc and the Channel Tunnel Group Ltd), joint operators of the Channel Tunnel railway link (Eurotunnel), brought proceedings against SeaFrance, a cross-channel maritime transport company and a subsidiary of SNCF acting under the trade mark 'Sealink', for infringement of EC competition law consisting of selling goods free of tax and excise duty on board its vessels and thus offsetting transport charges at below cost price. SeaFrance had already been found guilty of unfair competition by a French court in previous proceedings instituted by Eurotunnel. Consequently, Eurotunnel felt that anti-competitive practices of SeaFrance could only be stopped if art 28k of the Sixth Directive 77/388 of 17 May 1977 (on the harmonisation of the laws of the Member States relating to turnover taxes-Common system of value added tax) and art 28 of Directive 92/12 of 25 February 1992 were to be declared invalid by the ECJ. Those Articles authorise Member States to grant exemptions from value added tax and excise duty for supplies by tax-free shops located within an airport, port or Channel Tunnel terminal until 30 June 1999. The French Republic made use of this opportunity while implementing the Directives in question. The Parisian commercial court (tribunal de commerce) referred three questions to the ECJ:

1. the possibility for Eurotunnel to challenge the validity of arts 28k and 28 within the framework of art 177 EC, notwithstanding the fact that the plaintiffs did not bring an action for annulment under art 173 EC within the prescribed time-limit;
2. the assessment of validity of the challenged provisions; and
3. in the case of invalidity of the provisions, the consequences of a declaration of invalidity with respect to SeaFrance.

Held

The ECJ clarified its decision in *TWD* Case C–188/92 [1994] ECR I–833 regarding the conditions for a natural or legal person to challenge the validity of Community acts in the context of a preliminary ruling when no action for annulment has been brought pursuant to art 173 EC within a prescribed time-limit. In this respect the ECJ held that a natural or legal person may bring proceedings before a national court challenging the validity of a Community act, even though:

1. the act in question has not been addressed to that person;
2. that person has not brought an action for annulment pursuant to art 173 EC; and
3. a court of another Member State has already given judgment in separate proceedings.

The ECJ upheld the validity of transitional arrangements for tax-free shops based on Directive 91/680 and 92/12. In relation to the requirement for the European Parliament to be consulted again when the Council adopts a measure which substantially alters the Commission's proposal, the ECJ stated that such a consultation is not necessary if amendments correspond to the wishes of the European Parliament.

Judgment

'*Question 1*
By its first question the national court essentially asks whether a natural or legal person, such as Eurotunnel, may challenge before a national court the validity of provisions in directives, such as arts 28 and 28k, even though that person has not brought an action for annulment of those provisions pursuant to art 173 of the Treaty and even though a court of another Member State has already given judgment in separate proceedings.

In the case of Community directives whose contested provisions are addressed in general terms to Member States and not to natural or legal persons, it is not obvious that an action by Eurotunnel challenging arts 28 and 28k under art 173 of the Treaty would have been admissible.

In any event, Eurotunnel cannot be directly concerned by arts 28 and 28k. The exemption arrangements introduced by those provisions constitute no more than an option open to Member States. It follows that arts 28 and 28k are not directly applicable to the operators concerned, namely passenger transporters and travellers …

Question 2
The reasoning of the judgment making the reference and the wording of the second question make it clear that the only grounds of invalidity raised by the national court relate to the possibility that the procedure whereby arts 28 and 28k were adopted may have been irregular by reason of the alleged lack of a proposal from the Commission and failure to consult the Parliament again.

The lack of proposal from the Commission
As to that point, by virtue of its power to amend under, at that time, art 149(1) of the EEC Treaty (now art 189a(1) of the EC Treaty) the Council could amend the proposal from the Commission provided it acted unanimously, that requirement being imposed in any case by the legal basis of those directives, namely art 99 of the Treaty.

Moreover, the maintenance for a limited period of the system of exemption from value added tax and excise duty of supplies of goods by the tax-free shops, notwithstanding the Commission's opposition to that maintenance in the context of intra-Community travel, falls within the scope of Directives 91/680 and 92/12, which are intended to ensure that the conditions necessary for the movement of goods and services subject to value added tax or excise duty within an internal market without fiscal frontiers are implemented as from 1 January 1993.

Consequently, to the extent that the Council's amendments to the proposals for Directives 91/680 and 92/12 remained within the scope of those directives as defined in the original proposals from the Commission, the Council did not exceed its power to make amendments under art 149 of the Treaty.

The requirement for the Parliament to be consulted again
... It is to be remembered that due consultation of the Parliament in the cases provided for by the Treaty constitutes an essential formal requirement, breach of which renders the measure concerned void.

It is settled law that the requirement to consult the European Parliament in the legislative procedure, in the cases provided for by the Treaty, means that it must be consulted again whenever the text finally adopted, taken as a whole, differs in essence from the text on which the Parliament has already been consulted, except in cases in which the amendments substantially correspond to the wishes of the Parliament itself.

It must therefore be considered whether the amendments referred to by Eurotunnel and the Parliament go to the essence of the measures considered as a whole.

The purpose of the Commission's proposals for Directives 91/680 and 92/12 presented to the Parliament was to adjust the systems of value added tax and excise duty to the existence of an internal market, defined as an area without internal frontiers.

The object of arts 28 and 28k is to permit a pre-existing system to be maintained if the Member States so wish. Those articles must therefore be interpreted as optional exceptions of limited scope. The possibility of tax free sales is reserved for certain categories of traders and is limited in extent (ECU 90) and time (30 June 1999).

It follows that the changes made by arts 28 and 28k are not such as to affect the intrinsic tenor of the provisions introduced by Directives 91/680 and 92/12 and thus cannot be classed as changes in the essence of the measures.

In any event, the Parliament not only had an opportunity to express its opinion on the question of tax-free sales, it recommended that they should be maintained.

Consequently, by deciding to maintain tax-free sales until 30 June 1999 in order to deal with the social repercussions in that sector, the Council responded in substance to the wishes of the Parliament.

In those circumstances, it was not necessary for the Parliament to be consulted again on arts 28 and 28k.

It follows from all the foregoing that consideration of the questions raised has not disclosed any factor of such a kind as to affect the validity of art 28 and 28k.'

Comment
In the present case the ECJ clarified its decision in *TWD* Case C–188/92: if a Community act is addressed to natural or legal persons and thus they are directly and individually concerned they would be precluded from challenging the validity of those acts in the context of a preliminary ruling if they have not brought an action for annulment pursuant to art 173 EC within the prescribed time-limit. In this respect the ECJ transposes its solution regarding EC regulation to EC directives (*Accrington Beef* Case C–241/95 [1996] ECR 6699). In this case the challenged Community directives are addressed in general terms to Member States as they offer an option open to them which a priori excludes the existence of any link between the challenged directives and the applicants. As arts 28 and 28k are not directly applicable to the operators concerned, namely passenger transporters and travellers,

it would be extremely difficult for Eurotunnel to establish locus standi under art 173 EC even though in some cases the ECJ has accepted an action for annulment challenging EC directives addressed to the Member States provided the applicants were directly and individually concerned (*Gibraltar* Case C–298/89 [1993] ECR I–3605; *Asocarne* Case C–10/95P [1995] ECR I–4149).

In respect of the validity of arts 28 and 28k the ECJ held that the Council's amendments to the original proposals from the Commission remained within the scope of those Directives. Consequently, the Council did not exceed its powers to amend such proposals since under art 189a(1) EC the Council could amend the proposal provided it acted unanimously, which in fiscal matters is required anyway.

The requirement for the Parliament to be consulted again if the Commission's original proposal is substantially amended by the Council is essential from the point of view of the legality of an adopted act. Its infringement renders the adopted measure void. However, if substantial amendments made by the Council correspond to the wishes of the Parliament there is no need for the Parliament to be consulted again (this requirement has been clearly stated in *European Parliament* v *EC Council* Case C–65/90 [1992] ECR I–4593 and repeated in *Driessen en Zonen and Others* v *Minister van Verkeer en Waterstaat* Cases C–13–16/92 [1993] ECR I–4751 and *European Parliament* v *EC Council (Cabotage II)* Case C–388/92 [1994] ECR I–2067).

Firma Foto-Frost v *Haupzollamt Lubeck-Ost* Case 314/85 [1988] 3 CMLR 57 European Court of Justice

- *Referral on validity of Community acts – national courts have no jurisdiction to annul a Community act – exclusive jurisdiction of the ECJ to declare an act invalid*

Facts
Frost applied to a German municipal court to declare a decision issued by the Commission invalid on the grounds that it was in breach of the requirements set out in the Council regulation which delegated authority to the Commission to adopt decisions. The German court requested a preliminary ruling as to whether it could review the validity of the decision in question.

Held
The ECJ held that for the uniformity of Community law it is especially important that there are no divergences between Member States as to the validity of Community acts since they would jeopardise the very unity of the Community legal order as well as detract from the fundamental requirement of legal certainty. The ECJ drew comparison between its exclusive jurisdiction under art 173 EC and the preliminary ruling on validity of Community acts. It stated that the coherence of the system requires that where the validity of Community measures is challenged before a national court the jurisdiction to declare the act invalid must also be reserved to the ECJ. As a result the ECJ held that 'national courts have no jurisdiction themselves to declare the acts of Community Institutions invalid'.

Judgment
'In enabling national courts against whose decisions there is judicial remedy under national law to refer to the Court for a preliminary ruling questions on interpretation or validity, art 177 did not settle the question whether those courts themselves may declare that acts of Community institutions are invalid.

Those courts may consider the validity of a Community act and, if they consider that the grounds put forward before them by the parties in support of invalidity are unfounded, they may reject them, concluding that the measure is completely valid. By taking that action they are not calling the existence of the Community measure into question.

On the other hand, those courts do not have the power to declare acts of the Community institutions invalid. As the Court emphasised in the judgment of 13 May 1981 (Case 66/80 *International Chemical Corporation* v *Amministrazione delle Finanze* [1981] ECR 1191), the main purpose of the powers accorded to the Court by art 177 is to ensure that Community law is applied uniformly by national courts. That requirement of uniformity is particularly imperative when the validity of a Community act is in question. Divergencies between courts in the Member States as to the validity of Community acts would be liable to place in jeopardy the very unity of the Community legal order and detract from the fundamental requirement of legal certainty.

The same conclusion is dictated by consideration of the necessary coherence of the system of judicial protection established by the Treaty. In that regard it must be observed that requests for preliminary rulings, like actions for annulment, constitute means for reviewing the legality of acts of the Community institutions. As the Court pointed out in its judgment of 23 April 1986 (Case 294/83 *Partie Ecologiste "Les Verts"* v *European Parliament* [1986] ECR 1339), "in arts 173 and 184, on the one hand, and in art 177, on the other, the Treaty established a complete system of legal remedies and procedures designed to permit the Court of Justice to review the legality of measures adopted by the institutions".

Since art 173 gives the Court exclusive jurisdiction to declare void an act of a Community institution, the coherence of the system requires that where the validity of a Community act is challenged before a national court the power to declare the act invalid must also be reserved to the Court of Justice.

It must also be emphasised that the Court of Justice is in the best position to decide on the validity of Community acts. Under art 20 of the Protocol on the Statute of the Court of Justice of the [EC], Community institutions whose acts are challenged are entitled to participate in the proceedings in order to defend the validity of the acts in question. Furthermore, under the second paragraph of art 21 of that Protocol the Court may require the Member States and institutions which are not participating in the proceedings to supply all information which it considers necessary for the purpose of the case before it.

It should be added that the rule that national courts may not themselves declare Community acts invalid may have to be qualified in certain circumstances in the case of proceedings relating to an application for interim measures; however, that case is not referred to in the national court's question.

The answer to the first question must therefore be that national courts have no jurisdiction themselves to declare that acts of Community institutions are invalid.'

Comment

This case confirmed that the ECJ has exclusive jurisdiction to declare an act of a Community institution invalid. There is no distinction between national courts in matters relating to validity. Lower courts and the courts of final resort must refer to the ECJ if there are some doubts as to the validity of a Community measure.

Interim relief

Emesa Sugar (Free Zone) NV* v *European Commission Cases C–363 and 364/98P(R) Order of the ECJ of 17 December 1998 (not yet reported) European Court of Justice

• *Interim relief – conditions – urgency – discretionary power of the Commission – irreversible damage*

Facts

The company, Emesa, recognised as taking part in the Lomé agreement between the EU and the ACP countries, located on the island of Aruba, transforms sugar intended for export to the EU. The Council Decision 97/803/EC of 25 July 1997 provided for a revised system of imports quotas for sugar from ACP/PTOM limiting it to 30,000 tonnes per annum and thus modified its Decision 91/482/EEC regarding the terms of association of French overseas territories with the Community. Emesa challenged that decision under art 173 EC Treaty and in separate proceedings asked for its suspension on the ground of urgency and irreparable harm that its continuous application would cause to it, namely bankruptcy. The Court of First Instance (CFI) rejected the application for interim measures on the basis that damage would be purely financial and therefore could not be considered as irreparable and that Emesa did not submit any evidence as to the threat of bankruptcy even though one of its factories had already been closed and another temporarily ceased its activity as a result of the challenged decision. Emesa contested the decision of the CFI before the ECJ arguing that the CFI should have first examined the matter of urgency and then the question of harm and that the CFI erroneously assessed both conditions for granting interim measures, that is that damage would be an adequate remedy and that the matter of urgency must be incontestably proved by Emesa.

Held
The ECJ annulled the order of the CFI, although it referred back to the CFI. The Court confirmed that in the context of interim measures the CFI enjoyed a large measure of discretion and that it may examine the conditions for granting such measures in the order it prefers, that is the matter of urgency before the question of fumus bonu juris. The ECJ confirmed that the burden of proof is on the applicant.

Comment
In the present case the ECJ, instead of delivering itself a decision regarding interim measures by virtue of art 54(1) of its Statute referred the case back to the CFI. This meant that the question of interim measures would be further delayed which may result in the bankruptcy of Emesa. For Emesa the question of interim relief was vital if its rights under Community law were to have any substance. It seems that one has to take time in matters of urgency in order to be granted interim relief!

In the context of interim relief, the ECJ in *Zuckerfabrik Südderdithmarschen v Hauptzollamt Itzehoe* Cases C–143/88 and C–92/89 [1991] ECR I–415 established the conditions for obtaining interim relief which were further explained in *Atlanta Fruchthandelsgesellschaft v BEF* Case C–465/93 [1995] ECR I–3761. The ECJ stated that the interim legal protection which the national courts must afford to individuals under Community law must be the same, whether they seek suspension of enforcement of a national administrative measure adopted on the basis of a Community regulation or the grant of interim measures settling or regulating the disputed legal positions or relationships for their benefit. The Court held that a Community act may be suspended by a national court provided the latter has made reference to the ECJ under art 177 EC. As to the conditions they are very stringent:

1. the national court must justify why it considers that the ECJ should find the Community measure invalid;
2. the national court must take into consideration the extent of the discretion allowed to the Community institutions resulting from the ECJ's case law;
3. the national court must assess the Community interest in the light of the impact of suspension on the Community legal regime and the appropriateness of financial guarantees or security;
4. the national court must take into account any previous art 173 judgments concerning the disputed legislation.

6 Sources of Law and Principles of Interpretation

Primary sources

See Chapter 7: Fundamental Principles of European Community Law.

Treaties entered into by the European Community with third states

Hauptzollamt Mainz v *Kupferberg*
Case 104/81 [1982] ECR 3641; [1983] 1 CMLR 1 European Court of Justice

- *International agreements between the EC and third states – free trade agreement – conflict between national law and international agreements concluded by the EC with third states and national law of a Member State – supremacy of international agreements – direct effect of international agreements*

Facts
Prior to the accession of Portugal to the European Community, Kupferberg, a German undertaking, imported Portuguese wine into Germany. Duty was charged on these imports by the German customs authorities. Article 21 of the Portugal-EEC Free Trade Agreement contains provisions similar to those in the EC Treaty abolishing customs charges and charges having an equivalent effect. The plaintiff sought to have these charges abolished, arguing that art 21 of the Free Trade Agreement had direct effect in Community law and therefore prevailed over the inconsistent statute of German national law. If direct effect could be given to the provision, no customs duties would be payable on the imported wine from Portugal.

In fact, the German court of first instance (the Finanzgericht Rheinland-Pfalz) did give direct effect to art 21 and removed the duties accordingly. The German tax authorities, however, appealed the decision of this court to a higher court (the Bundesfinanzhof) which subsequently referred the matter to the ECJ for a preliminary ruling.

Held
The ECJ held that the relevant provisions of the Portugal-EEC Free Trade Agreement produced direct effect on the ground that international obligations assumed by the Community must be respected within the national legal systems of the Member States. However, such provisions must satisfy conditions similar to those for direct effect of provisions of Community Treaties, namely that the particular provision must be unconditional, sufficiently precise, and must not require legislative intervention on the part of the Community institutions or the Member States.

Judgment
'The Treaty establishing the Community has conferred upon the institutions the power not only of adopting measures applicable in the Community but also of making agreements with non-Member countries and international organisations in accordance with the provisions of the Treaty. According to art 228(2) these agreements are binding

on the institutions of the Community and on Member States. Consequently, it is incumbent upon the Community institutions, as well as upon the Member States, to ensure compliance with the obligations arising from such agreements.

The measures needed to implement the provisions of an agreement concluded by the Community are to be adopted, according to the state of Community law for the time being in the areas affected by the provisions of the agreement, either by the Community institutions or by the Member States. That is particularly true of agreements such as those concerning free trade where the obligations entered into extend to may areas of a very diverse nature.

In ensuring respect for commitments arising from an agreement concluded by the Community institutions the Member States fulfil an obligation not only in relation to the non-Member country concerned but also and above all in relation to the Community which has assumed responsibility for the due performance of the agreement. That is why the provisions of such an agreement, as the Court has already stated in its judgment in Case 181/73 *Haegeman* [1974] ECR 449, form an integral part of the Community legal system.

It follows from the Community nature of such provisions that their effect in the Community may not be allowed to vary according to whether their application is in practice the responsibility of the Community institutions or the Member States and, in the latter case, according to the effects in the internal legal order of each Member State which the law of that State assign to international agreements concluded by it. Therefore it is for the Court, within the framework of its jurisdiction in interpreting the provisions of agreements, to ensure their uniform application throughout the Community.

... Nevertheless the question whether such a stipulation is unconditional and sufficiently precise to have direct effect must be considered in the context of the Agreement of which it forms part. In order to reply to the question on the direct effect of the first paragraph of art 21 of the Agreement between the Community and Portugal it is necessary to analyse the provision in the light of both the object and purpose of the Agreement and its context.

The purpose of the Agreement is to create a system of free trade in which rules restricting commerce are eliminated in respect of virtually all trade in products originating in the territory of the parties, in particular by abolishing customs duties and charges having equivalent effect and eliminating quantitative restrictions and measures having equivalent effect.

Seen in context the first paragraph of art 21 of the Agreement seeks to promote the liberalisation of the trade in goods, through the abolition of customs duties and charges having equivalent effect and quantitative restrictions and measures having equivalent effect, from rendered nugatory by fiscal practices of the contracting parties. This would be so if the product imported from one party were taxed more heavily than the similar domestic products which it encounters on the market on the other party.

It appears from the foregoing that the first paragraph of art 21 of the Agreement imposes on the contracting parties un unconditional rule against discrimination in matters of taxation, which is dependent only on a finding that the products affected by a particular system of taxation are of like nature, and the limits of which are the direct consequence of the purpose of the Agreement. As such this provision may be applied by a court and thus produces direct effects throughout the Community.

The first part of the first question should be answered to the effect that the first paragraph of art 21 of the Agreement between the Community and Portugal is directly applicable and capable of conferring upon individual traders rights which the courts must protect.'

Comment

By virtue of art 228(2) EC Treaty international agreements entered into by the Community and third countries or international organisations are binding upon the EC institutions and

Member States. This provision has been inserted to underline that the principle of public international law, according to which only contracting parties to an international agreement are bound by its provisions, does not apply in the context of the Community. In addition, the principle of supremacy of Community law strengthens the peculiar position of the Member States vis-à-vis international agreements concluded between the Community and third parties. In *Haegeman* Case 181/73 [1974] ECR 449 the ECJ held that the provisions of international agreements, from their entry into force, form an integral part of the Community legal order. It means that international agreements acquire ipso facto, (ie solely because they are international agreements) and from the date of their entry into effect the force of law in the Community legal order. No express incorporation into Community law is required

In the hierarchy of sources of EC law international agreements concluded between the Communities and third countries or international organisations are situated below primary sources and general principles of EC law but above the secondary sources. Their secondary position vis-à-vis primary sources is justified on the grounds of art 228(7) EC (*Schroeder* Case 40/72 [1973] ECR 125).

In the present case the ECJ held that neither the nature nor the economy of an international agreement can prevent an individual from relying on its provisions in proceedings before national courts.

Secondary legislation

EC regulations

Bussone v Ministry of Agriculture
Case 31/78 [1978] ECR 2429; [1979] 3 CMLR 18 European Court of Justice

* *EC regulations – binding force – direct applicability – art 189 EC Treaty – national rules implementing EC directives*

Facts
The Council enacted a number of regulations concerning the marketing of eggs throughout the Community. These regulations were incorporated into Italian law by a domestic statute. One of the regulations specified a requirement that packs containing eggs were to have a band or a label, which could not be reused, to inform the consumer of certain important details, such as the sell-by date, the producer's name, the weight of the goods and the quality of the product. Under the Italian law, 'packing centres' were authorised to conduct this activity and only the government was entitled to issue these labels or bands.

An Italian businessman ran an egg-packing centre, and was required tp pay considerable sums to the Italian Ministry of Agriculture in order to acquire the labels. The businessman paid these charges, but challenged their legality under Community law, arguing that the regulation did not specify that a charge should be made for this service. In fact, the Italian legislation permitted the government to charge sums far in excess of the costs of supplying these bands and labels.

Held
The ECJ confirmed that direct applicability of regulations should not be compromised by implementing provisions of national law but did not believe that this effect had occurred in this particular case. The ECJ pointed out that the principle of direct applicability implies that the legal force of a regulation lies in the measure itself, independently of any implementing legislation.

Judgment
'The following third question is asked (by the Italian court):

"Must the said regulations be interpreted to mean that their direct applicability must not be jeopardised by the adoption of the national provisions which, whilst purporting to implement the regulations in question, introduce additional conditions, such as those reserving to the public authorities the right to prepare and distribute bands and labels and making the issue of such bands and labels subject to the payment of a pecuniary consideration?"

That question raises the point as to whether the fact that the preparation and distribution of labels is reserved to the public authorities and their issue is made conditional on payment of a pecuniary consideration is contrary to the directly applicable nature of the regulation, which would be prejudiced by the introduction of "additional considerations purporting to implement the regulation in question".

According to the second paragraph of art 189 of the Treaty a regulation shall have general application and shall be directly applicable in all Member States. By reason of its nature and its function in the system of sources of Community law, therefore, a regulation has direct effect. The direct applicability of a regulation requires that its entry into force and its application in favour of or against those subject to it must be independent of any measure of reception into national law. Proper compliance with that duty precludes the application of any legislative measure, even one adopted subsequently, which is incompatible with the provisions of that regulation.

That prohibition is, however, relaxed to the extent to which the regulation in question leaves it to the Member States themselves to adopt the necessary legislative, regulatory, administrative and financial measures to ensure the effective application of the provisions of that regulation.

The position is that established Regulations 1619/68 and 95/69, which provide inter alia that "large packs ... shall be provided with a band or label ... which shall be issued by or under the supervision of the official agencies ... appointed for the purpose in each Member State ... a list of [which] shall be forwarded to other Member States and to the Commission" (arts 17 and 26 of Regulation 1619/68) and that the latter shall be provided with "one or more specimens of the band or label ... which may be numbered [and] shall bear an official marking laid down by the competent authority" (art 5 of Regulation 95/69).

Nor is it ruled out that in that case the costs of printing and distributing the bands and labels, and those arising from the implementation of the specific checks required by the basic regulations, should be regarded as a service rendered to the user such as to justify the imposition of a pecuniary charge, on condition that it does not exceed the real costs of the supervisory system in question. Indeed, the fact that a Member State reserves to its public authorities the preparation of the bands and labels in no way disrupts the functioning of the common organisation and does not obstruct and is not of such a nature as to obstruct the free movement of the products.

The reply should therefore be given that the directly applicable nature of Regulation 1619/68, replaced by Regulation 2771/75 and Regulation 95/69, is not affected by the adoption of national rules required by the said regulations for their application which comply with the aim and objectives of the regulations by introducing additional conditions such as reserving to the public authorities the preparation and distribution of the bands and labels and making the issue thereof conditional on payment of a pecuniary consideration, on condition that the consideration is not disproportionate to the costs of the supervisory system in question.'

Comment

An EC regulation is binding in its entirety which means that its incomplete (*EC Commission* v *Italy* Case 39/72 [1973] ECR 101) or selective (*Granaria* Case 18/72 [1972] ECR 1172) application is prohibited under EC law. Also, the modification (*Norddeutsches Vieh- und Fleischkontor* Case 3/70 [1971] ECR 49) or introduction of any national legislation susceptible to affect its content or scope of application is contrary to EC law (*Bollmann* Case 40/69 [1970] ECR 69). These well established principles acquire a special importance in the case of an incomplete regulation. EC regulations are incomplete in the sense that they require Member States to adopt necessary measures to ensure their full application. Sometimes this requirement is expressly stated in a regulation itself, sometimes this obligation is based on art 5 EC which provides that Member States shall take all necessary measures to fulfil their obligations deriving out of the Treaty. In the present case the ECJ confirmed the principle that national measures enacted in relation to an incomplete EC regulation are subordinate to the provisions contained in that regulation and must neither alter them nor hinder their uniform application throughout the Community.

EC directives

Inter-Environmental Wallonie ASBL v Région Wallonne Case C–129/96 [1998] 1 CMLR 1057 European Court of Justice

- EC directives – obligations of Member States based on arts 5 and 189 EC Treaty before expiry of transposition period – adoption of national measures during a directive's transposition period likely to seriously compromise the result prescribed by the directive – entry into force of a directive at the time of its notification to the Member State concerned – broad interpretation of 'waste' under art 1(a) of Directive 75/442 as amended by Directive 91/156

Facts
In the framework of proceedings instituted by Inter-Environmental Wallonie ASBL (a non-profit-making organisation) requesting the Belgian Conseil d'Etat to annul the Decree of the Regional Council of 9 April 1992 on toxic or hazardous waste, the Belgian Conseil d'Etat (highest administrative court in Belgium) referred to the ECJ for a preliminary ruling under art 177 EC questions:

1. concerning the interpretation of art 5 and 189 EC Treaty and, in particular, whether those provisions preclude Member States from adopting national legislation contrary to an unimplemented EC directive before the period for its transposition has expired; and
2. concerning the interpretation of art 1(a) of Council Directive 75/442 of 15 July 1975 on waste as amended by Council Directive 91/156 of 18 March 1991.

Held
The ECJ held that a Member State to which an EC directive is addressed is required, during the period prescribed for its transposition, to refrain from adopting national measures liable to seriously compromise the result prescribed by that directive.

It also stated that a substance is not excluded from the definition of 'waste' contained in art 1(a) of Directive 75/44 as amended by Directive 91/156 merely because it directly or indirectly forms an integral part of an industrial production process.

Judgment
'It should be recalled at the outset that the obligation of a Member State to take all the measures necessary to achieve the result prescribed by a directive is a binding obligation imposed by the third paragraph of art 189 of the Treaty and by the directive itself.

The next point to note is that it follows from the second paragraph of art 191 of the [EC] Treaty, applicable at the material time, that a directive has legal effect with respect to the Member State to which it is addressed from the moment of its notification.

Here, and in accordance with current practice, Directive 91/156 itself laid down a period by the end of which the laws, regulations and administrative provisions necessary for compliance are to have been brought into force.

Since the purpose of such a period is, in particular, to give Member States the necessary time to adopt transposition measures, they cannot be faulted for not having transposed the directive into their internal legal order before expiry of that period.

Nevertheless, it is during the transposition period that the Member States must take the measures necessary to ensure that the result prescribed by the directive is achieved at the end of that period.

Although the Member States are not obliged to adopt those measures before the end of the period prescribed for transposition, it follows from the second paragraph of art 5 in conjunction with the third paragraph of art 189 of the Treaty and from the directive itself that during that period they must refrain from taking any measures liable seriously to compromise the result prescribed.

It is for the national court to assess whether that is the case as regards the national provisions whose legality it is called upon to consider.

If the provisions in issue are intended to constitute full and definitive transposition of the directive, their incompatibility with the directive might give rise to the presumption that the result prescribed by the directive will not be achieved within the period prescribed if it is impossible to amend them in time.

Conversely, the national court could take into account the right of a Member State to adopt transitional measures or to implement the directive in stages. In such cases, the incompatibility of the transitional national measures with the directive, or the non-transposition of certain of its provisions, would not necessarily compromise the result prescribed.'

Comment

The opportunities which individuals possess to enforce Community rights at the national level have been enriched by the ECJ in the present case. The practical implication of the ECJ decision in this case is that an individual is entitled, at a time when the period allowed by the directive for its transposition has not yet expired, to challenge national measures enacted during that period (whether or not they are intended to implement an EC directive) in the event of their incompatibility with the result prescribed by that directive. However, in relation to measures which purport to implement an EC directive a distinction must be made between national provisions intended to constitute full and definitive transposition of the directive and national provisions which introduce transitional measures or measures designed to implement the directive in stages. The ECJ addressed this question and held that in the case of the first-mentioned measures their incompatibility might indicate that the result prescribed by the directive would not be achieved within the prescribed time-limit as it would be impossible for a Member State to amend them in time and thus they should be struck down by a national court. In the case of the second-mentioned measures their incompatibility may only be temporary and therefore a national court should not declare them invalid before the end of the directive's transposition period.

This is a very important case as it specifies obligations imposed on Member States by EC directives before the expiry of the period for their transposition, and in particular the obligation of Member States to refrain from adopting measures which are likely to seriously compromise the result required by the directive. In the present case the ECJ has confirmed two important points.

First, that EC directives, whether published in the Official Journal of the European Communities or those not requiring publication (all other directives), enter into force (which means they are directly applicable) from the moment of their notification to Member States to which they are addressed, and not at the end of the transposition period laid down in the directive itself.

Second, the decision of the ECJ in the present case confirmed that a directive is directly applicable from the time of its notification to a Member State concerned, although it only becomes legally effective from the expiry of the implementation period. It has been well established (at least until this decision) that before the expiry of the prescribed time-limit no obligations or rights arise for a Member State or for individuals from a directive (*Ratti* Case 148/78 [1979] ECR 1629).

For that reason, it has been widely accepted that until the transposition of directives into national law or the expiry of the time-limit prescribed for their implementation, they do not exist from a legal point of view. They were not considered until this case as being directly applicable. This view has been seriously challenged by the decision of the ECJ in the present case.

General principles of law

Danisco Sugar AB v *Almänna Ombudet* Case C–27/96 [1997] ECR I–6653 European Court of Justice

• *Principles of international law – principle of good faith – accession of the Kingdom of Sweden to the European Union – common organisation of the markets in the sugar sector – national levy on sugar stocks*

Facts
Danisco Sugar AB, the only Swedish sugar producer and the largest importer of sugar, entered into a two-year agreement with the Swedish beet growers' association (SBC) which entitled the latter, in the event of accession of Sweden to the EU, to more than one-half of the difference between the 'minimum' Community price for sugar for the marketing year 1994/95 and the reference price for sugar applicable in Sweden during previous marketing years. When Danisco made a declaration in December 1994 that it held in stock 267,134 tonnes of sugar the Swedish government introduced new legislation which imposed a levy on sugar being held in stock in Sweden. Under the Sugar Law, Danisco was liable to pay approximately SKR 435 million in sugar tax. Danisco challenged the Sugar Law arguing that Sweden was in breach of Community law since the legislation in question was in fact a transitional measure which under art 149 of the Act of Accession could be adopted only by Community institutions. Furthermore, Sweden was not permitted, on the eve of its accession to the EU, to adopt measures liable to affect the functioning of the common organisation of the market in the sugar sector.

Held
The ECJ held that arts 137(2) and 145(2) of the Act of Accession of Austria, Finland, Norway and Sweden and the adjustment to the EU Treaties, in particular arts 39 and 40 EC, Council Regulation 1785/81 of 30 June 1981 on the common organisation of the markets in the sugar sector as well as the Commission Regulation 3330/94 of 21 December 1994 containing transitional measures in the sugar sector following the accession of Austria, Finland and Sweden did not preclude Sweden from adopting, on the eve of its accession to the EU, legislation imposing a levy on sugar stored within that State.

Judgment
'In order to establish whether a law introducing a levy on sugar stocks, such as the Lageravgiftslag, is contrary to the provisions of Community law concerning the common organisation of the markets in the sugar sector, it must be determined whether that law concerns an area for which the Community rules make exhaustive provision or interferes with the proper functioning of the mechanisms provided by the common organisation of the markets, in particular through its influence on price formation or on the structure of agricultural holdings.

As regards the sugar forming part of the normal carryover stocks, Regulation No 3300/94 provides that the provisions of Regulation No 1785/81 concerning the self-financing of the sector or the system of export refunds are not to apply to quantities of sugar produced before 1 July 1995 in the new Member States, since the entire sugar output of those States was produced under national arrangements and much of the sugar produced had already been disposed of before 1 January 1995.

As regards pricing, the levy on sugar stocks could not have had any effect on the position of sugar producers whose storage costs, including taxes, undoubtedly rose because of the levy, but whose selling price for the product increased commensurately by reason of accession, to come into line with the higher Community selling price for sugar. The impact of the levy on such persons was therefore neutral.

On the contrary, failure to charge a levy on sugar stocks at the time of accession would have placed Swedish sugar producers at an advantage compared with Community sugar producers, since they would have been able to benefit from the higher Community selling prices without, however, having contributed to the self-financing arrangements for the sector.'

Comment

The question raised in national proceedings concerned the compatibility of a Swedish law (which entered into force on 31 December 1994, that is one day before the accession of the Kingdom of Sweden to the European Union) with Community law. In the event that the legislation in question was contrary to the Act of Accession and the provisions of Community law concerning the common organisation of the markets in sugar, the Kingdom of Sweden was in breach of the principle of good faith contained in art 18 of the Vienna Convention on the Law of Treaties adopted on 23 May 1969 according to which a State, prior to the entry into force of an international treaty to which it is a contracting party, must refrain from adopting acts which would defeat that treaty's object and purpose. Unfortunately, in the present case it was not necessary for the ECJ to decide whether the Swedish law in question was contrary to the principle of good faith as the Court held that Swedish law was not in breach of EC law. This case leaves open the question whether the principle of good faith is to be considered as a general principle of EC law. In this respect it is interesting to note that in *Opel Austria* Case T–115/94 [1997] ECR II–39,

points 90 and 91 the Court of First Instance recognised the principle of good faith as a general principle of Community law. The Court stated that the principle of good faith is 'the corollary in public international law of the principle of protection of legitimate expectations which, according to the case law, forms part of the Community legal order [and on which] any economic operator to whom an institution has given justified hopes may rely.'

Nold and Others v *EC Commission*
Case 4/73 [1974] ECR 491; [1974] 2 CMLR 338 European Court of Justice

• *General principle of EC law – source of EC law – human rights – European Convention on Human Rights – relationship between EC law and human rights – ECSC Treaty*

Facts

In accordance with a Community decision made under the authority the ECSC Treaty, coal wholesalers were prohibited from directly purchasing Ruhr coal from the regional selling agency unless they purchased a certain minimum quantity. The applicant was a wholesale coal trader. The decision of the Commission prevented him from purchasing coal from the wholesale agency because he could not meet the minimum purchase requirement. As a result, he was forced to purchase coal via an intermediary and thereby incurred additional expenses.

The applicant argued that the Commission's decision was in breach of his fundamental human rights and sought to annul that decision. However, the Community Treaties do not refer to fundamental human rights as a source of law.

Held

The ECJ held that fundamental human rights form an integral part of the general principles of Community law and that the Court was the guardian of these principles insofar as they were adopted into Community law. The source of these principles of human rights was declared to be the constitutional traditions common to the Member States, together with the international agreements entered into by the Member States.

Judgment

'The applicant asserts finally that certain of its fundamental rights have been violated, in that the restrictions introduced by the new trading rules authorised by the Commission have the effect, by depriving it of direct supplies, of jeopardising both the profitability of the undertaking and the free development of its business activity to the point of endangering its very existence.

In this way the decision is said to violate, in respect of the applicant, a right akin to a proprietary right, as well as its right to the free pursuit of business activity, as protected by the Grundgesetz of the Federal Republic of Germany and by the Constitutions of other Member States and various international treaties, including in particular the Convention for the Protection of Human Rights and Fundamental Freedoms of 4 November 1950, and the Protocol to that Convention of 20 March 1952.

As the Court already stated, fundamental rights form an integral part of the general principles of law, the observance of which it ensures.

In safeguarding these rights, the Court is bound to draw inspiration from constitutional traditions common to the Member States, and it cannot therefore uphold measures which are incompatible with fundamental rights recognised and protected by the Constitutions of those States.

Similarly, international treaties for the protection of human rights on which the Member States have collaborated, or of which they are signatories, can supply guidelines which should be followed within the framework of Community law.

The submissions of the applicant must be examined in the light of these principles.

The rights of ownership are protected by the constitutional laws of all Member States and if similar guarantees are given in respect of their right freely to choose and practise their trade or profession, the rights thereby guaranteed, far from constituting unfettered prerogatives, must be viewed in the light of the social function of the property and activities protected thereunder.

For this reason, rights of this nature are protected by law subject always to limitations laid down in accordance with the public interest.

Within the Community legal order it likewise seems legitimate that these rights should, if necessary be subject to certain limits justified by the overall objectives pursued by the Community, on condition that the substance of these rights is left untouched.

As regards the guarantees accorded to a particular undertaking, they can in no respect be extended to protect mere commercial interests or opportunities, the uncertainties of which are part of the very essence of economic activity.

The disadvantages claimed by the applicant are in fact the result of economic change and not of the contested decision.

It was for the applicant, confronted by the economic changes brought about by the recession in coal production, to acknowledge the situation itself and carry out the necessary adaptations.

The submission must be dismissed for all the reasons outlined above.'

Comment

In the present case the ECJ, for the first time, made reference to the European Convention on Human Rights and Fundamental Freedoms signed in Rome on 4 November 1950 to which all Member States are contracting parties. The ECJ emphasised that the European Convention on Human Rights can supply guidelines which should be followed within the framework of Community law. However, the ECJ held that these rights are not absolute and 'far from constituting unfettered prerogatives, [they] must be viewed in the light of the social function'. Thus it is legitimate that 'these rights should, if necessary, be subject to certain limits justified by the overall objectives pursued by the Community, on condition that the substance of these rights is left untouched'. Although the ECJ has incorporated an important number of human rights within the general principle of Community law, the uneasy relationship between EC law and human rights persists (see Opinion 2/94 in Chapter 1).

Stephen Austin Saldanha and MTS Securities Corporation v Hiross Holding AG Case C–122/96 [1997] ECR I–5325 European Court of Justice

- Principle of non-discrimination on grounds of nationality contained in art 6 EC Treaty – dual nationality – security for costs

Facts
Mr Saldanha, a holder of dual nationality, ie UK and USA, domiciled in Florida and MTS Securities Corporation, an American company, both shareholders of Hiross Holding AG, an Austrian company, applied for an injunction to restrain Hiross from selling or transferring shares to its Italian subsidiary, or subsidiaries of that company established in Italy, without the approval of the general meeting of shareholders. Hiross applied to the Handelsgericht Wien (commercial court, Vienna) for an order requiring both Saldanha and MTS Securities Corporation to provide caution judicatum solvi, that is security for the costs of the proceedings as permitted under paragraph 57(1) of the Austrian Code of Civil Procedure. The interpretation of art 6(1) EC Treaty was at the heart of the dispute.

Held
The ECJ held that art 6 EC Treaty must be interpreted as precluding a Member State from imposing the cautio judicatum solvi (security for costs) on a national of a second Member State who is also a national of a non-Member State, in which he resides, where that national who is not resident and has no assets in the first Member State, has brought proceedings before one of its civil courts in his capacity as a shareholder against a company established in that Member State, if such a requirement is not imposed on its own nationals who are not resident and have no assets there.

Judgment
'In view of the fact that the Act of Accession contains no specific conditions whatsoever with regard to the application of art 6 of the Treaty, the latter provision must be regarded as being immediately applicable and binding on the Republic of Austria from the date of its accession, with the result that it applies to the future effects of situations arising prior to that new Member State's accession to the Communities. From the date of accession, therefore, nationals of another Member State can no longer be made subject to a procedural rule which discriminates on grounds of nationality, provided that such a rule comes within the scope ratione materiae of the EC Treaty.

[*The scope ratione materiae et personae of the first paragraph of art 6 of the Treaty*]
In the first place, the mere fact that a national of a Member State is also a national of a non-member country, in which he is resident, does not deprive him of the right, as a national of that Member State, to rely on the prohibition of discrimination on grounds of nationality enshrined in the first paragraph of art 6.

Since art 6 of the Treaty produces effects within the area covered by the Treaty, it is necessary to consider next whether that article applies to a provision in a Member State, such as that at issue in the main proceedings, which requires nationals of another Member State to provide security for costs where, in their capacity as shareholders, they bring proceedings against a company established in that Member State, even though its own nationals are not subject to such a requirement.

In that regard, whilst a rule of procedure such as that at issue in the main proceedings is in principle a matter for which Member States are responsible, the Court has consistently held that such a provision may not discriminate against persons to whom Community law gives the right to equal treatment or restrict the fundamental freedoms guaranteed by Community law.

In its judgments in Case C–43/95 *Data Delecta and Forsberg* v *MSL Dynamics* [1996] ECR I–4661, paragraph 15, and Case C–323/95 *Hayes* v *Kronenberger* [1997] ECR I–1711, paragraph 17, the Court held that a rule of domestic procedure requiring for judicial proceedings, such as those at issue in those cases, the provision of security for costs was liable to have an effect, even though indirect, on trade in goods and services between Member States and therefore fell within the scope of application of the Treaty.

The dispute in the main proceedings concerns the protection of interests relied on by a shareholder who is a national of one Member State against a company established in another Member State.

Article 54(3)(g) of the EC Treaty empowers the Council and the Commission, for the purpose of giving effect to the freedom of establishment, to co-ordinate to the necessary extent the safeguards which, for the protection of the interests of members and others, are required by Member States of companies or firms within the meaning of the second paragraph of art 58 of the EC Treaty with a view to making such safeguards equivalent throughout the Community. It follows that rules which, in the area of company law, seek to protect the interests of shareholders come within the scope of the Treaty and are for that reason subject to the prohibition of all discrimination based on nationality.

If Community law thus prohibits all discrimination based on nationality in regard to the safeguards required, in the Member States, of companies or firms within the meaning of the second paragraph of art 58 of the Treaty for the purpose of protecting the interests of shareholders, nationals of a Member State must also be in a position to seise the courts of another Member State of disputes to which their interests in companies there established may give rise, without being subject to discrimination vis-à-vis nationals of that State.

[*Discrimination within the meaning of the first paragraph of art 6 of the Treaty*]
By prohibiting "any discrimination on grounds of nationality", art 6 of the Treaty requires, in the Member States, complete equality of treatment between persons in a situation governed by Community law and nationals of the Member State in question.

It is clear that a provision such as that at issue in the main proceedings amounts to direct discrimination on grounds of nationality. Under that provision, a Member State does not require its own nationals to provide security, even if they are not resident and have no assets in that State.'

Comment
The interesting aspect of the present case is that Mr Saldanha had a double nationality. He held both British and American citizenship and had his domicile in Florida. In this context the question arose whether he was within the scope ratione personae of art 6 EC. In this respect, the ECJ confirmed its ruling in *Michelletti* Case C–369/90 [1992] ECR I–4239 in which it held that the determination of conditions governing the acquisition and loss of nationality constitute matters within the competence of each Member State, whose decision must be respected by the other Member State. As a result, the mere fact that a national of a Member State is also a national of a third country in which he resides does not affect his rights arising out of the Treaty.

The ECJ held that art 6 EC Treaty was directly applicable from the date of accession of Austria to the EU and, therefore, it applied to the future effects of a situation arising prior to the Austrian accession. The Court stated that the protection of the interests of shareholders is within the material scope of application of the EC Treaty. The ECJ declared a national procedural rule requiring EC nationals to provide security for costs in proceedings brought in another Member State to be contrary to art 6(1) EC if such a requirement is not imposed on its own nationals who are not resident and have no assets in that State (the ECJ has already condemned national procedural rules requiring the caution judicatum solvi under Swedish and German law (*Data Delecta and Forsberg* v *MSL Dynamics* Case C– 43/95 [1996] ECR I–4661 and *Hayes* v *Kronenberger* Case C–323/95 [1997] ECR I–1711).

United Kingdom v *EC Council (Re Working Time Directive)* Case C–84/94 [1996] ECR I–5758 European Court of Justice

- *Principles of subsidiarity and proportionality – legal base – Directive 93/104/ EC – arts 118a(2), 100 and 235 EC Treaty – misuse of powers – infringement of essential procedural requirements – social policy – working time – fixing of Sundays as the weekly rest day – annulment of the second paragraph of art 5 of the Directive*

Facts
The UK brought an action for either annulment of Council Directive 93/104 concerning certain aspects of the organisation of working time; or, for annulling its art 4, the first and second sentences of art 5 and all of arts 6(2) and art 7. The UK challenged the legal base of the Directive. First, the UK argued that the Directive should have been adopted under art 100 EC or art 235 EC which require unanimity within the Council instead of art 118A(2) which imposes only qualified majority voting (QMV) within the Council. Second, the UK claimed that the Directive was in breach of the principles of proportionality and subsidiarity since the Council failed to demonstrate that the objective of the Directive could better be achieved at Community level than at a national level. Finally, the UK contended that the Directive infringed essential procedural requirements by not providing sufficient reasons for its adoption in the preamble.

Held
The ECJ held that art 118A(2) was an appropriate legal base for the Directive since it refers to 'working environment', 'health' and 'safety' which should be interpreted broadly. In respect of the principles of subsidiarity and proportionality the ECJ confirmed that the principle of subsidiarity could be relied upon by the applicant, although in this case it was invoked to support the main claim and not as an autonomous ground for annulment. Thus, all disputes as to whether or not subsidiarity as such can be invoked before the ECJ seem settled. The ECJ annulled only the second sentence of art 5 of Directive 93/104 which stated that Sunday could be chosen as the weekly rest day. Taking into account cultural, ethnic and religious diversity in Member States the ECJ decided to leave to their discretion the choice of the weekly rest period. The remainder of the applicant was dismissed by the ECJ.

Judgment
'In support of its action, the applicant relied on four pleas, alleging, respectively, that the legal base of the directive is defective, breach of the principle of proportionality, misuse of powers, and infringement of essential procedural requirements.

[*The plea that the legal base of the directive is defective*]
The applicant contends that the directive should have been adopted on the basis of art 100 of the EC Treaty, or art 235 of the Treaty, which require unanimity within the Council.

The scope of art 118a
Article 118a(2), read in conjunction with art 118a(1), empowers the Council to adopt, by means of directives, minimum requirements for gradual implementation, having regard to the conditions and technical rules obtaining in each of the Member States, with a view to "encouraging improvements, especially in the working environment, as

regards the health and safety of workers" by harmonising conditions in this area, while maintaining the improvements made.

There is nothing in the wording of art 118a to indicate that the concepts of "working environment", "safety" and "health" as used in that provision should, in the absence of other indications, be interpreted restrictively, and not as embracing all factors, physical or otherwise, capable of affecting the health and safety of the worker in his working environment, including in particular certain aspects of the organisation of working time. On the contrary, the words "especially in the working environment" militate in favour of a broad interpretation of the powers which art 118a confers upon the Council for the protection of the health and safety of workers. Moreover, such an interpretation of the words "safety" and "health" derives support in particular from the preamble to the Constitution of the World Health Organisation to which all the Member States belong. Health is there defined as a state of complete physical, mental and social well-being that does not consist only in the absence of illness or infirmity.

It follows that, where the principal aim of the measure in question is the protection of the health and safety of workers, art 118a must be used, albeit such a measure may have ancillary effects on the establishment and functioning of the internal market.

Finally, it is to be remembered that it is not the function of the Court to review the expediency of measures adopted by the legislature. The review exercised under art 173 must be limited to the legality of the disputed measure.

[*The choice of legal basis for the directive*]
As part of the system of Community competence, the choice of the legal basis for a measure must be based on objective factors which are amenable to judicial review. Those factors include, in particular, the aim and content of the measure.

As regards the aim of the directive, the sixth recital in its preamble states that it constitutes a practical contribution towards creating the social dimension of the internal market. However, it does not follow from the fact that the directive falls within the scope of Community social policy that it cannot properly be based on art 118a, so long as it contributes to encouraging improvements as regards the health and safety of workers. Indeed, art 118a forms part of Chapter 1, headed "Social Provisions", of Title VIII of the Treaty, which deals in particular with "Social Policy". This led the Court to conclude that that provision conferred on the Community internal legislative competence in the area of social policy.

Furthermore, the organisation of working time is not necessarily conceived as an instrument of employment policy.

The approach taken by the directive, viewing the organisation of working time essentially in terms of the favourable impact it may have on the health and safety of workers, is apparent from several recitals in its preamble.

While it cannot be excluded that the directive may affect employment, that is clearly not its essential objective.

As regards the content of the directive, the applicant argues that the connection between the measures it lays down, on the one hand, and health and safety, on the other, is too tenuous for the directive to be based on art 118a of the Treaty.

A distinction must be drawn between the second sentence of art 5 of the directive and its other provisions.

As to the second sentence of art 5, whilst the question whether to include Sunday in the weekly rest period is ultimately left to the assessment of Member States, having regard, in particular, to the diversity of cultural, ethnic and religious factors in those States, the fact remains that the Council has failed to explain why Sunday, as a weekly rest day, is more closely connected with the health and safety of workers than any other day of the week. In those circumstances, the applicant's alternative claim must be upheld and the second sentence of art 5, which is severable from the other provisions of the directive, must be annulled.

The other measures laid down by the directive, which refer to minimum rest periods, length of work, night work, shift work and the pattern of work, relate to the "working environment"and reflect concern for the protection of "he health and safety of workers".

Since, in terms of its aim and content, the directive has as its principal objective the protection of the health and safety of workers by the imposition of minimum requirements for gradual implementation, neither art 100 nor art 100a could have constituted the appropriate legal basis for its adoption.

It must therefore be held that the directive was properly adopted on the basis of art 118a, save for the second sentence of art 5, which must accordingly be annulled.

[*The plea of breach of the principle of proportionality*]

... a measure will be proportionate only if it is consistent with the principle of subsidiarity. The applicant argues that it is for the Community institutions to demonstrate that the aims of the directive could better be achieved at Community level than by action on the part of the Member States. There has been no such demonstration in this case.

The argument of non-compliance with the principle of subsidiarity can be rejected at the outset. It is said that the Community legislature has not established that the aims of the directive would be better served at Community level than at national level. But that argument, as so formulated, really concerns the need for the Community action, which has already been examined [above].

As regards the principle of proportionality, the Court has held that, in order to establish whether a provision of Community law complies with that principle, it must be ascertained whether the means which it employs are suitable for the purpose of achieving the desired objective and whether they do not go beyond what is necessary to achieve it.

So far as concerns the first condition, it is sufficient that the measures on the organisation of working time which form the subject-matter of the directive, save for that contained in the second sentence of art 5, contribute directly to the improvement of health and safety protection for workers within the meaning of art 118a, and cannot therefore be regarded as unsuited to the purpose of achieving the objective pursued.

The second condition is also fulfilled. Contrary to the view taken by the applicant, the Council did not commit any manifest error in concluding that the contested measures were necessary to achieve the objective of protecting the health and safety of workers.

[*The plea of infringement of essential procedural requirements*]

As to those arguments, whilst the reasoning required by art 190 of the EC Treaty must show clearly and unequivocally the reasoning of the Community authority which adopted the contested measure so as to enable the persons concerned to ascertain the reasons for it and to enable the Court to exercise judicial review, the authority is not required to go into every relevant point of fact and law.

In the case of the directive, the preamble clearly shows that the measures introduced are intended to harmonise the protection of the health and safety of workers.

The argument that the Council should have included in the preamble to the directive specific references to scientific material justifying the adoption of the various measures which it contains must be rejected.

[*The plea of misuse of powers*]

... As is apparent from the court's examination of the plea of defective legal base, the Council could properly found the directive on Article 118a of the Treaty. The applicant has failed to establish that the directive was adopted with the exclusive or main purpose of achieving an end other than the protection of the health and safety of workers. In those circumstances, the plea of misuse of powers must be rejected.'

Comment

The principle of subsidiarity is not only a socio-political concept but also a fundamental principle of EC law. No special procedure has been established to bring an issue of subsidiarity before the ECJ although this solution was supported by the European Parliament.

In the present case the ECJ made a clear distinction between the principle of proportionality and the principle of subsidiarity. Advocate-General Leger emphasised that the principle of subsidiarity answers the question at which level, Community or national, the adoption of a legislative measure is more appropriate, while the principle of proportionality governs the intensity of the Community action. In the other words, the ECJ on the ground of subsidiarity would examine whether a measure adopted by a Member State would achieve the desired Community objective. Under the principle of proportionality the ECJ would examine whether less onerous, less restrictive measures adopted by the Community would achieve the aims pursued.

Principles of interpretation

Lister v *Forth Dock and Engineering Co* [1989] 2 WLR 634; [1989] 1 All ER 1134 House of Lords (Lords Keith of Kinkel, Brandon of Oakbrook, Templeman, Oliver and Jauncey of Tullichette)

- Interpretation – national measures implementing an EC directive – defective implementation – teleological interpretation.

Facts
The plaintiffs were employed in a ship repairing yard which fell into receivership and was subsequently sold. The employees were dismissed by the company in receivership one hour prior to the transfer of ownership in the yard to the purchasers.

According to the terms of the Transfer of Undertakings (Protection of Employment) Regulations, transfers of ownership do not automatically terminate contracts of employment if the employees were employed 'immediately before the transfer' of the business.

The plaintiffs claimed that, despite being dismissed by the company in receivership, the new owners were obliged to pay compensation for the statutory period of notice since they were employed immediately prior to the takeover, but the actual regulations were silent on this matter. The plaintiffs relied on the fact that the Regulations incorporated a Community directive into national law. Community legislation must be interpreted according to the 'purposive' or 'teleological' method of interpretation and not the 'literal' methods of interpretation commonly employed in British courts. If the literal method was employed, the plaintiffs would fail because the Regulations made no reference to legal principles in this situation. However, if the Regulations were given teleological interpretation, the plaintiffs could succed because the object and purpose of the legislation was to protect employees.

Held
The industrial tribunal upheld the claim of the plaintiffs and ordered the new employers to pay the compensation. However, this decision was overturned on appeal to the higher courts. Finally the matter came before the House of Lords which applied the teleological approach and allowed the claim.

Judgment
Lord Templeman:

'[I]t is said, since the workforce of Forth Dry Dock were dismissed at 3.30 pm, they were not employed "immediately before the transfer" at 4.30 pm and therefore Regulation 5(1) did not transfer any liability for the workforce from Forth Dock to Forth Estuary (the new owners). This argument is inconsistent with the directive. In *P Bork International A/S* v *Foreningen af Arbejdsledere i Danmark* Case 101/87 [1989] IRLR 41, at 44, the European Court ruled:

"... the only workers who may invoke

Directive 77/187 are those who have current employment relations or a contract of employment at the date of the transfer. The question whether or not a contract of employment or employment relationship exists at that date must be assessed under national law, subject, however, to the observance of the mandatory rules of the Directive concerning the protection of workers against dismissal by reason of transfer. It follows that the workers employed by the undertaking whose contract of employment or employment relationship has been terminated with effect from a date before that of the transfer, in breach of art 4(1) of the Directive, must be considered as still employed by the undertaking on the date of the transfer with the consequence, in particular, that the obligations of an employer towards them are fully transferred from the transferor to the transferee, in accordance with art 3(1) of the Directive ..."

In *Von Colson* v *Land Nordrhein-Westfalen* Case 14/83 [1984] ECR 1891, at 1909, the European Court, dealing with Council Directive 76/207 forbidding discrimination on grounds of sex regarding access to employment, ruled:

"... the Member States' obligations arising from a directive to achieve the result envisaged by the directive and their duty under art 5 of the Treaty to take all appropriate measures, whether general or particular, to ensure the fulfilment of that obligation, is binding on all the authorities of Member States including, for matters within their jurisdiction, the courts. It follows that, in applying the national law and in particular the provisions of national law specifically introduced in order to implement Directive 76/207, national courts are required to interpret their national law in the light of the wording and the purpose of the directive in order to achieve the result referred to in the third paragraph of art 189."

Thus the courts of the United Kingdom are under a duty to follow the practice of the European Court by giving a purposive construction to directives and to regulations for the purpose of complying with directives. In *Pickstone* v *Freemans plc* [1988] 2 All ER 803, this House implied words in a regulation designed to give effect to Council Directive 75/117 (1975) dealing with equal pay for women for doing work of equal value. If this House had not been able to make the necessary implication the Equal Pay (Amendments) Regulations 1983 would have failed in their object and the United Kingdom would have been in breach of its Treaty obligations to give effect to directives.

In the present case, in the light of Council Directive 77/187 and in the light of the ruling of the European Court in the *Bork* case, it seems to me, following the suggestion of my noble and learned friend Lord Keith, that Regulation 5(3) of the 1981 Regulations was not intended and ought not to be construe so as to limit the operation of Regulation 5 to persons employed immediately before the transfer in point of time. Regulation 5(3) must be construed on the footing that it applies to a person employed immediately before the transfer or who would have been so employed if he had not been unfairly dismissed before the transfer for a reason connected with the transfer. It would, of course, still be open for a new owner to show that the employee had been dismissed for an "economic, technical or organisational reason entailing changes in the workforce", but no such reason could be advanced in the present case where there was no complaint entailing changes in the workforce.

I would therefore allow the appeal and make the order proposed by my noble and learned friend Lord Oliver.'

Comment

In order to carry out its tasks the ECJ relies on a variety of methods of interpretation and a number of interpretive devices. Even though the interpretation of EC law is theoretically based on art 31 of the 1969 Vienna Convention on the Law of Treaties, which provides that the interpretation should be based on the ordinary meaning of the terms of a Treaty, in the context and in the light of its object and goal, the ECJ has given priority to interpretation 'in the general context' (systematic method) 'and in the light of its object and goal' (teleological method) over the literal interpretation of the Treaty (*Humblet* Case 6/60 [1960] ECR 1125). In Case 283/81 *CILFIT* the ECJ emphasised particular difficulties in the interpretation and application of EC law. The Community legislation is drafted in several languages and each version is authentic. Thus the comparison of different versions is sometimes necessary. Furthermore, Community law uses terminology and refers to legal concepts which are peculiar to it. It is autonomous and the meaning of legal concepts of the Community differs from those known under national laws of the Member States.

Also, the ECJ relies on other methods of interpretation depending upon the case and the degree to which the provision to be interpreted is ambiguous, obscure etc. The wide eclectism of the methods used to interpret EC law, combined with the willingness to draw from each of them the maximum effectiveness, are the salient feature of the interpretation of EC law by the ECJ.

In order to maintain the coherence of the Community system, and to ensure its unity and homogeneity, national courts must follow the methods of interpretation used by the ECJ. In the present case Lord Templeman emphasised that 'the courts of the United Kingdom are under a duty to follows the practice of the European Court by giving a purposive construction to directives'.

7 Fundamental Principles of European Community Law

Supremacy of EC law

Amministrazione delle Finanze dello Stato* v *Simmenthal SpA Case 106/77 [1978] ECR 629; [1978] 3 CMLR 263 European Court of Justice

* *Supremacy of EC law – national law subsequent to EC law – preliminary rulings – art 177 EC Treaty – charges equivalent to customs duties – art 12 EC Treaty – charges for veterinary and health inspection – art 30 EC Treaty – quantitative restrictions and measures having equivalent effect*

Facts
Simmenthal imported a consignment of beef from France to Italy. He was asked to pay for veterinary and public health inspections carried out at the frontier. He paid, but sued in the Italian court for reimbursement of money, arguing that the fees were contrary to Community law. After reference to the ECJ, which held that the inspections were contrary to art 30 EC as being of equivalent effect to quantitative restriction and consequently charges were unlawful under art 12 EC being charges equivalent to customs duties, the Italian court ordered the Italian Ministry to repay the fees. The ministry refused to pay claiming that the national statute of 1970 under which Simmenthal was liable to pay fees was still preventing any reimbursement and could only be set aside by the Italian Constitutional court. The question was referred once again to the ECJ under art 177 EC.

Held
The ECJ confirmed that in the event of incompatibility of a subsequent legislative measure enacted by a Member State with Community law all national judges must apply Community law in its entirety and must set aside any provision of national law, prior or subsequent, in conflict with Community law. National courts should not request or await the prior setting aside of an incompatible national provision by legislation or other constitutional means but of its own motion, if necessary, refuse the application of conflicting national law and instead apply Community law.

Judgment
'In accordance with the principle of the precedence of Community law, the relationship between provisions of the Treaty and directly applicable measures of the institutions on the one hand and the national law of the Member States on the other is such that those provisions and measures not only by their entry into force render automatically inapplicable any conflicting provision of current national law but – in so far as they are an integral part of, and take precedence in, the legal order applicable in the territory of each of the Member States – also preclude the valid adoption of new national legislative measures to the extent to which they would be incompatible with Community provisions.

Indeed any recognition that national legislative measures which encroach upon the field within which the Community exercises it legislative power or which are otherwise incompatible with the provisions of Community law had any legal effect would amount to a corresponding denial of the effectiveness of obligations undertaken unconditionally and irrevocably by Member States pursuant to the Treaty and would thus imperil the very foundations of the Community.

The same conclusion emerges from the structure of art 177 of the Treaty which provides that any court or tribunal of a Member State is entitled to make a reference to the Court whenever it considers that a preliminary ruling on a question of interpretation or validity relating to Community law is necessary to enable it to give judgment.

The effectiveness of that provision would be impaired if the national court were prevented from forthwith applying Community law in accordance with the decision or the case law of the Court.

It follows from the foregoing that every national court must, in a case within its jurisdiction, apply Community law in its entirety and protect rights which the latter confers on individuals and must accordingly set aside any provision of national law which may conflict with it, whether prior or subsequent to the Community rule.

Accordingly any provision of a national legal system and any legislative, administrative or judicial practice which may impair the effectiveness of Community law by withholding from the national court having jurisdiction to apply such law the power to do everything necessary at the moment of its application to set aside national legislative provisions which might prevent Community rules from having full force and effect are incompatible with those requirements which are the very essence of Community law.

This would be the case in the event of a conflict between a provision of Community law and a subsequent national law if the solution of the conflict were to be reserved for an authority with a discretion of its own, other than the court called upon to apply Community law, even if such an impediment to the full effectiveness of Community law were only temporary.

The first question should therefore be answered to the effect that a national court which is called upon, within the limits of its jurisdiction, to apply provisions of Community law is under a duty to give full effect to those provisions, if necessary refusing of its own motion to apply any conflicting provision of national legislation, even if adopted subsequently, and it is not necessary for the court to request or await the prior setting aside of such provision by legislative or other constitutional means.'

Comment

The obligation to give full effectiveness to Community law, and thus to protect rights which it confers upon individuals, empowers a national judge to suspend, as an interim measure, the application of national law which he suspects is in conflict with Community law although it might be contrary to national law to do so.

On the basis of supremacy of Community law national judges are able to resolve any difficulties which they may encounter while facing a conflict between national law and Community law. Similarly, administrative authorities are required to set aside any national provision incompatible with Community law (*Fratelli Costanzo* Case C–103/88 [1989] ECR 1839). In relation to sanctions, especially of a penal nature, ordered by virtue of national law and incompatible with Community law, those sanctions are considered as devoid of any legal base (*Schonenberg* Case 88/77 [1978] ECR 473; *Regina and Robert Tymen* Case 269/80 [1981] ECR 3079).

Costa v *ENEL* Case 6/64 [1964] ECR 585; [1964] CMLR 425
European Court of Justice

• *Supremacy of Community law – conflict between provisions of the constitutional treaties and national law – pre-existing national law*

Facts

Costa was a shareholder of one of the private undertakings nationalised by the Italian government on 6 September 1962 when the assets of some private undertakings were transferred to ENEL. Costa who was also a lawyer refused to pay an electricity bill for £1 sent by ENEL and was sued by the latter. He argued, inter alia, that the nationalisation legislation was contrary to various provisions of EC Treaty. The Milanese Giudice Conciliatore referred this question to the ECJ under art 177 EC. The Italian government claimed that the referral was 'absolutely inadmissible' since a national court which is obliged to apply national law cannot avail itself of art 177 EC.

Held

The ECJ rejected the arguments of the Italian government. The Court stated that the EC Treaty created a new legal order which was an integral element of the legal systems of the Member States. The national courts were required to apply Community law in all proceedings. Where a provision of national law was inconsistent with Community law, Community law took precedence, regardless of whether the national provision was enacted prior or subsequent to the date the EC Treaty took effect. The ECJ held that Community law because of its special and original nature, could not be overridden by domestic provisions, however framed, without being deprived of its character as Community law and without the legal basis of the Community itself being called into question.

Judgment

'By contrast with ordinary international treaties, the [EC] Treaty has created its own legal system which, on the entry into force of the Treaty, became an integral part of the legal systems of the Member States and which their courts are bound to apply.

By creating a Community of unlimited duration, having its own institutions, its own personality, its own legal capacity and capacity of representation on the international plane and, more particularly, real powers stemming from a limitation of sovereignty or a transfer of powers from the States to the Community, the Member States have limited their sovereign rights, albeit within limited fields, and have thus created a body of law which binds both their nationals and themselves.

The integration into the laws of each Member State of provisions which derive from the Community, and more generally the terms and the spirit of the Treaty, make it impossible for the States, as a corollary, to accord precedence to a unilateral and subsequent measure over a legal system accepted by them on a basis of reciprocity. Such a measure cannot therefore be inconsistent with that legal system. The executive force of Community laws, without jeopardising the attainment of the objectives of the Treaty set out in art 5(2) and giving rise to the discrimination prohibited by art [6].

The obligations undertaken under the Treaty establishing the Community would not be unconditional, but merely contingent, if they could be called in question by subsequent legislative acts of the signatories. Wherever the Treaty grants the States the right to act unilaterally, it does this by clear and precise provisions (for example arts 15, 93(3), 223, 224 and 225). Applications by Member States for authority to derogate from the Treaty are subject to a special authorisation procedure (for example arts 8(4), 17(4), 25, 26, 73, the third subparagraph of 93(2) and 226) which would lose their purpose if the Member States could renounce their obligations by means of an ordinary law.

The precedence of Community law is confirmed by art 189, whereby a regulation "shall be binding" and "directly applicable in all Member States". This provision, which is subject to no reservation, would be quite meaningless if a State could unilaterally nullify its effects by means of a legislative measure which could prevail over Community law.

It follows from all these observations that the law stemming from the Treaty, an independent source of law, could not, because of its special and original nature, be overridden by domestic legal provisions, however framed, without being deprived of its character as Community law and without the legal basis of the Community itself being called into question.

The transfer by the States from their domestic legal system to the Community legal system of the rights and obligations arising under the Treaty carries with it a permanent limitation of their sovereign rights, against which a subsequent unilateral act incompatible with the concept of the Community cannot prevail.'

Comment

In the present case the ECJ established the most important principle of Community law: the supremacy of EC Law. The ECJ based its reasoning on three arguments:

1. Direct applicability and direct effect of Community law would be meaningless if a Member State were permitted by subsequent legislation to nullify unilaterally its effects by means of a legislative measure which could prevail over Community law.
2. By transferring certain competences to the Community institutions the Member States have limited their sovereignty.
3. Uniformity of application of Community law, which ensures homogeneity of the Community legal order, requires that EC law prevails over conflicting national law.

The ECJ has summarised its reasoning in the following terms:

'... the law stemming from the Treaty, an independent source of law, could not, because of its special and original nature, be overridden by domestic legal provisions, however framed, without being deprived of its character as Community law and without the legal basis of the Community itself being called into question.'

This statement constitutes the essence of supremacy of Community law. The position of the ECJ has not changed since its decision in *Costa*. If anything, the ECJ has become more radical in confirming obvious implications of supremacy of Community law vis-à-vis the Member States. Indeed, whatever the reaction of the Member States, and no matter how long it takes to gain full recognition of this principle by the Member States, for the Community supremacy is a necessary requirement of its existence.

In the present case the ECJ resolved the conflict between national law enacted prior to the entry into force of the Treaties in favour of Community law. All pre-dating national law is deemed to be abrogated, or at least devoid of its legal effect, insofar as it is contrary to Community law.

Internationale Handelsgesellschaft GmbH v *Einfuhr und Vorratsstelle fur Getreide und Futtermittel* Case 11/70 [1970] ECR 1125; [1970] CMLR 255 European Court of Justice

• *Supremacy of EC law – conflict between provisions of the constitutional treaties and the German constitution – conflict avoided by interpreting both European and German constitutional law as enshrining the same constitutional safeguards – fundamental human rights*

Facts

EC regulations set up a system of export licences, guaranteed by a deposit, for certain agricultural products and required that the products were exported during the validity of the licence, failing which the deposit would be forfeited. The plaintiffs lost a deposit of DM 17,000 and argued that the system introduced by EC regulations, which was run by the West German National Cereals Intervention Agency, was in breach of the fundamental human rights' provisions contained in the German constitution and especially the principle of proportionality as it imposed obligations (the forfeited deposit) which were not necessary in order to achieve the objectives pursued by EC regulations, that is the regulation of the cereals market. The Frankfurt administrative court took the view that this type of deposit regulation was unconstitutional because it infringed the reasonable freedom of an individual to carry on business, and also contravened a fundamental principle of German legal theory that the compulsory payment of money cannot be imposed in the absence of fault on the part of the individual concerned. Nevertheless, the German court did refer the matter to the ECJ under art 177 EC.

Held
The ECJ held that Community law prevails over national constitutional law, including fundamental human rights enshrined in the constitution of a Member State. In order to avoid direct confrontation between EC law and fundamental human rights contained in the German constitution, the ECJ stated that fundamental human rights were a part of Community law and could therefore be enforced through the Community legal system. The ECJ upheld the regulation in question and declared the system of deposits as appropriate methods of attainment of the objectives of arts 40(3) EC and 43 EC concerning the common organisation of the agricultural markets.

Judgment
'Recourse to the legal rules or concepts of national law in order to judge the validity of measures adopted by the institutions of the Community would have an adverse effect on the uniformity and efficacy of Community law. The validity of such measures can only be judged in the light of Community law. In fact, the law stemming from the Treaty, an independent source of law, cannot because of its very nature be overridden by rules of national law, however framed, without being deprived of its character as Community law and without the legal basis of the Community itself being called in question. Therefore, the validity of a Community measure or its effect within a Member State cannot be affected by allegations that it runs counter to either fundamental rights as formulated by the constitution of that State or the principles of a national constitutional structure.

However, an examination should be made as to whether or not any analogous guarantee inherent in Community law has been disregarded. In fact, respect for fundamental human rights forms an integral part of the general principles of law protected by the Court of Justice. The protection of such rights, whilst inspired by the constitutional traditions common to the Member States, must be ensured within the framework of the structure and objectives of the Community.'

Comment
The ECJ confirmed that supremacy of Community law is unconditional and absolute, all Community law prevails over all national law.

It means that all sources of Community law, the provisions of the Treaties and secondary legislation – regulations (*Politi* Case 43/71 [1971] ECR 1039; *Marimex* Case 84/71 [1972] ECR 89), directives (*Rewe* Case 158/80 [1981] ECR 1805; *Becker* Case 8/81 [1982] ECR 53), decisions (*Salumificio di Cornuda* Case 130/78 [1979] ECR 867), general principles of Community law (*Wachauf* Case 5/88 [1989] ECR 2609), international agreements concluded between the Community and third countries (*Nederlandse Spoowegen* Case 38/75 [1975] ECR 1439; *SPI and SAMI* Cases 267–269/81 [1983] ECR 801) – irrespective whether or not they are directly effective, prevail over all national law. Also Community law is superior to all provisions of national law: legislative, administrative, jurisdictional and constitutional.

Ministero delle Finanze v *IN.CO.GE. '90 SRL and Others*
Joined Cases C–10–22/97 Judgment of 22 October 1998 (not yet reported) European Court of Justice

• *Supremacy of EC law – direct applicability of EC law – preliminary ruling – recovery of sums paid but not due – treatment of national charge incompatible with*

EC law

Facts
IN.CO.GE.'90 and 12 other Italian limited liability companies paid a special annual administrative charge for entering them on the register of companies (tassa do concessione governativa). This charge was declared unlawful by the ECJ in *Ponente Carni* Cases C–71 and 178/91 [1993] ECR I–1915. The companies subject to the charge sought to recover their payments. The Italian authorities refused the reimbursement. They argued that the Italian courts had no jurisdiction over fiscal matters and that the claims were time-barred. The Italian district magistarate's court at Rome referred to the ECJ the question relating to the consequences arising under Italian law from the incompatibility of the domestic charge with EC law. The questions of classification of the charge and of procedural law were at issue. If a national judge had to disapply national law which implemented EC law, including its provisions on the classification of the charge in question as contrary to EC law and classified the charge on the basis of Italian law, the charge in question would cease to be of a fiscal nature and would fall within the general rules for recovery of amounts paid but not due with a consequence of depriving the charge of any existence in law.

Held
The ECJ held that the incompatibility with EC law of a subsequently adopted rule of national law did not render that rule of national law non-existent. The national court must disapply that rule but uphold claims for repayment of a charge contrary to Community law. The national court may apply national procedural rules to any rights which are conferred by EC law, providing that they impose conditions no less favourable than for equivalent actions not involving EC law and that they do not make impossible or excessively difficult the exercise of rights conferred by Community law.

Judgment
'[*Jurisdiction*]
The Court has power to explain to the national court points of Community law which may help to solve the problem of jurisdiction with which that court is faced. To that end, it may, if appropriate, extract the relevant points from the wording of the question submitted and the facts set forth by the national court.

It appears from the order for reference that the Pretura di Roma is uncertain as to the consequences arising under national law from the incompatibility of a domestic charge with Community law. The Pretura bases its opinion that the disputes pending before it are not of a fiscal nature but fall, under Italian law, within the general rules for recovery of amounts paid but not due on the fact that such incompatibility, inasmuch as its effect is to disapply the relevant national provisions in their entirety and deprive the charge in question of any existence in law, necessarily has the effect of divesting it of its fiscal nature.

It follows that the Court does have jurisdiction to reply to the question submitted.

[*The question of supremacy*]
The Commission points out that, in its judgment in Case 106/77 *Amministrazione delle Finanze dello Stato* v *Simmenthal*, the Court held, inter alia, that the provisions of the Treaty and the directly applicable measures of the institutions have the effect, in their relationship with the domestic law of the Member States, not only of rendering automatically inapplicable any conflicting provision of national law in force but also of precluding the valid adoption of new national legislative measures which would be incompatible with Community provisions. From this, the Commission infers that a Member State has no power whatever to adopt a fiscal provision that is incompatible with Community law, with the result that such a provision and the corresponding fiscal obligation must be treated as non-existent.

That interpretation cannot be accepted.

It cannot therefore, contrary to the Commission's contention, be inferred from the judgment in *Simmenthal* that the incompatibility with Community law of a subsequently adopted rule of national law has the effect of rendering that rule of national law non-existent. Faced with such a situation, the national court is, however, obliged to disapply that rule, provided always that this obligation does not restrict the power of the competent national courts to apply, from among the various procedures available under national law, those which are appropriate for protecting the individual rights conferred by Community law.

It remains to be considered whether non-application, as the result of a judgment given by the Court, of national legislation which introduced a levy contrary to Community law has the result of depriving that levy retroactively of its character as a charge and thereby divesting of its fiscal nature the legal relationship established when that charge was levied between the national tax authority and the companies liable to pay it.

Entitlement to the recovery of sums levied in breach of Community law is a consequence of, and an adjunct to, the rights conferred on individuals by the relevant Community provisions as interpreted by the Court. A Member State is therefore in principle required to repay charges levied in breach of Community law.

In the absence of Community rules governing the matter, such repayment may be claimed only if the substantive and formal conditions laid down by the various national laws are complied with. Community law does not in principle preclude the legislation of a Member State from laying down, alongside a limitation period applicable under the ordinary law to actions between private individuals for the recovery of sums paid but not due, special detailed rules governing claims and legal proceedings to challenge the imposition of charges and other levies.

The possibility thus recognised by the Court of applying those special detailed rules to the repayment of charges and other levies found to be contrary to Community law would be deprived of any effect if the incompatibility between a domestic levy and Community law necessarily had the effect of depriving that levy of its character as a charge and divesting of its fiscal nature the legal relationship established, when the charge in question was levied, between the national tax authorities and the parties liable to pay it.'

Comment
In the present case the ECJ clarified its judgment in *Simmenthal*. The Commission argued that a national provision incompatible with EC law should be treated as non-existent and void. The ECJ disagreed. The Court held that inconsistent domestic law should be disregarded but any rights conferred by EC law have to be enforced under domestic procedure. Also the question of classification of the charge is a matter for national law when a domestic charge is found to be contrary to EC law provided the full effect is given to Community law.

R v Secretary of State for Transport, ex parte Factortame[1990] 2 AC 85
House of Lords

- Supremacy of EC law – national law subsequent to EC law – Merchant Shipping Act 1988 – absolute endorsement of the principle of supremacy in the UK – no qualifications for application of post-1972 statutes

Facts
The statutory requirements for registering vessels as British were radically altered by Part II of the Merchant Shipping Act 1988 and the Merchant Shipping (Registration of Fishing Vessels) Regulations 1988. Vessels which were previously registered as British under the 1984 statute required re-registration under the 1988 Act.

Ninety-five vessels owned by Community nationals failed to satisfy one or more of the conditions for registration under s14(1) of the Act and therefore failed to qualify as British vessels because they were managed or controlled from Spain or by Spanish nationals, or by reason of the proportion of the beneficial ownership of the shares in the applicant companies which was in Spanish hands.

The applicants sought judicial review of the relevant provisions of the Act on the ground that these provisions were in breach of EC law by depriving the applicants of enforceable Community rights. The Divisional Court of the Queen's Bench Division decided to request a preliminary ruling from the ECJ on the substantive question of Community law in order to enable it to determine the application. On a motion by the applicants for interim relief, the Divisional Court ordered that, pending final judgment of the case, the operation of the contested parts of the statute was to be disapplied and that the Secretary of State should be restrained from enforcing any rights under the legislation.

The Court of Appeal, on appeal from the Secretary of State, set aside the order made by the Divisional Court for interim relief. The applicants appealed the matter to the House of Lords.

Held

The House of Lords held that the remedy was not available under English law but in the light of the case law of the ECJ on interim measures a reference would be made to the ECJ under art 177 EC Treaty in respect of the award of interim protection.

Judgment

Lord Bridge:

'By virtue of s2(4) of the 1972 Act, Part II of the 1988 Act is to be construed and take effect subject to directly enforceable Community rights and those rights are, by s2(1) of the Act of 1972, to be "recognised and available in law, and ... enforced. allowed and followed accordingly ...". This has precisely the same effect as if a section were incorporated in Part II of the Act of 1988 which in terms enacted that the provisions with respect to registration of British fishing vessels were to be without prejudice to directly enforceable Community rights of nationals of any Member State of the EEC. Thus it is common ground that, in so far as the applicants succeed before the ECJ in obtaining a ruling in support of the Community rights which they claim, those rights will prevail over the restrictions imposed on registration of British vessels by Part II of the Act of 1988 and the Divisional Court will, in the final determination of the application for judicial review, be obliged to make appropriate declarations to give effect to those rights.

... I turn finally to consider the submission made on behalf of the appellants that, irrespective of the position under national law, there is an overriding principle of Community law which imposes an obligation on the national court to secure effective interim protection of rights having direct effect under Community law where a seriously arguable claim is advanced to be entitled to such rights and where the rights claimed will in substance be rendered nugatory or will be irremediably impaired if not effectively protected during any interim period which must elapse pending determination of a dispute as to the existence of those rights. The basic propositions of Community law on which the appellants rely in support of this submission may be quite shortly summarised. Directly enforceable Community rights are part of the legal heritage of every citizen of a Member State of the EEC. They arise from the Treaty of Rome itself and not from any judgment of the ECJ declaring their existence. Such rights are automatically available and must be given unrestricted retroactive effect. The persons entitled to the enjoyment of such rights are entitled to direct and immediate protection against possible infringement of them. The duty to provide such protection rests with the national court. The remedy to be provided against infringement must be effective, not merely symbolic or illusory. The rules of national law which render the exercise of directly enforceable Community rights excessively difficult or virtually impossible must be overridden.

Mr Vaughan, in a most impressive argument presented in opening this appeal, traced the progressive development of these principles of the jurisprudence of the ECJ through long series of reported decisions on which he relies. I must confess that at the conclusion of his argument I was strongly inclined to the view that, if English law could provide no effective remedy to secure the interim protection of the rights claimed by the appellants, it was nevertheless our duty under Community law to devise such a remedy. But the Solicitor General, in his equally impressive reply, and in his careful and thorough analysis of the case law, has persuaded me that none of the authorities on which Mr. Vaughan relies can properly be treated as determinative of the difficult question, which arises for the first time in the instant case, of providing interim protection of putative and disputed rights in Community law before their existence has been established. This is because the relevant decisions of the ECJ, from which the propositions of Community law asserted by Mr Vaughan are derived, were all made by reference to rights which the ECJ was itself then affirming or by reference to the protection of rights the existence of which had already been established by previous decisions of the ECJ.'

Comment

The House of Lords endorsed the principle of supremacy of Community law. The House of Lords held that if the applicants succeeded in their application before the ECJ, their rights protected under Community law would prevail over the restrictions imposed by the 1988 Act. However, the House of Lord made a reference to the ECJ regarding the obligation of the national court to provide an effective interlocutory remedy to protect rights having direct effect under Community law. This was a separate reference from one that had already been made by the Divisional Court.

R v Secretary of State for Transport, ex parte Factortame Case C–213/89 [1990] ECR I–2433; [1990] 3 CMLR 867 European Court of Justice

• *Supremacy of EC law – conflict between EC law and UK statute – granting of interim relief in the form of the suspension of the statute*

Facts

The House of Lords referred to the ECJ the question of whether or not Community law provides interim protection of rights under Community law in the event of the existence of inconsistent national legislation.

Held

The ECJ held that Community law required that a national court which, in a case before it involving a question of Community law, considered that the sole obstacle which precluded it from granting interim relief was a rule of national law should set aside that rule. As a result, the 1988 Act should be suspended pending the final judgment on its validity.

Judgment

'It is clear from the information before the Court, and in particular from the judgment making reference ... that the preliminary question raised by the House of Lords seeks essentially to ascertain whether a national court which, in a case before it concerning Community law, considers that the sole obstacle which precludes it from granting interim relief is a rule of national law, must disapply that rule.

For the purpose of replying to that question, it is necessary to point out that in its judgment in *Amministrazione delle Finanze dello Stato* v *Simmenthal SpA* [1978] ECR 629 the Court held that directly applicable rules of Community law "must be fully and uniformly applied in all Member States from the date of their entry into force and for so long as they continue in force" and that "in accordance with the principle of precedence of Community law, the relationship between provisions of the Treaty and directly applicable measures of the institutions on the one hand and the national law of the Member States on the other is such that those provisions and measures ... by their entry into force render automatically inapplicable any conflicting provision ... of national law."

In accordance with the case law of the Court, it is for the national court, in application of the principle of co-operation laid down in art 5 of the [EC] Treaty, to ensure the legal protection which persons derive from the direct effect of provisions of Community law.

The Court has also held that any provision of a national legal system and any legislative, administrative or judicial practice which might impair the effectiveness of Community law by withholding from the national court having jurisdiction to apply such law the power to do everything necessary at the moment of its application to set aside national legislative provisions which might prevent, even temporarily, Community rules from having full force and effect are incompatible with those requirements, which are the very essence of Community law.

It must be added that the full effectiveness of Community law would be just as much impaired if a rule of national law could prevent a court seised of a dispute governed by Community law from granting interim relief in order to ensure the full effectiveness of the judgment to be given on the existence of the rights claimed under Community law. It follows that a court which in those circumstances would grant interim relief, if it were not for a rule of national law, is obliged to set aside that rule.

That interpretation is reinforced by the system established by art 177 of the [EC] Treaty whose effectiveness would be impaired if a national court, having stayed proceedings pending the reply by the Court of Justice to the question referred to it for a preliminary ruling, were not able to grant interim relief until it delivered its judgment following the reply given by the Court of Justice.'

Comment

There should be no difficulties with the recognition of supremacy of Community law in the United Kingdom since when a State accedes to the Communities it must accept the "acquis communautaires". At the time of accession of the United Kingdom, the principle of supremacy was already well rooted in Community law. Furthermore, s2(4) of the European Communities Act 1972 provides that 'any enactment passed or to be passed ... shall be construed and have effect subject to the foregoing provisions of this section'. As a result, all legislative acts enacted subsequent to the European Communities Act 1972 are subject to Community law and thus any conflict between Community law and national subsequent legislation should be resolved in favour of the former on the grounds of supremacy of EC law. For many years, however, the judiciary tried to reconcile the irreconcilable: the principal of supremacy of EC law with Dicey's model of parliamentary sovereignty according to which there is no limit to the legislative power of Parliament subject to the exception that Parliament cannot limit its own powers for the future. It means that no legislation enacted by Parliament is irreversible. The present case confirmed the inevitable.

Their lordships accepted the decision of the ECJ gracefully. Lord Bridge said:

'If the supremacy within the European Community of Community law over national law of Member States was not always inherent in the EEC Treaty it was certainly well-established in the jurisprudence of the European Court of Justice long before the United Kingdom joined the Community. Thus, whatever limitation of its sovereignty Parliament accepted when it enacted the European Communities Act 1972 it was entirely voluntary. Under the terms of the Act of 1972 it has always been clear that it was the duty of a United Kingdom court, when delivering final judgment, to override any rule of national law found to be in conflict with any directly enforceable rule of Community law' (*Factortame (No 2)*).

Direct applicability and direct effect

Treaty articles

Gabrielle Defrenne v SABENA (No 1)
Case 43/75 [1976] ECR 455; [1976] 2 CMLR 98 European Court of Justice

- *Direct horizontal effect of EC Treaty – art 119 EC Treaty – direct and indirect discrimination – limitation ratione temporis of the judgment*

Facts
Miss Defrenne was employed as an air hostess by a Belgian airline company, SABENA. She claimed for loss she sustained in terms of pay she received as compared with male cabin stewards doing the same work. The Court de Travail referred to the ECJ under art 177 EC Treaty the question whether she could rely on art 119 EC which prohibits all discrimination between men and women workers and thus requires that they receive equal pay for performing the same task in the same establishment or service.

Held
The ECJ held that in her case it was not difficult to apply art 119 EC as the facts clearly showed that she was discriminated against. It stated that the prohibition on discrimination between men and women applies not only to the action of public authorities, but also extends to all agreements which are intended to regulate paid labour collectively, as contracts between individuals. However, in cases of discrimination which could not be easily identified, implementation measures based on art 119 EC Treaty may be necessary.

Judgment
'[*Direct horizontal effect of art 119 EC Treaty*]
The question of the direct effect of art 119 must be considered in the light of the nature of the principle of equal pay, the aim of this provision and its place in the scheme of the Treaty.

Article 119 pursues a double aim.

First, in the light of the different stages of the development of social legislation in the various Member States, the aim of art 119 is to avoid a situation in which undertakings established in States which have actually implemented the principle of equal pay suffer a competitive disadvantage in intra-Community competition as compared with undertakings established in States which have not yet eliminated discrimination against women workers as regards pay.

Secondly, this provision forms part of the social objectives of the Community, which is not merely an economic union, but is at the same time intended, by common action, to ensure social progress and seek the constant improvement of the living and working conditions of their peoples, as is emphasised by the preamble to the Treaty.

... This double aim, which is at once economic and social, shows that the principle of equal pay forms part of the foundations of the Community.

Furthermore, this explains why the Treaty has provided for the complete implementation of this principle by the end of the first stage of the transitional period.

Therefore, in interpreting this provision, it is impossible to base any argument on the dilatoriness and resistance which have delayed the actual implementation of this basic principle in certain Member States.

... Under the terms of the first paragraph of art 119, the Member States are bound to ensure and maintain "the application of the principle that men and women should receive equal pay for equal work".

The second and third paragraphs of the same article add a certain number of details concerning the concepts of pay and work referred to in the first paragraph.

For the purposes of the implementation of these provisions a distinction must be drawn within the whole area of application of art 119 between, first, direct and overt discrimination which may be identified solely with the aid of the criteria based on equal work and equal pay referred to by the article in question and, secondly, indirect and disguised discrimination which can only be identified by reference to more explicit implementing provisions of a Community or national character.

... Among the forms of direct discrimination which may be identified solely by reference to the criteria laid down by art 119 must be included in particular those which have their origin in legislative provisions or in collective labour agreements and which may be detected on the basis of a purely legal analysis of the situation.

This applies even more in cases where men and women receive unequal pay for equal work carried out in the same establishment or service, whether public or private.

... In such situation, at least, art 119 is directly applicable and may thus give rise to individual rights which the courts must protect.

[*Temporal effect of the judgment*]
The governments of Ireland and the United Kingdom have drawn the Court's attention to the possible economic consequences of attributing direct effect to the provisions of art 119, on the ground that such a decision might, in many branches of economic life, result in the introduction of claims dating back to the time at which such effect came into existence.

In view of the large number of people concerned such claims, which undertakings could not have foreseen, might seriously affect the financial situation of such undertakings and even drive some of them to bankruptcy.

... Therefore, the direct effect of art 119 cannot be relied on in order to support claims concerning pay periods prior to the date of this judgment, except as regards those workers who have already brought legal proceedings or made an equivalent claim.'

Comment
This case has established that some provisions of the Treaty may produce horizontal direct effect.

The case law of the ECJ has gradually elucidated which provisions of the Treaty have both direct vertical and horizontal effect. These are: art 119 EC Treaty, articles relating to competition policy (arts 85 and 86 EC), articles concerning the free movement of workers and self-employed (arts 48, 52, 59 and 60 EC), and art 6 EC which prohibits discrimination based on nationality,

In addition, art 30 EC Treaty which provides for the free movement of goods can be relied upon by an individual against another individual in proceedings before national courts (*Dansk Supermarket* Case 58/80 [1981] ECR 181).

Preliminary rulings have retroactive effect, that is they apply from the entry into force of the provision in question. For that reason in some cases the ECJ decided to take into consideration the fact that ex tunc effect may cause serious problems in respect of bona fides legal relationships established before the preliminary ruling was delivered and therefore restricted its temporal effects (see *Salumi* Cases 66, 127 and 128/79 [1980] ECR 1258; *Denkavit Italiana* Case 61/79 [1980] ECR 1205; *Blaizot* Case 24/86 [1988] ECR 379; *Barber* Case C–262/88 [1990] ECR I–889; *Société Bautiaa* Cases C–197 and 252/94 [1996] ECR I–505). Only the ECJ may limit it ex nunc and only in the case in which the ruling was given, not in any subsequent cases. In the present case the ECJ decided to limit ex tunc the temporal effect of its ruling.

Alfons Lütticke v *Hauptzollampt Saarloius* Case 57/65 [1966] ECR 205 European Court of Justice

• *Direct effect of EC Treaty – requirement of a clear and unconditional obligation imposed on Member States – art 95 EC Treaty – discriminatory taxation*

Facts

Lütticke imported whole milk powder from Luxembourg on which German customs levied duty and a turnover tax. Lütticke claimed that the imported product should be exempt from turnover tax as domestic natural milk and wholemilk powder were exempt from the turnover tax. The Finangericht des Saarlands referred the ECJ under art 177 to ascertain whether art 95 EC, which prohibits the imposition of such tax, has direct effect and thus confers rights upon individuals which a national court must protect.

Held

The ECJ held that art 95 EC Treaty was directly effective. The Court stated that this provision contained a general rule which imposed a clear and unconditional obligation on the Member State to refrain from adopting national measures introducing discriminatory internal taxation. The obligation is not qualified by any condition, or subject to the requirement of legislative intervention on the part of the Community institutions. Therefore, art 95 EC Treaty being directly effective created rights for individuals to which the national courts must give effect.

Judgment

'The first paragraph of art 95 contains a prohibition against discrimination, constituting a clear and unconditional obligation. With the exception of the third paragraph this obligation is not qualified by any condition, or subject, in its implementation or effects, to the taking of any measures either by the institutions of the Community or by the Member States. This prohibition is therefore complete, legally perfect and consequently capable of producing direct effects on the legal relationships between the Member States and persons within their jurisdiction. The fact that this article describes the Member States as being subject to the obligation of non-discrimination does not imply that individuals cannot benefit from it.

With regard to third paragraph of art 95, it indeed imposes an obligation on the Member States to "repeal" or "amend" any provisions which conflict with the rules set out in the preceding paragraphs. The said obligation however leaves no discretion to the Member States with regard to the date by which these obligations must be carried out, that is to say, before 1 January 1962. After this date it is sufficient for the national court to find, should the case arise, that the measures implementing the contested national rules of law were adopted after 1 January 1962, in order to be able to apply the first paragraph directly in any event. Thus the provisions of the third paragraph prevent the application of the general rule only with regard to implementing measures adopted before 1 January 1962, and founded upon provisions existing when the Treaty entered into force.

In the oral and written observations which have been submitted in the course of the proceedings, three governments have relied on art 97 in order to support a different interpretation of art 95.

In empowering Member States which levy a turnover tax calculated on a cumulative multi-stage tax system to establish average rates for products or groups of products, the said article constitutes a special rule for adopting art 95 and this rule is, by its nature, incapable of creating direct effect on the relationship between the Member States and persons subject to their jurisdiction. This situation is peculiar to art 97, and can in no circumstances influence the interpretation of art 95.

It follows from foregoing that, notwithstanding the exception in the third paragraph for provisions existing when the Treaty entered into force until 1 January 1962, the prohibition contained in art 95 produces direct effects and creates individual rights of which national courts must take account.'

Comment

The ECJ in *Van Gend en Loos* (below) held that direct effect of the Treaty's provisions is not automatic since they must be clear and precise. The question whether other provisions of EC Treaty could produce direct effect was confirmed in the present case in respect of art 95 EC Treaty.

Van Gend en Loos v Nederlandse Administratie der Belastingen Case 26/62 [1963] ECR 1; [1963] CMLR 105 European Court of Justice

- *Direct effect of EC Treaty – conditions for direct effect – customs duty – art 12 EC Treaty – jurisdiction of the ECJ*

Facts
In 1960 Van Gend imported from West Germany into The Netherlands the chemical product, unreaformaldehyde. In December 1959 The Netherlands enacted legislation which modified the Benelux tariff system and which brought into effect the Brussels Convention on Nomenclature unifying the classification of goods for custom purposes. Under the new nomenclature Van Gend's product was reclassified. It resulted in an increase in the duty payable on unreaformaldehyde to 8 per cent on an ad valorem basis as compared to 3 per cent payable previously under Dutch law. On the 14 January 1958 the EEC Treaty came into force. Its art 12 provided that:

> 'Member States shall refrain from introducing between themselves any new custom duties on imports or exports or any charge having equivalent effect, and from increasing those which they already apply in their trade with each other'

Van Gend challenged the increase as contrary to art 12 EC. When its claim was rejected by the customs inspector it appealed to the Dutch Tariecommissie (customs court) in Amsterdam. Under art 177 EC the customs court submitted two questions to the ECJ: first, whether art 12 EC could create rights for individuals as claimed by Van Gend; and, second, provided the answer to the first question was affirmative, whether the modification in custom duties was prohibited by art 12.

The governments of Belgium, West Germany and The Netherlands submitted additional memoranda to the ECJ claiming that art 12 EC created obligations for Member States and not rights for individuals. As a result, if a breach of EC law occurred the proceedings should solely be based on arts 169 and 170 EC.

Held
The ECJ held that art 12 EC Treaty should be interpreted as producing direct effects and creating individual rights which national courts must protect.

Judgment
'To ascertain whether the provisions of an international treaty extend so far in their effects it is necessary to consider the spirit, the general scheme and the wording of those provisions.

The objective of the Treaty, which is to establish a Common Market, the functioning of which is of direct concern to interested parties in the Community, implies that this Treaty is more than an agreement which merely creates mutual obligations between the contracting States. This view is confirmed by the preamble to the Treaty which refers not only to governments but to people. It is also confirmed more specifically by the establishment of institutions endowed with sovereign rights, the exercise of which affects Member States and also their citizens. Furthermore, it must be noted that the nationals of the States brought together in the Community are called upon to co-operate in the functioning of this Community through the intermediary of the European Parliament and the Economic and Social Committee.

In addition the task assigned to the Court of Justice under art 177, the object of which is to secure uniform interpretation of that Treaty by national courts and tribunals, confirms that the States have acknowledged that Community law has an authority which can be invoked by their nationals before those courts and tribunals.

The conclusion to be drawn from this is that the Community constitutes a new legal order of international law for the benefit of which the States have limited their sovereign rights, albeit within limited fields, and the subjects of which comprise not only Member States but also their nationals. Independently of the legislation of Member States. Community law therefore not only imposes legislation on individuals but is also intended to confer upon them rights which become part of their legal heritage. These rights arise not only where they are expressly granted by the Treaty, but also by reason of obligations which the Treaty imposes in a clearly defined way upon individuals as well as upon the Member States and upon the institutions of the Community.

With regard to the general scheme of the Treaty as it relates to customs duties and charges having equivalent effect it must be emphasised that art 9, which bases the Community upon a customs union, includes as essential provision the prohibition of these customs duties and charges. This provision is found at the beginning of the part of the Treaty which defines the "Foundations of the Community". It is applied and explained in art 12.

The wording of art 12 contains a clear and unconditional prohibition which is not a positive but a negative obligation. This obligation, moreover, is not qualified by any reservation on the part of States which would make its implementation conditional upon a positive legislative measure enacted under national law. The very nature of this prohibition makes it ideally adopted to produce direct effects in the legal relationship between Member States and their subjects.

The implementation of art 12 does not require any legislative intervention on the part of the States. The fact that under this article it is the Member States who are made the subject of the negative obligation does not imply that their nationals cannot benefit from this obligation.

In addition the argument based on arts 169 and 170 of the Treaty put forward by the three governments which have submitted observations to the Court in their statements of case is misconceived. The fact that these articles of the Treaty enable the Commission and the Member States to bring before the Court a State which has not fulfilled its obligations does not mean that individuals cannot plead these obligations, should the occasion arise, before a national court, any more than the fact that the Treaty placed at the disposal of the Commission ways of ensuring that obligations imposed upon those subject to the Treaty are observed, precludes the possibility, in actions between individuals before a national court, of pleading infringements of these obligations.

A restriction of the guarantees against an infringement of art 12 by Member States to the procedures under art 169 and 170 would remove all direct legal protection of the individual rights of their nationals. There is the risk that recourse to the procedure under thee Articles would be ineffective if it were to occur after the implementation of a national decision taken contrary to the provisions of the Treaty.

The vigilance of individuals concerned to protect their rights amounts to an effective supervision in addition to the supervision entrusted by arts 169 and 170 to the diligence of the Commission and of the Member States.

It follows from the foregoing considerations that, according to the spirit, the general scheme and the wording of the Treaty, art 12 must be interpreted as producing direct effects and creating individual rights which national courts must protect.'

Comment

In the present case the ECJ delivered one of the most important decisions from a point of view of development of Community law. The ECJ held Community law directly effective and thus creating rights and obligations for EC nationals enforceable before national courts.

The ECJ based its decision on a systematic and teleological interpretation of art 12 EC. The Court invoked a number of arguments in support of its decision. It stated that direct effect confirms the peculiar nature of

Community law. First, the objectives of the Treaty imply that the Treaty itself is 'more that an agreement which created mutual obligations between the contracting States'. Second, it stems from the Treaty's preamble, which refers not only to the Member States but also to its people as well as the institutional system, that Community law affects both the Member States and their citizens. Third, the Court invoked an argument drawn from art 177 EC that the Member States 'have acknowledged that Community law has an authority which can be invoked by their nationals before those courts and tribunals'. From all these arguments the ECJ inferred that Community law 'independently of the legislation of Member States ... not only imposes obligations on individuals but is also intended to confer upon them rights which become part of their legal heritage'. In addition, direct effect of Community law ensures its effectiveness since the vigilance of individuals concerned to protect their rights amounts to an effective supervision in addition to the supervision entrusted by arts 169 and 170 to the diligence of the Commission and of the Member States.

In the present case the ECJ established three conditions for a provision of the Treaty to produce direct effect. That provision must be clear, unconditional and self-executing, that is, no further implementing measures are necessary on the part of a Member State or Community institutions.

EC directives

Foster and Others v British Gas
Case C–188/89 [1990] ECR I–33/3; [1990] 3 CMLR 833 European Court of Justice

- *Direct effect – EC directives – emanation of the State – private corporations – degree of control exercised by the government over the activities of the corporation – Directive 76/207 – discrimination in retirement age between men and women*

Facts
Ms Foster and a number of other female employees were dismissed by the British Gas Corporation, an entity succeeded by British Gas plc, which latter company acquired the rights and liabilities of the former company. The plaintiffs were required to retire at the age of 60, but male employees were not required to retire until they attained the age of 65. An action was raised on the ground that British Gas plc had infringed art 5(1) of Council Directive 76/207 (1976) which had not been incorporated into United Kingdom domestic law.

The House of Lords referred to the ECJ the question whether British Gas plc could be considered an emanation of the State to which the doctrine of the direct effect of unimplemented directives would apply

Held
The ECJ held that the degree of State control over British Gas plc implied that it was an emanation of the State and the principle of vertical direct effect was applicable.

Judgment
'Before considering the question referred by the House of Lords, it must first be observed as a preliminary point that the United Kingdom has submitted that it is not a matter for the Court of Justice but for the national courts to determine, in the context of the national legal system, whether the provisions of a directive may be relied upon against a body such as the British Gas Corporation.

The question what effects measures adopted by Community institutions have and in particular whether those measures may be relied on against certain categories of persons necessarily involves interpretation of the Articles of the Treaty concerning measures adopted by the institutions and the Community measure in issue.

It follows that the Court of Justice has jurisdiction in proceedings for a preliminary ruling to determine the categories of persons against whom the provisions of a directive may be relied on. It is for the national courts, on the other hand, to decide whether a party before them falls within one of the categories so defined.

As the Court consistently held (see Case 8/81 *Becker* v *Finanzamt Münster-Innenstadt* [1982] ECR 53), where the Community authorities have, by means of a directive, placed Member States under a duty to adopt a certain course of action, the effectiveness of such a measure would be diminished if persons were prevented from relying upon it in proceedings before a court and national courts were prevented from taking into consideration as an element of Community law. Consequently, a Member State which has not adopted the implementing measures required by the directive within the prescribed period may not plead, as against individuals, its own failure to perform the obligations which the directive entails. Thus, wherever the provisions of a directive appear, as far as their subject matter is concerned, to be unconditional and sufficiently precise, those provisions may, in the absence of implementing measures adopted within the prescribed period, be relied upon as against any national provision which is incompatible with the directive or in so far as the provisions define rights which individuals are able to assert against the State.

The Court further held in the *Marshall* case [Case 152/84 [1986] ECR 723] that where a person is able to rely on a directive as against the State he may do so regardless of the capacity in which the latter is acting, whether as employer or as public authority. In either case it is necessary to prevent the State from taking advantage of its own failure to comply with Community law.

On the basis of those considerations, the Court has held in a series of cases that unconditional and sufficiently precise provisions of a directive could be relied on against organisations or bodies which were subject to the authority or control of the State or had special powers beyond those which result from the normal rules applicable to relations between individuals.

The Court has accordingly held that provisions of a directive could be relied on against tax authorities, local or regional authorities, constitutionally independent authorities responsible for the maintenance of public order and safety, and public authorities providing public health services.

It follows from the foregoing that a body, whatever its legal form, which has been made responsible, pursuant to a measure adopted by the State, for providing a public service under the control of the State and has for that purpose special powers beyond those which result from the normal rules applicable in relations between individuals, is included in any event among the bodies against which the provisions of a directive capable of having direct effect may be relied upon.

With regard to art 5(1) of Directive 76/207 it should be observed that in *Marshall* the Court held that that provision was unconditional and sufficiently precise to be relied on by an individual and to be applied by the national courts.

The answer to the question referred by the House of Lords must therefore be that art 5(1) of Council Directive 76/207 may be relied upon in a claim for damages against a body, whatever its legal form, which has been responsible, pursuant to a measure adopted by the State, for providing a public service under the control of that State and has for that purpose special powers beyond those which result from the normal rules applicable in relations between individuals.'

Comment

In the present case the ECJ elucidated the concept of a State and gave to it a wide interpretation. The ECJ provided a definition of a body which is an emanation of a State. It is a body

'... whatever its legal form, which has been made responsible pursuant to a measure adopted by a public authority, for providing a public service under the control of that authority and has for that purpose special powers beyond those which result from the normal rules applicable in relations between individuals.'

It results from this definition that three criteria should be satisfied in order to consider an organisation as an emanation of the State. First, it must be made responsible for providing a public service; second, it must provide that service under the control of the State; and, third, it must have special powers, beyond those normally applicable in relations between individuals, to provide that service.

Marshall v Southampton and South-West Hampshire Area Health Authority (No 1) Case 152/84 [1986] ECR 723 European Court of Justice

- *Direct vertical effect of EC directives – concept of a State – equal treatment – Directive 76/207/EEC – British Sex Discrimination Act 1975 – discrimination in retirement age between men and women*

Facts
Miss Marshall was an employee of Southampton and South-West Hampshire Area Health Authority (AHA) which maintained a policy of compulsory retirement for women over the age of 60 and men over the age of 65, with extensions in exceptional circumstances. Miss Marshall was dismissed at 62 on the ground that she had exceeded the normal retirement age for women. Miss Marshall wished to remain in employment. She argued that the British Sex Discrimination Act 1975, which excluded from its scope of application provision in relation to death and retirement, was contrary to Council Directive 76/207 on Equal Treatment. The UK had adopted this Directive but had not amended the 1975 Act believing that discrimination in retirement ages was allowed. The Court of Appeal asked the ECJ under art 177 EC whether the dismissal of Miss Marshall was unlawful and whether she was entitled in national courts to rely upon Directive 76/207.

Held
The ECJ held that the policy of the AHA was contrary to the terms of directive 76/207/EEC. The ECJ refused to give horizontal direct effect to EC directives but stated that the AHA was a public body regardless of the capacity in which it was acting, that is public authority or employer. The Court agreed with the argument submitted by the United Kingdom that the possibility of relying on provisions of the Directive against the respondent qua organ of the State would give rise to an arbitrary and unfair distinction between the rights of State employees and those of private employees. The ECJ added that such a distinction would have been avoided if the Member State concerned had correctly implemented the Directive into national law.

Judgment
'It is necessary to consider whether art 5(1) of Directive No 76/207 may be relied upon by an individual before national courts and tribunals.

The appellant and the Commission consider that the question must be answered in the affirmative. They contend in particular, with regard to arts 2(1) and 5(1) of Directive 76/207, that those provisions are sufficently clear to enable national courts to apply them without legislative intervention by the Member States, at least so far as overt discrimination is concerned.

In support of that view, the appellant points out that directives are capable of conferring rights on individuals which may be relied upon directly before the courts of the Member States; national courts are obliged by virtue of the binding nature of a directive, in conjunction with art 5 of the [EC] Treaty, to give effect to the provisions of directives where possible, in particular when construing or applying relevant provisions of national law (Case 14/83 *Von Colson and Kamann* v *Land Nordrhein-Westfalen* [1984] ECR 1891; [1986] 2 CMLR 430). Where there is any inconsistency between national law and Community law which cannot be removed by means of such a construction, the appellant submits that a national court is obliged to declare that the provision of national law is inconsistent with the directive is inapplicable.

The Commission is of the opinion that the provisions of art 5(1) of Directive No 76/207 are sufficiently clear and unconditional to be relied upon before a national court. They may therefore be set up against s6(4) of the Sex Discrimination Act, which, according to the decisions of the Court of Appeal, has been extended to the question of compulsory retirement and has therefore become ineffective to prevent dismissal based upon the difference in retirement ages for men and for women.

The respondent and the United Kingdom propose, conversely, that the second question should be answered in the negative. They admit that a directive may, in certain circumstances, have direct effect as against a Member State in so far as the latter may not rely on its failure to perform its obligations under the directive. However, they maintain that a directive can never impose obligations directly on individuals and that it can only have direct effect against a Member State qua public authority and not against a Member State qua employer. As an employer a State is no different from a provate employer. It would not therefore be proper to put persons employed by the State in a better position than those who are employed by a provate employer.

With regard to the legal position of the respondent's employees the United Kingdom states that they are in the same position as the employees of a private employer. Although according to United Kingdom constitutional law the health authorities, created by the National Health Service Act 1977, as amended by the Health Services Act 1980 and other legislation, are Crown bodies and their employees are Crown servants, nevertheless the administration of the National Health Service by the health authorities is regarded as being separate from the government's central administration and its employees are not regarded as civil servants.

Finally, both the respondent and the United Kingdom take the view that the provisions of Directive No76/207 are neither unconditional nor suffciently clear and precise to give rise to direct effect. The directives provides for a number of possible exceptions, the details of which are to be laid down by the Member States. Furthermore, the wording of art 5 is quite imprecise and requires the adoption of measures for its implementation.

It is necessary to recall that, according to a long line of decisions of the Court (in particular its judgment in Case 8/81 *Becker* v *Finanzamt Münster-Innenstadt* [1982] ECR 53; [1982] 1 CMLR 499), wherever the provisions of a directive appear, as far as their subject-matter is concerned, to be unconditional and sufficiently precise, those provisions may be relied upon by an individual against the State where that State fails to implement the directive in national law by the end of the period prescribed or where it fails to implement the directive correctly.

This view is based on the consideration that it would be incompatible with the binding nature which art 189 confers on the directive to hold as a matter of principle that the obligation imposed thereby cannot be relied on by those concerned. From that the Court deduced that a Member State which has not adopted the implementing measures required by the directive within the prescibed period may not plead, as against individuals, its own failure to perform the obligations which the directive entails.

With regard to the argument that a directive may not be relied upon against an individual, it must be emphasised that according to art 189 of the [EC] Treaty the binding nature of a directive, which constitutes the basis for the possibility of relying on the directive before a national court, exist only in relation to "each Member State to which it is addressed". It follows that a directive may not of itself impose obligations on an individual and that a provision of a directive may not be relied upon as such against such a person. It must therefore be examined whether, in this case, the respondent must be regarded as having acted as an individual.

Fundamental Principles of European Community Law 145

In that respect it must be pointed out that where a person involved in legal proceedings is able to rely on a directive as against the State he may do so regardless of the capacity in which the latter is acting, whether employer or public authority. In either case it is necessary to prevent the State from taking advantage of its own failure to comply with Community law.

It is for the national court to apply those considerations to the circumstances of each case; the Court of Appeal has, however, stated in the order for reference that the respondent, Southampton and South-West Hampshire Area Health Authority (Teaching), is a public authority.

The argument submitted by the United Kingdom that the possibility of relying on provisions of the directive against the respondent qua organ of the State would give rise to an arbitrary and unfair distinction between the rights of State employees and those of private employees does not justify any other conclusion. Such a distinction may easily be avoided if the Member State concerned has correctly implementd the directive in national law.

Finally, with regard to the question whether the provision contained in art 5(1) of Directive No 76/207, which implements the principle of equality of treatment set out in art 2(1) of the directive, may be considered, as far as its contents are concerned, to be unconditional and suficiently precise to be relied upon by an individual as against the State, it must be stated that the provision. taken by itself, prohibits any discrimination on grounds of sex with regard to working conditions, including the conditions governing dismissal, in a general manner and in unequivocal terms. The provision is therefore sufficiently precise to be relied on by an individual and to be applied by the national courts.

It is necessary to consider next whether the prohibition of discrimination laid down by the directive may be regarded as unconditional, in the light of the exceptions contained therein and of the fact that according to art 5(2) thereof the Member States are to take the measures necessary to ensure the application of the principal of equality of treatment in the context of national law.

With regard, in the first place, to the reservation contained in art 1(2) of Directive No 76/207 concerning the application of the principle of equality of treatment in matters of social security, it must be observed that, although the reservation limits the scope of the directive ratione materiae, it does not lay down any condition on the application of that principle in its field of operation and in particular in relation to art 5 of the directive. Similarly, the exceptions to Directive No 76/207 provided for in art 2 thereof are not relevant to this case.

It follows that art 5 of Directive No 76/207 does not confer on the Member States the right to limit the application of the principle of equality of treatment in its field of operation or to subject it to conditions and that that provision is sufficiently precise and unconditional to be capable of being relied upon by an individual before a national court in order to avoid the application of any national provision which does not conform to art 5(1).

Consequently, the answer to the second question must be that art 5(1) of Council Directive No 76/207 of 9 February 1976, which prohibits any discrimination on grounds of sex with regard to working conditions, including the conditions governing dismissal, may be relied upon as against a State authority acting in its capacity as employer, in order to avoid the application of any national provision which does not conform to art 5(1).'

Comment

In the present case the ECJ refused to confer on EC directives direct horizontal effect. Therefore, the ECJ restricted the application of the doctrine of the direct effect of EC directives by finding that the terms of unimplemented directives could only be relied upon against a State authority acting as an employer. In order to attenuate this restriction the ECJ extended the concept of a State. The obvious question that arises is what bodies should be considered as being an emanation of the State. In general, the answer is simple. The dichotomy of public/private body is well recognised under national laws of all Member States. Nevertheless, the ECJ in order to maximise the effect of EC directives has introduced an autonomous Community meaning of public body.

Pubblico Ministero v *Ratti* Case 148/78 [1979] ECR 1629; [1980] 1 CMLR 96 European Court of Justice

- *Directives – non-implemented – direct effect – conditions for direct effect – expiry of the time-limit for implementation – non-application of pre-existing national law where EC law harmonising measures introduced less rigorous standards*

Facts

Council directives were passed in 1973 and 1977 on the labelling and packaging of solvents and toxic substances respectively. Italy maintained even stricter requirements and failed to implement these directives into national law. Ratti was selling solvents and varnishes. He fixed labels to certain dangerous substances in conformity with Directive 73/173 and Directive 77/128 but contrary to Italian legislation of 1963. He was prosecuted by Italian authorities for breach of Italian legislation. Directive 73/173 was not implemented in Italy although the time-limit prescribed for its implementation elapsed on 8 December 1974. Also Directive 77/128 was not transposed into Italian law but the time-limit for its implementation had not yet expired. The Milan court asked the ECJ under art 177 EC which set of rules should be applied, national law or Directives 73/173 and 77/128.

Held

The ECJ held that if the provisions of an EC directive are sufficiently precise and unconditional, although not implemented within the prescribed period, an individual may rely upon them. However, if the time-limit for implementation into national law had not been reached at the relevant time, the obligation was not directly effective.

Judgment

'[T]he settled case law of the Court, last reaffirmed by the judgment of the Court in Case 51/76 *Nederlandse Ondernemingen* [1977] ECR 113, lays down that, whilst under art 189 regulations are directly applicable and, consequently, by their nature capable of producing direct effects, that does not mean that other categories of acts covered by that article can never produce similar effects.

It would be incompatible with the binding effect which art 189 ascribes to directives to exclude on principle the possibility of the obligations imposed by them being relied on by persons concerned.

Particularly in cases in which the Community authorities have, by means of directive, placed Member States under a duty to adopt a certain course of action, the effectiveness of such act would be weakened if persons concerned were prevented from relying on it in legal proceedings and national courts prevented from taking it into consideration as an element of Community law.

Consequently a Member State which has not adopted the implementing measures required by the directive in the prescribed periods may not rely, as against individuals, on its own failure to perform the obligations which the directive entails.

It follows that a national court requested by a person who has complied with the provisions of a directive not to apply a national provision incompatible with the directive not incorporated into the internal legal order of a defaulting Member State, must uphold the request if the obligation in question is unconditional and sufficently precise.

Therefore the answer to the first question must be that after the expiration of the period fixed for the implementaion of a directive a Member State may not apply its internal law – even if it is provided with penal sanctions – which has not yet been adopted in compliance with the directive, to a person who has complied with the requirements of the directive.

In the second question the national court asks, essentially, whether, in incorporating the provisions of the directive on solvents into its internal legal order, the State to which it is addressed may prescribe "obligations and limitations which are more precise and detailed than, or at all events different from, those set out in the directive", requiring in particular information not required by the directive to be affixed to the containers.

The combined effect of arts 3 to 8 of Directive 73/173 is that only solvents which "comply with the provisions of this directive and the annex thereto" may be placed on the market and that Member States are not entitled to maintain, parallel with the rules laid down by the said directive for imports, different rules for the domestic market.

Thus it is a consequence of the system introduced by Directive 73/173 that a Member State may not introduce into its national legislation conditions which are more restrictive than those laid down in the directive in question, or which are even more detailed or in any event different, as regards the classification, packaging and labelling of solvents, and that this prohibition on the imposition of restrictions not provided for applies both to the direct marketing of the products on the home market and to imported products.

The second question submitted by the national court must be answered in that way.'

Comment

In order to curtail non-implementation of EC directives by the Member States within a specific time-limit, usually laid down in the measures themselves, the ECJ held in the present case that after the expiration of the period fixed for the implementation of a directive a Member State may not apply its internal law which is not in conformity with Community law to a person who has complied with the requirements of the directive. A logical corollary to this principle is that a Member State which has failed to transpose an EC directive within the prescribed time-limit cannot rely on an unimplemented directive in proceedings against individuals.

Van Duyn v *Home Office* Case 41/74 [1974] ECR 1337 European Court of Justice

- *Direct vertical effect of EC directives – Directive 64/221/EEC – free movement of workers – art 48 EC Treaty – public policy exception*

Facts

Miss Van Duyn, a Dutch national, arrived at Gatwick Airport on 9 May 1973. She intended to work as a secretary at the British headquarters of the Church of Scientology of California. British immigration authorities refused her leave to enter on the grounds of public policy. Although it was not unlawful to work for the Church of Scientology, the government of the United Kingdom warned foreigners that the effect of the Church's activities were harmful to the mental health of those involved. Miss Van Duyn challenged the decision of the immigration authorities on two grounds: the basis of art 48 EC which grants workers the right to free movement between Member States subject to its paragraph 3 which imposes limitations on grounds of public policy, public security or public health; and on the basis of art 3(1) of Directive 64/221 which further implements art 48(3) EC and which provides that measures taken by Member States regarding public policy must be 'based exclusively on the personal conduct of the individual concerned'. She claimed that art 3(1) of Directive 64/221 was directly effective and that the refusal to allow her to enter the UK was not based on her conduct but on the general policy of the British government towards the Church of Scientology.

For the first time an English court referred

to the ECJ under art 177 EC. The High Court asked the question whether both art 48 EC and the Directive were directly effective.

Held

The ECJ held that both art 48 EC Treaty and the Directive produce direct effect. In particular, the ECJ held that given the nature, general scheme and wording of art 3(1) of Directive 64/221 its effectiveness would be greater if individuals were entitled to invoke it in national courts. Therefore, based on the principle of effect utile the ECJ decided that art 3(1) of Directive 64/221 was directly effective. The United Kingdom was entitled to rely on the public policy exception to refuse admission to Miss Van Duyn.

Judgment

'[*First question*]
By the first question, the Court is asked to say whether art 48 of the [EC] Treaty is directly applicable so as to confer on individuals rights enforceable by them in the courts of a Member State.

It is provided, in art 48(1) and (2), that freedom of movement for workers shall be secured by the end of the transitional period and that such freedom shall entail "the abolition of any discrimination based on nationality between workers of Member States as regards employment, remuneration and other conditions of work and employment".

These provisions impose on Member States a precise obligation which does not require the adoption of any further measure on the part either of the Community institutions or of the Member States and which leaves them, in relation to its implementation, no discretionary power.

Paragraph (3), which defines the rights implied by the principle of freedom of movement for workers, subjects them to limitations justified on grounds of public policy, public security or public heath. The application of these limitations is, however, subject to judicial control, so that a Member State's right to invoke the limitations does not prevent the provisions of art 48, which enshrine the principle of freedom of movement for workers, from conferring on individuals rights which are enforceable by them and which the national courts must protect.

The reply to the first question must therefore be in the affirmative.

[*Second question*]
The second question asks the Court to say whether Council Directive 64/221 of 25 February 1964 on the co-ordination of special measures concerning the movement and residence of foreign nationals which are justified on grounds of public policy, public security or public health is directly applicable so as to confer on individuals rights enforceable by them in courts of a Member State.

It emerges from the order making the reference that the only provision of the Directive which is relevant is that contained in art 3(1) which provides that "measures taken on grounds of public policy or public security shall be based exclusively on the personal conduct of the individual concerned".

The United Kingdom observes that, since art 189 of the Treaty distinguishes between the effects ascribed to regulations, directives and decisions, it must therefore be presumed that the Council in issuing a directive rather than making a regulation, must have intended that the directive should have an effect other than that of a regulation and accordingly that the former should not be directly applicable.

If, however, by virtue of the provisions of art 189, regulations are directly applicable and, consequently, may by their very nature have direct effects, it does not follow from this that other categories of acts mentioned in that art can never have similar effects. It would be incompatible with the binding effect attributed to a directive by art 189 to exclude, in principle, the possibility that the obligation which it imposes may be invoked by those concerned. In particular, where the Community authorities have, by directive, imposed on Member States the obligation to pursue a particular course of conduct, the useful effect of such an act would be weakened if individuals were prevented from relying on it before their national courts and if the latter were prevented from taking it into consideration as an element of Community law. Article 177, which empowers national courts to refer to the Court questions concerning the validity and interpretation of all acts of the Community institutions, without distinction, implies furthermore that these acts may be invoked by individuals in the national courts. It is necessary to examine, in every case, whether the nature, general scheme and wording of the provision in question are capable of having direct effects on the relations between Member States and individuals.

By providing that measures taken on grounds of public policy shall be based exclusively on the personal conduct of the individual concerned, art 3(1) of Directive 64/221 is intended to limit the discretionary power which national laws generally confer on the authorities responsible for the entry and expulsion of foreign nationals. First, the provision lays down an obligation which is not subject to any exception or condition and which, by its very nature, does not require the intervention of any act on the part either of the institutions of the Community or of Member State. Secondly, because Member States are thereby obliged, in implementing a clause which derogates from one of the fundamental principles of the Treaty in favour of individuals, not to take account of factors extraneous to personal conduct, legal certainty for the persons concerned requires that they should be able to rely on this obligation even though it has been laid down in a legislative act which has no automatic direct effect in its entirety.

If the meaning and exact scope of the provision raise questions of interpretation, these questions can be resolved by the courts, taking into account also the procedure under art 177 of the Treaty.

Accordingly, in reply to the second question, art 3(1) of Council Directive 64/221 of 25 February 1964 confers on individuals rights which are enforceable by them in the courts of a Member State and which the national courts must protect.'

Comment
The ECJ for the first time expressly recognised the direct effect of an EC directive.

The general principle is that EC directives should be correctly implemented into national law so that individuals can rely on their provisions before national courts through the national implementing measures. There should be no need to verify whether a provision of an EC directive satisfies the three criteria for direct effect, that is, it must be clear and precise, unconditional and self-executing. In this way, an individual may secure rights conferred by EC directives in the manner envisaged by art 189 EC. Therefore, the question of direct effect does not arise since the correct transposition of provisions of EC directives means that they are part of national law. The question whether an EC directive has been correctly implemented into national law concerns, in reality, the conformity of national law with EC law and not the question of direct effect. Thus, any provision of an EC directive transposed into national law may be invoked in any dispute (including a dispute between individuals) in order to verify whether national authorities have implemented it in accordance with requirements specified in the directive (*Nederlandse Ondernemingen* Case 51/76 [1977] ECR 113 at 127). Direct effect of EC directive becomes an issue only if the implementation measures adopted by a Member State are incompatible with its provisions (*Enka* Case 38/77 [1977] ECR 2203; *Fratelli Costanzo* Case 103/88 [1989] ECR 1839) or insufficient (*Rutili* Case 36/75 [1975] ECR 1219) or (as in *Ratti* Case 148/78) not implemented within the prescribed time-limit

Indirect effect

Marleasing SA v La Comercial Internacional de Alimentacion SA
Case C–106/89 [1990] ECR 4135; [1992] 1 CMLR 305 European Court of Justice

- EC directives – horizontal direct effect – interpretation of national law in conformity with EC law – arts 5 and 189 EC Treaty – company law – Directive 68/151 – grounds for annulment of a company – lack of cause – lack of consideration

Facts
A Spanish company was formed, allegedly to defraud the creditors of one of its founders. The company took over the assets of the individuals setting it up, and for legal purposes this process put the assets of those individuals beyond the reach of their creditors. Certain creditors sought to have the 'founders contract', which is one way of setting up a company in Spanish law, voided for lack of consideration or, in the alternative, on the ground that it was a sham transaction vitiated by the lack of a lawful cause.

The defendants argued that under art 11 of the EC First Company Directive 68/151, which provided an exhaustive list of the grounds on which the nullity of a company may be declared, lack of consideration or lack of lawful cause was not mentioned. Directive 68/151 was not implemented in Spain although the prescribed time-limit for its implementation had elapsed. The Spanish court asked the ECJ under art 177 proceedings whether art 11 of Directive 68/151 was directly effective and whether it prevented a declaration of nullity on grounds other than enumerated in that provision.

Held
The ECJ confirmed that EC directives could not produce horizontal direct effect, thus the defendants could not rely on art 11 in proceedings against another individual. Also art 11 of Directive 68/151 exhaustively listed the grounds of nullity and did not include the grounds on which Marleasing relied. Nevertheless, the ECJ held that, based on its judgment in *Von Colson*, a Spanish court was obliged 'so far as was possible' to interpret national law, whether it pre-dated or post-dated the Directive, in the light of its terms – meaning that a Spanish court had to interpret Spanish law in such a way as to disregard provisions of the Spanish Civil Code which pre-dated Directive 68/151. Therefore, the formation of the company could not be declared null or void for lack of consideration or lack of lawful cause.

Judgment
'With regard to the question whether an individual may rely on the directive against a national law, it should be observed that, as the Court has consistently held, a directive may not of itself impose obligations on an individual and, consequently, a provision of a directive may not be relied upon as such against such a person.

However, it is apparent from the documents before the Court that the national court seeks in substance to ascertain whether a national court hearing a case which falls within the scope of Directive 68/151 is required to interpret its national law in the light of the wording and purpose of that directive in order to preclude a declaration of nullity of a public limited company on a ground other than those listed in art 11 of the Directive.

In order to reply to that question, it should be observed that, as the Court pointed out in *Von Colson* v *Land Nordrhein-Westfalen* [1984] ECR 1891, the Member State's obligation arising from a directive to achieve the result envisaged by the directive and their duty under art 5 [EC] to take all appropriate measures, whether general or particular, to ensure the fulfilment of that obligation, is binding on all the authorities of Member States including, for matters within their jurisdiction, the courts. It follows that, in applying national law, whether the provisions in question were adopted before or after the directive, the national court called upon to intepret it is required to do so, so far as possible, in the light of the wording and the purpose of the directive in order to achieve the result pursued by the latter and thereby comply with the third paragraph of art 189 [EC].

It follows that the requirement that national law must be interpreted in conformity with art 11 of Directive 68/151 precludes the interpretation of provisions of national law relating to public limited companies in such a manner that the nullity of a public limited company may be ordered on grounds other than those exhaustively listed in art 11 of the directive in question.

With regard to the interpretation given to art 11 of the Directive, in particular art 11(2)(b), it should be observed that that provision prohibits the laws of the Member States from providing for a judicial declaration of nullity on grounds other than those exhaustively listed in the Directive, amongst which is the ground that the objects of the company are unlawful or contrary to public policy.

According to the Commission, the expression "objects of the comapny" must be interpreted as referring exclusively to the objects of the company as described in the instrument of incorporation or the articles od assiciation. It follows, in the Commission's view, that a declaration of nullity of a company cannot be made on the basis of the activity pursued by it, for instance defrauding the founder's creditors.

That argument must be upheld. As is clear from the preamble to Directive 65/151, its purpose was to limit the cases in which nullity can arise and the retroactive effect of a declaration of nullity in order to ensure "certainty in the law as regards relations between the company and third parties, and also between members". Furthermore, the protection of third parties "must be ensured by provisions which restrict to the greatest possible extent the grounds on which obligations entered into in the name of the company are not valid". It follows, therefore, that each ground of nullity provided in art 11 of the Directive must be interpreted strictly. In those circumstances the words "objects of the company" must be understood as referring to the objects of the company as described in the instrument of incorporation or the articles of assiciation.

The answer to the question submitted must therefore be that a national court hearing a case which falls within the scope of Directive 68/151 is required to interpret its national law in the light of the wording and purpose of that Directive in order to preclude a declaration of nullity of a public limited company on a ground other than those listed in art 11 of the Directive.'

Comment

Marleasing is a very controversial case. On the one hand, the ECJ stated that the obligation to interpret national law in conformity with EC law is demanded only 'as far as possible', on the other hand it did not require a national judge to interpret a national provision in the light of the Directive. It simply strikes down a conflicting national provision which was never intended to implement Directive 68/151.

Von Colson and Kamann v Land Nordrhein-Westfalen Case 14/83 [1984] ECR 1891 and **Harz v Deutsche Tradax GmbH** Case 79/83 [1984] ECR 1921 European Court of Justice

• *EC directives – interpretation of national law in conformity with EC law – arts 5 and 189 of EC Treaty – Directive 76/207 – sex discrimination – insufficient national remedy*

Facts

Both Von Colson and Harz were females discriminated against on grounds of gender when applying for a job. Von Colson was in the public service when she applied for the post of prison social worker and Harz was in the private sector when she applied to join a training programme with a commercial company. Under German law implementing Council Directive 76/207 they were entitled to receive only nominal damages, being reimbursement of their travel expenses. They claimed that the implementation was contrary to art 6 of Directive 76/207 which provided that:

> 'Member States shall introduced into their national legal systems such measures as are necessary to enable all persons who consider themselves wronged by failure to apply to them the principle of equal treatment ... to pursue their claims by judicial process after possible recourse to other competent authorities.'

Both applicants argued that they should be offered the post applied for or receive substantial damages. The German labour court referred under art 177 to ECJ the questions whether art 6 of Directive 76/207 was directly effective and whether under that Directive Member States were required to provide for particular sanctions or other legal consequences in cases of discrimination on grounds of sex against a person seeking employment.

Held

The ECJ avoided the question of direct effect of art 6 of Directive 76/207 and instead concentrated on the interpretation of national law in conformity with EC law. It held that national law must be interpreted in such a way as to achieve the result required by the Directive regardless of whether the defendant was the State or a private party.

Judgment

> '[This part of the judgment is identical in both cases]
> ... the Member States' obligation arising from a directive to achieve the result envisaged by the directive and their duty under art 5 of the Treaty to take all appropriate measures, whether general or particular, to ensure the fulfilment of that obligation, is binding on all authorities of Member States including, for matters within their jurisdiction, the courts. It follows that, in applying the national law and in particular the provisions of a national law specifically introduced in order to implement Directive No 76/207, national courts are required to interpret their national law in the light of the wording and the purpose of the Directive in order to achieve the result referred to in the third paragraph of art 189.
>
> On the other hand, as the above considerations show, the Directive does not include any unconditional and sufficiently precise obligation as regards sanctions for discrimination which, in the absence of implementing measures adopted in good time, may be relied on by individuals in order to obtain specific compensation under the Directive, where that is not provided for or permitted under national law.
>
> It should, however, be pointed out to the national court that although Directive No 76/207/EEC, for the purpose of imposing sanctions for the breach of the prohibition of discrimination, leaves the Member States free to choose between the different solutions suitable for achieving its objective, it nevertheless requires that if a Member State chooses to penalise breaches of that prohibition by the award of compensation, then in order to ensure that it is effective and that it has a deterrent effect, that compensation must in any event be adequate in relation to the damage sustained and must therefore amount to more than purely nominal compensation such as, for example, the reimbursement only of the expense incurred in connection with the application. It is for the national court to interpret and apply the legislation adopted for the implementation of the Directive in conformity with the requirements of Community law, in so far as it is given discretion to do so under national law.'

Comment

In *Von Colson* and *Harz* the ECJ provided a new solution to the problem of lessening the vertical/horizontal public/private dichotomy regarding EC directives. The ECJ held that national judges are required to interpret national law in the light of the text and objectives of Community law, in the present cases it was an EC directive. This solution is based on art 5 EC which applies to all national bodies, including national courts which have a duty to ensure that national law conforms with Community law and thus the requirement of the principle of effect utile is satisfied, that is, rights vested in individuals by Community law are protected by national courts.

The principle of interpretation of national law in conformity with EC law constitutes a logical consequence of the supremacy of EC law and applies in relation to all Community law irrespective of whether or not a provision of EC law is directly effective. National law whether anterior or subsequent must conform to Community law.

In *Von Colson* and *Harz* the interpretation of national law in conformity with the Directive resulted in providing an efficient remedy to the applicants tantamount to conferring on art 6 of Directive 76/207 horizontal direct effect. The German labour court found that it had power to award damages to both plaintiffs not exceeding six months' gross salary.

Webb v *EMO Air Cargo (UK) Ltd (No 2)* [1995] 4 All ER 577 House of Lords

- *EC directives – interpretation of national law in conformity with EC law – Directive 76/207 – unlawful dismissal – pregnancy – ss1(1)(a) and 5(3) of the Sex Discrimination Act 1975*

Facts
Ms Webb was offered a temporary job to replace her colleague who was taking maternity leave. Before the commencement of her employment Mrs Webb discovered that she was pregnant and as a result she was dismissed. She argued that her dismissal was unlawful under Directive 76/207 which prohibits discrimination based on sex. The House of Lords, called to interpret the Sex Discrimination Act 1975 which implemented Directive 76/207 asked, the ECJ under art 177 EC proceedings whether Ms Webb's dismissal was contrary to Directive 76/207.

Held
The ECJ held that Ms Webb's dismissal was in breach of Directive 76/207.

Judgment
Lord Keith of Kinkel (at p582 a–h):

'The provisions of the 1975 Act which your Lordships must endeavour to construe, so as to accord if at all possible with the ruling of the European Court, are ss1(1)(a) and 5(3).

Section 1(1)(a) provides:

"A person discriminates against a woman in any circumstances relevant for the purposes of any provisions of this Act if – (a) on the ground of her sex he treats her less favourably than he treats or would treat a man ..."

Section 5(3) provides:

"A comparison of the cases of persons of different sex and martial status under section 1(1) or 3(1) must be such that the relevant circumstances in the one case are the same or not materially different, in the other."

The reasoning in my speech in the earlier proceedings was to the effect that the relevant circumstances which existed in the present case, and which should be taken to be present in the case of the hypothetical man, was unavailability for work at the time when the worker was particularly required, and that the reason for the unavailability was not a relevant circumstance (see [1994] 4 All ER 929 at 933–935; [1993] 1 WLR 49 at 53–55). So it was not relevant that the reason for the woman's unavailability was pregnancy, a condition which could not be present in a man.

The ruling of the European Court proceeds on an interpretation of the broad principles dealt with in arts 2(1) and 5(1) of Directive 76/207. Sections 1(1)(a) and 5(3) of the 1975 Act set out a more precise test of unlawful discrimination, and the problem is how to fit the terms of that test into the ruling. It seems to me that the only way of doing so is to hold that, in a case where a woman is engaged for an indefinite period, the fact that the reason why she will be temporarily unavailable for work at a time when to her knowledge her services will be particularly required is pregnancy is a circumstance relevant to her case, being a circumstance which could not be present in the case of the hypothetical man. It does not necessarily follow that pregnancy would be a relevant circumstance in the situation where the woman is denied employment for a fixed period in the future during the whole of which her pregnancy would make her unavailable for work, nor in the situation where after engagement for such a period the discovery of her pregnancy leads to cancellation of the engagement.

My Lords, for these reasons I would allow the appeal and remit the case to the industrial tribunal to assess compensation.'

Comment

The House of Lords clearly accepted the decision of the ECJ in *Marleasing*, that is, that national legislation pre-dating Community law must be interpreted in conformity with the latter.

In order to interpret the Sex Discrimination Act 1975 as required by Directive 76/207 the House of Lords construed the s5(3) of the 1975 Act concept of 'relevant circumstances' as meaning in the case of Ms Webb her unavailability for work due to pregnancy and not as previously stated her unavailability to work (*Webb* v *EMO Air Cargo (UK) Ltd* [1992] 4 All ER 929 House of Lords). The House of Lords held that a male employee could not be dismissed on those grounds and thus Ms Webb's dismissal was discriminatory.

Limitations on indirect effect

Officier Van Justitie v *Kolpinghuis Nijmegen BV* Case 80/86 [1989] 2 CMLR 18 European Court of Justice

• *EC directives – non-implementation – right of State authorities to rely on non-implemented directives – criminal proceedings, interpretation of national law in conformity with EC law – Directive 80/777/EEC*

Facts

Directive 80/777/EEC on the approximation of the laws of the Member States relating to the exploitation and marketing of natural waters had not been implemented in The Netherlands within the prescribed time-limit. After its implementation period elapsed, but before the entry into force of national implementing measures, criminal proceedings were brought against Kolpinghuis Nijmengen for non-compliance of its beverage (intended for trade and human consumption which was called 'mineral water' but which consisted of tap water and carbon dioxide) with art 2 of the Dutch inspection regulation of the municipality of Nijmengen which prohibited the marketing of waters 'of unsound composition' as natural mineral waters. The problem with the Dutch regulation was that it did not define the expression 'unsound composition' although Directive 80/777/EEC contained specific provisions as to the composition of natural mineral water. The Dutch public prosecutor (the Officier van Justitie) argued that the Directive in question should have guided the national court in the interpretation of a national law which predated the Directive, since from the end of the transposition period the Directive had the force of law in The Netherlands.

Held

The ECJ held that a Member State in order to impose criminal liability on individuals could not rely on its own failure to fulfil an obligation arising out of the Treaty. This decision was based on the well established principle that EC dDirectives can never impose direct obligations on individuals since they are addressed to Member States and therefore individuals may only be bound by the legislation or regulations which a Member State to which the directive is addressed is obliged to adopt.

Judgment

'[*The obligation to interpret national law in conformity with EC law*]
As the Court stated in its judgment of 10 April 1984 in Case 14/83 *Von Colson and Kamann* v *Land Nordrhein-Westfalen* [1984] ECR 1891, the Member States' obligation arising from a directive to achieve the result envisaged by the directive and their duty under art 5 of the Treaty to take all appropriate measures, whether general or particular, to ensure the fulfilment of that obligation, is binding on all authorities of Member States including, for matters within their jurisdiction, the courts. It follows that, in applying the national law and in particular the provisions of a national law specifically introduced in order to implement the directive, national courts are required to interpret their national law in the light of the wording and the purpose of the directive in order to achieve the result referred to in the third paragraph of art 189 of the Treaty.

However, that obligation on the national court to refer to the content of the directive when interpreting the relevant rules of its national law is limited by the general principles of law which form part of Community law and in particular the principles of legal certainty and non-retroactivity. Thus the Court ruled in its judgment of 11 June 1987 in Case 14/86 *Pretore di Salo* v *X* [1987] ECR 2545 that a directive cannot, of itself and independently of a national law adopted by a Member State for its implementation, have the effect of determining or aggravating the liability in criminal law of persons who act in contravention of the provisions of that directive.

[*A Member State cannot base proceedings on an unimplemented directive when it failed to implement it within the prescribed time-limit*]
[A]ccording to the established case law of the Court whenever the provisions of a directive appear, as far as their subject matter is concerned, to be unconditional and sufficiently precise, those provisions may be relied upon by an individual against the State where that State fails to implement the directive into national law by the end of the period prescribed or where it fails to implement the directive correctly.

That view is based on the consideration that it would be incompatible with the binding nature which art 189 confers on the directive to hold as a matter of principle that the obligation imposed thereby cannot be relied on by those concerned. From that the Court deduced that a Member State which has not adopted the implementing measures required by the directive within the prescribed period may not plead, as against individuals, its own failure to perform the obligations which the directive entails.'

Comment

In the present case the ECJ defined the limit of a national court's obligation to interpret national law in conformity with EC law. The ECJ held that the uniform interpretation of Community law must be qualified in criminal proceedings where the effect of interpreting national legislation in the light of the Directive would be to impose criminal liability in circumstances where such liability would not arise under the national legislation taken alone. In the present case the ECJ stated that the obligation for a national judge to make reference to the terms of the Directive, when he interprets relevant provisions of national law, is limited by general principles of Community law and especially by the principles of legal certainty and non-retroactivity. This was further explained in *Criminal Proceedings against X* Joined Cases C–74 and 129/95 [1996] ECR I–6609 in which the ECJ held that:

'... the obligation on the national court to refer to the content of the Directive when interpreting the relevant rules of its national law is not unlimited, particularly where such interpretation would have the effect, on the basis of the Directive and independently of legislation adopted for its interpretation, of determining or aggravating the liability in criminal law of persons who act in contravention of its provisions' (Ibid, paragraph 24).

The ECJ explained that the principle of legality in relation to crime and punishment and especially the principle of legal certainty, its corollary, precludes bringing criminal proceedings in respect of conduct not clearly defined as culpable by law. In support of its decision the ECJ referred to the general principles of law which result from the common constitutional tradition of the Member States and art 7 of the European Convention on Human Rights.

Wagner Miret v Fondo de Garantia Salarial Case C–334/92 [1995] 2 CMLR 49 European Court of Justice

- *Directives – horizontal direct effect – interpretation of national law in conformity with EC law – arts 5 and 189 EC Treaty – Directive 80/987/EEC – State liability*

Facts

Wagner Miret was employed as a senior manager in a Spanish company that became insolvent. Under Directive 80/897 Member States were required to set up a fund compensating employees in the case of insolvency of their employer. Spain established such a fund but it did not apply to senior management staff. The referring court asked whether higher management staff were entitled, by virtue of Directive 80/897, to request payment of unpaid salary from the guarantee body established by national law for the other categories of employee or, if this was not the case, whether they were entitled to base their claims on the principle of State liability in tort for incorrect implementation of Directive 80/897.

Held

The ECJ held that Directive 80/897 was not precise enough to produce direct effect and that Spanish law clearly limited access to the fund. Spanish law could not be interpreted in such a way as to include senior management staff within a group of people to be compensated from that fund. As a result, the duty to interpret national law in conformity with Community law was not absolute so as to require interpretation of national law contra legem but only 'so far as possible'. However, Wagner Miret was not left without remedy as he could bring proceedings against Spain for incorrect implementation of Directive 80/897 as a result of which he suffered damage.

Judgment

'It should first be observed that Spain has established no guarantee institution other than the Fondo de Garantia Salarial.

Secondly, in its judgment of 19 November 1991 (Case C–6 and 9/90) *Francovich* v *Italian Republic* [1991] ECR I–5357), the Court held that under art 5 of the directive on the insolvency of employers, the Member States have a broad discretion with regard to the organisation, operation and financing of the guarantee institutions. The Court concluded that even though the provisions of the directive are sufficiently precise and unconditional as regards the determination of the persons entitled to the guarantee and as regards the content of that guarantee, those elements are not sufficient to enable individuals to rely, as against the State, on those provisions, before the national courts.

With regard, more particularly, to the problem raised by the national court, it should be pointed out that the directive on the insolvency of employers does not oblige the Member States to set up a single guarantee institution for all categories of employee, and consequently to bring higher management staff within the ambit of the guarantee institution established for the other categories of employee. Article 3(1) leaves it to the Member States to adopt the measures necessary to ensure that guarantee institutions guarantee payment of employees' outstanding claims.

From the discretion thus given to the Member States it must therefore be concluded that higher management staff cannot rely on the directive in order to request the payment of amounts owing by way of salary from the guarantee institution established for the other categories of employee.

Thirdly, it should be borne in mind that when it interprets and applies national law, every national court must presume that the State had the intention of nullifying entirely the obligations arising from the directive concerned. As the Court held in *Marleasing SA v La Commercial Internacional de Alimentacion SA* Case C–106/89, in applying national law, whether the provision in question was adopted before or after the directive, the national court called upon to interpret it is required to do so, as far as possible, in the light of the wording and the purpose of the directive in order to achieve the result pursued by the latter and thereby comply with the third paragraph of art 189 of the Treaty.

The principle of interpretation in conformity with directives must be followed in particular where a national court considers, as in the present case, that the pre-existing provisions of its national law satisfy the requirements of the directive concerned.

It would appear from the order for reference that the national provisions cannot be interpreted in a way which conforms with the directive on the insolvency of employers and therefore do not permit higher management staff to obtain the benefit of the guarantees for which it provides. If that is the case, it follows from the *Francovich* judgment, cited above, that the Member State concerned is obliged to make good the loss and damage sustained as a result of the failure to implement the directive in their respect.'

Comment

In the present case the ECJ limited the scope of *Marleasing*. National courts are under a duty to take into consideration all national law, whether adopted before or after the directive, concerning the matter in question in order to determine whether national legislation can be interpreted in the light of the wording and the purpose of the directive. The interpretation contra legem is required 'as far as possible'.

8 Free Movement of Goods

Articles 9 and 12 EC Treaty (now arts 23 and 25 EC Treaty

EC Commission* v *Belgium (Re Storage Charges) Case 132/82 [1983] ECR 1649; [1983] 3 CMLR 600 European Court of Justice

- *Free movement of goods – customs duties – arts 9 and 12 EC Treaty – charges having equivalent effect – concept – consideration for service rendered – criteria – storage charges levied on goods presented at public warehouses in the interior of a Member State – permissibility limits*

Facts
The Belgian authorities introduced a system whereby goods in Community transit could undergo customs clearance either at the border or in assigned warehouses within Belgium. If customs clearance in a warehouse was selected, the customs authorities imposed charges on the goods in respect of storage costs.

The Commission took exception to the levying of these costs, alleging that they were charges having an equivalent effect to customs duties and as such were prohibited under arts 9, 12, 13 and 16 of the EC Treaty. The Commission brought proceedings against Belgium before the ECJ.

Held
The ECJ held that charges which are assessed as part of the process of customs clearance on Community goods, or goods in free circulation within the Community, constitute charges having equivalent effect if they are imposed solely in connection with the completion of customs formalities.

Judgment
'The prohibition of charges having an effect equivalent to customs duties, laid down in provisions of the Treaty, is justified on the ground that pecuniary charges imposed by reason or on the occasion of the crossing of a frontier represent an obstacle to the free movement of goods.

It is in the light of those principles that the question whether the disputed storage charges may be classified as charges having an effect equivalent to customs duties must be assessed. It should therefore be noted, in the first place, that the placing of imported goods in temporary storage in the special stores of public warehouses represents a service rendered to traders. A decision to deposit the goods there can indeed be taken only at the request of the trader and then ensures their storage without payment of duties, until the trader has decided how they are to be dealt with.

However, it appears ... that the storage charges are payable equally when the goods are presented at the public warehouse solely for the completion of customs formalities, even though they have been exempted from storage and the importer has not requested that they be put in temporary storage.

Admittedly the Belgian government claims that even in that case a service is rendered to the importer.

It is always open to the latter to avoid payment to the disputed charges by choosing to have his goods cleared through customs at the frontier, where such procedure is free. Moreover, by using a public warehouse, the importer is entitled to have the goods declared through customs near the places for which his products are bound and he is therefore relieved of the necessity of himself either having at his own disposal premises suitable for their clearance or having recourse to private premises, the use of which is more expensive than that of the public warehouses. It is therefore legitimate, in the Belgian government's view, to impose a charge commensurate with that service.

That argument cannot be accepted. Whilst it is true that the use of a public warehouse in the interior of the country offers certain advantages to importers it seems clear first of all that such advantages are linked solely with the completion of customs formalities which, whatever the place, is always compulsory. It should moreover be noted that such advantages result from the scheme of Community transit ... in order to increase the fluidity of the movement of goods and to facilitate transport within the Community. There can therefore be no question of levying any charges for customs clearance facilities accorder in the interest of the Common Market.

It follows from the foregoing, that when payment of storage charges is demanded solely in connection with the completion of customs formalities, it cannot be regarded as the consideration for a service actually rendered to the importer.

Consequently, it must be declared that, by levying storage charges on goods which originate in a Member State or are in free circulation, and which are imported into Belgium, and presented merely for the completion of customs formalities at a special store, the Kingdom of Belgium failed to fulfil its obligations under arts 9 and 12 of the [EC] Treaty.'

Comment
It has been well established that any pecuniary charge, however small and whatever its designation and mode of application, which is imposed unilaterally on goods by reason of the fact that they cross a frontier and which is not a custom duty in the strict sense, is considered as a charge having equivalent effect to a custom duty and as such is prohibited under Community law as contrary to the free movement of goods (*EC Commission* v *Italy (Re Statistical Levy)* Case 24/68 [1969] ECR 193). The only justification for such a charge is when it is levied for a service actually rendered to the importer provided its amount is commensurate with that service (*Germany* v *EC Commission* Cases 52 and 55/65 [1966] ECR 159; *Rewe-Zentralfinanz* v *Landwirt-schaftskammer Westfalen-Lippe* Case 39/73 [1973] ECR 1039). In the present case the ECJ held that when a charge results from the storage of goods in connection with the completion of customs formalities carried out inland it would be in breach of art 13(2) EC Treaty.

EC Commission v *Germany (Re Animals Inspection Fees)* Case 18/87 [1990] 1 CMLR 561 European Court of Justice

- *Articles 9 and 12 EC Treaty – charges having equivalent effect to customs duties – veterinary inspection – Directive 81/389 – charges for inspection of animals for health reasons – charges must not exceed the value of the service*

Facts
Measures were brought into effect throughout the European Community by Council Directive 81/389 which permitted Member States to carry out veterinary inspections on live animals transported into or through their national territories. Certain German provinces, known as 'Länder', charged fees for the cost of conducting those inspections. The charges imposed were justified, according to the German government, to cover the actual costs incurred in maintaining the inspection facilities,

The Commission argued that these charges amounted to charges having an equivalent effect to customs duties and could not be justified under the Directive. Accordingly, the Commission brought an action against Germany before the ECJ.

Held

The ECJ held that the fees did not exceed the actual costs incurred as a consequence of the inspections. The inspections themselves were prescribed by Community law and had the objective of promoting the free movement of goods. Hence, imposing charges genuinely incurred for such services did not amount to charges having equivalent effect to customs duties.

Judgment

'It should be observed in the first place that, as the Court has held on a number of occasions, the justification for the prohibition of customs duties and any charges having an equivalent effect lies in the fact that any pecuniary charge, however small, imposed on goods by reason of the fact that they cross a frontier, constitutes an obstacle to the movement of goods which is aggravated by the resulting administrative formalities. It follows that any pecuniary charge, whatever its designation and mode of application, which is imposed unilaterally on goods by reason of the fact that they cross a frontier and is not a customs duty in the strict sense constitutes a charge having an equivalent effect to a customs duty within the meaning of arts 9, 12, 13, and 16 of the Treaty.

However, the Court has also held that such a charge escapes that classification if it relates to a general system of internal dues applied systematically and in accordance with the same criteria to domestic products and imported products alike (Case 132/78 *Denkavit* v *France* [1979] 3 CMLR 605), if it constitutes payment for a service in fact rendered to the economic operator of a sum in proportion to the service (Case 158/82 *EC Commission* v *Denmark* [1983] ECR 3573; [1984] 3 CMLR 658), or again, subject to certain conditions, if it attaches to inspections carried out to fulfil obligations impose by Community law (Case 4/76 *Bauhuis* v *Netherlands* [1977] ECR 5).

The contested fee, which is payable in importation and transit, cannot be regarded as relating to a general system of internal dues. Nor does it constitute payment for a service rendered to the operator, because this condition is satisfied only if the operator in question obtains a definite specific benefit (see Case 24/68 *EC Commission* v *Italy* [1969] ECR 193; [1971] CMLR 611), which is not the case if the inspection serves to guarantee, in the public interest, the health and life of animals in international transport (see Case 314/82 *EC Commission* v *Belgium* [1984] ECR 1543; [1985] 3 CMLR 134).

Since the contested fee was charged in connection with inspections carried out pursuant to a Community provision, it should be noted that according to the case law of the Court (*Bauhuis*, cited above; *EC Commission* v *Netherlands* [1977] ECR 1355; [1978] 3 CMLR 630; Case 1/83 *IFG* v *Freistaat Bayern* [1984] ECR 349; [1985] 1 CMLR 453) such fees may not be classified as charges having an effect equivalent to a customs duty if the following conditions are satisfied:

a) they do not exceed the actual costs of the inspections in connection with which they are charged;
b) the inspections in question are obligatory and uniform for all the products concerned in the Community;
c) they are prescribed by Community law in the general interest of the Community;
d) they promote the free movement of goods, in particular by neutralising obstacles which could arise from unilateral measures of inspection adopted in accordance with art 36 of the Treaty.

In this instance these conditions are satisfied by the contested fee. In the first place it has not been contested that it does not exceed the real cost of the inspections in connection with which it is charged.

Moreover, all the Member States of transit and destination are required, under, inter alia, art 2(1) of Directive 81/389, cited above, to carry out the veterinary inspections in question when animals are brought into their territories, and therefore the inspections are obligatory and uniform for all the animals concerned in the Community.

Those inspections are prescribed by Directive 81/389, which establishes the measures necessary for the implementation of Council Directive 77/489 on the protection of animals during international transport, with a view to the protection of live animals, an objective which is pursued in the general interest of the Community and not a specific interest of individual States.

Finally, it appears from the preambles to the two above-mentioned directives that they intended to harmonise the laws of the Member States regarding the protection of animals in international transport in order to eliminate technical barriers resulting from disparities in the national laws (see third, fourth and fifth recitals in the preamble to Directive 77/489 and third recital in the preamble to Directive 81/389).

In addition, failing such harmonisation, each Member State was entitled to maintain or introduce, under the conditions laid down in art 36 of the Treaty, measures restricting trade which were justified on grounds of the protection of the health and life of animals. It follows that the standardisation of the inspections in question is such as to promote the free movement of goods.

The Commission has claimed, however, that the contested fee is to be regarded as a charge having equivalent to a customs duty because, in so far as fees of this type have not been harmonised, such harmonisation, moreover, being unattainable in practice – their negative effect on the free movement of goods could not be compensated or, consequently, justified by the positive effects of the Community standardisation of inspections.

In this respect, it should be noted that since the fee in question is intended solely as the financially and economically justified compensation for an obligation imposed in equal measure on all the Member States by Community law, it cannot be regarded as equivalent to a customs duty; nor, consequently, can it fall within the ambit of the prohibition laid down in arts 9 and 12 of the Treaty.

The negative effects which such a fee may have on the free movement of goods in the Community can be eliminated only by virtue of Community provisions providing for the harmonisation of fees, or imposing the obligation on the Member States to bear the costs entailed in the inspections or, finally, establishing that the costs in question are to be paid out of the Community budget.

It follows from the foregoing that the Commission's application must be dismissed.'

Comment

The ECJ held that charges imposed in relation to health inspections required by Community law are not to be regarded as having equivalent effect to custom duties. In the present case the ECJ established strict conditions under which fees charged in connection with inspections prescribed by Community law are not to be considered as charges having an effect equivalent to a custom duty.

Articles 30 and 34 EC Treaty (now arts 28 and 29 EC Treaty)

EC Commission v French Republic
Case C–265/95 [1997] ECR I–6959
European Court of Justice

- *Free movement of goods – a Member State's responsibility for private blockades – obligations of the Member States under arts 30 and 5 EC Treaty*

Facts

The Commission brought proceedings under art 169 EC Treaty against France for failure to take all necessary and proportionate measures to prevent the free movement of fruit and vegetables from being obstructed by actions of private individuals. France had failed to fulfil its obligations under arts 30 and 5 EC Treaty, as well as its obligations flowing from the common organisation of the markets in agricultural products. For a decade the Commission received complaints regarding the passivity of the French government in face of acts of violence and vandalism such as: interception of lorries transporting agricultural products from other Member States and destruction of their loads; threats against French supermarkets, wholesalers and retailers dealing with those products; and damage to such products when on display in shops, etc, committed by French farmers. The Commission supported by the governments of Spain and the UK stated that on a number of occasions French authorities showed unjustifiable leniency vis-à-vis the French farmers, for example by not prosecuting the perpetrators of such acts when their identity was known to the police since often the incidents were filmed by television cameras and the demonstrators' faces were not covered. Furthermore, the French police were often not present on the spot, although the French authorities had been warned of the imminence of demonstrations or they did not interfere, as happened in June 1995 when Spanish lorries transporting strawberries were attacked by French farmers at the same place within a period of two weeks and the police who were present took no protective action. The government of France rejected the arguments submitted by the Commission as unjustified.

Held

The ECJ held that France was in breach of its obligations under art 30 EC Treaty, in conjunction with art 5 EC Treaty, and under the common organisation of the markets in agricultural products for failing to take all necessary and proportionate measures in order to prevent its citizens from interfering with the free movement of fruit and vegetables.

Judgment

'It should be stressed from the outset that the free movement of goods is one of the fundamental principles of the Treaty.

That fundamental principle is implemented by art 30 et seq of the Treaty.

That provision, taken in its context, must be understood as being intended to eliminate all barriers, whether direct or indirect, actual or potential, to flows of imports in intra-Community trade.

As an indispensable instrument for the realisation of a market without internal frontiers, art 30 therefore does not prohibit solely measures emanating from the State which, in themselves, create restrictions on trade between Member States. It also applies where a Member State abstains from adopting the measures required in order to deal with obstacles to the free movement of goods which are not caused by the State.

Article 30 therefore requires the Member States not merely themselves to abstain from adopting measures or engaging in conduct liable to constitute an obstacle to trade but also, when read with art 5 of the Treaty, to take all necessary and appropriate measures to ensure that fundamental freedom is respected on their territory.

In the latter context, the Member States, which retain exclusive competence as regards the maintenance of public order and the safeguarding of internal security, unquestionably enjoy a margin of discretion in determining what measures are most appropriate to eliminate barriers to the importation of products in a given situation.

However, it falls to the Court to verify, in cases brought before it, whether the Member State concerned has adopted appropriate measures for ensuring the free movement of goods.

As regards the present case, the facts which gave rise to the action brought by the Commission against the French Republic for failure to fulfil obligations are not in dispute.

It is therefore necessary to consider whether in the present case the French government complied with its obligations under art 30, in conjunction with art 5, of the Treaty, by adopting adequate and appropriate measures to deal with actions by private individuals which create obstacles to the free movement of certain agricultural products.

It should be stressed that the Commission's written pleadings show that the incidents to which it objects in the present proceedings have taken place regularly for more than ten years.

Moreover, in the present case the Commission reminded the French government on numerous occasions that Community law imposes an obligation to ensure de facto compliance with the principle of the free movement of goods by eliminating all restrictions on the freedom to trade in agricultural products from other Member States.

In the present case the French authorities therefore had ample time to adopt the measures necessary to ensure compliance with their obligations under Community law.

Since 1993 acts of violence and vandalism have not been directed solely at the means of transport of agricultural products but have extended to the wholesale and retail sector for those products.

Further serious incidents of the same type also occurred in 1996 and 1997.

Moreover, it is not denied that when such incidents occurred the French police were either not present on the spot, despite the fact that in certain cases the competent authorities had been warned of the imminence of demonstrations by farmers, or did not intervene, even where they far outnumbered the perpetrators of the disturbances.

As regards the numerous acts of vandalism committed between April and August 1993, the French authorities have been able to cite only a single case of criminal prosecution.

In the light of all the foregoing factors, the Court, while not discounting the difficulties faced by the competent authorities in dealing with situations of the type in question in this case, cannot but find that, having regard to the frequency and seriousness of the incidents cited by the Commission, the measures adopted by the French government were manifestly inadequate to ensure freedom of intra-Community trade in agricultural products on its territory by preventing and effectively dissuading the perpetrators of the offences in question from committing and repeating them.

Although it is not impossible that the threat of serious disruption to public order may, in appropriate cases, justify non-intervention by the police, that argument can, on any view, be put forward only with respect to a specific incident and not, as in this case, in a general way covering all the incidents cited by the Commission.

As regards the fact that the French Republic has assumed responsibility for the losses caused to the victims, this cannot be put forward as an argument by the French government in order to escape its obligations under Community law.

Nor is it possible to accept the arguments based on the very difficult socio-economic context of the French market in fruit and vegetables after the accession of the Kingdom of Spain.

It is settled case law that economic grounds can never serve as justification for barriers prohibited by art 30 of the Treaty.

Having regard to all the foregoing considerations, it must be concluded that in the present case the French government has manifestly and persistently abstained from adopting appropriate and adequate measures to put an end to the acts of vandalism which jeopardise the free movement on its territory of certain agricultural products originating in other Member States and to prevent the recurrence of such acts.'

Comment

This is one of the landmark decisions of the ECJ. Article 30 EC has been used by the ECJ as a principal tool for the removal of all barriers to the free movement of goods. Its scope of application has been gradually extended in order to respond to the development of the Community and its changing economic objectives. However, its remarkable evolution has not yet been completed . This has been confirmed by the ECJ in the present case. Article 30 EC is addressed to the Member States and concerns measures taken by them. The expression 'measures taken by the Member States' has been broadly interpreted to include measures taken by any public body (whether legislative, executive or judicial) as well as any semi-public body (*Apple and Pear Development Council* v *K J Lewis Ltd* Case 222/82 [1984] 3 CMLR 733) or a professional body which exercises regulatory and disciplinary powers conferred upon it by statutory instrument (*R* v *Royal Pharmaceutical Society of Great Britain* Cases 266 and 267/87 [1989] 2 CMLR 751) and even private companies when carrying out activities contrary to art 30 EC supported financially or otherwise by a Member State (*EC Commission* v *Ireland* Case 249/81 [1982] ECR 4005). It has always been accepted that the prohibition contained in art 30 EC concerns some activity, or some action taken by the Member State not passivity or inaction. The ECJ has decided otherwise. The ECJ inferred from the requirements imposed by art 3(c) EC and art 7a EC, which are implemented in art 30 EC, that the latter is also applicable where a Member State abstains from adopting the measures required in order to deal with obstacles to the free movement of goods which are not caused by the State.

Abstention constitutes a hindrance to the free movement of goods and is just as likely to obstruct intra-Community trade as a positive act. However, art 30 EC in itself is not sufficient to engage the responsibility of a Member State for acts committed by its citizens, but is so when read in the light of art 5 EC which requires the Member States not merely themselves to abstain from adopting measures or engaging in conduct liable to constitute an obstacle to trade but also to take all necessary and appropriate measures to ensure that fundamental freedom regarding the free movement of goods is respected on their territory.

Notwithstanding the fact that the ECJ recognises that a Member State has exclusive competences in relation to the maintenance of public order and the safeguard of internal security, it assesses the exercise of that competence by a Member State in the light of art 30 EC! As a result, the ECJ states that the French authorities failed to fulfil their obligations under the Treaty on two counts: first, they did not take necessary preventive and penal measures; and, second, the frequency and seriousness of the incidents taking into account the passivity of the French authorities not only made the importation of goods into France more difficult but also created a climate of insecurity which adversely affected the entire inter-Community trade.

The decision of the ECJ has far-reaching implications. It means that, a Member State may be liable under art 30 EC linked with art 5 EC if it does not prevent or adequately punish conduct of its economic operators which is capable of hindering the free movement of goods. Therefore, a Member State is forced to intervene in situations where, for example, private individuals decide to promote national products or otherwise obstruct inter-Community trade.

The ECJ rejected the three defences put forward by the French government.

Keck and Mithouard, Criminal Proceedings against Joined Cases C–267 and 268/91 [1993] ECR I–6097 European Court of Justice

• *Free movement of goods – measures having equivalent effect – concept – obstacles resulting from national provisions regulating selling arrangements not discriminatory – prohibition of resale at a loss – inapplicability of art 30 EC Treaty*

Facts

The French authorities commenced criminal proceedings against Keck and Methouard for selling goods at a price lower than their actual price (resale at a loss) which was in breach of French law of 1963, as amended in 1986, although that law did not ban sales at loss by the manufacturers. Both offenders argued that the law in question was contrary to fundamental freedoms under the EC Treaty: free movement of goods, persons, services and capital as well as in breach of EC competition law. The French court referred to the ECJ.

Held
The ECJ dismissed all arguments but one based on the free movement of goods. The ECJ held that French law concerned the selling arrangement and as such was outside the scope of art 30 EC Treaty.

Judgment
'By virtue of art 30, quantitative restrictions on imports and all measures having equivalent effect are prohibited between Member States. The Court has consistently held that any measure which is capable of directly or indirectly, actually or potentially, hindering intra-Community trade constitutes a measure having equivalent effect to a quantitative restriction.

It is not the purpose of national legislation imposing a general prohibition on resale at a loss to regulate trade in goods between Member States.

Such legislation may, admittedly, restrict the volume of sales, and hence the volume of sales of products from other Member States, in so far as it deprives traders of a method of sales promotion. But the question remains whether such a possibility is sufficient to characterise the legislation in question as a measure having equivalent effect to a quantitative restriction on imports.

In view of the increasing tendency of traders to invoke art 30 of the Treaty as a means of challenging any rules whose effect is to limit their commercial freedom even where such rules are not aimed at products from other Member States, the Court considers it necessary to re-examine and clarify its case law on this matter.

In 'Cassis de Dijon' (*Rewe-Zentral* v *Bundesmonopolverwaltung für Branntwein* Case 120/78 [1979] ECR 649) it was held that, in the absence of harmonisation of legislation, measures of equivalent effect prohibited by art 30 include obstacles to the free movement of goods where they are the consequence of applying rules that lay down requirements to be met by such goods (such as requirements as to designation, form, size, weight, composition, presentation, labelling, packaging) to goods from other Member States where they are lawfully manufactured and marketed, even if those rules apply without distinction to all products unless their application can be justified by a public-interest objective taking precedence over the free movement of goods.

However, contrary to what has previously been decided, the application to products from other Member States of national provisions restricting or prohibiting certain selling arrangements is not such as to hinder directly or indirectly, actually or potentially, trade between Member States within the meaning of the *Dassonville* judgment (Case 8/74 [1974] ECR 837), provided that those provisions apply to all affected traders operating within the national territory and provided that they affect in the same manner in law and in fact, the marketing of domestic products and of those from other Member States.

Where those conditions are fulfilled, the application of such rules to the sale of products from another Member State meeting the requirements laid down by that State is not by nature such as to prevent their access to the market or to impede access any more than it impedes the access of domestic products. Such rules therefore fall outside the scope of art 30 of the Treaty.'

Comment
The ECJ set new limits on art 30 EC Treaty. It re-examined and clarified its case law on the scope of art 30 EC Treaty and, at the same time departed from its earlier decision in *Dassonville* by stating that the *Dassonville* formula did not apply to selling arrangements if national rules prima facie contrary to art 30 EC Treaty affect all traders operating within the national territory and provided they affect in the same manner, in law and fact, the mar-

keting of both domestic and imported products, even though they may have some impact on the overall volume of sales. The main point made by the ECJ in the present case is a distinction between national rules which relate to the goods themselves and which are within the scope of art 30 EC Treaty and national rules relating to the selling agreements which fall outside the ambit of art 30 EC Treaty provided that the two conditions are satisfied: national rules must apply to all traders operating within the national territory and they must affect in the same manner, in law and fact, the marketing of domestic products and of those from other Member States. The main question is how to determine whether a particular national rule concerns the nature of the product itself or the selling arrangements for that product. In this respect there is still a lot of confusion.

René Kieffer and Romain Thill Case C–114/96 [1997] ECR I–3629
European Court of Justice

- *Free movement of goods – measures having equivalent effect to quantitative restrictions adopted by EC institutions – justification of measures restricting the free circulation of goods based on the principle of proportionality*

Facts
Criminal proceedings were brought against René Kieffer and Romain Thill for failing in 1993 and 1994 to provide information regarding statistical declarations required under Regulation 3330/91. The Regulation in question imposes upon the Member States the obligation to collect from every undertaking above a certain size detailed declarations of all intra-Community imports and exports. In order to gather necessary information undertakings concerned were obliged to incur costs and considerable effort since they had to provide for each transaction, whatever its value, complex data (in particular the eight-digit code from the combined nomenclature). The criminal court of Luxembourg (Tribunal de Police) referred two questions to the ECJ:

1. whether the obligation to provide detailed declarations imposed upon undertakings under Regulation 3330/91 may constitute a measure having equivalent effect to quantitative restrictions contrary to arts 30 and 34 EC Treaty; and
2. whether the obligation in question is in breach of the principle of proportionality as it constitutes an unjustified hindrance to the free movement of goods as well as going beyond what is necessary to achieve the objective of general interest pursued by Regulation 3330/91.

Held
The ECJ upheld the validity of Regulation 3330/91 on the ground that the aim it pursued, namely the completion of the internal market by establishing statistics on the trading of goods between Member States, justified the imposition upon undertakings of an obligation to provide complex data in relation to each intra-Community transaction. Although the obligation in question involved costs and inconvenience for the undertaking concerned, it was not disproportionate as it did not go beyond what was necessary to achieve the objective of general interest pursued by Regulation 3330/91.

Judgment
'It is settled law that the prohibition of quantitative restrictions and of all measures having equivalent effect applies not only to national measures but also to measures adopted by the Community institutions.

It is common ground that the detailed nature of the declarations required and the fact that it is obligatory to make a declaration in both the Member State of consignment and that of destination of the goods have restrictive effects with regard to the free movement of goods.

However, according to the first recital in its preamble, the aim of the Regulation is to promote completion of the internal market by establishing a satisfactory level of information on the trading of goods between Member States by means not involving checks at internal frontiers. Moreover, it appears from the third recital that certain Community policies must be based on statistical documentation providing the most up-to-date, accurate and detailed view of the internal market.

As the Court has already held, barriers to the free movement of goods may be accepted if they are essential in order to obtain reasonably complete and accurate information on movements of goods within the Community.

Consequently, the aim pursued by the Regulation, namely to promote completion of the internal market by establishing statistics on the trading of goods between Member States, appears justified. Moreover, its restrictive effects are commensurate with that aim. It remains to examine whether those restrictive effects are consistent with the principle of proportionality.

According to the Court's case law, in order to establish whether a Community measure complies with the principle of proportionality, it must be ascertained whether the means which it employs are suitable for the purpose of achieving the desired objective and whether they do not go beyond what is necessary to achieve it.

While the obligation to make declarations under the Regulation does specifically affect cross-frontier trade, and drawing up the declarations takes time and involves expense, particularly for small and medium-sized undertakings, it does not necessarily follow that those restrictive effects are disproportionate to the aim pursued.

First, even though undertakings are obliged to make declarations in respect of all transactions, different thresholds have been established precisely in order to enable account to be taken of their interests and not to impose a burden on them which is disproportionate to the results which users of the statistics are entitled to expect.

Second, the Community institutions have made available free of charge to undertakings modern data-processing tools such as the IDEP/CN8 data-capture software.

In view of the above considerations, it does not appear that the obligation to make declarations imposed by the Regulation goes beyond what is necessary to achieve the objective pursued, especially since, as the Court has frequently stated, the Community legislature enjoys a discretion in the framework of its powers of harmonisation.

With respect to the second point raised by the national court's questions, it follows precisely of this judgment that the obligation to make declarations under the Regulation is proportionate to the objective of general interest pursued.'

Comment

The ECJ confirmed that the prohibition of imposition of quantitative restrictions and measures having equivalent effect contained in arts 30 and 34 EC Treaty encompasses not only national measures (that is those enacted by the Member States) but also rules adopted by EC institutions. Although the ECJ has already stated in previous decisions such as *Denkavit Nederland* Case 18/83 [1984] ECR 2171 and *Mehuy and Schott* Case C–51/93 [1994] ECR I–3879 that measures adopted by Community institutions are capable of falling foul of arts 30 and 34 EC Treaty, in this case the ECJ appears to place a firmer emphasis on the possibility that Community acts of general application may hinder intra-Community trade. The ECJ held that Regulation 3330/91 may constitute a quantitative restriction prohibited by arts 30 and 34 EC Treaty and as such its validity may only be upheld if it can be shown that there are objectively justifiable reasons for the adoption of the rules in question. In the present case the ECJ stated that the restrictions imposed by Regulation 3330/91 are justified under the principle of proportionality.

Procureur du Roi v Dassonville Case 8/74 [1974] ECR 837; [1974] 2 CMLR 436 European Court of Justice

• Article 30 – measures having equivalent effect to quantitative restrictions – prohibition – trading rules capable of hindering trade – designation of origin of a product – Scotch whisky – admissibility of protective measures – conditions

Facts
A trader imported Scotch whisky into Belgium. The whisky had been purchased from a French distributor and had been in circulation in France. However, the Belgian authorities required a certificate of origin which could only be obtained from British customs, and which had to be made out in the name of the importers, before the goods could be legally imported into Belgium. As the certificate of origin could not be obtained for the consignment, the defendants went ahead with the transaction. They were charged by the Belgian authorities with the criminal offence of importing goods without the requisite certificate of origin.

The defendants claimed that the requirement of a certificate of origin in these circumstances was tantamount to a measure having an effect equivalent to a quantitative restriction and therefore was prohibited by art 30 of the EC Treaty. The Belgian court referred to the ECJ for a preliminary ruling on this question.

Held
The ECJ defined the concept of a measure having an equivalent effect to a quantitative restriction on imports and decided that the Belgian legislation fell into this classification. Consequently, the requirement of a certificate of origin, which is less easily obtainable by importers of an authentic product than importers of a product in free circulation, constitutes a prohibited measure of equivalent effect to a quantitative restriction.

Judgment
'It emerges from the file and from the oral proceedings that a trader, wishing to import into Belgium Scotch whisky which is already in free circulation in France, can obtain such a certificate only with great difficulty, unlike the importer who imports directly from the producer country.

All trading rules enacted by Member States which are capable of hindering directly or indirectly, actually or potentially, intra-Community trade are to be considered as measures having an effect equivalent to quantitative restrictions.

In the absence of a Community system guaranteeing for consumers the authenticity of a product's designation of origin, if a Member State takes measures to prevent unfair practices in this connection, it is however subject to the condition that these measures should be reasonable and that the means of proof required should not act as a hindrance to trade between Member States and should, in consequence, be accessible to all Community nationals.

Even without having to examine whether or not such measures are covered by art 36, they must not, in any case, by virtue of the principle expressed in the second sentence of that article, constitute a means of arbitrary discrimination or a disguised restriction on trade between Member States. That may be the case with formalities, required by a Member State for the purpose of proving the origin of a product, which only direct importers are really in a position to satisfy without facing serious difficulties.

Consequently, the requirement by a Member State of a certificate of authenticity which is less easily obtainable by importers of an authentic product which has been put into free circulation in a regular manner in another Member State than by importers of the same product coming directly from the country of origin constitutes a measure having an effect equivalent to a quantitative restriction as prohibited by the Treaty.'

Comment
This is one of the leading cases on the free movement of goods. The ECJ held that: 'All trading rules enacted by Member States which are capable of hindering directly or indirectly, actually or potentially, intra-Community trade are to be considered as measures having an effect equivalent to quantitative restrictions.' This is know as the *Dassonville* formula. This formula includes both distinctly applicable measures affecting imports and indistinctly applicable measures affecting imported and domestic products. The formula is very broad, the effect of the measure, including its potential effect (*EC Commission* v *Ireland (Re 'Buy Irish' Campaign)* Case 249/81 [1982] ECR 4005) is decisive in determining whether it should be considered as a measure having an equivalent effect to a quantitative restriction. Discrimin-atory intent is not required.

R v *Royal Pharmaceutical Society for Great Britain* Cases 266 and 267/87 [1989] 2 CMLR 751 European Court of Justice

- *Free movement of goods – rules enacted by professional bodies – statutory authority of such bodies – professional and ethical rules – contrary to art 30 EC – measures having equivalent effect to quantitative restrictions*

Facts
The Pharmaceutical Society of Great Britain is a professional body established to enforce rules of ethics for pharmacists throughout the United Kingdom. This organisation convenes periodic meetings of a committee which has statutory authority to impose disciplinary measures on pharmacists found to have violated these professional rules of ethics.

The Society enacted rules which prohibited a pharmacist from substituting one product for another with the same therapeutic effect, but bearing a different trade mark, when doctors refer to a particular brand of medication. Pharmacists were therefore required to dispense particular brand name products when these were specified in prescription. This rule was challenged as being a measure having an equivalent effect to a quantitative restriction as prohibited by art 30 EC Treaty.

Held
Rules prescribed by regulatory agencies and professional bodies established under statutory authority may constitute measures having an equivalent effect to quantitative restrictions within the meaning of art 30 EC Treaty even though the rules were not enacted by a national legislative body.

Judgment
'Before the question whether the measures at issue fall under the prohibition in art 30 of the Treaty or whether they are justified under art 36 of the Treaty is considered, the point raised by the national court's third question, which is whether a measure adopted by a professional body such as the Pharmaceutical Society of Great Britain may come within the scope of the said articles, should be resolved.

According to the documents before the Court, the Society, which was incorporated by Royal Charter in 1843 and whose existence is also recognised in United Kingdom legislation, is the sole professional body for pharmacy. It maintains the Register in which all pharmacists must be enrolled in order to carry on their business. As can be seen from the order for reference, it adopts rules of ethics applicable to pharmacists. Finally, United Kingdom legislation has established a disciplinary committee within the Society which may impose disciplinary sanctions on a pharmacist for professional misconduct; those sanctions may even involve his removal from the Register. An appeal lies to the High Court decisions of that committee.

It should be stated that measures adopted by a professional body on which national legislation has conferred powers of that nature may, if they are capable of affecting trade between Member States, constitute "measures" within the meaning of art 30 of the Treaty.

The reply to the third question should therefore be that measures adopted by a professional body, such as the Pharmaceutical Society of Great Britain, which lays down rules of ethics applicable to the members of the profession and has a committee upon which national legislation has conferred disciplinary powers that could involve removal from the register of person authorised to exercise the profession, may constitute "measures" within the meaning of art 30 of the [EC] Treaty.'

Comment

In the present case the ECJ held that art 30 EC Treaty applies not only to rules enacted by the Member States but also encompasses rules adopted by a professional body such as the Royal Pharmaceutical Society for Great Britain which exercises regulatory and disciplinary powers conferred upon it by statutory instrument. The ECJ stated that professional and ethical rules adopted by the society which required pharmacists to supply, under a prescription, only a particular brand name drug, may constitute measures having equivalent effect to quantitative restrictions in breach of art 30 EC Treaty. However, in the present case the measures were justified under art 36 EC Treaty.

Rewe-Zentral AG v Bundermonopolverwaltung für Branntwein *(Cassis de Dijon case)* Case 120/78 [1979] ECR 649; [1979] 3 CMLR 337 European Court of Justice

- *Free movement of goods – art 30 EC Treaty – mandatory requirements – legitimate objectives of such requirements – proportionality – rule of reason – rule of recognition*

Facts

German legislation governing the marketing of alcoholic beverages set a minimum alcohol strength of 25 per cent per litre for certain categories of alcoholic products. This regulation prevented an importer from marketing Cassis de Dijon, a French liqueur with an alcohol strength of between 15–20 per cent, into Germany.

The German government invoked human health and consumer protection concerns as the justification for the prohibition. The importer challenged the German legislation in the German court which referred the matter to the ECJ for a preliminary ruling.

Held

The ECJ held that the requirement was tantamount to a measure equivalent to a quantitative restriction and as such was prohibited by art 30 EC Treaty. Although the Court recognised that certain measures may be necessary to the protection of public health, the effectiveness of fiscal supervision, the fairness of commercial transactions and the defence of the consumer, this particular measure could not be justified on these grounds.

Judgment

'In the absence of common rules relating to the protection and marketing of alcohol – a proposal for a regulation submitted to the Council by the Commission on 7 December 1976 (OJ C309 p2) not yet having received the Council's approval – it is for the Member States to regulate all matters relating to the production and marketing of alcohol and alcoholic beverages on their own territory.

Obstacles to movement within the Community resulting from disparities between the national laws relating to the marketing of the products in question must be accepted in so far as those provisions may be recognised as being necessary in order to satisfy mandatory requirements relating in particular to the effectiveness of fiscal supervision, the protection of public health, the fairness of commercial transactions and the defence of the consumer.

The government of the Federal Republic of Germany, intervening in the proceedings, put forward various arguments which, in its view, justify the application of provisions relating to the minimum alcohol content of alcoholic beverages, adducing considerations relating on the one hand to the protection of public health and on the other to the protection of the consumer against unfair commercial practices.

As regards the protection of public health the German government states that the purpose of the fixing of minimum alcohol contents by national legislation is to avoid the proliferation of alcoholic beverages on the national market, in particular alcoholoc beverages with a low alcohol content since, in its view, such products may more easily induce a tolerance towards alcohol than more highly alcoholic beverages.

Such considerations are not decisive since the consumer can obtain on the market an extremely wide range of weakly or moderately alcoholic products and furthermore a large proportion of alcoholic beverages with a high alcohol content freely sold on the German market is generally in a diluted form.

The German government also claims that the fixing of a lower limit for the alcohol content of certain liqueurs is designed to protect the consumer against unfair practices on the part of producers and distributors of alcoholic beverages.

This argument is based on the consideration that the lowering of the alcohol content secures a competitive advantage in relation to beverages with a higher alcohol content, since alcohol constitutes by far the most expensive constituent of beverages by reason of the high rate of tax to which it is subject.

Furthermore, according to the German government, to allow alcoholic products into free circulation wherever, as regards their alcohol content, they comply with the rules laid down in the country of production would have the effect of imposing as a common standard within the Community the lowest alcohol content permitted in any of the Member States, and even of rendering any requirements in this field inoperative since a lower limit of this nature is foreign to the rules of several Member States.

As the Commission rightly observed, the fixing of limits in relation to the alcohol content of beverages may lead to the standardisation of products placed on the market and of their designations, in the interests of a greater transparency of commercial transactions and offers for sale to the public.

However, this line of argument cannot be taken so far as to regard the mandatory fixing of minimum alcohol contents as being as essential guarantee of the fairness of commercial transactions, since it is a simple matter to ensure that suitable information is conveyed to the purchaser by requiring the display of an indication of origin and of the alcohol content on the packaging of products.

It is clear from the foregoing that the requirements relating to the minimum alcohol content of alcoholic beverages do not serve a purpose which is in the general interest and such as to take precedence over the requirements of the free movement of goods, which constitutes one of the fundamental rules of the Community.

In practice, the principle effect of requirements of this nature is to promote alcoholic beverages having a high alcohol content by excluding from the national market products of other Member States which do not answer that description.

It therefore appears that the unilateral requirement imposed by the rules of a member States of a minimum alcohol content for the purposes of the sale of alcoholic beverages constitutes an obstacle to trade which is incompatible with the provisions of art 30 of the Treaty.

There is therefore no valid reason why, provided that they have been lawfully produced and marketed in one of the Member States, alcoholic beverages should not be introduced into any other Member State; the sale of such products may not be subject to a legal prohibition on the marketing of beverages with an alcohol content lower than the limit set by the national rules.

Consequently, the first question should be answered to the effect that the concept of "measures having an effect equivalent to quantitative restrictions on imports" contained in art 30 of the Treaty is to be understood to mean that the fixing of a minimum alcohol content for alcoholic beverages intended for human consumption by the legislation of a Member State also falls within the prohibition laid down in that provision where the importation of alcoholoc beverages lawfully produced and marketed in another Member State is concerned.'

Comment

This is one of the leading cases in the area of free movement of goods. In it the ECJ established two fundamental rules in respect of indistinctly applicable measures:

1. the rule of reason according to which, in the absence of common rules, obstacles to the free movement of goods resulting from disparities between national laws relating to the marketing of the products in question must be accepted in so far as those provisions may be recognised as necessary in order to satisfy mandatory requirements relating in particular to the effectiveness of fiscal supervision, the protection of public health, the fairness of commercial transactions and the defence of the consumer;
2. the rule of recognition which provides that there is no valid reason why goods which have been produced and marketed in one Member State should not be introduced into any other Member State.

The decision in the present case displaced the previous assumption that art 30 EC did not apply to a national measure unless it could be shown that the measure discriminated between imports and domestic products or between different forms of intra-Community trade.

Under the first rule, certain measures which are within the *Dassonville* formula will not infringe art 30 EC Treaty provided they are necessary to protect a mandatory requirement enumerated in the first rule. The list of mandatory requirements is not exhaustive. The ECJ may add additional justifications if necessary.

Under the second rule there is a presumption that goods which have been lawfully marketed in one Member State will comply with mandatory requirements of the State into which they are being imported. For that reason a national rule must not only pursue a legitimate objective but must be necessary and proportionate for the attainment of that objective

Stoke-on-Trent City Council v *B & Q plc* Case 169/91 [1993] 1 CMLR 426; [1993] 1 All ER 481 European Court of Justice

• *Free movent of goods – art 30 EC Treaty – restrictions on shops opening on Sundays – measures having equivalent effect to quantitative restrictions – legitimate socio-economic function – no discrimination caused on the ground of the origin of goods*

Facts

This case concerned the long-running saga of the compatibility of the Sunday trading laws of the United Kingdom with art 30 EC Treaty.

Section 47 of the Shops Act 1950 prohibits the opening of shops in England and Wales on Sundays except for the sale of certain items. The defendants were prosecuted by their local authority for opening their shop on Sundays contrary to this statute. In their defence, the defendants claimed that the prohibition of Sunday opening was contrary to art 30 EC Treaty because this entailed a restriction on trade which had a discriminatory effect on the sale of goods from other Member States.

The matter was finally appealed to the House of Lords which referred to the ECJ for a preliminary ruling along with a number of other cases pending before the lower courts concerning similar points of Community law.

Held

The ECJ held that the statute was not incompatible with art 30 EC Treaty. These restrictions had a legitimate socio-economic function which was recognised under Community law. At the same time, Community law recognised that the manner of achieving these social objectives was the primary responsibility of Member States as long as the means of achieving these objectives did not amount to discrimination and were not unreasonably restrictive.

Judgment

'Appraising the proportionality of national rules which pursue a legitimate aim under Community law involves weighing the national interest in attaining that aim against the Community interest in ensuring the free movement of goods. In that regard, in order to verify that the restrictive effects on intra-Community trade of the rules at issue do not exceed what is necessary to achieve the aim in view, it must be considered whether those effects are direct, indirect or purely speculative and whether those effects do not impede the marketing of imported products more than the marketing of national products.

It was on the basis of those considerations that in its judgments in the *Conforama* and *Marchandise* cases [*Marchandise* Case C–332/89 [1993] 3 CMLR 746; *Conforama* Case C–312/89 [1993] 3 CMLR 746] the Court ruled that the restrictive effects on trade of national rules prohibiting the employment of workers on Sundays in certain retailing activities were not excessive in relation to the aim pursued. For the same reasons, the Court must make the same finding with regard to national rules prohibiting shops from opening on Sundays.

It must therefore be stated in reply to the first question that art 30 of the Treaty is to be interpreted as meaning that the prohibition which it lays down does not apply to national legislation prohibiting retailers from opening their premises on Sundays.'

Comment

In the light of *Keck and Mithouard* the restriction on shops opening on Sundays concerns selling arrangements and as such is outside the scope of art 30 EC Treaty. In *Punto Casa SpA* v *Sindaco del Commune di Capena* Joined Cases C–69 and 258/93 [1994] ECR I–2355 the ECJ held that Italian legislation on the closure of retail outlets on Sundays related to selling arrangements and as such was outside the ambit of art 30 EC Treaty provided that the legislation in question applied equally to domestic and imported products, that is, affecting them in the same manner in law and fact. However, the present case was decided before *Keck and Mithouard* and for that reason the ECJ found justification for the UK Sundays trading laws in socio-economic objectives.

Article 36 EC Treaty (now art 30 EC Treaty)

D Bluhme (Brown Bees of Laesø)
Case C–67/97 Judgment of 3 December 1998 (not yet reported) European Court of Justice

• *Free movement of goods – application of art 30 to different parts of the territory of a Member State – prohibition of quantitative restrictions and measures having equivalent effect between Member States – derogations under art 36 EC – de minimis justification – protection of the health and life of animals – bees of the subspecies apis mellifera mellifera (Laesø brown bees)*

Facts

Criminal proceedings were instituted against Ditlev Bluhme for breach of Danish law prohibiting the keeping on the island of Læsø bees other than those of the subspecies *Apis mellifera mellifera* (brown bees of Laesø). Mr

Bluhme argued that the prohibition constituted a measure having equivalent effect to a quantitative restriction and as such was contrary to art 30, whilst the Dutch authorities claimed that such legislation, even if in breach of art 30 EC Treaty, was justified on the ground of the protection of the health and life of animals.

Held
The ECJ held that the Danish legislation prohibiting the keeping on the island of Læsø of any species of bee other than the subspecies Apis mellifera mellifera constituted a measure having an equivalent effect to a quantitative restriction within the meaning of art 30 EC but it was justified under art 36 EC on the ground of the protection of the health and life of animals.

Judgment
'In so far as art 6 of the [Danish legislation] at issue in the main proceedings involves a general prohibition on the importation onto Læsø and neighbouring islands of living bees and reproductive material for domestic bees, it also prohibits their importation from other Member States, so that it is capable of hindering intra-Community trade. It therefore constitutes a measure having an effect equivalent to a quantitative restriction.

It follows that a legislative measure prohibiting the keeping on an island such as Læsø of any species of bee other than the subspecies Apis mellifera mellifera (Læsø brown bee) constitutes a measure having an effect equivalent to a quantitative restriction within the meaning of art 30 of the Treaty.

Justification for legislation such as that at issue in the main proceedings

Measures to preserve an indigenous animal population with distinct characteristics contribute to the maintenance of biodiversity by ensuring the survival of the population concerned. By so doing, they are aimed at protecting the life of those animals and are capable of being justified under art 36 of the Treaty.

From the point of view of such conservation of biodiversity, it is immaterial whether the object of protection is a separate subspecies, a distinct strain within any given species or merely a local colony, so long as the populations in question have characteristics distinguishing them from others and are therefore judged worthy of protection either to shelter them from a risk of extinction that is more or less imminent, or, even in the absence of such risk, on account of a scientific or other interest in preserving the pure population at the location concerned.

As for the threat of the disappearance of the Læsø brown bee, it is undoubtedly genuine in the event of mating with golden bees by reason of the recessive nature of the genes of the brown bee. The establishment by the national legislation of a protection area within which the keeping of bees other than Læsø brown bees is prohibited, for the purpose of ensuring the survival of the latter, therefore constitutes an appropriate measure in relation to the aim pursued.'

Comment
It is interesting to note that this case confirms the confusion created by *Keck and Mithouard* Cases C–267 and 268/93. Indeed, the arguments submitted by the Danish government intended to exclude the application of art 30 EC Treaty rather than justifying national legislation on the ground of art 36 EC Treaty, in particular the protection of the health and life of animals. The ECJ did not examine the arguments submitted by the Danish government (supported by the Italian and Norwegian governments – the latter is permitted to submit written observations by virtue of of art 20 of the Statute of the ECJ as being a Member State of the EEA) probably because they were either patently wrong or contrary to the well established case law relating to art 30 EC Treaty. The argument that Danish legislation was applicable to a part of the territory was dismissed by the ECJ without any reference to *Aragonesa de Publicidad* Cases C–1 and 171/90 [1991] ECR I–4165 or *Ligur Carni* Cases C–277, 318 and 319/91 [1993] ECR I–6621. The argument based on the de

minimis rule was not discussed by the ECJ probably because it has been well established that art 30 EC Treaty applies to all obstacles to the free movement of goods without taking into account the extent to which they affect trade between Member States (see *Pranti* Case 16/83 [1984] ECR 1299). The argument based on the dichotomy introduced by *Keck and Mithouard* was dealt with in a particularly disappointing manner. In this respect the ECJ stated that the legislation in question focused on intrinsic characteristics of bees and therefore was not concerned with the modality of sale. Finally, the ECJ failed to fully explain the relationship between national measures and the protection of the health and life of animals within the meaning of art 36 EC Treaty. This approach would be welcomed, taking into account that in prior cases in this area the justifications based on the protection of the health and life of animals were made in the context of the prevention of propagation of animal diseases (*EC Commission v Germany* Case C–131/93 [1994] ECR I–3303) or the prevention of unnecessary suffering by animals (*Compassion in World Farming* Case C–1/96 [1998] ECR I–1251). In the present case the ECJ stated that such national measures 'contribute to the maintenance of biodiversity' and 'by so doing, they are aimed at protecting the life of those animals and are capable of being justified under art 36 of the Treaty'. The relationship between the maintenance of biodiversity and the protection of environment, which is outside the scope of art 36 EC Treaty should have been more clearly explained by the ECJ, taking into account that the ECJ has always emphasised that exceptions to art 30 EC Treaty must be strictly interpreted.

Conegate Limited v *HM Customs & Excise* Case 121/85 [1986] ECR 1007; [1986] 1 CMLR 739 European Court of Justice

- *Free movement of goods – art 36 EC Treaty – protection of public morality – abolishment of double morality standards*

Facts
A British company set up businesss importing inflatable dolls from Germany into the United Kingdom. A number of consignment of the products were seized by Customs officilas on the ground that the dolls were 'indecent and obscene', and accordingly subject to the prohibition on imports contained in the Customs Consolidation Act 1876. Although national rules prohibited the importation of these dolls, no regulation prevented their manufacture in the United Kingdom.

The company brought an action for recovery of the dolls. In particular, it was alleged that the prohibition order contravened art 30 EC Treaty, and was accordingly a measure having an effect equivalent to a quantitative restriction. In reply, the British authorities claimed that the measures were justified under art 36 in order to protect public morality.

Held
The ECJ held that the United Kingdom could not rely on art 36 to prohibit the importation of products, when no internal provisions had been enacted to prevent the manufacture and distribution of the offending products within the United Kingdom. To allow a Member State to prevent the importation of particular goods, while simultaniously allowing nationals to manufacture such products, would amount to discrimination on the ground of nationality.

Judgment
'The Court would observe that the first question raises, in the first place, the general problem of whether a prohibition on the importation of certain goods may be justified on grounds of public morality where the legislation of the Member State concerned contains no prohibition on the manufacture or marketing of the same products within the national territory.

So far as that problem is concerned, it must be borne in mind that according to art 36 of the [EC] Treaty the provisions relating to the free movement of goods within the

Community do not preclude prohibitions on imports justified "on grounds of public morality". As the Court held in its judgment of 14 December 1979, cited above [*R v Henn and Darby* Case 34/79 [1979] ECR 3795], in principle it is for each Member State to determine in accordance with its own scale of values and in the form selected by it the requirements of public morality in its territory.

However, although Community law leaves the Member States free to make their own assessment of the indecent or obscene character of certain articles, it must be pointed out that the fact that goods cause offence cannot be regarded as sufficiently serious to justify restrictions on the free movement of goods where the Member State concerned does not adopt, with respect to the same goods manufactured or marketed within its territory, penal measures or other serious and effective measures intended to prevent the distribution of such goods in its territory.

It follows that a Member State may not rely on grounds of public morality in order to prohibit the importation of goods from other Member States when its legislation contains no prohibition on the manufacture or marketing of the same goods on its territory.

It is not for the Court, within the framework of the powers conferred upon it by art 177 of the [EC] Treaty, to consider whether, and to what extent, the United Kingdom legislation contains such a prohibition. However, the question whether or not such a prohibition exists in a State comprised of different constituent parts which have their own legislation, can be resolved by taking into consideration all the relevant legislation. Although it is not necessary, for the purpose of the application of the above mentioned rule, that the manufacture and marketing of the products whose importation has been prohibited should be prohibited in the territory of all the constituent parts, it must at least be possible to conclude from the applicable rules, taken as a whole, that their purpose is, in substance, to prohibit the manufacture and marketing of those products.

In this instance, in the actual wording of its first question the High Court took care to define the substance of the national legislation the compatibility of which with Community law is a question which it proposes to determine. Thus it refers to rules in the importing Member State under which the goods in question may be manufactured freely and marketed subject only to certain restrictions, which it sets out explicitely, namely as absolute prohibition on the transmission of such goods by post, a restriction on their public display and, in certain areas of the Member State concerned, a system of licensing of premises for the sale of those goods to customers aged 18 years and over. Such restrictions cannot however be regarded as equivalent in substance to a prohibition on manufacture and marketing.

At the hearing, the United Kingdom again stressed the fact that at present no articles comparable to those imported by Conegate are manufactured on United Kingdom territory, but that fact, which does not exclude the posssibility of manufacturing such articles and which, moreover, was not referred to by the High Court, is not such as to lead to a different assessment of the situation.

In reply to the first question it must therefore be stated that a Member State may not rely on grounds of public morality within the meaning of art 36 of the Treaty in order to prohibit the importation of certain goods on the grounds that they are indecent or obscene, where the same goods may be manufactured freely on its territory and marketed on its territory subject to an absolute prohibition on their transmisssion by post, a restriction on their public display and, in certain regions, a system of licensing of premises for the sale of those goods to customers aged 18 and over.

That conclusion does not preclude the authorities of the Member State concerned from applying to those goods, once imported, the same restrictions on marketing which are applied to similar products manufactured and marketed within the country.'

Comment

In the light of the objective of completion of the common market, the ECJ decided to abolish double morality standards. In the present case the ECJ held that the United Kingdom could not rely on art 36 EC Treaty to prohibit the importation of inflatable sex dolls and other erotic materials, when no internal provisions had been enacted to prevent the manufacture and distribution of the offending products within the United Kingdom. To allow a Member State to prevent the importation of particular goods, while simultaneously allowing nationals to manufacture such products, would amount to discrimination based on nationality.

Dansk Denkavit v *Ministry of Agriculture* Case 29/87 [1988] ECR 2965; [1990] 1 CMLR 203 European Court of Justice

- *Free movement of goods – complete harmonisation of national laws – Directive 70/524 – identification and purity of additives in feed-stuffs – foreign products subject to more rigorous requirements than domestic products – art 36 EC Treaty – public health – levy charged to cover costs of control – taxation – arts 9 and 95 EC Treaty*

Facts

Directive 70/524 was enacted to harmonise all the national laws of the Member States as regards both the presence of additives and labelling requirements. However, Danish importers of animal feed-stuffs were required to obtain prior approval from the Danish authorities in order to import foreign feed-stuffs. In particular, foreign feed-stuffs were required to comply with certain procedural and labelling requirements which exceeded those specified in the Community directive harmonising procedures for such imports throughout the Community.

In addition Danish importers, as well as domestic producers of the product were charged an annual levy covering the costs of checking samples of the products. The importers challenged both the validity of these additional requirements and the annual levy imposed on all traders in feed-stuffs.

The national court was uncertain whether the annual levy was to be considered under art 12 or under art 95 EC Treaty.

Held

The ECJ held that Directive 70/524 harmonised the identification and the purity of the additives in feed-stuffs. Therefore, it precluded Member States from relying on art 36 in order to imposed national measures in this area, such as the requirement of a prior authorisation which constituted a measure having an effect equivalent to a quantitative restriction on imports. However, Directive 70/524 did not provide for harmonisation of such a nature as to deprive Member States of recourse to art 36 as regards measures of health control applicable to traders concerned.

The annual levy charged in like manner on importers and national producers of feed-stuffs intended to cover the costs incurred by the State in checking samples taken pursuant to Directive 70/524 was held compatible with arts 9 and 95 of the Treaty and of the provisions of that Directive.

Judgment

[*Additional restrictions imposed by Denmark in breach of Directive 70/524*]
Denkavit and the Commission maintain essentially that Directive 70/524 governs exhaustively the identification of additives and their purity in feed-stuffs so that they may circulate freely in the Community without Member States being able to impose health inspection measures not provided by the Directive itself. It follows that the national provisions at issue in the main proceedings cannot be justified under art 36 of the Treaty.

According to the Danish Ministry of Agriculture the presence of impurities in the additives used in feed-stuffs is likely to involve serious risks to public health. It maintains that neither the wording nor the context of Directive 70/524 or any other Community provision referred to the measures necessary for the protection of health. In its view it was only by the adoption of the third amending Directive 84/587 that the harmonisation of such measures was achieved. Prior to this it was for the Member States to take, by virtue of art 36 of the [EC], the measures needed to ensure the identification and purity of the products used as additives.

... [However], the directive expressly provided for the adoption at a Community level of criteria of quality for the substances authorised as additives in feed-stuffs and fixed for the adoption of such criteria a special procedure which may in particular be implemented at the request of a Member State. It follows that the Directive was intended to harmonise all the material conditions for marketing feed-stuffs as regards the presence or absence of additives and as regards marketing in that respect, including criteria of quality. Accordingly, the Member States no longer had the power to fix at national level such criteria of quality and if a Member State considered specific measures relating to the identification and purity of authorised substances to be necessary it had to have recourse to the Community procedure required for that purpose.

Accordingly, the answer to the first question put by the national court must be that Council Directive 70/524, as amended, provides for harmonisation which precludes Member States from relying on art 36 of the Treaty in order to impose, on the importation from other Member States of feed-stuffs containing additives, national measures intended to ensure the identification and the purity of the additives in question.

[*The lawfulness of an annual levy connected with measures of control applicable to traders*]
... the national court seeks essentially to ascertain whether an annual levy imposed in the same manner on importers of feed-stuffs containing additives and national manufacturers of such products and intended to cover the costs incurred by the State in checking samples taken pursuant to Directive 70/524 is compatible with arts 9 and 95 of the Treaty and the provisions of Directive 70/524.

As has been stated above, Directive 70/524, as amended up to the adoption of Directive 84/587, does not prevent Member States from requiring traders to obtain an authorisation. However, the exemption provided for in art 36 of the Treaty with regard to measures of control in regard to traders is solely concerned with restrictions on imports or exports and measures having an equivalent effect. It may not be extended to customs duties or charges having an equivalent effect which, for their part, fall outside the compass of art 36. It follows that the question whether such charges are permissible must be appraised in relation to art 9 or, as the case may be, art 95 of the Treaty.

In this respect the Court has consistently held that the prohibition laid down in art 9 of the Treaty of any customs duty and charge having an equivalent effect in relations between Member States covers any charge levied on the occasion or by reason of importation specifically affecting an imported product to the exclusion of a similar domestic product. Such a charge however does not fall within that classification if, as in the present case, it relates to a general system of internal dues applied systematically and in accordance with the same criteria to domestic products and imported products alike, in which case it does not come within the scope of art 9 but within that of art 95 of the Treaty.

With regard to art 95 Denkavit alleges that in relation to the annual levy the discrimination to the detriment of imports consists in the fact that there may be several buyers from a domestic producer without this involving him in additional charges whereas if a foreign producer has several importers each importer must again pay the charge in question.

That argument cannot be accepted where the burden of the charge in question is borne by traders as such, irrespective of the quantity of products imported or manufactured. As the Court held in its judgment of 28 January 1981 in Case 32/80 *Officier van Justitie* v *Kortmann* [1981] ECR 251, art 95 is complied with where an internal tax applies in accordance with the same criteria, objectively justified by the purpose for which the tax was introduced, to domestic products and imported products so that it does not result in the imported product's bearing a heavier charge than that borne by the similar domestic product.

The answer ... must therefore be that an annual levy charged in like manner on importers and national producers of feedstuffs containing additives and intended to cover the costs incurred by the State in checking samples taken pursuant to Diretive 70/524 is compatible with arts 9 and 95 of the Treaty and the provisions of that Directive.'

Comment
When national laws of the Member States have been harmonised at the Community level, the legality of additional requirements imposed by a Member State in the harmonised area depends upon whether or not the Community harmonisation is complete or partial. In the present case the ECJ held that Directive 70/524 was intended to harmonise all the material conditions for marketing feedstuffs, including the identification of additives and their purity. Consequently, a Member State was prohibited from imposing addditional requirement in this area. However, health inspections were not covered by the Directive. As a result the justification based on the protection of public health was accepted by the ECJ.

The interesting point in relation to the annual levy is that it is sometimes difficult to distinguish between charges under art 12 EC Treaty and discriminatory taxation covered by art 95 EC Treaty since both are fiscal barriers to trade. However, it has been well settled that arts 12 and 95 cannot apply to the same case (*Lutticke* v *HZA Saarlouis* Case 57/65 [1966] ECR 205). In the present case the ECJ held that the annual levy was within the scope of art 95 EC Treaty as it was related to a general system of internal taxation which applied systematically and in accordance with the same criteria to domestic and imported products.

Gunnar Nilsson, per Olov Hagelgren, Solweig Arrborn Case C–162/97 Judgment of 19 November 1998 (not yet reported) European Court of Justice

- *Free movement of goods – prohibition of quantitative restrictions and measures having equivalent effect – derogations under art 36 EC Treaty – protection of the life and health of animals – harmonisation of conditions on pure bred-breeding animals of the bovine species by EC directives – artificial insemination*

Facts
Swedish authorities brought criminal proceedings against a group of individuals who were selling bovine semen taken from Belgian bulls for insemination of Swedish cows. Swedish law prohibited the use of semen from bulls of breeds with specific genetic weaknesses and Belgian bulls were considered to be such a breed. The offenders argued that Swedish law was contrary to art 30 EC Treaty and that the product in question was subject to harmonised importation rules under EC law. The Swedish authorities claimed that national law was justified on the ground of the protection of animal health and in particular the protection of animals from any breeding liable to entail suffering for animals or to affect their behaviour. The Swedish court referred two questions to the ECJ:

1. whether art 30 of the Treaty or Directive 87/328 precludes national rules under which authorisation is required for insemination activities concerning bovine

animals, in particular the distribution of and insemination with semen; and
2. whether art 30 or Directive 87/328 precludes national rules prohibiting or subjecting to certain conditions the insemination and breeding of bovine animals where those activities are liable, in the opinion of the competent national authorities, to entail suffering for animals or affect their natural behaviour, or where the breed in question is regarded by those national authorities as carrying genetic defects.

Held
The ECJ held that Swedish law could be justified only if it intended to regulate the qualifications and operations of inseminators. The harmonisation of rules on trading in bull semen at EC level prevents a Member State from operating their own national rules on product quality as well as justifying national rules under the exception contained in art 36 EC, that is, the protection of health and life of animals.

Judgment
'[*First question*]
... an obligation on all traders to have their products distributed by a method authorised under national rules which apply without distinction as to the origin of the products in question, and so do not affect the marketing of products from other Member States differently from that of domestic products, does not fall within the scope of art 30 of the Treaty.

With respect in particular to the conditions of acceptance for breeding of pure-bred breeding animals of the bovine species and their semen, they have been harmonised, with a view to eliminating zootechnical barriers to the free movement of bovine semen, by Directives 77/504 and 87/328. It follows that a requirement whose purpose or effect is to control or verify imports of bovine semen by reference to zootechnical or pedigree considerations could be laid down only in conformity with those directives.

Having regard to that harmonisation, the requirement of authorisation for insemination activities may not be used for the purpose of controlling the genetic quality of breeding animals in a manner not provided for in the directives.

[*Second question*]
The zootechnical and pedigree conditions relating to intra-Community trade in bovine semen have been fully harmonised under Directives 87/328 and 91/174. It follows from that harmonisation that a Member State may not obstruct the use in its territory of the semen of pure-bred bulls where they have been accepted for artificial insemination in another Member State on the basis of tests carried out [in conformity with Community law].

The national authorities of a Member State of import therefore may not prevent the use of the semen of a breeding animal of the bovine species of a breed which has been accepted for artificial insemination on the ground that they regard that breed as carrying a genetic defect.'

Comment
It is not the first time that the ECJ had to resolve the question of compatibility of Directive 87/328 with art 30 EC Treaty (*Centre d'insémination de la Crespelle* Case C–387/93 [1994] ECR I–5077). In the present case the ECJ held that harmonisation of national rules at Community level as to the conditions of acceptance for breeding of pure-bred breeding animals of the bovine species and their semen precludes a Member State from imposing any supplementary requirement in relation to control of imports of bovine semen based on zootechical or pedigree considerations. The ECJ held that Directive 87/328 constituted a complete harmonisation of rules in this area and as such took into consideration legitimate interests of Member States. Consequently, a Member State cannot invoke any of the following arguments:

1. that the breed carries genetic defects;

2. that the use of semen would entail suffering for animals; and
3. that the use of semen would affect animals' natural behaviour

in order to justify national rules preventing the use of the semen from another Member State which on the basis of tests carried out in conformity with Community law accepted the semen of pure-bred bulls for artificial insemination.

However, neither art 30 EC Treaty nor Directive 87/328 impose any restrictions on a Member State in respect of the distribution of semen and on insemination activities provided that national rules in this area apply without distinction as to the origin of the product.

R v *Henn and Darby* Case 34/79 [1979] ECR 3795; [1980] CMLR 246 European Court of Justice

- *Free movement of goods – art 36 EC Treaty – protection of public morality – discretion granted to Member States to assess this standard*

Facts

The defendants imported a number of consignments of obscene films and publications into the UK from The Netherlands. They were caught by customs officials and charged with the criminal offence of being 'knowingly concerned in the fraudulent evasion of the prohibition of the importation of indecent or obscene articles'. In their defence, the defendants claimed that the prohibition on the importation of pornographic material was contrary to art 30 EC Treaty, as it constituted a measure having an equivalent effect to a quantitative restriction. The matter was referred to the ECJ.

Held

Article 30 is subject to a number of exceptions, one of which is contained in art 36 and relates to restrictions intended to protect public morality. The British legislation fell within the scope of this exception and consequently the criminal charges were consistent with Community law.

Judgment

[*First question*]
The first question asks whether a law of a Member State which prohibits the import into that State of pornographic articles is a measure having equivalent effect to a quantitative restriction on imports within the meaning of art 30 of the Treaty.

That article provides that "quantitative restrictions on imports and all measures having equivalent effect" shall be prohibited between Member States. It is clear that this provision includes a prohibition on imports inasmuch as this is the most extreme form of restriction. The expression used in art 30 must therefore be understood as being the equivalent of the expression "prohibitions or restrictions on imports" occurring in art 36.

The answer to the first question is therefore that a law such as that referred to in this case constitutes a quantitative restriction on imports within the meaning of art 30 of the Treaty.

[*Second and third questions*]
The second and third questions are framed in the following terms:

"2. If the answer to Question 1 is in the affirmative, does the first sentence of art 36 upon its true construction mean that a Member State may lawfully impose prohibitions on the importation of goods from another Member State which are of an indecent or obscene character as understood by the laws of that Member State?

3. In particular:

(i) is the Member State entitled to maintain such prohibitions in order to prevent, to guard against or to reduce the likelihood of breaches of the domestic law of all constituent parts of the customs territory of that State?

(ii) is the Member State entitled to maintain such prohibitions having regard to the national standards and characteristics of that State as demonstrated by the domestic laws of the constituent parts of the customs territory of that State including the law imposing the prohibition, notwithstanding variations between the laws of the constituent parts?"

It is covenient to consider these questions together.

Under the terms of art 36 of the Treaty the provisions relating to the free movement of goods within the Community are not to preclude prohibitions on imports which are justified inter alia "on grounds of public morality". In principle, it is for each Member State to determine in accordance with its own scale of values and in the form selected by it the requirements of public morality in its territory. In any event, it cannot be disputed that the statutory provisions applied by the United Kingdom in regard to the importation of articles having an indecent orobscene character come within the powers reserved to the Member States by the first sentence of art 36.

Each Member State is entitled to impose prohibitions on imports justified on grounds of public morality for the whole of its territory, as defined in art 227 of the Treaty, whatever the structure of its constitution may be and however the powers of legislating in regard to the subject in question may be distributed. The fact that certain differences exist between the laws enforced in different constituent parts of a Member State does not thereby prevent that State from applying a unitary concept in regard to prohibitions on imports imposed, on grounds of public morality, on trade with other Member States.

The answer to the second and third questions must therefore be that the first sentence of art 36 upon its true construction means that a Member State may, in principle, lawfully impose prohibitions on the importation from any other Member State of articles which are of an indecent or obscene character as understood by its domestic laws and that such prohibitions may lawfully be applied to the whole of its national territory even if, in regard to the field in question, variations exist between the laws in force in the different constituent parts of the Member State concerned.

[*Fourth, fifth and sixth questions*]
The fourth, fifth and sixth questions are framed in the following terms:

"4. If a prohibition on the importation of goods is justifiable on grounds of public morality or public policy, and imposed with that purpose, can that prohibition nevertheless amount to a means of arbitrary discrimination or disguised restriction on trade contrary to art 36?

5. If the answer to Question 4 is in the affirmative, does the fact that the prohibition imposed on the importation of such goods is different in scope from that imposed by the criminal law upon the possession and publication of such goods within the Member State or any part of it constitute a means of arbitrary discrimination or a disguised restriction on trade between Member States so as to conflict with the requirements of the second sentence of art 36?

6. If it be the fact that the prohibition imposed upon importation is, and a prohibition such as is imposed upon possession and publication is not, capable as a matter of administration of being applied by customs officials responsible for examining goods at the point of importation, would that fact have any bearing upon the answer to Question 5?"

In these questions the House of Lords takes account of the applicants' submissions based upon certain differences between, on the one hand, the prohibition on importing the goods in question, which is absolute and, on the other, the law in force in the various constituent parts of the United Kingdom, which appear to be less strict in the sense that the mere possession of obscene articles for non-commercial purposes does not constitute a criminal offence anywhere in the United Kingdom and that, even if it is generally forbidden, trade in such articles is subject to certain exceptions, notably those in favour of articles having scientific, literary, artistic or educational interest. Having regard to those differences the question has beeen raised whether the prohibition on imports might nor come within the second sentence of art 36.

According to the second sentence of art 36 the restrictions on imports referred to in the first sentence may not "constitute a means of arbitrary discrimination or a disguised restriction on trade between Member States".

In order to answer the questions which have been referred to the Court it is appropriate to have regard to the function of this provision, which is designed to prevent restrictions on trade based on the grounds mentioned in the first sentence of art 36 from being diverted from their proper purpose and used in such a way as either to create discrimination in respect of goods originating in other Member States or indirectly to protect certain national products. That is not the purport of a prohibition, such as that in force in the United Kingdom, on the importation of articles which are of an indecent or obscene character. Whatever may be the differences between the laws on this subject in force in the different parts of the United Kingdom, and notwithstanding the fact that they contain certain exceptions of limited scope, these laws, taken as a whole, have as their purpose the prohibition, or at least, the restraining, of the manufacture and marketing of publications or articles of an indecent or obscene character. In these circumstances it is permissible to conclude, on a comprehensive view, that there is no lawful trade in such goods in the United Kingdom. A prohibition on imports which may in certain respects be more strict than some of the laws applied within the United Kingdom cannot therefore be regarded as amounting to a measure designed to give protection to some national product or aimed at creating arbitrary discrimination between goods of this type depending on whether they are produced within the national territory or another Member State.

The answer to the fourth question must therefore be that if a prohibition on the importation of goods is justifiable on grounds of public morality and if it is imposed with that purpose the enforcement of that prohibition cannot, in the absence within the Member State concerned of a lawful trade in the same goods, constitute a means of arbitrary discrimination or a disguised restriction on trade contrary to art 36.

In these circumstances it is not necessary to answer the fifth and sixth questions.

Comment
In the present case, the ECJ upheld the arguments of the UK government. It is up to a Member State to determine, in accordance with its own scale of values and in the form selected by it, the requirements of public morality in its territory. The UK applied double standards; in the UK only pornographic materials likely to 'deprave or corrupt' were prohibited whilst it was lawful to trade in 'indecent or obscene' literature. The UK imposed more stringent conditions on imported goods than domestic goods which was contrary to the principle of non-discrimination based on nationality (but see *Conegate Limited* v *HM Customs & Excise* Case 121/85 [1986] ECR 1007).

Articles 37 and 90(2) EC Treaty (now arts 31 and 86 EC Treaty)

***Commission of the European Communities (supported by the United Kingdom of Great Britain and Northern Ireland)* v *Kingdom of The Netherlands, Italian Republic, French Republic and Kingdom of Spain* Joined Cases C–157–160/94 [1997] ECR I–5699 European Court of Justice**

• *State monopolies – common market in electricity and natural gas – conditions of application of art 90 EC – action for failure to fulfil an obligation based on arts 30, 34 and 37 of the EC Treaty*

Facts
The Commission brought proceedings under art 169 EC Treaty against The Netherlands, Italy, France and Spain for failure to fulfil their obligations under arts 30, 34 and 37 EC Treaty which failure consisted of establishing and maintaining, as part of a national monopoly of a commercial character, exclusive import and export rights in the electricity and gas industry. The Commission argued that those rights constituted measures equivalent to quantitative restrictions as they prevent producers in other Member States from selling their production in the Member States in question and deprived potential customers from freely choosing their sources of supply.

Held
The ECJ dismissed the application lodged by the Commission for a declaration that, by establishing and maintaining exclusive import and export rights in the electricity and gas industry, the Member States in question failed to fulfill their obligations under art 30, 34 and 37 EC Treaty.

Judgment
'[Case C–157/94 *Commission of the European Communities* v *Kingdom of The Netherlands,* the ECJ repeated the same arguments in all cases.]

'[*The conformity of the exclusive import rights with arts 30 and 37 of the Treaty*]

[*Article 37 of the Treaty*]
Accordingly, without requiring the abolition of those monopolies, that provision prescribes in mandatory terms that they must be adjusted in such a way as to ensure that when the transitional period has ended such discrimination shall cease to exist (paragraph 5). Moreover, even before the expiry of the transitional period, it prohibited the Member States from introducing further discrimination of the kind referred to in art 37(1).

As the Court held in Case 59/75 *Pubblico Ministero* v *Manghera* [1976] ECR 91, and Case C–347/88 *EC Commission* v *Greece* [1990] ECR I–4747, exclusive import rights give rise to discrimination prohibited by art 37(1) against exporters established in other Member States. Such rights are capable of directly affecting the conditions under which goods are marketed only as regards operators or sellers in other Member States.

[*Articles 30 and 36 of the Treaty*]
Since SEP's (NV Samenwerkende Elektriciteitsproduktiebedrijven (hereinafter "SEP") was holding monopoly in The Netherlands by virtue of Ministerial order of 20 March 1990), exclusive import rights are thus contrary to art 37 of the Treaty, it is unnecessary to consider whether they are contrary to art 30 or, consequently, whether they might possibly be justified under art 36 of the Treaty.

Nevertheless, it is still necessary to verify whether the exclusive rights at issue might be justified under art 90(2) of the Treaty.

[*Justification based on art 90(2) of the Treaty*]

The applicability of art 90(2) of the Treaty to State measures which infringe the Treaty rules on free movement of goods
Having regard to the scope to paragraphs 1 and 2 of art 90, and to their combined effect, paragraph 2 may be relied upon to justify the grant by a Member State to an undertaking entrusted with the operation of services of general economic interest of exclusive rights which are contrary to, in particular, art 37 of the Treaty, to the extent to which performance of the particular tasks assigned to it can be achieved only through the grant of such rights and provided that the development of trade is not affected to such an extent as would be contrary to the interests of the Community.

[*The necessity of the exclusive rights at issue for performance of SEP's tasks*]
For the Treaty rules not to be applicable to an undertaking entrusted with a service of general economic interest under art 90(2) of the Treaty, it is sufficient if the application of those rules obstructs the performance, in law or in fact, of the special obligations incumbent upon that undertaking. It is not

necessary for the survival of the undertaking itself to be under threat.

Moreover, it follows from the judgment in Case C–320/91 *Corbeau* [1993] ECR I–2533 that the conditions for the application of art 90(2) are fulfilled in particular if the maintenance of those rights is necessary to enable the holder of them to perform the tasks of general economic interest assigned to it under economically acceptable conditions.

It is undeniable that, if SEP's exclusive import rights were removed, not only certain customers but also the distribution companies would obtain supplies on foreign markets when the prices charged there were lower than those charged by SEP. That possibility would, in fact, be one of the main purposes of opening up the market.

In view of the intrinsic characteristics of electricity and the manner in which it is produced, transmitted and distributed in The Netherlands, it is also clear that such opening up of the market would involve substantial changes in the way the national supply system is run, particularly with regard to SEP's obligation to contribute, through the planning for which it is responsible, to the proper functioning of that system on the basis of costs that are as low as possible and in a socially responsible manner.

Furthermore, the Commission has not disputed that obvious fact but has merely listed, in general terms, certain alternative means which could have been adopted in place of the rights at issue, such as equalisation of the costs linked with public-service obligations as between SEP and the importers.

However, it must be noted that, by thus referring in general terms to certain means as alternatives to the rights at issue, the Commission did not take account of the particular features of the national electricity supply system highlighted by The Netherlands government and did not specifically consider whether those means would enable SEP to perform the tasks of general economic interest assigned to it in compliance with the obligations and constraints imposed upon it, of which the Commission has contested neither the legitimacy nor the legality.

Whilst it is true that it is incumbent upon a Member State relying upon art 90(2) to demonstrate that the conditions laid down by that provision are met, that onus of proof cannot be extended so far as to require the Member State, when setting out in detail the reasons for which, in the event of abolition of the contested measures, the performance, under economically acceptable conditions, of the tasks of general economic interest which it has entrusted to an undertaking would, in its view, be endangered, to go even further and prove, positively, that no other conceivable measure, which by definition would be hypothetical, could enable those tasks to be performed under the same conditions.

In proceedings under art 169 of the Treaty for failure to fulfil an obligation, it is incumbent upon the Commission to prove the allegation that the obligation has not been fulfilled and to place before the Court the information needed to enable the Court to establish that the obligation has not been fulfilled.

In view of the foregoing and, in particular, the fact that the Court has not adopted the legal approach on which both the Commission's reasoned opinion and its application were based, the Court is not in a position, in these proceedings, to consider whether, by granting exclusive import rights to SEP, The Netherlands government in fact went further than was necessary to enable that establishment to perform, under economically acceptably conditions, the tasks of general economic interest assigned to it.

It must however be borne in mind that, for the exclusive import rights of SEP to escape application of the Treaty rules under art 90(2) of the Treaty, the development of trade must not be affected to such an extent as would be contrary to the interests of the Community.

[*The effect on the development of intra-Community trade*]

The Commission has confined itself to pointing out that, for certain measures to be able to escape the application of the Treaty rules under art 90(2), it is necessary not only for the application of those rules directly or indirectly to obstruct performance of the particular task assigned to the undertaking but also that the Community interest should not be affected, but has provided no explanation to demonstrate that, because of SEP's exclusive import rights, the extent of the development of intra-Community trade in electricity has been and continues to be contrary to the interests of the Community.

It should have done so in this case.

Since the Commission took care to state expressly that its application is concerned only with SEP's exclusive import rights and not other rights relating in particular to transmission and distribution, it was under an obligation, in particular, to show how, in the absence of a common policy in the area concerned, development of direct trade between producers and consumers, in parallel with the development of trade between large grids, would have been possible having regard in particular to the existing capacity and arrangements for transmission and distribution.

Comment

The proceedings brought by the Commission in those cases prompted the Member States to adopt on 19 December 1996 Directive 96/92 on common rules for the internal market in electricity. For that reason, the decision of the ECJ in the present cases has lost its weight although the ECJ gave important indications as to the scope of application of arts 37 and 90(2) EC Treaty.

All defendants argued that the exclusive rights at issue might be justified under art 90(2) EC Treaty. The Commission answered that the Member States concerned could not rely on that provision for two reasons: first, because it is impossible to justify national provisions contrary to the rules contained in the EC Treaty under art 90(2) and, second, the conditions of the application of art 90(2) were not satisfied.

In respect to the first argument, contrary to the Commission submission, art 90 is clear and unambiguous. Under art 90(1) EC public undertakings or undertakings to which the Member States have conferred special or exclusive rights are subject to the provisions of the EC Treaty, especially the rules on competition. However, under art 90(2) they escape not only from the application of EC provisions regarding the free movement of goods but Community law as such if the performance of the particular tasks assigned to them can only be achieved through the grant of such rights and provided that the development of trade is not affected to such an extent as would be contrary to the interests of the Community. The ECJ held that taking into account the scope of application of paragraphs 1 and 2 of art 90 and their combined effect, paragraph 2 may be relied upon to justify the grant by a Member State, to an undertaking entrusted with the operation of services of general economic interest, of exclusive rights which are contrary to, in particular, art 37 of the Treaty.

The conditions of application of art 90(2) are the following: the holder of the exclusive rights must be entrusted with the operation of services of general economic interest; it must be impossible for the holder of such exclusive rights to perform the particular task assigned to him if the rules of the EC Treaty apply to him; and, finally, the derogation from the application of the EC Treaty granted to the holder of the exclusive rights must not affect intra-Community trade to such an extent that the interests of the Community are damaged.

Article 95 EC Treaty (now art 90)

EC Commission v Hellenic Republic
Case C–375/95 [1997] ECR I–5981
European Court of Justice

• *Failure to fulfil obligation –. breach of art 95 EC Treaty – prohibition of discriminatory internal taxation – 'similar products' under art 95 EC Treaty – objective justification for indirect taxation based on the protection of the environment*

Facts

The Commission brought proceedings against the Hellenic Republic for introducing and maintaining in force the following national rules contrary to art 95 EC Treaty:

Article 1 of Greek Law 363/1976, as amended by Law No 1676/1986, relating to a special consumer tax applicable to imported used cars under which in the assessment of their taxable value only a 5 per cent reduction of the price of equivalent new cars was permitted for each year of age of the used cars and the maximum reduction was fixed at 20 per cent of the value of equivalent new cars.

Article 3(1) of Law No 363/1976, which was replaced by art 2(7) of Law 2187/1994, concerning the determination of the taxable value of cars in order to levy the flat-rate added special duty which contained no reduction for used cars.

Article 1 of Law No 1858/1989, as amended many times, regarding the reduction of a special consumer tax for anti-pollution technology cars applied only to new cars and not to imported used cars with the same technology.

The Commission stated that the Greek government was in breach of art 95 EC since the above-mentioned legislation created a system of internal taxation which indirectly discriminated against used cars imported from the other Member States in comparison with cars bought in Greece.

The Greek government rejected the arguments of the Commission.

Held

The ECJ held that national rules for calculating special consumer tax and flat-rate added duty in order to determine the taxable value of imported used cars were in breach of art 95 EC. Also, national rules granting tax advantages (reducing the special consumer tax, which applied only to new anti-pollution technology cars and not to imported second-hand cars with the same technology) cannot be objectively justified under art 95 EC. As a result the ECJ held that the Hellenic Republic had failed to fulfil its obligations under art 95 EC Treaty.

The ECJ dismissed a complaint regarding the incompatibility of the old version of the rules regarding payment of the flat-rate added special duty contained in art 3(1) of Greek Law No 363/1976 on the basis that the Commission's reasoned opinion and the application submitted to the ECJ under art 169 EC must be based on identical grounds of complaint. However, it is not necessary that they are completely identical; it is sufficient so long as the essence of the complaint remains intact. For that reason, a complaint concerning a new version of the above mentioned legislation was declared admissible.

Judgment

'[*The first ground of complaint*]
Under its first ground of complaint, the Commission questions the compatibility with art 95 of the Treaty of the rules for calculating the basis of assessment to the special consumer tax for imported used cars inasmuch as they determine the taxable value of those cars by reducing the price of equivalent new cars by 5 per cent for each year of age of the vehicles in question, the maximum reduction allowed as a rule being 20 per cent.

The Greek government contends, primarily, that the Commission's comparison of the treatment of imported used cars and that of used cars bought in Greece is of no relevance on the ground that the latter have already borne the special consumer tax when new.

It should first of all be noted that the special consumer tax does not apply to domestic used-car transactions because it is charged only once, when the vehicle is first purchased within the country, and part of it remains incorporated in the value of those cars.

It is common ground that imported used cars and those bought locally constitute similar or competing products and art 95 therefore applies to the special consumer tax charged on the importation of used cars.

It follows that the Commission was correct in comparing, for the purpose of verifying compliance with art 95, the amount of the special consumer tax borne by imported used cars with the residual portion of the tax still incorporated in vehicles put into circulation in Greece when new before being resold in that country.

In the present case it is not disputed that as a result of the detailed rules for determining the taxable value of imported used cars, the special consumer tax on those vehicles, whatever their condition, is reduced for each year of use by only 5 per cent of the total of the tax charged on a new vehicle, and that reduction cannot as a rule be more than 20 per cent of the total of that tax, however old the vehicle in question may be. At the same time, the residual portion of the special consumer tax incorporated in the value of a used car bought in Greece decreases proportionately as the vehicle depreciates.

It should be noted that, in general, the annual depreciation in the value of cars is considerably more than 5 per cent, that depreciation is not linear, especially in the first years when it is much more marked than subsequently, and, finally, that vehicles continue to depreciate more than four years after being put into circulation.

It follows that the special consumer tax on imported used cars is usually higher than the proportion of the tax still incorporated in the value of used cars already registered and purchased on the Greek market.

Consequently, the Commission's first ground of complaint must be upheld.

[*The second ground of complaint*
Under its second ground of complaint the Commission submits that the detailed rules for calculating the flat-rate added special duty on imported used cars are incompatible with art 95 of the Treaty.

According to settled case law, an application under art 169 of the Treaty is circumscribed by the pre-litigation procedure provided for by that article and, consequently, the Commission's reasoned opinion and the application must be based on identical grounds of complaint.

The Court did, however, make it clear that requirement could not go so far as to make it necessary that, irrespective of the circumstances, the national provisions mentioned in the reasoned opinion and in the application should be completely identical. Where a change in the legislation occurred between those two phases of the procedure, it is sufficient that the system established by the legislation contested in the pre-litigation procedure has as a whole been maintained by the new measures which were adopted by the Member State after the issue of the reasoned opinion and have been challenged in the application.

That is exactly the case with respect to the Greek legislation on the flat-rate added special duty after the amendments introduced in 1994. Accordingly, the Commission's second ground of complaint, in so far as it relates to the new version of that duty, must be declared admissible.

As to the substance, it is sufficient to point out that since Law No 2187/1994 was adopted the detailed rules for determining the taxable value of imported used cars for the purposes of levying the flat-rate added special duty have been similar to those in force for the special consumer tax.

Thus they also give rise to discriminatory taxation of those vehicles.

In the circumstances, the Commission's second ground of complaint must be upheld in so far as it relates to the detailed rules for calculating the flat-rate special added duty on imported used cars as it has been structured since 1994.

[*The third ground of complaint*]
Under its third ground of complaint, the Commission charges the Hellenic Republic with excluding, in all events, imported used cars from the benefit of the reduced rates of special consumer tax applicable to anti-pollution technology cars.

It is not disputed that a Member State cannot, without offending against the prohibition on discrimination laid down in art

95 of the Treaty, confer tax advantages on less polluting cars while refusing those advantages to cars from the other Member States which nevertheless satisfy the same criteria as the domestic cars which do benefit from them.

In those circumstances the Commission's third ground of complaint must be upheld.'

Comment
In the present case the ECJ clarified an important procedural aspect of proceedings under art 169 EC concerning the need for the grounds of complaint and legal arguments to be identically set out in the letter of formal notice, the reasoned opinion and the application for declaration of violation of EC law. The ECJ decided to examine this question *ex officio*. The ECJ stated that the formal requirements could not be so strict as to impose upon the Commission the duty to commence the proceedings ab novo in circumstances where the legislation challenged in the pre-litigation procedure has, as a whole, been maintained by new legislation adopted by the Member State after the issue of the reasoned opinion.

As to the substance the ECJ examined the concept of 'similar products' under art 95 EC Treaty for the purposes of a tax comparison. Imported used cars and used cars bought locally constituted similar or competing products within the meaning of art 95 EC.

The ECJ analysed factors indicating indirect discrimination of imported products. In this respect, it has been well settled that art 95 EC encompasses not only national taxation systems that discriminate according to the origin of goods but also any tax which on its face discriminates on the basis of other factors and results in placing imported products at a disadvantage compared with domestic products (*Humblot* v *Directeur des Services Fiscaux* Case 112/84 [1985] ECR 1367; *Sequela* v *Administration des Impôts* Case 76/87 [1988] ECR 2397). Consequently, not only the rate of direct and indirect internal taxation on domestic and imported products but also the basis of assessment and rules regarding the imposition of the tax are important in determining whether there is a breach of art 95 EC. In this case it is clear that the rules for calculating the basis of assessment of the special consumer tax were discriminatory.

The ECJ rejected the justification for indirect discrimination of imported goods based on the protection of environment. The ECJ recognises that some tax arrangements which differentiate between domestic and imported products are lawful, despite their indirectly discriminatory effect against imported products, provided they are objectively justifiable, that is based on factors unconnected with the nationality (irrespective of origin of the products, see *EC Commission* v *Italy* Case 200/85 [1986] ECR 3953, and recently *Haahr Petroleum* Case C–90/94 [1997] ECR I–4085). In this case, the ECJ rejected the defence based on the protection of the environment since the benefit of the reduced rates of special consumer tax could not be objectively justified as it did not apply to used imported cars which satisfied the same technical criteria as new cars.

9 Intellectual Property

Bayerische Motorenwerke AG (BMW) and BMW Netherland BV v Ronald Karel Deenik Case C–63/97 [1999] 1 CMLR 1099 European Court of Justice

- *Trade mark – infringement – arts 5–7 of Directive 89/104 – unauthorised use of the BMW trade mark in advertisements for a garage business*

Facts

A German car manufacturer BMW and its Dutch branch BMW Netherlands brought an action against Mr Deenik, an independent owner of a garage specialising in the sale of second-hand BMW cars and repairs and maintenance of BMW cars, for using the BMW mark in advertisements of his business. The Hoge Raad (the Supreme Court of The Netherlands) considered that some of the advertisements might be unlawful as suggesting that Mr Deenik's business was affiliated to the trade-mark proprietor's distribution network, whilst other uses of the trade mark such as 'repairs and maintenance of BMW' 'BMW specialist' did not constitute infringement of that mark. The Hoge Raad referred to the ECJ five questions concerning the interpretation of arts 5–7 of Directive 89/104/EEC for a preliminary ruling.

Held

The ECJ held that arts 5–7 of Directive 89/104/EEC prevent the proprietor of a trade mark from prohibiting a third party from using the mark for informing the public that he carries out the repair and maintenance work of goods protected by that mark and put on the market under that mark by the proprietor or with his consent, or that he has specialised or is a specialist in the sale or repair of such goods. However, a reseller is not permitted to use the mark to lead the public to believe that his business is affiliated to the trade-mark proprietor's distribution network or that there is a special relationship between the two undertakings. The Court stated that the use of a trade mark, without the authorisation of its owner, for advertisement purposes such as described in the present case is within the scope of art 5 of Directive 89/104/EEC.

Judgment

'The Hoge Raad is asking the Court to interpret arts 5–7 of the directive so that it can decide whether use of the BMW mark in advertisements such as "Repairs and maintenance of BMWs", "BMW specialist" or "Specialised in BMWs" constitutes infringement of that mark.

It should be borne in mind that arts 6 and 7 of the directive contain rules limiting the right of the proprietor of a trade mark, under art 5, to prohibit a third party from using his mark. In this connection, art 6 provides, inter alia, that the proprietor of a trade mark may not prohibit a third party from using the mark where it is necessary to indicate the intended purpose of a product, provided that he uses it in accordance with honest practices in industrial or commercial matters. Article 7 provides that the proprietor is not entitled to prohibit the use of a trade mark in relation to goods which have been put on the market in the Community under that trade mark by the proprietor or with his consent, unless there exist legitimate reasons for him to oppose further commercialisation of the goods.

[*Questions 2 and 3*]
Whether the use of a trade mark, without the

proprietor's authorisation, in order to inform the public that another undertaking carries out repairs and maintenance of goods covered by that trade mark or that it has specialised, or is a specialist, in such goods constitutes a use of that mark for the purposes of one of the provisions of art 5 of the directive.

[*Questions 4 and 5*]
The national court is in substance asking whether arts 5–7 of the directive entitle the proprietor of a trade mark to prevent another person from using that mark for the purpose of informing the public that he carries out the repair and maintenance of goods covered by a trade mark and put on the market under that mark by the proprietor or with his consent, or that he has specialised or is a specialist in the sale or the repair and maintenance of such goods.

The Court is asked to rule, in particular, on the question whether the trade mark proprietor may prevent such use only where the advertiser creates the impression that his undertaking is affiliated to the trade mark proprietor's distribution network, or whether he may also prevent such use where, because of the manner in which the trade mark is used in the advertisements, there is a good chance that the public might be given the impression that the advertiser is using the trade mark in that regard to an appreciable extent for the purpose of advertising his own business as such, by creating a specific suggestion of quality.

That question must be considered, first, in relation to the advertisements for the sale of second-hand cars and, second, in relation to the advertisements for the repair and maintenance of cars.

[*The advertisements for the sale of second-hand BMW cars*]
Article 7 of the directive for the proprietor of the BMW mark to prohibit the use of its mark by another person for the purpose of informing the public that he has specialised or is a specialist in the sale of second-hand BMW cars, provided that the advertising concerns cars which have been put on the Community market under that mark by the proprietor or with its consent and that the way in which the mark is used in that advertising does not constitute a legitimate reason, within the meaning of art 7(2), for the proprietor's opposition.

The fact that the trade mark is used in a reseller's advertising in such a way that it may give rise to the impression that there is a commercial connection between the reseller and the trade mark proprietor, and in particular that the reseller's business is affiliated to the trade mark proprietor's distribution network or that there is a special relationship between the two undertakings, may constitute a legitimate reason within the meaning of art 7(2) of the directive.

If there is no risk that the public will be led to believe that there is a commercial connection between the reseller and the trade mark proprietor, the mere fact that the reseller derives an advantage from using the trade mark in that advertisements for the sale of goods covered by the mark, which are in other respects honest and fair, lend an aura of quality to his own business does not constitute a legitimate reason within the meaning of art 7(2) of the directive.

It is sufficient to state that a reseller who sells second-hand BMW cars and who genuinely has specialised or is a specialist in the sale of those vehicles cannot in practice communicate such information to his customers without using the BMW mark. In consequence, such an informative use of the BMW mark is necessary to guarantee the right of resale under art 7 of the directive and does not take unfair advantage of the distinctive character or repute of that trade mark.

The advertisements relating to repair and maintenance of BMW cars
So far as those advertisements are concerned, it is still necessary to consider whether use of the trade mark may be legitimate in the light of the rule laid down in art 6(1)(c) of the directive, that the proprietor may not prohibit a third party from using the trade mark to indicate the intended purpose of a product or service, in particular as accessories or spare parts, provided that the use is necessary to indicate that purpose and

is in accordance with honest practices in industrial or commercial matters.

If an independent trader carries out the maintenance and repair of BMW cars or is in fact a specialist in that field, that fact cannot in practice be communicated to his customers without using the BMW mark.'

Comment

In relation to art 5 of Directive 89/104/EEC the ECJ held that both the sale of second-hand BMW cars and the services such as repair and maintenance of BMW cars were within the scope of art 5 of the Directive. In order to determine whether the use of a trade mark is lawful for advertisement purposes the Court distinguished between the sale of goods covered by that trade mark and their repair and maintenance. In the first case, the ECJ confirmed its decision in *Parfums Christian Dior* Case C–337/95 (see below), that is that a reseller is entitled to make use of the trade mark to bring to the public's attention their further commercialisation, although the owner of a trade mark may stop a reseller from using his trade marks if advertisement damages the reputation of the trade marks. If the reseller advertises the goods covered by a trade mark in a manner customary to the resellers sector of trade, the owner of a trade mark may invoke art 7(2) of Directive 89/104/EEC to prohibit the use of its mark by a reseller in special circumstances. It occurs when a reseller advertises in such a manner as to induce the public to believe that there is a commercial connection between the two undertakings. This kind of advertisement is dishonest, unfair and harms legitimate interests of the trade mark owner. However, if there is no risk that the public will have the impression that there is a commercial connection between the two undertakings, the reseller may derive advantage from using the trade mark in the advertisement, in particular to enhance the quality of his business.

In respect of the advertisement for repair and maintenance of BMW cars, the rule of the 'exhaustion of rights' does not apply as there is no further commercialisation of goods. In this context art 6(1)(c) of the Directive lays down the conditions for using a trade mark. A third party is entitled to use the trade mark to indicated the intended purpose of products or services, in particular as accessories or spare parts, provided that the use is necessary to indicate that purpose. In this context, the use of a trade mark is lawful provided there is no risk that the public will be induced to believe that there is a commercial link between the two undertakings.

Parfums Christian Dior SA and Parfums Christian Dior BV v *Evora BV* Case C–337/95 [1997] ECR I–6013; [1998] 1 CMLR 234
European Court of Justice

• *Trade marks and the free movement of goods – meaning of 'exhaustion of rights' in relation to the further commercialisation of the protected goods by a non-authorised reseller – interpretation of arts 5–7 of the First Directive 89/104 on the approximation of the laws of the Member States relating to trade marks*

Facts

The French company Parfums Christian Dior SA (Dior France) and the Dutch company Parfums Christian Dior BV (Dior Netherlands) brought an action against the Dutch company Evora, which operates a chain of chemists' shops under the name of its subsidiary Kruidvat, for infringement of Dior trade marks and copyrights and applied for an order to stop Evora from advertising Dior products in a manner which damaged the luxurious image of Dior products. In a Christmas promotion in 1993 Kruidvat advertised some Dior products. Advertising leaflets of Evora depicted packaging and bottles of some Dior products which, according to the judgment of the referring court, related clearly and directly to the good offered for sale. The advertisement itself was carried out in a manner customary to retailers in this market sector. Kruidvat was neither a distributor of Dior France nor of Dior Netherlands. Dior products sold by the Kruidvat shops were supplied by Evora which obtained them by means of parallel imports.

The President of the Rechbank (lower court) granted Dior's application. On appeal by Evora against that order the Regional Court of Amsterdam set it aside. Dior appealed against that judgment to the Hoge Raad. The Supreme Court of The Netherlands (Hoge Raad) decided that the question of interpretation of the Uniform Benelux Law on Trade Marks should be dealt with by the Benelux Court and the questions on Community law should be referred to the ECJ. In this context the Hoge Raad referred to the ECJ the following questions:

1. Is the Benelux Court or the referring court to be regarded as the court or tribunal against whose decisions there is no judicial remedy under national law and therefore obliged to refer under art 177(3) EC Treaty?
2. On the interpretation of arts 5–7 of Directive 89/104/EEC and, in particular, whether a reseller is entitled to make use of the trade mark to bring to the public's attention the further commercialisation of goods when those trade-marked goods have been previously put on the Community market by or with the consent of the proprietor of the trade mark.
3. The application of the 'exhaustion of rights' rule in the light of art 7(2) of the Directive.
4. The rights of the owner of a trade mark or holder of copyright vis-à-vis a reseller in the context of the free movement of goods.

Held

The ECJ held that under arts 5 and 7 of Directive 89/104 when the owner of the trade mark, either directly or by the grant of licences to a third party, has put trade-marked goods on the Community market a reseller is entitled both to resell those goods and to make use of the trade mark in order to bring to the public's attention the further commercialisation of those goods. However, the owner of a trade mark may by virtue of art 7(2) of the Directive oppose the use of the trade mark for the further commercialisation of protected goods by a non-authorised reseller but only if it is established in the light of the specific circumstances of the case that the use of the trade mark for this purpose seriously damages the reputation of the trade mark.

Similarly, in the context of the free movement of goods, the owner of a trade mark or holder of copyright cannot prevent a reseller who habitually markets, in ways customary in the reseller's sector of trade, articles of the same kind as the protected goods, but not necessarily of the same quality, from using a trade mark or a copyright for the purpose of advertisement of protected goods unless it is established, taking into account the circumstances of a particular case, that the use of those goods for that purpose seriously damages their reputation.

Judgment

'[*The first question*]

By its first question, the Hoge Raad asks whether, in a case where a question relating to the interpretation of the Directive is raised in proceedings in one of the Benelux Member States concerning the interpretation of the Uniform Benelux Law on Trade Marks, it is the highest national court or the Benelux Court which is the national court against whose decisions there is no judicial remedy under national law and which is therefore obliged under the third paragraph of art 177 of the Treaty to make a reference to the Court of Justice.

First of all, it appears that the question submitted by the Hoge Raad is based, quite rightly, on the premises that a court such as the Benelux Court is a court which may submit questions to this Court for a preliminary ruling.

There is no good reason why such a court, common to a number of Member States, should not be able to submit questions to this Court, in the same way as courts or tribunals of any of those Member States.

In this regard, particular account must be taken of the fact that the Benelux Court has the task of ensuring that the legal rules common to the three Benelux States are applied uniformly and of the fact that the procedure before it is a step in the proceedings before the national courts leading to definitive interpretations of common Benelux legal rules.

To allow a court, like the Benelux Court, faced with the task of interpreting Community rules in the performance of its function, to follow the procedure provided for by art 177 of the Treaty would therefore serve the purpose of that provision, which is to ensure the uniform interpretation of Community law.

Next, as regards the question whether a court like the Benelux Court may be under an obligation to refer a question to the Court of Justice, it is to be remembered that, according to the third paragraph of art 177 of the Treaty, where a question of Community law is raised in a case pending before a court or tribunal of a Member State against whose decisions there is no judicial remedy under national law, that court or tribunal must bring the matter before the Court of Justice.

In these circumstances, in so far as no appeal lies against decisions of a court like the Benelux Court, which gives definitive rulings on questions of interpretation of uniform Benelux law, such a court may be obliged to make a reference to this Court under the third paragraph of art 177 where a question relating to the interpretation of the Directive is raised before it.

As regards, further, the question whether the Hoge Raad may be obliged to refer questions to this Court, there is no question that such a national supreme court, against whose decisions likewise no appeal lies under national law, may not give judgment without first making a reference to this Court under the third paragraph of art 177 of the Treaty when a question relating to the interpretation of Community law is raised before it.

However, it does not necessarily follow that, in a situation such as that described by the Hoge Raad, both courts are actually obliged to make a reference to this Court.

If, prior to making a reference to the Benelux Court, a court like the Hoge Raad has made use of its power to submit the question raised to the Court of Justice, the authority of the interpretation given by the latter may remove from a court like the Benelux Court its obligation to submit a question in substantially the same terms before giving its judgment. Conversely, if no reference has been made to the Court of Justice by a court like the Hoge Raad, a court like the Benelux Court must submit the question to the Court of Justice, whose ruling may then remove from the Hoge Raad the obligation to submit a question in substantially the same terms before giving its judgment.

[*The second question*]

By its second question, the Hoge Raad asks in substance whether, on a proper interpretation of arts 5–7 of the Directive, when trade-marked goods have been put on the Community market by or with the consent of the proprietor of the trade mark, a reseller, besides being free to resell those goods, is also free to make use of the trade mark to bring to the public's attention the further commercialisation of those goods.

If the right to prohibit the use of his trade mark in relation to goods, conferred on the proprietor of a trade mark under art 5 of the Directive, is exhausted once the goods have been put on the market by himself or with his consent, the same applies as regards the right to use the trade mark for the purpose of bringing to the public's attention the further commercialisation of those goods.

It follows from the case law of the Court that art 7 of the Directive is to be interpreted in the light of the rules of the Treaty relating to the free movement of goods, in particular art 36 and that the purpose of the "exhaustion of rights" rule is to prevent owners of trade marks from being allowed to partition national markets and thus facilitate the maintenance of price differences which may exist between Member States.

Even if the right to make use of a trade

mark in order to attract attention to further commercialisation were not exhausted in the same way as the right of resale, the latter would be made considerably more difficult and the purpose of the "exhaustion of rights" rule laid down in art 7 would thus be undermined.

[*The third question*]
According to art 7(2) of the Directive, the "exhaustion of rights" rule laid down in paragraph (1) is not applicable where there are legitimate reasons for the proprietor to oppose further commercialisation of trade-marked goods, especially where the condition of the goods is changed or impaired after they have been put on the market.

It follows that, where a reseller makes use of a trade mark in order to bring the public's attention to further commercialisation of trade-marked goods, a balance must be struck between the legitimate interest of the trade mark owner in being protected against resellers using his trade mark for advertising in a manner which could damage the reputation of the trade mark and the reseller's legitimate interest in being able to resell the goods in question by using advertising methods which are customary in his sector of trade.

As regards the instant case, which concerns prestigious, luxury goods, the reseller must not act unfairly in relation to the legitimate interests of the trade mark owner. He must therefore endeavour to prevent his advertising from affecting the value of the trade mark by detracting from the allure and prestigious image of the goods in question and from their aura of luxury.

For example, such serious damage to the reputation of the trade mark could occur if, in an advertising leaflet distributed by him, the reseller did not take care to avoid putting the trade mark in a context which might seriously detract from the image which the trade mark owner has succeeded in creating around his trade mark.

[*The fourth question*]
By its ... question the Hoge Raad asks in substance whether arts 30 and 36 of the Treaty preclude the owner of a trade mark or holder of copyright relating to the bottles and packaging which he uses for his goods from preventing a reseller, by invoking the trade mark right or copyright, from advertising the further commercialisation of those goods in a manner customary to retail traders in the relevant sector. It asks, further, whether this is also the case where the reseller, as a result of the manner in which he uses the trade mark in his advertising material, damages the luxurious and prestigious image of the trade mark, or where the publication or reproduction of the trade mark takes place in circumstances liable to cause damage to the person entitled to the copyright.

Contrary to Dior's contention, the national court is quite right in considering that a prohibition such as that envisaged in the main proceedings may constitute a measure having an effect equivalent to a quantitative restriction, in principle prohibited by art 30. In this regard, it is enough that, according to the judgment referring the questions for a preliminary ruling, the main proceedings concern goods which the reseller has procured through parallel imports and that a prohibition of advertising such as that sought in the main proceedings would render commercialisation, and consequently access to the market for those goods, appreciably more difficult.

As regards the question relating to trade mark rights, it is to be remembered that, according to the case law of the Court, art 36 of the Treaty and art 7 of the Directive are to be interpreted in the same way.

As regards the part of the ... question relating to copyright, it is to be remembered that, according to the case law of the Court, the grounds of protection of industrial and commercial property referred to in art 36 include the protection conferred by copyright.

Literary and artistic works may be the subject of commercial exploitation, whether by way of public performance or by way of the reproduction and marketing of the recordings made of them, and the two essential rights of the author, namely the exclusive right of performance and the exclusive right of reproduction, are not called in question by the rules of the Treaty.

It is also clear from the case law that, while the commercial exploitation of copyright is a source of remuneration for the copyright owner, it also constitutes a form of control on marketing exercisable by the owner and that, from this point of view, commercial exploitation of copyright raises the same issues as that of any other industrial or commercial property.

Having regard to that case-law – there being no need to consider the question whether copyright and trade mark rights may be relied on simultaneously in respect of the same product – it is sufficient to hold that, in circumstances such as those in point in the main proceedings, the protection conferred by copyright as regards the reproduction of protected works in a reseller's advertising may not, in any event, be broader than that which is conferred on a trade mark owner in the same circumstances.'

Comment

The most important question in this case concerned the meaning of the 'exhaustion of rights' in relation to trade marks and copyrights in the situation where a non-authorised reseller, who has obtained protected goods by means of parallel import, proceeds to their further commercialisation, particularly by using trade marks and copyrights to advertise those goods.

The ECJ held that a proper interpretation of arts 5–7 requires that when trade-marked goods have been put on the Community market by or with the consent of the owner of the trade mark, a reseller is entitled not only to resell those goods but also to make use of the trade mark to bring to the public's attention their further commercialisation. Although the rights to make use of a trade mark by the reseller for advertisement purposes are not exhausted in the same way as the right to their resale, the latter would be more difficult if further commercialisation of those goods is not covered by the concept of the 'exhaustion of rights'.

However, the ECJ held that in some circumstances the owner of a trade mark may stop a reseller from advertising the further commercialisation of goods. The legitimate interests of the trade-mark owner must be protected, especially when a reseller is using his trade marks for advertising in a manner which could damage the reputation of the trade marks. In this respect the ECJ emphasised that by virtue of art 7(2) of Directive 89/104 the trade-mark owner may prevent the reputation of his trade mark from being damaged by a reseller. This solution is not new (see for example *Bristol* Cases C–427, 429 and 436/93 [1996] ECR I–3457). However, the ECJ has not particularised the conditions in which the trade-mark owner may control a non-authorised reseller advertising the further commercialisation of protected goods under Community law. The ECJ based its conclusions on art 7(2) of Directive 89/104 and limited its reasoning to the present case. According to the ECJ in order to strike a balance between the legitimate interests of the trade-mark owner regarding the image of luxury which he has created around his trade mark and the right of a reseller to commercialise the protected goods by using advertising methods which are customary in his sector of trade, the reseller must endeavour to prevent his advertising from affecting the value of the trade mark by detracting from the allure and prestigious image of the goods in question and from their aura of luxury. This requirement is particularly difficult to satisfy, taking into account the fact that the reseller is not an authorised distributor of Dior products.

This may lead to surprising results under national law. In many Member States, for example in France, a non-authorised distributor is obliged not to follow too closely the methods of sale and advertisement put in place by the trade mark owner in relation to his network of exclusive distributors. Furthermore, this solution is particularly troublesome for manufacturers and exclusive distributors of luxury perfumes as it places them is a precarious situation. Community competition law has gradually determined the legal framework for agreements between manufacturers and exclusive distributors of perfumes (*Yves Saint-Laurent et Givenchy* Cases T–19 and 88/92 [1996] ECR II–1851, 1931 and 1961). However, now under the free movement of goods (as interpreted in this case), the ECJ introduces insecurity since it permits non-authorised distributors to advertise and to further commercialise the protected goods. The obvious consequence for the authorised distributors is that they may loose their customers.

The ECJ held that in the context of the free movement of goods (that is under arts 30 and 36 EC) the owner of the trade mark or holder of copyright is precluded in relation to bottles and packaging from preventing the reseller from advertising the further commercialisation of those goods in a manner customary to the reseller sector of trade unless it is established in the light of the specific circumstances of the case that the use of those goods for that purpose damages their reputation. The ECJ held that the restriction imposed upon a reseller regarding the advertisement of protected goods may constitute a quantitative restriction contrary to art 30 EC since it would render commercialisation and consequent access to the market for those goods more difficult. As a result, arts 36 EC and 7 of Directive 89/104 should be interpreted in the same way.

The ECJ transposes its solution in respect to trade marks to copyright. This solution is surprising since under Community law trade marks and copyrights are treated differently in the context of the 'exhaustion of rights'. In relation to copyright Community law has always made distinction between those rights which by their nature may be 'exhausted', for instance the right of parallel imports once literary and artistic works have been put into circulation in a Member State (*Musik-Vertrieb* v *GEMA* Case 78/70 [1971] ECR 147), and those which cannot be 'exhausted', such as the right to hire video cassettes in *EMI Electrola, Warner Brothers Inc* v *Christiansen* Case 158/86 [1988] ECR 2605, and see also *Coditel SA* v *Ciné Vog Films* Case 62/79 [1980] ECR 881. Also, a draft directive on copyright submitted on 10 December 1997 favours a more generous approach to copyright protection in the Community and proposes important limitations on the exhaustion principle. This is not the case with trade marks in respect of which Community law does not impose restrictions on the concept of the 'exhaustion of rights'. Therefore, it seems that copyrights and trade marks should not be treated in the same way. This is not the approach of the ECJ.

The ECJ held that the Benelux Court is within the scope of art 177(3) EC Treaty. The ECJ has also explained the circumstances in which both courts – the Hoge Raad and the Benelux Court – are obliged to make a referral. Subject to the *CILFIT* guidelines, the Benelux Court and the Hoge Raad, as courts of last resort, are obliged to refer to the ECJ. In the case of the Hoge Raad, the Supreme Court of The Netherlands if, prior to making a reference to the Benelux Court on matters of interpretation of the Benelux Treaties, it refers to the ECJ, the Benelux Court has to accept a preliminary ruling of the ECJ and is not obliged to submit to the ECJ a question in substantially the same terms before deciding the matter. However, the Benelux Court is obliged to refer to the ECJ if the Hoge Raad decides not to ask for a preliminary ruling.

SABEL BV v *Puma AG, Rudolf Dassler Sport* Case C–151/95 [1998] 1 CMLR 445 European Court of Justice

• *Trade marks and the free movement of goods – Directives 89/104 on approximation of laws relating to trade marks – conditions of validity of registration of trade marks – risk of confusion – likelihood of association*

Facts

Puma AG, a German company, brought proceedings against a Dutch company, SABEL BV, opposing the registration of a trade mark, under the international registration system of the Madrid Arrangement, by SABEL in Germany on the basis that ideas conveyed by the pictorial elements of the mark consisting of the name of SABEL and the representation of a running leopard conflicted with Puma's trade mark of a running puma. Both companies sold similar goods, that is leather and imitation leather products. The German Supreme Court, the Bundesgerichtshof, referred to the ECJ for a preliminary ruling a question on the interpretation of art 4(1) (b) of First Council Directive 89/104. This sets out the additional grounds on which registration of a trade mark may be refused or a registered mark declared invalid if, due to similarity or identity of an earlier registered trade mark with the trade mark to be registered (or already registered but later than the first trade mark) there is a likelihood of confusion of both trade marks on the part of the public, which includes the likelihood of association between the two marks. The German court asked the ECJ to clarify the meaning of the criterion 'likelihood of confusion ... which includes the likelihood of association with the earlier trade mark'.

Held

The ECJ held that the criterion of the 'likelihood of confusion ... which includes the likelihood of association with the earlier trade mark' contained in art 4(1)(b) of Directive 89/104 is to be interpreted as meaning that the mere association which the public might make between two trade marks resulting from a similarity of their semantic content does not constitute in itself a sufficient ground for concluding that there is a likelihood of confusion within the meaning of that provision. Consequently, the registration of a mark cannot be opposed on the ground that there is a similarity between it and another mark unless it is established that there is genuine and properly substantiated likelihood of confusion about the origin of the products or services in question, which should be assessed globally, taking into account all factors relevant to the circumstances of the case.

Judgment

'In its question the Bundesgerichtshof is essentially asking whether the criterion of the "likelihood of confusion ... which includes the likelihood of association with the earlier trade mark" contained in art 4(1) of the Directive is to be interpreted as meaning that the mere association which the public might make between the two marks as a result of a resemblance in their semantic content, is a sufficient ground for concluding that there exists a likelihood of confusion within the meaning of that provision, taking into account that one of those marks is composed of a combination of a word and a picture, whilst the other, consisting merely of a picture, is registered for identical and similar goods, and is not especially well known to the public.

Article 4(1)(b) of the Directive, which sets out the additional grounds on which registration may be refused or a registered mark declared invalid in the event of conflict with earlier marks, provides that a trade mark conflicts with an earlier trade mark if, because of the identity or similarity of both the trade marks and the goods or services covered, there exists a likelihood of confusion on the part of the public, which includes the likelihood of association between the two marks.

... In that connection, it is to be remembered that art 4(1)(b) of the Directive is designed to apply only if, by reason of the identity or similarity both of the marks and of the goods or services which they designate, "their exists a likelihood of confusion on the part of the public, which includes the likelihood of association with the earlier trade mark". It follows from that wording that the concept of likelihood of association is not an alternative to that of likelihood of confusion, but serves to define its scope. The terms of the provision itself exclude its application where there is no likelihood of confusion on the part of the public.

In that respect, it is clear from the tenth recital in the preamble to the Directive that the appreciation of the likelihood of confusion "depends on numerous elements and, in particular, on the recognition of the trade mark on the market, of the association which can be made with the used or registered sign, of the degree of similarity between the goods or services identified". The likelihood of confusion must therefore be appreciated globally, taking into account all factors relevant to the circumstances of the case.

The global appreciation of the visual, aural or conceptual similarity of the marks in question, must be based on the overall impression given by the marks, bearing in mind, in particular, their distinctive and dominant components.

In that perspective, the more distinctive the earlier mark, the greater will be the likelihood of confusion. It is therefore not impossible that the conceptual similarity resulting from the fact that two marks use images with analogous semantic content may give rise to a likelihood of confusion where the earlier mark has a particularly distinctive character, either per se or because of the reputation it enjoys with the public.

However. in circumstances such as those in point in the main proceedings, where the earlier mark is not especially well known to the public and consists of an image with little imaginative content, the mere fact that the two marks are conceptually similar is not sufficient to give rise to a likelihood of confusion.'

Comment

The ECJ held that the likelihood of confusion between the two trade marks depends upon the distinctiveness of the earlier mark either per se or because of the reputation its enjoys with the public. As a result, the criterion of 'likelihood of confusion which includes the likelihood of association with an earlier mark' means that the mere association which the consumers might make between two trade mark with analogous semantic content does not constitute in itself a sufficient ground for concluding that there is a likelihood of confusion.

The decision of the ECJ in the present case is in line with the objective of abolishing obstacles to the free movement of goos but at odds with its earlier decisions. For example in *CNL Sucal* v *Hag (Hag II)* Case C–10/89 [1990] ECR I–3711 the holder was allowed to rely on his trade mark to exclude products made by a third party but bearing a trade mark with a common origin to his, in a manner that would partition the common market. The likelihood of confusion between both products was an essential factor in deciding the case. In this respect the ECJ held that:

> 'To determine the exact effect of this exclusive right which is granted to the owner of the mark, it is necessary to take account of the essential function of the mark, which is to give the consumer or final user a guarantee of the identity of the origin of the marked product by enabling him to distinguish, without any possible confusion, that product from others of a different provenance.'

This approach was confirmed and intensified in *IHT Internationale Heiztechnik GmbH* v *Ideal Standard GmbH* Case C–9/93 [1994] ECR I–2789. The change of approach by the ECJ should be viewed in the light of considerable unification of intellectual property law by the Community. Furthermore, the change in attitude of the ECJ can be explained by the requirements of both the internal and the international market. In the context of the internal market the monopolistic tendencies of non-origin association is contrary to the free movement of goods and free competition. As to the international aspect this was discussed by Advocate-General Jacobs who placed Directive 89/104 and particularly the concept of confusion against the background of the Paris Convention for the Protection of Industrial Property of 20 March 1883 (as revised) and the GATT/TRIPs Agreement under which this concept is considered as the foundation for trade-mark protection.

Silhoutte International Schmied GmbH & Co KG v Hartlauer Handelsgesellschaft mbH Case C-355/96 [1998] ECR I-4799 European Court of Justice

- *Trade mark – exhaustion of trade mark – arts 5 and 7 of Directive 89/104/EEC, goods put on the market in the EEA and in a non-Member State – interpretation of national law in conformity with EC law – direct effect of Directive 89/104/96*

Facts
Silhoutte, a well known manufacturer of spectacles in the higher ranges, uses its trade mark 'Silhoutte' registered in Austria and most countries in the world to sell its product. In October 1995 Silhoutte sold 21,000 out-of-fashion spectacle frames to a Bulgarian company. Silhoutte instructed its representative to inform the purchaser that the frames were to be resold only in Bulgaria and the states of the former Soviet Union and not in the territory of the EU. However, this restriction was not inserted into the contract and it was not clear whether in fact the purchaser was aware of such a restriction. In December 1995 the frames were resold to Hartlauer, a retailer in Austria that sells spectacles and frames for low prices. Hartlauer offered frames bearing Silhoutte's trade mark for sale in Austria. Hartlauer was not supplied by Silhouette because that company considered that distribution of its products by Hartlauer would be harmful to its image as a manufacturer of top-quality fashion spectacles. Silhoutte brought an action for interim relief before the Landesgericht Steyr, seeking an injunction restraining Hartlauer from offering spectacles or spectacle frames for sale in Austria under its trade mark as the sale of cut-price and outmoded spectacle frames would damage its brand reputation within the EU. Silhoutte argued that its trade-mark rights were not exhausted, within the meaning of Directive 89/104/EEC, as they are exhausted only when the goods have been put on the market in the EEA by the proprietor or with his consent. Hautlauer's answer was that Silhouette had not sold the frames subject to any prohibition of or restriction on reimportation and that the Austrian law implementing the Directive did not grant a right to seek prohibitory injunctions. Silhouette's action was dismissed by the Landesgericht Steyr and, on appeal, by the Oberlandesgericht Linz. Silhouette appealed to the Oberster Gerichtshof on a point of law.

The Austrian Oberster Gerichtshof (Supreme Court) referred to ECJ for a preliminary ruling under art 177 EC two questions concerning the interpretation of art 7(1) of Directive 89/104. In particular, the Austrian court asked whether the holder of a trade mark who has consented to market the protected products in the Community and in the EEA can prevent a third party from using his trade mark outside the EEA, or whether he has exhausted his rights when the goods have been put in circulation, by or with his consent, in the Community and in the EEA.

Held
The ECJ held that national rules providing for exhaustion of trade-mark rights in respect of products put on the market outside the EEA under that mark by the proprietor or with its consent are contrary to art 7(1) of First Council Directive 89/104/EEC (as amended by the Agreement on the European Economic Area of 2 May 1992). The Court held that art 7(1) of Directive 89/104 cannot be interpreted as meaning that the proprietor of a trade mark is entitled, on the basis of that provision alone, to obtain an order restraining a third party from using his trade mark for products which have been put on the market outside the European Economic Area under that mark by the proprietor or with his consent.

Judgment
'[*Question 1*]
By its first question the Oberster Gerichtshof is in substance asking whether national

rules providing for exhaustion of trade-mark rights in respect of products put on the market outside the EEA under that mark by the proprietor or with his consent are contrary to art 7(1) of the Directive.

It is to be noted at the outset that art 5 of the Directive defines the "rights conferred by a trade mark" and art 7 contains the rule concerning "exhaustion of the rights conferred by a trade mark".

Like the rules laid down in art 6 of the Directive, which set certain limits to the effects of a trade mark, art 7 states that, in the circumstances which it specifies, the exclusive rights conferred by the trade mark are exhausted, with the result that the proprietor is no longer entitled to prohibit use of the mark. Exhaustion is subject first of all to the condition that the goods have been put on the market by the proprietor or with his consent. According to the text of the Directive itself, exhaustion occurs only where the products have been put on the market in the Community (in the EEA since the EEA Agreement entered into force).

No argument has been presented to the Court that the Directive could be interpreted as providing for the exhaustion of the rights conferred by a trade mark in respect of goods put on the market by the proprietor or with his consent irrespective of where they were put on the market.

In that respect, although the third recital in the preamble to the Directive states that "it does not appear to be necessary at present to undertake full-scale approximation of the trade mark laws of the Member States", the Directive none the less provides for harmonisation in relation to substantive rules of central importance in this sphere, that is to say, according to that same recital, the rules concerning those provisions of national law which most directly affect the functioning of the internal market, and that that recital does not preclude the harmonisation relating to those rules from being complete.

Articles 5–7 of the Directive must be construed as embodying a complete harmonisation of the rules relating to the rights conferred by a trade mark.

Accordingly, the Directive cannot be interpreted as leaving it open to the Member States to provide in their domestic law for exhaustion of the rights conferred by a trade mark in respect of products put on the market in non-member countries.

This, moreover, is the only interpretation which is fully capable of ensuring that the purpose of the Directive is achieved, namely to safeguard the functioning of the internal market.

Finally, the Community authorities could always extend the exhaustion provided for by art 7 to products put on the market in non-member countries by entering into international agreements in that sphere, as was done in the context of the EEA Agreement.

[Question 2]
By its second question the Oberster Gerichtshof is in substance asking whether art 7(1) of the Directive can be construed as meaning that the proprietor of a trade mark is entitled, on the basis of that provision alone, to obtain an order restraining a third party from using its mark for products which have been put on the market outside the EEA under that mark by the proprietor or with his consent.

While it is undeniable that the Directive requires Member States to implement provisions on the basis of which the proprietor of a trade mark, when his rights are infringed, must be able to obtain an order restraining third parties from making use of his mark, that requirement is imposed, not by art 7, but by art 5 of the Directive.

That being so, it is to be remembered, first, that, according to settled case law of the Court, a directive cannot of itself impose obligations on an individual and cannot therefore be relied upon as such against an individual. Second, according to the same case law, when applying domestic law, whether adopted before or after the directive, the national court that has to interpret that law must do so, as far as possible, in the light of the wording and the purpose of the directive so as to achieve the result it has in view and thereby comply with the third paragraph of art 189 of the Treaty. '

Comment
At the time of the dispute Austria was only a member of the EEA. Its national law prior to the implementation of the Directive recognised the principle of international exhaustion according to which once goods had been marketed anywhere by or with the consent of the owner his rights were exhausted and therefore he had no control over the goods. Austrian rules implementing the Directive restricted the exhaustion principle to first marketing within the EEA. For that reason Hartlauer argued that the Directive applied only to the EEA and the question of international exhaustion was left to national law of Member States. The ECJ rejected this argument. The Court considered that art 7 of the Directive had comprehensively resolved the question of exhaustion in the sense that it harmonised law in this area in all Member States. This solution ensures uniformity and is in conformity with the objectives of the Directive. The ECJ emphasised that if some Member States recognised the principle of international exhaustion while others did not, the result may be barriers to the free movement of goods and services within the EEA.

The decision of the ECJ in the present case reinforces the protection conferred upon the proprietor of a trade mark under Community law. Now, he is entitled to stop parallel imports. As a result, there is nothing to prevent him from setting up whatever differing commercial arrangements he likes inside and outside the EEA. However, this solution yields surprising results in the context of competition law, in particular in relation to elimination of obstacles to parallel imports. In *Javico* Case C–306/96 [1998] ECR I–28 April the ECJ held that a clause prohibiting parallel export to the EU of products put into circulation in third countries was prima facie in breach of art 85(1) EC Treaty. Therefore, an undertaking such as Silhoutte can on the basis of art 7 of the Directive alone prevent parallel imports, while an undertaking such as Yves Saint-Laurent Parfums (see *Javico*) which has concluded a commercial agreement with an undertaking situated in a third country will not only be stopped from doing this but in addition will face proceedings under art 85(1) EC Treaty!

Furthermore, the decision of the ECJ in the present case means that consumers in the EEA are no longer able to buy branded goods imported from outside the EEA and obtained from unauthorised sources at a low price.

It is interesting to note, that in the present case the ECJ held that art 5 of the Directive did require Member States to provide the remedy of an injunction in their domestic laws. The ECJ left national court to resolve the question of injunctive relief but brought to their attention the obligation imposed upon them to interpret national law in conformity with Community law taking into account that EC directives cannot have horizontal direct effect and therefore Silhoutte international had no remedy against Hartlauer.

10 Free Movement of Workers: Articles 49–51 EC Treaty (now Articles 39–42 EC Treaty)

Ibiyinka Awoyemi Case C–230/97 Judgment of 29 October 1998 (not yet reported) European Court of Justice

- *Directive – transposition – direct effect – retroactive application of penal law in mitius – free movement of persons – failure to exchange a driving licence issued by one Member State to a national of a non-Member country for a licence from another Member State in which that person is now resident – criminal penalties*

Facts
Criminal proceedings were commenced against Ibiyinka Awoyemi, a Turkish national, for not exchanging his Community driving licence issued by one Member State for a driving licence of the Member State of his current residence, Belgium, within the prescribed time-limit as required under Directive 80/1263. Although Directive 80/1263 did not impose any penalties in the event of failure to comply with the exchange of a driving licence within the prescribed time-limit, Belgian implementing legislation specified such a failure as a criminal offence. The obligation to exchange was abolished by Directive 91/439. The Belgian court asked the ECJ whether it was allowed to apply retroactively to the offender the more favourable provisions of Directive 91/439, even though the offence took place before the expiry of the time-limit prescribed for the implementation of Directive 91/439 and in the absence of national implementing legislation.

Held
The ECJ held that in the above circumstances a Member State was not precluded from treating the national of the non-Member State as driving without a licence liable to imprisonment or fine. The ECJ stated that a non-national of a Member State is entitled to rely on directly effective provisions of Directive 91/439 and that Community law does not prevent a national court from applying retroactively the more favourable criminal provisions of Directive 91/439 even where the offence took place before the date set for compliance with that Directive and in the absence of national measures intended to implement that Directive.

Judgment
'Directive 80/1263 makes no provision for the penalties to be imposed in the event of breach of the obligation laid down in the first subparagraph of art 8(1) to exchange driving licences.

Accordingly, in the absence of Community rules governing the matter, the Member States remain competent in principle to impose penalties for breach of such an obligation.

Moreover, the Member States may not impose a criminal penalty in this area so disproportionate to the gravity of the infringement as to become an obstacle to the free movement of persons (judgment in *Skanavi and Chryssanthakopoulos* of 29 February 1996).

However, a person such as Mr Awoyemi may not rely on that case law.

It follows from the judgment in *Skanavi and Chryssanthakopoulos*, that the justification for the restriction imposed on the power of the Member States to provide for criminal penalties in the event of breach of the obligation to exchange driving licences is the free movement of persons established by the Treaty.

... with regard to the question whether [arts 1(2) and 8(1) of Directive 91/439] are sufficiently precise and unconditional to be capable of being relied upon by an individual in proceedings before a national court, it should be noted, in the first place, that art 1(2) provides for mutual recognition, without any formality, of driving licences issued by Member States and secondly, that art 8(1) replaces simply with a right, conferred on the holder of a valid driving licence issued by one Member State where that person has taken up normal residence in another Member State, the obligation to exchange driving licences within the one-year period referred to in the first subparagraph of art 8(1) of Directive 80/1263.

As the Advocate-General has stressed in points 37 to 41 of his Opinion, those provisions thus impose on Member States clear and precise obligations which consist in the mutual recognition of Community model driving licences and in the prohibition on requiring the exchange of driving licences issued by another Member State, regardless of the nationality of the holder, since the Member States have no discretion as to the measures to be adopted in order to comply with those requirements.

It may be inferred from the direct effect which should therefore be attributed to arts 1(2) and 8(1) of Directive 91/439 that individuals are entitled to rely on them in proceedings before the national courts.'

Comment
The offender was a national of a third country and as such could not invoke the principle of free movement of persons in order to challenge penal sanctions imposed under Belgian law. In *Skanavi* Case C–193/94 (29 February 1996) where a national of a Member State was prosecuted for a similar offence in Belgium, the ECJ held that a Member State was precluded from imposing a criminal penalty in this area so disproportionate to the gravity of the infringement as to become an obstacle to the free movement of persons.

The retroactive application of Community law in order to attenuate the application of penal law has already been permitted by the ECJ in relation to the free movement of capital (see *Bordessa* Cases C–358 and 416/93 [1995] ECR I–361; *Sanz de Lera* Case C–163/94 [1995] ECR I–4821). Its extension to other areas of EC law is not surprising, especially if a Member State has a well established principle of the retroactive effect of more favourable provisions of criminal law.

Bonsignore v *Oberstadtdirektor of the City of Cologne* Case 67/74 [1975] ECR 297 European Court of Justice

• *Free movement of persons – limitation on ground of public policy – arts 3(1) of Directive 64/221 – deportation – general preventive measure*

Facts
An Italian national permanently residing in Germany, Carmelo Bonsignore, shot his brother by accident. The weapon he used was a pistol he had illegally acquired. He was fined for this offence but no punishment was imposed for the accidental killing of his brother. The German authorities ordered his deportation for 'reasons of a general preventive nature' based on 'the deterrent effect which the deportation of an alien found in illegal possession of a firearm would have in immigration circles having regard to the resurgence of violence in the large urban cities'.

The German court referred to the ECJ a question whether art 3 of Directive 64/221/EEC prohibits deportation for reasons of a general preventive nature when it is clear that the individual concerned would not commit further offences.

Held
The ECJ held that art 3(1) and (2) of Directive 64/221/EEC prevents the deportation of a national of a Member State if such deportation is ordered for the purpose of deterring other aliens as a general preventive measure.

Judgment
'According to art 3(1) and (2) of Directive No 64/221 "measures taken on grounds of public policy or of public security shall be based exclusively on the personal conduct of the individual concerned" and "previous criminal convictions shall not in themselves constitute grounds for the taking of such measures".

These provisions must be interpreted in the light of the objectives of the directive which seeks in particular to co-ordinate the measures justified on grounds of public policy and for maintenance of public security envisaged by arts 48 and 56 of the Treaty, in order to reconcile the application of these measures with the basic principle of the free movement of persons within the Community and the elimination of all discrimination, in the application of the Treaty, between the nationals of the State in question and those of the other Member States.

With this view, art 3 of the directive provides that measures adopted on grounds of public policy and for the maintenance of public security against the nationals of Member States of the Community cannot be justified on grounds extraneous to the individual case, as is shown in particular by the requirement set out in paragraph (1) that "only" the "personal conduct" of those affected by the measures is to be regarded as determinative.

As departures from the rules concerning the free movement of persons constitute exceptions which must be strictly construed, the concept of "personal conduct" expresses the requirement that a deportation order may only be made for breaches of the peace and public security which might be committed by the individual affected.

The reply to the question referred should therefore be that art 3(1) and (2) of Directive No 64/221 prevents the deportation of a national of a Member State if such deportation is ordered for the purpose of deterring other aliens, that is, if it is based, in the words of the national court, on reasons of a "general preventive nature".'

Comment
The ECJ held that any departure from the rule concerning free movement of persons must be strictly interpreted. A Member State should base the decision on deportation solely on the requirements embodied in art 3(1) of Directive 64/221, that is taking into account exclusively the personal conduct of the individual concerned. Future behaviour is only relevant in so far as there are clear indications that the individual would commit further offences. In *R* v *Bouchereau* Case 30/77 [1977] ECR 1999 the ECJ held that a likelihood of re-offending may be found in past conduct, although previous criminal convictions do not in themselves constitute grounds for taking measures on the basis of public policy or public security. The Court stated that it is possible that past conduct alone may constitute such a threat to the requirements of public policy when the individual concerned has a 'propensity to act in the same way in the future' as he did in the past.

Lawrie-Blum v *Land Baden-Württenberg* Case 66/85 [1986] ECR 2121 European Court of Justice

• *Freedom of movement of workers – definition of a worker – discrimination based on nationality – employment in public service – art 48(4) EC Treaty*

Facts

Deborah Lawrie-Blum, a British national, was, after successfully passing her examination for the profession of teacher, refused admission to the period of probationary service which had to be completed in order to become a teacher in Germany. During the probationary period a trainee teacher is considered as a civil servant and receives remuneration for conducting classes. Under the German law of Länder Baden-Württenberg only German nationals were admitted to probationary service. Deborah Lawrie-Blum challenged the decision of the German authorities on the basis of art 6 EC Treaty and art 48(2) EC Treaty. The Länder authorities contended that a trainee teacher is not a 'worker' within the meaning of art 48 and that the probationary service should be regarded as employment in the public service within the meaning of art 48(4) EC Treaty.

Held

The ECJ held that a trainee teacher who, under the direction and supervision of the school authorities, is undergoing a period of service in preparation for the teaching profession during which he provides services by conducting classes and receives remuneration must be considered as a 'worker' under art 48(1) EC Treaty irrespective of the legal nature of the employment relationship. The ECJ stated that a trainee teacher cannot be regarded as employed in the public service within the meaning of art 48(4) EC Treaty.

Judgment

'[*The concept of a "worker" under art 48(1) EC Treaty*]

Since freedom of movement for workers constitutes one of the fundamental principles of the Community, the term "worker" in art 48 may not be interpreted differently according to the law of each Member State but has a Community meaning. Since it defines the scope of that fundamental freedom, the Community concept of a "worker" must be interpreted broadly (judgment of 23 March 1982 in *Levin* v *Staatssecretaris van Justitie* Case 53/81 [1982] ECR 1053).

That concept must be defined in accordance with objective criteria which distinguish the employment relationship by reference to the rights and duties of the persons concerned. The essential feature of an employment relationship, however, is that for a certain period of time a person performs services for and under the direction of another person in return for which he receives remuneration.

In the present case it is clear that during the entire period of preparatory service the trainee teacher is under the direction and supervision of the school to which he is assigned. It is the school that determines the services to be performed by him and his working hours and it is the school's instructions that he must carry out and its rules that he must observe. During a substantial part of the preparatory service he is required to give lessons to the school's pupils and thus provides a service of some economic value to the school. The amounts which he receives may be regarded as remuneration for the services provided and for the duties involved in completing the period of preparatory service. Consequently the three criteria for the existence of an employment relationship are fulfilled in this case ...

The fact that trainee teachers give lessons for only a few hours a week and are paid remuneration below the starting salary of a qualified teacher does not prevent them from being regarded as workers. In its judgment in *Levin*, cited above, the Court held that the expression "worker" and "activity as an employed person" must be understood as including persons who, because they are not employed full time, receive pay lower than that for full-time employment provided that the activities performed are effective and genuine. The latter requirement is not called into question in this case.

Consequently the reply to the first part of the question must be that a trainee teacher who under the direction and supervision of the school authorities is undergoing a period of service in preparation for the teaching profession during which he provides services by giving lessons and receives remuneration must be regarded as a worker within the meaning of art 48(1) of the EEC Treaty irrespective of the legal nature of the employment relationship.

[*The concept of "employment in the public service" under art 48(4) EC Treaty*]

... access to certain posts may be limited by reason of the fact that in a given Member State person appointed to such posts have the status of civil servants. To make the application of art 48(4) dependant on the legal nature of the relationship between the employee and the administration would enable the Member States to determine at will the post covered by the exception laid down in that provision.

As the Court has already stated in its judgment of 17 December 1980 in *EC Commission* v *Belgium* Case 149/79 [1980] ECR 3881 and of 26 May in *EC Commission* v *Belgium (No 2)* Case 149/79 [1982] ECR 1845, "employment in the public service" within the meaning of art 48(4), which is excluded from the ambit of art 48(1), (2) and (3), must be understood as meaning those posts which involve direct or indirect participation in the exercise of powers conferred by public law and in the discharge of functions whose purpose is to safeguard the general interest of the State or of other public authorities and which therefore require a special relationship of allegiance to the State on the part of persons occupying them and reciprocity of rights and duties which form the foundation of the bond of nationality. The posts excluded are confined to those which, having regard to the tasks and responsibilities involved, are apt to display the characteristics of the specific activities of the public service in the sphere described above.

Those very strict conditions are not fulfilled in the case of a trainee teacher, even if he does in fact take the decisions described by the Länder Baden-Württemberg.

Consequently, the reply to the second part of the question must be that the period of preparatory service for the teaching profession cannot be regarded as employment in the public service within the meaning of art 48(4) to which nationals of other Member States may be denied access.'

Comment

The ECJ established an autonomous Community definition of a worker. A 'worker' within the meaning of art 48 EC Treaty is a person who performs services of some economic value for and under the direction of another person, in return for which she/he receives remuneration.

In the present case the ECJ provided a Community meaning in respect of the notion of 'employment in the public service' contained in art 48(4) EC Treaty. Two elements are necessary in order to invoke the exception embodied in art 48(4) EC Treaty: the post in question must involve both the exercise of power conferred by public law and the safeguarding of the general interest of the State. As with any exception to a general rule the ECJ restrictively interpreted the notion of 'employment in the public service'. The Member States have tried unsuccessfully to challenge the restrictive approach of the ECJ in a number of cases (see *EC Commission* v *Belgium (No 2)* Case 149/79 [1982] ECR 1845; *EC Commission* v *Italy* Case 225/85 [1986] ECR 2625).

***R* v *Immigration Appeal Tribunal and Surinder Singh, ex parte Secretary of State for the Home Department* Case C-370/90 [1992] 3 CMLR 335 European Court of Justice**

- *Free movement of workers – family members' rights – non-EC spouse – divorce – deportation*

Facts

Mr Singh, an Indian national, married a British citizen in the United Kingdom in 1982. The couple then left the UK to work in Germany for three years where both obtained employment. They subsequently returned to the UK to start a private business. However, at no time during this period did Mr Singh acquire British nationality.

Decree nisi of divorce was made against Mr Singh in July 1987 and the date of expiry of his temporary leave to stay in the UK, which had been periodically extended during his marriage, was brought forward to September of that year. After the expiry of his temporary leave, Mr Singh remained in the UK without permission and, in December 1988, the Secretary of State for the Home Department issued a deportation order against him. In February 1989, after the deportation proceedings had commenced, decree absolute was pronounced in the divorce hearing.

The issue of deportation came before the Immigration Appeal Tribunal, before decree absolute had been pronounced, which held that Mr Singh was entitled to remain in the UK on the ground that he had Community rights, as a spouse of a British citizen, under the principles of the free movement of persons and the right of establishment.

The Secretary of State applied to the High Court for judicial review of this decision and that court referred the question of Mr Singh's right to remain in the UK under Community law to the ECJ for a preliminary ruling.

Held

Where a national of one Member State travels to another for the purpose of obtaining employment the whole gambit of Community rights under the principle of the free movement of workers is activated. These rights are contained not only in art 48 of the EC Treaty but also in secondary legislation including Regulation 1612/68, Directive 68/360 and Directive 73/148.

These measures confer rights on both the worker and his or her spouse and family. In particular, even a non-EC spouse is entitled to such rights as the relevant legislation makes no distinction between EC national spouses and non-EC national spouses.

If these rights have been activated, an individual may rely on the rights stemming from the principle of free movement when returning to his or her own country. This includes the right to be accompanied by a non- EC spouse under the same conditions as other migrant workers.

Once inside the home country, the Community national has the right to establish a business under art 52 and the non-EC spouse is entitled to enjoy at least the same rights in this respect as would be available under Community law on entering and residing in another Member State.

The Court did not rule whether Mr Singh was entitled to remain in the UK after the decree absolute but confined its decision to the interpretation of the rights of Mr Singh during the period before then, since proceedings were commenced before the date of decree absolute.

Judgment

'The provisions of the Council regulations and directives on freedom of movement within the Community for employed and self-employed persons, in particular art 10 of Regulation 1612/68, arts 1 and 4 of Directive 68/360 and arts 1(c) and 4 of Directive 73/148, provide that the Member States must grant the spouse and children of such a person rights of residence equivalent to that granted to the person himself.

A national of a Member State might be deterred from leaving his country of origin in order to pursue an activity as an employed or self-employed person as envisaged by the Treaty in the territory of another Member State if, on returning to the Member State of which he is a national in order to pursue an activity there as an employed or self-employed person, the conditions of his entry and residence were not at least equivalent to those which he would enjoy under the Treaty or secondary law in the territory of another Member State.

He would in particular be deterred from so doing if his spouse and children were not also permitted to enter and reside in the territory of his Member State of origin under conditions at least equivalent to those granted them by Community law in the territory of another Member State.

It follows that a national of a Member State who has gone to another Member State in order to work there as an employed person pursuant to art 48 [EC] and returns to establish himself in order to pursue an activity as a self-employed person in the territory of the Member State of which he is a national has the right, under art 52 [EC] Treaty, to be accompanied in the territory of the latter State by his spouse, a national of a non-Member country, under the same conditions as are laid down by Regulation 1612/68, Directive 68/360 or Directive 73/148.

Admittedly, as the United Kingdom submits, a national of a Member State enters and resides in the territory of that State by virtue of the rights attendant upon his nationality and not by virtue of those conferred on him by Community law. In particular, as is provided, moreover, by art 3 of the Fourth Protocol to the European Convention on Human Rights, a State may not expel one of its own nationals or deny him entry to its territory.

However, this case is concerned not with a right under national law but with the rights of movement and establishment granted to a Community national by arts 48 and 52 [EC] Treaty. These rights cannot be fully effective id such a person may be deterred from exercising them by obstacles raised in his or her country of origin to the entry and residence of his or her spouse. Accordingly, when a Community national who has availed himself or herself of those rights returns to his or her country of origin, his or her spouse must enjoy at least the same rights of entry and residence as would be granted to him or her under Community law if his or her spouse chose to enter and reside in another Member State. Nevertheless, arts 48 and 52 [EC] do not prevent Member States from applying to foreign spouses of their own nationals rules on entry and residence more favourable than those provided for by Community law ...'

Comment

So far the ECJ has not decided on the right of residence of a divorced spouse who is a non-EC national and who was married to an EC national. In the present case the deportation proceedings had been instituted before the decree nisi of divorce was made. Therefore, it is still uncertain to what extent Community law will assist a divorced non-EC national in securing his right of permanent residence, in particular in the light of the principle set up in *Morson and Jhanjan (Re Surinam Mothers)* Cases 35 and 36/82 [1982] ECR 3723 that Community law does not apply to 'wholly internal situations'. In this case two Dutch nationals working and residing in The Netherlands wanted to bring their mothers of Surinamese nationality to reside with them in The Netherlands. Under Dutch law they were not permitted to do so and the ECJ held that Community law did not apply to their situation as there was no link connecting it with EC law.

It is submitted that both the above situations should be resolved on the basis of art 8 of the European Convention on Human Rights taking into account that fundamental principles of human rights are part of Community law. In this respect the European Court of Human Rights in *Berrehab* (21 June 1988, series A no 138, pp15 and 16) held that the expulsion of a divorced husband whose child remained in Belgium was contrary to art 8 the ECHR. The European Court of Human Rights did not grant an automatic right of residence to a divorced spouse but took into consideration the degree of contact between the divorced parent and the child. This solution is also in line which the ECJ judgment in *Kus* v *Landeshaupt Stadt Wiesbaden* Case C–237/91 [1992] ECR I–6781 in which it was decided that a Turkish national who married an EC national (and on that basis was granted the right of residence in a Member State) was allowed to reside after his divorce on two grounds: first, he was lawfully working in that Member State and, second, on the basis of certain provisions of the EEC-Turkey

Association Agreement. In this case the ECJ held that the divorce did not affect the legality of his continuing residence.

R v Secretary of State for the Home Department, ex parte Mann Singh Shingara; R v Secretary of State for the Home Department, ex parte Abbas Radiom Joined Cases C-65 and 111/95 Judgment of 17 June 1997 (not yet reported) European Court of Justice

- *Derogations from the freedom of movement based on public policy – public security – right of entry – legal remedies – arts 8 and 9 of Directive 64/221/EEC*

Facts
In separate proceedings for judicial review each applicant was refused leave to enter the United Kingdom. Mr Shingara, a holder of French citizenship, was refused entry to the UK in 1991 on the grounds of public policy and public security. The notice refusing him entry specified that the Secretary of State had personally decided that it would be contrary to the interests of public policy and public security to admit him to the UK and that under s15(3) of the Immigration Act 1971 he was not entitled to appeal against this decision. In 1993 Mr Shingara was admitted to the UK on the basis of his French identity card but seven days later was arrested in Birmingham and detained as an illegal entrant and duly returned to France. The Secretary of State indicated that the deportation decision was based on the fact that Mr Shingara was promoting Sikh terrorism. On that occasion he was granted leave to apply for judicial review, but in fact did not apply.

Mr Radiom, a holder of Iranian and Irish nationality, who by some legal means obtained an indefinite residence permit for the UK in 1983, worked in the UK for the Iranian consular services from 1983 to 1989. Following the severing of diplomatic relations between the UK and the Islamic Republic of Iran in 1989 Mr Radiom was asked by the Home Office to leave the UK within seven days, after which time, if he stayed within the country, he would be detained and deported on the grounds of public security. He decided to voluntarily leave the UK but subsequently submitted an application to the Home Office for a residence permit claiming that as an EC national he was entitled to work in the UK. The application was refused and Mr Radiom was informed by the Secretary of State that it was considered that his presence in the UK would still pose a threat to public security since he was a supporter of violence against dissidents as advocated by the Iranian government. He was also refused a right of appeal against this decision notwithstanding the fact that he was an EC national.

Both applicants argued that the United Kingdom law refusing them the opportunity of an appeal against the decision of the Secretary of State to deny them entry to the UK on the grounds of public policy and public security was contrary to Community law, in particular arts 8 and 9 of Directive 64/221/EEC. They both applied for judicial review of Home Office decisions.

Held
The ECJ held that English law was in conformity with arts 8 and 9 of Directive 64/221/EEC.

In respect of art 8 of the Directive (which requires that a Member State provide the same remedies for nationals of other Member States as those available to its own nationals in respect of decisions concerning entry, renewal of residence permit or expulsion), the ECJ held that art 8 did not impose on a Member State an obligation to introduce specific appeal provisions against such decisions. It is sufficient that there is a general system of judicial review available to nationals from other Member States under the same conditions as to nationals of that Member State

The ECJ held that the three situations mentioned in art 9(1) (that is, 'where there is no right of appeal to a court of law, or where such appeal may be only in respect of the decisions, or where the appeal cannot have suspensory effect') in which a Member State has an obligation to delay the implementation of a decision to refuse the renewal of residence permit or the expulsion of the holder of such permit until a competent authority of the host country gives an opinion, constitute the conditions under which rights provided for in art 9(2) are to be exercised. Under art 9(2) in the event of a refusal to issue a first residence permit, or a decision ordering expulsion before the issue of such a permit, a national of another Member State is entitled to ask an independent authority to review such a decision.

The ECJ held that a national of a Member State who had been refused entry into another Member State on the grounds of public policy, public security or public order but did not appeal against the decision had a right of appeal against a second decision preventing him from entering or remaining in that Member State within a reasonable time of it having been made although he did not appeal against the first decision.

Judgment

'[*First and second questions*]
The first part of the first question asks in substance whether, on a proper construction of art 8 of the directive, where under the national legislation of a Member State (i) remedies are available in respect of acts of the administration generally and (ii) different remedies are available in respect of decisions concerning entry by nationals of the State concerned, the obligation imposed on the Member State by that provision is satisfied if nationals of other Member States enjoy the same remedies as those available against acts of the administration generally in that Member State.

The Court notes that art 8 does not govern the ways in which remedies are to be made available, for instance by stipulating the courts from which such remedies may be sought, such details being dependent upon the organisation of the courts in each Member State.

However, the obligation to grant the person concerned the same legal remedies in respect of any decision concerning entry, or refusing the issue or renewal of a residence permit, or ordering expulsion from the territory as are available to nationals in respect of acts of the administration, means that a Member State cannot, without being in breach of the obligation imposed by art 8, organise, for persons covered by the directive, legal remedies governed by special procedures affording lesser safeguards than those pertaining to remedies available to nationals in respect of acts of the administration.

As regards the main proceedings here, the national legislation provides for remedies in respect of acts of the administration generally and another kind of remedy in respect of decisions concerning entry of nationals of the Member State concerned. In addition, the order for reference states that the latter remedy is also available to non-nationals regarding entry, with the exception, however, of refusals of entry on grounds of the public good.

The reservations contained in arts 48 and 56 of the EC Treaty permit Member States to adopt, with respect to the nationals of other Member States and on the grounds specified in those provisions, in particular grounds justified by the requirements of public policy, measures which they cannot apply to their own nationals, inasmuch as they have no authority to expel the latter from the national territory or to deny them access thereto.

It follows that the remedies available to nationals of other Member States in the circumstances defined by the directive cannot be assessed by reference to the remedies available to nationals concerning the right of entry.

The two situations are indeed in no way comparable: whereas in the case of nationals the right of entry is a consequence of the status of national, so that there can be no margin of discretion for the State as regards the exercise of that right, the special circumstances which may justify reliance on the concept of public policy as against nationals of other Member States may vary over time and from one country to another, and it is therefore necessary to allow the competent national authorities a margin of discretion.

In the light of that reply it is not necessary to answer either the second part of the first question or the second question.

[*Third question*]
The third question asks whether, on a proper construction of art 9 of the directive, the three hypotheses mentioned in art 9(1) (namely "where there is no right of appeal to a court of law, or where such appeal may be only in respect of the legal validity of the decision, or where the appeal cannot have suspensory effect") apply equally as regards art 9(2), that is to say, where the decision challenged is a refusal to issue a first residence permit or a decision ordering expulsion before the issue of such a permit.

The provisions of art 9 of the directive complement those of art 8. Their purpose is to provide minimum procedural guarantees for persons affected by one of the measures referred to in the three cases defined in art 9(1). Where the right of appeal is restricted to the legality of the decision, the purpose of the intervention of the competent authority referred to in art 9(1) is to enable an exhaustive examination of all the facts and circumstances, including the expediency of the proposed measure, to be carried out before the decision is finally taken.

If art 9(2) of the directive were to be interpreted as meaning that the addressee of a decision refusing to issue a first residence permit or a decision ordering expulsion before the issue of such a permit was entitled to obtain an opinion from the competent authority mentioned in art 9(1) in circumstances other than those defined in that paragraph, he would be entitled to do so even where the remedies available entailed a review of the substance and an exhaustive examination of all the facts and circumstances. Such an interpretation would not be in accordance with the purpose of the provisions, since the procedure of referral for consideration and an opinion provided for in art 9 is intended to mitigate the effect of deficiencies in the remedies referred to in art 8 of the directive.

[*Fourth and fifth questions*]
The fourth and fifth questions ask in substance whether a national of a Member State who has been refused entry into another Member State for reasons of public order or public security has a right of appeal in respect of measures adopted subsequently which prevent his entering that State, even if the first decision has not been the subject of an appeal or an opinion.

A Community national expelled from a Member State may apply for a fresh residence permit, and, if that application is made after a reasonable time, it must be examined by the competent administrative authority in that State, which must take into account, in particular, the arguments put forward to establish that there has been a material change in the circumstances which justified the first decision ordering expulsion.

Decisions prohibiting entry into a Member State of a national of another Member State constitute derogations from the fundamental principle of freedom of movement. Consequently, such a decision cannot be of unlimited duration. A Community national against whom such a prohibition has been issued must therefore be entitled to apply to have his situation re-examined if he considers that the circumstances which justified prohibiting him from entering the country no longer exist.

When a fresh application has been made for entry or a residence permit, after a reasonable time has elapsed since the preceding decision, the person concerned is entitled to a new decision, which may be the subject of an appeal on the basis of art 8 and, where appropriate, art 9 of the directive.'

Comment
Directive 64/221/EEC regulates the application of the three derogations from the right to freedom of movement conferred on EC nationals by Community law. Those derogations based on the grounds of public policy,

public security and public health, as exceptions to the provisions of the EC Treaty, must be interpreted restrictively. No Community definition is provided in respect of those three derogations. The Directive only describes the situations in which a Member State may prevent an EC national from exercising his right to enter the territory of another Member State on the grounds of public policy, public security and public order. Consequently, the Directive permits a Member State a certain discretion in the application of those derogations, provided its exercise is within the limits of the EC Treaty. Furthermore, Directive 64/221/EEC provides procedural safeguards for EC nationals from other Member States seeking to enforce their rights of entry and residence in a Member State. Articles 8 and 9 of Directive 64/221/EEC establish requirements for remedies against immigration decisions excluding an EC national from the territory of a host Member State.

The main issue under art 8 of the Directive was that a decision made by the Secretary of State under s13 of the Immigration Act 1970, which excluded an EC national from that State's territory on the grounds of 'public good', was not subject to appeal although it remained subject to judicial review as does any act of administration. The ECJ emphasised that the requirements of art 8 of the Directive are satisfied if EC nationals from other Member State have the same legal remedies as are available to nationals of a host State, in the present cases consisting of general judicial review provisions.

Article 9 of Directive 64/221/EEC poses a problem of interpretation. Under art 9(1) of the Directive a decision refusing renewal of a residence permit or ordering the expulsion of the holder of a residence permit from the territory of a host State should be suspended (save in cases of urgency) until an opinion has been obtained from a competent authority of the host State different from that which has taken the challenged decision. Before that competent authority the applicant must have a right of defence and of assistance and representation in three situations: 'where there is no right of appeal to a court of law, where such an appeal may be only in respect of validity of the decision, or where the appeal cannot have suspensory effect'. Article 9(2) of the Directive concerns a decision in respect of a refusal to issue a first residence permit or a decision ordering expulsion before the issue of such a permit, but does not indicate the conditions precedent to the exercise of that right. The ECJ held that the right of appeal against decisions enumerated in art 9(2) applies in the three situations mentioned in art 9(1). This interpretation is consistent with the objective of art 9 of the Directive which intends to mitigate the effect of deficiencies in the remedies referred to in art 8 of the Directive.

The ECJ held that where an EC national is refused entry into the territory of another Member State on the grounds of public security, and does not challenge this decision, and later applies for a residence permit, and a new decision confirming the previous one is issued against him, he has a right of appeal within a reasonable time against a second decision, notwithstanding the fact that he did not appeal against the first.

Roland Rutili v *Minister of the Interior* Case 36/75 [1975] ECR 1219; [1976] 1 CMLR 140 European Court of Justice

- *Free movement of workers – art 48(3) of EC Treaty – residence permit – restriction on entry and residence within a Member State – public policy*

Facts
Rutili was an Italian national who resided in France and, between 1967 and 1968, he actively participated in political and trade union activities. The French authorities grew increasingly concerned with his activities, and issued a deportation order. This was subsequently altered to a restriction order requiring him to remain in certain provinces of France.

In particular, the order prohibited him from residing in the province in which he was habitually resident and in which his family resided.

The plaintiff challenged the legality of these measures on the ground that they interfered with his right of freedom of movement. The question was referred to the ECJ for a preliminary ruling.

Held

The ECJ interpreted the right of a Member State to limit the free movement of workers on the ground of public policy and concluded that this right must be construed strictly. In particular, a Member State cannot, in the case of a national of another Member State, impose prohibitions on residence which are territorially limited except in circumstances where such prohibitions may be imposed on its own nationals.

Judgment

'[*Justification of measures adopted on grounds of public policy from the point of view of substantive law*]

By virtue of the reservation contained in art 48(3), Member States continue to be, in principle, free to determine the requirements of public policy in the light of their national needs.

Nevertheless, the concept of public policy must, in the Community context and where, in particular, it is used as a justification for derogating from the fundamental principles of equality of treatment and freedom of movement for workers, be interpreted strictly, so that its scope cannot be determined unilaterally by each Member State without being subject to control by the institutions of the Community.

Accordingly, restrictions cannot be imposed on the right of a national of any Member State to enter the territory of another Member State, to stay there and to move within it unless his presence or conduct constitutes a genuine and sufficiently serious threat to public policy.

In this connection art 3 of Directive 64/221 imposes on Member States the duty to base their decision on the individual circumstances of any person under the protection of Community law and not on general considerations.

[*The justifiaction for, in particular, a prohibition on residence in part of the national territory*]

The questions put by the Tribunal Administratif were raised in connection with a measure prohibiting residence in a limited part of the national territory.

In reply to a question from the Court, the government of the French Republic stated that such measures may be taken in the case of its own nationals either, in the case of certain criminal convictions, as an additional penalty, or following the declaration of a state of emergency.

The provisions enabling certain areas of the national territory to be prohibited to foreign nationals are, however, based on legislative instruments specifically concerning them.

In this connection, the government of the French Republic draws attention to art 4 of the Council Directive 64/220 of 25 February 1964 on the abolition of restrictions on movement and residence within the Community for nationals of Member States with regard to establishment and the provision of services

Right of entry into the territory of Member States and the right to stay there and to move freely within it is defined in the Treaty by reference to the whole territory of these States and not by reference to its internal subdivisions.

The reservation contained in art 48(3) concerning the protection of public policy has the same scope as the rights the exercise of which may, under that paragraph, be subject to limitations.

It follows that prohibitions on residence under the reservation inserted to this effect in art 48(3) may be imposed only in respect of the whole of the national territory.

On the other hand, in the case of partial prohibitions on residence, limited to certain areasof the territory, persons covered by Community law must, under art [6] of the

Treaty and within the field of application of that provision, be treated on a footing of equality with the nationals of the Member State concerned.

It follows that a Member State cannot, in the case of a national of another Member State covered by the provisions of the Treaty, impose prohibitions on residence which are territorially limited exept in circumstances where such prohibitions may be imposed on its own nationals.'

Comment
In the present case the ECJ clarified the scope of art 48(3) of EC Treaty which provides for an exception to the free movement of workers based on the grounds of public policy, public security and public health. The ECJ stated that the exception must be interpreted restrictively so as not to undermine the fundamental principle of the free movement of workers.

The interesting aspect of the present case is that a Member State may only impose partial prohibitions on residence, that is restrict the residence of an EC migrant worker to certain areas of its territory if such a restriction may be imposed on its own nationals. If a Member State has no power to restrict the residence of its own nationals to a specific area then it has only two options in relation to an EC migrant worker: to refuse his entry or to permit him to reside in the whole of the national territory.

As to restrictions on admission to or residence within a Member State for nationals of other Member States based on types of activities they intend to carry on once admitted and which are lawful when conducted by host State nationals, the ECJ did confirm its previous decision in *Van Duyn* v *Home Office* Case 41/74. The ECJ reversed its position in *Andoui and Cornuaille* v *Belgian State* Joined Cases 115 and 116/81 [1982] ECR 1665 in which the Court held that a Member State may only justify such restrictions on the admission to or residence within its territory of nationals of another Member State if it adopted, with respect to the same conduct on the part of its own nationals, repressive measures or other genuine and effective measure intended to combat such conduct.

The State v *Jean Noel Royer* Case 48/75 [1976] ECR 497; [1976] 2 CMLR 619 European Court of Justice

• *Free movement of workers – art 48(3) EC Treaty – direct effect – art 1 Regulation 1612/68 – art 4 Directive 68/360 – expulsion – public policy*

Facts
Royer was a French national who had been convicted of minor offences and prosecuted for a number of armed robberies but never convicted. His wife was also a French national, but worked in Liège in Belgium. He visited his wife in Belgium, but omitted to comply with the administrative formalities upon entry into the country. He was subsequently convicted of illegal entry and residence in Belgium and left the country.

Some time later, Royer returned to Belgium, but again failed to comply with the necessary administrative formalities. He was served with a ministerial decree of expulsion which alleged that his presence was a danger to public policy in Belgium. As a defence, Royer invoked art 48 of the [EC] Treaty, and the related Community directives, to establish that he was entitled to enter and remain in Belgium as a worker.

Held
The ECJ gave direct effect to art 48 and relied on the directives implementing the right of workers and their families to reside in other Member States to reject the need for a permit in order to acquire residency in other Member States. In addition, the failure of a Community national to comply with the administrative formalities upon entry into another Member State did not justify expuslsion.

Judgment

'[*Referring to the rights granted by arts 48, 52 and 59 of the Treaty*]

These provisions, which may be construed as prohibiting Member States from setting up restrictions or obstacles to the entry into and residence in their territory of nationals of other Member State, have the effect of conferring rights directly on all persons falling within the ambit of the above-mentioned articles, as later given closer articulation by regulations or directives implementing the Treaty.

This interpretation has been recognised by all the measures of secondary law adopted for the purpose of implementing the above-mentioned provisions of the Treaty.

Thus art 1 of Regulation 1612/68 provides that any national of a Member State, shall, irrespective of his place of residence, have "the right to take up activity as an employed person and to pursue such activity within the territory of another Member State" and art 10 of the same regulation extends the "right to instal themselves" to the members of the family of such a national.

Article 4 of Directive 68/360 provides that "Member State shall grant the right of residence in their territory" to the persons referred to and further states that as "proof" of this right an individual residence permit shall be issued.

Further the preamble to Directive 73/148 states that freedom of establishment can be fully attained only "if a right of permanent residence is granted to the persons who are to enjoy freedom of establishment" and that freedom to provide services entails that persons providing and receiving services should have "the right of residence for the time during which the services are being provided".

These provisions show that the legislative authorities of the Community were aware that, while not creating new rights in favour of persons protected by Community law, the regulation and directives concerned determined the scope and detailed rules for the exercise of rights conferred directly by the Treaty.

... (a) It follows from the foregoing that the right of nationals of a Member State to enter the territory of another Member State and reside there for the purposes intended by the Treaty – in particular to look for or pursue an occupation or activities as employed or self-employed persons, or to rejoin their spouse or family – is a right conferred directly by the Treaty, or, as the case may be, by the provisions adopted for its implementation.

It must therefore be concluded that the right is acquired independently of the issue of a residence permit by the competent authority of a Member State.

The grant of this permit is therefore to be regarded not as a measure giving rise to rights but as a measure by a Member State serving to prove the individual position of a national of another Member State with regard to provisions of Community law.

(b) Article 4(1) and (2) of Directive 68/360 provides, without prejudice to art 10 thereof, that Member States shall "grant" the right of residence in their territory to persons who are able to produce the documents listed in the directive and that "proof" of the right of residence shall be constituted by issue of a special residence permit.

The above-mentioned provisions of the directive are intended to determine details regulating the exercise of rights conferred directly by the Treaty.

It follows, therefore, that the right of residence must be granted by the authorities of the Member States to any person falling within the categories set out in art 1 of the Directive and who is able to prove, by producing the documents specified in art 4(3), that he falls within one of these categories.

The answer to the question put should therefore be that art 4 of Directive 68/360 entails an obligation for Member States to issue a residence permit to any person who provides proof, by means of the appropriate documents, that he belongs to one of the categories set out in art 1 of the directive.

(c) The logical consequence of the foregoing is that the mere failure by a national of a Member State to complete the legal formalities concerninng access, movement and residence of aliens does not justify a decision ordering expulsion.'

Comment
The ECJ held that the right to entry and residence is granted directly by art 48 EC Treaty and is therefore independent from the question of a residence permit. The latter has only declaratory and probatory force. Consequently, a failure to comply with formalities regarding entry and residence cannot justify a decision ordering expulsion from the territory of a host Member State or temporary imprisonment. In respect of sanctions that a Member State may impose on nationals from other Member States for failure to comply with administrative requirements regarding entry and residence such sanctions are subject to the principle of proportionality. Any national measures which are disproportionate to the objectives of the Treaty in the area of free movement of persons will be struck out by the ECJ as contrary to Community law.

In the present case the ECJ held that art 48(3) EC Treaty encompasses the right to enter in search of work although it did not fix any time-limit for such a search. It seems that a six-months' period can be considered as a reasonable time for the purpose of seeking employment. This was implied from the ECJ decision in *R* v *Immigration Appeal Tribunal, ex parte Antonissen* Case C–292/89 [1991] 2 CMLR 373 in which the ECJ accepted that if after a six-month stay in a host Member State for the purpose of seeking employment, an EC migrant had failed to find employment a deportation order could be issued, unless the migrant provided evidence that he was actively seeking employment and had a genuine chance of being employed.

11 Social Policy

Margaret Boyle and Others v Equal Opportunities Commission Case C–411/96 [1998] 3 CMLR 1133 European Court of Justice

• Social policy – sex discrimination – equal pay and equal treatment for men and women – maternity leave – rights of pregnant women in respect of sick leave – annual leave – accrual of pension rights – obligation to repay maternity pay received

Facts

Margaret Boyle and five other applicants brought proceedings before the Industrial Tribunal against their employer, the Equal Opportunities Commission, for a declaration that some provisions of the maternity scheme applied to them by their employer were contrary to Community law in so far as they discriminated against female employees. In particular the following clauses of the maternity scheme were called into question.

First, a clause which makes the payment, during the period of maternity leave, of pay higher than the statutory payment but requires repayment of the difference if the worker fails to return to work after childbirth.

Second, a clause requiring an employee who has expressed her intention to commence her maternity leave during the six weeks preceding the expected confinement, and is on sick leave with a pregnancy-related illness immediately before that date and gives birth during the period of sick leave, to bring forward the date on which her paid maternity leave commences, either to the beginning of the six weeks preceding the expected week of childbirth or to the beginning of the period of sick leave, whichever is later.

Third, a clause prohibiting a woman from taking sick leave during the minimum period of 14 weeks' maternity leave to which a female worker is entitled pursuant to art 8 of Directive 92/85, or any supplementary period of maternity leave granted to her by the employer, unless she elects to return to work and thus terminates her maternity leave.

Fourth, a clause limiting the period during which annual leave accrues to the minimum period of 14 weeks' maternity leave to which female workers are entitled under the directive.

Fifth, a clause limiting, in the context of an occupational scheme wholly financed by the employer, the accrual of pension rights during maternity leave to the period during which the woman receives the pay provided for by that employment contract or national legislation.

Held

The ECJ held that only the clause that prohibits a woman from taking sick leave during the minimum period of 14 weeks' maternity leave and the clause limiting, in the context of an occupational scheme wholly financed by the employer, the accrual of pension rights during the period of maternity leave to the period during which the woman receives the pay provided for by her employment contract or national legislation were in breach of Community law.

Judgment

'[*The first question*]
In that respect, it should be noted that it was in view of the risk that the provisions relating to maternity leave would be ineffective if rights connected with the employment contract were not maintained, that the Community legislature provided that "maintenance of a payment to, and/or entitlement

to an adequate allowance" for workers to whom the Directive applies must be ensured in the case of the maternity leave.

The concept of allowance to which that provision refers ... includes all income received by the worker during her maternity leave which is not paid to her by her employer pursuant to the employment relationship.

In this respect, the provisions of the Directive are intended to ensure that, during her maternity leave, the worker receives an income at least equivalent to the sickness allowance provided for by national social security legislation in the event of a break in her activities on health grounds.

Female workers must be guaranteed an income of that level during their maternity leave, irrespective of whether it is paid in the form of an allowance, pay or a combination of the two.

However, the Directive is not intended to guarantee her any higher income which the employer may have undertaken to pay her, under the employment contract, should she be on sick leave.

It follows that a clause in an employment contract according to which a worker who does not return to work after childbirth is required to repay the difference between the pay received by her during her maternity leave and the statutory payments to which she was entitled in respect of maternity leave is compatible with Directive 92/85 in so far as the level of those payments is not lower than the income which the worker concerned would receive, under the relevant national social security legislation, in the event of a break in her activities on grounds connected with her state of health.

A clause in an employment contract which makes the application of a more favourable set of rules than that prescribed by national legislation conditional on the pregnant woman, unlike any worker on sick leave, returning to work after childbirth, failing which she must repay the contractual maternity pay in so far as it exceeds the level of the statutory payments in respect of that leave, therefore does not constitute discrimination on grounds of sex.

[*The second question*]
... In that respect, art 8 of Directive 92/85 leaves it open to the Member States to determine the date on which maternity leave is to commence.

National legislation may therefore, as here, provide that the period of maternity leave commences with the date notified by the person concerned to her employer as the date on which she intends to commence her period of absence, or the first day after the beginning of the sixth week preceding the expected week of childbirth during which the employee is wholly or partly absent because of pregnancy, should that day fall on an earlier date.

The clause to which the second question relates merely reflects the choice made in such national legislation.

[*The third question*]
... In that respect, although the Member States are required to take the necessary measures to ensure that workers are entitled to a period of maternity leave of at least 14 weeks, those workers may waive that right, with the exception of the two weeks compulsory maternity leave which, in the United Kingdom, commence on the day on which the child is born.

In contrast, if a woman becomes ill during the period of maternity leave referred to by Directive 92/85 and places herself under the sick leave arrangements, and that sick leave ends before the expiry of the period of maternity leave, she cannot be deprived of the right to continued enjoyment, after that date, of the maternity leave provided for by the aforementioned provision until the expiry of the minimum period of 14 weeks, that period being calculated from the date on which the maternity leave commenced.

The third question need be examined only in so far as the clause of the employment contract referred to therein applies to the supplementary period of maternity leave granted by the employer to female workers.

In that respect, the principle of non-discrimination laid down by the equal treatment directive does not require a woman to be able to exercise simultaneously both the right to supplementary maternity leave granted to her by the employer and the right to sick leave.

Consequently, in order for a woman on maternity leave to qualify for sick leave, she may be required to terminate the period of supplementary maternity leave granted to her by the employer.

[*The fourth question*]

... It should be noted that substantially more women than men take periods of unpaid leave during their career because they take supplementary maternity leave, so that, in practice, the clause at issue applies to a greater percentage of women than men.

However, the fact that such a clause applies more frequently to women results from the exercise of the right to unpaid maternity leave granted to them by their employers in addition to the period of protection guaranteed by Directive 92/85.

The supplementary unpaid maternity leave constitutes a special advantage, over and above the protection provided for by Directive 92/85 and is available only to women, so that the fact that annual leave ceases to accrue during that period of leave cannot amount to less favourable treatment of women.

[*The fifth question*]

... The accrual of pension rights in the context of an occupational scheme wholly financed by the employer constitutes one of the rights connected with the employment contracts of the workers.

Such rights must, in accordance with Directive 92/85, be ensured during the period of maternity leave of at least 14 weeks to which female workers are entitled.

Although, in accordance with Directive 92/85, it is open to Member States to make entitlement to pay or the adequate allowance conditional upon the worker concerned fulfilling the conditions of eligibility for such benefits laid down under national legislation, no such possibility exists in respect of rights connected with the employment contract.

The accrual of pension rights under an occupational scheme during the period of maternity leave referred to by Directive 92/85 cannot therefore be made conditional upon the woman's receiving the pay provided for by her employment contract or SMP [statutory maternity pay] during that period.'

Comment

In the present case the ECJ defined some aspects of the financial arrangements and other rights to which women are entitled during the period of maternity leave.

Mary Brown v *Rentokil Ltd* Case C–394/96 [1998] ECR I–4185; [1998] 2 CMLR 1049 European Court of Justice

• *Social policy – sex discrimination – Directive 76/207/EEC – equal treatment for men and women – pregnant woman – dismissal – absences due to illness connected to pregnancy*

Facts

Mary Brown worked for Rentokil as a driver. Rentokil's contract of employment contained a clause stipulating that if an employee was absent from work due to illness for more than 26 weeks continuously, the employee would be dismissed. In August 1990 Mary Brown informed her employer that she was pregnant. Shortly afterwards, she suffered from health problems connected with her pregnancy. From 16 August 1990 she submitted a succession of four-week medical certificates mentioning various pregnancy-related disorders. She did not return to work. In accordance with her contract she was informed by a letter of 30 January 1991 that she would be dismissed on 8 February 1991. Mary Brown was therefore dismissed while pregnant. Her child was born on 22 March 1991. She challenged her dismissal, as contrary to Community law, before the Industrial Tribunal which rejected her application. She appealed to the House of Lords, which referred two questions on the interpretation of Directive 76/207/EEC, namely its arts 2(1) and 5(1) regarding the implementation of the principle of equal treatment for men and woman in relation to employment, vocational training and working conditions, to the ECJ for a preliminary ruling:

Held

The ECJ held that Community law precludes dismissal of a woman at any time during her pregnancy for absences due to incapacity for work caused by illness resulting from her pregnancy, even if the dismissal was based on a contractual provision permitting the employer to dismiss an employee, regardless of gender, after a certain number of weeks of continuous absence.

Judgment

'According to settled case law of the Court of Justice, the dismissal of a female worker on account of pregnancy, or essentially on account of pregnancy, can affect only women and therefore constitutes direct discrimination on grounds of sex.

It is clear from the documents before the Court that the question concerns the dismissal of a female worker during her pregnancy as a result of absences through incapacity for work arising from her pregnant condition. As Rentokil points out, the cause of Mrs Brown's dismissal lies in the fact that she was ill during her pregnancy to such an extent that she was unfit for work for 26 weeks. It is common ground that her illness was attributable to her pregnancy.

However, dismissal of a woman during pregnancy cannot be based on her inability, as a result of her condition, to perform the duties which she is contractually bound to carry out. If such an interpretation were adopted, the protection afforded by Community law to a woman during pregnancy would be available only to pregnant women who were able to comply with the conditions of their employment contracts, with the result that the provisions of Directive 76/207 would be rendered ineffective.

Although pregnancy is not in any way comparable to a pathological condition, the fact remains, that pregnancy is a period during which disorders and complications may arise compelling a woman to undergo strict medical supervision and, in some cases, to rest absolutely for all or part of her pregnancy. Those disorders and complications, which may cause incapacity for work, form part of the risks inherent in the condition of pregnancy and are thus a specific feature of that condition.

In its judgment in Case C–179/88 *Handels- og Kontorfunktionaerernes Forbund i Danmark* v *Dansk Arbejdsgiverforening* [1990] ECR I–3979, the Court concluded that, during the maternity leave accorded to her under national law, a woman is protected against dismissal on the grounds of her absence.

If such protection against dismissal must be afforded to women during maternity leave, the principle of non-discrimination, for its part, requires similar protection throughout the period of pregnancy. Finally, dismissal of a female worker during pregnancy for absences due to incapacity for work resulting from her pregnancy is linked to the occurrence of risks inherent in pregnancy and must therefore be regarded as essentially based on the fact of pregnancy. Such a dismissal can affect only women and therefore constitutes direct discrimination on grounds of sex.

It follows that arts 2(1) and 5(1) of the Directive preclude dismissal of a female worker at any time during her pregnancy for absences due to incapacity for work caused by an illness resulting from that pregnancy.

It is clear from all the foregoing considerations that, contrary to the Court's ruling in Case C–400/95 *Larsson* v *Føtex Supermarked* [1997] ECR I–2757, where a woman is absent owing to illness resulting from pregnancy or childbirth, and that illness arose during pregnancy and persisted during and after maternity leave, her absence not only during maternity leave but also during the period extending from the start of her pregnancy to the start of her maternity leave cannot be taken into account for computation of the period justifying her dismissal under national law. As to her absence after maternity leave, this may be taken into account under the same conditions as a man's absence, of the same duration, through incapacity for work.'

Comment
In the present case the ECJ extended the scope of protection for pregnant female workers. It held that the principle of non-discrimination prohibits their dismissed at any time during their pregnancy if the dismissal is based on absences due to incapacity for work caused by an illness resulting from their pregnancy. A contractual provision which permits the employer to dismiss any worker, regardless of gender, after a stipulated number of weeks of continuous absence affects a female and a male worker differently. In the case of a pregnant female worker the application of such a contractual provision amounts to direct sex discrimination if her absence is caused by pregnancy-related illness.

Nils Draempachl v *Urania Immobilienservice OHP* Case C–180/95 [1997] ECR I–2195
European Court of Justice

- *Right to reparation in the event of discrimination in respect of access to employment – choice of sanctions by the Member State for breaches of Directive 76/207 – ceiling of compensation awards – aggregate compensation*

Facts
Nils Draempachl claimed to be a victim of discrimination based on sex in respect of recruitment. According to him a job advertisement in a daily newspaper was exclusively addressed to women. The employer, a private company, did not even acknowledge his application. The German court had no problem in finding that the advertisement was contrary to the prohibition against unequal treatment under Directive 76/209. The conditions for compensation of victims of discrimination formed the subject-matter of the preliminary ruling under art 177 EC proceedings. Under art 611a, para 2 BGB (German Civil Code) a victim of discrimination was entitled to pecuniary compensation not exceeding three months' salary in cases where the employer was not at fault and, under art 61b, para 1 of the German Law regarding the organisation of Labour courts (Arb GG), in the case of multiple proceedings the amount of compensation was limited to six months' salary.

Held
The ECJ held that the German system which limits the amount of compensation for victims of discrimination based on sex is contrary to Community law.

Judgment
'[*Question 1*]
By its first question the national court asks in substance whether the Directive and, in particular, arts 2(1) and 3(1) thereof, preclude provisions of domestic law which make reparation of damage suffered as a result of discrimination on grounds of sex in the making of an appointment subject to the requirement of fault.

In paragraph 22 of its judgment in *Dekker* Case C–177/88 [1990] ECR I–3941 the Court held that the Directive does not make liability on the part of the person guilty of discrimination conditional on proof of fault or on the absence of any ground discharging such liability.

In paragraph 25 of that judgment the Court also stated that, when the sanction chosen by the Member State is provided for in rules governing employers' civil liability, any breach of the prohibition of discrimination must, in itself, be sufficient to render the employer fully liable, without there being any possibility of invoking the grounds of exemption provided for by domestic law.

It must therefore be concluded that the Directive precludes provisions of domestic law which make reparation of damage suffered as a result of discrimination on grounds of sex in the making of an appointment subject to the requirement of fault.

[*Questions 2 and 3*]

By these questions, which should be examined together, the Arbeitsgericht asks in substance whether the Directive precludes provisions of domestic law which place a ceiling of three months' salary on the amount of compensation which may be claimed by applicants discriminated against on grounds of their sex in the making of appointments. It also asks whether the answer to that question applies equally to applicants who were discriminated against in the recruitment procedure but who, owing to the superior qualifications of the applicant engaged, would not have obtained the position even if the selection process had been free of discrimination and to those who were discriminated against in the recruitment procedure and who would have obtained the position to be filled if selection had been carried out without discrimination.

In this regard, it must be pointed out first of all that, even though the Directive does not impose a specific sanction on the Member States, nevertheless art 6 obliges them to adopt measures which are sufficiently effective for achieving the aim of the Directive and to ensure that those measures may be effectively relied on before the national courts by the persons concerned.

Moreover, the Directive requires that, if a Member State chooses to penalise breach of the prohibition of discrimination by the award of compensation, that compensation must be such as to guarantee real and effective judicial protection, have a real deterrent effect on the employer and must in any event be adequate in relation to the damage sustained. Purely nominal compensation would not satisfy the requirements of an effective transposition of the Directive.

In choosing the appropriate solution for guaranteeing that the objective of the Directive is attained, the Member States must ensure that infringements of Community law are penalised under conditions, both procedural and substantive, which are analogous to those applicable to infringements of domestic law of a similar nature and importance.

It follows from the foregoing that provisions of domestic law which, unlike other provisions of domestic civil law and labour law, prescribe an upper limit of three months' salary for the compensation which may be obtained in the event of discrimination on grounds of sex in the making of an appointment do not fulfil those requirements.

The question which must therefore be considered is whether that answer applies equally to job applicants who, because the successful applicant had superior qualifications, would not have obtained the position, even if the selection process had been free of discrimination, and to those who would have obtained the position if selection process had been carried out without discrimination.

In this regard, it must be borne in mind that reparation must be adequate in relation to the damage sustained.

Nevertheless, such reparation may take account of the fact that, even if there had been no discrimination in the selection process, some applicants would not have obtained the position to be filled since the applicant appointed had superior qualifications. It is indisputable that such applicants, not having suffered any damage through exclusion from the recruitment procedure, cannot claim that the extent of the damage they have sustained is the same as that sustained by applicants who would have obtained the position if there had been no discrimination in the selection process.

Having regard to those considerations, it does not seem unreasonable for a Member State to lay down a statutory presumption that the damage suffered by an applicant may not exceed a ceiling of three months' salary.

In this regard, it must be made clear it is for the employer, who has in his possession all the applications submitted, to adduce proof that the applicant would not have obtained the vacant position even if there had been no discrimination.

[Question 4]
By its fourth question the Arbeitsgericht asks in substance whether the Directive precludes provisions of domestic law imposing a ceiling on the aggregate amount of compensation payable to several applicants discriminated against on the grounds of their sex in the making of an appointment.

As the Court held in its judgment in *Von Colson and Kamann*, the Directive entails that the sanction chosen by the Member States must have a real dissuasive effect on the employer and must be adequate in relation to the damage sustained in order to ensure real and effective judicial protection.

It is clear that a provision which places a ceiling of six months' salary on the aggregate amount of compensation for all applicants harmed by discrimination on grounds of sex in the making of an appointment, where several applicants claim compensation, may lead to the award of reduced compensation and may have the effect of dissuading applicants so harmed from asserting their rights. Such a consequence would not represent real and effective judicial protection and would have no really dissuasive effect on the employer, as required by the Directive.

Moreover, such a ceiling on the aggregate compensation is not prescribed by other provisions of domestic civil law or labour law.

However, as the Court has already held, the procedures and conditions governing a right to reparation based on Community law must not be less favourable than those laid down by comparable national rules.'

Comment

The ECJ clarified the conditions upon which a Member State can impose sanctions for breaches of Directive 76/207 regarding equal treatment of men and women. The Court held that irrespective of the grounds on which a Member State chooses to base liability under Directive 76/207 proof of fault is not required. As a result, any breach of the prohibition of discrimination renders the employer fully liable without there being any possibility of invoking grounds of exemption provided for by domestic law.

In respect of statutory presumptions laid down by a Member State regarding the amount of compensation which may be claimed by applicants discriminated against on grounds of their sex during the recruitment procedure, the ECJ emphasised that in order to achieve the objective of Directive 76/207 the Member State must ensure that breaches of Community law are penalised under the same procedural and substantive conditions as infringements of domestic law of a similar nature and importance (see *EC Commission* v *Greece* Case 68/88 [1989] ECR 2965). Second, the compensation must be:

1. such as to guarantee real and effective judicial protection for victims of discrimination;
2. a real deterrent to the employer;
3. adequate in relation to the damage sustained by applicants discriminated against on grounds of their sex in the process of appointments (see *Von Colson and Kamann* Case 14/83 [1984] ECR 1891).

As to a ceiling of three months' salary on the amount of compensation, the ECJ made a distinction between potentially successful and potentially unsuccessful candidates in the situation in which the selection process had been carried out without discrimination. In the case of an applicant who would not have obtained the position to be filled since the applicant appointed had superior qualifications, the former had not suffered damage through exclusion from the recruitment procedure and thus the limitation of three months' salary placed on the amount of compensation is reasonable. However, a Member State is precluded from placing a ceiling of three months' salary on the amount of compensation in the case of an applicant who would have obtained the position if there had been no discrimination in the selection process.

In respect of the aggregate amount of compensation payable to several applicants discriminated against in the appointment procedure on the ground of their sex, a Member State is precluded from imposing a priori a ceiling of six months' salary since this limitation may lead to the award of reduced compensation and thus prevent applicants so harmed from asserting their rights under Community law.

Handels- og Kontorfunktionaerernes Forbund v *Fællesforeningen for Danmarks Brugsforeninger* Case C–66/96 Judgment of 19 November 1998 (not yet reported) European Court of Justice

- *Social policy – art 119 EC Treaty – equal treatment for men and women – Directive 76/207/EEC – remuneration – working conditions for a pregnant woman – Directive 92/85/EEC*

Facts
A group of Danish female employees brought proceedings against their respective employers in relation to maintenance of their wages during absences from work connected with their pregnancy. All applicants (whose pregnancy followed an abnormal course during the three months preceding the expected date of confinement) challenged Danish law as contrary to Community law. The contested Danish law provided that in the event of incapacity for work, or legitimate impediment for a particular reason linked with the pregnancy, arising before the three months' period prior the confinement, the employee was not entitled to receive her wages but would receive benefits in accordance with the Law on Benefits and Danish Administrative Instruction No 191 of 27 October 1994, which benefits did not equal the full pay. The Danish court referred to the ECJ a number of question relating to the contested Danish law which law made a distinction between incapacity for work on grounds of pregnancy/confinement and on grounds of illness. The ECJ placed those questions in three groups relating to the conformity of Danish law with Community law in the following situations:

First, Danish law stipulates that for a maximum of five weeks' absence over a period beginning not earlier than three months before the confinement and ending not later than three months after the confinement, the employee is entitled to receive half pay from her employer whilst in the event of incapacity for work on grounds of illness a worker is in principle entitled to receive full pay from his or her employer;

Second, Danish law provides that a pregnant woman is not entitled to receive pay from her employer where, before the beginning of her maternity leave, she is absent from work due to routine pregnancy-related inconveniences or mere medical recommendation where there is no risk to the unborn child or any actual pathological condition, while any worker who is unfit for work on the ground of illness is entitled to full pay from his/her employer.

Third, Danish law provides that an employer when he considers that he cannot provide work for a woman who is pregnant although not unfit for work, may send her home without paying her full wages.

Held
The ECJ held Danish law in breach of Community law when it stipulated that a pregnant woman who, before the beginning of her maternity leave, was unfit for work due to a pathological condition connected with her pregnancy, as attested by a medical certificate, was not entitled to receive full pay from her employer but only benefits paid by a local authority when, in the event of incapacity for work on grounds of illness, as attested by a medical certificate, a worker was entitled to receive full pay from his/her employer. The Court stated that it was lawful for national law to provide that a pregnant woman was not entitled to receive her pay from her employer where, before the beginning of her maternity leave, she is absent from work by reason either of routine pregnancy-related inconveniences, when there is in fact no incapacity for work, or of medical recommendation intended to protect the unborn child but not based on an

actual pathological condition or on any special risks for the unborn child, while any worker who is unfit for work on the grounds of illness is in principle entitled to full pay from his/her employer. The Court held that it was contrary to Community law for national legislation to provide that an employer could send home a woman who was pregnant although not unfit for work, without paying her salary in full, when he considers that he cannot provide work for her.

Judgment

'[*The first situation*]
In this case, it is clear from the case file that all workers are in principle entitled, under the legislation at issue in the main proceedings, to continue to be paid in full in the event of incapacity for work.

Thus, the fact that a woman is deprived, before the beginning of her maternity leave, of her full pay when her incapacity for work is the result of a pathological condition connected with the pregnancy must be regarded as treatment based essentially on the pregnancy and thus as discriminatory.

It follows that the application of legislative provisions such as those at issue in the main proceedings involves discrimination against women, in breach of art 119 of the Treaty and of Directive 75/117.

[*The second situation*]
The next point is that the pay received by a worker while on sick leave constitutes pay within the meaning of art 119 of the Treaty.

In contrast to the [first situation] outlined by the national court, the pregnant woman is absent from her work before the beginning of her maternity leave not because of a pathological condition or of any special risks for the unborn child giving rise to an incapacity for work attested by a medical certificate but by reason either of routine pregnancy-related inconveniences or of mere medical recommendation, without there being any incapacity for work in either of those two situations.

Consequently, the fact that the employee forfeits some, or even all, of her salary by reason of such absences which are not based on an incapacity for work cannot be regarded as treatment based essentially on the pregnancy but rather as based on the choice made by the employee not to work.

[*The third situation*]
By reserving to Member States the right to retain or introduce provisions which are intended to protect women in connection with "pregnancy and maternity", Directive 76/207 recognises the legitimacy, in terms of the principle of equal treatment, of protecting a woman's biological condition during and after pregnancy.

However, legislation such as that at issue in the main proceedings cannot fall within the scope of that provision.

It appears from the order for reference that the Danish legislation is aimed not so much at protecting the pregnant woman's biological condition as at preserving the interests of her employer. Given the nature of the employment, the employer may impose requirements with regard to the employee's working capacity which justify her ceasing work at a date prior to the three-month period preceding the confinement.

Directive 92/85 sets up an assessment and information procedure in respect of activities liable to involve a risk to safety or health or an effect on workers who are pregnant or breastfeeding. That procedure can lead to the employer making a temporary adjustment in working conditions and/or working hours or, if such an adjustment is not feasible, a move to another job. It is only when such a move is also not feasible that the worker is granted leave in accordance with national legislation or national practice for the whole of the period necessary to protect her safety or health.

That legislation such as that at issue does not satisfy the substantive and formal conditions laid down in Directive 92/85 for granting the worker leave from her duties since, first, the reason for giving leave to the employee is based on the interest of the employer and, secondly, that decision can be taken by the employer without first examining the possibility of adjusting the employee's working conditions and/or working hours or even the possibility of moving her to another job.'

Comment
It is interesting to note that the ECJ confirmed the right of an employer to forfeit some or even all of the salary of a pregnant worker who is absent from work before her maternity leave not because of a pathological condition or any special risk for the unborn child but for reasons either of routine pregnancy-related inconveniences or of mere medical recommendation, without there being any incapacity for work in either of those two situations. In such a case it is her choice not to work. Although this distinction is well justified as it protects the employer against possible abuses of the rights conferred upon pregnant workers by Community law, in practice its usefulness is limited. It is very difficult to distinguish between routine-related inconveniences and more serious medical problems resulting from pregnancy.

Lisa Jacqueline Grant v *South West Trains Ltd* Case C–249/96 [1998] ECR I–621; [1998] 1 CMLR 993 European Court of Justice

- *Sex discrimination – sexual orientation – art 119 EC Treaty – discrimination based on sexual orientation not equivalent to discrimination between the sexes – homosexuality outside the scope of equal pay legislation*

Facts
A British woman employed by the rail operator South West Trains Ltd. challenged the decision of her employer who refused free travel and travel concessions on its network for her lesbian partner. Such benefits are granted to an employee's spouse, or to a partner of the opposite sex of an employee, provided there has been a meaningful relationship between them for at least two years. The plaintiff argued that the restrictions regarding 'opposite sex' were contrary to art 119 EC as supplemented by Directive 75/117 on Equal Pay since travel concessions amounted to pay.

Held
The ECJ held that discrimination in employment based on sexual orientation is outside the scope of application of the EC Treaty.

Judgment
'First, it should be observed that the regulations of the undertaking in which Ms Grant works provide for travel concessions for the worker, for the worker's "spouse", that is, the person to whom he or she is married and from whom he or she is not legally separated, or the person of the opposite sex with whom he or she has had a "meaningful" relationship for at least two years, and for the children, dependent members of the family, and surviving spouse of the worker.

The refusal to allow Ms Grant the concessions is based on the fact that she does not satisfy the conditions prescribed in those regulations, more particularly on the fact that she does not live with a "spouse" or a person of the opposite sex with whom she has had a "meaningful" relationship for at least two years.

That condition, the effect of which is that the worker must live in a stable relationship with a person of the opposite sex in order to benefit from the travel concessions, is, like the other alternative conditions prescribed in the undertaking's regulations, applied regardless of the sex of the worker concerned. Thus travel concessions are refused to a male worker if he is living with a person of the same sex, just as they are to a female worker if she is living with a person of the same sex.

Since the condition imposed by the undertaking's regulations applies in the same way to female and male workers, it cannot be regarded as constituting discrimination directly based on sex.

Second, the Court must consider whether, with respect to the application of a condition such as that in issue in the main proceedings, persons who have a stable relationship with a partner of the same sex are in the same situation as those who are married or have a stable relationship outside marriage with a partner of the opposite sex.

While the European Parliament, as Ms Grant observes, has indeed declared that it deplores all forms of discrimination based on an individual's sexual orientation, it is nevertheless the case that the Community has not as yet adopted rules providing for such equivalence.

As for the laws of the Member States, while in some of them cohabitation by two persons of the same sex is treated as equivalent to marriage, although not completely, in most of them it is treated as equivalent to a stable heterosexual relationship outside marriage only with respect to a limited number of rights, or else is not recognised in any particular way.

The European Commission of Human Rights for its part considers that despite the modern evolution of attitudes towards homosexuality, stable homosexual relationships do not fall within the scope of the right to respect for family life under art 8 of the Convention and that national provisions which, for the purpose of protecting the family, accord more favourable treatment to married persons and persons of opposite sex living together as man and wife than to persons of the same sex in a stable relationship are not contrary to art 14 of the Convention, which prohibits inter alia discrimination on the ground of sex.

In another context, the European Court of Human Rights has interpreted art 12 of the Convention as applying only to the traditional marriage between two persons of opposite biological sex.

It follows that, in the present state of the law within the Community, stable relationships between two persons of the same sex are not regarded as equivalent to marriages or stable relationships outside marriage between persons of opposite sex. Consequently, an employer is not required by Community law to treat the situation of a person who has a stable relationship with a partner of the same sex as equivalent to that of a person who is married to or has a stable relationship outside marriage with a partner of the opposite sex.

In those circumstances, it is for the legislature alone to adopt, if appropriate, measures which may affect that position.

Finally, Ms Grant submits that it follows from *P v S* [*P v S and Cornwall County Council* Case C–13/94 [1996] ECR I–2143] that differences of treatment based on sexual orientation are included in the "discrimination based on sex" prohibited by art 119 of the Treaty.

The Court stated that the provisions of the directive prohibiting discrimination between men and women were simply the expression, in their limited field of application, of the principle of equality, which is one of the fundamental principles of Community law. It considered that that circumstance argued against a restrictive interpretation of the scope of those provisions and in favour of applying them to discrimination based on the worker's gender reassignment.

The Court considered that such discrimination was in fact based, essentially if not exclusively, on the sex of the person concerned. That reasoning, which leads to the conclusion that such discrimination is to be prohibited just as is discrimination based on the fact that a person belongs to a particular sex, is limited to the case of a worker's gender reassignment and does not therefore apply to differences of treatment based on a person's sexual orientation ...'

Comment

The ECJ did not follow the opinion of the Advocate-General although it was widely expected that the ECJ would include discrimination based on sexual orientation within the scope of the EC Treaty. The ECJ decided that the employers were neither in breach of art 119 EC nor of Directive 75/117 on Equal Pay and that they had not indirectly discriminated against the plaintiff.

The ECJ held that art 119 EC applies only if men and women are treated differently. In this present case there was no discrimination based on sex as the same rule applied to female and male workers.

The ECJ refused to recognise stable homosexual relationships as equivalent to stable heterosexual relationships and dismissed the argument based on indirect discrimination accepted in *Cornwall* Case C–13/94 [1996] ECR I–2143 in which the ECJ held that the dismissal of a worker on the ground of that worker's sex change constituted unlawful discrimination. The ECJ refused to extend this decision to the present case. Also, the ECJ refused to take into consideration art 28 of the United Nations' Covenant on International Civil and Political Rights 1966 which states that sexual orientation forms an element of sex. Although international instruments such as the Covenant on International Civil and Political Rights 1966 contains international human rights principles they are not part of EC law and therefore outside its material scope of application.

The decision of the ECJ in *Grant* should be assessed in the light of a new art 13 of the Treaty of Amsterdam which requires the Council to adopt, by unanimity, measures removing all forms of discrimination, including discrimination based on sexual orientation. Therefore, the matter is only settled temporarily and the Treaty of Amsterdam will certainly call into question the present position. Nevertheless, Community measures in this area will be difficult to adopt taking into account the divergencies existing in treatment of homosexual relationships under national laws of the Member States.

Kalanke v *Freie Hansestadt Bremen* Case C–450/93 [1995] ECR I–3051 European Court of Justice

- *Discrimination based on sex on promotion – art 119 EC Treaty – Directive 76/207/EEC – equally qualified male and female – compatibility of affirmative schemes – prohibited when implemented too restrictively*

Facts
The city of Bremen, in Germany, enacted a law which promoted positive discrimination in the appointment of staff to certain public positions. The aim of the legislation was to increase the number of female staff in these positions. In essence, where two employees or job applicants had the same qualifications or the same levels of experience, the female employees were to be appointed to the post.

The applicant was a candidate for a post in the city's parks department. At the final selection both he and a female candidate were interviewed. The interview panel found the two candidates to have approximately the same qualifications and levels of experience. In the circumstances, they appointed the female applicant in compliance with the terms of law.

The applicant brought proceedings in a German court which referred a question to the ECJ seeking clarification of the compatibility of positive discrimination with art 119 EC Treaty and Community measures introducing equal pay between genders.

Held
The ECJ held that Community law precludes a Member State from introducing legislation discriminating in favour of female employees. National rules which guarantee women absolute and unconditional priority for appointments or promotion exceed the objective of equal opportunities between genders which is the objective of Community law in this area. The challenged legislation was too excessive in its structure and had the direct effect of unconditionally discriminating against men.

Judgment
'Paragraph 4 of the Landesgleichstellungsgesetz of 20 November 1990 (Bremen Law on Equal Treatment for Men and Women in the Public Service, hereinafter "the LGG") provides:

"Appointment, assignment to an official post and promotion

(1) In the case of an appointment (including establishment as a civil servant or judge) which is not made for training purposes, women who have the same qualifications as men applying for the same post are to be given priority in sectors where they are under-represented ...

(2) There is under-representation if women do not make up at least half of the staff in the individual pay, remuneration and salary brackets in the relevant group within a department ..."

The national court asks, essentially, whether art 2(1) and (4) of the Directive precludes national rules such as these in the present case which, where candidates of different sexes shortlisted for promotion are equally qualified, automatically give priority to women in sectors where they are under-represented, under-representation being deemed to exist when women do not make up at least half of the staff in the individual pay brackets in the relevant group or in the function levels provided for in the organisation chart ...

A national rule that, where men and women who are candidates for the same promotion are equally qualified, women are automatically to be given priority in sectors where they are under-represented, involves discrimination on grounds of sex.

It must, however, be considered whether such a national rule is permissible under art 2(4), which provides that the Directive "shall be without prejudice to measures to promote equal opportunities for men and women, particularly by removing existing inequalities which affect women's opportunities" ...

[A]s a derogation from an individual right laid down in Directive, art 2(4) must be interpreted strictly.

National rules which guarantee women absolute and unconditional priority for appointment or promotion go beyond promoting equal opportunities and overstep the limits of the exception in art 2(4) of the Directive.

Furthermore, in so far as it seeks to achieve equal representation of men and women in all grades and levels within a department, such a system substitutes for equality of opportunity as envisaged in art 2(4) the result which is only to be arrived at by providing such equality of opportunity.

The answer to the national court's question must therefore be that art 2(1) and (4) of the Directive preclude national rules such as those in the present case which, where candidates of different sexes shortlisted for promotion are equally qualified, automatically give priority to women in sectors where they are under-represented, under-representation being deemed to exist where women do not make up at least half of the staff in the individual brackets in the relevant personnel group or in the function levels provided for in the organisation chart.'

Comment

In the present case a national rule giving automatic priority to women candidates over equally qualified male candidates for the same promotion in a work sector in which there are fewer women than men was declared by the ECJ to be in breach of art 2(4) of Directive 76/207. The ECJ held that the discretion granted to Member States under art 2(4) of Directive 76/207 must be exercised within the confines laid down by that Directive and being a derogation from an individual right must be interpreted strictly (*Johnston* v *Chief Constable of the Royal Ulster Constabulary* Case 222/84 [1986] ECR 1651). Consequently, national law giving women absolute and unconditional priority for promotion went beyond promoting equal opportunities and overstepped the limit of exception provided for in art 2(4) of Directive 76/207.

B S Levez v T H Jennings (Harlow Pools) Ltd Case C–326/96 Judgment of 1 December 1998 (not yet reported) European Court of Justice

• *Social policy – men and women – equal pay – art 119 EC Treaty – Directive 75/117/EEC – remedies for breach of the prohibition on discrimination – pay arrears – domestic legislation placing a two-year limit on awards for the period prior to the institution of proceedings – similar domestic actions*

Facts
In February 1991 Mrs Levez was employed at a salary of £10,000 per annum as the manager of a betting shop owned by Jennings. In December 1991 she was appointed at a salary of £ 10,800 per annum as the manager of another betting shop belonging to Jennings. She replaced a man who was subject to the same contract terms and performed the same job but was paid £11,400 per annum. At the time of her appointment, she was told by Mr Jennings that her salary was the same as the salary paid to her predecessor. Her salary reached £ 11,400 in April 1992. When Mrs Levez was leaving her employment with Jennings in March 1993 she discovered that until her rise in April 1992 she was paid less then her male predecessor. In September 1993 Mrs Levez brought proceedings before the industrial tribunal under the Equal Pay Act 1970 against Mr Jennings claiming breach of the deemed equality clause implied into her contract by the Equal Pay Act 1970 under which she would be entitled to a salary of £11,400 from February 1991. She also claimed payment of the corresponding salary arrears. Mr Jennings argued that she was not entitled, in proceedings brought for breach of an equality clause, to be awarded any payment by way of arrears of remuneration or damages in respect of a time earlier than two years before the date on which the proceedings had been instituted. The tribunal dismissed her application as time-barred and held that it had no power to extend the time-limit. Mrs Levez appealed claiming that a two-year time limit was contrary to Community law. The referring court asked the ECJ whether the national limitation period was contrary to EC law and whether the fact that Mrs Levez had available to her an alternative cause of action (that is breach of contract and deceit in the county court for which the time-limit is six years) justified a two-year limitation period for claims under the Equal Pay Act 1970.

Held
The ECJ held that Community law precludes the application of a rule of national law which limits an employee's entitlement to arrears of remuneration or damages for breach of the principle of equal pay to a period of two years prior to the date on which the proceedings were instituted, there being no possibility of extending that period, where the delay in bringing a claim is attributable to the fact that the employer deliberately misrepresented to the employee the level of remuneration received by persons of the opposite sex performing like work. That was so even where another remedy was available, if that remedy entailed procedural rules or other conditions less favourable than those applicable to similar domestic actions.

Judgment
'[*The first question*]
The first point to note is that, according to established case law, in the absence of Community rules governing the matter it is for the domestic legal system of each Member State to designate the courts and tribunals having jurisdiction and to lay down the detailed procedural rules governing actions for safeguarding rights which individuals derive from Community law, provided, however, that such rules are not less favourable than those governing similar domestic actions (the principle of equivalence) and do not render virtually impossible or excessively difficult the exercise of rights conferred by Community law (the principle of effectiveness).

The Court has thus recognised that it is compatible with Community law for national rules to prescribe, in the interests of legal certainty, reasonable limitation periods for bringing proceedings.

Consequently, a national rule under which entitlement to arrears of remuneration is restricted to the two years preceding the date on which the proceedings were instituted is not in itself open to criticism.

However, with respect to the main proceedings, it is clear from the order for reference that Jennings misinformed Mrs Levez in stating that her male predecessor had been paid a salary of £10,800, which accordingly was the amount to which her salary was increased with effect from 30 December 1991. It was not until April 1992 that her salary was increased to £11,400.

It is clear, therefore, that it was because of that inaccurate or, indeed, deliberately misleading information provided by the employer that Mrs Levez was in no position to realise that, even after December 1991, she had been the victim of sex discrimination.

As regards the period preceding December 1991, it was not until April 1993 that Mrs Levez discovered the extent of the discrimination against her.

Where an employer provides an employee with inaccurate information as to the level of remuneration received by employees of the opposite sex performing like work, the employee so informed has no way of determining whether he is being discriminated against or, if so, to what extent. Consequently, by relying on the rule at issue in that situation, the employer would be able to deprive his employee of the means provided for by the Directive of enforcing the principle of equal pay before the courts.

In short, to allow an employer to rely on a national rule such as the rule at issue would, in the circumstances of the case before the national court, be manifestly incompatible with the principle of effectiveness referred to above. Application of the rule at issue is likely, in the circumstances of the present case, to make it virtually impossible or excessively difficult to obtain arrears of remuneration in respect of sex discrimination. It is plain that the ultimate effect of this rule would be to facilitate the breach of Community law by an employer whose deceit caused the employee's delay in bringing proceedings for enforcement of the principle of equal pay.

[*The second question*]

The second question should be construed as seeking to ascertain whether Community law precludes the application of the rule at issue even when another remedy is available but, compared with other domestic actions which may be regarded as similar, is likely to entail procedural rules or other conditions which are less favourable.

In view of the explanations given by the United Kingdom government, it must be held that, where an employee can rely on the rights derived from art 119 of the Treaty and the Directive before another court, the rule at issue does not compromise the principle of effectiveness. It remains to be determined whether, in the circumstances of the case before the national court, proceedings such as those which may be brought before the county court comply with the principle of equivalence.

In principle, it is for the national courts to ascertain whether the procedural rules intended to ensure that the rights derived by individuals from Community law are safeguarded under national law comply with the principle of equivalence.

In order to determine whether the principle of equivalence has been complied with in the present case, the national court which alone has direct knowledge of the procedural rules governing actions in the field of employment law must consider both the purpose and the essential characteristics of allegedly similar domestic actions.

It is necessary to consider the possibilities contemplated by the order for reference. It is there suggested that claims similar to those based on the Act may include those linked to breach of a contract of employment, to discrimination in terms of pay on grounds of race, to unlawful deductions from wages or to sex discrimination in matters other than pay.

If it transpires that a claim under the Act which is brought before the county court is similar to one or more of the forms of action listed by the national court, it would remain for that court to determine whether the first-mentioned form of action is governed by procedural rules or other requirements which are less favourable.

On that point, it is appropriate to consider whether, in order fully to assert rights conferred by Community law before the county court, an employee in circumstances such as those of Mrs Levez will incur additional costs and delay by comparison with a claimant who, because he is relying on what may be regarded as a similar right under domestic law, may bring an action before the Industrial Tribunal, which is simpler and, in principle, less costly.'

Comment
In the present case the ECJ applied the principle of equivalence and the principle of effectiveness to national procedural rules for enforcing Community law in the area of equal pay. The ECJ held that domestic limitation periods which comply with those principles are permissible. As a result the two-year time-limit was not open to criticism as it is consistent with EC law. Nevertheless its application to the present circumstances was contrary to Community law since there had been misrepresentation by the employer, the claim submitted by Mrs Levez was time-barred, and the national court had no jurisdiction to extend the two-year limitation period. Consequently, the rule in question was in breach of both principles. In relation to the second question, the ECJ left to the national court the task of assessing whether an alternative cause of action, for breach of contract and deceit, in the county court with a six-year time-limit complies with the principle of equivalence. In this respect, the ECJ enumerated factors, such as additional costs and delays incurred by the applicant, that should be taken into consideration by a national court in deciding whether or not an action brought before a county court is less favourable than an action brought before an Industrial Tribunal.

Mary Teresa Magorrian and Irene Patricia Cunningham v Eastern Health and Social Services Board and Department of Health and Social Services Case C–246/96 [1997] ECR I–7153 European Court of Justice

- *Article 119 EC – Protocol 2 annexed to the Treaty on European Union – equal pay for male and female – part-time workers – occupational social security pension scheme – additional pension benefits – its exclusion of part-time workers – backdating of the claims under art 119 EC – national procedural time-limits contrary to Community law*

Facts
Two British women were employed as nurses in the public sector in Northern Ireland. At the beginning of their careers they worked as full-time nurses, Mrs M for nine years and Mrs C for 18 years. At that time they were considered as mental health officers (MHO). Later, and until their retirement, they both worked on a part-time basis – Mrs M from 1979 to 1992, thus accumulating the equivalent of 11 years' full-time pensionable service, and Mrs C from 1980 to 1994 thus accumulating the equivalent of over 11 years' full-time pensionable service. Both (as part-time workers) were no longer considered as MHOs. The change of status had two important consequences. First, an MHO was entitled to retire at 55 rather than 60 and every year served after 20 years' service or after reaching the age of 50 counted as double for pension purposes. Second, the employer was party to a voluntary contributory contracted-out pension scheme which was open to part-time workers provided that they worked the minimum hours. When they retired they obtained their basic pensions but were deprived of some additional benefits which they would have received had they worked full-time throughout their careers as MHOs. Before their retirement both brought

proceedings against their employer under art 119 EC. They argued that they were discriminated against in respect of their pay on the ground of sex by reason of their period of part-time work being discounted in the calculation of their pensions. According to s2(5) of the Equal Pay (Northern Ireland) Act 1970 any compensation awarded for breach of the equal pay rules in that Act is to be limited to two years immediately before the date on which the proceedings were commenced. Substantive provisions of the Equal Pay (Northern Ireland) Act 1970 are identical to the UK Equal Pay Act 1970.

In this context three questions arose: first, whether both claimants were discriminated against on the ground of sex contrary to art 119 EC; second, whether the two years' cut-off in s2(5) of the Equal Pay (Northern Ireland) Act 1970 could be enforced; and, third, in the event that this rule was invalid it was necessary to determine the date to which the claims could be backdated. The industrial tribunal in Northern Ireland had no problem in finding that both claimants were discriminated against in respect of their pay in breach of art 119 EC and that there was indirect discrimination on the ground of sex given that more women than men worked part-time and thus did not qualify for MHO status. However, the two remaining issues were referred to the ECJ under art 177 EC.

Held

The ECJ held that both claimants were entitled to additional benefits

Judgment

'[*First question*]
In *Defrenne*, the Court held that the principle of equal pay under art 119 may be relied on before national courts and that those courts have a duty to ensure the protection of the rights which that provision vests in individuals. However, the Court also stated that judgment, that important considerations of legal certainty affecting all the interests involved, both public and private, meant that the direct effect of art 119 could not be relied on in order to support claims concerning pay periods prior to the date of that judgment, 8 April 1976, except as regards workers who had already brought legal proceedings or made an equivalent claim.

Although those principles were upheld in the judgment in *Barber* in relation to "contracted-out" occupational pension schemes, the Court also stated that overriding considerations of legal certainty precluded reliance being placed on the direct effect of art 119 of the Treaty in order to claim entitlement to a pension with effect from a date prior to delivery of the judgment in that case, except in the case of persons who had in the meantime taken steps to safeguard their rights.

However, in *Vroege* and *Fisscher* [*Vroege* Case C–57/93 [1994] ECR I–4541; *Fisscher* Case C–128/93 [1994] ECR I–4583] the Court took the view that the limitation of the effects in time of the *Barber* judgment concerned only those kinds of discrimination which, owing to the transitional derogations for which Community law provided and which were capable of being applied to occupational pensions, employers and pension schemes could reasonably have considered to be permissible.

As the judgment in *Bilka* [*Bilka-Kaufhaus GmbH* v *Karin Weber von Hartz* Case 170/84 [1986] ECR 1607] included no limitation of its effects in time, the direct effect of art 119 may be relied on, as from 8 April 1976, the date of the judgment in *Defrenne*, in which that article was first held to have direct effect, in order retroactively to claim equal treatment in relation to the right to join an occupational pension scheme.

As regards the right to receive benefits additional to a retirement pension under an occupational scheme such as that involved in the main proceedings, the Court finds that, even if the persons concerned have always been entitled to a retirement pension under the Superannuation Scheme, nevertheless they were not fully admitted to that contributory scheme. Solely on account of the fact that they worked part-time, they were specifically excluded from MHO status which gives access to a special scheme under the Superannuation Scheme.

It is sufficient to recall in this regard that in its judgment of 24 October 1996, *Dietz*, the Court stated that membership of a scheme would be of no interest to employees if it did not confer entitlement to the benefits provided by the scheme in question. In a situation such as that involved in that case, the Court took the view that entitlement to a retirement pension under an occupational scheme was indissolubly linked to the right to join such a scheme.

The same is true where the discrimination suffered by part-time workers stems from discrimination concerning access to a special scheme which confers entitlement to additional benefits.

[*Question 2*]
By its second question the national court is asking essentially whether Community law precludes the application to a claim based on art 119 of the Treaty of a national rule under which entitlement, in the event of a successful claim, is limited to a period which starts to run from a point in time two years prior to commencement of proceedings in connection with the claim.

As far as this issue is concerned, it must be stated that application of a procedural rule such as regulation 12 of the Occupational Pensions Regulations whereby, in proceedings concerning access to membership of occupational pension schemes, the right to be admitted to a scheme may have effect from a date no earlier than two years before the institution of proceedings would deprive the applicants in the main proceedings of the additional benefits under the scheme to which they are entitled to be affiliated, since those benefits could be calculated only by reference to periods of service completed by them as from 1990, that is to say two years prior to commencement of proceedings by them.

However, it should be noted that, in such a case, the claim is not for the retroactive award of certain additional benefits but for recognition of entitlement to full membership of an occupational scheme through acquisition of MHO status which confers entitlement to the additional benefits.

Whereas the rules at issue in *Johnston* [Case 222/84 [1986] ECR 1651] merely limited the period, prior to commencement of proceedings, in respect of which backdated benefits could be obtained, the rule at issue in the main proceedings in this case prevents the entire record of service completed by those concerned after 8 April 1976 until 1990 from being taken into account for the purposes of calculating the additional benefits which would be payable even after the date of the claim.

Consequently, a rule such as that before the national court in this case is such as to render any action by individuals relying on Community law impossible in practice.

Moreover, the effect of that national rule is to limit in time the direct effect of art 119 of the Treaty in cases in which no such limitation has been laid down either in the Court's case law or in Protocol No 2 annexed to the Treaty on European Union.'

Comment
The complexity of the solution imposed by the ECJ in respect of temporal effects of art 119 EC has engendered many disputes. In the present case the same uncertainty emerges from the questions as to what dates should any backdating of the claim be calculated – the date indicated in *Defrenne* v *Sabena* Case 43/75, that is 8 April 1976, or the date of the judgment as in *Barber* v *Guardian Royal Exchange Assurance Group* Case C–262/88, that is 17 May 1990?

The ECJ held that the date applicable in the present case was that indicated in the case of *Defrenne* (8 April 1976) and therefore for both claimants the pensionable employment commenced on that date. The ECJ explained that considerations for the limitation of the temporal effect of art 119 EC were no longer applicable since 'there was no reason to suppose that those concerned could have been mistaken as to the applicability of art 119'. The ECJ emphasised that in this case access to the status of MHO which conferred certain benefits to the claimants under their pension scheme was at issue and not the amount of pension payable to them.

The question of validity of s2(5) of the Equal Pay (Northern Ireland) Act 1970 was then examined by the ECJ. The ECJ invoked the principles of effectiveness and equivalence in order to determine whether national procedural rules were in conformity with EC law. In the present case they were in breach of those principles. The ECJ emphasised that even though both claimants were successful in their action, national procedural rules would deprive them of the benefit of art 119 EC. For that reason, s2(5) of the Equal Pay (Northern Ireland) Act 1970 is incompatible with Community law as it renders the enforcement of rights conferred by Community law impossible in practice.

This solution has important financial implications. Part-time female employees of health services who have been deprived of additional benefits from the occupational pension scheme will welcome the decision in the present case while the Treasury, no doubt, will be less pleased!

Hellmut Marschall v *Land Nordrhein-Westfalen* Case C–409/95 [1997] ECR I–6363; [1998] 1 CMLR 547 European Court of Justice

- *Discrimination based on sex in promotion – equally qualified male and female candidates – priority for female candidates – saving clause*

Facts

Hellmut Marschall, a tenured teacher (teacher qualified for teaching in first-grade secondary school and so employed) for the Länder of North Rhine-Westphalia applied for a higher grade post. He was informed by the District Authorities that they intended to appoint a female candidate to that position. When Marschall challenged the decision, the District Authorities replied that the female candidate must necessarily be promoted as according to their official assessment both candidates were equally qualified but there were fewer women than men at the level of the relevant post. The preference of a female candidate was based on art 25(5), para 2 of the German Law on Civil Servants of the Land which states that:

> 'Where, in the sector of the authority responsible for promotion, there are fewer women than men in the particular higher grade post in the career bracket, women are to be given priority for promotion in the event of equal suitability, competence and professional performance, unless reasons specific to an individual (male) candidate tilt the balance in his favour'.

Marschall brought proceedings before a German Administrative court. The latter referred to the ECJ for a preliminary ruling on the interpretation of art 2(1) and 2(4) of Directive 76/207.

Held

The ECJ held that where there are fewer women than men in a particular level of seniority, and the male and female candidates for a post at that level were equally qualified in terms of suitability, competence and performance, it is permissible for national law to provide that the woman is to be appointed unless there are reasons specific to the male candidate which tilt the balance in his favour.

Judgment

'... unlike the provision in question in *Kalanke*, the provision in question in this case contains a clause ("Öffnungsklausel", hereinafter "saving clause") to the effect that women are not to be given priority if reasons specific to an individual male candidate tilt the balance in his favour.

It is therefore necessary to consider whether a national rule containing such a clause is designed to promote equality of opportunity between men and women within the meaning of art 2(4) of the Directive.

Article 2(4) is specifically and exclusively designed to authorise measures which, although discriminatory in appearance, are in fact intended to eliminate or reduce actual instances of inequality which may exist in the reality of social life

It thus authorises national measures relating to access to employment, including promotion, which gives a specific advantage to women with a view to improving their ability to compete on the labour market and to pursue a career on an equal footing with men.

It appears that even where male and female candidates are equally qualified, male candidates tend to be promoted in preference to female candidates particularly because of prejudices and stereotypes concerning the role and capacities of women in working life and the fear, for example, that women will interrupt their careers more frequently, that owing to household and family duties they will be less flexible in their working hours, or that they will be absent from work more frequently because of pregnancy, childbirth and breastfeeding.

For those reasons, the mere fact that male candidates are equally qualified does not mean that they have the same chances.

It follows that a national rule in terms of which, subject to the application of the saving clause, female candidates for promotion who are equally as qualified as the male candidates are to be treated preferentially in sectors where they are under-represented may fall within the scope of art 2(4) if such a rule may counteract the prejudicial effects on female candidates of the attitudes and behaviour described above and thus reduce actual instances of inequality which may exist in the real world.'

Comment
Advocate-General Jacobs recommended the same solution as in *Kalanke* Case C–450/93, that is, that the German law in question was contrary to art 2(4) of Directive 76/207 although it contained a 'saving clause' providing that women are not to be given priority in promotion if reasons specific to a male candidate tilt the balance in his favour. The ECJ disagreed. The Court held that for many reasons, especially because of prejudices and stereotypes relating to the role and capacity of women in working life, there is a tendency to promote male candidates to the disadvantage of female candidates and that 'the mere fact that a male candidate and a female candidate are equally qualified does not mean that they have the same chances'. However, in this particular instance, the saving clause was sufficient to fall within the scope of art 2(4) of Directive 76/207 provided it is strictly interpreted as an exception to the general rule. As a result, the German law in question is in conformity with the Community law since it does not confer automatic and unconditional priority to female candidates and since it provides that male candidates who are as equally qualified as female candidates will be subject to an objective assessment which will take into consideration all criteria specific to both female and male candidates and will override the priority given to female candidates where one or more of those criteria tilt the balance in favour of the male candidate, and that those criteria are not such as to discriminate against the female candidates.

This solution seems fair: while encouraging the promotion of women candidates it ensures equal opportunities for both sexes. It also softens the decision of the ECJ in *Kalanke* which has been strongly criticised especially by Northern European Member States which are already more committed to combat the prejudicial effects on women in employment. It is interesting to note that art 13 of the Treaty of Amsterdam, which prohibits any discrimination, may change the approach of the ECJ towards national measures which appear discriminatory even though they intend to reduce or eliminate actual inequality between men and women.

R v *Secretary of State for Employment, ex parte Seymour-Smith and Perez* Case C–167/97 Judgment of 9 February 1999 (not yet reported) European Court of Justice

• *Social policy – men and women – equal treatment – compensation for unfair dismissal – concept of pay – right of a worker not to be unfairly dismissed – whether falling under art 119 EC Treaty or Directive 76/207/EEC – test for determining whether a national measure constitutes indirect discrimination under art 119 EC Treaty – objective justification*

Facts

Both applicants, Nicole Seymour-Smith and Laura Perez, worked for their respective employers from February 1990 to May 1991, when they were dismissed. Their claims for unfair dismissal were rejected by the Industrial Tribunal on the grounds that the condition of two years' employment (that is, only employees continuously employed for a minimum period of two years were entitled to bring claims for unfair dismissal) provided for by the amended s54 of the Employment Protection (Consolidation) Act 1978 was not satisfied. The applicants applied to the High Court for judicial review of the two years' rule, arguing that it was in breach of Community law in so far as it discriminated against women since statistics proved that the proportion of women satisfying the two years' employment rule is lower than the proportion of men satisfying it. The High Court dismissed the application on the grounds that the statistics did not show that the challenged rule affected more women than men. On appeal, the Court of Appeal decided that the rule was indirectly discriminatory and was not objectively justified. Both parties appealed to the House of Lords which referred five questions to the ECJ for a preliminary ruling

First, whether a judicial award for compensation (which an industrial tribunal that found a complaint of unfair dismissal well justified could, if no reinstatement or re-engagement order was to be made, make in respect of employees with more than two years' continuous employment) for breach of the right not to be unfairly dismissed constituted 'pay' within the meaning of art 119 EC Treaty

Second, whether the conditions determining whether an employee is entitled, where he has been unfairly dismissed, to obtain reinstatement or re-engagement, or else compensation, fall within the scope of art 119 of the Treaty or that of Directive 76/207.

Third, whether the legality of a rule of the kind at issue must be assessed as at the time of its adoption, the time when it entered into force or the time when the employee is dismissed.

Fourth, a question concerning the legal test establishing whether a measure adopted by a Member State has disparate effect as between men and women to such a degree as to amount to indirect discrimination for the purposes of art 119 of the Treaty.

Fifth, a question concerning the legal criteria for establishing the objective justification, for the purposes of indirect discrimination under art 119 of the Treaty, of a measure adopted by a Member State in pursuance of its social policy.

Held

The ECJ held that a judicial award of compensation for breach of the right not to be unfairly dismissed constitutes 'pay' within the meaning of art 119 EC Treaty. The ECJ stated that a national court should assess whether a national measure had disparate effect on men and women to such an extent as to amount to indirect discrimination taking into account the relevant statistics. If so, it was also a task of a national court to decide whether that measure had been justified by objective factors unrelated to any discrimination based on sex. Finally, it was for the national court to determine the point in time at which the legality of the challenged rule had to be assessed.

Judgment

'[*Question 1*]
According to settled case law, the concept of pay, within the meaning of the second paragraph of art 119, comprises any other consideration, whether in cash or in kind, whether immediate or future, provided that the worker receives it, albeit indirectly, in respect of his employment from his employer.

The Court has also held that the fact that certain benefits are paid after the termination of the employment relationship does not prevent them from being in the nature of pay, within the meaning of art 119 of the Treaty.

In this case, the compensation awarded to an employee for unfair dismissal, which comprises a basic award and a compensatory award, is designed in particular to give the employee what he would have earned if the employer had not unlawfully terminated the employment relationship.

The basic award refers directly to the remuneration which the employee would have received had he not been dismissed. The compensatory award covers the loss sustained by him as a result of the dismissal, including any expenses reasonably incurred by him in consequence thereof and, subject to certain conditions, the loss of any benefit which he might reasonably be expected to have gained but for the dismissal.

It follows that compensation for unfair dismissal is paid to the employee by reason of his employment, which would have continued but for the unfair dismissal. That compensation therefore falls within the definition of pay for the purposes of art 119 of the Treaty.

[*Question 2*]
... On that point it should be noted that where the claim is for compensation, the condition laid down by the disputed rule concerns access to a form of pay to which art 119 and Directive 75/117 apply.

In this case, the proceedings brought by Ms Seymour-Smith and Ms Perez before the Industrial Tribunal do not relate to the possible consequences of a working condition, namely the right not to be unfairly dismissed, but seek compensation as such, which is a matter falling under art 119 of the Treaty rather than Directive 76/207.

It would be otherwise if the dismissed employee were to seek reinstatement or re-engagement. In such a case, the conditions laid down by national law would concern working conditions or the right to take up employment and would therefore fall under Directive 76/207.

[*Question 3*]
... It should be noted at the outset that the requirements of Community law must be complied with at all relevant times, whether that is the time when the measure is adopted, when it is implemented or when it is applied to the case in point.

However, the point in time at which the legality of a rule of the kind at issue in this case is to be assessed by the national court may depend on various circumstances, both legal and factual.

Thus, where the authority which adopted the act is alleged to have acted ultra vires, the legality of that act must, in principle, be assessed at the point in time at which it was adopted.

On the other hand, in circumstances involving the application to an individual situation of a national measure which was lawfully adopted, it may be appropriate to examine whether, at the time of its application, the measure is still in conformity with Community law.

[*Question 4*]
... Article 119 of the Treaty sets out the principle that men and women should receive equal pay for equal work. That principle excludes not only the application of provisions leading to direct sex discrimination, but also the application of provisions which maintain different treatment between men and women at work as a result of the application of criteria not based on sex where those differences of treatment are not attributable to objective factors unrelated to sex discrimination.

It is common ground that the disputed rule does not entail direct sex discrimination. It must therefore be considered whether the rule may constitute indirect discrimination incompatible with art 119 of the Treaty.

As regards the establishment of indirect discrimination, the first question is whether a measure such as the rule at issue has a more unfavourable impact on women than on men.

Next, the best approach to the comparison of statistics is to consider, on the one hand, the respective proportions of men in the workforce able to satisfy the requirement of two years' employment under the disputed rule and of those unable to do so, and, on the other, to compare those proportions as regards women in the workforce. It is not sufficient to consider the number of persons affected, since that depends on the number of working people in the Member State as a whole as well as the percentages of men and women employed in that State.

It must be ascertained whether the statistics available indicate that a considerably smaller percentage of women than men is able to satisfy the condition of two years' employment required by the disputed rule. That situation would be evidence of apparent sex discrimination unless the disputed rule were justified by objective factors unrelated to any discrimination based on sex.

It is also for the national court to assess whether the statistics concerning the situation of the workforce whether they cover enough individuals, whether they illustrate purely fortuitous or short-term phenomena, and whether, in general, they appear to be significant.

In this case, it appears from the order for reference that in 1985, the year in which the requirement of two years' employment was introduced, 77.4 per cent of men and 68.9 per cent of women fulfilled that condition.

Such statistics do not appear, on the face of it, to show that a considerably smaller percentage of women than men is able to fulfil the requirement imposed by the disputed rule.

[Question 5]
... It is settled case law that if a Member State is able to show that the measures chosen reflect a necessary aim of its social policy and are suitable and necessary for achieving that aim, the mere fact that the legislative provision affects far more women than men at work cannot be regarded as a breach of art 119 of the Treaty.

Although social policy is essentially a matter for the Member States under Community law as it stands, the fact remains that the broad margin of discretion available to the Member States in that connection cannot have the effect of frustrating the implementation of a fundamental principle of Community law such as that of equal pay for men and women.

Mere generalisations concerning the capacity of a specific measure to encourage recruitment are not enough to show that the aim of the disputed rule is unrelated to any discrimination based on sex nor to provide evidence on the basis of which it could reasonably be considered that the means chosen were suitable for achieving that aim.'

Comment

The question to resolve for the ECJ was whether there was indirect discrimination involved as all parties agreed that the applicants were not directly discriminated against. The ECJ applied its usual test in order to determine indirect discrimination. The Court considered whether the challenged national provision had produced more disadvantageous effects on female workers than on male workers, taking into account the relevant statistics concerning, on the one hand, the respective proportions of men in the workforce able to satisfy the requirement of two years' employment and those unable to do so, and, on the other hand, compared those proportions in respect of women in the workplace. The ECJ has recourse to the statistics provided they are reliable and significative (*Enderby* Case C–123/92 [1993] ECR I–5535). In the present case, the statistics for 1985 indicated that 77.4 per cent of men and 68.9 per cent of women fulfilled the condition of the two years' employment. Therefore statistically the impact of the challenged provision was, on the face of it, non-significative. Even if the contested provision had more detrimental impact on women than on men it might be justified by objective reasons unrelated to any discrimination based on sex. It is for the Member State to prove that the measure chosen reflects a necessary aim of its social policy and is suitable and necessary for achieving that aim which must be unrelated to any discrimination based on sex (*Freers and Speckmann* Case C–278/93 [1996] ECR I–1165). The ECJ agreed that the aim of the UK's social policy was legitimate but rejected the means chosen, that is the challenged rule, as suitable and necessary to achieve that aim.

The ECJ held that although social policy is essentially within the competence of a Member State, the aims of national rules pursuing a social policy aim cannot have the effect of frustrating the implementation of a fundamental principle of EC law, in this case that of equal pay for men and women.

12 The Right of Establishment and the Right to Supply and Receive Services: Articles 52–58 EC Treaty (now Articles 43–58 EC Treaty)

Right of establishment

Centros Ltd v Erhvervs-og Selskabsstyrelsen Case C–212/97 Judgment of 9 March 1999 (not yet reported) European Court of Justice

- Freedom of establishment – arts 56 and 58 EC Treaty – establishment of a branch by a company not carrying on any actual business – circumvention of national law – refusal to register – fraud – free movement of workers – art 52 EC Treaty

Facts

In May 1992 Mrs Bryde, a Danish national, registered her company Centros in the UK, taking advantage of the UK law which did not impose any requirement on limited liability companies as to the paying-up of a minimum share capital.

During the summer of 1992 Mrs Bryde requested the Danish Trade and Companies Board to register a branch of Centros in Denmark. The Board refused on the grounds that Centros had never traded since its formation and that Mrs Bryde was, in fact, seeking to establish in Denmark not a branch but a principal establishment by circumventing Danish rules concerning the paying-up of minimum capital fixed at DKK 200,000.

Centros challenged the decision of the Danish Trade and Companies Board.

Held

The ECJ held that it was contrary to arts 52 and 58 of the EC Treaty for a Member State to refuse on the above-mentioned grounds to register a branch of a company formed in accordance with the law of another Member State in which it had its registered office but in which the company itself was not engaged in any business activities.

Judgment

'By its question, the national court is in substance asking whether it is contrary to arts 52 and 58 of the Treaty for a Member State to refuse to register a branch of a company formed in accordance with the legislation of another Member State in which it has its registered office but where it does not carry on any business when the purpose of the branch is to enable the company concerned to carry on its entire business in the State in which that branch is to be set up, while avoiding the formation of a company in that State, thus evading application of the rules governing the formation of companies which are, in that State, more restrictive so far as minimum paid-up share capital is concerned.

According to the Court, a situation in which a company formed in accordance with the law of a Member State in which it has its registered office desires to set up a branch in another Member State falls within the scope of Community law. In that regard, it is immaterial that the company was formed in the first Member State only for the purpose of establishing itself in the second, where its main, or indeed entire, business is to be conducted.

The fact that Mrs and Mrs Bryde formed the company Centros in the United Kingdom for the purpose of avoiding Danish legislation requiring that a minimum amount of share capital be paid up does not, however, mean that the formation by that British company of a branch in Denmark is not covered by freedom of establishment for the purposes of art 52 and 58 of the Treaty. The question of the application of those articles of the Treaty is different from the question whether or not a Member State may adopt measures in order to prevent attempts by certain of its nationals to evade domestic legislation by having recourse to the possibilities offered by the Treaty.

Where it is the practice of a Member State, in certain circumstances, to refuse to register a branch of a company having its registered office in another Member State, the result is that companies formed in accordance with the law of that other Member State are prevented from exercising the freedom of establishment conferred on them by arts 52 and 58 of the Treaty.

Consequently, that practice constitutes an obstacle to the exercise of the freedoms guaranteed by those provisions.

A Member State is entitled to take measures designed to prevent certain of its nationals from attempting, under cover of the rights created by the Treaty, improperly to circumvent their national legislation or to prevent individuals from improperly or fraudulently taking advantage of provisions of Community law.

However, the national courts must nevertheless assess such conduct in the light of the objectives pursued by those provisions.

In the present case, the provisions of national law, application of which the parties concerned have sought to avoid, are rules governing the formation of companies and not rules concerning the carrying on of certain trades, professions or businesses. The provisions of the Treaty on freedom of establishment are intended specifically to enable companies formed in accordance with the law of a Member State and having their registered office, central administration or principal place of business within the Community to pursue activities in other Member States through an agency, branch or subsidiary.

That being so, the fact that a national of a Member State who wishes to set up a company chooses to form it in the Member State whose rules of company law seem to him the least restrictive and to set up branches in other Member States cannot, in itself, constitute an abuse of the right of establishment. The right to form a company in accordance with the law of a Member State and to set up branches in other Member States is inherent in the exercise, in a single market, of the freedom of establishment guaranteed by the Treaty.

In this connection, the fact that company law is not completely harmonised in the Community is of little consequence. Moreover, it is always open to the Council, on the basis of the powers conferred upon it by art 54(3)(g) of the EC Treaty, to achieve complete harmonisation.

The fact that a company does not conduct any business in the Member State in which it has its registered office and pursues its activities only in the Member State where its branch is established is not sufficient to prove the existence of abuse or fraudulent conduct which would entitle the latter Member State to deny that company the benefit of the provisions of Community law relating to the right of establishment.

Accordingly, the refusal of a Member State to register a branch of a company formed in accordance with the law of another Member State in which it has its registered office on the grounds that the branch is intended to enable the company to carry on all its economic activity in the host State, with the result that the secondary establishment escapes national rules on the provision for and the paying-up of a minimum capital, is incompatible with arts 52 and 58 of the Treaty, in so far as it prevents any exercise of the right freely to set up a secondary establishment which arts 52 and 58 are specifically intended to guarantee.

The national measures liable to hinder or make less attractive the exercise of fundamental freedoms guaranteed by the Treaty must fulfill four conditions: they must be applied in a non-discriminatory manner; they must be justified by imperative requirements in the general interest; they must be suitable for securing the attainment of the objective which they pursue; and they must not go beyond what is necessary in order to attain it.

Those conditions are not fulfilled in the case in the main proceedings. First, the practice in question is not such as to attain the objective of protecting creditors which it purports to pursue since, if the company concerned had conducted business in the United Kingdom, its branch would have been registered in Denmark, even though Danish creditors might have been equally exposed to risk.

Second, it is possible to adopt measures which are less restrictive, or which interfere less with fundamental freedoms, by, for example, making it possible in law for public creditors to obtain the necessary guarantees.

Lastly, the fact that a Member State may not refuse to register a branch of a company formed in accordance with the law of another Member State in which it has its registered office does not preclude that first State from adopting any appropriate measure for preventing or penalising fraud, either in relation to the company itself, if need be in cooperation with the Member State in which it was formed, or in relation to its members, where it has been established that they are in fact attempting, by means of the formation of the company, to evade their obligations towards private or public creditors established on the territory of a Member State concerned. In any event, combating fraud cannot justify a practice of refusing to register a branch of a company which has its registered office in another Member State.'

Comment
The ECJ confirmed its liberal approach towards the freedom of establishment by stating that national rules regarding the prevention of fraud cannot justify restrictions which impair the freedom of establishment of companies. In its advisory opinion, Advocate-General La Pergola suggested that in the light of the evolution of the Community the freedom of establishment should be approached in the same manner as the free movement of goods, that is, the principles of *Cassis de Dijon* should apply. The echo of his suggestion can be found in the statement of the ECJ that only 'imperative requirements' in the general interest may justify national measures hindering the exercise of the right to freely set up a branch in other Member States.

The ECJ did not 'look behind the veil' of a company, it applied the provisions relating to the right of establishment. Therefore, the fact that Mrs Bryde was taking advantage of more lenient company law in the UK permitting her to avoid paying the capital required by Danish law for the establishment of the company, and that the main purpose of establishing her company in the UK was to open a branch in Denmark which actually was intended to be a principal establishment, did not constitute an abuse of right of establishment. The decision in the present case in not surprising taking into account that the ECJ in previous cases applied a restrictive approach to national measures intended to fight fraud which imposed restrictions on the freedom of establishment (*EC Commission* v *France* Case 270/83 [1986] ECR 273 in which the right of establishment was exercised in order to benefit from tax advantages in another Member State; and *Segers* v *Bestuur van de Bedrifsvereniging voor bank-en verzekeringswezen* Case C–79/85 [1986] ECR 2375 concerning social security benefits).

The only danger of this approach is that it might create the so-called 'Delaware 'effect within the EU. Under the 'Delaware' effect many states in the USA have introduced very lenient rules in respect of the formation of companies (in particular in relation to the protection of creditors) in order to attract new companies. In the context of the EU it will be necessary to harmonise national laws of the Member States in this area in order to prevent some Member States from introducing new legislation aimed at attracting businesses from other Member States but at the cost of weaker protection for creditors.

EC Commission v Luxembourg (Re Access to the Medical Profession)
Case C–351/90 [1992] 3 CMLR 124
European Court of Justice

- *Freedom of establishment for medical profession – arts 48 and 52 EC Treaty – prohibition on maintaining multiple practices in different Member States – national measures amounted to discrimination – no justification for national measures*

Facts
Under Luxembourg law, doctors, dentists and veterinary surgeons with practices in other Member States were prohibited from practising in Luxembourg without the express permission of the Luxembourg authorities. However, this prohibition did not apply to members of these professions from Luxembourg.

The Commission brought proceedings against Luxembourg on the grounds that the requirement to obtain express permission was in breach of arts 48 and 52 of the Treaty as it discriminated between nationals and non-nationals.

Held
The ECJ held that Luxembourg was in breach of its obligations under arts 48 and 52 EC Treaty by requiring nationals of Member States to obtain a special permission before practising in Luxembourg. Any derogations from the terms of these articles must be justified on objective grounds and must not be unduly harsh or restrictive. In the circumstances of the present case, the restrictions were considered to be too restrictive and therefore unjustified.

Judgment
'It should be observed that the so-called single-practice rule for doctors, dentists and veterinary surgeons has the effect of restricting the freedom of movement of workers and the right of establishment which are guaranteed by arts 48 and 52 [EC].

In accordance with the Court's settled case law, the right of establishment includes freedom to set up and maintain, subject to observance of the professional rules of conduct, more than one place of work within the Community.

This is just as true where a person who is employed or self-employed and established in one Member State wishes to work in another Member State, irrespective of whether he proposes to do so as an employed or self-employed person.

As the Court pointed out in *EC Commission v France* [1986] ECR 1475, with regard to the medical and dental professions, the professional rules of conduct which must be observed are those which reflect a concern to ensure that individuals enjoy the most effective and complete health protection possible. The rules governing the profession of veterinary surgeon likewise have the same objective of health.

However, it follows from the same judgment that those rules, in so far as they have the effect of restricting the right of establishment and freedom of movement of workers, are compatible with the Treaty only if the restrictions they entail are actually justified by general obligations inherent in good professional practice and if the restrictions are imposed without distinction on nationals of the Member State in question and those of other Member States. In this connection the Court found that this was not the case where the restrictions were likely to create discrimination against practitioners established in other Member States or obstacles to entering the profession which go beyond what is necessary to attain the above-mentioned objectives.

On this point it must be said that the single-practice rule, which the Luxembourg Government describes as essential for continuity of patient care, is applied more strictly to doctors and dentists practising in other Member States than to those working in Luxembourg. In effect, s16, sentence 2 of the Act permits an exception to the single-practice rule only in favour of persons practising in Luxembourg.

In this connection the Luxembourg government contends that the exception can be extended by ministerial decisions, in special cases, to persons established in other Member States.

This argument cannot succeed. Firstly, s16 of the Act refers only to practitioners established in Luxembourg. Secondly, observance of the principles of equal treatment which find expression in arts 48 and 52 [EC] should not depend on the unilateral will of national authorities.

Accordingly it must be said that, although the legal position is clear in the sense that arts 48 and 52 [EC] are directly applicable in the Member States, nevertheless the continued existence of s16 of the Act in question gives rise to an ambiguous de facto situation by keeping the individuals concerned in a state of uncertainty with regard to their rights under Community law.

It should be added that a general prohibition on practitioners established or employed in another Member State from working from an establishment in Luxembourg is unduly restrictive.

On this point the Luxembourg government argues that the single practice rule is objectively justified on grounds of public health and public policy, and by the general interest. It adds that the relationship between practitioner and patient is inherently personal and requires continuity of attendance by the practitioner at his surgery or place of employment in order to provide continuous care, and that the emergency service would be disorganised if practitioners with more than one place of work were involved.

These arguments likewise cannot succeed.

Firstly, there is no need for a practitioner, whether a general practitioner, dentist or veterinary surgeon, or even a specialist, to be close to the patient or client continuously. Secondly, the single-practice rule does not necessarily ensure that the same practitioner is continuously available if, for example, he has to be elsewhere, works part-time or belongs to a group practice. Finally, continuity of patient care and efficient organisation of the emergency service can be secured by less restrictive means, such as requirements for minimum attendance or arrangements to provide substitutes.

These considerations show that the prohibition is too absolute and too general to be justified by the need to provide continuity of patient care.

Therefore, it must be found that, by preventing medical practitioners, dentists and veterinary surgeons established in another Member State or working as employed persons there from establishing themselves in Luxembourg or working there as employed persons while retaining their practice or employment in the other Member State, the Grand Duchy of Luxembourg has failed to fulfill its obligations under arts 48 and 52 [EC].'

Comment
National rules imposing restrictions on the right of establishment must fulfill four criteria in order to be justified. They must apply without distinction to nationals and non-nationals, they must be justified by imperative requirements in the general interest, they must be suitable for the attainment of the objective which they pursue, and they must not go beyond what is necessary to attain that objective. In the present case, these criteria were not fulfilled.

Imperial Chemical Industries* v *Colmer (Inspector of Taxes) Case C–264/96 [1998] 3 CMLR 293
European Court of Justice

• *Freedom of establishment – art 52 EC Treaty – companies – foreign holdings –*

direct taxation – tax relief – maintenance of the cohesion of tax system – tax evasion – scope of application of EC law – preliminary reference – art 5 EC Treaty – supremacy of EC law

Facts

ICI, together with another company, both residents in the UK, formed a consortium through which they beneficially owned Coopers Animal Health (Holdings) Ltd. The sole business of this company was to hold shares in 23 trading companies which were its subsidiaries. Some of the subsidiaries were resident in the UK (four), some in other Member States (six) and some outside the territory of the EU. Within the subsidiary companies residing in the UK was Coopers Animal Health Ltd (CAH). ICI applied for tax relief under ss258–264 of the Income and Corporation Taxes Act 1970 in order to set off losses incurred by CAH. This was refused on the ground that CAH (Holdings) Ltd was not a holding company within the meaning of s258(7) of the Act since the majority of the subsidiaries were not resident in the UK. ICI challenged that decision and argued that the residence requirement under the Act was contrary to arts 52 and 58 of EC Treaty. The House of Lords referred two questions to the ECJ: first, whether the residency requirement under the Income and Corporation Taxes Act 1970 was in conformity with arts 52 and 58 of EC Treaty; and, second, concerning the scope of application of EC law where the subsidiaries were established in non-Member States.

Held

Article 52 EC precludes legislation of a Member State which, in the case of companies established in that State belonging to a consortium through which they control a holding company, by means of which they exercise their right to freedom of establishment in order to set up subsidiaries in other Member States, makes a particular form of tax relief subject to the requirement that the holding company's business consists wholly or mainly in the holding of shares in subsidiaries that were established in the Member State concerned. In relation to the second question the ECJ held that art 5 of EC Treaty did not require the national court to interpret its legislation in conformity with EC law or to disapply the legislation to situations falling outside the scope of EC law.

Judgment

'[*The first question*]

Under the legislation at issue in the main proceedings, companies belonging to a resident consortium which have, through a holding company, exercised their right to freedom of establishment in order to set up subsidiaries in other Member States are denied tax relief on losses incurred by a resident subsidiary where the majority of the subsidiaries controlled by the holding company have their seat outside the United Kingdom.

It is therefore necessary to determine whether there is any justification for such inequality of treatment under the Treaty's provisions on freedom of establishment.

As regards the justification based on the risk of tax avoidance, suffice it to note that the legislation at issue in the main proceedings does not have the specific purpose of preventing wholly artificial arrangements, set up to circumvent United Kingdom tax legislation, from attracting tax benefits, but applies generally to all situations in which the majority of a group's subsidiaries are established, for whatever reason, outside the United Kingdom. However, the establishment of a company outside the United Kingdom does not, of itself, necessarily entail tax avoidance, since that company will in any event be subject to the tax legislation of the State of establishment.

Furthermore, the risk of charges being transferred, which the legislation at issue is designed to prevent, is entirely independent of whether or not the majority of subsidiaries are resident in the United Kingdom. The existence of only one non-resident subsidiary is enough to create the risk invoked by the United Kingdom government.

In answer to the argument that revenue lost through the granting of tax relief on losses incurred by resident subsidiaries cannot be offset by taxing the profits of non-resident subsidiaries, it must be pointed out that diminution of tax revenue occurring in this way is not one of the grounds listed in art 56 of the Treaty and cannot be regarded as a matter of overriding general interest which may be relied upon in order to justify unequal treatment that is, in principle, incompatible with art 52 of the Treaty.

It is true that in the past the Court has accepted that the need to maintain the cohesion of tax systems could, in certain circumstances, provide sufficient justification for maintaining rules restricting fundamental freedoms. Nevertheless, in the cases cited, there was a direct link between the deductibility of contributions from taxable income and the taxation of sums payable by insurers under old-age and life assurance policies, and that link had to be maintained in order to preserve the cohesion of the tax system in question. In the present case, there is no such direct link between the consortium relief granted for losses incurred by a resident subsidary and the taxation of profits made by non-resident subsidiaries.

[*The second question*]
By its second question the House of Lords essentially asks the Court to explain the scope of the duty to cooperate in good faith, laid down by art 5 of the Treaty.

It must be emphasised that the difference of treatment applied according to whether or not the business of the holding company belonging to the consortium consists wholly or mainly in holding shares in subsidiaries having their seat in non-member countries lies outside the scope of Community law.

Consequently, arts 52 and 58 of the Treaty do not preclude domestic legislation under which tax relief is not granted to a resident consortium member where the business of the holding company owned by that consortium consists wholly or mainly in holding shares in subsidiaries which have their seat in non-member countries. Nor does art 5 of the Treaty apply.

Accordingly, when deciding an issue concerning a situation which lies outside the scope of Community law, the national court is not required, under Community law, either to interpret its legislation in a way conforming with Community law or to disapply that legislation. Where a particular provision must be disapplied in a situation covered by Community law, but that same provision could remain applicable to a situation not so covered, it is for the competent body of the State concerned to remove that legal uncertainty in so far as it might affect rights deriving from Community rules.'

Comment

In *Futura Participation* Case C–250/95 [1997] ECR I–2471 the ECJ was more inclined to favour the maintenance of a national tax system. In the present case it held that although direct taxation was in principle within the competence of the Member State, the latter must nevertheless exercise its powers of direct taxation in conformity with Community law (see *Schumacker* Case C–279/93 [1995] ECR I–225). In circumstances such as those in the present case, national legislation hindered the freedom of establishment since it set up differential tax treatment of consortium companies established in the UK as compared with those established in other Member States. The justifications provided by the UK were rejected by the ECJ (see above). Also, the argument based on the maintenance of cohesion of the national tax system submitted by the government of the UK was rejected as neither satisfying the conditions established in *Hans-Martin Bachmann* v *Belgian State* Case C–204/90 [1992] ECR I–249 nor fulfilling the criterion of proportionality. The ECJ confirmed that while a particular provision of national law must be disapplied in relation to a situation covered by EC law the same provision could be applied in a situation falling outside the scope of EC law. However, this may create legal uncertainty which a Member

State should avoid in so far as it might affect rights deriving from EC law.

Jean Reyners v The Belgian State
Case 2/74 [1974] ECR 631; [1974] 2 CMLR 305 European Court of Justice

* Freedom of establishment – art 52 EC Treaty – national restrictions based on nationality preventing foreign nationals practising law – discrimination contrary to arts 6 and 52 EC Treaty – direct effect of art 52 EC Treaty – need for professional qualification – art 55 EC Treaty – advocates do not exercise official authority

Facts
Jean Reyners, a Dutch national born and bred in Belgium, a holder of the Belgian doctorate in law (docteur en droit), sat the necessary examinations to become an advocate in Belgium. The Belgian legislation provided that only Belgian nationals could be called to the Belgian Bar. Reyners challenged the compatibility of this legislation with art 52 EC Treaty. The Belgian Conseil d'Etat referred the matter to the ECJ under the preliminary ruling procedure. During these proceedings, the Belgian Bar and the government of Luxembourg submitted that the profession of advocate was excluded from art 52 EC Treaty as its activities were connected with the exercise of official authority within the meaning of art 55 EC Treaty. In Belgium an advocate may be called upon to sit as a judge in certain cases, and a judge exercises official authority.

Held
The rule established in art 52 EC Treaty had to be interpreted in the light of the whole scheme of the EC Treaty, including art 6 which prohibits any discrimination on the grounds of nationality. The ECJ held that art 52 EC Treaty was directly effective. The Court stated that the exception to freedom of establishment contained in art 55 EC Treaty did not apply to the profession of advocate as it was restricted to activities which involved a direct and specific connection with the exercise of official authority.

Judgment
'[*On the interpretation of art 52 EC Treaty*] The rule on equal treatment with nationals is one of the fundamental legal provisions of the Community.

As a reference to a set of legislative provisions effectively applied by the country of establishment to its own nationals, this rule is, by its essence, capable of being directly invoked by nationals of all the other Member States.

In laying down that freedom of establishment shall be attained at the end of the transitional period, art 52 thus imposes an obligation to attain a precise result, the fulfilment of which had to made easier by, but not made dependent on, the implementation of a programme of progressive measures.

The fact that this progression has not been adhered to leaves the obligation itself intact beyond the end of the period provided for its fulfilment.

This interpretation is in accordance with art 8(7) of the Treaty, according to which the expiry of the transitional period shall constitute the latest date by which all the rules laid down must enter into force and all the measures required for establishing the Common Market must be implemented.

It is not possible to invoke against such an effect the fact that the Council has failed to issue the directives provided for by arts 54 and 57 or the fact that certain of the directives actually issued have not fully attained the objective of non-discrimination required by art 52.

After the expiry of the transitional period the directives provided for by the Chapter on the right of establishment have become superfluous with regard to implementing the rule on nationality, since this is henceforth sanctioned by the Treaty itself with direct effect.

These directives have however not lost all interest since they preserve an important scope in the field of measures intended to make easier the effective exercise of the right of freedom of establishment.

It is therefore to reply to the question raised that, since the end of the transitional period, art 52 of the Treaty is a directly applicable provision despite the absence in a particular sphere of the directives prescribed by arts 54(2) and 57(1) of the Treaty.

[*On the interpretation of art 55 EC Treaty*]
The Conseil d'Etat has also requested a definition of what is meant in the first paragraph of art 55 by "activities which in that State are connected, even occasionally, with the exercise of official authority".

... Professional activities involving contacts, even regular and organic, with the courts, including even compulsory co-operation in their functioning, do not constitute, as such, connection with the exercise of official authority.

The most typical activities of the profession of avocat, in particular, such as consultation and legal assistance and also representation and the defence of parties in court, even when the intervention or assistance of the avocat is compulsory or is a legal monopoly, cannot be considered as connected with the exercise of judicial authority.

The exercise of these activities leaves the discretion of judicial authority and the free exercise of judicial power intact.

It is therefore right to reply to the question raised that the exception to freedom of establishment provided for by the first paragraph of art 55 must be restricted to those activities referred to in art 52 which in themselves involve a direct and specific connection with the exercise of official authority.

In any case it is not possible to give this description, in the context of a profession such as that of avocat, to activities such as consultation and legal assistance or the representation and defence of parties in court, even if the performance of these activities is compulsory or there is a legal monopoly in respect of it.'

Comment
In the present case the ECJ held that art 52 EC Treaty was directly effective and the fact that this provision stated that the restrictions on the freedom of establishment 'shall be abolished by progressive stages in the course of the transitional period' did not affect the rights of nationals of one Member State wishing to establish themselves in another Member State to enjoy immediate protection. The ECJ held that art 52 EC Treaty imposed an obligation to attain a precise result which was not conditional upon the implementation of a programme of progressive measures. The latter would only facilitate the attainment of the prescribed result.

The ECJ also stated that the legal profession is within the scope of art 52 EC Treaty and therefore the exception to freedom of establishment based on art 55 EC Treaty can not be invoked (the situation is uncertain in respect of the notariat of the Member States of continental Europe).

Jean Thieffry v *Conseil de l'Ordre des Avocats à la Cour de Paris* Case 71/76 [1977] ECR 765; [1977] 2 CMLR 373 European Court of Justice

• *Free movement of lawyers – art 52 of EC Treaty – discrimination on the grounds of nationality – art 57 of EC Treaty – recognition of professional qualification – national practice or legislation – admission to professional bodies*

Facts
Jean Thieffry, a Belgian advocate and a holder of a Belgian diploma of Doctor of Laws which was recognised by a French University as equivalent to the French licentiate's degree of law, applied for admission to the training stage required for an advocate at the Paris Bar. He satisfied the condition for admission to the training stage as he sat and successfully passed the French examination for the Certificat d'Aptitude à la Profession d'Avocat (Qualifying Certificate for the Profession of Advocate). The Paris Bar refused to call him

to the bar. The refusal was justified on the ground that he 'offers no French diploma evidencing a licentiate's degree or a doctor's degree'. He challenged the decision of the Paris Bar Council before the French Court of Appeal (Cour d'Appel) which referred to the ECJ a question concerning the interpretation of art 57 of the Treaty, which relates to the mutual recognition of evidence of professional qualifications for the purpose of access to activities as self-employed persons, with regard, in particular, to admission to exercise the profession of advocate.

Held
The ECJ held that national authorities, including national professional bodies such as the Paris Bar Council, have a duty to ensure that national practices and legislation are compatible which the objectives of the Treaty. Even in the absence of Community measures adopted under art 57 EC Treaty for a particular profession, by virtue of art 52 EC Treaty a person cannot be denied the practical benefit of the freedom of establishment on the ground that national legislation providing for the recognition of equivalence of diplomas limits such recognition to university purposes, in particular in circumstances when the applicant had also obtained a professional qualifying certificate in accordance with legislation of the State of establishment.

Judgment
'... if the freedom of establishment provided for by art 52 can be ensured in a Member State either under the provisions of laws and regulations in force, or by virtue of the practices of the public service or of professional bodies, a person subject to Community law cannot be denied the practical benefit of that freedom solely by virtue of the fact that, for a particular profession, the directives provided for by art 57 of the Treaty have not yet been adopted.

Since the practical enjoyment of freedom of establishment can thus in certain circumstances depend upon national practice or legislation, it is incumbent upon the competent public authorities – including legally recognised professional bodies – to ensure that such practice or legislation [is] applied in accordance with the objective defined by the provisions of the Treaty relating to freedom of establishment.

In particular, there is an unjustified restriction on that freedom where, in a Member State, admission to a particular profession is refused to a person covered by the Treaty who holds a diploma which has been recognised as an equivalent qualification by the competent authority of the country of establishment and who furthermore has fulfilled the specific conditions regarding professional training in force in that country, solely by reason of the fact that the person concerned does not possess the national diploma corresponding to the diploma which he holds and which has been recognised as an equivalent qualification.

The national court specifically referred to the effect of a recognition of equivalence "by the university authority of the country of establishment", and in the course of the proceedings the question has been raised whether a distinction should be drawn, as regards the equivalence of diplomas, between university recognition, granted with a view to permitting the pursuit of certain studies, and a recognition having "civil effect", granted with a view to permitting the pursuit of professional activity.

It emerges from the information supplied in this connection by the Commission and the governments which took part in the proceedings that the distinction between the academic effect and the civil effect of the recognition of foreign diplomas is acknowledged, in various forms, in the legislation and practice of several Member States.

Since the distinction falls within the ambit of the national law of the different States, it is for the national authorities to assess the consequences thereof, taking account, however, of the objectives of Community law.

In this connection it is important that, in each Member State, the recognition of evidence of a professional qualification for the purposes of establishment may be accepted to the full extent compatible with the observance of the professional requirements mentioned above.

Consequently, it is for the competent national authorities, taking account of the requirements of Community law set out above, to make such assessments of the facts as will enable them to judge whether a recognition granted by a university authority can, in addition to its academic effect, constitute valid evidence of a professional qualification.

The fact that a national legislation provides for recognition of equivalence only for university purposes does not of itself justify the refusal to recognise such equivalence as evidence of a professional qualification.

This is particularly so when a diploma recognised for university purposes is supplemented by a professional qualifying certificate obtained according to the legislation of the country of establishment.

In these circumstances, the answer to the question referred to the Court should be that when a national of one Member State desirous of exercising a professional activity such as the profession of advocate in another Member State has obtained a diploma in his country of origin which has been recognised as an equivalent qualification by the competent authority under the legislation of the country of establishment and which has thus enabled him to sit and pass the special qualifying examination for the profession in question, the act of demanding the national diploma prescribed by the legislation of the country of establishment constitutes, even in the absence of the directives provided for in art 57, a restriction incompatible with the freedom of establishment guaranteed by art 52 of the Treaty.'

Comment

In the context of the present case it is interesting to note that at last in 1998 the European Parliament and the Council adopted Directive 98/5/EC on the right of establishment for lawyers who have obtained professional qualifications in the home Member State and wish to practise their profession on a permanent basis in any other Member State. The Directive must be implemented by 14 March 2000. The Directive applies to employed and self-employed lawyers and in the UK encompasses solicitors, barristers and advocates. The main features of Directive 98/5/EC are that:

1. A lawyer establishing himself in another Member State must use the professional title which he has obtained in his home Member State. This restriction was deemed necessary in order to avoid confusion between the lawyer's home State qualification and the qualification required by the host Member State. The professional title must be expressed in the official language of the home Member State.
2. A lawyer who wishes to establish himself in another Member State must register with the competent authorities of the host Member State.
3. There are no restrictions as to the areas of law in which a lawyer is permitted to practise in the host Member State. The above means that such a lawyer can give legal advice on both the law of the host and home Member States as well as EC law and international law. This is subject to two exceptions. First, if a host Member State reserves some activities such as the preparation of deeds, the administration of estates or the creation and transfer of interests in land for certain categories of lawyers, and in other Member States those activities are performed by non-lawyers, a host Member State is permitted to exclude lawyers from other Member States from carrying out those activities. Second, the requirement for a lawyer from another Member State to act in conjunction with a lawyer from a host Member State while representing a client in the courts of a host Member State has been maintained.

It should be noted that:

1. The rules of personal conduct and etiquette of both a home and a host Member

State apply to a lawyer wishing to practise in a host Member State.
2. The competent authorities of a host Member State are entitled to bring disciplinary proceedings against a lawyer from another Member State registered in the host State who fails to meet the professional standards required by that State under the same conditions as applied to lawyers qualified in the host Member State.
3. The Directive has substantially revised the conditions under which a lawyer from another Member State may qualify as a lawyer in a host Member State: first, if he effectively and regularly pursues his practice in the host Member State in the law of that State for three years; second, even if he practises the law of his home Member State or EC law or international law, he may obtain the host Member State's qualification provided he carries out his professional activities in a host Member State for three years and satisfies the host Member State's authorities as to his competence with regard to that State's law.

Freedom to supply services

EC Commission v Germany (Re Restrictions on the Legal Profession) Case 427/85 [1988] ECR 1123; [1989] 2 CMLR 677 European Court of Justice

• *Freedom to provide legal services – Directive 77/249 – its implementation in Member States – additional requirements added by a national authority when implementing Directive 77/249 – clarification of the term 'work in conjunction with' – unjustifiable restrictions*

Facts
The Council of Ministers enacted Directive 77/249 (1977) to facilitate the effective exercise by lawyers of the freedom to provide legal services in Member States other than those in which their professional qualifications had been obtained. The German government gave effect to this Directive through a law passed in 1980. However, this legislation, while allowing lawyers from other Member States to provide legal services in Germany, required that such foreign lawyers could only act 'in conjunction' with a German host lawyer. A number of other restrictions were also imposed on foreign lawyers. The German lawyer, and not the visiting foreign lawyer, had to be the authorised representative of the client and the foreign lawyer could not appear in oral hearings or in criminal trials.

The Commission argued that these restrictions were in breach of Directive 77/249 and brought proceedings against Germany under art 169 EC Treaty for a declaration that Germany failed to fulfil its obligations arising out of the Treaty.

Held
The ECJ held that Germany failed to effectively implement Directive 77/249 into its national law by imposing too restrictive conditions on the supply of legal services in Germany by lawyers from other Member States. In particular, the ECJ found that the requirement that foreign lawyers act in conjunction with a German lawyer at all material times was disproportionate to the objective sought by the Directive, that is the protection of individuals from inappropriately qualified legal representatives.

Judgment
'The Commission criticises the Federal Republic of Germany in general terms for having determined the meaning of "work in conjunction" in the 1980 Act in such a way that it goes beyond the limits laid down by the Directive and by arts 59 and 60 of the EC Treaty. The complaints relate in particular to the requirements concerning proof of work in conjunction, the role attributed to

the German lawyer in conjunction with whom the foreign lawyer is to work and contacts between the lawyer providing services and persons held in custody.

According to the German government, the detailed rules governing work in conjunction laid down in the 1980 Act are a direct consequence of art 5 of the Directive, which provides that the German lawyer with whom the work in conjunction is to be carried out must practise before the judicial authority in question and is, "where necessary, answerable to that authority". A German lawyer can only be so answerable if he is familiar with all the steps taken by the lawyer providing services and becomes aware of them at the right time, namely before they have taken effect. For that reason, the German lawyer must be constantly involved in the development of the case; such involvement in the case can be ensured only if the judicial authority in question can be certain that that is the case at all times, if the German lawyer is present at the oral stage of the proceedings and if he can claim the status of authorised representative or defending counsel.

The German government also claims that the freedom to provide services should not interfere with the proper administration of justice. Unlimited access by foreign lawyers to proceedings before German courts would be likely to create difficulties arising from insufficient knowledge of the rules of substantive and procedural law applied by those courts. Only the involvement of a local lawyer can ensure that cases are properly presented to the court.

It must be observed in the first place, with respect to the German government's first argument, that the Directive does not in fact explain the meaning of the expressions "work in conjunction" and "answerable to [the judicial] authority" used in art 5. Those expressions must therefore be interpreted in the light of the purposes of the Directive, which is "to facilitate the effective exercise by lawyers of freedom to provide services".

Consequently, whilst the Directive allows national legislation to require a lawyer providing services to work in conjunction with a local lawyer, it is intended to make it possible for the former to carry out the tasks entrusted to him by his client, whilst at the same time having due regard for the proper administration of justice. Seen from that viewpoint, the obligation imposed upon him to act in conjunction with a local lawyer is intended to provide him with the support necessary to enable him to act within a judicial system different from that to which he is accustomed and to assure the judicial authority concerned that the lawyer providing the services actually has that support and is thus in a position fully to comply with the procedural and ethical rules that apply.

Accordingly, the lawyer providing services and the local lawyer, both being subject to the ethical rules applicable in the host Member State, must be regarded as being capable, in compliance with those ethical rules and in the exercise of their professional independence, of agreeing upon a form of cooperation appropriate to their client's instructions.

That does not mean that it would not be open to the national legislature to lay down a general framework for the operation between the two lawyers. However, the resultant obligations must not be disproportionate in relation to the objectives of the duty to work in conjunction as defined above.

It must, however, be pointed out that the German Act of 1980 imposes upon the two lawyers who are required to work in conjunction obligations which go further than is necessary for the attainment of those objectives. Neither the presence of the German lawyer throughout the oral proceedings nor the requirement that the German lawyer must himself be the authorised representative or defending counsel nor the detailed provisions concerning process of work in conjunction are in general necessary or even useful for the provision of the support required by the lawyer providing services.

It must be added that art 5 of the Directive, in referring to the local lawyer's being "answerable", is referring, as stated above, to answerability to the judicial authority concerned and not to the client.

However, the problem of possibly inadequate knowledge of German law referred to by the German government to justify the requirements of the 1980 Act forms part of the responsibility of the lawyer providing services vis-à-vis his client who is free to entrust his interests to a lawyer of his choice.

It should also be pointed out that the German Government's argument that only the forms of work in conjunction provided for by the German legislation make it possible to ensure that lawyers pursue their activities in such a way as to maintain sufficient contact with their clients and the judicial authorities is untenable. As the Court stated in Case 107/83, *Ordre Des Avocats* v *Klopp* [1984] ECR 2971, modern methods of transport and telecommunications enable lawyers to ensure the necessary contact in an appropriate manner.

The reasons for considering that the detailed arrangements for work in conjunction laid down by the 1980 Act are, by reason of their disproportionality, incompatible with the Treaty do not however apply in the same way to the provisions of that Act concerning visits to persons held in custody. Such visits are of a special nature, specific to the relationship which is established between persons in custody and the competent court, which does not exist in the case of other persons.

Moreover, it must be recognised that there may be cogent reasons, in particular those which relate to public security the appraisal of which is a matter for the Member State concerned, for a Member State to lay down rules governing contacts between lawyers and persons in custody.

Those considerations also apply where representation by a lawyer is not compulsory. Consequently, it must be stated that the German Act which imposes an obligation to work in conjunction for the purpose of contacts with persons in custody, even where representation by a lawyer is not mandatory, is not, in that respect, contrary to the provisions of the Directive.

However, in so far as the German Act provides that a lawyer providing services may not, as defending counsel, visit a person in custody unless accompanied by a German lawyer with whom he is working in conjunction, and cannot correspond with a person held in custody except through that German lawyer, without any exception being allowed, even with the authorization of the court or the authority responsible for contacts with persons in custody, the restrictions laid down by that Act go further than is necessary to achieve the legitimate objectives which that Act pursues.

Accordingly, the Commission's complaints concerning the procedures for work in conjunction must be upheld.'

Comment
The ECJ clarified the concept of 'work in conjunction' used in Directive 77/249 concerning the obligation of a lawyer from one Member State who provides legal services in another to act in conjunction with a local lawyer. The ECJ interpreted this concept restrictively. The Court stated that the concept must be interpreted in the light of the objective of the Directive, which was to facilitate the freedom to supply services by lawyers. Thus, any restriction must be justified and not excessive. Taking into account that a foreign lawyer may have linguistic problems as well as insufficient knowledge of substantive and procedural rules of a host Member State in some circumstances, it would be necessary for him to seek support of a local lawyer, in particular when national law requires representation of a client in its courts by a lawyer.

Van Binsbergen v *Bestuur van de Bedrijfsvereniging Voor de Metaalnijverheid* Case 33/74 [1974] ECR 1299; [1973] 1 CMLR 298 European Court of Justice

• *Freedom to supply services – arts 50 and 60 EC Treaty – requirement of permanent residence in a host Member State – rules of conduct and professional ethics*

Facts

Van Binsbergen was represented before the Dutch social security court by Kortmann, a Dutch national. During the proceedings Kortmann, a legal adviser and representative in social security matters, moved from The Netherlands to Belgium and from there he corresponded with the Dutch court. He was informed by the court registrar that only persons established in The Netherlands were permitted to represent their clients before the Dutch social security court and as a permanent resident of Belgium he could no longer act for Van Binsbergen. Kortmann challenged this provision of the relevant Netherlands statute on procedure in social security matters as incompatible with art 59 EC Treaty.

Held

The ECJ held that arts 59 and 60 EC Treaty were directly effective. The Court stated that those provisions must be interpreted as meaning that the national law of a Member State cannot, by imposing a requirement as to habitual residence within that State, deny persons established in another Member State the right to provide services, where the provision of such services is not subject to any special condition under the national law applicable.

However, the ECJ held that a residence requirement would be compatible with arts 59 and 60 of the Treaty if it were objectively justified by the need to ensure observance of professional rules of conduct, provided such rules are non-discriminatory, objectively justified and proportionate.

Judgment

'[*Professional rules of conduct*]
... The question put by the national court therefore seeks to determine whether the requirement that legal representatives be permanently established within the territory of the State where the service is to be provided can be reconciled with the prohibition, under arts 59 and 60, on all restrictions on freedom to provide services within the Community.

The restrictions to be abolished pursuant to arts 59 and 60 include all requirements imposed on the person providing the service by reason in particular of his nationality or the fact that he does not habitually reside in the State where the service is provided, which do not apply to persons established within the national territory or which may prevent or otherwise obstruct the activities of the person providing the service.

In particular, a requirement that the person providing the service must be habitually resident within the territory of the State where the service is to be provided may, according to the circumstances, have the result of depriving art 59 of all useful effect, in view of the fact that the precise object of that article is to abolish restrictions on freedom to provide services imposed on persons who are not established in the State where the service is to be provided.

However, taking into account the particular nature of the services to be provided, specific requirements imposed on the person providing the service cannot be considered incompatible with the Treaty where they have as their purpose the application of professional rules justified by the general good – in particular rules relating to organisation, qualifications, professional ethics, supervision and liability – which are binding upon any person established in the State in which the service is provided, where the person providing the service would escape from the ambit of those rules by being established in another Member State.

Likewise, a Member State cannot be denied the right to take measures to prevent the exercise by a person providing services whose activity is entirely or principally directed towards its territory of the freedom guaranteed by art 59 for the purpose of avoiding the professional rules of conduct which would be applicable to him if he were established within that State; such a situation may be subject to judicial control under the provisions of the chapter relating to the right of establishment and not of that on the provision of service.

In accordance with these principles, the requirement that persons whose functions are to assist the administration of justice must be permanently established for professional purposes within the jurisdiction of certain courts or tribunals cannot be considered incompatible with the provisions of art 59 and 60, where such requirement is objectively justified by the need to ensure observance of professional rules of conduct connected, in particular, with the administration of justice and with respect for professional ethics.

That cannot, however, be the case when the provision of certain services in a Member State is not subject to any sort of qualification or professional regulation and when the requirement of habitual residence is fixed by reference to the territory of the State in question.

In relation to a professional activity the exercise of which is similarly unrestricted within the territory of a particular Member State, the requirement of residence within that State constitutes a restriction which is incompatible with arts 59 and 60 of the Treaty if the administration of justice can satisfactorily be ensured by measures which are less restrictive, such as the choosing of an address for service.

It must therefore be stated in reply to the question put to the Court that the first paragraph of art 59 and the third paragraph of art 60 of the [EC] Treaty must be interpreted as meaning that the national law of a Member State cannot, by imposing a requirement as to habitual residence within that State, deny persons established in another Member State the right to provide services, where the provision of services is not subject to any special condition under the national law applicable ...

[*Direct effect of arts 59 and 60 EC Treaty*]
... as regards at least the specific requirement of nationality or of residence, arts 59 and 60 impose well-defined obligations, the fulfilment of which by the Member States cannot be delayed or jeopardised by the absence of powers which were to be adopted in pursuance of powers conferred under arts 63 and 66.

Accordingly, the reply should be that the first paragraph of art 59 and the third paragraph of art 60 have direct effect and may therefore be relied on before national courts, at least in so far as they seek to abolish any discrimination against a person providing a service by reason of his nationality or the fact that he resides in a Member State other than that in which the service is provided.'

Comment
The ECJ held that arts 59 and 60 EC Treaty are directly effective. The Court emphasised that both provisions are subject to the principle of non-discrimination based on the ground of nationality. However, the concept of the free movement of services goes beyond mere discrimination as it covers disproportionate and unjustified restrictions. National restrictions should be assessed in the light of these three criteria, that is they should be non-discriminatory, proportional and objectively justified. In the present case, the requirement of permanent residence applied without discrimination to nationals and non-nationals; it is objectively justified by the general good, that is, by the need to ensure observance of professional rules of conduct especially connected with the administration of justice and with respect for professional ethics. In respect to the third criterion the ECJ held that the requirement of permanent residence would, in the present case, be disproportionate as the objective of the proper administration of justice can be achieved by less restrictive measures such as the choosing of an address in the Member State in which the service is provided. This test has clear parallels with the *Cassis de Dijon* case, although the ECJ has refused to adopt a Keck case limitation to the freedom to provide services (*Alpine Investments* Case C–384/93 [1995] ECR I–1141).

It is also interesting to note that the present case concerned a Dutch national who provided services in The Netherlands acting for a Dutch client before a Dutch court. The fact that he was established in Belgium brought the case within the scope of Community law. Therefore, in some cases EC law protects nationals of a Member State against their own State!

Freedom to receive services

Cowan v Trésor Public Case 186/87 [1989] ECR 195; [1990] 2 CMLR 613 European Court of Justice

• *Freedom to provide services includes freedom to receive services – discrimination on the ground of nationality – art 7 EC Treaty – assault on tourist – criminal compensation*

Facts

A British national, Ian Cowan, was violently assaulted outside a Metro station in Paris. The perpetrators of the offence were never apprehended. Mr Cowan applied to the Commission d'Indeminsation des Victims d'Infraction, the French equivalent of the Criminal Injuries Compensation Board, for compensation for his injuries. The French Code of Criminal Procedure allows compensation to be paid to victims of assaults if physical injury has been sustained and compensation cannot be sought from another source. However, the same Code of Criminal Procedure restricted the payment of compensation to French nationals and holders of French residence permits. On this grounds Mr Cowan's application for compensation was refused by the French Treasury.

Mr Cowen challenged this decision relying on art 6 of the Treaty. He argued that art 6 prohibited discrimination based on nationality and that such discrimination prevented tourists from going freely to other Member States to receive services.

Held

The ECJ held that the freedom to provide services also entailed the right to receive services. Since the right to receive services was embodied in the EC Treaty, it was subject to the prohibition of discrimination on the grounds of nationality as prescribed by art 6. Laws and regulations which prevent the exercise of this right were declared to be incompatible with Community law and, in the circumstances of this case, the requirement of French nationality or a French residence permit, in order to claim compensation for criminal injuries constituted unjustifiable discrimination.

Judgment

'Under art [6] of the [EC] Treaty the prohibition of discrimination applies "within the scope of application of this Treaty" and "without prejudice to any special provisions contained therein". This latter expression refers particularly to other provisions of the Treaty in which the application of the general principle set out in that article is given concrete form in respect of specific situations. Examples of that are the provisions concerning free movement of workers, the right of establishment and the freedom to provide services.

On that last point, in its judgment of 31 January 1984 in Joined Cases 286/82 and 26/83 (*Luisi and Carbone* v *Ministero del Tesoro* [1984] ECR 377), the Court held that the freedom to provide services includes the freedom for the recipient of the services to go to another Member State in order to receive a service there, without being obstructed by restrictions, and that tourists, among others, must be regarded as recipients of services.

When Community law guarantees a natural person the freedom to go to another Member State the protection of that person from harm in the Member State in question, on the same basis as that of nationals and persons residing there, is a corollary of that freedom of movement. It follows that the prohibition of discrimination is applicable to recipients of services within the meaning of the Treaty as regards protection against the risk of assault and the right to obtain financial compensation provided for by national law when the risk materialises. The fact that the compensation at issue is financed by the Public Treasury cannot alter the rules regarding the protection of the rights guaranteed by the Treaty.

In the light of all the foregoing the answer to the question submitted must be that the prohibition of discrimination laid down in particular in art [6] of the EC Treaty must be interpreted as meaning that in respect of persons whose freedom to travel to a Member State, in particular as recipients of services, is guaranteed by Community law that State may not make the award of State compensation for harm caused in that State to the victim of an assault resulting in physical injury subject to the condition that he holds a residence permit or be a national of the country which has entered into a reciprocal agreement with that Member State.'

Comment
The ECJ held that the freedom to provide services included the freedom to receive services and that tourists were within the scope of art 59 as recipients of services. In the present case the ECJ, by virtue of the prohibition of discrimination contained in art 6 EC Treaty, extended the category of persons protected under Community law. The combined effect of arts 59 and 6 EC Treaty permitted Cowan to act against the French State.

Criminal Proceedings against Calfa
Case C–348/96 Judgment of 19 January 1999 (not yet reported)
European Court of Justice

- *Freedom to provide service – free movement of persons – public policy – prohibited drugs – exclusion for life from a Member State's territory – personal conduct in the light of art 3(1) of Directive 64/221/EEC*

Facts
Donatella Calfa, an Italian national, went for holidays to Crete where she was convicted of the possession and use of prohibited drugs. She was sentenced by a Greek court to three months' imprisonment and expulsion for life from Greek territory. Under Greek penal law, foreign nationals convicted of certain drug offences were automatically subject to an expulsion order for life unless for some compelling reasons, particularly family matters, their continued residence in Greece was allowed. Donatella Calfa challenged the expulsion order as contrary to a number of provisions of the EC Treaty, especially arts 48, 52 and 59 of EC Treaty, as well as Council Directive 64/221/EEC of 25 February 1964 on the Co-ordination of Special Measures Concerning the Movement and Residence of Foreign Nationals which Are Justified on Grounds of Public Policy, Public Security or Public Health.

Held
The ECJ held that arts 48, 52 and 59 of EC Treaty and art 3(1) of Directive 64/21/EEC precluded legislation which (with certain exceptions, in particular where they were family reasons) required a Member State's courts to order expulsion for life from its territory of nationals of other Member States found guilty on that territory of the offences of obtaining and being in possession of drugs for their own personal use.

Judgment
'Although in principle criminal legislation is a matter for which the Member States are responsible, the Court has consistently held that Community law sets certain limits to their power, and such legislation may not restrict the fundamental freedoms guaranteed by Community law.

In the present case, the penalty of expulsion for life from the territory, which is applicable to the nationals of other Member States in the event of conviction for obtaining and being in possession of drugs for their own use, clearly constitutes an obstacle to the freedom to provide services. This would also be true for the other fundamental freedoms.

Article 56 permits Member States to adopt, with respect to nationals of other Member States, and in particular on the grounds of public policy, measures which they cannot apply to their own nationals, inasmuch as they have no authority to expel the latter from the territory or to deny them access thereto.

The concept of public policy may be relied upon in the event of a genuine and sufficiently serious threat to the requirements of public policy affecting one of the fundamental interests of society.

In this respect, it must be accepted that a Member State may consider that the use of drugs constitutes a danger for society such as to justify special measures against foreign nationals who contravene its laws on drugs, in order to maintain public order.

However, as the Court has repeatedly stated, the public policy exception, like all derogations from a fundamental principle of the Treaty, must be interpreted restrictively.

In that regard, Directive 64/221 sets certain limits on the right of Member States to expel foreign nationals on the grounds of public policy and states that measures taken on grounds of public policy or of public security that have the effect of restricting the residence of a national of another Member State must be based exclusively on the personal conduct of the individual concerned. In addition, previous criminal convictions cannot in themselves constitute grounds for the taking of such measures. It follows that the existence of a previous criminal conviction can, therefore, only be taken into account in so far as the circumstances which gave rise to that conviction are evidence of personal conduct constituting a present threat to the requirements of public policy.

In the present case, the legislation at issue in the main proceedings requires nationals of other Member States found guilty, on the national territory in which that legislation applies, of an offence under the drugs laws, to be expelled for life from that territory, unless compelling reasons, in particular family reasons, justify their continued residence in the country. The penalty can be revoked only by a decision taken at the discretion of the Minister for Justice after a period of three years?.

Therefore, expulsion for life automatically follows a criminal conviction, without any account being taken of the personal conduct of the offender or of the danger which that person represents for the requirements of public policy.

It follows that the conditions for the application of the public policy exception provided for in Directive 64/221, as interpreted by the Court of Justice, are not fulfilled and that the public policy exception cannot be successfully relied upon.'

Comment

The ECJ held that Donatella Calfa, as a tourist, was a recipient of services in another Member State and as such within the scope of application of art 59 of EC Treaty (see *Cowan* Case 186/87). The ECJ emphasised that although national legislation in criminal matters is within the competence of a Member State the requirements of EC law set limitations on Member States' powers. Such legislation should not limit the fundamental freedoms guaranteed by Community law. The ECJ held that the expulsion for life from a territory of a Member State was an obstacle to the freedom to receive services under art 59 as well as the freedom of establishment under art 52 and the free movement of workers contained in art 48 EC. In those circumstances it was necessary to examine whether the expulsion order could be justified under art 56 EC Treaty and art 3(1) of Directive 64/221 on the ground of public policy. The ECJ emphasised that the exception to the free movement of persons should be interpreted restrictively and decided that the expulsion order could not be justified on the ground of public policy since the Greek legislation provided for an automatic expulsion for life following a criminal conviction without taking into account the personal conduct of the offender or whether that conduct created a genuine and sufficiently serious threat affecting one of the fundamental interests of society (see *Bouchereau* Case 30/77 [1977] ECR 1999).

13 EC Competition Law

Article 85 EC Treaty (now art 81 EC Treaty)

Ahlström and Others v Commission (Re Wood Pulp Cartel) Joined Cases 89, 104, 114, 116, 117 and 125–129/85 [1993] 4 CMLR 407 European Court of Justice

- *Extraterritorial application of EC Treaty – effects doctrine – undertakings from third countries – art 85(1) EC Treaty – quarterly price announcements – parallel behaviour – concerted price-fixing – oligopolistic market*

Facts
The Commission found more than 40 suppliers of wood pulp in violation of Community competition law despite the fact that none of these companies was resident within the European Community. Fines were imposed on 36 of these companies for violation of art 85(1) EC Treaty. A number of these companies appealed against the decision to the ECJ. They challenged the Commission's finding that they breached art 85(1) through concertation on prices for their products by means of a system of quarterly price announcements.

Held
The Court annulled the decision of the Commission that the undertakings concerned infringed art 85(1) through concertation on prices for their products, on the grounds that the Commission had not provided a firm, precise and consistent body of evidence in this respect.

Judgment
'[*The system of quarterly price announcements*]
First, the Commission considers that the system was deliberately introduced by the pulp producers in order to enable them to ascertain the prices that would be charged by their competitors in the following quarters. The disclosure of prices to third parties, especially to the press and agents working for several producers, well before their application at the beginning of a new quarter gave the other producers sufficient time to announce their own, corresponding, new prices before the quarter and to apply them from the commencement of that quarter.

Secondly, the Commission considers that the implementation of that mechanism had the effect of making the market artificially transparent by enabling producers to obtain a rapid and accurate picture of the prices quoted by their competitors.

In deciding on that point, it must be borne in mind that art 85(1) [EC] prohibits all agreements between undertakings, decisions by associations of undertakings and concerted practices which may affect trade between Member States and which have as their object or effect the prevention, restriction or distortion of competition within the Common Market.

According to the Court's judgment in *Suiker Unie* (Cases 40–48, 50, 54–56, 111, 113–114/73 [1975] ECR 1663) a concerted practice refers to a form of co-operation between undertakings which, without having been taken to the stage where an agreement properly so-called has been concluded, knowingly substitutes for the risk of competition practical co-operation between them. In the same judgment, the Court added that the criteria of co-ordination and co-operation must be understood in the light of the concept inherent in the provision of the Treaty relating to competition that each economic operator must determine independently the policy which he intends to adopt on the Common Market.

In this case, the communications arise from the price announcements made to users. They constitute in themselves market behaviour which does not lessen each undertaking's uncertainty as to the future attitude of its competitors. At the time when each undertaking engages in such behaviour, it cannot be sure of the future conduct of the others.

Accordingly, the system of quarterly price announcements on the pulp market is not regarded as constituting in itself an infringement of art 85(1) [EC].

... it must be stated that, in this case, concertation is not the only plausible explanation for the parallel conduct. To begin with, the system of price announcements may be regarded as constituting a rational response to the fact that the pulp market constituted a long-term market and to the need felt by both buyers and sellers to limit commercial risks. Further, the similarity in the dates of price announcements may be regarded as a direct result of the high degree of market transparency, which does not have to be described as artificial. Finally, the parallelism of prices and the price trends may be satisfactorily explained by the oligopolistic tendencies of the market and by the specific circumstances prevailing in certain periods. Accordingly, the parallel conduct established by the Commission does not constitute evidence of concertation.'

Comment

The Commission based its decision on the economic analysis of the wood pulp market as it was not able to find physical evidence of concertation. The factors that the Commission took into account, inter alia, were: the system of early announcements of prices which made prices transparent; the uniform fluctuation of prices; and the uniform approach to prices which could be explained in a narrow oligopolistic situation where undertakings had to follow a market leader, but in the present situation there were more than 50 producers of wood pulp and therefore the market was not oligopolistic. The Commission concluded that such uniform market behaviour could be explained only by a concerted practice of the undertakings concerned. The ECJ decided otherwise. The ECJ held that parallel conduct could not be regarded as furnishing proof of concertation unless concertation constituted the only plausible explanation. The ECJ appointed its own experts to analyse the market. Their findings convinced the ECJ that there may be explanations of parallel behaviour other than concertation, such as the natural structure of the market. In the present case the market was cyclical. In respect of transparency of prices, the early announcements were requested by customers – taking into account the cyclical nature of the market, they wanted to know as soon as possible the price for wood pulp.

Automec (II) v *EC Commission* Case T–24/90 [1992] 5 CMLR 431 Court of First Instance

- *Investigation of complaints – discretion of the Commission – refusal of the Commission to conduct investigation – requirement of sufficient Community interest – remedies available in national courts*

Facts

The applicant was a company competing with the motor vehicle producer, BMW. It complained to the Commission that BMW Italia's distribution system was incompatible with art 85(1) EC Treaty. The Commission refused to pursue the complaint because it considered that the matter was not of sufficient Community importance or significance to merit an investigation. In response, the applicant requested the CFI to grant an interim order to require the Commission to conduct an investigation and to permit the applicant, Automec, to use some of BMW's trademarks.

Held

The CFI held that art 85(1) EC Treaty prohibited certain anti-competitive practices and, when these had a mainly national effect, the proper procedure was to seek a remedy in the appropriate national courts. National courts are authorised to grant damages for injury caused to private parties as a consequence of violations of art 85(1) and to restrain further violation if proved.

The CFI confirmed that the Commission was correct in refusing to investigate the matter, in deciding its own investigative priorities and to point the complaint in the direction of the national court for the purposes of seeking an appropriate remedy.

Judgment

'It is for the Court to verify, first, whether the Commission has carried out the examination of the complaint which it is required to do by evaluating with all the requisite care the factual and legal aspects adduced by the applicant in his complaint and, secondly, whether the Commission has given proper reasons for closing the file on the complaint on the basis of its power to accord degrees of priority to pursuing the matters referred to it on the one hand, and on the basis of the Community interest in the matter a criterion of priority on the other.

In this connection the Court finds, first, that the Commission carried out a careful examination of the complaint, in the course of which it not only took account of the factual and legal aspects adduced in the complaint itself, but also conducted an information exchange of views and information with the applicant and its lawyers. The Commission rejected the complaint only after noting the further details supplied by the applicant in this way and the observations submitted in reply to the letter sent pursuant to art 6 of Regulation 99/63. Therefore, having regard to the factual and legal aspects contained in the complaint, the Commission carried out an appropriate examination thereof and it cannot be charged with a want of diligence.

Secondly, concerning the reasons for the contested decision to close the file, the Court points out in the first place that the Commission is entitled to accord different degrees of priority to examining the complaints it receives.

The second point to be considered is whether it is legitimate, as the Commission contends, to refer to the Community interest of a matter as a criterion of priority.

In this connection it should be observed that, unlike the civil courts, whose task is to safeguard the subjective rights of private persons in their mutual relations, an administrative authority must act in the public interest. Consequently it is legitimate for the Commission to refer to the Community interest in order to determine the degree of priority to be accorded to the different matters before it. This does not mean removing the Commission's acts from judicial review: as art 190 requires the reasons on which decisions are based to be stated, the Commission cannot merely refer to the Community interest in isolation. It must set out the legal and factual considerations which lead it to conclude that there is not a sufficient Community interest which would justify the adoption of measures of investigation. Thus by reviewing the legality of those reasons the Court can review the Commission's acts.

To assess the Community interest in pursuing the examination of a matter, the Commission must take account of the circumstances of the particular case, particularly the legal and factual aspects set out in the complaint referred to it. It is for the Commission in particular to weigh up the importance of the alleged infringement for the functioning of the Common Market, the probability of being able to establish the existence of the infringement and the extent of the investigation measures necessary in order to fulfil successfully its task of securing compliance with arts 85 and 86.

In this context the question for the Court is whether the Commission was right, in this particular case, to conclude that there was not a sufficient Community interest in pursuing the examination of the matter on the ground that the applicant, who had already referred to the Italian courts the dispute concerning the termination of the distribution agreement, could also submit to those courts the question of whether BMW Italia's distribution system was compatible with art 85(1) EC ...

However, to assess the legality of the contested decision to close the file, the Court must determine whether, in referring the complainant enterprise to the national court, the Commission misconstrued the extent of the protection which the national court can provide to safeguard the rights derived by the applicant from art 85(1) EC.

In this connection it should be observed that arts 85(1) and 86 take direct effect in relations between individuals and create rights for individuals which the national courts must safeguard. The power to apply those provisions is vested simultaneously in the Commission and the national courts. Such co-operation is however characterised by the obligation of loyal co-operation between the Commission and the national courts arising from art 5 EC.

Therefore the Court must consider whether the Commission could rely upon such co-operation to ensure as assessment of the question whether BMW Italia's distribution system is compatible with art 85 (1) EC.

To this end, the Italian court is in position to determine, first, whether the system entails restrictions of competition within the meaning of art 85(1). In the event of doubt, it can seek a preliminary ruling from the Court of Justice. If it finds that there is a restriction of competition contrary to art 85(1), it must next consider whether the system has the benefit of a group exemption under Regulation 123/85.This question is also within its jurisdiction. If there is any doubt as to the validity or interpretation of the Regulation, the Court may also make a reference to the Court of Justice pursuant to art 177 EC. In each of these situations the national court is able to give a ruling on the conformity of the distribution system within art 85(1) EC ...

Consequently, in referring the applicant to the national court, the Commission has not misconstrued the extent of the protection which the latter can give to the rights which the applicant derives from art 85(1) and (2) EC.

It follows from what has been said that the Court's examination of the contested decision reveals no mistake in law or in fact and no manifest error in assessment. It follows that the objection based on the contravention of Community law, particularly art 155 EC, art 3 of Regulation 17 and art 6 of Regulation 99/63 is unfounded.'

Comment

Under art 3(2)(b) of Regulation 17/62 (OJ SpEd 1959–62 p87) any natural or legal person who claims a 'legitimate interest' may ask the Commission to investigate an alleged infringement of arts 85 and 86 EC Treaty. The form is not important, it may be a simple letter, provided it is signed and the address and name of the complaining person are included or it may be a formal letter of complaint written on the official form ('Form C').

The Commission is under a duty to reply (*Demo-Studio Schmidt* Case 210/81 [1983] ECR 3045) but an applicant is not entitled to obtain a decision within the meaning of art 189 EC Treaty (*GEMA* v *EC Commission* Case 125/78 [1979] ECR 3173). The Commission's failure provide a reply, may result in an action for failure to act under art 175 EC Treaty. In the present case, the Commission refused to pursue the complaint. In such event, the Commission must inform the applicant of its reasons and fix a time limit for him to submit any further comments in writing (Regulation 99/63, art 6). The Commission's refusal was based on the lack of Community interest and the applicant was referred to a national court to enforce his rights. The CFI approved the Commission's right to prioritise its workload and stated that the co-operation between the Commission and the national courts ensures the enforcement of EC Competition law, taking into account that arts 85 and 86 EC Treaty are directly effective and that the ECJ can assist (under the preliminary ruling procedure) national courts in the event of difficulties in the interpretation of those provisions. The judgment in the present case implies that a reply of the Commission refusing to take action in response to a complaint lodged by a natural or legal person is reviewable under art 173 EC Treaty. This solution has been reinforced by the ECJ in *Guerin Automobiles v EC Commission* Case C–282/95P [1997] 5 CMLR 447.

Consten SA and Grundig-Verkaufs GmbH v *EC Commission* Cases 56 and 58/64 [1966] ECR 299; [1966] CMLR 418 European Court of Justice

- *Article 85(1) EC Treaty – exclusive distributorship agreements – vertical restraints – absolute territorial protection – effect on trade between Member States – restriction on competition – extent of prohibition in art 85(1)*

Facts

Grundig, a large German manufacturer of electrical equipment, entered into an agreement with a French distributor, Consten, according to which Consten was appointed as Grundig's exclusive agent in France, Corsica and the Saar region. The distribution agreement contained terms which, inter alia, allowed Consten to employ the Grundig trade mark 'GINT' and emblem in its promotions. On the basis of this authority, Consten registered the Grundig trade mark in France. A French competitor imported a number of Grundig products from Germany and attempted to sell these in the French market. Consten raised an action for infringement of a trade mark against this rival, relying on the earlier registration of the trade mark. The Commission objected to these proceedings and commenced an investigation into the functioning of the exclusive distribution agreement

The Commission found that the agreement was contrary to art 85(1) of the [EC] Treaty, being an agreement which had the object of distorting competition within the Community by restricting trade. The plaintiffs brought an action in the ECJ contesting these findings.

Held

The ECJ severed the offending clauses of the agreement and declared them void under art 85(2) EC Treaty. In respect of the agreement, the only clauses which were prohibited under art 85 were those giving absolute territorial protection The ECJ annulled the decision of the Commission in so far as it declared void all clauses of the agreement.

Judgment

'[*Vertical agreements*]

The applicants submit that the prohibition in art 85(1) applies only to so-called horizontal agreements. The Italian government submits furthermore that sole distributorship contracts do not constitute "agreements between undertakings" within the meaning of that provision, since the parties are not on a footing of equality. With regard to these contracts, freedom of competition may only be protected by virtue of art 86 of the Treaty.

Neither the wording of art 85 nor that of art 86 gives any ground for holding that distinct areas of application are to be assigned to each of the two articles according to the level in the economy at which the contracting parties operate. Article 85 refers in a general way to all agreements which distort competition within the Common Market and does not lay down any distinction between those agreements based on whether they are made between competitors operating at the same level in the economic process or between non-competing persons operating at a different level. In principle, no distinction can be made where the Treaty does not make any distinction.

Furthermore, the possible application of art 85 to a sole distributorship contract cannot be excluded merely because the grantor and the concessionaire are not competitors inter se and not on a footing of equality. Competition may be distorted within the meaning of art 85(1) not only by agreements which limit it as between the parties, but also by agreements which prevent or restrict the competition which might take place between one of them and third parties. For this purpose, it is irrelevant whether the parties to the agreement are or are not on a footing of equality as regards their position and function in the economy. This applies all the more, since, by such an agreement, the parties might seek, by preventing or limiting the competition of third parties in respect of the products, to create or guarantee for their benefit an unjustified advantage at the expense of the consumer or user, contrary to the general aims of art 85.'

Comment
This is the first case concerning exclusive distribution agreements and the first judgment of the ECJ on appeal from the decision of the Commission. It is also the first case in which the ECJ held that art 85(1) applies not only to undertakings at horizontal level but also to undertakings at vertical level, that is between undertakings which do not compete with each other as they operate at different levels of the market. The ECJ restrictively interpreted art 85 EC Treaty. It held that the agreement intended to isolate the French market for Grundig products and therefore partition the common market along national lines which in itself distorted competition in the common market. For that reason, without examining other factors, such as economic data, the correctness of criteria which the Commission had applied in order to compare the French market with the German market, etc, the ECJ held that the agreement was in breach of art 85(1) and upheld the Commission's position in this matter.

In relation to the effect of the agreement, the German government submitted that the Commission should have analysed the competition between similar competing products (inter-brand competition and not the competition between various distributors of Grundig products (intra-brand)). The ECJ confirmed the Commission approach and held that the benefit of inter-brand over intra-brand competition should not mean that an agreement tending to restrict intra-brand competition could escape the prohibition contained in art 85(1) merely because it might increase inter-brand-competition

In respect of the requirement that the practice 'may affect trade between Member States' the argument submitted by the parties that the agreement would increase the trade in Grundig products between the Member States was rejected by the ECJ. The Court stated that the fact that an agreement favours an increase, even a large one, in the volume of trade between Member States is not sufficient to exclude the possibility that the agreement may 'affect' such trade as it may constitute a threat, either direct or indirect, actual or potential to freedom of trade in a manner that harms the objectives of the Common Market

In the Commission Green Paper on *Vertical Restraints in Competition Policy* (COM(96) 721 final, 22 January 1997) it was emphasised that absolute territorial protection 'which may affect trade between Member States will not only continue to fall per se within art 85(1) but [is] unlikely to be exempted'. However, the Commission stressed that agreements between producers and distributors can be used pro-competitively and anti-competitively and for that reason the scope of block exemptions should be increased while the current system should be maintained.

In relation to the trade mark, the ECJ held that the trade-mark owner, Grundig, could not grant a licence to Consten resulting in absolute territorial protection for the licensee. For that reason, Consten could not rely on its trade mark to prevent parallel import of Grundig products from other Member States. The use of the mark 'GINT' was for the purpose of partitioning the common market alongside the national market and as such in breach of art 85(1) EC Treaty.

Imperial Chemical Industries Ltd v EC Commission (Dyestuffs) Case 48/69 [1972] ECR 619 European Court of Justice

- *Article 85(1) – agreements – decisions and concerted practices – parallel behaviour – oligopoly – exchange of information*

Facts
ICI was one of a number of undertakings which manufactured aniline dyestuffs. The leading producers of aniline dyestuffs increased their prices almost simultaneously on three occasion: in 1964 by 10 per cent; in 1965 by 10–15 per cent; and in 1967 by 8 per cent. The Commission decided that these three general and uniform increases in prices indicated that there had been a concerted practice between the undertakings concerned contrary to art 85(1) EC Treaty and imposed fines on them. ICI challenged the Commission's decision on the grounds that the price increase merely reflected parallel behaviour in an oligopolistic market and did not result from concerted practices.

Held
The ECJ dismissed the application of ICI.

Judgment
'[*The concept of a concerted practice*]
Article 85 draws a distinction between the concept of "concerted practices" and that of "agreements between undertakings" or a "decision by associations of undertakings"; the object is to bring within the prohibition of that article a form of co-ordination between undertakings which, without having reached the stage where an agreement properly so-called has been concluded, knowingly substitutes practical co-operation between them for the risks of competition.

By its very nature, then, a concerted practice does not have all the elements of a contract but may inter alia arise out of co-ordination which becomes apparent from the behaviour of the participants.

Although parallel behaviour may not by itself be identified with a concerted practice, it may however amount to strong evidence of such a practice if it leads to conditions of competition which do not correspond to the normal conditions of the market, having regard to the nature of the products, the size and number of the undertakings, and the volume of the said market.

This is especially the case if the parallel conduct is such as to enable those concerned to attempt to stabilise prices at a level different from that to which competition would have led, and to consolidate positions to the detriment of effective freedom of movement of the products in the Common Market and of the freedom of consumers to choose their suppliers.

Therefore the question whether there was a concerted action in this case can only be correctly determined if the evidence upon which the contested decision is based is considered, not in isolation, but as a whole, account being taken of the specific features of the market in the products in question.

... The general and uniform increase on those different markets can only be explained by a common intention on the part of those undertakings, first, to adjust the level of prices and the situation resulting from competition in the form of discounts, and secondly, to avoid the risk, which is inherent in any price increase, of changing the conditions of competition.

... Although every producer is free to change his prices, taking into account in so doing the present or foreseeable conduct of his competition, nevertheless it is contrary to the rules on competition contained in the Treaty for a producer to co-operate with his competitors, in a way whatsoever, in order to determine a co-ordinated course of action resulting to a price increase and to ensure its success by prior elimination of all uncertainty as to each other's conduct regarding the essential elements of that action, such as the amount, subject-matter, date and place of the increase.

... In these circumstances and taking into

account the nature of the market in the products in question, the conduct of the applicant, in conjunction with other undertakings against which proceedings have been taken, was designed to replace the risks of competition and the hazards of competitors' spontaneous reactions by co-operation constituting a concerted practice prohibited by art 85(1) of the Treaty.'

Comment

Concerted practices are most difficult to evidence. In the present case the ECJ defined a concept of concerted practice which with some modifications introduced in *Suiker Unie* Cases 40–48, 50, 54–56, 111 and 113–114/73 [1976] 1 CMLR 295 can be described as a form of co-ordination between undertakings which, without having been taken to the stage where an agreement properly so-called exists, knowingly substitutes practical co-operation between them for the risks of competition. In the situation of an oligopolistic market, in which the market in dominated by a small number of large concerns, it is extremely difficult to establish collusive practices as it is expected that when one producer changes its prices others will follow. Therefore, it is difficult to distinguish between parallel behaviour and a concerted practice. The case law of the ECJ indicates that the distinction is made on the basis of an external observation of the market. Parallelism in prices can often be explained by the structure of the market. In the *Wood Pulp* cases the ECJ emphasised that inference cannot be made unless it is the only plausible explanation of the observed conduct of undertakings and decided that the oligopolistic tendencies of the market in wood pulp explained the behaviour of the undertaking concerned. However, in the present case the ECJ held that the market in the products in question was not oligopolistic.

Sarrio SA v *EC Commission* Case T–334/94 [1998] ECR II–1727; [1998] 5 CMLR 195 Court of First Instance

• *Article 85(1) EC Treaty – participation in concerted practices – liability established by participating in meetings with anti-competitive object – price agreement – market sharing – exchange of information, definition of cartel – not necessary to participate in all elements of infringement where collusion part of overall plan – aggravating circumstances – concealment of a cartel – right to defence – fines*

Facts

The decision of the Commission of 13 July 1994 in so-called 'cartonboard' cases in which 19 suppliers of cartonboard were found in breach of art 85(1) EC Treaty as they operated a price-fixing and market sharing cartel was challenged by 17 of them, including Sarrio. The Commission had found that the undertakings concerned fixed prices for cartonboard through committees set up under the auspices of the Product Group Paperboard (PGP), their trade association. In this respect a number of structures were set up comprising the President's Working Group (PWG) that took general decisions concerning the timing and level of price increases by producers and which submitted reports to the President's Conference (PC), the latter bringing together managing directors and managers of the undertaking twice a year. In 1987 the undertakings set up the Joint Marketing Committee (JMC) which essentially defined the mode of price policy decided by PWG, country-by-country, and for the major customers in order to achieve a system of equivalent prices in Europe. The Commission also discovered that there was a systematic exchange of information between the cartonboard suppliers operated by a secretarial company, Fides, registered in Switzerland which collated all reports on orders, production, sales and capacity utilisations by the undertakings concerned and sent back to them aggregated data. On appeal the undertakings submitted similar arguments concerning: the proof of their participation in an agreement prohibited under art 85(1) EC, the infringement of their right of defence in the Commission's proceedings, and the fining policy of the Commission. Taking into account the outcome of the case, as well as the similarity of arguments presented by the parties, only Sarrio's appeal is examined. Sarrio argued that it had not participated in any agreement either to set prices (as it charged different prices for each transaction) or to fix the market shares and outputs of the participants. Sarrio also argued that the fines imposed by the Commission were unjustified and that its right to defence in the proceedings was infringed as the Commission submitted as evidence a document not notified to them and consequently they had no opportunity to make comment on it.

Held

The CFI confirmed the Commission decision in *Sarrio*.

Judgment

'[*Error committed by the Commission in considering that there was one overall infringement and that Sarrió was responsible for it as a whole*]
First of all, the Commission found that the applicant had infringed art 85(1) of the Treaty by participating, from mid-1986 until at least April 1991, in an agreement and a concerted practice which started in mid-1986 and which consisted of several separate constituent elements.

According to the second paragraph of point 116 of the Decision, the "whole gravamen of the infringement lies in the combination of the producers over several years in a joint unlawful enterprise pursuant to a common design". That view of the infringement is also expressed in point 128 of the Decision: "It would however be artificial to subdivide what is clearly a continuing common enterprise having one and the same overall objective into several discrete infringements."

Consequently, even though the Commission did not expressly use the concept of a "single infringement" in the Decision, it implicitly referred to that concept, as is shown by the reference to paragraph 260 of the judgment of this Court in *ICI* v *Commission*.

Furthermore, the Commission's repeated use of the word "cartel" to cover the various kinds of anti-competitive conduct which it found expresses a comprehensive view of the infringements of art 85(1) of the Treaty. As is clear, in fact, from point 117 of the Decision, the Commission's view is as follows:

"The proper approach in a case such as the present one is to demonstrate the existence, operation and salient features of the cartel as a whole and then to determine (a) whether there is credible and persuasive proof to link each individual producer to the common scheme and (b) for what period each producer participated."

It adds:

"The Commission ... is not required to compartimentalise the various constituent elements of the infringement by identifying each separate occasion during the duration of the cartel on which a consensus was reached on one or another matter or each individual example of collusive behaviour and the[n] exonerating from involvement on that occasion or in that particular manifestation of the cartel any producer not implicated on that occasion by direct evidence."

It also states (in point 118): "There is ample direct evidence to prove the adherence of each suspected participant to the infringement", without distinguishing between the constituent elements of the overall infringement.

Thus, the single infringement, as conceived by the Commission, is bound up with "the cartel as a whole" or "the overall cartel" and is characterised by a continuous course of action adopted by a number of undertakings pursuing a common unlawful objective. That view of a single infringement gives rise to the system of proof set out in point 117 of the Decision and to unitary responsibility, in the sense that any undertaking "linked" to the overall cartel is held responsible for it whatever the constituent elements in which it is proved to have participated.

In order to be entitled to hold each addressee of a decision, such as the present decision, responsible for an overall cartel during a given period, the Commission must demonstrate that each undertaking concerned either consented to the adoption of an overall plan comprising the constituent elements of the cartel or that it participated directly in all those elements during that period. An undertaking may also be held responsible for an overall cartel even though it is shown that it participated directly only in one or some of the constituent elements of that cartel, if it is shown that it knew, or must have known, that the collusion in which it participated was part of an overall plan and that the overall plan included all the constituent elements of the cartel.

Where that is the case, the fact that the undertaking concerned did not participate directly in all the constituent elements of the overall cartel cannot relieve it of responsibility for the infringement of art 85(1) of the Treaty. Such a circumstance may nevertheless be taken into account when assessing the seriousness of the infringement which it is found to have committed.

In the present case, it is apparent from the Decision that the infringement found in art 1 consisted of collusion on three matters which were different but which pursued a common objective. Those three types of collusion must be regarded as the constituent elements of the overall cartel. According to that article, each of the undertakings mentioned infringed art 85(1) of the Treaty by participating in an agreement and concerted practice by which the undertakings: (a) agreed regular price increases for each grade of the product in each national currency and planned and implemented those increases; (b) reached an understanding on maintaining the market shares of the major producers at constant levels, subject to modification from time to time; and (c) increasingly, from early 1990, took concerted measures to control the supply of the product in the Community in order to ensure the implementation of the concerted price rises.

Despite its view that there was a "single" infringement, the Commission explains in the Decision that

"[t]he 'core' documents which prove the existence of the overall cartel or individual manifestations thereof often identify participants by name, and there is also a vast body of further documentary evidence showing the role of each producer in the cartel and the extent of its involvement" (point 118, first paragraph, of the Decision).

The Court must therefore consider, in the light of the foregoing considerations, whether the Commission has proved the applicant's participation in the cartel, as found in art 1 of the Decision.

As has already been held the Commission has proved that, as an undertaking which took part in the meetings of the PWG from its establishment, the applicant participated, from mid-1986, in collusion on prices and, from the end of 1987, in collusion on market shares and in collusion on downtime, that is to say, in the three constituent elements of the infringement found in art 1 of the Decision. It was therefore fully entitled to decide to hold the applicant responsible for an infringement consisting of those three types of collusion pursuing the same objective.

So the Commission did not place on the applicant responsibility for the conduct of other producers and did not hold it responsible on the sole basis of its participation in the PG Paperboard.

[*The application for annulment of art 2 of the Decision*]

It will be recalled that art 2 of the Decision provides as follows:

"The undertakings named in art 1 shall forthwith bring the said infringement to an end, if they have not already done so. They shall henceforth refrain in relation to their cartonboard activities from any agreement or concerted practice which may have the same or a similar object or effect, including any exchange of commercial information:

(a) by which the participants are directly or indirectly informed of the production, sales, order backlog, machine utilisation rates, selling prices, costs or marketing plans of other individual producers; or

(b) by which, even if no individual information is disclosed, a common industry response to economic conditions as regards price or the control of production is promoted, facilitated or encouraged; or

(c) by which they might be able to monitor adherence to or compliance with any express or tacit agreement regarding prices or market sharing in the Community.

Any scheme for the exchange of general information to which they subscribe, such as the Fides system or its successor, shall be so conducted as to exclude not only any information from which the behaviour of individual producers can be identified but also any data concerning the present state of the order inflow and backlog, the forecast utilisation rate of production capacity (in both cases, even if aggregated) or the production capacity of each machine.

Any such exchange system shall be limited to the collection and dissemination in aggregated form of production and sales statistics which cannot be used to promote or facilitate common industry behaviour.

The undertakings are also required to abstain from any exchange of information of competitive significance in addition to such permitted exchange and from any meetings or other contact in order to discuss the significance of the information exchanged or the possible or likely reaction of the industry or of individual producers to that information.

A period of three months from the date of the communication of this Decision shall be allowed for the necessary modifications to be made to any system of information exchange."

As is apparent from point 165 of the Decision, art 2 was adopted in accordance with art 3(1) of Regulation No 17. By virtue of that provision, where the Commission finds that there is an infringement, inter alia, of art 85 of the Treaty, it may require the undertakings concerned to bring the infringement to an end.

It is settled law that art 3(1) of Regulation No 17 may be applied so as to include an order directed at bringing an end to certain acts, practices or situations which have been found to be unlawful.

Moreover, since art 3(1) of Regulation No 17 is to be applied according to the nature of the infringement found, the Commission has the power to specify the extent of the obligations on the undertakings concerned in order to bring an infringement to an end. Such obligations on the part of the undertakings may not, however, exceed what is appropriate and necessary to attain the objective sought, namely to restore compliance with the rules infringed.

In the present case, in order to verify whether, as the applicant claims, the scope of the direction in art 2 of the Decision is too wide, it is necessary to consider the extent of the various prohibitions it places on the undertakings.

The prohibition in the second sentence of the first paragraph of art 2, requiring the undertakings to refrain in future from any agreement or concerted practice which may have an effect which is the same as, or similar to, those of the infringements found in art 1 of the Decision, is aimed solely at preventing the undertakings from repeating the behaviour found to be unlawful. Consequently, in adopting such directions, the Commission has not exceeded the powers conferred on it by art 3 of Regulation No 17.

The provisions of subparagraphs (a), (b) and (c) of the first paragraph of art 2 are directed more specifically at prohibiting future exchange of commercial information.

The direction in subparagraph (a) of the first paragraph of art 2, which prohibits any future exchange of commercial information by which the participants directly or indirectly obtain individual information on competitors, presupposes a finding by the Commission in the Decision that an information e exchange of such a nature is unlawful under art 85(1) of the Treaty.

It should be noted that art 1 of the Decision does not state that the exchange of individual commercial information in itself constitutes an infringement of art 85(1) of the Treaty.

It states more generally that the undertakings infringed that article of the Treaty by participating in an agreement and concerted practice whereby the undertakings, inter alia, "exchanged commercial information on deliveries, prices, plant standstills, order backlogs and machine utilisation rates in support of the above measures".

However, since the operative part of a decision must be interpreted in the light of the statement of reasons for it, it should be noted that the second paragraph of point 134 of the Decision states:

> "The exchanging by producers of normally confidential and sensitive individual commercial information in meetings of the PG Paperboard (mainly the JMC) on order backlog, machine closures and production rates was patently anti-competitive, being intended to ensure that the conditions for implementing agreed price initiatives were as propitious as possible."

Consequently, as the Commission duly found in the Decision that the exchange of individual commercial information in itself constituted an infringement of art 85(1) of the Treaty, the future prohibition of such an exchange of information satisfies the conditions for the application of art 3(1) of Regulation No 17.

The prohibitions relating to the exchanges of commercial information referred to in subparagraphs (b) and (c) of the first paragraph of art 2 of the Decision must be considered in the light of the second, third and fourth paragraphs of that article, which support what is expressed in those subparagraphs. It is in this context that it is necessary to determine whether, and if so to what extent, the Commission considered the exchanges in question to be illegal, since the extent of the obligations on the undertakings must be restricted to that which is necessary in order to bring their conduct into line with what is lawful under art 85(1) of the Treaty.

The Decision must be interpreted as meaning that the Commission considered the Fides system to be contrary to art 85(1) of the Treaty in that it underpinned the cartel (point 134, third paragraph, of the Decision). Such an interpretation is borne out by the wording of art 1 of the Decision, from which it is apparent that the commercial information was exchanged between the undertakings "in support of the ... measures" considered to be contrary to art 85(1) of the Treaty.

The scope of the future prohibitions set out in subparagraphs (b) and (c) of the first paragraph of art 2 of the Decision must be assessed in the light of that interpretation by the Commission of the compatibility, in the present case, of the Fides system with art 85 of the Treaty.

In that regard, first, the prohibitions in question are not restricted to exchanges of individual commercial information, but relate also to certain aggregated statistical data (art 2, first paragraph, (b), and second paragraph, of the Decision). Second, subparagraphs (b) and (c) of the first paragraph of art 2 prohibit the exchange of certain statistical information in order to prevent the establishment of a possible support for future anti-competitive conduct.

Such a prohibition exceeds what is necessary in order to bring the conduct in question into line with what is lawful because it seeks to prevent the exchange of purely statistical information which is not in, or capable of being put into, the form of individual information on the ground that the information exchanged might be used for anti-competitive purposes. First, it is not apparent from the Decision that the Commission considered the exchange of statistical data to be in itself an infringement of art 85(1) of the Treaty. Second, the mere fact that a system for the exchange of statistical information might be used for anti-competitive purposes does not make it contrary to art 85(1) of the Treaty, since in such circumstances it is necessary to establish its actual anti-competitive effect. It follows that the Commission's argument that art 2 of the Decision is purely declaratory in nature is unfounded.

Consequently, the first to fourth paragraphs of art 2 of the Decision must be annulled, save and except as regards the following passages:

> "The undertakings named in art 1 shall forthwith bring the said infringement to an end, if they have not already done so. They shall henceforth refrain in relation to their cartonboard activities from any agreement or concerted practice which may have the same or a similar object or effect, including any exchange of commercial information:
>
> (a) by which the participants are directly or indirectly informed of the production, sales, order backlog, machine utilisation rates, selling prices, costs or marketing plans of other individual producers.
>
> Any scheme for the exchange of general information to which they subscribe, such as the Fides system or its successor, shall be so conducted as to exclude any information from which the behaviour of individual producers can be identified."

[*The claim for annulment or reduction of the amount of the fine*]

[*Error of appraisal by the Commission in that it considered that the cartel "was largely successful in achieving its objectives" and infringement of the obligation to state reasons in that regard*]

According to the seventh indent of point 168 of the Decision, the Commission determined the general level of fines by taking into account, inter alia, the fact that the cartel "was largely successful in achieving its objectives". It is common ground that this consideration refers to the effects on the market of the infringement found in art 1 of the Decision.

In order to review the Commission's appraisal of the effects of the infringement, the Court considers that it suffices to consider the appraisal of the effects of the collusion on prices. First, it is apparent from the Decision that the finding concerning the large measure of success in achieving objectives is essentially based on the effects of collusion on prices. While those effects are considered in points 100 to 102, 115, and 135 to 137 of the Decision, the question whether the collusion on market shares and collusion on downtime affected the market was, by contrast, not specifically examined in it.

Second, consideration of the effects of the collusion on prices also makes it possible, in any event, to assess whether the objective of the collusion on downtime was achieved, as the aim of that collusion was to prevent the concerted price initiatives from being undermined by an excess of supply.

Third, as regards collusion on market shares, the Commission does not submit that the objective of the undertakings which participated in the meetings of the PWG was an absolute freezing of their market shares. According to the second paragraph of point 60 of the Decision, the agreement on market shares was not static "but was subject to periodic adjustment and re-negotiation". In view of that point, the fact that the Commission took the view that the cartel was largely successful in achieving its objectives without specifically examining in the Decision the success of that collusion on market shares is not therefore open to objection.

As regards collusion on prices, the Commission appraised the general effects of this collusion. Consequently, even assuming that the individual data supplied by the applicant show, as it claims, that the effects of collusion on prices were, in its case, less significant than those found on the European cartonboard market taken as a whole, such individual data cannot in themselves suffice to call into question the Commission's assessment.

It is apparent from the Decision, as the Commission confirmed at the hearing, that a distinction was drawn between three types of effects. Moreover, the Commission relied on the fact that the price initiatives were considered by the producers themselves to have been an overall success.'

Comment
In the 'cartonboard' cases the CFI clearly defined the conditions under which an undertaking may be held responsible for an overall cartel. Sarrio argued that it had participated only in some, not all, aspects of the agreement. The CFI held that it was possible for a member of a cartel to be held liable for the overall cartel once it has become aware of the overall plan of the cartel, although its limited participation may constitute a mitigating factor in relation to the fine imposed by the Commission.

The CFI rejected the argument that although Sarrio had participated in an agreement which co-ordinated price changes it had applied its own prices to each individual transaction. The CFI held that the agreement had impact on transaction prices as it provided the bases for price negotiation in each transaction and that Sarrio infringed art 85(1) EC solely by participating in the agreement. The CFI followed the same line of reasoning while rejecting Sarrio's argument concerning no implementation of the agreement. The CFI stated that a serious anti-competitive intent is contrary to art 85(1) whether or not the agreement was in fact implemented.

In relation to the fine imposed by the Commission, the CFI confirmed the Commission decision. It stated that the cartel had been successful in co-ordinating prices, and that even though there were variations in prices, all prices were based on announced prices and that market shares had been regulated although not absolutely frozen. The CFI also approved the increase in fines based on the fact that the undertakings tried to conceal the operation of the cartel. Sarrio argued that secrecy was essential for the operation of a cartel. The Commission and the CFI disagreed, especially in the light of the fact that there were no minutes or other internal or external memos of the meetings of the JMC.

Völk v Etablissements Vervaecke SPRL Case 5/69 [1969] ECR 295 European Court of Justice

- *Article 85(1) – exclusive distribution agreement – absolute territorial protection – effect on inter-State trade – the de minimis rule*

Facts
Völk, a small undertaking manufacturing washing machines, concluded an exclusive distribution agreement with Vervaecke, a Dutch distributor. Völk's share of the market in washing machines was less than 1 per cent. When a dispute arose between the parties, a Dutch court referred to the ECJ a question whether art 85(1) should apply taking into account the small share of the market held by Völk.

Held
The ECJ held that even an exclusive distributorship agreement ensuring absolute territorial protection was outside the scope of art 85(1) EC Treaty as the effects produced on trade between Member States were not appreciable.

Judgment
'If an agreement is to be capable of affecting trade between Member States it must be possible to foresee with a sufficient degree of probability on the basis of set of objective factors of law or of fact that the agreement in question may have an influence, direct or indirect, actual or potential, on the pattern of trade between Member States in such a way that it might hinder the attainment of the objectives of a single market between States. Moreover the prohibition in art 85(1) is applicable only if the agreement in question also has as its object or effect the prevention, restriction or distortion of competition within the Common Market. Those conditions must be understood by reference to the actual circumstances of the agreement. Consequently an agreements falls outside the prohibition in art 85 when it has

only an insignificant effect on the markets, taking into account the weak position which the persons concerned have on the market of the product in question. Thus an exclusive dealing agreement even with absolute territorial protection may, having regard to the weak position of the persons concerned on the market in the product in question in the area covered by the absolute protection, escape the prohibition laid down in art 85(1).'

Comment
In the present case the ECJ established the de minimis rule under which some agreements prima facie in breach of art 85 (1) EC Treaty are, nevertheless, outside its scope of application where the market share of the parties is minimal so their agreement has no effect on intra-Community trade. The manufacturer's share of the market (0.6 per cent) was considered by the ECJ as insignificant and the agreement itself concerned only 600 units.

In order to help businesses to assess whether the de minimis rule applies to their agreement the Commission has published a Notice on Agreements of Minor Importance, which has been recently revised (OJ C373 9.12.1997 pp13–15)

The Notice is not binding but very useful for undertakings since if their agreement falls below the fixed thresholds they can proceed and do not have to notify it to the Commission. The Commission states in its Notice that no infringement proceedings will be commenced in respect of any such agreement, and if the parties mistakenly, but in good faith, fail to notify their agreement, believing that it is within the scope of the Notice, the Commission will not impose fines on them. If the parties are uncertain whether or not their agreement is excluded from art 85(1) EC they should notify it to the Commission in the usual way. Horizontal agreements which are within the scope of the de minimus rule but have as their object price-fixing, restriction of production or sales or market sharing being per se contrary to art 86(1) EC are excluded from the scope of the Notice. Although the Commission in general will not commence proceedings in respect of such agreements, unless the interests of the Community require it, they should be notified to the Commission. Similar treatment is applied to vertical agreements which are (by their nature) in breach of art 85(1), that is those which either fix resale prices or confer territorial protection upon the participating undertakings or third undertakings.

The Notice distinguishes between three types of agreement:

1. Horizontal agreements. In the case of undertakings operating at the same level of production or marketing a threshold is fixed at 5 per cent, ie the aggregate market shares held by participating undertakings in any of the relevant market must not exceed 5 per cent.
2. Vertical agreements. Agreements between undertakings operating at different economic level in the distribution process are within the scope of the Notice if the aggregate market shares of participating undertakings do not exceed in any of the relevant market a threshold of 10 per cent.
3. Mixed agreements. In a mixed horizontal/vertical agreement (or in the event that the classification of an agreement is difficult) a threshold of 5 per cent is applicable.

The Commission will consider agreements, whether horizontal, vertical or mixed, as protected by the Notice if they exceed the fixed threshold by no more that one-tenth in relation to market shares over two successive financial years.

Article 86 EC Treaty (now art 82 EC Treaty)

AKZO Chemie BV v *EC Commission Case C–62/86* Case C–62/86 [1991] ECR I–3359; [1993] 5 CMLR 197 European Court of Justice

- *Article 86 EC Treaty – relevant market share – relevant product market – relevant geographical market – determination of dominant position – predatory pricing*

Facts

Benzoyl peroxide is a chemical that can be used for bleaching flour and as a catalyst in plastic manufacture. Engineering and Chemical Supplies Ltd (ECS), an English undertaking producing benzoyl peroxide, which had mainly operated in the flour additive sector, decided to expand its sales into the larger plastics sector in the United Kingdom and Ireland. The plastic sector was dominated by AKZO, a producer of organic peroxides including benzoyl peroxide (one of the main organic peroxides) which was also present in the flour additive sector. When one of the largest customers of AKZO in the plastics sector became a customer of ECS, AKZO threatened to reduce prices in the UK flour sector. ECS complained to the Commission. The Commission ordered interim measures under which AKZO's branch in the UK was to stay within the profit levels prior to ECS's expansion to the plastics sector. The Commission found a memo prepared by one of the AKZO's directors stating that the ECS managing director was informed that 'aggressive commercial action would be taken on the milling side unless he refrained from selling his products to the plastics industry'.

The Commission found that AKZO abused its dominant position in the market for organic peroxides by engaging in predatory pricing in order to eliminate ECS. AKZO challenged the methodology employed by the Commission in assessing the existence of a dominant position, in particular in the determination of the relevant product market and the geographical market, and claimed that its prices were not abusive as they always included an element of profit.

Held

The allegations of AKZO were rejected. The ECJ upheld the Commission's assessment of the relevant product market and relevant geographical market.

Judgment

'[*Identification of the relevant product market*]

In the decision it is primarily the organic peroxide market (including benzoyl peroxide used in the plastic industry) that is held to be the relevant market, because that was the market from which AKZO sought in the long-term to exclude ECS. Alternatively, according to the decision, the abuse took place in the flour additives market in the United Kingdom and Ireland.

It must be determined, firstly, whether the Commission was right to define the relevant market as the organic peroxides market.

AKZO disputes this definition in view of the subject-matter of the decision, which relates solely to its allegedly unlawful behaviour in the flour additive sector. It points out in this respect that in *Commercial Solvents* v *EC Commission* [1974] 1 CMLR 309, the Court held that the market in which the effects of the abuse appear is "irrelevant as regards the determination of the relevant market to be considered for the purpose of a finding that a dominant position exists".

That argument must be examined in the light of the particular circumstances of this case.

In that respect it must be observed that benzoyl peroxide, one of the main organic peroxides used in the manufacture of plastics, is also one of the main additives for flour because of its use as a bleaching agent for flour in the United Kingdom and Ireland.

Secondly, it should be pointed out that before 1979 ECS operated solely in the flour additive sector. It was only in the course of that year that it decided to extend its activities to the plastics sector. Consequently, when the dispute arose, ECS had only an extremely small share in that sector.

Moreover, it is not disputed that the plastic sector was more important to AKZO than the flour additives sector, since it had much higher turnover in that sector.

AKZO therefore applied price reductions in a sector (that of flour additives) which was vital to ECS but only of limited importance to itself. Furthermore, AKZO was able to set off any losses that it incurred in the flour additives sector against profits from its activity in the plastic sector, a possibility not available to ECS.

Finally, according to statements made by a manager of AKZO, which will be considered when the complaint relating to the threats is examined, AKZO did not adopt its behaviour in order to strengthen its position in the flour additive sector, but to preserve its position in the plastic sector by preventing ECS from extending its activities to that sector.

The Commission was in those circumstances justified in regarding the organic peroxides market as the relevant market, even though the abusive behaviour alleged was intended to damage ECS's main business activity in a different market.

[*Predatory pricing*]
... Prices below average variable costs (that is to say, those which vary depending on the quantities produced) by means of which a dominant undertaking seeks to eliminate a competitor must be regarded as abusive. A dominant undertaking has no interest in applying such prices except that of eliminating competitors so as to enable it subsequently to raise its prices by taking advantage of its monopolistic position, since each sale generates a loss, namely the total amount of the fixed costs (that is to say, those which remain constant regardless of the quantities produced) and, at least, part of the variable costs relating to the unit produced.

Moreover, prices below average total costs, that is to say, fixed costs plus variable costs, but above average variable costs must be regarded as abusive if they are determined as part of a plan for eliminating a competitor. Such prices can drive from the market undertakings which are perhaps as efficient as the dominant undertaking but which, because of their smaller resources, are incapable of withstanding the competition waged against them.'

Comment
The divergencies between the Commission and the undertaking under investigation in the determination of the relevant product market followed a not unusual pattern, bearing in mind that undertakings always seek a broad interpretation and the Commission always seeks the opposite. The narrower the definition of a product market the greater the market share of any one undertaking. In the present case, the ECJ defined the relevant product market not by reference to demand and supply substitutability but focused on AKZO's behaviour in relation to the flour additives market. The practices of AKZO in that market, which practices were allegedly abusive, would not be financially viable if AKZO was not in a dominant position. Therefore, by its action AKZO defined the relevant product market.

In respect of predatory prices, in the present case the Commission based its conclusion that AKZO applied predatory prices on an internal memorandum and the desire of AKZO to eliminate the expansion of ECS to the plastics market. There is neither a Community definition of predatory pricing nor a recognised test under EC law for determining what prices should be considered as such. In *Tetra Pak International SA v EC Commission (No 2)* Case C–333/94P [1997] 4 CMLR 662 the ECJ stated that prices which were considerably lower than average variable cost are per se predatory and in such a case no proof of intention to eliminate competitors was necessary. However, if there is over-capacity or over-supply in the relevant product market, or if there is a restructuring of the market, an undertaking applying such prices would be able to escape the prohibition contained in art 86 EC Treaty.

Oscar Bronner GmbH & Co KG v Mediaprint Zeitungs-und Eitschriftenverlag GmbH & Co KG
Case C–7/97 Judgment of 26 November 1998 (not yet reported) European Court of Justice

- *Article 86 EC Treaty – abuse of a dominant position – newspaper home-delivery scheme – refusal of an undertaking holding a dominant position to include another undertaking in the scheme*

Facts
The Austrian Regional Court in Vienna referred to the ECJ for a preliminary ruling two questions on the interpretation of art 86 of the Treaty which had been raised in proceedings between two Austrian undertakings. They were Oscar Bronner, editor, publisher, manufacturer and distributor of the daily newspaper *Der Standard* which in 1994 held 3.6 per cent of circulation and 6 per cent of advertising share of the Austrian daily newspaper market and Mediaprint Zeitungs, publisher of two daily newspapers which in 1994 held 46.8 per cent of the Austrian daily newspaper market in terms of circulation and 42 per cent in terms of advertising revenues. Mediaprint Zeitungs' two newspapers reached 53.3 per cent of the population from the age of 14 in private households and 71 per cent of all newspaper readers. Mediaprint set up a nationwide delivery system consisting of delivering the newspapers directly to subscribers in the early hours of the morning. Oscar Bronner (for financial reasons) was not able to set up a similar system of delivery on its own and had to use postal service for delivery of its newspaper which took place late in the mornings. Brunner sought an order requiring Mediaprint to cease abusing Mediaprint's alleged dominant position in the market by including Bronner's newspaper, *Der Standard*, in its home-delivery service against payment of reasonable remuneration. Mediaprint refused to do so.

Held
The ECJ held that the refusal by a press undertaking which held a very large share of the daily newspaper market in a Member State and operated the only nationwide newspaper home-delivery scheme in that Member State to allow the publisher of a rival newspaper, which by reason of its small circulation was unable either alone or in co-operation with other publishers to set up and operate its own home-delivery scheme in economically reasonable conditions, to have access to that scheme for appropriate remuneration did not constitute abuse of a dominant position within the meaning of art 86 of the EC Treaty.

Judgment
'In examining whether an undertaking holds a dominant position within the meaning of art 86 of the Treaty, it is of fundamental importance, as the Court has emphasised many times, to define the market in question and to define the substantial part of the common market in which the undertaking may be able to engage in abuses which hinder effective competition.

As regards the definition of the market at issue in the main proceedings, it is therefore for the national court to determine, inter alia, whether home-delivery schemes constitute a separate market, or whether other methods of distributing daily newspapers, such as sale in shops or at kiosks or delivery by post, are sufficiently interchangeable with them to have to be taken into account also.

The case law indicates that the territory of a Member State over which a dominant position extends is capable of constituting a substantial part of the common market.

Finally, it would need to be determined whether the refusal by the owner of the only nationwide home-delivery scheme in the territory of a Member State, which uses that scheme to distribute its own daily newspapers, to allow the publisher of a rival daily newspaper access to it constitutes an abuse of a dominant position within the meaning of art 86 of the Treaty, on the ground that such refusal deprives that competitor of a means of distribution judged essential for the sale of its newspaper.

It would still be necessary not only that the refusal of the service comprised in home delivery be likely to eliminate all competition in the daily newspaper market on the part of the person requesting the service and that such refusal be incapable of being objectively justified, but also that the service in itself be indispensable to carrying on that person's business, inasmuch as there is no actual or potential substitute in existence for that home-delivery scheme.

That is certainly not the case.

In the first place, it is undisputed that other methods of distributing daily newspapers, such as by post and through sale in shops and at kiosks, even though they may be less advantageous for the distribution of certain newspapers, exist and are used by the publishers of those daily newspapers.

Moreover, it does not appear that there are any technical, legal or even economic obstacles capable of making it impossible, or even unreasonably difficult, for any other publisher of daily newspapers to establish, alone or in cooperation with other publishers, its own nationwide home-delivery scheme and use it to distribute its own daily newspapers.

It should be emphasised in that respect that, in order to demonstrate that the creation of such a system is not a realistic potential alternative and that access to the existing system is therefore indispensable, it is not enough to argue that it is not economically viable by reason of the small circulation of the daily newspaper or newspapers to be distributed.'

Comment

The ECJ distinguished the present case from others where the refusal of a dominant undertaking in a particular sector to supply or to give access to its facilities were considered as an abuse of that position on the market. In particular, in *Commercial Solvents* v *EC Commission* Cases 6 and 7/73 [1974] ECR 223 the refusal of Commercial Solvents, the world's only large-scale producer of raw materials from which the drug ethambutol could be made (and as such holding a dominant position in that sector), to supply raw materials to Zoja, one of the three makers of ethambutol in the EC, was considered as contrary to art 86(1)(d) EC Treaty. In *Télé-marketing* Case 311/84 an undertaking registered in Luxembourg and dominant over the transmission of advertisements to Belgium refused to transmit telemarketing spots unless its own answering services were used was condemned by the ECJ for abusing its dominant position (see also *Independent Television Publications Limited* v *EC Commission* Case T–76/89 [1991] 4 CMLR 745). It seems that the restrictive approach of the ECJ to the refusal of an undertaking enjoying a dominant position to supply or to give access to its facilities has been relaxed.

In the present case the ECJ specifies two conditions under which the refusal of the dominant undertaking cannot be justified: first, if the refusal of participation in the service comprising home delivery would be likely to eliminate all competition in the daily newspaper market; and, second, if there is no actual or potential substitute in existence for that home-delivery scheme. These two conditions were not satisfied in the present case and therefore, the ECJ held that there was no abuse of a dominant position on the part of Mediaprint.

Hilti v *EC Commission* Case T–30/89 [1992] 4 CMLR 16 Court of First Instance

• Article 86 EC Treaty – relevant product market – substitutability of different component products

Facts

Hilti manufactured nail guns and the nails and cartridge strips for such equipment. After an investigation by the Commission Hilti was found to have abused its dominant position within the EC market for each of these products, namely the market in nail guns, the market in cartridge strips and the market in nails.

The Commission stated that Hilti abused its position, inter alia, by pursuing a policy of supplying cartridge strips to certain end users or distributors only when such cartridge strips were purchased with the necessary complement of nails ('tying' of cartridge strips and nails), by blocking the sale of competitors' nails by a policy of reducing discounts for orders of cartridges without nails (the reduction of discounts was based essentially on the fact that the customer was purchasing nails from Hilti's competitors), by exercising pressure on independent distributors (mainly in The Netherlands) not to fulfil certain export orders (notably to the UK), by refusing to supply cartridges to independent nail manufactures (mainly to the undertakings that complained to the Commission), etc.

Hilti challenged the Commission's definition of the relevant product market. Hilti argued that these three markets must be regarded as constituting a single indivisible market because each of the products could not be used by consumers without the others.

Held
The CFI upheld the decision of the Commission. The CFI stated that the Commission was correct in identifying three separate product markets because all the products could be manufactured separately and could be purchased by consumers without them having to buy the other products. The relevant product market was therefore the three distinct product markets and the relevant geographical market was the Community as a whole.

Judgment
'[*The relevant geographical market*]
The documents before the Court show that there are large price differences for Hilti products between the Member States and that transport costs for nails are low.

Those two factors make parallel trading highly likely between the national markets of the Community. It must therefore be concluded that the Commission was right in taking the view that the relevant geographical market in this case is the Community as a whole.

The applicant's argument on this point must therefore be rejected.

[*The relevant product market*]
... In order to determine ... whether Hilti, as a supplier of nail guns and of consumables designed for them, enjoys such power over the relevant product market as to give it a dominant position within the meaning of art 86, the first question to be answered is whether the relevant market in the market for all construction fastening systems or whether the relevant markets are for power-actuated fastening (PAF) tools and the consumables designed for them, namely cartridge strips and nails.

The Court takes the view that nail guns, cartridge strips and nails constitute three specific markets. Since cartridge strips and nails are specifically manufactured, and purchased by users, for a single brand of gun, it must be concluded that there are separate markets for Hilti-compatible strips and nails, as the Commission found in its decision.

With particular regard to the nails whose use in Hilti is essential element of the dispute, it is common ground that since the 1960 there have been independent producers, including the interveners, making nails for use in nail guns. Some of those producers are specialised and produce only nails, and indeed some make only nails designed for Hilti tools. That fact in itself is sound evidence that there is a specific market for Hilti-compatible nails.

Hilti's contention that guns, cartridge strips and nails should be regarded as forming an indivisible whole, a "powder-actuated fastening system" is in practice tantamount to permitting producers of nail guns to exclude the use of consumables other than their own branded products in their tools. However, in the absence of general and binding statements or rules, any independent producer is quite free, as far as Community competition law is concerned, to manufacture consumables intended for use in equipment manufactured by others, unless in doing so it infringes a patent or some other industrial or intellectual property right.

Even on the assumption that, as the applicant has argued, components of different makes cannot be interchanged without the system characteristics being influenced, the solution should lie in the adoption of appropriate laws and regulations, not in unilateral measures taken by nail gun producers which have the effect of preventing independent producers from pursuing the bulk of their business.

Hilti's argument that PAF tools and consumables form part of the market in PAF systems for the construction industry generally cannot be accepted either. The Court finds the PAF systems differ from other fastening systems in several important respects. The specific features of PAF systems, set out in Paragraph 62 of the Decision, are such as to make them the obvious choice in a number of cases. It is evident from the documents before the Court that in many cases there is no realistic alternative either for a qualified operator carrying out a job on site or for a technician instructed to select the fastening methods to be used in a given situation.

The Court considers that the Commission's description of those features in its decision is sufficiently clear and convincing to provide solid legal justification for the conclusions drawn from it.

Those findings leave no real doubt as to the existence, in practice, of a variety of situations, some of which inherently favour the use of a PAF system whilst others favour one or more other fastening systems. As the Commission notes, the fact that several different fastening methods have each continued for long periods to account for an important share of total demand for fastening systems shows that there is only a relatively low degree of substitutability between them.

In such circumstances the Commission was entitled to base its conclusions on arguments which took account of the qualitative characteristics of the products at issue.

[*Factors indicating dominance*]
The Commission has proved that Hilti holds a market share of around 70 per cent to 80 per cent in the relevant market for nails. That figure was supplied to the Commission by Hilti following a request by the Commission for information pursuant to art 11 of Regulation No 17. As the Commission has rightly emphasised, Hilti was therefore obliged to supply information which, to the best of its knowledge, was as accurate as possible. Hilti's subsequent assertion that the figure were unsound is not corroborated by any evidence or by any examples showing them to be unreliable. The argument of the applicant must therefore be rejected.

... With particular reference to market shares, the Court of Justice has held ... that very large shares are in themselves, and save in exceptional circumstances, evidence of a dominant position.

In this case it is established that Hilti holds a share of between 70 per cent and 80 per cent in the relevant market. Such a share is, in itself, a clear indication of the existence of a dominant position in the relevant market ...'

Comment
In the context of the present case it should be noted that the Commission published its Notice on the Definition of the Relevant Market for the Purposes of Community Competition Law (OJ C37 1997 p5) based on the then existing practices of both the Commission and the ECJ.

The Notice identifies three main factors of competitive constraints to which undertakings are subject and which identify the relevant market: demand substitutability, supply substitutability and potential competition. In relation to demand and supply substitutability the Notice provides examples in order to illustrate the reasoning of the Commission. Thus, to assess the demand substitutability a hypothetical situation is examined in which a small (up to 10 per cent) and permanent price increase is applied: if the existence of other products within the geographical markets would make the price rise unprofitable due to loss of sales, those products are part of the market since in those circumstances the consumer would substitute one product for another.

The supply substitutability is determined by reference to the ability of competitors to switch their resources to manufacture a product which has been subject to a small and permanent price rise without significant increase in cost and risk for such an undertaking. If switching the production involves major investment, or risks then there is no supply substitutability for the product in question. The Notice suggests that the third constraint, the impact of potential competition, is not applied when determining markets but in a later stage when the relevant market has been defined in order to assess whether the presence of potential competition might influence the market strength in relation to the undertaking concerned.

According to the Notice a product market: 'comprises all those products and/or services which are regarded as interchangeable or substitutable by the consumer by reason of the products' characteristics, their prices and their intended use'.

In order to establish whether there are possible relevant markets the Commission will take into consideration the following evidence:

1. evidence of substitution in the recent past such as price changes and introduction of new products on the market;
2. views of customers and competitors in relation to the effect on the product market of a small and permanent price increase;
3. consumer preference which may be assessed conducting surveys among consumers and retailers. Also information gathered by the undertaking concerned may be useful;
4. costs and obstacles involved in switching demand to potential substitutes;
5. the category of consumers and price discrimination which is important where there is a clearly defined group of consumers.

In relation to a geographical market the Notice states that it 'comprises the area in which the undertakings concerned are involved in the supply and demand of products or services, in which the conditions of competition are sufficiently homogenous and which can be distinguished from neighbouring areas because the conditions of competition are appreciably different in those areas'.

Criteria very similar to those regarding a relevant product market are to be applied in order to identify a geographical market, although not all of them will be relevant in any one case. The heads of evidence are: past evidence of diversion of orders to other areas; basic demand characteristics, ie whether there are local preferences based on brand, language, culture and the need for a local presence; views of customers and retailers; current geographical pattern of purchase; trade flow pattern of shipment when ascertaining actual geographical pattern in the context of a large number of customers; and barriers and cost associated with switching orders to companies situated in other areas.

The Commission also provides a useful note on the range of evidence which it examines in each case for market definition purposes. It includes information forwarded by the undertakings under inquiry, by competitors, by customers and by trade associations. Visits and inspections are also part of the evidence-gathering procedure. Furthermore, the Notice specifies that in the determination of market share both volume sales and value sales are to be taken into consideration.

Merger control

Gencor Ltd v Commission of the European Communities Case T–102/96 Judgment of 25 March 1999 (not yet reported) Court of First Instance

• *Competition – merger – Regulation 4064/89 – decision declaring a concentration incompatible with the common market – collective dominant position – extraterritorial scope of application of Regulation 4064/89 – principle of public international law – commitments – admissibility of an action for annulment – legal interest in bringing proceedings*

Facts
Gencor Ltd, a company incorporated under South African law operating mainly in the mineral resources and metals industries, held 46.5 per cent of Impala Platinum Holdings (Implats), also a company registered in South Africa, which brought together Gencor's activities in the platinum group metal ('PGM') sector. Lonrho, an English company operating in various sectors such as mining, metals, hotels, agriculture and general trade, held 73 per cent of Eastern Platinum Ltd and Western Platinum Ltd (LPD), both incorporated under South African law which brought together Lonrho's activities in the PGM sector. The remaining 27 per cent of LPD was held by Gencor.

Gencor and Lonrho proposed to acquire joint control of Implats in order to control LPD. As a result of that transaction Implats was to be held as to 32 per cent by Gencor, 32 per cent by Lonrho and 36 per cent by the public. In practical terms, the concentration would eliminate competition between Gencor and Lonrho not only in the PGM sector in South Africa but also in the marketing of PGMs in the Community where Implats and LPD are important suppliers in this sector, which instead of being supplied by three South African companies would have only two suppliers, Implats/LPD and Amplats (the leading worldwide suppliers in the PGM sector.

The proposed concentration was approved on 22 August 1995 by the South African Competition Board.

On 17 November 1995 Gencor and Lonrho jointly notified the Commission of the above agreements. The Commission declared that the concentration was incompatible with the common market and the functioning of the EEA Agreement, because it would have led to the creation of a dominant duopoly position between Amplats and Implats/LPD in the world platinum and rhodium market as a result of which effective competition would have been significantly impeded in the common market.

On 28 June 1996 the applicant brought this action for the annulment of the contested decision, on the grounds that the Commission had no jurisdiction under Regulation 4064/89 since the transaction was carried out outside the Community and, in the alternative, if the Regulation did apply, it was unlawful and therefore inapplicable pursuant to art 184 of the Treaty.

Held
The CFI dismissed the application.

Judgment
[*Assessment of the territorial scope of the Regulation*]
The Regulation, in accordance with art 1 thereof, applies to all concentrations with a Community dimension, that is to say to all concentrations between undertakings which do not each achieve more than two-thirds of their aggregate Community-wide turnover within one and the same Member State, where the combined aggregate worldwide turnover of those undertakings is more than ECU 5,000 million and the aggregate Community-wide turnover of at least two of them is more than ECU 250 million.

Article 1 does not require that, in order

for a concentration to be regarded as having a Community dimension, the undertakings in question must be established in the Community or that the production activities covered by the concentration must be carried out within Community territory.

With regard to the criterion of turnover, it must be stated that the concentration at issue has a Community dimension within the meaning of the Regulation. The undertakings concerned have an aggregate worldwide turnover of more than ECU 10,000 million, above the ECU 5,000 million threshold laid down by the Regulation. Gencor and Lonrho each had a Community-wide turnover of more than ECU 250 million in the latest financial year. Finally, they do not each achieve more than two-thirds of their aggregate Community-wide turnover within one and the same Member State.

The legal bases for the Regulation (namely arts 87 and 235 of the Treaty, as well as arts 3(g) and 85 and 86 thereof) as well as the first to fifth, ninth and eleventh recitals in the preamble to the Regulation, merely point to the need to ensure that competition is not distorted in the common market, in particular by concentrations which result in the creation or strengthening of a dominant position. They in no way exclude from the Regulation's field of application concentrations which, while relating to mining and/or production activities outside the Community, have the effect of creating or strengthening a dominant position as a result of which effective competition in the common market is significantly impeded.

By referring, in general terms, to the concept of substantial operations, the Regulation does not, for the purpose of defining its territorial scope, ascribe greater importance to production operations than to sales operations. On the contrary, by setting quantitative thresholds which are based on the worldwide and Community turnover of the undertakings concerned, it rather ascribes greater importance to sales operations within the common market as a factor linking the concentration to the Community.

[*Compatibility of the contested decision with public international law*]
Application of the Regulation is justified under public international law when it is foreseeable that a proposed concentration will have an immediate and substantial effect in the Community.

The Court of First Instance states that it was in fact foreseeable that the immediate and substantial effect of creating a dominant duopoly position in a world market would also be to impede competition significantly in the Community, an integral part of that market.

In those circumstances, the contested decision is not inconsistent with either the Regulation or the rules of public international law relied on by the applicant.

Secondly, the applicant maintains that the creation or strengthening of a collective dominant position cannot be prohibited under the Regulation.

The question thus arises as to whether the words 'which creates or strengthens a dominant position' cover only the creation or strengthening of an individual dominant position or whether they also refer to the creation or strengthening of a collective dominant position, that is to say one held by two or more undertakings.

The reference in the fifteenth recital in the preamble to the Regulation to a 25 per cent threshold for market share cannot justify a restrictive interpretation of the Regulation. Since oligopolistic markets in which one of the jointly dominant undertakings has a market share of less than 25 per cent are relatively rare, that reference cannot remove cases of joint dominance from the scope of the Regulation. It is more common to find oligopolistic markets in which the dominant undertakings hold market shares of more than 25 per cent. Thus, the market structures which encourage oligopolistic conduct most are those in which two, three or four suppliers each hold approximately the same market share.

That threshold is given purely by way of guidance, as is made clear by the fifteenth recital itself, and it is not incorporated in any way in the provisions of the Regulation.

Since the interpretations of the Regulation based on their wording and the history and the scheme of the Regulation do not permit their precise scope to be assessed as regards the type of dominant position concerned, the legislation in question must be interpreted by reference to its purpose.

It follows from the sixth, seventh, tenth and eleventh recitals in the preamble to the Regulation that it, unlike arts 85 and 86 of the Treaty, is intended to apply to all concentrations with a Community dimension in so far as, because of their effect on the structure of competition within the Community, they may prove incompatible with the system of undistorted competition envisaged by the Treaty.

A concentration which creates or strengthens a dominant position on the part of the parties to the concentration with an entity not involved in the concentration is liable to prove incompatible with the system of undistorted competition laid down by the Treaty. Consequently, if it were accepted that only concentrations creating or strengthening a dominant position on the part of the parties to the concentration were covered by the Regulation, its purpose as indicated by the abovementioned recitals would be partially frustrated. The Regulation would thus be deprived of a not insignificant aspect of its effectiveness, without that being necessary from the perspective of the general structure of the Community system of control of concentrations.

According to the Court of First Instance, the Commission was fully entitled to conclude that the concentration would have led to the creation of a dominant duopoly on the part of Amplats and Implats/LPD in the platinum and rhodium market, as a result of which effective competition would have been significantly impeded in the common market within the meaning of art 2 of the Regulation. It also follows that the reasoning in the contested decision fulfils the requirements laid down by art 190 of the Treaty.

Finally, the Court of First Instance considers what type of commitment (in particular, behavioural) may be accepted under the Regulation.

Where the Commission concludes that the concentration is such as to create or strengthen a dominant position, it is required to prohibit it, even if the undertakings concerned by the proposed concentration pledge themselves vis-à-vis the Commission not to abuse that position.

Consequently, the Commission has power to accept only such commitments as are capable of rendering the notified transaction compatible with the common market.

Since the commitments as a whole were not capable of eliminating the impediment to effective competition caused by the concentration, the Commission was justified in rejecting them, even if there were no particular difficulties in verifying whether they had been carried out.'

Comment
The extra-territorial application of EC competition law is in the present case less controversial than in *Re Wood Pulp Cartel* as Lonrho is a company incorporated in the UK. Therefore under the principle of nationality the jurisdiction of the EC competition authorities is justified. Juridiction based on nationality is recognised under public international law, while jurisdiction based on the effects doctrine is still contested. From a practical point of view the strict application of the effects doctrine may create international disputes and is likely to disrupt good international relations. For that reason, the courts in the USA since the mid-1970s have imposed important limitations based on international comity (non-binding rules of goodwill and civility, founded on the moral right of each State to receive courtesy from others) on the application of the effects doctrine under which an anti-competitive practice must have direct and substantial effect in the USA, and the court should balance interests involved in order to determine whether or not the extra-territorial jurisdiction should be upheld (especially see *Mannington Mills Inc* v *Congoleum Corp* 595 F 2d 1287 (3d Cir 1979) and *United*

States v *Nippon Paper Indust Co* 109 F3d (1st Cir 1997)).

The Commission enjoys a large measure of discretion in relation to the enforcement of arts 85 and 86 EC Treaty and has used it to avoid international disputes (see Boeing/ McDonnell Douglas 97/816 (1997) OJ L336 p16). This is not the case in relation to merger control under Regulation 4064/89. It seems that once the envisaged merger satisfies the threshold requirements, the Commission must act, or at least assess the proposed merger from the point of view of Community interests.

It is interesting to note that Merger Regulation 4064/89 which was updated on 26 June 1997 by Regulation 1310/97/EC (entered into force on 1 March 1998) was applied to the present case.

The main changes introduced by the 1997 Merger Regulation concern the thresholds triggering its application and the abolition of a distinction between 'co-operative' and 'concentrative' ventures. The basic rule set out in art 1 of the old Merger Regulation remains, that is a concentration has a 'Community dimension' where, first, the combined aggregate worldwide turnover of all undertakings concerned is over ECU 5 billion and, second, the aggregate Community-wide turnover of each of at least two undertakings concerned is more than ECU 250 million unless each of the undertakings concerned achieves more than two-thirds of its aggregate Community-wide turnover within one and the same Member State. The 1997 Regulation introduces a 'one-stop-shop' EU notification procedure for cross-border merger agreements involving at least three Member States and meeting a slightly lower turnover criteria

In relation to joint-ventures the 97 Regulation abolishes the distinction between 'co-operative' and 'concentrative' ventures and establishes only one category for all of them – the 'full- function' joint-ventures. There is one notification procedure for all joint-ventures carried out within the same time-limit as applicable to merger agreements, that is at the maximum five months (one month for the initial examination followed, if necessary, by a four-months' inquiry). As a result, the full-function joint-ventures will obtain a decision from the Commission in a very short period of time as compared with the old rules. Also, under new rules commitments may be made by the undertakings concerned during the first stage of the investigation in order to allay the Commission's reservations on competition grounds.

Procedural rights and duties

Baustahlgewebe GmbH* v *Commission of the European Communities Case C–185/95P Judgment of 17 December 1998 (not yet reported) European Court of Justice

- *Competition – appeal – excessive duration of the procedure before the CFI – art 6 of the European Convention on Human Rights – reasonable satisfaction for the excessive duration of proceedings – access to the file – general principle of Community law – independent assessment of fines by the CFI*

Facts
On 20 October 1989 Baustahlgewebe brought action for annulment of the Commission Decision 89/515/EEC which imposed fines on 14 producers of welded steel mesh for infringement of art 85(1) EC Treaty. After five years and six months the CFI delivered its decision reducing the fine from ECU 4.4 million to ECU 3 million and partially annulling the Commission decision. The applicant claimed, inter alia, that the CFI was in breach of the principle that proceedings must be disposed of within a reasonable time as enshrined in art 6 of the European Convention on Human Rights, that the CFI

infringed its rights of defence by refusing access to the file, and that a disproportionate fine was imposed upon it.

Held
The ECJ held that the proceedings before the CFI were excessively protracted. For that reason the ECJ partially annulled the decision of the CFI. The ECJ stated that the excessive duration of proceedings before the CFI had no impact on the outcome of the case and decided that ECU 50,000 constituted fair satisfaction for a procedural irregularity of that kind. The fine imposed on the applicants was reduced to 2,950,000. The right to consult the CFI's file is governed by the EC Statute of the Court of Justice and by the Rules of Proceedings of the Court of First Instance and not by the general principles of Community law. Consequently, the refusal of the CFI was justified by virtue of art 64 of its rules of procedure. The ECJ held that the CFI had unlimited jurisdiction to determine the amount of fines.

Judgment
'[*Breach of the principle that proceedings must be disposed of within a reasonable time*]
First, it must be noted that the proceedings being considered by the Court of Justice in this case, in order to determine whether a procedural irregularity was committed to the detriment of the appellant's interests, commenced on 20 October 1989, the date on which the application for annulment was lodged, and closed on 6 April 1995, the date on which the contested judgment was delivered. Consequently, the duration of the proceedings now being considered by the Court of Justice was about five years and six months.

It must first be stated that such a duration is, at first sight, considerable. However, the reasonableness of such a period must be appraised in the light of the circumstances specific to each case and, in particular, the importance of the case for the person concerned, its complexity and the conduct of the applicant and of the competent authorities.

As regards the importance of the proceedings to the appellant, it must be emphasised that its economic survival was not directly endangered by the proceedings. The fact nevertheless remains that, in the case of proceedings concerning infringement of competition rules, the fundamental requirement of legal certainty on which economic operators must be able to rely and the aim of ensuring that competition is not distorted in the internal market are of considerable importance not only for an applicant himself and his competitors but also for third parties in view of the large number of persons concerned and the financial interests involved.

It must be held that the procedure before the Court of First Instance was of genuine importance to the appellant.

As regards the complexity of the case, it must be borne in mind that, in its decision, the Commission concluded that 14 manufacturers of welded steel mesh had infringed art 85 of the Treaty by a series of agreements or concerted practices concerning delivery quotas and the prices of that product. The appellant's application was one of 11, submitted in three different languages, which were formally joined for the purposes of the oral procedure.

In that regard, it is clear from the documents before the Court and from the contested judgment that the procedure concerning the appellant called for a detailed examination of relatively voluminous documents and points of fact and law of some complexity.

It has not been established that the appellant contributed, in any significant way, to the protraction of the proceedings.

As regards the conduct of the competent authorities, it must be borne in mind that the purpose of attaching the Court of First Instance to the Court of Justice and of introducing two levels of jurisdiction was, first, to improve the judicial protection of individual interests, in particular in proceedings necessitating close examination of complex facts, and, second, to maintain the quality and effectiveness of judicial review in the

Community legal order, by enabling the Court of Justice to concentrate on its essential task, namely to ensure that in the interpretation and application of Community law the law is observed.

That is why the structure of the Community judicial system justifies, in certain respects, the Court of First Instance, which is responsible for establishing the facts and undertaking a substantive examination of the dispute, being allowed a relatively longer period to investigate actions calling for a close examination of complex facts. However, that task does not relieve the Community court established especially for that purpose from the obligation of observing reasonable time-limits in dealing with cases before it.

Account must also be taken of the constraints inherent in proceedings before the Community judicature, associated in particular with the use of languages provided for in art 35 of the Rules of Procedure of the Court of First Instance, and of the obligation, laid down in art 30(2) of those rules, to publish judgments in the languages referred to in art 1 of Regulation No 1 of the Council of 15 April 1958 determining the languages to be used by the European Economic Community.

However, it must be held that the circumstances of this case are not such as to indicate that constraints of that kind can provide justification for the time which the proceedings took before the Court of First Instance.

It must be emphasised, as far as the principle of a reasonable time is concerned, that two periods are of significance with respect to the proceedings before the Court of First Instance. Thus, about 32 months elapsed between the end of the written procedure and the decision to open the oral procedure. Admittedly, it was decided by order of 13 October 1992 to join the 11 cases for the purposes of the oral procedure. It must be pointed out, however, that, in that period, no other measure of organisation of procedure or of inquiry was adopted. In addition, 22 months elapsed between the close of the oral procedure and the delivery of the judgment of the Court of First Instance.

Even if account is taken of the constraints inherent in proceedings before the Community judicature, investigation and deliberations of such a duration can be justified only by exceptional circumstances. Since there was no stay of the proceedings before the Court of First Instance, under arts 77 and 78 of its Rules of Procedure or otherwise, it must be concluded that no such circumstances exist in this case.

In the light of the foregoing considerations, it must be held, notwithstanding the relative complexity of the case, that the proceedings before the Court of First Instance did not satisfy the requirements concerning completion within a reasonable time.

For reasons of economy of procedure and in order to ensure an immediate and effective remedy regarding a procedural irregularity of that kind, it must be held that the plea alleging excessive duration of the proceedings is well founded for the purposes of setting aside the contested judgment in so far as it set the amount of the fine imposed on the appellant at ECU 3 million.

However, in the absence of any indication that the length of the proceedings affected their outcome in any way, that plea cannot result in the contested judgment being set aside in its entirety.

[*Breach of the principle of promptitude*]
It must be noted, first, that, contrary to the appellant's submission at the hearing, neither art 55(1) of the Rules of Procedure of the Court of First Instance nor any other provision of those rules or of the EC Statute of the Court of Justice provides that the judgments of the Court of First Instance must be delivered within a specified period after the oral procedure.

Also, it must be emphasised that the appellant has not established that the duration of the deliberations had any impact on the outcome of the proceedings before the Court of First Instance, in particular as far as any impairment of evidence is concerned.

In those circumstances, this plea must be rejected as unfounded.

[*Breach of the principles applicable in the taking of evidence*]
There is no ground for finding that the Court of First Instance failed to consider evidence submitted by the appellant when examining that submitted by the Commission.

The Court of First Instance was right in considering that the offers of evidence submitted in the reply were out of time and in refusing them on the ground that the appellant had not given reasons for the delay in submitting them.

Consequently, the plea that the Court of First Instance infringed the rules of evidence must be rejected.

[*Infringement of the right to consult certain documents*]
The appellant claims that the Court of First Instance infringed the rights of the defence by refusing to accede to its request that all the documents in the administrative procedure be produced, even though the right of access to the file derives from a fundamental principle of Community law which must be observed in all circumstances.

It must be observed that access to the file in competition cases is intended in particular to enable the addressees of a statement of objections to acquaint themselves with the evidence in the Commission's file so that they can express their views effectively on the basis of that evidence on the conclusions reached by the Commission in its statement of objections

However, contrary to the appellant's assertion, the general principles of Community law governing the right of access to the Commission's file do not apply, as such, to court proceedings, the latter being governed by the EC Statute of the Court of Justice and by the Rules of Procedure of the Court of First Instance.

The appellant was entitled to ask the Court of First Instance to order the opposite party to produce documents which were in its possession. Nevertheless, to enable the Court of First Instance to determine whether it was conducive to proper conduct of the procedure to order the production of certain documents, the party requesting production must identify the documents requested and provide the Court with at least minimum information indicating the utility of those documents for the purposes of the proceedings.

It must be held that it is clear from the contested judgment and from the documents before the Court of First Instance that, although the Commission submitted to it a list of all the documents in the file concerning it, the appellant did not sufficiently identify, in its request to the Court of First Instance, the documents in the file of which it sought production.

The Court of First Instance was therefore right to reject the request for the production of documents. Accordingly, this plea must be rejected as unfounded.

[*The pleas alleging infringement of art 15 of Regulation No 17*]
As regards the allegedly disproportionate nature of the fine, it must be borne in mind that it is not for the Court of Justice, when ruling on questions of law in the context of an appeal, to substitute, on grounds of fairness, its own assessment for that of the Court of First Instance exercising its unlimited jurisdiction to rule on the amount of fines imposed on undertakings for infringements of Community law.

As regards the finding that the appellant participated in the ... cartel, it need merely be stated that, since the appellant was penalised because of agreements which were not inseparably linked with constitution of the cartel and were intended to protect the German market against uncontrolled imports from other Member States, the Court of First Instance was fully entitled, in law, to conclude that the existence of that authorised cartel could not be regarded as a general mitigating circumstance in relation to that action by the appellant, which had assumed particular responsibility in that connection by reason of the functions exercised by its director.

The factors on the basis of which the gravity of an infringement may be assessed may include the volume and value of the goods in respect of which the infringement was committed and the size and economic power of the undertaking and, consequently, the influence which the undertaking was able to exert on the market.

Accordingly, this complaint must be rejected.

[*The consequences of annulment of the contested judgment to the extent to which it determines the amount of the fine*]

Having regard to all the circumstances of the case, the Court considers that a sum of ECU 50,000 constitutes reasonable satisfaction for the excessive duration of the proceedings.

Consequently, since the contested judgment is to be annulled to the extent to which it determined the fine ... the Court of Justice, giving final judgment, in accordance with art 54 of its Statute, sets that fine at ECU 2,950,000.'

Comment

In the present case, for the first time, the ECJ held that a Community court was in breach of the principle that the proceedings must be disposed of within a reasonable time. In order to determine whether or not the duration of the proceedings before the CFI had been excessive the ECJ made reference to art 6 of the European Convention on Human Rights and Fundamental Freedoms and the case law of the European Court of Human Rights in this area. Subsequently, the ECJ assessed the reasonableness of such period in the light of the circumstances of this case, in particular four criteria were taken into account: the importance of the case for the person concerned; its complexity; the conduct of the applicant; and the conduct of the competent authorities. The ECJ concluded the case was of considerable importance, not only to the applicant but also to third parties, in view of: the large number of persons concerned; the amount of the fine; the complexity of the case; and the fact that the applicant did not contribute to the protraction of the proceedings. Consequently, the ECJ implicitly confirmed that pecuniary sanctions imposed on legal persons for breach of EC Competition law are within the scope of criminal matters in the sense of art 6 of the ECHR.

In the present case, the ECJ for the first time held that it was entitled to award 'reasonable satisfaction' within the meaning of art 50 of the ECHR for the excessive duration of the proceedings and consequently reduced the amount of the fine imposed on the applicants.

Hoechst AG v *EC Commission*
Cases 46/87 and 227/88 [1989] ECR 2859; [1991] 4 CMLR 10 European Court of Justice

• *Competition procedure – right of the Commission to enter premises and remove evidence – refusal of the undertaking to co-operate with the Commission – safeguards against abusive behaviour of the Commission – European Convention on Human Rights – assistance of national authorities – respect for the national procedural guarantees*

Facts

The Commission made decisions authorising search and seizure operations at the headquarters and premises of the plaintiff under art 14 of Regulation 17/62, which concerns procedure for conducting investigations into infringements of Community competition policy. These decisions were adopted after the plaintiff had refused to accede to the Commission's request to hand over certain confidential documentation. In response to the refusal to disclose information, the Commission also imposed fines against the plaintiff.

The plaintiff objected to the conduct of the search on the ground that it had infringed general principles of Community law. The plaintiff submitted a number of grounds in support of his contentions, the majority of which concerned the need to respect due process of law, particularly as enshrined in the European Convention on Human Rights.

Regulation 17/62 was silent on a number of important issues concerning the rights of the suspects in such investigations. The Commission was required to derive applicable rules from the general principles of Community law.

Held
The ECJ held that Regulation 17/62 must be interpreted in such matter as to protect the rights of individuals against abuse of legal processes, particularly as regards the principles contained in the European Convention on Human Rights. Such rights included the protection of lawyer-client confidentiality, the privileged nature of legal correspondence between them, and the right to legal representation. The Court recognised that it was a general principle of Community law that individuals should be protected from arbitrary and disproportionate intervention by public authorities in the sphere of private activities.

Judgment

'The applicant considers that the contested decision is unlawful inasmuch as it permitted the Commission's officials to take steps which the applicant describes as search, which are not provided for under art 14 of Regulation 17/62 and which infringe fundamental rights recognised by Community law. It adds that if that provision is to be interpreted as empowering the Commission to carry out searches, it is unlawful on the ground that it is incompatible with fundamental rights, for the protection of which it is necessary that searches should be carried out only on the basis of a judicial warrant issued in advance.

The Commission contends that its powers under art 14 of Regulation 17/62 extend to the adoption of measures which, under the law of some Member States, would be regarded as searches. It nonetheless considers that the requirements of judicial protection deriving from fundamental rights, which it does not contest in principle, are fulfilled in so far as the addressees of decisions ordering investigations have an opportunity, on the one hand, to contest those decisions before the Court and, on the other, to apply for suspension of their operation by way of interim order, which permits the Court to check rapidly that the investigations ordered are not arbitrary in nature. Such review is equivalent to a judicial warrant issued in advance.

It should be noted, before the nature and scope of the Commission's powers of investigation under art 14 of Regulation are examined, that that article cannot be interpreted in such a way as to give rise to results which are incompatible with the general principles of Community law and in particular with fundamental rights.

The Court has consistently held that fundamental rights are an integral part of the general principles of law the observance of which the Court ensures, in accordance with the constitutional traditions common to the Member States, and the international treaties on which the Member States have collaborated or of which they are signatories. The European Convention for the Protection of Human Rights 1950 is of particular significance in that regard.

The interpreting art 14 of Regulation 17/62, regard must be had in particular to the rights of the defence, a principle whose fundamental nature has been stressed on numerous occasions in the Court's decisions (see in particular Case 322/81, *Michelin* v *EC Commission* [1983] ECR 361).

In that judgment, the Court pointed out that the rights of the defence must be observed in administrative procedures which may lead to the imposition of penalties. But it is also necessary to prevent those rights from being irremediably impaired during preliminary inquiry procedures including, in particular, investigations which may be decisive in providing evidence of the unlawful nature of conduct engaged in by undertakings for which they may be liable.

Consequently, although certain rights of the defence relate only to the contentious proceedings which follow the delivery of the statement of objections, other rights, such as the right to legal representation and the privileged nature of correspondence between lawyer and client must be respected as from the preliminary-inquiry stage.

Since the applicant has also relied on the requirements stemming from the fundamental rights to the inviolability of the home, it should be observed that, although the existence of such a right must be recognised in the Community legal order as a principle common to the laws of the Member States in regard to the private dwellings of natural persons, the same is not true in regard to undertakings, because there are not inconsiderable divergencies between the legal systems of the Member States in regard to the nature and degree of protection afforded to business premises against intervention by the public authorities.

No other inference is to be drawn from art 8(1) of the European Convention on Human Rights which provides that: "Everyone has the right to respect for his private and family life, his home and his correspondence." The protective scope of that article is concerned with the development of man's personal freedom and may not therefore be extended to business premises. Furthermore, it should be noted that there is no case law of the European Court of Human Rights on that subject.

Nonetheless, in all the legal systems of the Member States, any intervention by the public authorities in the sphere of private activities of any person, whether natural or legal, must have a legal basis and be justified on the grounds laid down by law, and, consequently, those systems provide, albeit in different forms, protection against arbitrary or disproportionate intervention. The need for such protection must be recognised as a general principle of Community law. In that regard, it should be pointed out that the Court has held that it has the power to determine whether measures of investigation taken by the Commission under the ECSC Treaty are excessive (Joined Cases 5–11/62 *San Michele and ors* v *EC Commission* [1962] ECR 449).

The nature ans scope of the Commission's powers of investigation under art 14 of Regulation 17/62 should therefore be considered in the light of the general principles set out above.

Article 14(1) authorises the Commission to undertake all necessary investigations into undertakings and associations of undertakings and provide that:

To this end the officials authorised by the Commission are empowered:

a) to examine the books and other business records;
b) to take copies of or extracts from the books and business records;
c) to ask for oral explanations on the spot;
d) to enter any premises, land and means of transport of undertakings;

Article 14(2) and (3) provide that investigations may be carried out upon production of an authorisation in writing or of a decision requiring undertakings to submit to the investigation. As the Court has already decided, the Commission may choose between those two possibilities in the light of the special features of each case (Case 136/79 *National Panasonic* v *EC Commission* [1980] ECR 2033). Both the written authorisation and the decisions must specify the subject matter and purpose of the investigation. Whichever procedure is followed, the Commission is required to inform, in advance, the competent authority of the Member State in whose territory the investigation is to be carried out and, according to art 14(4), that authority must be consulted before the decision ordering the investigation is adopted.

According to art 14(5), the Commission's officials may be assisted in carrying out their duties by officials of the competent authority of the Member State in whose territory the investigation is to be made. Such assistance may be provided either at the request of that authority or of the Commission.

Finally, according to art 14(6), the assistance of the national authorities is necessary for the carrying out of the investigation where it is opposed by an undertaking.

It follows from the seventh and eighth recitals in the preamble to Regulation 17/62 that the aim of the powers given to the

Commission by art 14 of that Regulation is to enable it to carry out its duty under the [EC] Treaty of ensuring that the rules on competition are applied in the Common Market. The function of those rules is, as follows from the fourth recital in the preamble to the Treaty, art 3(f) and arts 85 and 86, to prevent competition being distorted to the detriment of the public interest, individual undertakings and consumers. The exercise of the power given to the Commission by Regulation 17 thus contributes to the maintenance of the system of competition intended by the Treaty with which undertakings are absolutely bound to comply. The eighth recital states that for that purpose the Commission must be empowered throughout the Common Market, to require such information to be supplied and to undertake such investigations "as are necessary" to bring to light any infringement of art 85 and 86.

Both the purpose of Regulation 17/62 and the list of powers conferred on the Commission's officials by art 14 thereof show that the scope of investigations may be very wide. In that regard, the right to enter any premises, land and means of transport of undertakings is of particular importance inasmuch as it is intended to permit the Commission to obtain evidence of infringements of the competition rules in the places in which such evidence is normally to be found, that is to say, on the business premises of undertakings.

That right of access would serve no useful purpose if the Commission's officials could do no more than ask for information or files which they could identify precisely in advance. On the contrary, such a right implies the power to search for various items of information which are not already known or fully identified. Without such a power, it would be impossible for the Commission to obtain information necessary to carry out the investigation if the undertakings concerned refused to co-operate or adopted an obstructive attitude.

Although art 14 of Regulation 17/62 thus confers wide powers of investigation on the Commission, the exercise of these powers is subject to conditions serving to ensure that the rights of the undertakings concerned are respected.

In that regard, it should be noted first that the Commission is required to specify the subject matter and purpose of the investigation. That obligation is a fundamental not merely in order to show that the investigation to be carried out on the premises of the undertaking concerned is justified but also to enable those undertakings to assess the scope of their duty to co-operate while at the same time safeguarding the rights of the defence.

It should be pointed out that the conditions for the exercise of the Commission's investigative powers vary according to the procedure which the Commission has chosen, the attitude of the undertakings concerned and the intervention of the national authorities.

Article 14 of Regulation 17/62 deals in the first place with investigations carried out without the co-operation of the undertakings concerned, either voluntarily, where there is a written authorisation, or by virtue of an obligation arising under a decision ordering an investigation. In the latter case, which is the situation here, the Commission officials have, inter alia, the power to have shown to them the documents they request, to enter such premises as they choose, and to have shown to them the contents of any piece of furniture which they indicate. On the other hand, they may not obtain access to premises or furniture by force or oblige the staff of the undertaking to give them such access, or carry out search without the permission of the management of the undertaking.

The situation is completely different if the undertakings concerned oppose the Commission's investigation. In that case, the Commission's officials may, on the basis of art 14(6) and without the co-operation of the undertakings, search for any information necessary for the investigation with the assistance of the national authorities, which are required to afford them the assistance necessary for the performance of their duties. Although such assistance is required only if the undertaking expresses its opposition, it may also be requested as a precautionary measure, in order to overcome any opposition on the part of the undertaking.

It follows from art 14 (6) that it is for each Member State to determine the conditions under which the national authorities will afford assistance to the Commission's officials. In that regard, the Member States are required to ensure that the Commission's action is effective, while respecting the general principles set out above. It follows that, within those limits, the appropriate procedural rules designed to ensure respect for the rights of undertakings are those laid down by national law.

Consequently, if the Commission intends, with the assistance of the national authorities, to carry out an investigation other than with the co-operation of the undertakings concerned, it is required to respect the relevant procedural guarantees laid down by national law.'

Comment

The present case illustrates the relationship between national law and EC law in relation to enforcement powers conferred upon the Commission in competition matters. The Commission may decide to carry out investigations under an authorisation from the Commission or under a formal decision, with or without prior notification to the undertaking concerned. The Commission officials may decide to carry out so called 'dawn raids' – that is arrive at the undertaking's premises without warning. In such event, the undertaking under investigation is entitled to refuse to submit to the investigation although this attitude is not sensible since, first, it implies that the undertaking under investigation has something to hide and, second, the obstruction of investigation will be taken into account in the determination of a fine. In the present case the Commission imposed a fine of ECU 55,000 on Hoechst. Under EC law alone, the Commission official are not entitled to enter the premises of the undertaking under investigation. They have to respect the relevant procedural guarantees laid down in the national law of the undertaking under investigation. For that reason, art 14(6) of Regulation 17/62 provides that when an undertaking refuses to submit to investigations national authorities are required to provide necessary assistance to enable the Commission to make their investigation. In the UK the Crown must obtain an injunction (for example a search order) from the commercial court to assist the Commission. National authorities are not entitled to call into question the need for the investigations since only the ECJ can review the acts of the Commission, but it is for them to decide upon the appropriate procedure to be applied in the investigations. The present case clarifies the rights of an undertaking in such investigations. The Commission is not permitted to carry out 'fishing expeditions'. The subject of the investigations must be specified in the above-mentioned authorisation or decision, that is, the suspicion which the Commission is seeking to verify must be clearly indicated, but, as the ECJ held in the present case, the Commission is not obliged to provide the addressee with all information at its disposal in relation to the alleged infringement.

Samenwerkende Elektriciteits Produktiebedrijven (SEP) NV v *Commission of the European Communities* Case C–36/92P [1994] ECR I–1911 European Court of Justice

• *Competition procedure – powers of the Commission to compel production of documents – relevancy of documents requested to the investigation – transmission to the competent authorities of the Member State of information obtained by the Commission – professional secrecy – obligation of the authorities of the Member State to observe the confidentiality of the information transmitted by the Commission – extent – limits*

Facts

The Commission opened an investigation into the commercial relationship between a Dutch electricity production company and its state-controlled gas supplier (Gasunie). This relationship was governed by a code of conduct. During the investigation, the Commission requested the electricity company to provide a copy of a contract with a Norwegian gas company (Statoil). The contract with the Norwegian supplier was not specifically the subject of the investigation. Nevertheless, the agreement infringed the rights of the Dutch gas supplier which had a State-sponsored monopoly on the supply of gas in The Netherlands.

The electricity company refused to provide a copy of the agreement to the Commission on two grounds. First, the production of the agreement was not necessary for the investigation. Second, the national authorities might obtain a copy and thereafter commence proceedings for infringing the national monopoly in the supply of gas.

The Commission issued an order compelling the disclosure of the contract and the applicant appealed against this decision. The CFI held that the Commission was entitled to have sight of the contract in order to assess the legality of related agreements under investigation. In this particular situation, the contract between the Dutch company and the Norwegian supplier was required by the Commission to identify a pattern of business conduct being pursued by the Dutch company.

Referring to the applicant's claim that the disclosure of the contract might result in it falling into the hands of the national authorities, the Court held that the business activities of the company were adequately protected by the duty of confidentiality imposed by art 20 of Regulation 17/62 . The applicant appealed to the ECJ.

Held

The ECJ did not share the CFI opinion that art 20 of Regulation 17/62 adequately protected the applicant against an action of the national authorities who had legitimately pursued the contract. They cannot be required to disregard it; in particular if it fell to them to determine the commercial policy of the competing undertaking supervised by them. In these circumstances it is for the Commission to decide whether or not a particular document contains business secrets. If so, the Commission must issue a reasoned decision informing the applicant that it intends to transmit a document to the national authorities notwithstanding the claim that that document is of a confidential nature with respect to those authorities. Before implementing this decision, the Commission must give the applicant an opportunity to bring an action before the Court with a view to having the assessments made reviewed by it and to prevent the contested disclosure.

As a result, an action for annulment brought under art 173 EC Treaty and not an action against the decision under art 11 of Regulation 17/62 ordering the document to be produced to the Commission should be commenced in order to protect business secrets of the applicant. The obligation to produce the document does not necessarily mean that it can be automatically transmitted to the competent national authorities.

Judgment

'In reaching the conclusion that art 20 provides an adequate safeguard for [SEP], the Court of First Instance held that:

> "The protection provided by art 20 is twofold. First, paragraph 2 of that Article prohibits the disclosure of information acquired as a result of the application of Regulation No 17 and of the kind covered by the obligation of professional secrecy. Secondly, art 20(1) prohibits the use of information acquired as a result of the application of Regulation No 17 for any purpose other than that for which it has been requested. Those two safeguards, which are of a complementary nature, are intended to ensure the confidential treatment of information transmitted to Member States as a result of the application of art 10(1) of Regulation No 17."

The Court of First Instance thus held, in paragraph 56, that the twofold protection provided by art 20 prohibited national officials not only from disclosing the contents of the Statoil contract but also from "using the information contained in it in order to establish the commercial policy pursued by certain public undertakings".

It should be noted that according to art 20(2) the competent authorities of the Member States, their officials and other servants are required not to disclose information which is acquired by them as a result of the application of Regulation No 17 and which is of the kind covered by the obligation of professional secrecy (judgment in Case C–67/91 *Dirección General de Defensa de la Competencia* v *Associación Española de Banca Privada and Others* [1992] ECR I–4785, paragraph 21). That prohibition of disclosure does not, however, guarantee that the information in question will not be taken into consideration by the authorities which receive it or the officials who learn of it in the performance of their duties.

As regards art 20(1), which states that "information acquired as a result of the application of arts 11, 12, 13 and 14 [of Regulation 17] shall be used only for the purpose of the relevant request or investigation", the Court of Justice held in its judgment in *Associación Española de Banca Privada* (cited above, paragraph 37) that professional secrecy involves the need for authorities lawfully in possession of information to be unable to use it for a reason other than that for which it has been obtained. It concluded (paragraph 42) that such information may not be relied on by the authorities of the Member States either in a preliminary investigation procedure or to justify a decision based on provisions of competition law.

The procedural safeguard thus given to undertakings may not, however, go so far as to call for the information transmitted to be actually ignored by the national authorities. Thus, the Court also held in that judgment that the authorities of the Member States were not required to ignore the information disclosed to them and thereby suffer "acute amnesia"; that information constituted circumstantial evidence which might, if necessary, be taken into account in order to justify the initiation of a national procedure (paragraph 39).

In the present case the restriction imposed by art 20(1) on the use of the information received could not avert the irreversible consequences of the mere fact that a supplier (or its supervisory authority) has knowledge of the terms of business accorded to its customer by a rival supplier. Thus in the present case the Dutch authorities and officials who had legitimately consulted the Statoil contract transmitted by the Commission could not effectively be required to disregard the terms granted by Statoil to SEP, if it fell to them to determine the commercial policy of Gasunie.

Whichever paragraph is referred to, art 20, contrary to what was held by the Court of First Instance, therefore does not prevent the use of that information in connection with the determination of the commercial policy of Gasunie, with the possible consequence that damage might be caused to SEP. That article therefore does not constitute an effective safeguard for SEP.

By interpreting art 20 as it did, the Court of First Instance therefore infringed Community law.

It does not necessarily follow that the appeal must be upheld. As the Court of Justice held in its judgment in Case C–30/91P *Lestelle* v *EC Commission* [1992] ECR I–3755 (paragraph 28), if the grounds of a judgment of the Court of First Instance disclose a breach of Community law but the operative part appears well founded for other reasons of law, the appeal must be dismissed.

In the appeal, the appellant wrongly assumes that art 10 of Regulation No 17, which states that "the Commission shall forthwith transmit to the competent authorities of the Member States ... copies of the most important documents lodged with the Commission", obliges the Commission automatically to transmit the Statoil contract to the Netherlands authorities.

Firstly, the wording of art 10 itself gives the Commission power to determine which are the most important documents, with a view to transmitting them to the authorities of the Member States.

Secondly, art 10(1) must be interpreted in the light of the general principles of the right of undertakings to the protection of their business secrets, a principle which finds expression in art 214 of the Treaty and various provisions of Regulation No 17, such as arts 19(3), 20(2) and 21(2) (see the judgment in Case 53/85 *AKZO Chemie* v *EC Commission* [1986] ECR 1965, paragraph 28).

In cases such as the present one where an undertaking has expressly raised before the Commission the confidential nature of a document as against the competent national authorities, on the ground that it contains business secrets, and where that argument is not irrelevant, the general principle of the protection of business secrets, referred above, may limit the Commission's obligation under art 10(1) to transmit the document to the competent national authorities.

In proceedings between the Commission and an undertaking relating to the communication by the Commission to a third party who had submitted a complaint of documents which the undertaking claimed were of a confidential nature, the Court held that it is for the Commission to judge whether or not a particular document contains business secrets. After giving an undertaking an opportunity to state its views, the Commission is required to adopt a decision in that connection which contains an adequate statement of the reasons on which it is based and which must be notified to the undertaking concerned. Having regard to the extremely serious damage which could result from improper communication of documents to a competitor, the Commission must, before implementing its decision, give the undertaking an opportunity to bring an action before the Court with a view to having the assessments made reviewed by it and to preventing disclosure of the documents in question (*AKZO Chemie* v *EC Commission,* cited above, paragraph 29).

In the present case, analogous considerations require the Commission, if it wishes to transmit a document to the competent national authorities, notwithstanding the claim that in the particular circumstances of the case that document is of a confidential nature with respect to those authorities, to adopt a properly reasoned decision amenable to judicial review by means of an action for annulment.

It is an action for the annulment of such a decision that SEP might effectively rely on its right to protection of its business secrets.

It follows that the obligation to produce the Statoil contract, imposed on SEP by the contested decision, does not necessarily mean that the contract can be transmitted to the Netherlands authorities.

Accordingly, notwithstanding legally defective reasoning, the judgment under appeal rightly rejected the plea alleging breach of the principle of proportionality.

The appeal must therefore be dismissed in its entirety.'

Comment

SEP provided two reasons for its refusal. The Commission did not accept them and issued an order compelling the disclosure of the contract. An undertaking may challenge such a decision under art 173 EC Treaty.

In relation to the first reason, under art 11 of Regulation 17/62 the Commission is entitled to obtain all necessary information from an undertaking. It is up to the Commission to decide which documents are relevant and which are not. The CFI held that 'necessary information' related to anything which is connected to or has some relationship between the information requested and the infringement under investigation (also *Orkem* v *EC Commission* Case 374/87 [1989] ECR 3238.

As to the second justification provided by SEP, under art 11(2) of Regulation 17/62 the Commission is obliged to send a copy of any request for information to the competent national authorities of the Member State in which the undertaking concerned has its seat, and copies of the most important documents submitted to the Commission within the framework of competition proceedings. In the present case the CFI stated that the Commission may exercise it discretion whether or not to send the contested document to the national authorities, in particular when the undertaking concerned has raised the question of the document's confidentiality before the Commission. The question whether or not national authorities may base national proceedings on such documents was answered in the negative by the ECJ in *Dirección General de Defensa de la Competencia* v *Associación Española de Banca Privada* Case C–67/91 [1992] ECR I–4785. The ECJ held that art 20(2) of Regulation 17/62 prevented national authorities from using information received from the Commission for purposes other than those for which it was obtained, although it may be used in order to assess whether to institute national proceedings.

Fines

EC Community v *Volkswagen AG and Others* European Commission Decision 98/273/EC of 28 January 1998 [1998] 5 CMLR 33 (subject to appeal at the time of writing)

- *Restrictive practices – selective distribution agreements – art 85(1) EC Treaty – market partitioning – export ban imposed on Italian dealers – obstacles to the free movement of goods – art 30 EC Treaty – fine*

Facts

Volkswagen AG and its subsidiaries Audi AG and Autogerma SpA were in persistent breach of arts 85 and 86 EC as they prevented its franchise dealers in Italy from selling VW models to German and Austrian nationals who wished to purchase them in Italy where sale prices were lower than in Germany and Austria. The Commission stated that Volkswagen AG was in breach of the principle of the prohibition of discrimination on the grounds of nationality as embodied in art 6 EC.

Volkswagen AG challenged the fine as disproportionate.

Held

On 28 January 1998 the Commission imposed the biggest ever fine on a single party of ECU 102 million on the German car manufacturer Volkswagen AG. The fine represents 10 per cent of VW's net annual profit.

Decision

'... in fixing the amount of the fine, the Commission must have regard to all relevant circumstances and in particular to the gravity and duration of the infringement. The gravity depends on the type of infringement, on its effects on the market and on the size of the market concerned.

The obstruction of parallel exports of vehicles by final consumers and of cross deliveries within the dealer network hampers the objective of the creation of the Common Market, a principle of the Treaty, and is already for that reason to be classified as a particularly serious infringement.

The Commission has already examined numerous cases of obstruction of parallel imports; the relevant rules have been settled for many years.

The Volkswagen group has the highest market share of any motor vehicle manufacturer in the Community.

The infringement has had direct effects on the Italian market for the sale of new motor vehicles, by rendering considerably more difficult, and even temporarily impeding altogether, sales of vehicles for parallel export by final consumers. Correspondingly, the infringement has also had effects on the market for new motor vehicles, in particular in Germany and Austria, but also on the markets in all other Member States. The dealers in these markets have been sheltered against price competition from Italy.

Volkswagen knew that the measures aimed to or at least were liable to obstruct parallel exports of vehicles from Italy by final consumers, and intermediaries, and restrict competition. Volkswagen was also aware that its behaviour was infringing art 85. This is evident from the internal memo "Reimporte Italien" (Reimports from Italy) of 23 February 1995 ... According to this, Volkswagen was aware of the effect of the margins policy and regarded the scheme itself as "very likely to attract a fine". The deliberate nature of this policy can be seen further in the measures for monitoring and penalising dealers ... Altogether, it can be concluded from this that Volkswagen has committed the infringement against art 85(1) deliberately.

... Another factor determining the amount of the fine is, pursuant to art 15(2) of Regulation 17, the duration of the violation. The infringement committed by Volkswagen can be established at least from 30 December 1987. It has not been completely terminated at the present date.

The infringement lasted more than ten years and was therefore of very long duration. In accordance with the guidelines on the method of setting fines imposed pursuant to art 15(2) of Regulation 17 and of art 65(5) ECSC, the amount fixed for the gravity of an infringement can be increased by a percentage of up to 10 per cent per year of the infringement. For the period between 1988 and 1992, and for the year 1997, the Commission considers that an increase of 5 per cent per year is appropriate. The infringement was intensified during the period between 1993 and 1996, during which a great number of reinforcing measures were introduced. For each of those years, the Commission considers that an increase of the maximum percentage of 10 per cent is appropriate. This justifies an increase of the amount mentioned ... of ECU 35 million – which results in a base figure of ECU 85 million.

Further, the determination of the fine must take into account aggravating and attenuating factors.

With regard specifically to the situation in Italy, the Commission actually pointed out to Volkswagen, in two letters ... that the prevention and/or obstruction of parallel imports from Italy would be an infringement of the Community's competition rules. It is clear from the memo "Reimporte Italien" (Reimports from Italy) dated 24 March 1995, found by the Commission in the course of the investigation ... that at least the first letter from the Commission was subject of discussions at VW and Audi, but that the two firms did not draw the legally necessary conclusions. It is true that Autogerma addressed a circular to the dealers dated 16 March 1995 ... of which a copy was also sent to the Commission, in which the dealers were reminded of the provisions of Regulation 123/85 and of their dealers contracts. In fact, however, steps were not taken to ensure that the previously imposed impediments to sales to final consumers and intermediaries were removed. In particular, the dealer contracts have not been modified accordingly. The fact that Volkswagen has not terminated the infringement following the letters of the Commission, and at the same time has given the Commission to believe that the violation had been ended, is being regarded as an aggravating factor in determining the amount of the fine.

A further aggravating factor is that Volkswagen has used the economic dependence existing between a motor vehicle manufacturer and its dealers for obstructing and preventing sales by the dealers to final consumers who are not resident in their contract territory. Thus, a great number of Italian contract dealers, who are legally and economically independent undertakings, have suffered, in some cases quite substantial, turnover losses. The pressure exerted on the dealers by Volkswagen and the companies in the group culminated in more than 50 contract dealers being threatened with the termination of their contract in the event that they continued to sell vehicles to foreign customers, including final consumers. Finally, dealers contracts were terminated in 10 cases, substantially endangering the existence of the businesses concerned.

With regard to these aggravating factors, an increase of the basic amount of the fine by 20 per cent, ie ECU 17 million, appears justified.

Comment

It is interesting to note that the Commission has recently published a Notice regarding its fining policy under arts 85 and 86 EC with a view to ensuring the transparency and impartiality of its decisions (OJ C9 1998 p3; [1998] 3 CMLR 472). The principles set up in the Notice were applied to the present case.

The Notice is not binding. The Commission enjoys a wide discretion in the determination of the amount of fine in each case. The maximum fine that can be imposed is 10 per cent of an undertaking's turnover (which includes all group turnover) in the preceding financial year. In practice, the Commission, in determining the amount of fine, takes into consideration two criteria: the gravity of the infringement and the duration of the infringement. The guidelines provide that the Commission's first task in assessing the amount of fine is to determine the basic amount by applying both criteria. The next step consists of adjusting the basic amount in the light of two sets of circumstances: it is increased by reference to aggravating circumstances or reduced by reference to attenuating circumstances.

The Commission identifies five sets of aggravating circumstances but its list is not exhaustive. There are:

1. repeated infringements of the same type by the same undertaking;
2. refusal of the undertaking to co-operate with the Commission during its investigation or the obstruction of the investigation by an undertaking;
3. being the leader, or an instigator, of any infringement;
4. if an undertaking has made a substantial profit due to its anti-competitive conduct, the Commission would tend to increase the fine in order to encompass the profit;
5. if an undertaking applies retaliatory measures against any other undertaking in order to enforce its anti-competitive conduct.

The list of extenuating circumstances (also not exhaustive) enumerates the following situations:

1. the passive role of an undertaking consisting of the following of other undertakings in their infringement;
2. non-implementation in practice of an anti-competitive agreement or practice;
3. termination of the infringement as soon as the Commission notifies it to an undertaking;
4. existence of reasonable doubt on the part of an undertaking as to its anti-competitive conduct;
5. unintentional or negligent infringement;
6. in the case of a cartel, effective co-operation of an undertaking who is party to the cartel with the Commission.

The Commission will take into consideration the economic context of the infringement and the ability of an undertaking to actually pay the fine. The Commission stated that in the context of trade associations it would, if possible, impose fines on individual members of the association rather than the trade association itself. A symbolic fine of ECU 1,000 may be imposed if the infringement is technical or relatively trivial.

LAW OF THE EUROPEAN CONVENTION
ON HUMAN RIGHTS

14 The Right to Life: Article 2

Ogur v Turkey Judgment of 20 May 1999 (not yet reported) Grand Chamber of the European Court of Human Rights

- *Use of lethal force by a State in order to achieve legitimate aims – absolute necessity – the force used neither proportionate nor absolutely necessary – non-intentional killing within the scope of art 2*

Facts

Musa Ogur, a Turkish national who was working at a mine as a night-watchman near the village of Dagkonak in the province of Sirak, was killed on 24 December 1990 by Turkish security forces carrying out an armed operation near the site where Musa Ogur was working. The victim was about to come off duty when he was hit by bullets fired by the security forces.

At that time, a state of emergency was in force in this area. The applicant (mother of the victim) claimed that security forces opened fire without warning. The government of Turkey submitted that the security forces were after four terrorists, members of the PKK (Worker's Party of Kurdistan) who had used the site as a shelter and that Musa Ogur was hit by bullets from warning shots.

The public prosecutor of the province of Sirnak declared on 26 December 1990 that he had no jurisdiction to commence proceedings against security forces, and forwarded the file to the Administrative Council of the province which on 15 August 1991 held that no proceedings should be brought against the members of the security forces in the criminal courts taking into account that the victim died after warning shots were fired and that it was impossible to identify the person who had fired at him. This decision was upheld by the Supreme Administrative Court of Turkey.

The applicant claimed that her son's right to life guaranteed under art 2 of the Convention was violated and that the investigations of her son death by the national authorities were ineffective and she was deprived of her right to participate in the proceedings.

Held

The Court held Turkey in breach of art 2 as regards the planning and execution of the security operation that resulted in the death of the applicant's son (16:1 votes) and as regards the investigations conducted by the national authorities (unanimously). The Court awarded the applicant a specified sum for non-pecuniary damage and legal costs and expenses under art 41 of the Convention.

The Commission decided that there was violation of art 2 of the Convention (32:1 votes) and after attempting unsuccessfully to secure a friendly settlement referred the case to the European Court of Human Rights.

Judgment

'No intention to kill on the part of the security forces had been established. It was thanks to their considerable numbers that, despite a major armed attack, further, even more serious incidents had been avoided, a fact that showed the operation had been well organised, despite very adverse weather and terrain. It had by no means been proved that the use of force by the security forces had not been absolutely necessary.

… The Court, further, reiterates that the exceptions delineated in paragraph 2 of art 2 of the Convention indicate that this provision extends to, but is not concerned exclusively with, intentional killing. The text of art 2, read as a whole, demonstrates that paragraph 2 does not primarily define instances where it is permitted intentionally to kill an individual, but describes the situations where it is permitted to "use force" which may result, as an unintended outcome, in the deprivation of life. The use of force, however, must be no more than "absolutely necessary" for the achievement of one of the purposes set out in sub-paragraphs (a), (b) or (c).

In this respect the use of the term 'absolutely necessary' in art 2 paragraph 2 indicates that a stricter and more compelling test of necessity must be employed than that normally applicable when determining whether State action is "necessary in a democratic society" under paragraph 2 of arts 8 to 11 of the Convention. In particular, the force used must be strictly proportionate to the achievement of the aims set out in sub-paragraphs 2(a), (b) and (c) of art 2.

In keeping with the importance of this provision in a democratic society, the Court must, in making its assessment, subject deprivations of life to the most careful scrutiny, particularly where deliberate lethal force is used, taking into consideration not only the actions of the agents of the State who actually administer the force but also all the surrounding circumstances including such matters as the planning and control of the actions under examination (see *McCann and Others* v *the United Kingdom*, judgment of 27 September 1995, Series A no 324, p46, paragraphs 148–50).

... The Court must therefore now consider whether in the instant case the force used against the victim by the security forces could be said to be absolutely necessary and therefore strictly proportionate to the achievement of one of the aims set out in paragraph 2 of art 2, the only relevant ones of which, in the circumstances of the case, are the "defence of any person from unlawful violence" and "effect[ing] a lawful arrest".

In this connection, it should be remembered that, according to the government, the objective of the members of the security forces had been to apprehend the victim, who was thought to be a terrorist. On that occasion they had had to face a "major armed response", to which they had replied with warning shots, one of which had hit Musa Ogur, who had allegedly been running away. That accident was explained, in particular, by the poor visibility at the scene of the events, due to fog and the lie of the land, which was sloping.

Like the Commission, the Court notes, however, that of all the witnesses interviewed, only the members of the security forces stated that they had been the target of an armed attack ... Admittedly, in his report, the technical expert appointed by the Sirnak public prosecutor also noted "an exchange of fire between the security forces and members of the PKK terrorist movement who were firing from the shelter and seeking to escape", but he gave no indication of the facts on which that statement was based ...

On the other hand, in its decision of 26 December 1990, the public prosecutor's office made no mention of any attack on the security forces, noting merely that when Musa Ogur left the shelter and squatted down to answer a call of nature, "the security forces gained the impression that the suspect was escaping and they opened fire and killed him" (see paragraph 12 above).

The night-watchmen who were with the victim just before the incident all stated that he had gone out of the shelter alone, to answer a call of nature, and that neither before nor after the shot which fatally wounded Musa Ogur had they used the shotguns that were in the shelter (see paragraphs 20 and 24 above). In this connection, the Court notes that, according to the Sirnak public prosecutor, there were no cartridges or cartridge cases at the spot where the victim's body lay ... that was a finding which the prosecutor confirmed orally ... Only eight spent shotgun cartridges were found by the prosecutor in the dugouts, but they were two or three days old ... Three shotguns were apparently also found in the shelter, but it was only a matter of surmise that the night-watchmen had used them against the security forces (see paragraphs 20 and 30 above). Lastly, it would appear that no member of the security forces was wounded during the operation in question.

The Court consequently considers that there is insufficient evidence to establish that the security forces came under any armed attack at the scene of the incident.

The Court notes, further, that according to Celal Uymaz, the gendarmerie lieutenant-colonel appointed in the case by the governor as investigating officer, the security forces are under instructions, in circumstances such as those of the instant case, to give at least three verbal warnings to the suspects by loud hailer ... In the Court's view, such precautions are all the more necessary where, as in this instance, the operations take place in darkness and fog, on hilly ground.

Only one of the witnesses questioned, however, stated that verbal warnings had been given on this occasion ... while another indicated that no warning had been given and a third witness said that he could not remember what had happened ...

The Court concludes that there is not sufficient evidence to establish that the security forces gave the warnings usual in such cases.

The Court points out that, by definition, warning shots are fired into the air, with the gun almost vertical, so as to ensure that the suspect is not hit ... That was all the more essential in the instant case as visibility was very poor. It is accordingly difficult to imagine that a genuine warning shot could have struck the victim in the neck. In this context, it should also be noted that according to one of the members of the security forces, the men had taken up position fifty metres apart from each other but were not linked by radio; that must necessarily have made it difficult to transmit orders and to control the operations ...

The Court consequently considers that, even supposing that Musa Ogur was killed by a bullet fired as a warning, the firing of that shot was badly executed, to the point of constituting gross negligence, whether the victim was running away or not.

In sum, all the deficiencies so far noted in the planning and execution of the operation in issue suffice for it to be concluded that the use of force against Musa Ogur was neither proportionate nor, accordingly, absolutely necessary in defence of any person from unlawful violence or to arrest the victim. There has therefore been a violation of art 2 on that account.

2. The investigations by the national authorities

The applicant stated that the Administrative Council – composed of persons who are not lawyers and are answerable to the executive – did everything to protect those responsible for the incident of 24 December 1990, relying on the law governing the prosecution of civil servants ... In her submission, the administrative authorities' efforts to protect those responsible for the crime were obvious. In that connection, she referred to several witness statements, including that of the investigating officer, who had said that he had not considered it necessary to identify and question the members of the security forces who had taken part in the operation ... and that made by Mehmet Akay, according to which revealing the identity of the soldiers in question could have put their lives at risk ...

The Commission considered that the investigation carried out at national level into the death of the applicant's son had not been conducted by independent authorities, had not been thorough and had taken place without the applicant's being able to take part. In the Commission's view, such a situation amounted to a breach by the State of its obligation to "protect the right to life by law".

The government did not make any observations on the circumstances in which the investigation into Musa Ogur's death was carried out.

The Court reiterates that the obligation to protect the right to life under art 2 of the Convention, read in conjunction with the State's general duty under art 1 of the Convention to "secure to everyone within [its] jurisdiction the rights and freedoms defined in [the] Convention", requires by implication that there should be some form of effective official investigation when individuals have been killed as a result of the use of force. This investigation should be capable of leading to the identification and punishment of those responsible ...

The Court observes that when he inspected the scene of the incident, the Sirnak public prosecutor confined himself to noting findings in respect of the victim's body, making an inspection and a sketch of the scene, reconstructing the events and interviewing three witnesses, all of them night-watchmen colleagues of the victim ...

In his report the prosecutor indicated, in particular: "Since the gunshot wound was the certain cause of death and no other finding was made that could suggest any other cause, it was not considered necessary to carry out a full post-mortem" ... It should be pointed out here, however, that in a case of this kind a proper post-mortem examination – if it had been carried out – could have provided valuable information about the approximate positions of the person who fired and the victim, and the distance between them, at the moment of the shot.

The same report merely mentions the discovery of eight cartridges, three shotguns and a quantity of powder, but none of that evidence was subsequently subjected to detailed examination. On the subject of the cartridges the report does no more than state that they "must have been two or three days old"; in respect of the powder, it states that it was "impossible to say whether it was fresh powder or not" ... Here too a proper examination, in particular a ballistic test, could have revealed exactly when those items had been used.

As to the witnesses questioned at the scene by the prosecutor, they were all members of the night-watchmen's team. No member of the security forces that took part in the operation was interviewed on that occasion.

Lastly, the expert report prepared at the prosecutor's request contains information that is very imprecise and findings mostly unsupported by any established facts.

The subsequent investigation carried out by the administrative investigation authorities scarcely remedied the deficiencies noted above in that, again, no post-mortem or other forensic examination, notably in the form of ballistic tests, was ordered and no members of the security forces that took part in the operation were questioned, although their names were known ... Thus no serious attempt to identify the person who had fired the fatal shot was made, although several of the witness statements indicated that the shot came from the security forces.

At all events, serious doubts arise as to the ability of the administrative authorities concerned to carry out an independent investigation, as required by art 2 of the Convention. The Court notes that the investigating officer appointed by the governor was a gendarmerie lieutenant-colonel and, as such, was subordinate to the same chain of command as the security forces he was investigating. As to the Administrative Council, whose responsibility it was to decide whether proceedings should be instituted against the security forces concerned, it was composed of senior officials from the province and was chaired by the governor, who, in this instance, was administratively in charge of the operation by the security forces. In this connection, the evidence of one of the members of the Sirnak Administrative Council should be noted, according to which, in practice, it was not possible to oppose the governor: either the members signed the decision prepared by him or they were replaced by other members who were willing to do so (see paragraph 48 above).

It must be noted, lastly, that during the administrative investigation, the case file was inaccessible to the victim's close relatives, who had no means of learning what was in it (see paragraph 15 above). The Supreme Administrative Court ruled on the decision of 15 August 1991 on the sole basis of the papers in the case, and this part of the proceedings was likewise inaccessible to the victim's relatives. Nor was the decision of 15 August 1991 served on the applicant's lawyer, with the result that the applicant was deprived of the possibility of herself appealing to the Supreme Administrative Court.

In conclusion, the investigations in this case cannot be regarded as effective investigations capable of leading to the identification and punishment of those responsible for the events in question. There has therefore been a violation of art 2 on this account also.'

Comment
Under art 2 of the Convention contracting States have a positive obligation to preserve life of persons within their jurisdiction. The killing of people by the State outside the judicial process is only permitted in exceptional circumstances enumerated in art 2(2)(a), (b) and (c) which (as any exceptions) must be strictly interpreted so as not to undermine the fundamental right to life protected under the Convention. Failure to interpret strictly would amount to granting to national authorities a right to kill.

In the present case, the Court clearly stated that unintentional killing of a person by agents of the State is within the scope of art 2 of the Convention (see also Application No 10044/82 Dec 10.7.84. DR 32, 190). The Court held that even if the victim was killed by a bullet fired as a warning, the firing of that shot was badly executed, to the point of constituting gross negligence irrespective of whether the victim was running away or not.

In order to determine whether the use of lethal force was lawful the Court applied its usual test based on "absolute necessity". The use of lethal force is lawful if proportionate to the achievement of the objective set out in art 2(2), in this case, "defence of any person from unlawful violence" and to "effect a lawful arrest". Indeed, there should be a balance between the duty of the State to protect life of its nationals and the requirement that the use of lethal force must be absolutely necessary. Turkey failed the test. The force used by security forces was neither proportionate nor absolutely necessary.

It is also interesting to note that the Court examined the investigation carried out by the Turkish authority in the light of art 2 of the Convention. The Court Stated that the combined effect of arts 1 and 2 implies that there should be some form of effective official investigation when individuals have been killed as a result of the use of force. That investigation should result in the identification and punishment of those responsible.

Paton v *United Kingdom* (1980) 3 EHRR 408 European Commission on Human Rights

• *The right to life of a foetus – whether protected by art 2 – no such protection – abortion – life and health of the mother paramount*

Facts
The applicant attempted to have his wife's abortion prevented by an injunction from the High Court. The High Court refused to grant the injunction on the ground that the abortion was permitted under the Abortion Act 1967.

An application was lodged with the European Court complaining that the 1967 Act contravened, inter alia, art 2 of the Convention which protects the right to life. The essence of the complaint was that a foetus is entitled to the protection of this right as a 'person' within the meaning of the article.

Held
The Commission held that the term 'person' did not encompass a foetus because the life of a pregnant woman was deemed paramount. To extend the protection of art 2 to unborn children would be to place a higher value on such life than on the life of the mother.

Judgment
'Article 2(1), first sentence, provides: "Everyone's right to life shall be protected by law" (in the French text: "Le droit de toute personne a la vie est protege par la loi"). The Commission, in its interpretation of this clause and, in particular, of the terms

"everyone" and "life", has examined the ordinary meaning of the provision in the context both of art 2 and of the Convention as a whole, taking into account the object and purpose of the Convention.

The Commission first notes that the term "everyone" ("toute personne") is not defined in the Convention. It appears in art 1 and in Section I, apart from art 2(1), in arts 5, 6, 8 and 11 and 13. In nearly all these instances the use of the word is such that it can apply only postnatally. None indicates clearly that it has any possible prenatal application, although such application in a rare case – eg under art 6(1) – cannot be entirely excluded.

As regards, more particularly, art 2, it contains the following limitations of "everyone's" right to life enounced in the first sentence of paragraph (1):

- a clause permitting the death penalty in paragraph (1), second sentence: "No one shall be deprived of his life intentionally save in the execution of a sentence of a court following his conviction of a crime for which this penalty is provided by law"; and
- the provision, in paragraph (2), that deprivation of life shall not be regarded as inflicted in contravention of art 2 when it results from "the use of force which is no more than absolutely necessary" in the following three cases: "In defence of any person from unlawful violence"; "in order to effect a lawful arrest or to prevent the escape of a person lawfully detained"; "in action lawfully taken for the purpose of quelling a riot or insurrection".

All the above limitations, by their nature, concern persons already born and cannot be applied to the foetus.

Thus both the general usage of the term "everyone" ("toute personne") of the Convention (paragraph 7 above) and the context in which this term is employed in art 2 (paragraph 8 above) tend to support the view that it does not include the unborn.

The Commission has next examined, in the light of the above considerations, whether the term "life" in art 2(1), first sentence, is to be interpreted as covering only the life of persons already born or also the "unborn life" of the foetus. The Commission notes that the term "life", too, is not defined in the Convention.

It further observes that another, more recent international instrument for the protection of human rights, the American Convention on Human Rights of 1969, contains in art 4(1), first and second sentences, the following provisions expressly extending the right to life to the unborn:

Every person has the right to have his life respected. This right shall be protected by law and, in general, from the moment of conception.

The Commission is aware of the wide divergence of thinking on the question of where life begins. While some believe that it starts already with conception others tend to focus upon the moment of nidation, upon the point that the foetus becomes "viable", or upon live birth.

The German Federal Constitutional Court, when interpreting the provision "everyone has a right to life" in art 2(2) of the Basic Law, stated as follows (Judgment of 25 February 1975, Appendix VI to the Commissioner's Report in the *Brüggemann and Scheuten Case* CI 1b of the grounds):

"Life in the sense of the historical existence of a human individual exists according to established biological and physiological knowledge at least from the 14th day after conception (Nidation, Individuation) ... The process of development beginning from this point is a continuous one so that no sharp divisions or exact distinction between the various stages of development of human life can be made. It does not end at birth: for example, the particular type of consciousness peculiar to the human personality only appears a considerable time after the birth."

The protection conferred by art 2(2) first sentence of the Basic Law can therefore be limited neither to the "complete" person after birth nor to the foetus capable of independent existence prior to birth. The right to life is guaranteed to every one who "lives"; in this context no distinction can be made between the various stages of developing life before birth or between born and unborn children. "Everyone" in the meaning of art 2(2) of the Basic Law is "every living human being", in other words: every human individual possessing life; "everyone" therefore includes unborn human beings.

The Commission also notes that, in a case arising under the Constitution of the United States, *Roe* v *Wade*, 410 US 113 (1973), the State of Texas argued before the Supreme Court that, in general, life begins at conception and is present throughout pregnancy. The Court, while not resolving the difficult question where life begins, found that, "with respect to the State's important and legitimate interest in potential life, the 'compelling' point is at viability".

The Commission finally recalls the decision of the Austrian Constitutional Court mentioned in paragraph 6 above which, while also given in the framework of constitutional litigation, had to apply, like the Commission in the present case, art 2 of the European Convention on Human Rights.

The Commission considers with the Austrian Constitutional Court that, in interpreting the scope of the term "life" in art 2(1), first sentence, of the Convention, particular regard must be had to the context of the article as a whole. It also observes that the term "life" may be subject to different interpretations in different legal instruments, depending on the context in which it is used in the instrument concerned.

The Commission has already noted, when discussing the meaning of the term "everyone" in art 2 (paragraph 8 above), that the limitations, in paragraphs (1) and (2) of the article, of "everyone's" right to "life", by their nature, concern persons already born and cannot be applied to the foetus. The Commission must therefore examine whether art 2, in the absence of any express limitation concerning the foetus, is to be interpreted:

- as not covering the foetus at all;
- as recognising a "right to life" of the foetus with certain implied limitations; or
- as recognising an absolute "right to life" of the foetus.

The Commission has first considered whether art 2 is to be construed as recognising an absolute "right to life" of the foetus and has excluded such an interpretation on the following grounds.

The "life" of the foetus is intimately connected with, and cannot be regarded in isolation from, the life of the pregnant woman. If art 2 were held to cover the foetus and its protection under this article were, in the absence of any express limitation, seen as absolute, an abortion would have to be considered as prohibited even where the continuance of the pregnancy would involve a serious risk to the life of the pregnant woman. This would mean that the "unborn life" of the foetus would be regarded as being of a higher value than the life of the pregnant woman. The "right to life" of a person already born would thus be considered as subject not only to the express limitations mentioned in paragraph 8 above but also to a further, implied limitation.

The Commission finds that such an interpretation would be contrary to the object and purpose of the Convention. It notes that, already at the time of the signature of the Convention (4 November 1950), all High Contracting Parties, with one possible exception, permitted abortion where necessary to save the life of the mother and that, in the meanwhile, the national law on termination of pregnancy has shown a tendency towards further liberalisation.'

Comment

The question whether art 2 of the Convention protects life of unborn children is irrevocably linked with that of abortion. Abortion is so controversial, taking into account wide disparities of national laws, that the Court has avoided, so far successfully, delivering any decision on the matter. In the case of *Open Door Counselling Ltd and Dublin Well Women Centre Ltd* v *Ireland* (1993) 15 EHRR 244 the Court held that the injunction of the Irish Attorney-General restraining the applicant from providing abortion advice was in breach of the Convention (15:8 votes). The Court examined the injunction in the light of art 10 (the right to impart information) ignoring the argument submitted by the Irish government that the injunction was justified in order to protect rights of unborn children and as such was within the scope of art 2.

For the Commission the prevailing consideration is the life, health and well being of the mother. In this respect in *H* v *Norway* (No 17004/90 (1992) unreported) the Commission stated that Norwegian law which permitted abortion up to 14 weeks of pregnancy on the ground that 'pregnancy, birth and care for the child may place the woman in a difficult situation of life' was not in violation of art 2 of the Convention. It seems that this is the position of the Commission on the matter of abortion.

Another interesting aspect is the determination of the 'victim' in abortion cases. In this regard, locus standi has been granted to the 'potential father', a husband in the present case, a partner of a pregnant woman in *H* v *Norway*, or a pregnant woman herself (*Brüggemann and Scheuten* v *FRG* No 6959/75 (1978) 10 DR 100), although she made her claim under art 8 arguing that the right to abortion constituted an aspect of her right to privacy. However, locus standi has been refused to a member of the public challenging national legislation permitting abortion (*X* v *Austria* No 70451/75 (1976) 7 DR 87, *X* v *Norway* No 867/60 (1961) 6 CD 34) as not being personally affected, or a church minister although he was dismissed from his office when he refused to perform his functions as a result his opposition (*Knudsen* v *Norway* No 11045/84 (1985) 42 DR 247).

15 The Right to Freedom from Torture and Inhuman and Degrading Treatment: Article 3

Soering v *United Kingdom* (1989) 11 EHRR 439 European Court of Human Rights

* Inhuman treatment or punishment – degrading treatment or punishment – death penalty – extradition – the 'death row' phenomenon

Facts
Soering, a German national from West Germany, was accused of committing a multiple murder in Virginia (USA). He was found in the United Kingdom and a request was made by the United States government for his extradition to stand trial on charges of murder. Soering faced the very real prospect of the death penalty if sentenced to death in Virginia. An application was made on Soering's behalf to stay the extradition on the ground that, by sending him to face the possibility of the death sentence, the United Kingdom would be in violation of art 3 of the Convention.

Held
The Court held that to extradite Soering to the United States to face the death row phenomenon would be a violation of art 3 of the Convention for which the United Kingdom would be responsible. Consequently, the UK stayed the extradition of the applicant to the United States.

Judgment
'The applicant alleged that the decision by the Secretary of State for the Home Department to surrender him to the authorities of the United States of American would, if implemented, give rise to a breach by the United Kingdom of art 3 of the Convention, which provides:

"No one shall be subjected to torture or to inhuman or degrading treatment or punishment."

The alleged breach derives from the applicant's exposure to the so-called "death row phenomenon." This phenomenon may be described as consisting in a combination of circumstances to which the applicant would be exposed if, after having been extradited to Virginia to face a capital murder charge, he were sentenced to death.

Article 3 makes no provision for exceptions and no derogation from it is permissible under art 15 in time of war or other national emergency. This absolute prohibition on torture and on inhuman or degrading treatment or punishment under the terms of the Convention shows that art 3 enshrines one of the fundamental values of the democratic societies making up the Council of Europe. It is also to be found in similar terms in other international instruments such as the 1966 International Covenant on Civil and Political Rights and the 1969 American Convention on Human Rights and is generally recognised as an internationally accepted standard.

The question remains whether the extradition of a fugitive to another State where he would be subjected or be likely to be subjected to torture or to inhuman or degrading treatment or punishment would itself engage the responsibility of a Contracting State under art 3 ... It would hardly be compatible with the underlying values of the Convention, that "common heritage of political traditions, ideals, freedom and the rule of law" to which the Preamble refers, were a Contracting State knowingly to surrender a fugitive to another State where there were substantial grounds for believing that he would be in danger of being subjected to torture, however heinous the crime allegedly committed. Extradition in such circumstances, while not explicitly referred to in the brief and general wording of art 3, would plainly be contrary to the spirit and intention of the article, and in the Court's view this inherent obligation not to extradite also extends to cases in which the fugitive would be faced in the receiving State by a real risk of exposure to inhuman or degrading treatment or punishment proscribed by that article ...

Capital punishment is permitted under certain conditions by art 2(1) of the Convention, which reads:

> "Everyone's right to life shall be protected by law. No one shall be deprived of his life intentionally save in the execution of a sentence of a court following his conviction of a crime from which this penalty is provided by law."

In view of this wording, the applicant did not suggest that the death penalty per se violated art 3. He, like the two government parties [the United Kingdom and the Federal Republic of Germany as intervenor], agreed with the Commission that the death penalty does not in itself raise an issue under art 2 or art 3 ...

That does not mean however that circumstances relating to a death sentence can never give rise to an issue under art 3. The manner in which it is imposed or executed, the personal circumstances of the condemned person and a disproportionality to the gravity of the crime committed, as well as the conditions of detention awaiting execution, are examples of factors capable of bringing the treatment or punishment received by the condemned person within the proscription under art 3.

The applicant submitted that the circumstances to which he would be exposed as a consequence of the implementation of the Secretary of State's decision to return him to the United States, namely the "death row phenomenon", cumulatively constitute such serious treatment that his extradition would be contrary to art 3. He cited in particular the delays in the appeal and review procedures following a death sentence, during which time he would be subject to increasing tension and psychological trauma; the fact, so he said, that the judge or jury in determining sentence is not obliged to take into account the defendant's age and mental state at the time of the offence; the extreme conditions of his future detention in "death row", where he expects to be the victim of violence and sexual abuse because of his age, colour and nationality; the constant spectre of the execution itself, including the ritual of execution.

For any prisoner condemned to death, some element of delay between imposition and execution of the sentence and the experience of severe stress in conditions necessary for strict incarceration are inevitable. The democratic character of the Virginia legal system in general and the positive features of Virginia trial, sentencing and appeal procedures in particular are beyond doubt. The Court agrees with the Commission that the machinery of justice to which the applicant would be subject in the United States is in itself neither arbitrary nor unreasonable, but, rather, respects to the rule of law and affords not inconsiderable procedural safeguards to the defendant in a capital trial.

However, in the Court's view, having regard to the very long period of time spent on death row in such extreme conditions, with the ever-present and mounting anguish of awaiting execution of the death penalty, and to the personal circumstances of the applicant, especially his age and mental state at the time of the offence, the applicant's extradition to the United States would expose him to a real risk of treatment going beyond the threshold set by art 3. A further consideration of relevance is that in the particular instance the legitimate purpose of extradition could be achieved by another means which would not involve suffering of such exceptional intensity or duration [extradition to the Federal Republic of Germany for trial].

Accordingly, the Secretary of State's decision to extradite the applicant to the United States would, if implemented, give rise to a breach of art 3.'

Comment
The death penalty is permitted under art 2 of the Convention although prohibited under Protocol 6 to the ECHR. In this respect it is interesting to note that at the summit meeting of the European Council held at Amsterdam in June 1998, the Member States of the European Union issued a Declaration on the Abolition of the Death Penalty (recommending abolition) which penalty has already been abolished in most of the Member States and has not been applied in any of them for many years.

Article 3 of the Convention has been applied to extradition and deportation in cases where the applicant claimed that he would be subjected to inhuman or degrading treatment or punishment if sent abroad.

In the present case, the Court held that the possibility of six to eight years' incarceration on death row in a prison in Virginia prior to the execution of the death sentence was contrary to art 3 of the Convention but that the death penalty itself was not. The Court took into consideration many factors in deciding in favour of the applicant. These were: evidence of his mental illness at the time of the alleged commitment of the offence; his young age at that time (he was 18 years old); the conditions in a prison in Virginia where the applicant was to be sent, ie known for its particularly draconian custodial regime, homosexual abuse and physical violence among the death row inmates; and the fact that West Germany had requested his return in order to ensure that the applicant would have a fair trial and would not risk the death penalty.

In order to protect the applicant from the serious and irreparable nature of the suffering risked if extradited to the USA, the Court held that his extradition was in violation of art 3 of the Convention. After the judgment of the Court the government of the UK informed the USA that the extradition of Soering on charges for which the death penalty may be imposed was refused. The government of the USA in a diplomatic note ensured the UK government that it would prohibit the applicant's prosecution in Virginia for the offence of capital murder. Subsequently, Soering was extradited to the USA.

It is submitted that the possibility that Europe may become a safe haven for dangerous criminals under threat of execution by the relevant authorities should not be allowed to prevail over the objectives of art 3 of the Convention.

16 The Right to Liberty and Security of the Person: Article 5

Brogan and Others v United Kingdom (1989) 11 EHRR 117
European Court of Human Rights

• *Detention of suspected terrorists – length of permissible period of detention without being charged with an offence – period of four days held to be excessive*

Facts
Four suspects were arrested and detained under s12 of the Prevention of Terrorism Act. Although all were eventually released, each spent a minimum of four days without being charged with any offence or being brought before a magistrate. They complained that the UK was in breach of art 5(3) and (4) of the Convention.

Held
The Court held that the UK was in breach of both provisions as the applicants were not brought 'promptly' before a court after having been detained.

Judgment
'Under the [Prevention of Terrorism Act 1984], a person arrested under s12 on reasonable suspicion of involvement in acts of terrorism may be detained by police for an initial period of 48 hours, and, on the authorisation of the Secretary of State for Northern Ireland, for a further period or periods of up to five days.

The applicants claimed, as a consequence of their arrest and detention under this legislation, to have been the victims of a violation of art 5(3) which provides:

"Everyone arrested or detained in accordance with the provisions of paragraph (1)(c) of this article shall be brought promptly before a judge or other officer authorised by law to exercise judicial power and shall be entitled to trial within a reasonable time or to release pending trial. Release may be conditioned by guarantees to appear for trial."

The applicants noted that a person arrested under the ordinary law of Northern Ireland must be brought before a Magistrates' Court within 48 hours; and that under the ordinary law in England and Wales the maximum period of detention permitted without charge is four days, judicial approval being required at the 36-hour stage. In their submission, there was no plausible reason why a seven-day detention period was necessary, marking as it did such a radical departure from ordinary law and even from the three-day period permitted under the special powers of detention embodied in the Northern Ireland (Emergency Provisions) Act 1978. Nor was there any justification for not entrusting such decisions to the judiciary of Northern Ireland.

The [British] government has argued that in view of the nature and extent of the terrorist threat and the resulting problems in obtaining evidence sufficient to bring charges, the maximum statutory period of detention of seven days was an indispensable part of the effort to combat that threat, as successive parliamentary debates and reviews of the legislation had confirmed. In particular, they drew attention to the difficulty faced by the security forces in obtaining evidence which is both admissible and usable in consequence of training in anti-interrogation techniques adopted by those engaged in terrorism. Time was also needed to undertake necessary scientific examinations, to correlate information from other detainees and to liaise with other security forces ...

The fact that a detained person is not charged or brought before a court does not in itself amount to a violation of the first part of art 5(3). No violation of art 5(3) can arise if the arrested person is released "promptly" before any judicial control of his detention would have been feasible. If the arrested person is not released promptly, he is entitled to a prompt appearance before a judge or judicial officer.

The assessment of "promptness" has to be made in the light of the object and purpose of art 5. The Court has regard to the importance of this article in the Convention system: it enshrines a fundamental human right, namely the protection of the individual against arbitrary interferences by the State with his right to liberty. Judicial control of interferences by the executive with the individual's right to liberty is an essential feature of the guarantee embodied in art 5(3), which is intended to minimise the risk of arbitrariness. Judicial control is implied by the rule of law, "one of the fundamental principles of a democratic society ... which is expressly referred to in the Preamble to the Convention" and "from which the whole Convention draws its inspiration."

The issue to be decided is therefore whether, having regard to the special features relied on by the government, each applicant's release can be considered "prompt" for the purposes of art 5(3).

The investigation of terrorist offences undoubtedly presents the authorities with special problems, partial reference to which has already been made ... The Court takes full judicial notice of the factors adverted to by the [British] government in this connection. It is also true that in Northern Ireland the referral of police requests for extended detention to the Secretary of State and the individual scrutiny of each police request by a Minister do provide a form of executive control. In addition, the need for the continuation of the special powers has been constantly monitored by Parliament and their operation regularly reviewed by independent personalities. The Court accepts that, subject to the existence of adequate safeguards, the context of terrorism in Northern Ireland has the effect of prolonging the period during which the authorities may, without violating art 5(3), keep a person suspected of serious terrorism offences in custody before bringing him before a judge or other judicial officer.

The difficulties, alluded to by the government, of judicial control over decisions to arrest and detain suspected terrorists may affect the manner of implementation of art 5(3), for example in calling for appropriate procedural precautions in view of the nature of the suspected offences. However, they cannot justify, under art 5(3), dispensing altogether with "prompt" judicial control.

[T]he scope for flexibility in interpreting and applying the notion of "promptness" is very limited. In the Court's view, even the shortest of the four periods of detention, namely the four days and six hours spent in police custody by Mr McFadden, falls outside the strict constraints as to time permitted by the first part of art 5(3). To attach such importance to the special features of this case as to justify so lengthy a period of detention without appearance before a judge or other judicial officer would be an unacceptably wide interpretation of the plain meaning of the word "promptly". An interpretation to this effect would import into art 5(3) a serious weakening of a procedural guarantee to the detriment of the individual and would entail consequences impairing the very essence of the right protected by this provision. The Court thus has to conclude that none of the applicants was either brought "promptly" before a judicial authority or released "promptly" following his arrest. The undoubted fact that the arrest and detention of the applicants were inspired by the legitimate aim of protecting the community as a whole from terrorism is not on its own sufficient to ensure compliance with the specific requirements of art 5(3).

There has thus been a breach of art 5(3) in respect of all four applicants.'

Comment

Under art 5 of the Convention everyone has the right to liberty and security. However, this right in not absolute as the Convention permits detention of individuals in certain circumstances on the ground of the public interest, and by virtue of art 15 in time of an emergency threatening the life of the nation a contracting State may derogate from its obligations contained in art 5 of the Convention.

By providing procedural guarantees for detained individuals suspected of having committed criminal offences, art 5(3) of the Convention crystallises the protection of individuals against arbitrary interference by the State with an individual's right to liberty. Article 5(3) imposes two separate obligations: first, a duty to promptly produce the detainee before a judicial officer; and, second, a duty to arrange the trial within a reasonable time irrespective of whether the individual concerned is still in detention or has been released prior to a trial.

In the present case the Court clarified the obligation of a contracting State to promptly bring a detainee before a competent authority. The interpretation of promptness in terms of length of time spent in detention without appearance before a judge or other judicial authority was examined by the Court. In this respect the Court held that its flexibility in interpreting the concept of 'promptness' is very limited taking into account, on the one hand, the plain meaning of the word 'prompt' which clearly means 'at once' or immediately' and, on the other hand, the main objective of art 5(3) which is to ensure efficient and speedy justice, especially in respect of pre-trial detention when due regard to the presumption of innocence must be taken. The Court stated that even though the special circumstances in Northern Ireland, especially the obligation of the UK to protect the community as a whole from terrorism, justified the arrest and detention of the applicants, the period of the shortest detention of all applicants (McFadden for four days and six hours) fell outside the strict constraints required by the concept of promptness.

It is interesting to note that in *Arrowsmith v UK* (1978) 19 DR 5 the Court emphasised that the right protected under art 5 'comprises the guarantee that an individual will be arrested and detained only for reasons and according to the procedure prescribed by law'. In the present case the lawfulness of detention was not challenged as the Prevention of Terrorism (Temporary Provisions) Act 1984 permitted the detention of the individual for seven days without charge. It is clear from the judgment of the Court that in the case of national emergency a contracting State should by virtue of art 15 of the Convention invoke a derogation from art 5 rather than stretch the concept of 'promptness' to its limits and thus frustrate the objective of art 5(3) of the Convention. This was also the understanding of the government of the UK as it subsequently invoked the derogation from art 5 following the decision of the Court delivered in the present case.

Hood v *United Kingdom* Judgment of 18 February 1999 (not yet reported) European Court of Human Rights

- *Deprivation of liberty – the role of 'convening officer' – judge or other official exercising judicial power – independence of a tribunal – Army Act 1955*

Facts

The applicant, David Hood, was a British national and, when a soldier in the British Army, was tried and convicted under the Army Act 1955 by court-martial on a number of charges of a criminal nature. He challenged the role of the 'convening officer' who is central to the court-martial proceedings. He is in charge of convening the court-martial, appointing its members and the prosecuting officer, deciding whether or not a plea to a lesser charge, submitted by the offender, could be accepted, and under certain circumstances is entitled to dissolve the court-martial before or during the trial. He usually acts as confirming officer and confirms the court-martial's findings. The applicant challenged the decision of his commanding officer who under the 1955 Act is entitled to decide whether or not the accused should be detained prior to the trial. The applicant was detained and could not initiate habeas corpus proceedings contesting the lawfulness of his detention as neither military nor civilian legal aid were available to him.

The applicant claimed: that he had not been brought promptly before a judge or other judicial officer; that he had not had available to him the procedure prescribed by art 5(4) of the Convention permitting him to challenge his continuing detention; that he had not had enforceable rights to compensation or an effective domestic remedy as required under art 13; and that he had been denied a fair and public hearing by an independent and impartial tribunal established by law as required by art 6(1) and (3) of the Convention.

Held

The Court held unanimously that the United Kingdom had violated art 5(3) and (5) (right to liberty) and art 6(1) (right to a fair trial) of the Convention. The Court awarded the applicant £10,500 for legal costs and expenses.

Judgment

'A. *Applicability of art 5(3)*
51. The parties did not contest the applicability of art 5(3) and the Court finds that it clearly does apply. Given the nature of the relevant charges and the penalty imposed, the applicant was arrested on reasonable suspicion of having committed an "offence" within the meaning of art 5(1)(c) (see, for example, *De Jong, Baljet and Van den Brink* v *The Netherlands*, judgment of 22 May 1984, Series A no 77, pp21–22, paragraphs 42–44). Moreover, the applicant's close arrest amounted to detention in view of his confinement to a cell in the unit guardroom under the supervision of a guard (see *Engel and Others* v T*he Netherlands*, judgment of 8 June 1976, Series A no 22, p26, paragraph 63).

B. *Compliance with art 5(3)*
52. The applicant contended before the Court that he was not brought before his commanding officer on 29 November 1994 pursuant to Rule 4 of the 1972 Rules (see paragraph 29 above), submitting that he had no recollection of any such hearing and that there was no entry for that date in his diary or any written record of any such hearing. In the alternative, he argued that, even if there had been such a hearing pursuant to Rule 4 of the 1972 Rules, his commanding officer could not be considered to be impartial because of that officer's additional role in the prosecution of cases and his responsibility for discipline and order in his command. The applicant also referred in this context to the commanding officer's lack of legal qualifications.

53. Finally, the applicant asserted that the Rule 4 procedure was deficient for other reasons, including the lack of any written record and the absence of any provision for the accused to be informed of the reasons for his proposed pre-trial detention or for the accused to make submissions against such detention.

54. The Commission found in its report that the applicant had not disputed that he was brought before his commanding officer on 29 November 1994 pursuant to Rule 4 of the 1972 Rules. However, since it was satisfied that the commanding officer's impartiality was capable of appearing open to doubt because of that officer's other powers and duties to which the applicant adverted, it concluded that there had been a violation of art 5(3). In view of this conclusion, the Commission did not find it necessary to examine the applicant's remaining complaints under art 5(3).

55. The government maintained that the applicant's Rule 4 hearing did take place on 29 November 1994 and pointed out at the hearing before the Court that the applicant had not disputed that fact before the Commission or raised the point in his habeas corpus application to the High Court. They accepted the Commission's conclusion of a violation of art 5(3) and they took the view that it was not necessary to con-

sider separately the applicant's additional complaints under this article.

56. With regard to the factual dispute between the parties as to whether the applicant was brought before his commanding officer on 29 November 1994 in accordance with Rule 4 of the 1972 Rules, the Court finds the submissions of the government persuasive. The applicant could have raised the matter before the Commission after its decision on the admissibility of his application but he did not do so. In addition, any failure to fulfil the requirements of Rule 4 of the 1972 Rules would fall within the scope of habeas corpus proceedings. The applicant did not plead any such omission in the habeas corpus proceedings which he instituted in relation to another alleged non-compliance with domestic law and for which proceedings he was advised by the same legal representative as appeared before this Court (see paragraph 18 above). In such circumstances, the Court has examined the complaint under art 5(3) on the basis that the applicant was brought before his commanding officer on 29 November 1994 pursuant to Rule 4 of the 1972 Rules.

57. As to the applicant's substantive complaint about the commanding officer's impartiality in the context of the Rule 4 hearing, according to the case law of the Convention bodies, if it appears at the time the decision on pre-trial detention is taken that the "officer authorised by law to exercise judicial power" is liable to intervene in the subsequent proceedings as a representative of the prosecuting authority, then he could not be regarded as independent of the parties at that preliminary stage as it is possible for him to become one of the parties at a later stage (see *Huber* v *Switzerland*, judgment of 23 October 1990, Series A no 188, p18, paragraphs 42–43 and *Brincat* v *Italy*, judgment of 26 November 1992, Series A no 249–A, pp11–12, paragraphs 20–21).

The Court has noted the powers and duties of the commanding officer outlined, in particular, at paragraphs 23, 27, 28, 32 and 34 above, which would arise subsequent to that officer's conduct of the hearing pursuant to Rule 4 of the 1972 Rules. This being so, the commanding officer was liable to play a central role in the subsequent prosecution of the case against the applicant. Although the unit adjutant often carries out certain of these functions of the commanding officer (and, indeed, did so in the present case), it is clear that the adjutant does so on behalf of the commanding officer to whom he is directly subordinate in rank. Moreover, the judge advocate confirmed during the applicant's court martial that the unit adjutant is generally nominated prosecuting or assistant prosecuting officer and, in the present case, he carried out the latter function.

In such circumstances, the Court concludes that the applicant's misgivings about his commanding officer's impartiality must be taken to be objectively justified.

58. The Court also considers, as did the Commission, that the commanding officer's concurrent responsibility for discipline and order in his command would provide an additional reason for an accused reasonably to doubt that officer's impartiality when deciding on the necessity of the pre-trial detention of an accused in his command. This view is reinforced by paragraph 6.005 of the Queen's Regulations (see paragraph 36 above), which allows for the commanding officer to refuse the pre-trial release of an accused if he is of the view that it is undesirable "in the interests of discipline" that the accused be at large or be allowed to consort with his comrades.

59. The foregoing conclusion renders it unnecessary to address the applicant's related argument about his commanding officer's lack of legal qualifications.

60. Finally, as to the applicant's submission that the Rule 4 procedure was deficient in other respects (see paragraph 53 above), the government submitted before the Commission that the Rule 4 procedure had provided the applicant with the "opportunity" to be heard and that the applicant had been informed by his commanding officer of the reasons for his pre-trial detention. In this connection the Court recalls the procedural and substantive requirements of art

5(3) obliging the "officer", inter alia, to hear himself the accused, to examine all the facts militating for and against pre-trial detention and to set out in the decision on detention the facts upon which that decision is based (see *Schiesser* v *Switzerland*, judgment of 4 December 1979, Series A no 34, p13–14, paragraph 31 and *Letellier* v *France*, judgment of 26 June 1991, Series A no 207, p18, paragraph 35). The Court further stressed, in its *Duinhof and Duijf* v *The Netherlands* judgment, the importance of "formal, visible requirements stated in the 'law'" as opposed to standard practices in determining whether a national procedure for deciding on the liberty of an individual satisfies the requirements of art 5(3) (judgment of 22 May 1984, Series A no 79, pp15–16, paragraph 34).

However, given its conclusions at paragraphs 57 and 58 above, the Court is of the view that it is not necessary to rule on this additional complaint.

61. In sum, the Court finds that there has been a violation of art 5(3) of the Convention since the commanding officer could not be regarded as independent of the parties at the relevant time. ...

V. Alleged violation of art 6(1) and (3) of the Convention

74. The applicant's main challenge before the Court was to the independence and impartiality of the court martial.

The Commission found that the applicant had not been given a hearing by an independent and impartial tribunal.

In view of the decision and reasoning of the Court in the above-mentioned *Findlay* judgment [*Reports of Judgments and Decisions* 1997–I, p276] (at pp279–83, paragraphs 68–80) and in *Coyne* v *United Kingdom*, judgment of 24 September 1997 (*Reports of Judgments and Decisions* 1997–V, pp1854–55, paragraphs 54–58), the government did not contest the Commission's conclusion.

75. The applicant also contended that the court martial was not a tribunal "established by law". He further complained under art 6(1) and (3)(c) about the alleged inadequacy of the military legal aid system, arguing that he would not have submitted his and his girlfriend's statements to the unit adjutant if he had had legal representation.

The Commission did not find it necessary to consider these complaints.

The government pointed out that the applicant had received legal aid from the military authorities and that the court martial had rejected his objection to the admission of the statements and submitted that the Court should adopt the same position as the Commission on these complaints.

76. The Court recalls that in its above-mentioned *Findlay* judgment it found that a general court martial convened pursuant to the Army Act 1955 did not meet the requirements of independence and impartiality laid down by art 6(1) of the Convention, in view in particular of the central part played in the prosecution by the convening officer, who was closely linked to the prosecuting authorities, was superior in rank to the members of the court martial and had the power, albeit in prescribed circumstances, to dissolve the court martial and to refuse to confirm its decision (see the above-cited *Findlay* judgment at pp279–83, paragraphs 68–80, together with paragraph 45 above). In its above-mentioned *Coyne* judgment, it came to a similar conclusion in respect of a district court martial convened under the Air Force Act 1955.

77. The Court can find no reason for distinguishing the present case from the cases of Mr Findlay and Mr Coyne as regards the part played by the convening officer in the organisation of the court martial. It follows that, for the reasons expressed in the above-mentioned *Findlay* judgment, the court martial which considered the applicant's case was not "independent and impartial" within the meaning of art 6(1).

78. As in the above-mentioned *Findlay* judgment (at p283, paragraph 80), the Court does not judge it necessary to examine separately the applicant's submission under art 6(1) that the court martial was not a tribunal "established by law". The Court comes to a similar conclusion in relation to the applicant's complaint about the alleged inadequacy of the military legal aid system in view of the above findings and the particular

circumstances of the present case, including the submission of the statements in question following specific legal advice obtained by the applicant.

79. In conclusion, the Court finds that there has been a violation of art 6(1) since the court martial did not meet the requirements of independence and impartiality.'

Comment
The judgment of the Court is not surprising taking into account its previous decision of 25 February 1997 in *Findlay* v *United Kingdom* in which it held that a court martial convened under the Army Act 1955 did not comply with the requirements of independence and impartiality contained in art 6(1) of the Convention. The Court found no reason to distinguish the present case and in each of two judgments unanimously condemned the role of the "convening officer". One judgment being in the present case and the other being in the case of *Cable and Others* v *United Kingdom* where the judgment was given by a Grand Chamber of the European Court of Human Rights on 18 February 1999. The Court held unanimously that there had been a violation of art 6(1) of the Convention. The case originated in thirty-five separate applications brought by British citizens, all of them soldiers in the British military forces, charged, convicted and sentenced by courts-martial under either the Air Force Act 1955 or the Army Act 1955. The proceedings before the Court contributed to the amendment of the challenged Acts, inter alia, by the Armed Forces Act 1966 and by the Investigation and Summary Dealing (Army) Regulations 1997 in order to comply with art 6(1) of the Convention.

17 The Right to Privacy and Family Life: Article 8

Dudgeon* v *United Kingdom (1981) 4 EHHR 149 European Court of Human Rights

• *Respect for family life and for private life – restrictions on sexual acts between males whether in public or private – not necessary in a democratic society – violation of art 8 of the Convention*

Facts

The applicant complained that under the law in force at the time in Northern Ireland, homosexual conduct was prosecuted in violation of the right of privacy contrary to art 8. In fact, homosexuality was not prohibited but it was a criminal offence for two consenting males over 21 years of age to commit homosexual acts whether in private or public.

Held

The Court found that the United Kingdom had unjustifiably interfered with the applicant's right to privacy contrary to art 8 of the Convention.

Judgment

'In the government's submission, the law in Northern Ireland relating to homosexual acts does not give rise to a breach of art 8, in that it is justified by the terms of paragraph 2 of the article. This contention was disputed by both the applicant and the Commission.

An interference with the exercise of an art 8 right will not be compatible with paragraph 2 unless it is "in accordance with the law", has an aim or aims that is or are legitimate under that paragraph and is "necessary in democratic society" for the aforesaid aim or aims (see, mutatis mutandis, *Young, James and Webster*, judgment of 13 August 1981, Series A no 44, p24, paragraph 59).

It has not been contested that the first of these three conditions was met. As the Commission pointed out in paragraph 99 of its report, the interference is plainly "in accordance with the law" since it results from the existence of certain provisions in the 1861 and 1885 Acts and the common law.

It next falls to be determined whether the interference is aimed at "the protection of morals" or "the protection of the rights and freedoms of others", the two purposes relied on by the government.

The 1861 and 1885 Acts were passed in order to enforce the then prevailing conception of sexual morality. Originally they applied to England and Wales, to all Ireland, then unpartitioned, and also, in the case of the 1885 Act, to Scotland. In recent years the scope of the legislation has been restricted in England and Wales (with the 1967 Act) and subsequently in Scotland (with the 1980 Act): with certain exceptions it is no longer a criminal offence for two consenting males over 21 years of age to commit homosexual acts in private. In Northern Ireland, in contrast, the law has remained unchanged. The decision announced in July 1979 to take no further action in relation to the proposal to amend the existing law was, the Court accepts, prompted by what the United Kingdom government judged to be the strength of feeling in Northern Ireland against the proposed change, and in particular the strength of the view that it would be seriously damaging to the moral fabric of Northern Irish society. This being so, the general aim pursued by the legislation remains the protection of morals in the sense of moral standards obtaining in Northern Ireland.

Both the Commission and the government took the view that, in so far as the legislation seeks to safeguard young persons from undesirable and harmful pressures and attentions, it is also aimed at "the protection of the rights and freedoms of others". The Court recognises that one of the purposes of the legislation is to afford safeguards for vulnerable members of society, such as the young, against the consequences of homosexual practices. However, it is somewhat artificial in this context to draw a rigid distinction between "protection of the rights and freedoms of others" and "protection of morals". The latter may imply safeguarding the moral ethos or moral standards of a society as a whole, but may also, as the Government pointed out, cover protection of the moral interests and welfare of a particular section of society, for example schoolchildren (see *Handyside*, judgment of 7 December 1976, Series A no 24, p25, paragraph 52 in fine – in relation to art 10(2) of the Convention). Thus, "protection of the rights and freedoms of others", when meaning the safeguarding of the moral interests and welfare of certain individuals or classes of individuals who are in need of special protection for reasons such as lack of maturity, mental disability or state of dependence, amounts to one aspect of "protection of morals" (see, mutatis mutandis, *Sunday Times*, judgment of 26 April 1979, Series A no 30, p34, paragraph 56). The Court will therefore take account of the two aims on this basis.

As the Commission rightly observed in its report, the cardinal issue arising under art 8 in this case is to what extent, if at all, the maintenance in force of the legislation is "necessary in a democratic society" for these aims.

There can be no denial that some degree of regulation of male homosexual conduct, as indeed of other forms of sexual conduct, by means of the criminal law can be justified as "necessary in a democratic society". The overall function served by the criminal law in this field is, in the words of the Wolfenden report, "to preserve public order and decency [and] to protect the citizen from what is offensive or injurious". Furthermore, this necessity for some degree of control may even extend to consensual acts committed in private, notably where there is call – to quote the Wolfenden report once more – "to provide sufficient safeguards against exploitation and corruption of others, particularly those who are specially vulnerable because they are young, weak in body or mind, inexperienced, or in a state of special physical, official or economic dependence". In practice there is legislation on the matter in all the member States of the Council of Europe, but what distinguishes the law in Northern Ireland from that existing in the great majority of the member States is that it prohibits generally gross indecency between males and buggery whatever the circumstances. It being accepted that some form of legislation is "necessary" to protect particular sections of society as well as the moral ethos of society as a whole, the question in the present case is whether the contested provisions of the law of Northern Ireland and their enforcement remain within the bounds of what, in a democratic society, may be regarded as necessary in order to accomplish those aims.

A number of principles relevant to the assessment of the "necessity", "in a democratic society", of a measure taken in furtherance of an aim that is legitimate under the Convention have been stated by the Court in previous judgments.

Firstly, "necessary" in this context does not have the flexibility of such expressions as "useful", "reasonable", or "desirable", but implies the existence of a "pressing social need" for the interference in question (see the above-mentioned *Handyside* judgment, p22, paragraph 48).

In the second place, it is for the national authorities to make the initial assessment of the pressing social need in each case;

accordingly, a margin of appreciation is left to them (ibid). However, their decision remains subject to review by the Court (ibid, p23, paragraph 49).

As was illustrated by the Sunday Times judgment, the scope of the margin of appreciation is not identical in respect of each of the aims justifying restrictions on a right (p36, paragraph 50). The government inferred from the *Handyside* judgment that the margin of appreciation will be more extensive where the protection of morals is in issue. It is an indisputable fact, as the Court stated in the *Handyside* judgment, that "the view taken ... of the requirements of morals varies from time to time and from place to place, especially in our era," and that "by reason of their direct and continuous contact with the vital forces of their countries. State authorities are in principle in a better position than the international judge to give an opinion on the exact content of those requirements" (p22, paragraph 48).

However, not only the nature of the aim of the restriction but also the nature of the activities involved will affect the scope of the margin of appreciation. The present case concerns a most intimate aspect of private life. Accordingly, there must exist particularly serious reasons before interferences on the part of the public authorities can be legitimate for the purposes of paragraph 2 of art 8.

Finally, in art 8 as in several other articles of the Convention, the notion of "necessity" is linked to that of a "democratic society". According to the Court's case law, a restriction on a Convention right cannot be regarded as "necessary in a democratic society" – two hallmarks of which are tolerance and broadmindedness – unless, amongst other things, it is proportionate to the legitimate aim pursued (see the above-mentioned *Handyside* judgment, p23, paragraph 49, and the above-mentioned *Young, James and Webster* judgment, p25, paragraph 63).

The Court's task is to determine on the basis of the aforestated principles whether the reasons purporting to justify the "interference" in question are relevant and sufficient under art 8(2) (see the above-mentioned *Handyside* judgment, pp23–24, paragraph 50). The Court is not concerned with making any value-judgment as to the morality of homosexual relations between adult males.

It is convenient to begin by examining the reasons set out by the government in their arguments contesting the Commission's conclusion that the penal prohibition of private consensual homosexual acts involving male persons over 21 years of age is not justified under art 8(2).

In the first place, the government drew attention to what they described as profound differences of attitude and public opinion between Northern Ireland and Great Britain in relation to questions of morality. Northern Irish society was said to be more conservative and to place greater emphasis on religious factors, as was illustrated by more restrictive laws even in the field of heterosexual conduct.

Although the applicant qualified this account of the facts as grossly exaggerated, the Court acknowledges that such differences do exist to a certain extent and are a relevant factor. As the government and the Commission both emphasised, in assessing the requirements of the protection of morals in Northern Ireland, the contested measures must be seen in the context of Northern Irish society.

The fact that similar measures are not considered necessary in other parts of the United Kingdom or in other Member States of the Council of Europe does not mean that they cannot be necessary in Northern Ireland (see, mutatis mutandis, the above-mentioned *Sunday Times* judgment, pp37–38, paragraph 61: cf also the above-mentioned *Handyside* judgment, pp26–28, paragraphs 54 and 57). Where there are disparate cultural communities residing within the same State, it may well be that different requirements both moral and social, will face the governing authorities.

As the government correctly submitted, it follows that the moral climate in Northern Ireland in sexual matters, in particular as evidenced by the opposition to the proposed legislative change, is one of the matters which the national authorities may legitimately take into account in exercising their discretion. There is, the Court accepts, a strong body of opposition stemming from a genuine and sincere conviction shared by a large number of responsible members of the Northern Irish community that a change in the law would be seriously damaging to the moral fabric of society. This opposition reflects –as do in another way the recommendations made in 1977 by the Advisory Commission – a view both of the requirements of morals in Northern Ireland and of the measures thought within the community to be necessary to preserve prevailing moral standards.

Whether this point of view be right or wrong, and although it may be out of line with current attitudes in other communities, its existence among an important sector of Northern Irish society is certainly relevant for the purposes of art 8(2).

The government argued that this conclusion is further strengthened by the special constitutional circumstances of Northern Ireland. In the period between 1921 (when the Northern Ireland Parliament first met) and 1972 (when it last sat), legislation in the social field was regarded as a devolved matter within the exclusive domain of that Parliament. As a result of the introduction of "direct rule" from Westminster, the United Kingdom Government, it was said, had a special responsibility to take full account of the wishes of the people of Northern Ireland before legislating on such matters.

In the present circumstances of direct rule, the need for caution and for sensitivity to public opinion in Northern Ireland is evident. However, the Court does not consider it conclusive in assessing the "necessity", for the purposes of the Convention, of maintaining the impugned legislation that the decision was taken, not by the former Northern Ireland government and Parliament, but by the United Kingdom authorities during what they hope to be an interim period of direct rule.

Without any doubt, faced with these various considerations, the United Kingdom government acted carefully and in good faith; what is more, they made every effort to arrive at a balanced judgment between the differing viewpoints before reaching the conclusion that such a substantial body of opinion in Northern Ireland was opposed to a change in the law that no further action should be taken. Nevertheless, this cannot of itself be decisive as to the necessity for the interference with the applicant's private life resulting from the measures being challenged (see the above-mentioned *Sunday Times* judgment, p36, paragraph 59). Notwithstanding the margin of appreciation left to the national authorities, it is for the Court to make the final evaluation as to whether the reasons it has found to be relevant were sufficient in the circumstances, in particular whether the interference complained of was proportionate to the social need claimed for it.'

Comment

In was recognised by the Court in *Norris* v *Ireland* (1988) 13 EHHR 186 that sexual life constitutes an integral part of the private life of the individual. However, homosexual relationships are not included in the definition of family life within the meaning of art 8 of the Convention although they are considered as forming part of 'private life' (DR 32/220). In the present case the Court held that a blanket criminalisation of all homosexual activity between all men regardless of age was too broad to be justified under art 8(2) of the Convention although the Commission confirmed that under certain circumstances the total prohibition of all homosexual relations between consenting adult males (for example in the context of the armed forces) is justified on the grounds of protection of morals and the prevention of disorder (DR 34/68). Although each contracting State has its own perception of what is necessary to protect morals the criminalisation of homosexuality seems to be a thing of the past as there is a broad European consensus in this respect (see *Modinos* v *Cyprus* A 259 (1993) Com Rep, paragraph 45).

The Homosexual Offences (Northern Ireland) Order 1982 'decriminalised' homosexual acts conducted in private between consenting adults, subject to exceptions concerning mental patients and members of the armed forces and merchant seamen. The Order entered into force on 9 December 1982.

Golder v *United Kingdom* (1975) 1 EHRR 524 European Court of Human Rights

- *Respect for correspondence – the right to communicate with solicitor – interference prescribed by law – not necessary in a democratic society – violation of art 8 – fair hearing – access to court – violation of art 6(1) of the Convention*

Facts
A prisoner addressed a petition to the Home Secretary requesting the right to consult with a solicitor on the subject of a possible libel suit against a prison officer. The prison officer had alleged that the applicant was a participant in a serious disturbance at the prison. The request was refused.

The applicant claimed that the interference by the authorities, that is the Home Secretary's refusal of his petition, infringed his right to communicate and that the UK was in breach of arts 6(1) and 8 of the Convention

Held
The Court held that the actions of the authorities amounted to an unlawful interference with the prisoner's right to communicate under art 8 of the Convention. The same facts constituted a violation of art 6(1) of the Convention.

Judgment
'*On the alleged violation of art 8*
In the opinion of the majority of the Commission "the same facts which constitute a violation of art 6(1) constitute also a violation of art 8". The government disagree with this opinion.

Article 8 of the Convention reads as follows:
"1. Everyone has the right to respect for his private and family life, his home and his correspondence.
2. There shall be no interference by a public authority with the exercise of this right except such as is in accordance with the law and is necessary in a democratic society in the interests of national security, public safety or the economic well-being of the country, for the prevention of disorder or crime, for the protection of health or morals, or for the protection of the rights and freedoms of others."

The Home Secretary's refusal of the petition of 20 March 1970 had the direct and immediate effect of preventing Golder from contacting a solicitor by any means whatever, including that which in the ordinary way he would have used to begin with, correspondence. While there was certainly neither stopping nor censorship of any message, such as a letter, which Golder would have written to a solicitor – or vice versa – and which would have been a piece of correspondence within the meaning of paragraph 1 of art 8, it would be wrong to conclude therefrom, as do the government, that this text is inapplicable. Impeding someone from even initiating correspondence constitutes the most far-reaching form of "interference" with the exercise of the "right to respect for correspondence"; it is inconceivable that that should fall outside the scope of art 8 while mere supervision indisputably falls within it. In any event, if Golder had attempted to write to a solicitor notwithstanding the Home Secretary's decision or without requesting the required permission, that correspondence would have been stopped and he could have invoked art 8; one would arrive at a paradoxical and hardly equitable result, if it were considered that in complying with the requirements of the Prison Rules 1964 he lost the benefit of the protection of art 8.

The Court accordingly finds itself called upon to ascertain whether or not the refusal of the applicant's petition violated art 8.

In the submission of the government, the right to respect for correspondence is subject, apart from interference covered by paragraph 2 of art 8, to implied limitations resulting, inter alia, from the terms of art 5(1)(a): a sentence of imprisonment passed after conviction by a competent court inevitably entails consequences affecting the operation of other articles of the Convention, including art 8.

As the Commission have emphasised that submission is not in keeping with the manner in which the Court dealt with the issue raised under art 8 in the *"Vagrancy"* cases (*De Wilde, Ooms and Versyp*, judgment of 18 June 1971, Series A no 12, pp45–46, paragraph 93). In addition and more particularly, that submission conflicts with the explicit text of art 8. The restrictive formulation used at paragraph 2 ("There shall be no interference ... except such as ...") leaves no room for the concept of implied limitations. In this regard, the legal status of the right to respect for correspondence, which is defined by art 8 with some precision, provides a clear contrast to that of the right to a court.

The government have submitted in the alternative that the interference complained of satisfied the explicit conditions laid down in paragraph 2 of art 8.

It is beyond doubt that the interference was "in accordance with the law", that is Rules 33(2) and 34(8) of the Prison Rules 1964 (paragraph 17 above).

The Court accepts, moreover, that the "necessity" for interference with the exercise of the right of a convicted prisoner to respect for his correspondence must be appreciated having regard to the ordinary and reasonable requirements of imprisonment. The "prevention of disorder or crime", for example, may justify wider measures of interference in the case of such a prisoner than in that of a person at liberty. To this extent, but to this extent only, lawful deprivation of liberty within the meaning of art 5 does not fail to impinge on the application of art 8.

In its judgment of 18 June 1971 cited above, the Court held that "even in cases of persons detained for vagrancy" (paragraph 1(e) of art 5) – and not imprisoned after conviction by a court – the competent national authorities may have "sufficient reason to believe that it (is) 'necessary' to impose restrictions for the purpose of the prevention of disorder or crime, the protection of health or morals, and the protection of the rights and freedoms of others". However, in those particular cases there was no question of preventing the applicants from even initiating correspondence; there was only supervision which in any event did not apply in a series of instances, including in particular correspondence between detained vagrants and the counsel of their choice (Series A no 12, p26, paragraph 39, and p45, paragraph 93).

In order to show why the interference complained of by Golder was "necessary", the government advanced the prevention of disorder or crime and, up to a certain point, the interests of public safety and the protection of the rights and freedoms of others. Even having regard to the power of appreciation left to the Contracting States, the Court cannot discern how these considerations, as they are understood "in a democratic society", could oblige the Home Secretary to prevent Golder from corresponding with a solicitor with a view to suing Laird for libel. The Court again lays stress on the fact that Golder was seeking to exculpate himself of a charge made against him by that prison officer acting in the course of his duties and relating to an incident in prison. In these circumstances, Golder could justifiably wish to write to a solicitor. It was not for the Home Secretary himself to appraise – no more than it is for the Court today – the prospects of the action contemplated; it was for a solicitor to advise the applicant on his rights and then for a court to rule on any action that might be brought.

The Home Secretary's decision proves to be all the less "necessary in a democratic society" in that the applicant's correspondence with a solicitor would have been a preparatory step to the institution of civil legal proceedings and, therefore, to the exercise of a right embodied in another article of the Convention, that is, art 6.

The Court thus reaches the conclusion that there has been a violation of art 8.'

Comment

This is a straightforward decision of the Court. A contracting State is prohibited from interfering with correspondence between a prisoner and his lawyer and between a lawyer and a detained prisoner. Taking into account the special relationship between them no restrictions whatsoever are permitted, including the refusal to send a letter by the prison authorities. The right to respect for legal correspondence is unqualified and extends to the situation where the lawyer is not appointed by the prisoner and to the situation where the lawyer is advising the detainee to remain silent (*Schöenberger and Durmaz* v *Switzerland* 11 EHRR 202). As the Court stated in the present case, even impeding someone from initiating correspondence constituted the most far-reaching form of 'interference' with the exercise of the right to respect for correspondence. The Court has been consistent in upholding the special lawyer-client relationship (*Campbell* v *UK* (1993) 15 EHRR 137) based, on the one hand, on a lawyer's duty of confidentiality in the context of all lawyer-client relationships (see *Niemietz* v *Germany* A 251–B (1992)) and, on the other hand, on the prisoner's need to communicate with the outside world, especially with someone he can trust. As a result of the decisions of the Court and the Commission the UK rules governing correspondence between a prisoner and his lawyer have been amended on a number of occasions.

Johnston v *Ireland* (1986) 9 EHRR 203 European Court of Human Rights

- *Prohibition on divorce and prevention of remarrying – respect for family life – no right to divorce under the Convention – no violation of art 8 of the Convention*

Facts

The applicant wished to divorce his spouse and marry another woman. Divorce, as a concept, was not recognised under Irish law. Since the applicant's first marriage could not be legally terminated, any second marriage would constitute bigamy. He was therefore effectively prevented from remarrying.

The complaint alleged that the prohibition on divorce violated the applicant's right to have a family life. The right to found a family, it was alleged, was frustrated by the Irish authorities by the extent of the prohibition on divorce. The main issue was whether Ireland was required to amend its laws to permit divorce.

Held

The Court found that the rights alleged by the applicant were too liberal an interpretation of art 8(1). There was consequently no failure on the part of the Irish authorities to respect the applicant's right to a family life.

Judgment

'Article 8
The principles which emerge from the Court's case law on art 8 include the following.

a) By guaranteeing the right to respect for family life, art 8 presupposes the existence of a family (see the above-mentioned *Marckx* judgment, Series A no 31, p14, paragraph 31).

b) Article 8 applies to the "family life" of the "illegitimate" family as well as to that of the "legitimate" family (ibid).

c) Although the essential object of art 8 is to protect the individual against arbitrary interference by the public authorities, there may in addition be positive obligations inherent in an effective "respect" for family life. However, especially as far as those positive obligations are concerned, the notion of "respect" is not clear-cut: having regard to the diversity of the practices followed and the situations obtaining in the contracting States, the notion's requirements will vary considerably from case to case. Accordingly, this is an area in which the contracting parties enjoy a wide margin of appreciation in determining the steps to be taken to ensure compliance with the Convention with due regard to the needs and resources of the community and of individuals (see *Abdulaziz, Cabales and Balkandali*, judgment of 28 May 1985, Series A no 94, pp33–34, paragraph 67).

In the present case, it is clear that the applicants, the first and second of whom have lived together for some fifteen years, constitute a "family" for the purposes of art 8. They are thus entitled to its protection, notwithstanding the fact that their relationship exists outside marriage (see paragraph 55(b) above).

The question that arises, as regards this part of the case, is whether an effective "respect" for the applicants' family life imposes on Ireland a positive obligation to introduce measures that would permit divorce.

It is true that, on this question, art 8, with its reference to the somewhat vague notion of "respect" for family life, might appear to lend itself more readily to an evolutive interpretation than does art 12. Nevertheless, the Convention must be read as a whole and the Court does not consider that a right to divorce, which it has found to be excluded from art 12 (see paragraph 54 above), can, with consistency, be derived from art 8, a provision of more general purpose and scope. The Court is not oblivious to the plight of the first and second applicants. However, it is of the opinion that, although the protection of private or family life may sometimes necessitate means whereby spouses can be relieved from the duty to live together (see the above-mentioned *Airey* judgment, Series A no 32, p 17 paragraph 33), the engagements undertaken by Ireland under art 8 cannot be regarded as extending to an obligation on its part to introduce measures permitting the divorce and the re-marriage which the applicants seek.

On this point, there is therefore no failure to respect the family life of the first and second applicants.

Article 14, taken in conjunction with art 8
The first and second applicants complained of the fact that whereas Roy Johnston was unable to obtain a divorce in order subsequently to marry Janice Williams-Johnston, other persons resident in Ireland and having the necessary means could obtain abroad a divorce which would be recognised de jure or de facto in Ireland. They alleged that on this account they had been victims of discrimination, on the ground of financial means, in the enjoyment of the rights set forth in art 8, contrary to art 14, which reads as follows:

> "The enjoyment of the rights and freedoms set forth in [the] Convention shall be secured without discrimination on any ground such as sex, race, colour, language, religion, political or other opinion, national or social origin, association with a national minority, property, birth or other status."

This allegation, contested by the government, was rejected by the Commission.

Article 14 safeguards persons who are "placed in analogous situations" against discriminatory differences of treatment in the exercise of the rights and freedoms recognised by the Convention (see, as the most recent authority, *Lithgow and Others*, judgment of 8 July 1986, Series A no 102, p66, paragraph 177).

The Court notes that under the general Irish rules of private international law foreign divorces will be recognised in Ireland only if they have been obtained by persons domiciled abroad (see paragraph 20 above). It does not find it to have been established that these rules are departed from in practice. In its view, the situations of such persons and of the first and second applicants cannot be regarded as analogous.

There is, accordingly, no discrimination, within the meaning of art 14.

Article 9
The first applicant also alleged that his inability to live with the second applicant other than in an extra-marital relationship

was contrary to his conscience and that on that account he was the victim of a violation of art 9 of the Convention, which guarantees to everyone the "right to freedom of thought, conscience and religion".

The applicant supplemented this allegation, which was contested by the government and rejected by the Commission, by a claim of discrimination in relation to conscience and religion, contrary to art 14 taken in conjunction with art 9.

It is clear that Roy Johnston's freedom to have and manifest his convictions is not in issue. His complaint derives, in essence, from the non-availability of divorce under Irish law, a matter to which, in the Court's view, art 9 cannot, in its ordinary meaning, be taken to extend.

Accordingly, that provision, and hence art 14 also, are not applicable.

Conclusion
The Court thus concludes that the complaints related to the inability to divorce and re-marry are not well-founded.'

Comment
In this case the Court had to decide whether the Convention guarantees the right to divorce. The Court held that the Convention does not include this right. The Court emphasised that although the Convention should be interpreted in the light of international conventions and social changes in contracting States that interpretation has its limits. Even the evolutive interpretation cannot infer from the Convention a right that is not originally included, especially taking into account that the omission was deliberate.

In the light of the judgment in *Airey* v *Ireland* A (1979) Series A no 32, in which the Court stated (somewhat perversely) that the protection of family life of spouses may sometimes necessitate them being relieved from the duty of living together, and that a State is in the best position to decide how to ensure that right, the requirements of art 8 are satisfied when a State recognises the institution of judicial separation.

It is interesting to note that the right to divorce is recognised under art 16 of the Universal Declaration of Human Rights which states that spouses should be treated equally 'in marriage and during its dissolution'.

Laskey, Jaggard and Brown v *United Kingdom* Judgment of 19 February 1997 (not yet reported) European Court of Human Rights

• *Sado-masochistic activities – interference necessary in a democratic society – protection of health – no violation of art 8 of the convention*

Facts
The applicants, members of a group of homosexual men who participated in sado-masochistic activities involving maltreatments of the genitals, ritualistic beating and branding, were making videos of their gatherings for private use. One of these tapes fell into the hands of the police who charged them with a number of offences, in particular causing bodily harm and wounding contrary to ss47 and 20 of the Offences against the Person Act 1861.

The applicants were all adults, their activities were consensual, conducted in private and subject to certain rules, in particular in relation to the infliction of pain which was stopped when a certain code word was used. No applicant suffered permanent injury or infection resulting from their activities.

The applicants based their defence on the consent of the alleged 'victim' to the assault. Their defence was rejected. They pleaded guilty and on 19 December 1990 were sentenced: Mr Laskey to 12 months' imprisonment, Mr Jaggard to three years and Mr Brown to two years nine months.Their appeal to the Court of Appeal was dismissed although their sentences were considerably reduced. On appeal to the House of Lords, the law Lords held that the consent of a 'victim' constituted no defence under the 1861 Act, and that it would be contrary to the public interest to create an exception to that rule based on sado-masochistic activities (two of five Law Lords dissenting)

As a result of the national proceedings all the applicants lost their jobs, Mr Jaggard required extensive psychiatric treatment and Mr Laskey died in 1995.

The applicants claimed violation of their right to private life and discrimination based on their sexual orientation under art 14 of the Convention.

Held

Contrary to the decision of the Commission which held that there was violation of art 8 of the Convention (11 votes to seven) the Court unanimously held that the UK was neither in breach of art 8 nor of art 14 of the Convention.

Judgment

'Alleged violation of art 8 of the Convention
The Court observes that not every sexual activity carried out behind closed doors necessarily falls within the scope of art 8 ... In the present case, the applicants were involved in consensual sado-masochistic activities for purposes of sexual gratification. There can be no doubt that sexual orientation and activity concern an intimate aspect of private life (see, mutatis mutandis, *Dudgeon* v *United Kingdom*, judgment of 22 October 1981, Series A no 45, p21, paragraph 52). However, a considerable number of people were involved in the activities in question which included, inter alia, the recruitment of new "members", the provision of several specially equipped "chambers", and the shooting of many videotapes which were distributed among the "members" (see paragraphs 8 and 9 above). It may thus be open to question whether the sexual activities of the applicants fell entirely within the notion of "private life" in the particular circumstances of the case.

However, since this point has not been disputed by those appearing before it, the Court sees no reason to examine it of its own motion in the present case. Assuming, therefore, that the prosecution and conviction of the applicants amounted to an interference with their private life, the question arises whether such an interference was 'necessary in a democratic society' within the meaning of the second paragraph of art 8 ...

Necessary in a democratic society
37. The applicants maintained that the interference in issue could not be regarded as "necessary in a democratic society". This submission was contested by the government and by a majority of the Commission.

38. In support of their submission, the applicants alleged that all those involved in the sado-masochistic encounters were willing adult participants; that participation in the acts complained of was carefully restricted and controlled and was limited to persons with like-minded sado-masochistic proclivities; that the acts were not witnessed by the public at large and that there was no danger or likelihood that they would ever be so witnessed; that no serious or permanent injury had been sustained, no infection had been caused to the wounds, and that no medical treatment had been required. Furthermore, no complaint was ever made to the police – who learnt about the applicants' activities by chance (see paragraph 8 above).

The potential for severe injury or for moral corruption was regarded by the applicants as a matter of speculation. To the extent that issues of public morality had arisen – with reference to Mr Laskey's conviction for keeping a disorderly house and for the possession of an indecent photograph of a child (see paragraph 11 above) – these had been dealt with under the relevant sexual offences provisions and appropriately punished. In any event, such issues fell outside the scope of the case as presented before the Court.

39. The applicants submitted that their case should be viewed as one involving matters of sexual expression, rather than violence. With due regard to this consideration, the line beyond which consent is no

defence to physical injury should only be drawn at the level of intentional or reckless causing of serious disabling injury.

40. For the government, the State was entitled to punish acts of violence, such as those for which the applicants were convicted, that could not be considered of a trifling or transient nature, irrespective of the consent of the victim. In fact, in the present case, some of these acts could well be compared to "genital torture" and a Contracting State could not be said to have an obligation to tolerate acts of torture because they are committed in the context of a consenting sexual relationship. The State was moreover entitled to prohibit activities because of their potential danger.

The government further contended that the criminal law should seek to deter certain forms of behaviour on public-health grounds but also for broader moral reasons. In this respect, acts of torture – such as those in issue in the present case – may be banned also on the ground that they undermine the respect which human beings should confer upon each other. In any event, the whole issue of the role of consent in the criminal law is of great complexity and the contracting States should enjoy a wide margin of appreciation to consider all the public-policy options.

41. The Commission noted that the injuries that were or could be caused by the applicants' activities were of a significant nature and degree, and that the conduct in question was, on any view, of an extreme character. The State authorities therefore acted within their margin of appreciation in order to protect its citizens from real risk of serious physical harm or injury.

42. According to the Court's established case-law, the notion of necessity implies that the interference corresponds to a pressing social need and, in particular, that it is proportionate to the legitimate aim pursued; in determining whether an interference is 'necessary in a democratic society', the Court will take into account that a margin of appreciation is left to the national authorities (see, inter alia, *Olsson* v *Sweden (No 1)*, judgment of 24 March 1988, Series A no 130, pp31–32, paragraph 67), whose decision remains subject to review by the Court for conformity with the requirements of the Convention.

The scope of this margin of appreciation is not identical in each case but will vary according to the context. Relevant factors include the nature of the Convention right in issue, its importance for the individual and the nature of the activities concerned (see *Buckley* v *United Kingdom*, judgment of 25 September 1996, *Reports of Judgments and Decisions* 1996–IV, pp1291–92, paragraph. 74).

43. The Court considers that one of the roles which the State is unquestionably entitled to undertake is to seek to regulate, through the operation of the criminal law, activities which involve the infliction of physical harm. This is so whether the activities in question occur in the course of sexual conduct or otherwise.

44. The determination of the level of harm that should be tolerated by the law in situations where the victim consents is in the first instance a matter for the State concerned since what is at stake is related, on the one hand, to public health considerations and to the general deterrent effect of the criminal law, and, on the other, to the personal autonomy of the individual.

45. The applicants have contended that, in the circumstances of the case, the behaviour in question formed part of private morality which is not the State's business to regulate. In their submission the matters for which they were prosecuted and convicted concerned only private sexual behaviour.

The Court is not persuaded by this submission. It is evident from the facts established by the national courts that the applicants' sado-masochistic activities involved a significant degree of injury or wounding which could not be characterised as trifling or transient. This, in itself, suffices to distinguish the present case from those applications which have previously been examined by the Court concerning consensual homosexual behaviour in private between adults where no such feature was present (see the *Dudgeon* judgment cited above, *Norris* v

Ireland, judgment of 26 October 1988, Series A no 142, and *Modinos v Cyprus*, judgment of 22 April 1993, Series A no 259).

46. Nor does the Court accept the applicants' submission that no prosecution should have been brought against them since their injuries were not severe and since no medical treatment had been required.

In deciding whether or not to prosecute, the State authorities were entitled to have regard not only to the actual seriousness of the harm caused – which as noted above was considered to be significant – but also, as stated by Lord Jauncey of Tullichettle (see paragraph 21 above), to the potential for harm inherent in the acts in question. In this respect it is recalled that the activities were considered by Lord Templeman to be "unpredictably dangerous" (see paragraph 20 above).

47. The applicants have further submitted that they were singled out partly because of the authorities' bias against homosexuals. They referred to the recent judgment in the Wilson case (see paragraph 30 above), where, in their view, similar behaviour in the context of a heterosexual couple was not considered to deserve criminal punishment.

The Court finds no evidence in support of the applicants' allegations in either the conduct of the proceedings against them or the judgment of the House of Lords. In this respect it recalls the remark of the trial judge when passing sentence that "the unlawful conduct now before the court would be dealt with equally in the prosecution of heterosexuals or bisexuals if carried out by them" (see paragraph 11 above).

Moreover, it is clear from the judgment of the House of Lords that the opinions of the majority were based on the extreme nature of the practices involved and not the sexual proclivities of the applicants (see paragraphs 20 and 21 above).

In any event, like the Court of Appeal, the Court does not consider that the facts in the Wilson case were at all comparable in seriousness to those in the present case (see paragraph 30 above).

48. Accordingly, the Court considers that the reasons given by the national authorities for the measures taken in respect of the applicants were relevant and sufficient for the purposes of art 8 paragraph 2 ...

49. It remains to be ascertained whether these measures were proportionate to the legitimate aim or aims pursued.

The Court notes that the charges of assault were numerous and referred to illegal activities which had taken place over more than ten years. However, only a few charges were selected for inclusion in the prosecution case. It further notes that, in recognition of the fact that the applicants did not appreciate their actions to be criminal, reduced sentences were imposed on appeal (see paragraphs 15–17 above). In these circumstances, bearing in mind the degree of organisation involved in the offences, the measures taken against the applicants cannot be regarded as disproportionate.

50. In sum, the Court finds that the national authorities were entitled to consider that the prosecution and conviction of the applicants were necessary in a democratic society for the protection of health within the meaning of art 8 paragraph 2 of the Convention ...'

Comment

The main question before the Court was to established whether interference by the State was 'necessary in a democratic society' as other requirements of the four-tier test applied by the Court under arts 8–12 of the Convention were satisfied.

The Court held that determination of the tolerable level of harm, where the victim consented, was left to the appreciation of a State and that the justifications provided by the national authorities were relevant and sufficient taking into account that the activities of the applicants involved a significant degree of injury and that the national authorities were entitled to consider not only actual harm but also the potential for more serious injury resulting from the applicants activities.

The Court held that the interference was 'necessary in a democratic society' for the protection of health and it stated that the fact that the sentences were reduced on appeal demonstrated that the interference was not disproportionate.

This case confirms that a State enjoys a large margin of appreciation in matters relating to morality.

Marckx v *Belgium* (1979) 2 EHRR 330 European Court of Human Rights

- *Respect for family life – distinction between legitimate and illegitimate children unjustified – positive obligation of a State to ensure the effective protection of rights guaranteed under the Convention – violation of arts 8 and 14 and Protocol 1(1) by Belgium*

Facts
Under Belgian law, the applicant was deemed to be an illegitimate child and therefore deprived of certain rights. In particular, illegitimate children were described as such on their birth certificates and identified by their mother's name. Such an entry could not be altered after birth.

In addition, the law of succession discriminated against illegitimate children. Both restrictions were challenged as being unlawful interference with family life contrary to art 8 of the Convention.

Held
The law discriminating against illegitimate children was based on a distinction which lacked objective and reasonable justification. Accordingly there was a violation of art 8 and the right to family relationship.

Judgment

'On the manner of establishing Alexandra Marckx's maternal affiliation
Under Belgian law, the maternal affiliation of an "illegitimate" child is established neither by his birth alone nor even by the entry – obligatory under art 57 of the Civil Code – of the mother's name on the birth certificate; arts 334 and 341a require either a voluntary recognition or a court declaration as to maternity. On the other hand, under art 319, the affiliation of a married woman's child is proved simply by the birth certificate recorded at the registry office (see paragraph 14 above).

The applicants see this system as violating, with respect to them, art 8 of the Convention, taken both alone and in conjunction with art 14. This is contested by the Government. The Commission, for its part, finds a breach of art 8, taken both alone and in conjunction with art 14, with respect to Alexandra, and a breach of art 14, taken in conjunction with art 8, with respect to Paula Marckx.

On the alleged violation of art 8 of the Convention, taken alone
Paula Marckx was able to establish Alexandra's affiliation only by the means afforded by art 334 of the Civil Code, namely recognition. The effect of recognition is declaratory and not attributive: it does not create by records the child's status. It is irrevocable and retroactive to the date of birth. Furthermore, the procedure to be followed hardly presents difficulties: the declaration may take the form of a notarial deed, but it may also be added, at any time and without expense, to the record of the birth at the registry office (see paragraph 14 above).

Nevertheless, the necessity to have recourse to such an expedient derived from a refusal to acknowledge fully Paula Marckx's maternity from the moment of the birth. Moreover, in Belgium an unmarried mother is faced with an alternative: if she recognises her child (assuming she wishes to do so), she will at the same time prejudice him since her capacity to give or bequeath her property to him will be restricted; if she desires to retain the possibility of making such dispositions as she chooses in her child's favour, she will be obliged to renounce establishing a family tie with him in law (see paragraph 18 above). Admittedly, that possibility, which is now open to her in the absence of recognition, would disappear entirely under the current Civil Code (art 908) if, as is the applicants' wish, the mere mention of the mother's name on the birth certificate were to constitute proof of any "illegitimate" child's maternal affiliation. However, the dilemma which exists at present is not consonant with "respect" for family life; it thwarts and impedes the normal development of such life (see paragraph 31 above). Furthermore, it appears from paragraph 60 to 65 below that the unfavourable consequences of recognition in the area of patrimonial rights are of themselves contrary to art 14 of the Convention taken in conjunction with art 8 and with art 1 of Protocol No 1.

The Court thus concludes that there has been a violation of art 8 taken alone, with respect to the first applicant.

As regards Alexandra Marckx, only one method of establishing her maternal affiliation was available to her under Belgian law, namely to take legal proceedings for the purpose (recherche de maternite), arts 341a–341c of the Civil Code). Although a judgment declaring the affiliation of an "illegitimate" child has the same effects as a voluntary recognition, the procedure applicable is, in the nature of things, far more complex. Quite apart from the conditions of proof that have to be satisfied, the legal representative of an infant needs the consent of the family council before he can bring, assuming he wishes to do so, an action for a declaration as to status; it is only after attaining majority that the child can bring such an action himself (see paragraph 14 above). There is thus a risk that the establishment of affiliation will be time-consuming and that, in the interim, the child will remain separated in law from his mother. This system resulted in a lack of respect for the family life of Alexandra Marckx who, in the eyes of the law, was motherless from 16 to 29 October 1973. Despite the brevity of this period, there was thus also a violation of art 8 with respect to the second applicant.

On the alleged violation of art 14 of the Convention, taken in conjunction with art 8
The Court also had to determine whether, as regards the manner of establishing Alexandra's maternal affiliation, one or both of the applicants have been victims of discrimination contrary to art 14 taken in conjunction with art 8.

The government, relying on the difference between the situations of the unmarried and the married mother, advance the following arguments: whilst the married mother and her husband "mutually undertake ... the obligation to feed, keep and educate their children" (art 203 of the Civil Code), there is no certainty that the unmarried mother will be willing to bear on her own the responsibilities of motherhood; by leaving the unmarried mother the choice between recognising her child or dissociating herself from him, the law is prompted by a concern for protection of the child, for it would be dangerous to entrust him to the custody and authority of someone who has shown no inclination to care for him; many unmarried mothers do not recognise their child (see paragraph 14 above).

In the Court's judgment, the fact that some unmarried mothers, unlike Paula Marckx, do not wish to take care of their child cannot justify the rule of Belgian law whereby the establishment of their maternity is conditional on voluntary recognition or a court declaration. In fact, such an attitude is not a general feature of the relationship between unmarried mothers and their children; besides, this is neither claimed by the Government nor proved by the figures which they advance. As the Commission points out, it may happen that also a married mother might not wish to bring up her child, and yet, as far as she is concerned, the birth alone will have created the legal bond of affiliation.

Again, the interest of an "illegitimate" child in having such a bond established is no less than that of a "legitimate" child. However, the "illegitimate" child is likely to remain motherless in the eyes of Belgian law. If an "illegitimate" child is not recognised voluntarily, he has only one expedient, namely an action to establish maternal affiliation (arts 341a–341c of the Civil Code; see paragraph 14 above). A married woman's child also is entitled to institute such an action (arts 326–330), but in the vast majority of cases the entries on the birth certificate (art 319) or, failing that, the constant and factual enjoyment of the status of a legitimate child (une possession d'etat constante; art 320 render this unnecessary.

The government do not deny that the present law favours the traditional family but they maintain that the law aims at ensuring that family's full development and is thereby founded on objective and reasonable grounds relating to morals and public order (ordre public).

The Court recognises that support and encouragement of the traditional family is in itself legitimate or even praiseworthy. However, in the achievement of this end recourse must not be had to measures whose object or result is, as in the present case, to prejudice the "illegitimate" family; the members of the "illegitimate" family enjoy the guarantees of art 8 on an equal footing with the members of the traditional family.

The government concede that the law at issue may appear open to criticism but plead that the problem of reforming it arose only several years after the entry into force of the European Convention on Human Rights in respect of Belgium (14 June 1955), that is with the adoption of the Brussels Convention of 12 September 1962 on the Establishment of Maternal Affiliation of Natural Children (see paragraph 20 above).

It is true that, at the time when the Convention of 4 November 1950 was drafted, it was regarded as permissible and normal in many European countries to draw a distinction in this area between the "illegitimate" and the "legitimate" family. However, the Court recalls that this Convention must be interpreted in the light of present-day conditions (*Tyrer*, judgment of 25 April 1978, Series A no 26, p15, paragraph 31). In the instant case, the Court cannot but be struck by the fact that the domestic law of the great majority of the member States of the Council of Europe has evolved and is continuing to evolve, in company with the relevant international instruments, towards full juridical recognition of the maxim "mater semper certa est".

Admittedly, of the ten States that drew up the Brussels Convention, only eight have signed and only four have ratified it to date. The European Convention of 15 October 1975 on the Legal Status of Children born out of Wedlock has at present been signed by only ten and ratified by only four members of the Council of Europe. Furthermore, art 14 paragraph 1 of the latter Convention permits any State to make, at the most, three reservations, one of which could theoretically concern precisely the manner of establishing the maternal affiliation of a child born out of wedlock (art 2).

However, this state of affairs cannot be relied on in opposition to the evolution noted above. Both the relevant Conventions are in force and there is no reason to attribute the currently small number of contracting States to a refusal to admit equality between "illegitimate" and "legitimate" children on the point under consideration. In fact, the existence of these two treaties denotes that there is a clear measure of common ground in this area amongst modern societies.

The official statement of reasons accompanying the Bill submitted by the Belgian government to the Senate on 15 February 1978 (see paragraph 21 above) provides an illustration of this evolution of rules and attitudes. Amongst other things, the statement points out that "in recent years several Western European countries, including the Federal Republic of Germany, Great Britain, the Netherlands, France, Italy and Switzerland, have adopted new legislation radically altering the traditional structure of the law of affiliation and establishing almost complete equality between legitimate and illegitimate children". It is also noted that "the desire to put an end to all discrimination and abolish all inequalities based on birth is ... apparent in the work of various international institutions". As regards Belgium itself, the statement stresses that the difference of treatment between Belgian citizens, depending on whether their affiliation is established in or out of wedlock, amounts to a "flagrant exception" to the fundamental principle of the equality of everyone before the law (art 6 of the Constitution). It adds that "lawyers and public opinion are becoming increasingly convinced that the discrimination against (illegitimate) children should be ended".

The government maintain, finally, that the introduction of the rule "mater semper certa est" should be accompanied, as is contemplated in the 1978 Bill, by a reform of the provisions on the establishment of paternity, failing which there would be a considerable and one-sided increase in the responsibilities of the unmarried mother. Thus, for the government, there is a comprehensive problem and any piecemeal solution would be dangerous.

The Court confines itself to noting that it is required to rule only on certain aspects of the maternal affiliation of "illegitimate" children under Belgian law. It does not exclude that a judgment finding a breach of the Convention on one of those aspects might render desirable or necessary a reform of the law on other matters not submitted for examination in the present proceedings. It is for the respondent State, and the respondent State alone, to take the measures it considered appropriate to ensure that its domestic law is coherent and consistent.

The distinction complained of therefore lacks objective and reasonable justification. Accordingly, the manner of establishing Alexandra Marckx's maternal affiliation violated, with respect to both applicants, art 14 taken in conjunction with art 8.'

Comment

This is one of the landmark decisions of the Court. The Court held that a contracting State had positive obligations under art 8 of the Convention, namely to ensure the effective protection and enjoyment of rights guaranteed under the Convention, which in the present case required abolition of discriminatory laws in force in Belgium. It should be noted that non-interference by the State which results in a disregard of guaranteed rights may amount to violation of art 8 of the Convention.

The Court confirmed that national legislation discriminating against illegitimate children was within the scope of art 8 of the Convention. In order to determine whether the challenged legislation was justified, the Court applied the proportionality test. Even though the objective of the Belgian social policy consisting of encouraging traditional family life was legitimate, the contested legislation was disproportionate since it prejudiced the 'illegitimate' families and therefore violated rights of individuals. The objectives pursued by Belgium could have been achieved by less draconian means.

The decision of the Court should be examined in the context of changing moral values in Europe.

Nowadays one-third of all children born in Europe are illegitimate, many live in uniparental families or multi-parental environments, including partners of their parents and their children. The evolutive interpretation of the Convention permits adjustment of the Strasbourg system to the changing conditions and moral values in contracting States.

It took Belgium eight years to change the contested legislation On 31 March 1987 Belgium enacted national legislation eliminating all discrimination between legitimate and illegitimate children

18 Freedom of Thought, Conscience and Religion: Article 9

Buscarini and Others v San Marino
Judgment of 18 February 1999 (not yet reported) Grand Chamber of the European Court of Human Rights

- *Freedom of conscience and religion – mandatory oath which referred to the gospels for new members of the national Parliament – justification based on national traditions rejected*

Facts
The applicants, nationals of San Marino, were elected to the San Marino Parliament in 1993. There was a procedural rule in s55 of the San Marino Elections Act requiring that before taking their places elected members had to take an oath involving a mandatory reference to the Gospels. The applicants took their oath of office in writing omitting the reference to the Gospels. On 26 July 1993 the Parliament ordered them to retake the oath, this time on the Gospels on threat of losing their seats. The applicants complied with the order of Parliament but claimed the violation of their rights to freedom of religion and conscience protected under art 9 of the Convention.

In October 1993 San Marino Law No 115 changed s55 of the San Marino Elections Act so as to permit Members of Parliament, but not other public servants, to replace the reference to the Gospels by the words 'on my honour'.

Held
The Court held unanimously that San Marino was in breach of art 9 of the Convention.

Judgment
'30. Mr Buscarini and Mr Della Balda submitted that the obligation which the General Grand Council imposed on them on 26 July 1993 demonstrated that in the Republic of San Marino at the material time the exercise of a fundamental political right, such as holding parliamentary office, was subject to publicly professing a particular faith, in breach of art 9.

31. The Commission agreed with that analysis; the government contested it.

32. The government maintained that the wording of the oath in question was not religious but, rather, historical and social in significance and based on tradition. The Republic of San Marino had, admittedly, been founded by a man of religion but it was a secular State in which freedom of religion was expressly enshrined in law (art 4 of the Declaration of Rights of 1974). The form of words in issue had lost its original religious character, as had certain religious feast-days which the State recognised as public holidays.

The act complained of therefore did not amount to a limitation on the applicants' freedom of religion.

33. The applicants and the Commission rejected that assertion.

34. The Court reiterates that, "as enshrined in art 9, freedom of thought, conscience and religion is one of the foundations of a 'democratic society' within the meaning of the Convention. It is, in its religious dimension, one of the most vital elements that go to make up the identity of believers and their conception of life, but it is also a precious asset for atheists, agnostics, sceptics and the unconcerned. The plu-

ralism indissociable from a democratic society, which has been dearly won over the centuries, depends on it" (see *Kokkinakis* v *Greece*, judgment of 25 May 1993, Series A no 260–A, p17, paragraph 31). That freedom entails, inter alia, freedom to hold or not to hold religious beliefs and to practise or not to practise a religion.

In the instant case, requiring Mr Buscarini and Mr Della Balda to take an oath on the Gospels did indeed constitute a limitation within the meaning of the second paragraph of art 9, since it required them to swear allegiance to a particular religion on pain of forfeiting their parliamentary seats. Such interference will be contrary to art 9 unless it is "prescribed by law", pursues one or more of the legitimate aims set out in paragraph 2 and is "necessary in a democratic society".

1. "Prescribed by law"
35. As the Commission noted in its report (paragraph 38), "the interference in question was based on s55 of the Elections Act, Law no 36 of 1958, which referred to the decree of 27 June 1909 laying down the wording of the oath to be sworn by Members of Parliament ...". Therefore, it was "prescribed by law" within the meaning of the second paragraph of art 9 of the Convention. That point was not disputed.

2. Legitimate aim and whether "necessary in a democratic society"
36. The government emphasised the importance, in any democracy, of the oath taken by elected representatives of the people, which, in their view, was a pledge of loyalty to republican values. Regard being had to the special character of San Marino, deriving from its history, traditions and social fabric, the reaffirmation of traditional values represented by the taking of the oath was necessary in order to maintain public order.

The history and traditions of San Marino were linked to Christianity, since the State had been founded by a saint; today, however, the oath's religious significance had been replaced by "the need to preserve public order, in the form of social cohesion and the citizens' trust in their traditional institutions".

It would therefore be inappropriate for the Court to criticise the margin of appreciation which San Marino had to have in this matter.

In any event, the government maintained, the applicants had had no legal interest in pursuing the Strasbourg proceedings since the entry into force of Law no 115 of 29 October 1993 ("Law no 115/1993"), which did not require persons elected to the General Grand Council to take the oath on the Gospels.

37. According to Mr Buscarini and Mr Della Balda, the resolution requiring them to take the oath in issue was in the nature of a "premeditated act of coercion" directed at their freedom of conscience and religion. It aimed to humiliate them as persons who, immediately after being elected, had requested that the wording of the oath should be altered so as to conform with, inter alia, art 9 of the Convention.

38. The Court considers it unnecessary in the present case to determine whether the aims referred to by the government were legitimate within the meaning of the second paragraph of art 9, since the limitation in question is in any event incompatible with that provision in other respects.

39. The Court notes that at the hearing on 10 December 1998 the government sought to demonstrate that the Republic of San Marino guaranteed freedom of religion; in support of that submission they cited its founding Statutes of 1600, its Declaration of Rights of 1974, its ratification of the European Convention in 1989 and a whole array of provisions of criminal law, family law, employment law and education law which prohibited any discrimination on the grounds of religion. It is not in doubt that, in general, San Marinese law guarantees freedom of conscience and religion. In the instant case, however, requiring the applicants to take the oath on the Gospels was tantamount to requiring two elected representatives of the people to swear allegiance to a particular religion, a requirement which is not compatible with art 9.

As the Commission rightly stated in its report, it would be contradictory to make the exercise of a mandate intended to represent different views of society within Parliament subject to a prior declaration of commitment to a particular set of beliefs.

40. The limitation complained of accordingly cannot be regarded as "necessary in a democratic society". As to the government's argument that the application ceased to have any purpose when Law no 115/1993 was enacted, the Court notes that the oath in issue was taken before the passing of that legislation.

41. In the light of the foregoing, there has been a violation of art 9 of the Convention.'

Comment

Judgments under art 9 of the Convention are rare. This case is interesting from two points of view. First, in relation to the parties involved in the dispute. The complaint was lodged by Members of the San Marino Parliament against the government of San Marino. It is certainly unusual to see individuals, who have been elected to a parliamentary body taking proceedings against the State of whose governing body they form part.

Second, the justification of the government based on the history and national traditions of San Marino as being closely linked with Christianity (the Republic had been founded by a saint), was rejected by the Court. The Court held that the Constitution of San Marino enshrines the freedom of conscience and religion and that, as the Commission rightly pointed out, there was a contradiction between the mandatory requirement of an oath referring to a particular religion and the exercise of their parliamentary mandate by San Marino's MPs who represent different views of society and therefore should not be obliged to make commitment to a particular set of beliefs.

19 The Right to Freedom of Expression: Article 10

Handyside v United Kingdom (1976)
1 EHRR 737 European Court of Human Rights

- *Freedom of expression – limitation in the case of obscenity – interference necessary in a democratic society – protection of health – protection of morals – interference prescribed by law – no violation of art 10 – no violation of arts 14 and 18 – no violation of Protocol 1(1)*

Facts
The applicant was convicted of publishing obscene literature, and all materials relating to the publication were seized and subsequently destroyed. The Court was asked whether the statutes under which the applicant was prosecuted were consistent with the right to freedom of expression and whether interference by the national authorities was necessary in a democratic society for the protection of morals.

Held
The Court held that the prosecution had legitimate objectives, namely the protection of the morals of the public and especially the young. In addition, the statute under which the prosecutions had been made had a similarly valid purpose and objective. Therefore, the UK was not in breach of arts 10, 14 and 18 nor of Protocol 1(1).

Judgment
'The Commission's report and the subsequent hearings before the Court in June 1976 brought to light clear-cut differences of opinion on a crucial problem, namely, how to determine whether the actual "restrictions" and "penalties" complained of by the applicant were "necessary in a democratic society", "for the protection of morals". According to the government and the majority of the Commission, the Court has only to ensure that the English courts acted reasonably, in good faith and within the limits of the margin of appreciation left to the Contracting States by art 10 paragraph 2. On the other hand, the minority of the Commission sees the Court's task as being not to review the Inner London Quarter Sessions judgment but to examine the Schoolbook directly in the light of the Convention and of nothing but the Convention.

The Court points out that the machinery of protection established by the Convention is subsidiary to the national systems safeguarding human rights (judgment of 23 July 1968 on the merits of the *"Belgian Linguistic"* case, Series A no 6, p35, paragraph 10 in fine). The Convention leaves to each Contracting State, in the first place, the task of securing the rights and freedoms it enshrines. The institutions created by it make their own contribution to this task but they become involved only through contentious proceedings and once all domestic remedies have been exhausted (art 26).

These observations apply, notably, to art 10 paragraph 2. In particular, it is not possible to find in the domestic law of the various Contracting States a uniform European conception of morals. The view taken by their respective laws of the requirements of morals varies from time to time and from place to place, especially in our era which is characterised by a rapid and far-reaching evolution of opinions on the subject. By reason of their direct and continuous contact with the vital forces of their countries, State authorities are in principle in a better position than the international judge to give an opinion on the exact content of these requirements as well as on the "necessity" of a "restriction" or "penalty" intended to meet them. The Court notes at this juncture that, whilst the adjective "necessary", within the meaning of art 10 paragraph 2, is not synonymous with "indispensable" (cf, in arts 2 paragraph 2 and 6 paragraph 1, the words "absolutely necessary" and "strictly necessary" and, in art 15 paragraph I, the phrase "to the extent strictly required by the exigencies of the situation"), neither has it the flexibility of such expressions as "admissible", "ordinary" (cf art 4 paragraph 3), "useful" (cf the French text of the first paragraph of art 1 of Protocol No 1), "reasonable" (cf arts 5 paragraph 3 and 6 paragraph 1) or "desirable". Nevertheless, it is for the national authorities to make the initial assessment of the reality of the pressing social need implied by the notion of "necessity" in this context.

Consequently, art 10 paragraph 2 leaves to the contracting States a margin of appreciation. This margin is given both to the domestic legislator ("prescribed by law") and to the bodies, judicial amongst others, that are called upon to interpret and apply the laws in force (*Engel and Others*, judgment of 8 June 1976, Series A no 22, pp41–42, paragraph 100; cf, for art 8 paragraph 2, *De Wilde, Ooms and Versyp*, judgment of 18 June 1971, Series A no 12, pp45–46, paragraph 93, and *Golder*, judgment of 21 February 1975, Series A no 18, pp21–22, paragraph 45).

Nevertheless, art 10 paragraph 2 does not give the contracting States an unlimited power of appreciation. The Court, which, with the Commission, is responsible for ensuring the observance of those States' engagements (art 19), is empowered to give the final ruling on whether a "restriction" or "penalty" is reconcilable with freedom of expression as protected by art 10. The domestic margin of appreciation thus goes hand in hand with a European supervision. Such supervision concerns both the aim of the measure challenged and its "necessity"; it covers not only the basic legislation but also the decision applying it, even one given by an independent court. In this respect, the Court refers to art 50 of the Convention ("decision or ... measure taken by a legal authority or any other authority") as well as to its own case-law (*Engel and Others*, judgment of 8 June 1976, Series A no 22, pp41–42, paragraph 100).

The Court's supervisory functions oblige it to pay the utmost attention to the principles characterising a "democratic society". Freedom of expression constitutes one of the essential foundations of such a society, one of the basic conditions for its progress and for the development of every man. Subject to paragraph 2 of art 10, it is applicable not only to "information" or "ideas" that are favourably received or regarded as inoffensive or as a matter of indifference, but also to those that offend, shock or disturb the State or any sector of the population. Such are the demands of that pluralism, tolerance and broadmindedness without which there is no "democratic society". This means, amongst other things, that every "formality", "condition", "restriction" or "penalty" imposed in this sphere must be proportionate to the legitimate aim pursued.

From another standpoint, whoever exercises his freedom of expression undertakes "duties and responsibilities" the scope of which depends on his situation and the technical means he uses. The Court cannot overlook such a person's "duties" and "responsibilities" when it enquires, as in this case, whether "restrictions" or "penalties" were conducive to the "protection of morals" which made them "necessary" in a "democratic society".

It follows from this that it is in no way the Court's task to take the place of the competent national courts but rather to review under art 10 the decisions they delivered in the exercise of their power of appreciation.

However, the Court's supervision would generally prove illusory if it did not more than examine these decisions in isolation; it must view them in the light of the case as a whole, including the publication in question and the arguments and evidence adduced by the applicant in the domestic legal system and then at the international level. The Court must decide, on the basis of the different data available to it, whether the reasons given by the national authorities to justify the actual measures of "interference" they take are relevant and sufficient under art 10 paragraph 2 (cf, for art 5 paragraph 3, *Wemhoff*, judgment of 27 June 1968, Series A no 7, pp24–25, paragraph 12, *Neumeister*, judgment of 27 June 1968, Series A no 8, p37, paragraph 5, *Stögmüller*, judgment of 10 November 1969, Series A no 9, p39, paragraph 3, *Matznetter*, judgment of 10 November 1969, Series A no 10, p31, paragraph 3, and *Ringeisen*, judgment of 16 July 1971, Series A no 13, p42, paragraph 104).

Following the method set out above, the Court scrutinised under art 10 paragraph 2 the individual decisions complained of, in particular, the judgment of the Inner London Quarter Sessions.

The Court reviewed the said judgment in the light of the case as a whole; in addition to the pleadings before the Court and the Commission's report, the memorials and oral explanations presented to the Commission between June 1973 and August 1974 and the transcript of the proceedings before the Quarter Sessions were, *inter alia,* taken into consideration.

The Court attaches particular importance to a factor to which the judgment of 29 October 1971 did not fail to draw attention, that is, the intended readership of the Schoolbook. It was aimed above all at children and adolescents aged from twelve to eighteen. Being direct, factual and reduced to essentials in style, it was easily within the comprehension of even the youngest of such readers. The applicant had made it clear that he planned a wide-spread circulation. He had sent the book, with a press release, to numerous daily papers and periodicals for review or for advertising purposes. What is more, he had set a modest sale price (thirty pence), arranged for a reprint of 50,000 copies shortly after the first impression of 20,000 and chosen a title suggesting that the work was some kind of handbook for use in schools.

Basically the book contained purely factual information that was generally correct and often useful, as the Quarter Sessions recognised. However, it also included, above all in the section on sex and in the passage headed "Be yourself" in the chapter on pupils, sentences or paragraphs that young people at a critical stage of their development could have interpreted as an encouragement to indulge in precocious activities harmful for them or even to commit certain criminal offences. In these circumstances, despite the variety and the constant evolution in the United Kingdom of views on ethics and education, the competent English judges were entitled, in the exercise of their discretion, to think at the relevant time that the Schoolbook would have pernicious effects on the morals of many of the children and adolescents who would read it.

However, the applicant maintained, in substance, that the demands of the "protection of morals" or, to use the wording of the 1959/1964 Acts, of the war against publications likely to "deprave and corrupt", were but a pretext in his case. The truth of the matter, he alleged, was that an attempt had been made to muzzle a small-scale publisher whose political learnings met with the disapproval of a fragment of public opinion. Proceedings were set in motion, said he, in an atmosphere little short of "hysteria", stirred up and kept alive by ultra-conservative elements. The accent in the judgment of 29 October 1971 on the anti-authoritarian aspects of the Schoolbook showed, according to the applicant, exactly what lay behind the case.

The information supplied by Mr Handyside seems, in fact, to show that letters from members of the public, articles in the press and action by Members of Parliament were not without some influence in the decision to seize the Schoolbook and to take criminal proceedings against its publisher. However, the government drew attention to the fact that such initiatives could well have been explained not by some dark plot but by the genuine emotion felt by citizens faithful to traditional moral values when, towards the end of March 1971, they read in certain newspapers extracts from the book which was due to appear on 1 April. The Government also emphasised that the proceedings ended several months after the "campaign" denounced by the applicant and that he did not claim that it had continued in the intervening period. From this the Government concluded that the "campaign" in no way impaired dispassionate deliberation at the Quarter Sessions.

For its part the Court finds that the anti-authoritarian aspects of the Schoolbook as such were not held in the judgment of 29 October 1971 to fall foul of the 1959/1964 Acts. Those aspects were taken into account only insofar as the appeal court considered that, by undermining the moderating influence of parents, teachers, the Churches and youth organisations, they aggravated the tendency to "deprave and corrupt" which in its opinion resulted from other parts of the work. It should be added that the revised edition was allowed to circulate freely by the British authorities despite the fact that the anti-authoritarian passages again appeared there in full and even, in some cases, in stronger terms. As the Government noted, this is hard to reconcile with the theory of a political intrigue.

The Court thus allows that the fundamental aim of the judgment of 29 October 1971, applying the 1959/1964 Acts, was the protection of the morals of the young, a legitimate purpose under art 10 paragraph 2. Consequently the seizures effected on 31 March and 1 April 1971, pending the outcome of the proceedings that were about to open, also had this aim.'

Comment
The Court held that the right to freedom of expression is fundamental in a democratic society. The Court stated that the main features of a democratic society are pluralism, tolerance and broad-mindness.

The right to freedom of expression applies to all types of expression including, subject to art 10(2), information and ideas that 'offend, shock or disturb' the State or some sector of the population. Under art 10(2) of the Convention a State enjoys a wide margin of discretion in deciding what is necessary to protect morals. Therefore, initially a State assesses the reality of the pressing social need for its interference. Nevertheless, a State's power of appreciation is not unlimited as the Court is entitled to review a State's power of appreciation in the light of the case as a whole, including the publication itself, the arguments and evidence submitted by the applicant and the international law relevant to the case at issue, in particular art 19 of the UN International Covenant on Civil and Political Rights which ensures the respect of the right to freedom of expression in much stronger terms than those of art 10 of the Convention.

The Sunday Times v *United Kingdom* (1980) 3 EHRR 317
European Court of Human Rights

• *Freedom of expression – interference prescribed by law – the authority and impartiality of the judiciary – measures not necessary in a democratic society – protection of the rights and freedoms of others – violation of art 10 of the Convention*

Facts
The Sunday Times intended to publish a series of articles exposing the danger of the drug thalidomide. An injunction was granted by the Divisional Court and upheld by the House of Lords which prevented publication of further material on the subject. The newspaper complained that the injunction was an interference with the right to freedom of expression for which the United Kingdom was responsible as the authority who permitted the granting of such an order.

Held

The Court held that granting the injunction was an interference with the right of freedom of expression.

Judgment

'Was the interference "prescribed by law"?
... In the Court's opinion, the following are two of the requirements that flow from the expression "prescribed by law". Firstly, the law must be adequately accessible: the citizen must be able to have an indication that is adequate in the circumstances of the legal rules applicable to a given case. Secondly, a norm cannot be regarded as a "law" unless it is formulated with sufficient precision to enable the citizen to regulate his conduct: he must be able – if need be with appropriate advice – to foresee, to a degree that is reasonable in the circumstances, the consequences which a given action may entail. Those consequences need not be foreseeable with absolute certainty: experience shows this to be unattainable. Again, whilst certainty is highly desirable, it may bring in its train excessive rigidity and the law must be able to keep pace with changing circumstances. Accordingly, many laws are inevitably couched in terms which, to a greater or lesser extent, are vague and whose interpretation and application are questions of practice.

In the present case, the question whether these requirements of accessibility and foreseeability were satisfied is complicated by the fact that different principles were relied on by the various Law Lords concerned. The Divisional Court had applied the principle that a deliberate attempt to influence the settlement of pending proceedings by bringing public pressure to bear on a party constitutes contempt of court (the "pressure principle"). Certain members of the House of Lords also alluded to this principle whereas others preferred the principle that it is contempt of court to publish material which prejudges, or is likely to cause public prejudgment of, the issues raised in pending litigation (the "prejudgment principle").

The applicants do not claim to have been without an indication that was adequate in the circumstances of the "pressure principle". Indeed, the existence of this principle had been recognised by counsel for Times Newspapers Ltd who is reported as saying before the Divisional Court: "Even if it applies pressure to a party, the article is not contempt at all because (the higher public interest) overcomes any question of wrongdoing. Alternatively, if the article is prima facia contempt, the higher public interest provides a defence against what would otherwise be contempt." Again, Lord Justice Phillimore in the Court of Appeal referred to "the mass of authority ... showing that an attempt to stir up public feeling against a party is a serious contempt".

The Court also considers that there can be no doubt that the "pressure principle" was formulated with sufficient precision to enable the applicants to foresee to the appropriate degree the consequences which publication of the draft article might entail. In *Vine Products Ltd v Green* [1966] Ch 484 at p495, Mr Justice Buckley had formulated the law in this way: "It is a contempt of this court for any newspaper to comment on pending legal proceedings in any way which is likely to prejudice the fair trial of the action. That may arise in various ways. It may be that the comment is one which is likely in some way or other to bring pressure to bear upon one or other of the parties to the action, so as to prevent that party from prosecuting or from defending the action, or encourage that party to submit to terms of compromise which he otherwise might not have been prepared to entertain, or influence him in some other way in his conduct in the action, which he ought to be free to prosecute or to defend, as he is advised, without being subject to such pressure."

The applicants contend, on the other hand, that the prejudgment principle was novel and that they therefore could not have had an adequate indication of its existence. Support for this view is to be found in several authorities cited by the applicants, including the Phillimore report which stated that the House of Lords "formulated a rather different test". Nevertheless, the Court has also noted the following:

- in the applicants' memorial it is submitted; "the 'prejudgment principle' as applied by the House of Lords to the facts of the present case has never before constituted the 'ratio' of an English judicial decision *in a comparable case*" (emphasis added);
- In 1969 the Interdepartmental Committee on the Law of Contempt as it affects Tribunals of Inquiry stated in paragraph 26 of its report: "There is no reported case of anyone being found guilty of contempt of court in respect of comment made about the subject matter of a trial before a judge alone ... There are however dicta which support the view that such comment may amount to contempt";
- the third edition of *Halsbury's Laws of England* (vol 8, pp7 et seq, paragraphs 11–13) contains the following passages which are accompanied by references to previous case-law: "... writings ... prejudicing the public for or against a party are contempts ... there (is nothing) of more pernicious consequence than to prejudice the minds of the public against persons concerned as parties in causes before the cause is finally heard ... It is a contempt to publish an article in a newspaper commenting on the proceedings in a pending ... civil action ... In such cases the mischievous tendency of a trial by the newspapers when a trial by one of the regular tribunals of the country is going on is to be considered ... On the other hand, the summary jurisdiction (to punish contempt) ought only to be exercised when it is probable that the publication will substantially interfere with a fair trial."

As regards the formulation of the "prejudgment principle", the Court notes that reference was made in the House of Lords to various authorities and, in particular, to *Hunt* v *Clarke* (1889), where Lord Justice Cotton had stated the law in this way: "If any one discusses in a paper the rights of a case or the evidence to be given before the case comes on, that, in my opinion, would be a very serious attempt to interfere with the proper administration of justice. It is not necessary that the court should come to the conclusion that a judge or a jury will be prejudiced, but if it is calculated to prejudice the proper trial of a cause, that is a contempt, and would be met with the necessary punishment in order to restrain such conduct." Moreover, the editor of *The Sunday Times* said in his affidavit filed in the Divisional Court proceedings: "... I was given legal advice that the (proposed) article ... was in a category different from that of the articles published hitherto in that in addition to presenting information which strengthened the moral argument for a fairer settlement it included evidence which related to the issue of liability in the pending thalidomide proceedings."

To sum up, the Court does not consider that the applicants were without an indication that was adequate in the circumstances of the existence of the "prejudgment principle". Even if the Court does have certain doubts concerning the precision with which that principle was formulated at the relevant time, it considers that the applicants were able to foresee to a degree that was reasonable in the circumstances, a risk that publication of the draft article might fall foul of the principle.

The interference with the applicants' freedom of expression was thus "prescribed by law" within the meaning of art 10 paragraph 2.

Did the interference have aims that are legitimate under art 10 paragraph 2?
In the view of the applicants, the Government and the minority of the Commission, the law of contempt of court serves the purpose of safeguarding not only the impartiality and authority of the judiciary but also the rights and interests of litigants.

The majority of the Commission, on the other hand, whilst accepting that the law of contempt has the general aim of securing the fair administration of justice and that it thereby seeks to achieve purposes similar to those envisaged in art 10 paragraph 2 where it speaks of maintaining the authority and impartiality of the judiciary, considered that it was not called upon to examine separately whether that law has the further purpose of protecting the rights of others.

The Court first emphasises that the expression "authority and impartiality of the judiciary" has to be understood "within the meaning of the Convention" (see, mutatis mutandis, *Konig*, judgment of 28 June 1987, Series A no 27, pp29–30, paragraph 88). For this purpose, account must be taken of the central position occupied in this context by art 6 which reflects the fundamental principle of the rule of law (see, for example, *Golder*, judgment of 21 February 1975, Series A no 18, p17, paragraph 34).

The term "judiciary" ("pouvoir judiciaire") comprises the machinery of justice or the judicial branch of government as well as the judges in their official capacity. The phrase "authority of the judiciary" includes, in particular, the notion that the courts are, and are accepted by the public at large as being, the proper form for the ascertainment of legal rights and obligations and the settlement of disputes relative thereto; further, that the public at large have respect for and confidence in the courts' capacity to fulfil that function.

It suffices, in this context, to adopt the description of the general purpose of the law of contempt given by the Phillimore report. As can be seen from paragraph 18 above, the majority of the categories of conduct covered by the law of contempt relate either to the position of the judges or to the functioning of the courts and of the machinery of justice: "maintaining the authority and impartiality of the judiciary" is therefore one purpose of that law.

In the present case, the Court shares the view of the majority of the Commission that, insofar as the law of contempt may serve to protect the rights of litigants, this purpose is already included in the phrase "maintaining the authority and impartiality of the judiciary": the rights so protected are the rights of individuals in their capacity as litigants, that is as persons involved in the machinery of justice, and the authority of that machinery will not be maintained unless protection is afforded to all those involved in or having recourse to it. It is therefore not necessary to consider as a separate issue whether the law of contempt has the further purpose of safeguarding "the rights of others".

It remains to be examined whether the aim of the interference with the applicants' freedom of expression was the maintenance of the authority and impartiality of the judiciary.

None of the Law Lords concerned based his decision on the ground that the proposed article might have an influence on the "impartiality" of the judiciary. This ground was also not pleaded before the Court and can be left out of account.

The reasons why the draft article was regarded as objectionable by the House of Lords may be briefly summarised as follows:

- by "prejudicing" the issue of negligence, it would have led to disrespect for the processes of the law or interfered with the administration of justice;
- it was a kind that would expose Distillers to public and prejudicial discussion of the merits of their case, such exposure being objectionable as it inhibits suitors generally from having recourse to the courts;
- it would subject Distillers to pressure and to the prejudicies of prejudgment of the issues in the litigation and the law of contempt was designed to prevent interference with recourse to the courts;
- prejudgment by the press would have led inevitably in this case to replies by the parties, thereby creating the danger of a "trial by newspaper" incompatible with the proper administration of justice;
- the courts owe it to the parties to protect them from the prejudices of prejudgment which involves their having to participate in the flurries of pre-trial publicity.

The Court regards all these various reasons as falling within the aim of maintaining the "authority ... of the judiciary" as interpreted by the Court in the second sub-paragraph of paragraph 55 above.

Accordingly, the interference with the applicants' freedom of expression had an aim that is legitimate under art 10 paragraph 2.'

Comment

The Court examined the scope of the margin of appreciation enjoyed by a State. The margin of appreciation is wider in matters relating to morality, taking into account that the requirements of morals vary according to the time and place and, therefore, the national authorities are in a better position than the Court to assess the content of these requirements. However, in relation to more objective concepts such as the 'authority of judiciary', which is more or less the same in all contracting States, a State has a lesser power of appreciation and the Court supervision is more extensive.

The Court emphasised the importance of free press in a democratic society. It is incumbent on the press to impart information as the public has a right to receive it.

The Court held that the interference of the UK was disproportionate, taking into account that the publication was a well balanced reporting of the thalidomide tragedy, that there was substantial legitimate public interest in the case, and that the public had the right to be properly informed.

The Court examined the requirement imposed by art 10(2) of the Convention that the interference must be prescribed by public law, which means that it must be based on domestic law. This was necessary as the Court was faced which the common law rule on contempt of court, in particular whether the article should be considered as a prejudgment of an issue before the domestic court (see above).

It is interesting that the Court found the House of Lords in breach of art 10 of the Convention. The Law Lords unanimously although for different reasons upheld the injunction.

As a result of the judgment the UK changed its law on contempt of court. Contempt of court is now governed by the Contempt of Court Act of 27 July 1981.

20 The Right of Association with Others: Article 11

Socialist Party and Others v Turkey
Judgment of 25 May 1998 (not yet reported) Grand Chamber of the European Court of Human Rights

• *Right of association – includes political parties – dissolution of Turkish Socialist Party by the Constitutional Court of Turkey – non-compliance of Turkey with art 11 – dissolution not necessary in a democratic society – measure disproportionate*

Facts

When the Socialist Party of Turkey (SP) was set up on 1 February 1988 its constitution and programme were submitted to the Office of Principal State Counsel at the Court of Cassation for determination of their compatibility with the Turkish constitution and Law 2820 concerning the regulation of political parties. Two weeks later the Office of Principal State Counsel applied to the Turkish Constitutional Court for an order dissolving the SP on the ground that its programme was contrary to the Turkish constitution as it sought to establish a dictatorship of the proletariat. The Constitutional Court dismissed the application. In response, the Turkish authorities brought criminal proceedings before the National Security Court against leaders of the SP, including Mr Perinçek based on art 142 (of the Criminal Code) prohibiting Marxist-Leninist activities. Mr Perinçek was accused of spreading harmful propaganda concerning the establishment of domination of the working class evidenced by his speeches before his election as Chairman of the SP. All accused were acquitted when art 142 of the Criminal Code was repealed (see *Hazar, Hazar and Acik v Turkey* Nos 16311-16313/90 (1992) 72 DR 200.

On 26 August 1991 the High Electoral Committee in charge of supervision of national elections decided that SP satisfied all requirements necessary to participate in the general election of 20 October 1991. Consequently, the SP ran an election campaign.

On 14 November 1991 the office of the Principal State Counsel applied to the Constitutional Court for a second time seeking an order dissolving the SP on the ground that the party carried out activities likely to undermine the territorial integrity of Turkey and the unity of the nation contrary to the Turkish constitution. The application was based on statements made by Mr Perinçek in which he stated that the Kurdish problem should be resolved by peaceful means with respect to the principles of democracy and freedom. He also recognised the right of Kurdish people to self-determination and advocated the creation of a federal State in Turkey guaranteeing equal right for Kurds and Turks.

The Constitutional Court dissolved the SP on 10 July 1992. This measure entailed ipso jure the liquidation of the SP and the transfer of its assets to the Treasury. The Constitutional Court decided that statements made by Mr Perinçek bound his party and that there was no contradiction between the dismissal of the first application for an order dissolving the SP and its present decision because, first, this case was based on different facts and, second, the repeal of art 142 of the Criminal Code did not mean that similar conduct no longer constituted a valid ground for dissolution under Law 2820 regulating activities of political parties in Turkey.

Held

The court unanimously held Turkey in breach of art 11 of the Convention.

Judgment

'Alleged violation of art 11 of the Convention

41. The Court reiterates that notwithstanding its autonomous role and particular sphere of application, art 11 must also be considered in the light of art 10. The protection of opinions and the freedom to express them is one of the objectives of the freedoms of assembly and association as enshrined in art 11. That applies all the more in relation to political parties in view of their essential role in ensuring pluralism and the proper functioning of democracy.

As the Court has emphasised many times, there can be no democracy without pluralism. It is for that reason that freedom of expression as enshrined in art 10 is applicable, subject to paragraph 2, not only to "information" or "ideas" that are favourably received or regarded as inoffensive or as a matter of indifference, but also to those that offend, shock or disturb. The fact that their activities form part of a collective exercise of freedom of expression in itself entitles political parties to seek the protection of arts 10 and 11 of the Convention (see, among other authorities, *United Communist Party of Turkey and Others*, judgment cited above [*Reports of Judgments and Decisions* 1998–I, p17], pp20–21, paragraphs 42–43).

42. In the instant case it must first be noted that in its judgment of 10 July 1992 the Constitutional Court held that on that occasion it no longer had to consider whether the SP's programme and constitution were lawful, but only whether its political activities contravened the statutory prohibitions. In dissolving the party, the Constitutional Court had had regard to public statements – some of them in written form – made by Mr Perinçek which it considered to constitute new facts and evidence that were binding on the SP (see paragraph 15 above). Consequently, the Court may confine itself to examining those statements.

43. The Constitutional Court noted that, by distinguishing two nations –the Kurdish nation and the Turkish nation – Mr Perinçek had advocated the creation of minorities within Turkey and, ultimately, the establishment of a Kurdish-Turkish federation, to the detriment of the unity of the Turkish nation and the territorial integrity of the State. The SP was ideologically opposed to the nationalism of Atatürk, which was the most fundamental principle underpinning the Republic of Turkey. Although different methods were used, the aim of the SP's political activity was similar to that of terrorist organisations. As the SP promoted separatism and revolt its dissolution was justified (see paragraph 15 above).

44. In the light of these factors, the Court must firstly consider the content of the statements in issue and then determine whether they justified the dissolution of the SP.

With regard to the first issue the Court reiterates that when it carries out its scrutiny, its task is not to substitute its own view for that of the relevant national authorities but rather to review under art 11 the decisions they delivered in the exercise of their discretion. In so doing, the Court has to satisfy itself that the national authorities based their decisions on an acceptable assessment of the relevant facts (see, mutatis mutandis, the *United Communist Party of Turkey and Others* judgment cited above, p22, paragraph 47).

45. Further, the Court has previously held that one of the principal characteristics of democracy is the possibility it offers of resolving a country's problems through dialogue, without recourse to violence, even when they are irksome. Democracy thrives on freedom of expression. From that point of view, there can be no justification for hindering a political group solely because it seeks to debate in public the situation of part of the State's population and to take part in the nation's political life in order to find, according to democratic rules, solutions capable of satisfying everyone concerned

(see the *United Communist Party of Turkey and Others* judgment cited above, p27, paragraph 57).

46. Having analysed Mr Perinçek's statements, the Court finds nothing in them that can be considered a call for the use of violence, an uprising or any other form of rejection of democratic principles. On the contrary, he stressed on a number of occasions the need to achieve the proposed political reform in accordance with democratic rules, through the ballot box and by holding referenda. At the same time, he spoke out against 'the former culture idolising violence and advocating the use of force to solve problems between nations and in society' (see paragraph 13 above).

At the hearing the Agent for the Government stated that Mr Perinçek had "justified the use of violent and terrorist methods" by saying in particular: "The Kurd has proved himself through the fight of impoverished peasants by linking its destiny [to theirs]. By holding meetings with thousands of people in the towns and provinces, the Kurd had proved himself and broken down the barriers of fear." Furthermore, by calling on those present to "sow courage, rather than watermelons", Mr Perinçek had, in the Government's submission, "exhorted them to stop all activities other than the destruction of order". Lastly, by using the phrase "The Kurdish people are standing up" he had called upon them to revolt.

While the Court accepts that these phrases were directed at citizens of Kurdish origin and constituted an invitation to them to rally together and assert certain political claims, it finds no trace of any incitement to use violence or infringe the rules of democracy. In that regard, the relevant statements were scarcely any different from those made by other political groups that were active in other countries of the Council of Europe.

47. The Constitutional Court had also criticised Mr Perinçek for having drawn a distinction between two nations, the Kurdish nation and the Turkish nation, in his speeches and of thereby pleading in favour of creating minorities and the establishment of a Kurdish-Turkish federation, to the detriment of the unity of the Turkish nation and the territorial integrity of the State. Ultimately, the SP had advocated separatism.

The Court notes that, read together, the statements put forward a political programme with the essential aim being the establishment, in accordance with democratic rules, of a federal system in which Turks and Kurds would be represented on an equal footing and on a voluntary basis. Admittedly, reference is made to the right to self-determination of the "Kurdish nation" and its right to "secede"; however, read in their context, the statements using these words do not encourage secession from Turkey but seek rather to stress that the proposed federal system could not come about without the Kurds' freely given consent, which should be expressed through a referendum.

In the Court's view, the fact that such a political programme is considered incompatible with the current principles and structures of the Turkish State does not make it incompatible with the rules of democracy. It is of the essence of democracy to allow diverse political programmes to be proposed and debated, even those that call into question the way a State is currently organised, provided that they do not harm democracy itself.

48. It is true here too that, as was the case with the TBKP (see the *United Communist Party of Turkey and Others* judgment cited above, p27, paragraph 58), it cannot be ruled out that the statements in issue concealed objectives and intentions different from the ones proclaimed in public. In the absence of concrete actions belying Mr Perinçek's sincerity in what he said, however, that sincerity should not be doubted. The SP was thus penalised for conduct relating solely to the exercise of freedom of expression.

49. The Court also notes that Mr Perinçek was acquitted in the National Security Courts where he had been prosecuted in respect of the same statements (see paragraph 11 above). In that connection the government stressed that the two types of proceedings were entirely different, one con-

cerning the application of criminal law, the other the application of constitutional law. The Court merely notes that the Turkish courts had divergent views as to the effect of Mr Perinçek's statements.

It is now important to determine whether, in the light of the above considerations, the SP's dissolution can be considered to have been necessary in a democratic society, that is to say whether it met a 'pressing social need' and was 'proportionate to the legitimate aim pursued' (see, among many other authorities and mutatis mutandis, *Vogt v Germany*, judgment of 26 September 1995, Series A no 323, pp25–26, paragraph 52).

50. The Court reiterates that, having regard to the essential role of political parties in the proper functioning of democracy (see the *United Communist Party of Turkey and Others* judgment cited above, p17, paragraph 25), the exceptions set out in art 11 are, where political parties are concerned, to be construed strictly; only convincing and compelling reasons can justify restrictions on such parties' freedom of association. In determining whether a necessity within the meaning of art 11 paragraph 2 exists, the contracting States have only a limited margin of appreciation, which goes hand in hand with rigorous European supervision embracing both the law and the decisions applying it, including those given by independent courts (see the *United Communist Party of Turkey and Others* judgment cited above, p22, paragraph 46).

51. The Court observes that the interference in question was radical: the SP was dissolved with immediate and permanent effect, its assets were liquidated and transferred ipso jure to the Treasury and its leaders – who admittedly did not include Mr Perinçek when the party was dissolved (see paragraph 14 above) – were banned from carrying on certain similar political activities. Measures as severe as those may only be applied in the most serious cases.

52. The Court has already noted that Mr Perinçek's statements, though critical and full of demands, did not appear to it to call into question the need for compliance with democratic principles and rules.

The Court is prepared to take into account the background of cases before it, in particular the difficulties associated with the prevention of terrorism (see, among other authorities, the *United Communist Party of Turkey and Others* judgment cited above, p27, paragraph 59). In the present case, however, it has not been established how, in spite of the fact that in making them their author declared attachment to democracy and expressed rejection of violence, the statements in issue could be considered to have been in any way responsible for the problems which terrorism poses in Turkey.

53. In view of the findings referred to above, there is no need either to bring art 17 into play, as nothing in the statements warrants the conclusion that their author relied on the Convention to engage in activity or perform acts aimed at the destruction of any of the rights and freedoms set forth in it (see, mutatis mutandis, the *United Communist Party of Turkey and Others* judgment cited above, p.7, paragraph 60).

54. In conclusion, the dissolution of the SP was disproportionate to the aim pursued and consequently unnecessary in a democratic society. It follows that there has been a violation of art 11 of the Convention.'

Comment

The Court confirmed its earlier judgments recognising political parties as a form of association necessary to ensure the proper functioning of democracy (*KPD v FRG* No 250/57, 1 YB 222 (1957) (*German Communist Party Case*)), and confirmed its then recent decision of 30 January 1998 in the *United Communist Party of Turkey and Others v Turkey*. The Court held that political parties are not only protected under art 11 of the Convention but they constitute the most important form of association. The Court emphasised that a political party cannot be excluded from the protection of art 11 simply because its activities are regarded by national authorities as undermining the constitutional structure of the State.

The Court examined the compliance of the dissolution order with art 11. The Court applied the usual four-tier test: first, it stated that there was interference by the State authorities with the right to association of the applicants; second, it found that the interference was 'prescribed by law'; third, that it pursued at least one legitimate aim set out in art 11, that is the protection of national security.

The fourth requirement was whether the interference was 'necessary in a democratic society'. Here the Court emphasised that the assessment of the political programme of the SP as contrary to the Turkish constitution did not make it incompatible with the rules of democracy, the essence of which is the existence of plurality of political programmes, including those that challenge the current structure of a State, provided they do not harm democracy and are pursued by peaceful means. The Court held that a State has a limited margin of appreciation under art 11(2) of the Convention and therefore only convincing and compelling reasons can justify restrictions imposed by a State on such party's freedom. That was not the case here as measures applied by the Turkish government were disproportionate and consequently unnecessary in a democratic society.

21 The Right to Marry: Article 12

Sheffield and Horsham v United Kingdom (1998) 27 EHRR 163
European Court of Human Rights

- *Post-operative transsexuals – no obligation for a State to recognise for legal purposes new sexual identities of applicants*

Facts

The applicants, Miss Kristina Sheffield and Miss Rachel Horsham, born in the UK, were registered at birth as being of the male sex. Both underwent gender re-assignment surgery. They claimed that the UK was in breach of arts 8, 12, 13 and 14 of the Convention as the UK failed to recognise in law, in particular by amending or updating the register of birth, the change of their gender.

Miss Sheffield, residing in London, was previously married and had a daughter from that marriage. Before her gender re-assignment operation she was required to obtain a divorce. After the operation her former spouse applied to the court to terminate all contacts between Miss Sheffield and her daughter as being contrary to the child's interest. The application was granted. As a result the applicant had not seen her daughter for a period of 12 years. Also, on a number of occasions the applicant had to reveal her previous gender as registered in the birth certificate which caused her deep distress and embarrassment.

Miss Horsham, a holder of dual nationality (British and Dutch), claimed that she had to live in exile in The Netherlands and had been prevented from marrying her male partner because of the refusal of the UK to change her gender in the register of birth. Miss Horsham after her gender re-assignment surgery, under an order granted by the Amsterdam Regional Court, was issued with a birth certificate showing her new name and sex. Under Dutch law she can marry her male partner. She claimed that on her return to the UK her marriage would be nullified and she would be subject to distress and public humiliation because of the refusal of the UK to update her birth certificate.

Held

The Court held (11 votes to nine) that the United Kingdom had not violated the Convention. The Court also held by a majority of 18 votes to two, in relation to the application of Miss Horsham, that the UK had not violated art 12 of the Convention.

Judgment

'*Alleged violation of art 8 of the Convention*

The Commission

49. The Commission considered that the applicants, even if they do not suffer daily humiliation and embarrassment, are nevertheless subject to a real and continuous risk of intrusive and distressing enquiries and to an obligation to make embarrassing disclosures. Miss Sheffield's case showed that this risk was not theoretical.

50. The Commission had regard in particular to the clear trend in European legal systems towards legal acknowledgment of gender reassignment. It also found it significant that the medical profession has reached a consensus that transsexualism is an identifiable medical condition, gender dysphoria, in respect of which gender reassignment treatment is ethically permissible and can be recommended for improving the quality of life and, moreover, is State-funded in certain Member States. In view of these developments, the Government's

concerns about the difficulties in assimilating the phenomenon of transsexualism readily into existing legal frameworks cannot be of decisive weight. In the view of the Commission, appropriate ways could be found to provide for transsexuals to be given prospective legal recognition of their gender reassignment without destroying the historical nature of the register of births. The Commission considered that the concerns put forward by the government, even having regard to their margin of appreciation in this area, were not sufficient to outweigh the interests of the applicants and for that reason there had been a violation of art 8 of the Convention.

2. *The Court's assessment*

51. The Court observes that it is common ground that the applicants' complaints fall to be considered from the standpoint of whether or not the respondent State has failed to comply with a positive obligation to ensure respect for their rights to respect for their private lives. It has not been contended that the failure of the authorities to afford them recognition for legal purposes, in particular by altering the register of births to reflect their new gender status or issuing them with birth certificates whose contents and nature differ from the entries made at the time of their birth, constitutes an 'interference'.

Accordingly, as in the above-mentioned *Rees* and *Cossey* cases [*Rees* v *UK* (1987) 9 EHRR 56; *Cossey* v *UK* (1991) 13 EHRR 622], the issue raised by the applicants before the Court is not that the respondent State should abstain from acting to their detriment but that it has failed to take positive steps to modify a system which they claim operates to their prejudice. The Court will therefore proceed on that basis.

52. The Court reiterates that the notion of "respect" is not clear-cut, especially as far as the positive obligations inherent in that concept are concerned: having regard to the diversity of the practices followed and the situations obtaining in the contracting States, the notion's requirements will vary considerably from case to case. In determining whether or not a positive obligation exists, regard must be had to the fair balance that has to be struck between the general interest of the community and the interests of the individual, the search for which balance is inherent in the whole of the Convention (see the above-mentioned *Rees* judgment, p15, paragraph 37; and the above-mentioned *Cossey* judgment, p15, paragraph 37).

53. It is to be noted that in applying the above principle in both the *Rees* and *Cossey* cases, the Court concluded that the same respondent State was under no positive obligation to modify its system of birth registration in order to allow those applicants the right to have the register of births updated or annotated to record their new sexual identities or to provide them with a copy birth certificate or a short-form certificate excluding any reference to sex at all or sex at the time of birth.

Although the applicants in the instant case have formulated their complaints in terms which are wider than those invoked by Mr Rees and Miss Cossey since they contend that their rights under art 8 of the Convention have been violated on account of the failure of the respondent State to recognise for legal purposes generally their post-operative gender, it is nonetheless the case that the essence of their complaints concerns the continuing insistence by the authorities on the determination of gender according to biological criteria alone and the immutability of the gender information once it is entered on the register of births.

54. The government have relied in continuing defence of the current system of births registration on the general interest grounds which were accepted by the Court in its *Rees* and *Cossey* judgments as justification for preserving the register of births as a historical record of facts subject neither to alteration so as to record an entrant's change of sex nor to abridgement in the form of an extract containing no indication of the bearer's registered gender (see, in particular, the *Cossey* judgment, pp15–16, paragraphs 38 and 39), as well as to the wide margin of appreciation which they claim in respect of the treatment to be accorded in law to post-

operative transsexuals. It is the applicants' contention that that defence is no longer tenable having regard to significant scientific and legal developments and to the clear detriment which the maintenance in force of the current system has on their personal situation, factors which, in their view, tilt the balance away from public-interest considerations in favour of the need to take action to safeguard their own individual interests.

55. The Court notes that in its *Cossey* judgment it considered that there had been no noteworthy scientific developments in the area of transsexualism in the period since the date of adoption of its *Rees* judgment which would compel it to depart from the decision reached in the latter case. This view was confirmed subsequently in ... *B v France*, judgment of 25 March 1992 (Series A no 232–C) in which it observed that there still remained uncertainty as to the essential nature of transsexualism and that the legitimacy of surgical intervention in such cases is sometimes questioned (p49, paragraph 48). As to legal developments occurring since the date of the *Cossey* judgment, the Court in the *B* case stated that there was, as yet, no sufficiently broad consensus among the member States on how to deal with a range of complex legal matters resulting from a change of sex.

56. In the view of the Court, the applicants have not shown that since the date of adoption of its *Cossey* judgment in 1990 there have been any findings in the area of medical science which settle conclusively the doubts concerning the causes of the condition of transsexualism. While Professor Gooren's research into the role of the brain in conditioning transsexualism may be seen as an important contribution to the debate in this area (see paragraph 43 above), it cannot be said that his views enjoy the universal support of the medico-scientific profession. Accordingly, the non-acceptance by the authorities of the respondent State for the time being of the sex of the brain as a crucial determinant of gender cannot be criticised as being unreasonable. The Court would add that, as at the time of adoption of the *Cossey* judgment, it still remains established that gender reassignment surgery does not result in the acquisition of all the biological characteristics of the other sex despite the increased scientific advances in the handling of gender reassignment procedures.

57. As to legal developments in this area, the Court has examined the comparative study which has been submitted by Liberty (see paragraph 35 above). However, the Court is not fully satisfied that the legislative trends outlined by amicus suffice to establish the existence of any common European approach to the problems created by the recognition in law of post-operative gender status. In particular, the survey does not indicate that there is as yet any common approach as to how to address the repercussions which the legal recognition of a change of sex may entail for other areas of law such as marriage, filiation, privacy or data protection, or the circumstances in which a transsexual may be compelled by law to reveal his or her pre-operative gender.

58. The Court is accordingly not persuaded that it should depart from its *Rees* and *Cossey* decisions and conclude that on the basis of scientific and legal developments alone the respondent State can no longer rely on a margin of appreciation to defend its continuing refusal to recognise in law a transsexual's post-operative gender. For the Court, it continues to be the case that transsexualism raises complex scientific, legal, moral and social issues, in respect of which there is no generally shared approach among the Contracting States (see *X, Y and Z v United Kingdom*, judgment of 22 April 1997, *Reports of Judgments and Decisions* 1997–II, p635, paragraph 52).

59. Nor is the Court persuaded that the applicants' case histories demonstrate that the failure of the authorities to recognise their new gender gives rise to detriment of sufficient seriousness as to override the respondent State's margin of appreciation in this area (cf the above-mentioned *B v France* judgment). It cannot be denied that the incidents alluded to by Miss Sheffield

were a source of embarrassment and distress to her and that Miss Horsham, if she were to return to the United Kingdom, would equally run the risk of having on occasion to identify herself in her pre-operative gender. At the same time, it must be acknowledged that an individual may with justification be required on occasion to provide proof of gender as well as medical history. This is certainly the case of life assurance contracts which are uberrimae fidei. It may possibly be true of motor insurance where the insurer may need to have regard to the sex of the driver in order to make an actuarial assessment of the risk. Furthermore, it would appear appropriate for a court to run a check on whether a person has a criminal record, either under his or her present name or former name, before accepting that person as a surety for a defendant in criminal proceedings. However, quite apart from these considerations the situations in which the applicants may be required to disclose their pre-operative gender do not occur with a degree of frequency which could be said to impinge to a disproportionate extent on their right to respect for their private lives. The Court observes also that the respondent State has endeavoured to some extent to minimise intrusive enquiries as to their gender status by allowing transsexuals to be issued with driving licences, passports and other types of official documents in their new name and gender, and that the use of birth certificates as a means of identification is officially discouraged (see paragraphs 26 and 31 above).

60. Having reached those conclusions, the Court cannot but note that despite its statements in the *Rees* and *Cossey* cases on the importance of keeping the need for appropriate legal measures in this area under review having regard in particular to scientific and societal developments (see, respectively, pp18–19, paragraph 47, and p41, paragraph 42), it would appear that the respondent State has not taken any steps to do so. The fact that a transsexual is able to record his or her new sexual identity on a driving licence or passport or to change a first name are not innovative facilities. They obtained even at the time of the *Rees* case. Even if there have been no significant scientific developments since the date of the *Cossey* judgment which make it possible to reach a firm conclusion on the aetiology of transsexualism, it is nevertheless the case that there is an increased social acceptance of transsexualism and an increased recognition of the problems which post-operative transsexuals encounter. Even if it finds no breach of art 8 in this case, the Court reiterates that this area needs to be kept under review by Contracting States.

61. For the above reasons, the Court considers that the applicants have not established that the respondent State has a positive obligation under art 8 of the Convention to recognise in law their post-operative gender. Accordingly, there is no breach of that provision in the instant case.

II. Alleged violation of art 12 of the Convention

62. The applicants submitted that any marriage which a male-to-female post-operative transsexual contracted with a man would be void under English law having regard to the fact that a male-to-female transsexual is still considered for legal purposes as male. While they addressed the prejudice which they suffered in respect of their right to marry in the context of their more general complaint under art 8 of the Convention, before the Commission they relied on art 12 of the Convention, which provides:

> "Men and women of marriageable age have the right to marry and to found a family, according to the national laws governing the exercise of this right."

63. Miss Horsham stated in particular that she intended to marry her male partner in The Netherlands, where the validity of her marriage would be recognised. However, she feared that she would be unable to settle subsequently in the United Kingdom since it was doubtful whether the English courts would recognise the validity of the marriage. This situation meant that she would have to live her married life in forced exile outside the United Kingdom.

64. The government contended that there was no breach of the applicants' rights under art 12 of the Convention and requested the Court to endorse this view on the basis of the reasoning which led it to conclude in the above-mentioned *Rees* and *Cossey* cases that there had been no breach of that provision. As to Miss Horsham's situation, the government further submitted that she had never sought to test the validity of her proposed marriage, which might well be recognised by the English courts in application of the rules of private international law. She must be considered to have failed to exhaust domestic remedies in respect of this complaint.

65. The Commission found that the applicants' allegations gave rise to no separate issue having regard to the substance of their complaints under art 8 of the Convention.

66. The Court recalls that the right to marry guaranteed by art 12 refers to the traditional marriage between persons of opposite biological sex. This appears also from the wording of the article which makes it clear that art 12 is mainly concerned to protect marriage as the basis of the family. Furthermore, art 12 lays down that the exercise of this right shall be subject to the national laws of the Contracting States. The limitations thereby introduced must not restrict or reduce the right in such a way or to such an extent that the very essence of the right is impaired. However, the legal impediment in the United Kingdom on the marriage of persons who are not of the opposite biological sex cannot be said to have an effect of this kind (see the above-mentioned *Rees* judgment, p19, paragraphs 49 and 50).

67. The Court recalls further that in its *Cossey* judgment it found that the attachment to the traditional concept of marriage which underpins art 12 of the Convention provides sufficient reason for the continued adoption by the respondent State of biological criteria for determining a person's sex for the purposes of marriage, this being a matter encompassed within the power of the contracting States to regulate by national law the exercise of the right to marry (p18, paragraph 46).

68. In light of the above considerations, the Court finds that the inability of either applicant to contract a valid marriage under the domestic law of the respondent State having regard to the conditions imposed by the Matrimonial Causes Act 1973 (see paragraph 27 above) cannot be said to constitute a violation of art 12 of the Convention.

69. The Court is not persuaded that Miss Horsham's complaint raises an issue under art 12 which engages the responsibility of the respondent State since it relates to the recognition by that State of a post-operative transsexual's foreign marriage rather than the law governing the right to marry of individuals within its jurisdiction. In any event, this applicant has not provided any evidence that she intends to set up her matrimonial home in the United Kingdom and to enjoy married life there. Furthermore, it cannot be said with certainty what the outcome would be were the validity of her marriage to be tested in the English courts.

70. The Court concludes that there has been no violation of art 12.'

Comment
It is interesting to note that the Court did not change its previous position that a State is entitled to rely on a margin of appreciation to refuse in law the new sexual identity of post-operative transsexuals' (*Rees* v *United Kingdom* (1987) 9 EHRR 56; *Cossey* v *United Kingdom* (1991) 13 EHRR 622; *X, Y, Z* v *United Kingdom* Judgment of 22 April 1997, *Reports of Judgments and Decisions* 1997–II, p635). The Court did not share the opinion of the Commission which declared that there had been a violation of art 8 of the Convention (15 votes to one), although compared to the Court's previous judgment as many as nine judges recognised the need for changes in favour of transsexuals as compared to only three in the case of *Rees* and eight in the case of *Cossey*. The Court refused to take into consideration new medical evidence, although it recognised the increased social acceptance of transsexualism.

It is interesting to note that the Council of Europe in its Recommendation 1117 (1989) has invited Member States to introduce legislation permitting, in the case of irreversible transsexualism, rectification of the register of birth and identity papers of such persons.

In the UK (one of the four remaining contracting States refusing to update the birth certificates of post-operative transsexuals), the government introduced the Gender Identity (Registration and Civil Status) Bill 1996 which recognises the possibility of amending the register of births for post-operative transsexuals.

22 The Right to Freedom from Discrimination: Article 14

Abdulaziz, Cabales and Balkandali* v *United Kingdom (1985) 7 EHRR 471
European Court of Human Rights

- *Respect for family life – sexual and racial discrimination – degrading treatment or punishment – violation of arts 14 and 8 of the Convention – no discrimination based on race of the applicants*

Facts
The applicants claimed that they had been victims of racial and sexual discrimination as a consequence of the application of the immigration laws of the United Kingdom. Discrimination was alleged because it was easier for a male to immigrate to the United Kingdom than for a woman already settled in the United Kingdom to obtain permission for her non-national spouse to enter and remain in the country.

Racial discrimination was allegedly perpetrated through the United Kingdom immigration laws themselves. These rules were administered in such a manner as to lower the number of coloured immigrants entering the United Kingdom.

The United Kingdom argued that both forms of discrimination were based on objective and reasonable grounds.

Held
On the allegation of sexual discrimination, the Court found in favour of the applicants. As regards racial discrimination, the court found against the applicants. Discrimination had not been perpetrated against certain ethnic groups, such as those from the New Commonwealth and Pakistan.

Judgment
'*Alleged discrimination on the ground of sex*
As regards the alleged discrimination on the ground of sex, it was not disputed that under the 1980 Rules it was easier for a man settled in the United Kingdom than for a woman so settled to obtain permission for his or her non-national spouse to enter or remain in the country for settlement. Argument centred on the question whether this difference had an objective and reasonable justification.

According to the government, the difference of treatment complained of had the aim of limiting "primary immigration" and was justified by the need to protect the domestic labour market at a time of high unemployment. They placed strong reliance on the margin of appreciation enjoyed by the Contracting States in this area and laid particular stress on what they described as a statistical fact: men were more likely to seek work than women, with the result that male immigrants would have a greater impact than female immigrants on the said market. Furthermore, the reduction, attributed by the Government to the 1980 Rules, of approximately 5,700 per annum in the number of husbands accepted for settlement in the United Kingdom was claimed to be significant. This was said to be so especially when the reduction was viewed in relation to its cumulative effect over the years and to the total number of acceptances for settlement.

This view was contested by the applicants. For them, the government's plea ignored the modern role of women and the fact that men may be self-employed and also, as was exemplified by the case of Mr Balkandali, create rather than seek jobs. Furthermore, the government's figure of 5,700 was said to be insignificant and, for a number of reasons, in any event unreliable.

The government further contended that the measures in question were justified by the need to maintain effective immigration control, which benefited settled immigrants as well as the indigenous population. Immigration caused strains on society; the government's aim was to advance public tranquillity, and a firm and fair control secured good relations between the different communities living in the United Kingdom.

To this, the applicants replied that the racial prejudice of the United Kingdom population could not be advanced as a justification for the measures.

In its report, the Commission considered that, when seen in the context of the immigration of other groups, annual emigration and unemployment and economic activity rates, the impact on the domestic labour market of an annual reduction of 2,000 (as then estimated by the government) in the number of husbands accepted for settlement in the United Kingdom was not of a size or importance to justify a difference of treatment on the ground of sex and the detrimental consequences thereof on the family life of the women concerned. Furthermore, the long-standing commitment to the reunification of the families of male immigrants, to which the government had referred as a reason for accepting wives whilst excluding husbands, no longer corresponded to modern requirements as to the equal treatment of the sexes. Neither was it established that race relations or immigration controls were enhanced by the rules; they might create resentment in part of the immigrant population and it had not been shown that it was more difficult to limit abuses by non-national husbands than by other immigrant groups. The Commission unanimously concluded that there had been discrimination on the ground of sex, contrary to art 14, in securing the applicants' right to respect for family life, the application of the relevant rules being disproportionate to the purported aims.

At the hearings before the Court, the Commission's Delegate stated that this conclusion was not affected by the government's revised figure (about 5,700) for the annual reduction in the number of husbands accepted for settlement.

The Court accepts that the 1980 Rules had the aim of protecting the domestic labour market. The fact that, as was suggested by the applicants, this aim might have been further advanced by the abolition of the "United Kingdom ancestry" and the "working holiday" rules in no way alters this finding. Neither does the Court perceive any conclusive evidence to contradict it in the Parliamentary debates, on which the applicants also relied. It is true, as they pointed out, that unemployment in the United Kingdom in 1980 was lower than in subsequent years, but it had nevertheless already attained a significant level and there was a considerable increase as compared with previous years.

Whilst the aforesaid aim was without doubt legitimate, this does not in itself establish the legitimacy of the difference made in the 1980 Rules as to the possibility for male and female immigrants settled in the United Kingdom to obtain permission for, on the one hand, their non-national wives or fiancees and, on the other hand, their non-national husbands or fiances to enter or remain in the country.

Although the contracting States enjoy a certain "margin of appreciation" in assessing whether and to what extent differences in otherwise similar situations justify a different treatment, the scope of this margin will vary according to the circumstances, the subject-matter and its background (see the above mentioned *Rasmussen* judgment, Series A no 87, p 15, paragraph 40).

As to the present matter, it can be said that the advancement of the equality of the sexes is today a major goal in the Member States of the Council of Europe. This means that very weighty reasons would have to be advanced before a difference of treatment on the ground of sex could be regarded as compatible with the Convention.

In the Court's opinion, the government's arguments summarised in para 75 above are not convincing.

It may be correct that on average there is a greater percentage of men of working age than of women of working age who are "economically active" (for Great Britain 90 per cent of the men and 63 per cent of the women) and that comparable figures hold good for immigrants (according to the statistics, 86 per cent for men and 41 per cent for women for immigrants from the Indian subcontinent and 90 per cent for men and 70 per cent for women for immigrants from the West Indies and Guyana).

Nevertheless, this does not show that similar differences in fact exist – or would but for the effect of the 1980 Rules have existed – as regards the respective impact on the United Kingdom labour market of immigrant wives and of immigrant husbands. In this connection, other factors must also be taken into account. Being "economically active" does not always mean that one is seeking to be employed by someone else. Moreover, although a greater number of men than of women may be inclined to seek employment, immigrant husbands were already by far outnumbered, before the introduction of the 1980 Rules, by immigrant wives, many of whom were also "economically active". Whilst a considerable proportion of those wives, in so far as they were "economically active", were engaged in part-time work, the impact on the domestic labour market of women immigrants as compared with men ought not to be underestimated.

In any event, the Court is not convinced that the difference that may nevertheless exist between the respective impact of men and of women on the domestic labour market is sufficiently important to justify the difference of treatment, complained of by the applicants, as to the possibility for a person settled in the United Kingdom to be joined by, as the case may be, his wife or her husband.

In this context the Government stressed the importance of the effect on the immigration of husbands of the restrictions contained in the 1980 Rules, which had led, according to their estimate, to an annual reduction of 5,700 (rather than 2,000, as mentioned in the Commission's report) in the number of husbands accepted for settlement.

Without expressing a conclusion on the correctness of the figure of 5,700, the Court notes that in point of time the claimed reduction coincided with a significant increase in unemployment in the United Kingdom and that the government accepted that some part of the reduction was due to economic conditions rather than to the 1980 Rules themselves.

In any event, for the reasons stated in para 79 above, the reduction achieved does not justify the difference in treatment between men and women.

The Court accepts that the 1980 Rules also had, as the government stated, the aim of advancing public tranquillity. However, it is not persuaded that this aim was served by the distinction drawn in those rules between husbands and wives.

There remains a more general argument advanced by the government, namely that the United Kingdom was not in violation of art 14 by reason of the fact that it acted more generously in some respects – that is, as regards the admission of non-national wives and fiancees of men settled in the country – than the Convention required.

The Court cannot accept this argument. It would point out that art 14 is concerned with the avoidance of discrimination in the enjoyment of the Convention rights in so far as the requirements of the Convention as to those rights can be complied with in different ways. The notion of discrimination within the meaning of art 14 includes in general cases where a person or group is treated, without proper justification, less favourably than another, even though the more favourable treatment is not called for by the Convention.

The Court thus concludes that the applicants have been victims of discrimination on the ground of sex, in violation of art 14 taken together with art 8.

Alleged discrimination on the ground of race

As regards the alleged discrimination on the ground of race, the applicants relied on the opinion of a minority of the Commission. They referred, inter alia, to the whole history of and background to the United Kingdom immigration legislation and to the Parliamentary debates on the immigration rules.

In contesting this claim, the government submitted that the 1980 Rules were not racially motivated, their aim being to limit "primary immigration".

A majority of the Commission concluded that there had been no violation of art 14 under this head. Most immigration policies – restricting, as they do, free entry – differentiated on the basis of people's nationality, and indirectly their race, ethnic origin and possibly their colour. Whilst a Contracting State could not implement "policies of a purely racist nature", to give preferential treatment to its nationals or to persons from countries with which it had the closest links did not constitute "racial discrimination". The effect in practice of the United Kingdom rules did not mean that they were abhorrent on the grounds of racial discrimination, there being no evidence of an actual difference of treatment on grounds of race.

A minority of the Commission, on the other hand, noted that the main effect of the rules was to prevent immigration from the New Commonwealth and Pakistan. This was not coincidental: the legislative history showed that the intention was to "lower the number of coloured immigrants". By their effect and purpose, the rules were indirectly racist and there had thus been a violation of art 14 under this head in the cases of Mrs Abdulaziz and Mrs Cabales.

The Court agrees in this respect with the majority of the Commission.

The 1980 Rules, which were applicable in general to all "non-patrials" wanting to enter and settle in the United Kingdom, did not contain regulations differentiating between persons or groups on the ground of their race or ethnic origin. The rules included in paragraph 2 a specific instruction to immigration officers to carry out their duties without regard to the race, colour or religion of the intending entrant , and they were applicable across the board to intending immigrants from all parts of the world, irrespective of their race or origin.

As the Court has already accepted, the main and essential purpose of the 1980 Rules was to curtail "primary immigration" in order to protect the labour market at a time of high unemployment. This means that their reinforcement of the restrictions on immigration was grounded not on objections regarding the origin of the non-nationals wanting to enter the country but on the need to stem the flow of immigrants at the relevant time.

That the mass immigration against which the rules were directed consisted mainly of would-be immigrants from the New Commonwealth and Pakistan, and that as a result they affected at the material time fewer white people than others, is not a sufficient reason to consider them as racist in character: it is an effect which derives not from the content of the 1980 Rules but from the fact that, among those wishing to immigrate, some ethnic groups outnumbered others.

The Court concludes from the foregoing that the 1980 Rules made no distinction on the ground of race and were therefore not discriminatory on that account. This conclusion is not altered by the following two arguments on which the applicants relied.

a) The requirement that the wife or fiancee of the intending entrant be born or have a parent born in the United Kingdom and also the "United Kingdom ancestry rule" were said to favour persons of a particular ethnic origin. However, the Court regards these provisions as being exceptions designed for the benefit of persons having close links with the United Kingdom, which do not affect the general tenor of the rules.

b) The requirement that the parties to the marriage or intended marriage must have met was said to operate to the disadvantage of individuals from the Indian subcontinent, where the practice of arranged marriages is customary. In the Court's view, however, such a requirement cannot be taken as an indication of racial discrimination: its main purpose was to prevent evasion of the rules by means of bogus marriages or engagements. It is, besides, a requirement that has nothing to do with the present cases.

The Court accordingly holds that the applicants have not been victims of discrimination on the ground of race.'

Comment

The Court stated that the advancement of equality of sexes constituted a major objective in the contracting States to the Convention and for that reason the Court would require 'very weighty' justifications from a State in order to justify discrimination based on sex as compatible with the Convention. Both justifications provided by the UK, namely the necessity for the UK to protect the labour market (since men were more likely than woman to seek employment in the UK) and the need to secure peaceful relations between different communities in the UK, were rejected by the Court as unconvincing.

As a result of the judgment the immigration rules were amended on 26 August 1985. The new rules eliminated the distinction between married men and women settled in the UK in relation to 'admission' or 'leave to remain' in respect of their spouses on the basis of marriage.

23 The Right to Participate in Elections to Choose Legislature: Article 3 of Protocol 1

Matthews v *United Kingdom*
Judgment of 18 February 1999 (not yet reported) Grand Chamber of the New European Court of Human Rights

• *Right to participate in elections to choose the legislature – art 3 of Protocol 1 – the recognition of the European Parliament as a legislative body – the UK responsible for the lack of elections to the European Parliament in Gibraltar*

Facts
In April 1994 Ms Denise Matthews, a British citizen residing in Gibraltar, applied to the Electoral Office for Gibraltar to be registered as a voter in the elections to the European Parliament (EP). Her application was refused on the ground that Gibraltar was not included under the EC Act on Direct Elections 1976 in the franchise for those elections.

Ms Matthews claimed that the absence of elections to the EP in Gibraltar violated art 3 of Protocol 1 to the Convention which guarantees the right to participate in elections to choose the legislature, and art 14 of the Convention which ensures freedom from discrimination. Her ground was that she, as a citizen of the European Union, was entitled to vote in the elections to the European Parliament in any Member State of her residence but not in Gibraltar.

Held
The Court held by 15 votes to two that the United Kingdom was in breach of art 3 of Protocol 1.

Judgment
'*A. Whether the United Kingdom can be held responsible under the Convention for the lack of elections to the European Parliament in Gibraltar*
26. According to the government, the applicant's real objection was to Council Decision 76/787 and to the 1976 Act concerning elections to the European Parliament (see paragraph 18 above). That Act, which had the status of a treaty, was adopted in the Community framework and could not be revoked or varied unilaterally by the United Kingdom. The government underlined that the European Commission of Human Rights had refused on a number of occasions to subject measures falling within the Community legal order to scrutiny under the Convention. Whilst they accepted that there might be circumstances in which a contracting party might infringe its obligations under the Convention by entering into treaty obligations which were incompatible with the Convention, they considered that in the present case, which concerned texts adopted in the framework of the European Community, the position was not the same. Thus, acts adopted by the Community or consequent to its requirements could not be imputed to the Member States, together or individually, particularly when those acts concerned elections to a

constitutional organ of the Community itself. At the hearing, the government suggested that to engage the responsibility of any State under the Convention, that State must have a power of effective control over the act complained of. In the case of the provisions relating to the elections to the European Parliament, the United Kingdom Government had no such control.

27. The applicant disagreed. For her, the Council Decision and 1976 Act constituted an international treaty, rather than an act of an institution whose decisions were not subject to Convention review. She thus considered that the government remained responsible under the Convention for the effects of the Council Decision and 1976 Act. In the alternative – that is, if the Council Decision and 1976 Act were to be interpreted as involving a transfer of powers to the Community organs – the applicant argued, by reference to Commission case-law, that in the absence of any equivalent protection of her rights under art 3 of Protocol No 1, the government in any event retained responsibility under the Convention.

28. The majority of the Commission took no stand on the point, although it was referred to in concurring and dissenting opinions.

29. Article 1 of the Convention requires the High Contracting Parties to "secure to everyone within their jurisdiction the rights and freedoms defined in ... [the] Convention". Article 1 makes no distinction as to the type of rule or measure concerned, and does not exclude any part of the Member States' "jurisdiction" from scrutiny under the Convention (see *United Communist Party of Turkey and Others* v *Turkey*, judgment of 30 January 1998, *Reports of Judgments and Decisions* 1998–I, pp17–18, paragraph 29).

30. The Court notes that the parties do not dispute that art 3 of Protocol No 1 applies in Gibraltar. It recalls that the Convention was extended to the territory of Gibraltar by the United Kingdom's declaration of 23 October 1953 (see paragraph 19 above), and Protocol No 1 has been applicable in Gibraltar since 25 February 1988. There is therefore clearly territorial "jurisdiction" within the meaning of art 1 of the Convention.

31. The Court must nevertheless consider whether, notwithstanding the nature of the elections to the European Parliament as an organ of the EC, the United Kingdom can be held responsible under art 1 of the Convention for the absence of elections to the European Parliament in Gibraltar, that is, whether the United Kingdom is required to "secure" elections to the European Parliament notwithstanding the Community character of those elections.

32. The Court observes that acts of the EC as such cannot be challenged before the Court because the EC is not a contracting party. The Convention does not exclude the transfer of competences to international organisations provided that Convention rights continue to be "secured". Member States' responsibility therefore continues even after such a transfer.

33. In the present case, the alleged violation of the Convention flows from an annex to the 1976 Act, entered into by the United Kingdom, together with the extension to the European Parliament's competences brought about by the Maastricht Treaty. The Council Decision and the 1976 Act (see paragraph 18 above), and the Maastricht Treaty, with its changes to the [EC] Treaty, all constituted international instruments which were freely entered into by the United Kingdom. Indeed, the 1976 Act cannot be challenged before the European Court of Justice for the very reason that it is not a "normal" act of the Community, but is a treaty within the Community legal order. The Maastricht Treaty, too, is not an act of the Community, but a treaty by which a revision of the [EC] Treaty was brought about. The United Kingdom, together with all the other parties to the Maastricht Treaty, is responsible ratione materiae under art 1 of the Convention and, in particular, under art 3 of Protocol No 1, for the consequences of that Treaty.

34. In determining to what extent the United Kingdom is responsible for "secur-

ing" the rights in art 3 of Protocol No 1 in respect of elections to the European Parliament in Gibraltar, the Court recalls that the Convention is intended to guarantee rights that are not theoretical or illusory, but practical and effective (see, for example, the above-mentioned *United Communist Party of Turkey and Others* judgment, pp18–19, paragraph 33). It is uncontested that legislation emanating from the legislative process of the European Community affects the population of Gibraltar in the same way as legislation which enters the domestic legal order exclusively via the House of Assembly. To this extent, there is no difference between European and domestic legislation, and no reason why the United Kingdom should not be required to "secure" the rights in art 3 of Protocol No 1 in respect of European legislation, in the same way as those rights are required to be "secured" in respect of purely domestic legislation. In particular, the suggestion that the United Kingdom may not have effective control over the state of affairs complained of cannot affect the position, as the United Kingdom's responsibility derives from its having entered into treaty commitments subsequent to the applicability of art 3 of Protocol No 1 to Gibraltar, namely the Maastricht Treaty taken together with its obligations under the Council Decision and the 1976 Act. Further, the Court notes that on acceding to the EC Treaty, the United Kingdom chose, by virtue of art 227(4) of the Treaty, to have substantial areas of EC legislation applied to Gibraltar (see paragraphs 11 to 14 above).

35. It follows that the United Kingdom is responsible under art 1 of the Convention for securing the rights guaranteed by art 3 of Protocol No 1 in Gibraltar regardless of whether the elections were purely domestic or European.

B. Whether art 3 of Protocol No 1 is applicable to an organ such as the European Parliament

36. The government claimed that the undertaking in art 3 of Protocol No 1 was necessarily limited to matters falling within the power of the parties to the Convention, that is, sovereign States. They submitted that the "legislature" in Gibraltar was the House of Assembly, and that it was to that body that art 3 of Protocol No 1 applied in the context of Gibraltar. For the government, there was no basis upon which the Convention could place obligations on contracting parties in relation to elections for the parliament of a distinct, supranational organisation, and they contended that this was particularly so when the Member States of the European Community had limited their own sovereignty in respect of it and when both the European Parliament itself and its basic electoral procedures were provided for under its own legal system, rather than the legal systems of its member States.

37. The applicant referred to previous decisions of the European Commission of Human Rights in which complaints concerning the European Parliament were dealt with on the merits, so that the Commission in effect assumed that art 3 of Protocol No 1 applied to elections to the European Parliament (see, for example, *Lindsay* v *United Kingdom*, application No 8364/78, decision of 8 March 1978, *Decisions and Reports* (DR) 15, p247, and *Tête* v *France*, application No 11123/84, decision of 9 December 1987, DR 54, p52). She agreed with the dissenting members of the Commission who did not accept that because the European Parliament did not exist when Protocol No 1 was drafted, it necessarily fell outside the ambit of art 3 of that Protocol.

38. The majority of the Commission based its reasoning on this jurisdictional point. It considered that "to hold art 3 of Protocol No 1 to be applicable to supranational representative organs would be to extend the scope of art 3 beyond what was intended by the drafters of the Convention and beyond the object and purpose of the provision. ...[T]he role of art 3 is to ensure that elections take place at regular intervals to the national or local legislative assembly, that is, in the case of Gibraltar, to the House of Assembly" (see paragraph 63 of the Commission's report).

39. That the Convention is a living instrument which must be interpreted in the light of present-day conditions is firmly rooted in the Court's case-law (see, inter alia, *Loizidou* v *Turkey*, judgment of 23 March 1995 (preliminary objections), Series A no 310, pp26–27, paragraph 71, with further reference). The mere fact that a body was not envisaged by the drafters of the Convention cannot prevent that body from falling within the scope of the Convention. To the extent that contracting States organise common constitutional or parliamentary structures by international treaties, the Court must take these mutually agreed structural changes into account in interpreting the Convention and its Protocols.

The question remains whether an organ such as the European Parliament nevertheless falls outside the ambit of art 3 of Protocol No 1.

40. The Court recalls that the word "legislature" in art 3 of Protocol No 1 does not necessarily mean the national parliament: the word has to be interpreted in the light of the constitutional structure of the State in question. In the case of *Mathieu-Mohin and Clerfayt* v *Belgium*, the 1980 constitutional reform had vested in the Flemish Council sufficient competence and powers to make it, alongside the French Community Council and the Walloon Regional Council, a constituent part of the Belgian "legislature", in addition to the House of Representatives and the Senate (see *Mathieu-Mohin and Clerfayt* v *Belgium*, judgment of 2 March 1987, Series A no 113, p23, paragraph 53; see also the Commission's decisions on the application of art 3 of Protocol No 1 to regional parliaments in Austria (application No 7008/75, decision of 12 July 1976, DR 6, p120) and in Germany (application No 27311/95, decision of 11 September 1995, DR 82-A, p158)).

41. According to the case law of the European Court of Justice, it is an inherent aspect of EC law that such law sits alongside, and indeed has precedence over, domestic law (see, for example, *Costa* v *ENEL*, 6/64 [1964] ECR 585, and *Amministrazione delle Finanze dello Stato* v *Simmenthal SpA*, 106/77 [1978] ECR 629). In this regard, Gibraltar is in the same position as other parts of the European Union.

42. The Court reiterates that art 3 of Protocol No 1 enshrines a characteristic of an effective political democracy (see the above-mentioned *Mathieu-Mohin and Clerfayt* judgment, p22, paragraph 47, and the above-mentioned *United Communist Party of Turkey and Others* judgment, pp21–22, paragraph 45). In the present case, there has been no submission that there exist alternative means of providing for electoral representation of the population of Gibraltar in the European Parliament, and the Court finds no indication of any.

43. The Court thus considers that to accept the government's contention that the sphere of activities of the European Parliament falls outside the scope of art 3 of Protocol No 1 would risk undermining one of the fundamental tools by which "effective political democracy" can be maintained.

44. It follows that no reason has been made out which could justify excluding the European Parliament from the ambit of the elections referred to in art 3 of Protocol No 1 on the ground that it is a supranational, rather than a purely domestic, representative organ.

C. Whether the European Parliament, at the relevant time, had the characteristics of a "legislature" in Gibraltar

45. The government contended that the European Parliament continued to lack both of the most fundamental attributes of a legislature: the power to initiate legislation and the power to adopt it. They were of the opinion that the only change to the powers and functions of the European Parliament since the Commission last considered the issue in the above-mentioned *Tête* decision (see paragraph 37 above) – the procedure under art 189b of the EC Treaty – offered less than even a power of co-decision with the Council, and in any event applied only to a tiny proportion of the Community's legislative output.

46. The applicant took as her starting-

point in this respect that the European Commission of Human Rights had found that the entry into force of the Single European Act in 1986 did not furnish the European Parliament with the necessary powers and functions for it to be considered as a "legislature" (see the above-mentioned *Tête* decision). She contended that the Maastricht Treaty increased those powers to such an extent that the European Parliament was now transformed from a mere advisory and supervisory organ to a body which assumed, or assumed at least in part, the powers and functions of legislative bodies within the meaning of art 3 of Protocol No 1. The High Contracting Parties had undertaken to hold free elections at reasonable intervals by secret ballot, under conditions which would ensure the free expression of the opinion of the people in the choice of the legislature. She described the powers of the European Parliament not solely in terms of the new matters added by the Maastricht Treaty, but also by reference to its pre-existing powers, in particular those which were added by the Single European Act in 1986.

47. The Commission did not examine this point, as it found art 3 not to be applicable to supranational representative organs.

48. In determining whether the European Parliament falls to be considered as the 'legislature', or part of it, in Gibraltar for the purposes of art 3 of Protocol No 1, the Court must bear in mind the sui generis nature of the European Community, which does not follow in every respect the pattern common in many States of a more or less strict division of powers between the executive and the legislature. Rather, the legislative process in the EC involves the participation of the European Parliament, the Council and the European Commission.

49. The Court must ensure that 'effective political democracy' is properly served in the territories to which the Convention applies, and in this context, it must have regard not solely to the strictly legislative powers which a body has, but also to that body's role in the overall legislative process.

50. Since the Maastricht Treaty, the European Parliament's powers are no longer expressed to be "advisory and supervisory". The removal of these words must be taken as an indication that the European Parliament has moved away from being a purely consultative body, and has moved towards being a body with a decisive role to play in the legislative process of the European Community. The amendment to art 137 of the EC Treaty cannot, however, be taken as any more than an indication as to the intentions of the drafters of the Maastricht Treaty. Only on examination of the European Parliament's actual powers in the context of the European Community legislative process as a whole can the Court determine whether the European Parliament acts as the "legislature", or part of it, in Gibraltar.

51. The European Parliament's role in the Community legislative process depends on the issues concerned (see paragraphs 15–16 above).

Where a regulation or directive is adopted by means of the consultation procedure (for example under arts 99 or 100 of the EC Treaty) the European Parliament may, depending on the specific provision, have to be consulted. In such cases, the European Parliament's role is limited. Where the EC Treaty requires the procedure set out in art 189c to be used, the European Parliament's position on a matter can be overruled by a unanimous Council. Where the EC Treaty requires the art 189b procedure to be followed, however, it is not open to the Council to pass measures against the will of the European Parliament. Finally, where the so-called "assent procedure" is used (as referred to in the first paragraph of art 138b of the EC Treaty), in relation to matters such as the accession of new Member States and the conclusion of certain types of international agreements, the consent of the European Parliament is needed before a measure can be passed.

In addition to this involvement in the passage of legislation, the European Parliament also has functions in relation to the appointment and removal of the European Commission. Thus, it has a power of censure over the European Commission, which can ultimately lead to the European Commission having to resign as a body (art 144); its consent is necessary for the appointment of the European Commission (art 158); its consent is necessary before the budget can be adopted (art 203); and it gives a discharge to the European Commission in the implementation of the budget, and here has supervisory powers over the European Commission (art 206).

Further, whilst the European Parliament has no formal right to initiate legislation, it has the right to request the European Commission to submit proposals on matters on which it considers that a Community act is required (art 138b).

52. As to the context in which the European Parliament operates, the Court is of the view that the European Parliament represents the principal form of democratic, political accountability in the Community system. The Court considers that whatever its limitations, the European Parliament, which derives democratic legitimation from the direct elections by universal suffrage, must be seen as that part of the European Community structure which best reflects concerns as to 'effective political democracy'.

53. Even when due allowance is made for the fact that Gibraltar is excluded from certain areas of Community activity (see paragraph 12 above), there remain significant areas where Community activity has a direct impact in Gibraltar. Further, as the applicant points out, measures taken under art 189b of the EC Treaty and which affect Gibraltar relate to important matters such as road safety, unfair contract terms and air pollution by emissions from motor vehicles and to all measures in relation to the completion of the internal market.

54. The Court thus finds that the European Parliament is sufficiently involved in the specific legislative processes leading to the passage of legislation under arts 189b and 189c of the EC Treaty, and is sufficiently involved in the general democratic supervision of the activities of the European Community, to constitute part of the 'legislature' of Gibraltar for the purposes of art 3 of Protocol No 1.

D. *The application of art 56 of the Convention to the case*

55. art 56 paragraphs 1 and 3 of the Convention provide as follows:

"1. Any State may at the time of its ratification or at any time thereafter declare by notification addressed to the Secretary General of the Council of Europe that the ... Convention shall, subject to paragraph 4 of this article, extend to all or any of the territories for whose international relations it is responsible. ...

3. The provisions of [the] Convention shall be applied in such territories with due regard, however, to local requirements."

56. The government noted, without relying formally on the point, that two members of the Commission had emphasised the constitutional position of Gibraltar as a dependent territory in the context of art 56 (formerly art 63) of the Convention.

57. The applicant was of the view that the "local requirements" referred to in art 56 paragraph 3 of the Convention could not be interpreted so as to restrict the application of art 3 of Protocol No 1 in the case.

58. The Commission, which found art 3 not to be applicable on other grounds, did not consider this point. Two members of the Commission, in separate concurring opinions, both found that art 56 of the Convention had a role to play in the case.

59. The Court recalls that in *Tyrer* v *United Kingdom*, judgment 25 April 1978, Series A no 26, pp18–19, paragraph 38) it found that before the former art 63 paragraph 3 could apply, there would have to be "positive and conclusive proof of a requirement". Local requirements, if they refer to the specific legal status of a territory, must be of a compelling nature if they are to justify the application of art 56 of the Convention. In the present case, the government do not contend that the status of Gibraltar is such as to give rise to "local requirements" which could limit the application of the Convention, and the Court

finds no indication that there are any such requirements.

E. Whether the absence of elections to the European Parliament in Gibraltar in 1994 was compatible with art 3 of Protocol No 1

60. The government submitted that, even if art 3 of Protocol No 1 could be said to apply to the European Parliament, the absence of elections in Gibraltar in 1994 did not give rise to a violation of that provision but instead fell within the State's margin of appreciation. They pointed out that in the 1994 elections the United Kingdom had used a single-member constituency, "first-past-the-post" system. It would have distorted the electoral process to constitute Gibraltar as a separate constituency, since its population of approximately 30,000 was less than 5 per cent of the average population per European Parliament seat in the United Kingdom. The alternative of redrawing constituency boundaries so as to include Gibraltar within a new or existing constituency was no more feasible, as Gibraltar did not form part of the United Kingdom and had no strong historical or other link with any particular United Kingdom constituency.

61. The applicant submitted that she had been completely deprived of the right to vote in the 1994 elections. She stated that the protection of fundamental rights could not depend on whether or not there were attractive alternatives to the current system.

62. The Commission, since it did not find art 3 of Protocol No 1 to be applicable, did not examine whether or not the absence of elections in Gibraltar was compatible with that provision.

63. The Court recalls that the rights set out in art 3 of Protocol No 1 are not absolute, but may be subject to limitations. The contracting States enjoy a wide margin of appreciation in imposing conditions on the right to vote, but it is for the Court to determine in the last resort whether the requirements of Protocol No 1 have been complied with. It has to satisfy itself that the conditions do not curtail the right to vote to such an extent as to impair its very essence and deprive it of effectiveness; that they are imposed in pursuit of a legitimate aim; and that the means employed are not disproportionate. In particular, such conditions must not thwart "the free expression of the people in the choice of the legislature" (see the above-mentioned *Mathieu-Mohin and Clerfayt* judgment, p23, paragraph 52).

64. The Court makes it clear at the outset that the choice of electoral system by which the free expression of the opinion of the people in the choice of the legislature is ensured – whether it be based on proportional representation, the 'first-past-the-post' system or some other arrangement – is a matter in which the State enjoys a wide margin of appreciation. However, in the present case the applicant, as a resident of Gibraltar, was completely denied any opportunity to express her opinion in the choice of the members of the European Parliament. The position is not analogous to that of persons who are unable to take part in elections because they live outside the jurisdiction, as such individuals have weakened the link between themselves and the jurisdiction. In the present case, as the Court has found (see paragraph 34 above), the legislation which emanates from the European Community forms part of the legislation in Gibraltar, and the applicant is directly affected by it.

65. In the circumstances of the present case, the very essence of the applicant's right to vote, as guaranteed by art 3 of Protocol No 1, was denied.

It follows that there has been a violation of that provision.'

Comment

The Court, contrary to the Commission (11 votes to six), recognised the European Parliament as a legislative body within the meaning of art 3 of Protocol 1. In a number of applications previously submitted to it the Commission refused to consider the EP as a legislative body on the ground that it lacked identifiable legislative functions (*Tête* v *France* No 11123/84 (1987) 54 DR 52, *Fournier* v *France* No 11406/85 (1988) 55

DR 130). In order to decide whether the EP is a 'legislature' within the meaning of art 3 of Protocol 1 the Court examined the EP's role in the decision-making procedures of the EC in the light of the Treaty on European Union, its supervisory powers and, most importantly, the fact that the EP is the only democratically elected institution of the EC. The Court emphasised that art 3 of Protocol 1 applies not only to domestic representative organs, including regional bodies (such as regional councils in Belgium, in addition to both houses of the national Parliament: *Mathieu-Mohin* v *Belgium* (1987) Series A no 113) but also to a supra-national bodies such as the EP.

Another interesting aspect of the judgment is that rather than complaining to the Commission the applicants ought to have challenged Council Directive 76/787 and the 1976 Act concerning elections to the EP before the judicial bodies of the European Community or before national courts. Only the ECJ is empowered to declare acts of the EC institutions invalid. In this respect the European Court of Human Rights stated that Community acts cannot be challenged before the European Court of Human Rights as the EC is not a contracting party to the ECHR. However, the Court stated that the transfer of competences by a Member State to EC institutions is subject to that State's previous international obligations and that the Convention and its Protocols clearly state that a contracting State is responsible for the consequences of international treaties entered into subsequent to the ratification of the Convention in securing the rights guaranteed under the Convention and its Protocols. In addition, taking into account that EC legislation affects the population of Gibraltar in the same manner as legislation enacted by the Gibraltar House of Assembly, there was no reason why the UK should not have extended the right to participate in elections to the EP to Gibraltar. For the above-mentioned reasons the UK was held responsible for breach of art 3 of Protocol 1.

Appendix

Numbering of the Treaty on European Union and the EC Treaty articles before and after entry into force of the Amsterdam Treaty

Treaty on European Union

Before	After	Before	After
TITLE I	TITLE I	Article J.16	Article 26
Article A	Article 1	Article J.17	Article 27
Article B	Article 2	Article J.18	Article 28
Article C	Article 3	TITLE VI (***)	TITLE VI*
Article D	Article 4	Article K.1	Article 29
Article E	Article 5	Article K.2	Article 30
Article F	Article 6	Article K.3	Article 31
Article F.1 (*)	Article 7	Article K.4	Article 32
TITLE II	TITLE II	Article K.5	Article 33
Article G	Article 8	Article K.6	Article 34
		Article K.7	Article 35
TITLE III	TITLE III	Article K.8	Article 36
Article H	Article 9	Article K.9	Article 37
TITLE IV	TITLE IV	Article K.10	Article 38
Article I	Article 10	Article K.11	Article 39
		Article K.12	Article 40
TITLE V (***)	TITLE V	Article K.13	Article 41
Article J.1	Article 11	Article K.14	Article 42
Article J.2	Article 12	TITLE VIa (**)	TITLE VII
Article J.3	Article 13	Article K.15 (*)	Article 43
Article J.4	Article 14	Article K.16 (*)	Article 44
Article J.5	Article 15	Article K.17 (*)	Article 45
Article J.6	Article 16	TITLE VII	TITLE VIII
Article J.7	Article 17	Article L	Article 46
Article J.8	Article 18	Article M	Article 47
Article J.9	Article 19	Article N	Article 48
Article J.10	Article 20	Article O	Article 49
Article J.11	Article 21	Article P	Article 50
Article J.12	Article 22	Article Q	Article 51
Article J.13	Article 23	Article R	Article 52
Article J.14	Article 24	Article S	Article 53
Article J.15	Article 25		

Treaty Establishing the European Community

Before	After	Before	After
PART ONE	*PART ONE*	Article 18 (repealed)	–
Article 1	Article 1	Article 19 (repealed)	–
Article 2	Article 2	Article 20 (repealed)	–
Article 3	Article 3	Article 21 (repealed)	–
Article 3a	Article 4	Article 22 (repealed)	–
Article 3b	Article 5	Article 23 (repealed)	–
Article 3c (*)	Article 6	Article 24 (repealed)	–
Article 4	Article 7	Article 25 (repealed)	–
Article 4a	Article 8	Article 26 (repealed)	–
Article 4b	Article 9	Article 27 (repealed)	–
Article 5	Article 10	Article 28	Article 26
Article 5a (*)	Article 11	Article 29	Article 27
Article 6	Article 12	CHAPTER 2	CHAPTER 2
Article 6a	Article 13	Article 30	Article 28
Article 7 (repealed)	–	Article 31 (repealed)	–
Article 7a	Article 14	Article 32 (repealed)	–
Article 7b (repealed)	–	Article 33 (repealed)	–
Article 7c	Article 15	Article 34	Article 29
Article 7d (*)	Article 16	Article 35 (repealed)	–
PART TWO	*PART TWO*	Article 36	Article 30
Article 8	Article 17	Article 37	Article 31
Article 8a	Article 18	TITLE II	TITLE II
Article 8b	Article 19	Article 38	Article 32
Article 8c	Article 20	Article 39	Article 33
Article 8d	Article 21	Article 40	Article 34
Article 8e	Article 22	Article 41	Article 35
PART THREE	*PART THREE*	Article 42	Article 36
TITLE I	TITLE I	Article 43	Article 37
Article 9	Article 23	Article 44 (repealed)	–
Article 10	Article 24	Article 45 (repealed)	–
Article 11 (repealed)	–	Article 46	Article 38
CHAPTER 1	CHAPTER 1	Article 47 (repealed)	–
SECTION 1 (deleted)	–	TITLE III	TITLE III
Article 12	Article 25	CHAPTER 1	CHAPTER 1
Article 13 (repealed)	–	Article 48	Article 39
Article 14 (repealed)	–	Article 49	Article 40
Article 15 (repealed)	–	Article 50	Article 41
Article 16 (repealed)	–	Article 51	Article 42
Article 17 (repealed)	–	CHAPTER 2	CHAPTER 2
SECTION 2 (deleted)	–	Article 52	Article 43
		Article 53 (repealed)	–

Appendix 375

Before	After	Before	After
Article 54	Article 44	Article 76	Article 72
Article 55	Article 45	Article 77	Article 73
Article 56	Article 46	Article 78	Article 74
Article 57	Article 47	Article 79	Article 75
Article 58	Article 48	Article 80	Article 76
CHAPTER 3	CHAPTER 3	Article 81	Article 77
Article 59	Article 49	Article 82	Article 78
Article 60	Article 50	Article 83	Article 79
Article 61	Article 51	Article 84	Article 80
Article 62 (repealed)	–	TITLE V	TITLE VI
Article 63	Article 52	CHAPTER 1	CHAPTER 1
Article 64	Article 53	SECTION 1	SECTION 1
Article 65	Article 54	Article 85	Article 81
Article 56	Article 55	Article 86	Article 82
CHAPTER 4	CHAPTER 4	Article 87	Article 83
Article 67 (repealed)	–	Article 88	Article 84
Article 68 (repealed)	–	Article 89	Article 85
Article 69 (repealed)	–	Article 90	Article 86
Article 70 (repealed)	–	SECTION 2 (deleted)	–
Article 71 (repealed)	–	Article 91 (repealed)	–
Article 72 (repealed)	–	SECTION 3	SECTION 2
Article 73 (repealed)	–	Article 92	Article 87
Article 73a (repealed)	–	Article 93	Article 88
Article 73b	Article 56	Article 94	Article 89
Article 73c	Article 57	CHAPTER 2	CHAPTER 2
Article 73d	Article 58	Article 95	Article 90
Article 73e (repealed)	–	Article 96	Article 91
Article 73f	Article 59	Article 97 (repealed)	–
Article 73g	Article 60	Article 98	Article 92
Article 73h (repealed)	–	Article 99	Article 93
TITLE IIIa (**)	TITLE IV	CHAPTER 3	CHAPTER 3
Article 73i (*)	Article 61	Article 100	Article 94
Article 73j (*)	Article 62	Article 100a	Article 95
Article 73k (*)	Article 63	Article 100b (repealed)	–
Article 73l (*)	Article 64	Article 100c (repealed)	–
Article 73m (*)	Article 65	Article 100d (repealed)	–
Article 73n (*)	Article 66	Article 101	Article 96
Article 73o (*)	Article 67	Article 102	Article 97
Article 73p (*)	Article 68	TITLE VI	TITLE VII
Article 73q (*)	Article 69	CHAPTER 1	CHAPTER 1
TITLE IV (**)	TITLE V	Article 102a	Article 98
Article 74	Article 70		
Article 75	Article 71		

Before	After	Before	After
Article 103	Article 99	TITLE VIIa	TITLE X
Article 103a	Article 100	Article 116 (*)	Article 135
Article 104	Article 101	TITLE VIII	TITLE XI
Article 104a	Article 102	CHAPTER 1 (***)	CHAPTER 1
Article 104b	Article 103	Article 117	Article 136
Article 104c	Article 104	Article 118	Article 137
CHAPTER 2	CHAPTER 2	Article 118a	Article 138
Article 105	Article 105	Article 118b	Article 139
Article 105a	Article 106	Article 118c	Article 140
Article 106	Article 107	Article 119	Article 141
Article 107	Article 108	Article 119a	Article 142
Article 108	Article 109	Article 120	Article 143
Article 108a	Article 110	Article 121	Article 144
Article 109	Article 111	Article 122	Article 145
CHAPTER 3	CHAPTER 3	CHAPTER 2	CHAPTER 2
Article 109a	Article 112	Article 123	Article 146
Article 109b	Article 113	Article 124	Article 147
Article 109c	Article 114	Article 125	Article 148
Article 109d	Article 115	CHAPTER 3	CHAPTER 3
CHAPTER 4	CHAPTER 4	Article 126	Article 149
Article 109e	Article 116	Article 127	Article 150
Article 109f	Article 117	TITLE IX	TITLE XII
Article 109g	Article 118	Article 128	Article 151
Article 109h	Article 119	TITLE X	TITLE XIII
Article 109i	Article 120	Article 129	Article 152
Article 109j	Article 121	TITLE XI	TITLE XIV
Article 109k	Article 122	Article 129a	Article 153
Article 109l	Article 123	TITLE XII	TITLE XV
Article 109m	Article 124	Article 129b	Article 154
TITLE VIa (**)	TITLE VIII	Article 129c	Article 155
Article 109n (*)	Article 125	Article 129d	Article 156
Article 109o (*)	Article 126	TITLE XIII	TITLE XVI
Article 109p (*)	Article 127	Article 130	Article 157
Article 109q (*)	Article 128	TITLE XIV	TITLE XVII
Article 109r (*)	Article 129	Article 130a	Article 158
Article 109s (*)	Article 130	Article 130b	Article 159
TITLE VII	TITLE IX	Article 130c	Article 160
Article 110	Article 131		
Article 111 (repealed)	–		
Article 112	Article 132		
Article 113	Article 133		
Article 114 (repealed)	–		
Article 115	Article 134		

Appendix 377

Before	After	Before	After
Article 130d	Article 161	Article 138c	Article 193
Article 130e	Article 162	Article 138d	Article 194
TITLE XV	TITLE XVIII	Article 138e	Article 195
		Article 139	Article 196
Article 130f	Article 163	Article 140	Article 197
Article 130g	Article 164	Article 141	Article 198
Article 130h	Article 165	Article 142	Article 199
Article 130i	Article 166	Article 143	Article 200
Article 130j	Article 167	Article 144	Article 201
Article 130k	Article 168	SECTION 2	SECTION 2
Article 130l	Article 169		
Article 130m	Article 170	Article 145	Article 202
Article 130n	Article 171	Article 146	Article 203
Article 130o	Article 172	Article 147	Article 204
Article 130p	Article 173	Article 148	Article 205
Article 130q (repealed)	–	Article 149 (repealed)	–
TITLE XVI	TITLE XIX	Article 150	Article 206
		Article 151	Article 207
Article 130r	Article 174	Article 152	Article 208
Article 130s	Article 175	Article 153	Article 209
Article 130t	Article 176	Article 154	Article 210
TITLE XVII	TITLE XX	SECTION 3	SECTION 3
Article 130u	Article 177	Article 155	Article 211
Article 130v	Article 178	Article 156	Article 212
Article 130w	Article 179	Article 157	Article 213
Article 130x	Article 180	Article 158	Article 214
Article 130y	Article 181	Article 159	Article 215
PART FOUR	PART FOUR	Article 160	Article 216
		Article 161	Article 217
Article 131	Article 182	Article 162	Article 218
Article 132	Article 183	Article 163	Article 219
Article 133	Article 184	SECTION 4	SECTION 4
Article 134	Article 185		
Article 135	Article 186	Article 164	Article 220
Article 136	Article 187	Article 165	Article 221
Article 136a	Article 188	Article 166	Article 222
PART FIVE	PART FIVE	Article 167	Article 223
TITLE I	TITLE I	Article 168	Article 224
CHAPTER 1	CHAPTER 1	Article 168a	Article 225
SECTION 1	SECTION 1	Article 169	Article 226
		Article 170	Article 227
Article 137	Article 189	Article 171	Article 228
Article 138	Article 190	Article 172	Article 229
Article 138a	Article 191	Article 173	Article 230
Article 138b	Article 192	Article 174	Article 231
		Article 175	Article 232

Before	After	Before	After
Article 176	Article 233	TITLE II	TITLE II
Article 177	Article 234	Article 199	Article 268
Article 178	Article 235	Article 200 (repealed)	–
Article 179	Article 236	Article 201	Article 269
Article 180	Article 237	Article 201a	Article 270
Article 181	Article 238	Article 202	Article 271
Article 182	Article 239	Article 203	Article 272
Article 183	Article 240	Article 204	Article 273
Article 184	Article 241	Article 205	Article 274
Article 185	Article 242	Article 205a	Article 275
Article 186	Article 243	Article 206	Article 276
Article 187	Article 244	Article 206a (repealed)	–
Article 188	Article 245	Article 207	Article 277
SECTION 5	SECTION 5	Article 208	Article 278
Article 188a	Article 246	Article 209	Article 279
Article 188b	Article 247	Article 209a	Article 280
Article 188c	Article 248	PART SIX	PART SIX
CHAPTER 2	CHAPTER 2	Article 210	Article 281
Article 189	Article 249	Article 211	Article 282
Article 189a	Article 250	Article 212 (*)	Article 283
Article 189b	Article 251	Article 213	Article 284
Article 189c	Article 252	Article 213a (*)	Article 285
Article 190	Article 253	Article 213b (*)	Article 286
Article 191	Article 254	Article 214	Article 287
Article 191a (*)	Article 255	Article 215	Article 288
Article 192	Article 256	Article 216	Article 289
CHAPTER 3	CHAPTER 3	Article 217	Article 290
Article 193	Article 257	Article 218 (*)	Article 291
Article 194	Article 258	Article 219	Article 292
Article 195	Article 259	Article 220	Article 293
Article 196	Article 260	Article 221	Article 294
Article 197	Article 261	Article 222	Article 295
Article 198	Article 262	Article 223	Article 296
CHAPTER 4	CHAPTER 4	Article 224	Article 297
Article 198a	Article 263	Article 225	Article 298
Article 198b	Article 264	Article 226 (repealed)	–
Article 198c	Article 265	Article 227	Article 299
CHAPTER 5	CHAPTER 5	Article 228	Article 300
Article 198d	Article 266	Article 228a	Article 301
Article 198e	Article 267	Article 229	Article 302
		Article 230	Article 303
		Article 231	Article 304
		Article 232	Article 305
		Article 233	Article 306
		Article 234	Article 307
		Article 235	Article 308

Before	After	Before	After
Article 236 (*)	Article 309	FINAL PROVISIONS	FINAL PROVISIONS
Article 237 (repealed)	–	Article 247	Article 313
Article 238	Article 310	Article 248	Article 314
Article 239	Article 311		
Article 240	Article 312		
Article 241 (repealed)	–		
Article 242 (repealed)	–		
Article 243 (repealed)	–		
Article 244 (repealed)	–		
Article 245 (repealed)	–		
Article 246 (repealed)	–		

(*)   New Article introduced by the Treaty of Amsterdam
(**) New Title introduced by the Treaty of Amsterdam
(***) Chapter 1 restructured by the Treaty of Amsterdam

EU Law Today

Alina Kaczorowska, BCL, DEA, PhD, Barrister at the Paris Bar, Principal Lecturer in Law, Southampton Institute

The book is designed for law students and non-law students with EU Law elements in their courses. Further, it is a useful reference work for legal practitioners.

Since EU Law has become a compulsory subject for undergraduate students on qualifying law degrees, this book is an ideal core text for any semesterised course on EU Law (one chapter can be studied each week).

The text examines the conceptual apparatus of the EU, the general objectives which the EU performs and the methods and techniques employed by the Community Institutions and the Members States for the achievement of those ends. It includes a number of topics not found in standard textbooks, eg the general historical background of European integration, the requirements for admission of new members, the challenge of enlargements and internal and external competencies of the European Union since the Treaty of Maastricht.

Particular attention is paid to areas in which students find most difficulty including direct effect, direct applicability and supremacy of EU Law, direct actions before the Court of Justice of the European Communities (ECJ), together with newly introduced sanctions for non-compliance under art 171(2) EC.

The text, which includes the most recent developments in the EU and its law, is a succinct exposition of the letter and spirit of the institutional law of the European Communities and the European Union.

For further information on contents, please contact:

Mail Order
Old Bailey Press
200 Greyhound Road
London
W14 9RY
United Kingdom

Telephone No: 00 44 (0) 20 7385 3377
Fax No: 00 44 (0) 20 7381 3377

ISBN 1 85836 271 7
Soft cover 246 x 175 mm
444 pages   £14.95
Published 1998

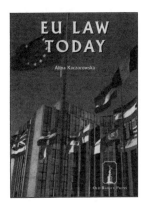

Research on the Net

Kevin McGuinness, Steele Raymond Professor of Business Law at Bournemouth University and Tom Short, Principal Lecturer and Research Fellow at Bournemouth University

Research on the Net is the essential tool for anyone seeking to find reliable academic information on the Net. It goes far beyond the point where search engines fade out, offering direct links to more than 4,000 current sites for primary research information, connecting to hundreds of thousands of other sites. All 4,000 links were verified three times, to ensure that they remained accurate and live at the date of publication.

Locating specific information on the Internet is a time-consuming, frustrating process. This book simplifies this process by (a) describing and analysing in detail the information that can be found at each site; (b) focusing on full text resources and primary research data where available; (c) excluding peripheral, publicity and vanity sites that bog down other methods of Net research; (d) employing a thematic organisation; and (e) linking to relevant sources of information around the world. To assist access, a Mac OS and Windows-compatible disc is included with the text, providing hypertext links to all sites listed.

This book is a vital tool for project students, doctoral students, lecturers, journalists and others carrying out academic research in business, law, the social sciences and humanities in this Internet Age.

For further information on contents, please contact:

Mail Order
Old Bailey Press
200 Greyhound Road
London
W14 9RY
United Kingdom

Telephone No: 00 44 (0) 20 7385 3377
Fax No: 00 44 (0) 20 7381 3377

ISBN 1 85836 269 5
Soft cover 246 x 175 mm
444 pages   £19.95
Published 1998

Law Update 1999

Law Update 2000 edition – due March 2000

An annual review of the most recent developments in specific legal subject areas, useful for law students at degree and professional levels, others with law elements in their courses and also practitioners seeking a quick update.

Published around March every year, the Law Update summarises the major legal developments during the course of the previous year. In conjunction with Old Bailey Press textbooks it gives the student a significant advantage when revising for examinations.

Contents
Administrative Law • Civil and Criminal Procedure • Commercial Law • Company Law • Conflict of Laws • Constitutional Law • Contract Law • Conveyancing • Criminal Law • Criminology • English Legal System • Equity and Trusts • European Union Law • Evidence • Family Law • Jurisprudence • Land Law • Law of International Trade • Public International Law • Revenue Law • Succession • Tort

For further information on contents, please contact:

Mail Order
Old Bailey Press
200 Greyhound Road
London
W14 9RY
United Kingdom

Telephone No: 00 44 (0) 20 7385 3377
Fax No: 00 44 (0) 20 7381 3377

ISBN 1 85836 303 9
Soft cover 246 x 175 mm
408 pages   £9.95
Published March 1999

Old Bailey Press

The Old Bailey Press integrated student library is planned and written to help you at every stage of your studies. Each of our range of Textbooks, Casebooks, Revision WorkBooks and Statutes are all designed to work together and are regularly revised and updated.

We are also able to offer you Suggested Solutions which provide you with past examination questions and solutions for most of the subject areas listed below.

You can buy Old Bailey Press books from your University Bookshop or your local Bookshop, or in case of difficulty, order direct using this form.

Here is the selection of modules covered by our series:

Administrative Law; Commercial Law; Company Law (no Single Paper 1997); Conflict of Laws (no Suggested Solutions Pack); Constitutional Law: The Machinery of Government; Obligations: Contract Law; Conveyancing (no Revision Workbook); Criminology (Sourcebook in place of a Casebook or Revision WorkBook); Criminal Law; English Legal System; Equity and Trusts; Law of The European Union; Evidence; Family Law; Jurisprudence: The Philosophy of Law (Sourcebook in place of a Casebook); Land: The Law of Real Property; Law of International Trade; Legal Skills and System (Textbook only); Public International Law; Revenue Law (no Casebook); Succession: The Law of Wills and Estates; Obligations: The Law of Tort.

Mail order prices:

Textbook £11.95

Casebook £9.95

Revision WorkBook £7.95

Statutes £9.95

Suggested Solutions Pack (1991–1995) £6.95

Single Paper 1996 £3.00

Single Paper 1997 £3.00

To complete your order, please fill in the form below:

Module	Books required	Quantity	Price	Cost
		Postage		
		TOTAL		

For Europe, add 15% postage and packing (£20 maximum).
For the rest of the world, add 40% for airmail.

ORDERING

By telephone to Mail Order at 020 7385 3377, with your credit card to hand.

By fax to 020 7381 3377 (giving your credit card details).

By post to:
Old Bailey Press, 200 Greyhound Road, London W14 9RY.

When ordering by post, please enclose full payment by cheque or banker's draft, or complete the credit card details below.

We aim to despatch your books within 3 working days of receiving your order.

Name

Address

Postcode   Telephone

Total value of order, including postage: £

I enclose a cheque/banker's draft for the above sum, or

charge my   ☐ Access/Mastercard   ☐ Visa   ☐ American Express
Card number

☐☐☐☐ ☐☐☐☐ ☐☐☐☐ ☐☐☐☐

Expiry date   ☐☐☐☐

Signature: ....Date: ....